ROUTLEDGE HANDBOOK TO LUIGI NONO AND MUSICAL THOUGHT

Of the post-war, post-serialist generation of European composers, it was Luigi Nono who succeeded not only in identifying and addressing aesthetic and technical questions of his time, but in showing a way ahead to a new condition of music in the twenty-first century. His music has found a listenership beyond the ageing constituency of 'contemporary music'. In Nono's work, the audiences of sound art, improvisation, electronic, experimental and radical musics of many kinds find common cause with those concerned with the renewal of Western art music. His work explores the individually and socially transformative role of music; its relationship with history and with language; the nature of the musical work as distributed through text, time, technology and individuals; the nature and performativity of the act of composition; and, above all, the role and nature of listening as a cultural activity. In many respects his music anticipates the new technological state of culture of the twenty-first century while radically reconnecting with our past. His work is itself a case study in the evolution of musical activity and the musical object: from the period of an apparently stable place for art music in Western culture to its manifold new states in our century. *Routledge Handbook to Luigi Nono and Musical Thought* seeks to trace the evolution of Nono's musical thought through detailed examination of the vast body of sketches, and to situate this narrative in its personal, cultural and political contexts.

Jonathan Impett is a trumpet player and composer. He is Director of Research at the Orpheus Institute, Ghent, where he leads the research group 'Music, Thought and Technology', and Associate Professor at Middlesex University, London. His work is concerned with the resituating and redistributing of musical activity. It explores the spaces between score and improvisation, musician and technology, the use of interactive and intelligent systems, the cultural role of models from science and the nature of the contemporary technologically situated musical artefact. He is also a member of the Orchestra of the Eighteenth Century.

ROUTLEDGE HANDBOOK TO LUIGI NONO AND MUSICAL THOUGHT

Jonathan Impett

First published 2019
by Routledge
2 Park Square, Milton Park, Abingdon, Oxon OX14 4RN

and by Routledge
711 Third Avenue, New York, NY 10017

Routledge is an imprint of the Taylor & Francis Group, an informa business

© 2019 Jonathan Impett

The right of Jonathan Impett to be identified as author of this work has been asserted by them in accordance with sections 77 and 78 of the Copyright, Designs and Patents Act 1988.

All rights reserved. No part of this book may be reprinted or reproduced or utilised in any form or by any electronic, mechanical, or other means, now known or hereafter invented, including photocopying and recording, or in any information storage or retrieval system, without permission in writing from the publishers.

Trademark notice: Product or corporate names may be trademarks or registered trademarks, and are used only for identification and explanation without intent to infringe.

British Library Cataloguing-in-Publication Data
A catalogue record for this book is available from the British Library

Library of Congress Cataloging-in-Publication Data
Names: Impett, Jonathan, author.
Title: Routledge handbook to Luigi Nono and musical thought / Jonathan Impett.
Description: Abingdon, Oxon ; New York, NY : Routledge, 2019. |
Includes bibliographical references and index.
Identifiers: LCCN 2018021573| ISBN 9781409455974 (hardback) |
ISBN 9780429485732 (ebook)
Subjects: LCSH: Nono, Luigi—Criticism and interpretation. |
Music—20th century—History and criticism.
Classification: LCC ML410.N667 I66 2019 | DDC 780.92—dc23
LC record available at https://lccn.loc.gov/2018021573

ISBN: 978-1-4094-5597-4 (hbk)
ISBN: 978-0-429-48573-2 (ebk)

Typeset in Bembo and Bach
by Florence Production Ltd, Stoodleigh, Devon, UK.

Bach musicological font developed by © Yo Tomita

This book is dedicated to the memory of my father,
Norman Impett – 'Non', to all who loved him.

CONTENTS

List of figures	xii
List of plates	xvi
Notes	xvii
Acknowledgements	xviii
Foreword	xix
Introduction	xx

1 Prolegomena: a Venetian pre-biography — 1

2 Accelerated learning: years of study, 1942–50 — 9

A classical education	9
Encounters	15
Gian Francesco Malipiero	15
Bruno Maderna	17
Hermann Scherchen	22
Eunice Katunda	25
René Leibowitz	27
Luigi Dallapiccola	28
'Due liriche greche'	29

3 Confronting modernism: Darmstadt — 36

The emergence of a language	36
'Variazioni canoniche sulla serie dell'op. 41 di Arnold Schönberg'	37
Dodecaphonic variations	47
'Fučík'	47
'Polifonica – Monodia – Ritmica'	49

vii

Contents

'*Composizione per orchestra [n. 1]*'	59
Engagement	63
Lorca: drama, struggle and reference: 'Epitaffio n. 1–3 per Federico Garcia Lorca'	66
'*Epitaffio n. 1: España en el corazón*'	66
'*Epitaffio n. 2: Y su sangre ya viene cantando*'	72
'*Epitaffio n. 3: Memento − Romance de la Guardia Civil Española*'	74

4 Taking positions: song — **83**

Traveller . . .	83
Expressions	87
'*Due espressioni*'	87
'*La Victoire de Guernica*'	93
'*Liebeslied*'	98
Into the theatre: 'Der rote Mantel, Was ihr wollt'	100
Integration	105
'*Canti*'	105
'*Incontri*'	112

5 'Docere e movere': *Il canto sospeso* — **122**

Genesis	122
Text	124
Music	125
Instrumental movements 1, 4 and 8	127
Solo vocal movements 3, 5 and 7	129
Choral movement 2, 6 and 9	134
Song	139

6 Poetry and drama — **147**

'Varianti'	147
Collaboration	147
Reflection	148
Composition	150
Earth and sea	158
'*La terra e la compagna*'	159
'*Cori di Didone*'	168
Diary and design: 'Composizione per orchestra n. 2: Diario polacco '58'	175
Inception	175
Space and movement	178
Historical presence and present tensions	185
Helmut Lachenmann	187
Melos reborn	189

Contents

'Sarà dolce tacere	191
'"Ha venido". Canciones para Silvia'	194
Into the studio: 'Omaggio a Emilio Vedova'	196

7 Intolleranza 1960   **204**

Gestation	204
Composition	211
Production	215
Resonance	217

8 New spaces: studio, street, factory   **221**

'Canti di vita e d'amore: Sul ponte di Hiroshima'	221
'Canciones a Guiomar'	232
Possibility of a new theatre . . .	237
Evolving projects	237
'Un diario italiano'	239
'La fabbrica illuminata'	245
Locating the work	245
The sonic factory	246
American journey	253
The inferno: 'Die Ermittlung' and 'Ricorda cosa ti hanno fatto in Auschwitz'	254
Internationalism	260
The living studio	260
'A floresta é jovem e cheja de vida'	263

9 Manifestos   **276**

Anti-revisionism: 'Per Bastiana – Tai-Yang Cheng'	276
Political engagement at home and abroad	279
Situated action and Venetian counterpoint: 'Contrappunto dialettico alla mente'	282
The soundtrack of struggle	285
'Il Manifesto'	287
Direct action	292
'Musica-Manifesto n. 1: Un volto, e del mare – Non consumiamo Marx'	292
'Y entonces comprendió'	297
The institutional performance of protest: 'Voci destroying muros, Ein Gespenst geht um in der Welt'	301
Solidarity in a new culture	308
Music and reality	308
A wave of strength and light	311

Contents

10 *Al gran sole carico d'amore*   **320**

A long-awaited sunrise   320
Operatic architecture   322
A national event   328
A Gramscian opera?   330
Under a common flag: 'Für Paul Dessau'   333

11 Waves   **337**

'..... sofferte onde serene ...'   337
    Exploring piano and pianist   337
    '. . . the infinite smile of the waves'   339
    '. . . a man searching for truth'   341
    Aftershock: 'I Turcs tal Friúl'   344
'Con Luigi Dallapiccola'   345
'Fragmente-Stille, an Diotima'   349
    The process of knowledge   349
    Waves of memory   352
    'Fragmente' and criticism   361
    'Fragmente', Hölderlin and the caesura   362
    'Fragmente', Hölderlin and Marx   363

12 *Prometeo*   **368**

'Das atmende Klarsein'   368
    Breathing anew   368
    '. . . a sense of the possible'   371
'Io, frammento dal Prometeo'   376
'Quando stanno morendo, Diario polacco n. 2'   381
    Music of continuous resistance   381
    Subversive humanism   387
'. . . peace is doubtful disquiet'   388
    Reconciliation   388
    'Omaggio a György Kurtág'   388
    'Guai ai gelidi mostri'   390
    Physical, virtual and historical spaces   394

13 *A tragedy of listening*   **399**

Inception   399
Production   407
'Prometeo. Tragedia dell'ascolto'   412
    'Prologo'   412
    'Isola 1°'   419
    'Isola 2° (Io-Prometeo, Hölderlin, Stasimo 1°)'   421

Contents

'Interludio 1°'	425
'3 voci (a)'	426
'Isola 3° – 4° – 5°'	427
'3 voci (b)'	429
'Interludio 2°'	430
'Stasimo 2°'	431

14 Resonances 435

Echoes 435

The architecture of silence: 'A Carlo Scarpa, architetto, ai suoi
infiniti possibili' 435

'A Pierre: Dell'azzurro silenzio, inquietum' 439

'Risonanze erranti. Liederzyklus a Massimo Cacciari' 441

Musical precursors 441

Poetic catalysis 443

'Der Wanderer' 448

15 Possible worlds 452

'1° Caminantes . . . Ayacucho' 452

'. . . in an infinite space and with innumerable voices' 452

'Ars combinatoria' 453

The word and its absence 462

'Découvrir la subversion. Hommage à Edmond Jabès' 462

The blank page 465

'Post-prae-ludium n. 1 "per Donau"' 467

'2° No hay caminos, hay que caminar . . . Andrej Tarkovskij' 468

Distillation 468

Expansion 471

Sun, sacrifice and angels 475

Berlin 478

'La lontananza nostalgica future' 480

A short history: Berlin 480

A long history: Freiburg 481

The folds of memory 485

'Post-prae-ludium n. 3 "BAAB-ARR"' 489

'"Hay que caminar" Soñando' 491

Unexplored worlds 494

References	502
Index	516

FIGURES

2.1	*Liriche d'Ungaretti*: sketch for *Eterno*	22
2.2	*Due liriche greche*: pitch material	31
3.1	*Variazioni canoniche*: series from Schönberg op. 41 as notated by Nono	37
3.2	*Variazioni canoniche*: third derived row	38
3.3	*Variazioni canoniche*: rhythm base and variant	38
3.4	*Variazioni canoniche*: remapping of series	39
3.5	*Variazioni canoniche*: contrapuntal basis	40
3.6	*Variazioni canoniche*: combination scheme	41
3.7	*Variazioni canoniche*: mirror-canon, filtering and retranscription	42
3.8	*Variazioni canoniche*: derivation of new voices from canon on ritmo base	43
3.9	*Variazioni canoniche*: second voice from Figure 3.8, in bars 95–8	43
3.10	*Variazioni canoniche*: pitch structure of *Lento* (bars 217–83)	44
3.11	*Variazioni canoniche*: *Lento*	45
3.12	*Fučík*: pitch series	48
3.13	*Polifonica*: series substitution process	50
3.14	*Polifonica*: opening, bars 1–14	51
3.15	*Polifonica*: root rhythm from *Andante*	52
3.16	*Polifonica*: retranscription of opening of *Andante*	53
3.17	*Polifonica*: rhythm from Katunda	54
3.18	Interval circles: 'melodic' and 'harmonic'	55
3.19	*Monodia*, bars 1–6	57
3.20	*Ritmica*: rhythmic seed	58
3.21	*Composizione per orchestra [n. 1]*: interval/duration mappings	60
3.22	*Composizione per orchestra [n. 1]*: derivation of episode 1, bars 17–21	61
3.23	*Composizione per orchestra [n. 1]*: II episodio, monody bars 71–8	62
3.24	*Epitaffio n. 1: Tarde*: derivation of opening	68
3.25	*Epitaffio n. 1: Lenin*: extracts from *Bandiera rossa*	69
3.26	*Epitaffio n. 1: La Guerra*: opening	71
3.27	*Y su sangre*: formal plan	73
3.28	*Y su sangre*: Sarabanda rhythms A and B	74
3.29	*Y su sangre*: fandango	74
3.30	*Memento*: form and dances	76
3.31	*Memento*: bars 102–7, 110–12, 118–21	77

Figures

3.32	*Memento*: bars 163–75, first four sequences of *Baille*	79
4.1	*Due espressioni*: evolution of pitch series	89
4.2	*Due espressioni, 2*: derivation of Furlana rhythms	91
4.3	Symmetrical/directional figure, common in Nono's early sketches	92
4.4	*La Victoire de Guernica*: derivation of series	96
4.5	*Guernica*: timpani duet, bars 90–2	97
4.6	*Liebeslied*: pitch material	99
4.7	*Liebeslied*: rhythmic material for first stanza	100
4.8	*Liebeslied*: coda	100
4.9	*Der rote Mantel*: *Amore* series and derivatives	103
4.10	*Canti per 13*: densities	109
4.11	*Canti per 13*: derivation of bars 19–22	110
4.12	*Incontri*: series (Nono's annotation)	113
4.13	Nono's diagram of distribution of materials A and B through the first half of *Incontri*	114
4.14	From sketches for *Incontri*	114
4.15	*Incontri*: derivation of bars 32–9	116
5.1	*Il canto sospeso*: all-interval series as notated by Nono	125
5.2	*Il canto sospeso*: formal balance	126
5.3	*Il canto sospeso No. 1*: opening	128
5.4	*Il canto sospeso No. 1*: final melody, bars 96–107	129
5.5	*Il canto sospeso No. 5*: bars 288–98, quintuplet layer	130
5.6	*Il canto sospeso No. 7*: derivation of series	133
5.7	*Il canto sospeso No. 7*: form scheme	133
5.8	*Il canto sospeso No. 7*: bars 443–55	134
5.9	*Il canto sospeso No. 6a*: pitch structure	137
5.10	*Il canto sospeso No. 6b*: density scheme	138
5.11	*Il canto sospeso No. 9*: rhythmic process	138
5.12	*From a letter to Stockhausen*, 4 September 1952	142
6.1	*Varianti*: diagrams from preparatory sketch	148
6.2	*Varianti*: initial number path and Latin square	151
6.3	*Varianti*: lines 1–4 show pattern of bars 1–80, reversed in bars 155–234	152
6.4	*Varianti*: sound-complex shapes from sketches	153
6.5	*Varianti*: bars 1–3, annotated by Kolisch	154
6.6	*Varianti*: solo violin, bars 116–25	156
6.7	*La terra e la compagna*: successive text analyses	160
6.8a	*La terra e la compagna*: offset pattern	164
6.8b	*La terra e la compagna*: bars 31–4	165
6.9	*Cori di Didone*: rhythm base and sound complex patterns from sketches	172
6.10	*Cori di Didone*: bars 1–9, reduction of rhythm and pitch	173
6.11	*Composizione per orchestra n. 2: Diario polacco '58* – spatial concept	179
6.12	*Composizione per orchestra n. 2: Diario polacco '58* – arrangement of materials in bars 108–239	182
6.13	Nono's studio, late 1950s	184
6.14	*Sarà dolce tacere*: group structure of bars 89–91 – transcription of sketch and final score	193
6.15	*"Ha venido". Canciones para Silvia* – bars 88–97	195
7.1	*Intolleranza 1960*: plan, October 1960 (aggregate of several sketches)	208

xiii

Figures

7.2	*Intolleranza 1960*: final form	210
7.3	*Intolleranza 1960*: initial series for the soloists, with Nono's interval notation	212
7.4	*Intolleranza 1960*: bars 173–5	213
8.1	*Canti di vita e d'amore: Sul ponte di Hiroshima*: sound shapes	223
8.2	*Sul ponte di Hiroshima*: rhythm layers from bars 11–13	225
8.3	*Djamila Boupachà*: opening	227
8.4	*Tu*: Nono's structural plan	229
8.5	*Canciones a Guiomar*: soprano, bars 1–4	234
8.6	*Canciones a Guiomar*: reduction of bars 12–16	234
8.7	*Canciones a Guiomar*: reduction of bars 59–64	235
8.8	Nono working on *Un diario italiano*, mid-1960s	241
8.9	*La fabbrica illuminata*: choral fragment 1, pitch field	247
8.10	*La fabbrica illuminata*: beginning of *Finale* – derivation of pitch material in three stages	250
8.11	*La fabbrica illuminata*: timeline sketch of opening	251
8.12	*Musica per "Die Ermittlung" di Peter Weiss*: correspondence between dramatic structure and Nono's tape cues	256
8.13	*Musica per "Die Ermittlung" di Peter Weiss*: spectrogram of cue 10	257
8.14	*Musica per "Die Ermittlung" di Peter Weiss*: transcription of cue 13	257
8.14	*Ricorda cosa ti hanno fatto in Auschwitz*: sonogram	258
8.16	*A floresta é jovem e cheja de vida*: part-book of Kadigia Bove, opening	269
9.1	*Per Bastiana – Tai-Yang Cheng*: pattern of blocks in orchestral groups 1–3	278
9.2	*Musica-Manifesto n. 1*: sonograms of *Un volto, e del mare* and *Non consumiamo Marx*	294
9.3	*Y entonces comprendió*: page from *Noche* in part book of Mary Lindsey	300
9.4	*Ein Gespenst geht um in der Welt*	307
9.5a	Monteverdi: *Lamento d'Arianna*: opening	313
9.5b	*Como una ola de fuerza y luz*: soprano, 2'30"–2'55"	313
10.1	*Al gran sole carico d'amore*: Act I, bars 379–81	325
10.2a	From *Non siam più la commune di Parigi*	326
10.2b	Pitch sets	326
10.2c	Basic durations	326
10.2d	Segments 7–12	326
10.2e	From Act II, Scene 4	327
10.2	*Al gran sole carico d'amore*: derivation of Deola material, Act II	327
11.1	*..... sofferte onde serene ...*: initial pitch material	340
11.2	*..... sofferte onde serene ...*: bars 1–5	341
11.3a	*Fragmente-Stille, an Diotima*: Nono's articulation of the 'scala enigmatica'	344
11.3b	*..... sofferte onde serene ...*: rationalization of Figure 10.1	344
11.4a	*Con Luigi Dallapiccola*: three-dimensional number square	347
11.4b	*Con Luigi Dallapiccola*: *B calmo* material, derived from square	347
11.4c	*Con Luigi Dallapiccola*: Crotales 1, bars 29–34	347
11.4	*Con Luigi Dallapiccola*: derivation and use of *B calmo* rhythm matrix	347
11.5	Ockeghem: *Malor me bat* from Petrucci *Odhecaton*, 1501	353
11.6	*Fragmente-Stille, an Diotima*: scala enigmatica	353
11.7	*Fragmente-Stille, an Diotima*: fragment patterns	354
11.8a	Six-part rhythm matrix	356
11.8b	From lines 2–3 of Figure 11.8a	356

xiv

Figures

11.8c	Intermediate stage	356
11.8d	Final score	357
11.8	*Fragmente-Stille, an Diotima*: derivation of violin I, opening	357
12.1	*Das atmende Klarsein*: bars 1–7	373
12.2a	Early sketch	379
12.2b	Text fragments 20 and 21	379
12.2c	Section 1, bar 10–11	379
12.2d	Section VI, opening – sopranos	379
12.2e	Section VI, opening – bass flute	379
12.2	*Io, frammento dal Prometeo*: development from *Das atmende Klarsein*	379
13.1	*Prometeo*: early plan of first part	402
13.2	*Prometeo*: drawing by Cacciari, 1978	402
13.3	*Prometeo*: map of final structure	405
13.4	*Prometeo*: form	411
13.5	*Prometeo*: *Prologo* early sketch	413
13.6	*Prometeo*: interval material for *Prologo*	413
13.7	*Prometeo*: mythological strata of *Prologo*	416
13.8a	Frieze from Corfu	417
13.8b	Temple at Selinunte	417
13.8c	Frieze from the Parthenon (British Museum)	417
13.8	*Prometeo*: annotated photographs from Nono's sketches	417
13.9	*Prometeo*: *Prologo*, bars 129–31, solo SAT	418
13.10	*Prometeo*: *Isola 1°*, bars 111–12, coro lontanissimo	421
13.11	*Isola 3° – 4° – 5°*: alto soloists, bars 36–41	428
14.1	*A Carlo Scarpa, architetto, ai suoi infiniti possibili*: evolution of form (tempo ♩ = 30 except where noted)	437
14.2a	*Risonanze erranti*: Ockeghem *Malheur me bat*, fragmented and filtered	445
14.2b	*Risonanze erranti*: bars 21–2 of *Machaut-Ockeghem-Josquin*	445
14.2c	*Risonanze erranti*: crotales, bars 38–9	445
14.2	*Risonanze erranti*: use of *Machaut-Ockeghem-Josquin* material	445
14.3a	*Risonanze erranti*: samples 1–2 of *Machaut-Ockeghem-Josquin*	445
14.3b	*Risonanze erranti*: alto, bars 1–8	445
14.3	*Risonanze erranti*: opening – derivation from *Machaut-Ockeghem-Josquin* samples	445
15.1	*1° Caminantes . . . Ayacucho* – spatial distribution (from draft score)	455
15.2	*1° Caminantes . . . Ayacucho* – basic pitch material	455
15.3	*1° Caminantes . . . Ayacucho* – trumpets, bars 36–40	457
15.4a	*1° Caminantes . . . Ayacucho* – monody from sketches for *Quando stanno morendo*	458
15.4b	*1° Caminantes . . . Ayacucho* – alto solo, bars 78–115	458
15.5	*1° Caminantes . . . Ayacucho*: distribution of Bruno's text	459
15.6	*Découvrir la subversion* – outline pitch structure	464
15.7	*2° No hay caminos, hay que caminar . . . Andrej Tarkovskij*: structure	472
15.8	*2° No hay caminos, hay que caminar . . . Andrej Tarkovskij*: bars 2–3	474
15.9	*Varianti*: solo violin, bars 83–4	485
15.10	*La lontananza nostalgica utopica futura*: leggio I, bar 1	485
15.11	*La lontananza nostalgica utopica futura*: leggio I, bars 23–5	486
15.12	*La lontananza nostalgica utopica futura*: leggio II, 'intonatio' figures	487
15.13	Nono's annotation of Mondrian *Composition, 1916*	496

PLATES

1   *Al gran sole carico d'amore*: sketch
2   *..... sofferte onde serene ...*: bars 1–5. (Reproduced by kind permission of Casa Ricordi.)
3   *Quando stanno morendo/Omaggio a György Kurtág*: pitch material
4   *Guai ai gelidi mostri*: Nono's postcard of Giovanni Bellini *Sacra Conversazione*
5–7 Photographs by Nono of his working spaces during the composition of *Prometeo*, 1983–4
8   *Prometeo*: Nono at the mixing desk, showing part of Piano's performance space in San Lorenzo, Venice, 1984
9   *Prometeo*: sketch of disposition and colours of *isole* in San Lorenzo

NOTES

Abbreviations

ALN Archivio Luigi Nono, Venice. Documents are referred to by their catalogue number.

LNI, LNII *Luigi Nono: Scrittti e colloqui*, vols I and II. Angela Ida De Benedictis and Veniero Rizzardi (eds), LIM, Lucca/Ricordi, Milan, 2001.

Extracts from correspondence are reproduced by kind permission of the respective copyright owners. In particular, thanks are due to:

The heirs of Luigi Nono
The heirs of Bruno Maderna
Stockhausen-Stiftung für Musik, Kürten.

Translations are by the author except where noted.
Where no author is given, texts cited in endnotes are by Nono.

ACKNOWLEDGEMENTS

I would like to gratefully acknowledge the support of The British Academy and the Orpheus Institute, Ghent. This research was carried out in the context of the 'Music, Thought and Technology' group at the Orpheus Institute. It has been greatly facilitated by all the colleagues and staff there, in particular Director Peter Dejans. I would especially like to thank Nuria Schoenberg Nono, Giovanna Boscarino, Giorgio Mastinu, Erika Schaller and Claudia Vincis of the Archivio Luigi Nono, Venice, for their expert and generous wisdom, help and patience. Finally, the assistance, encouragement and patience of Annie Vaughan at Routledge and the meticulous editing of Emma Brown have been invaluable in the realisation of this project.

FOREWORD

From 2003 to the present, Jonathan Impett has spent long periods of study in Venice at the Archive of the Luigi Nono Foundation (*Fondazione Archivio Luigi Nono*). It was immediately obvious to me that he intended to write a book that encompassed the creative work of Luigi Nono set in the context of his life: of the composer's extensive musical interests, his constant search for what was 'new' in the arts, in theatre and literature, as well as his social–political awareness and cultural ties around the world.

The Archive could provide him with the sources for his research on the compositions and on Nono's life. And Jonathan took advantage of all of these possibilities. The result is a volume that reads like a biography and is at the same time a scholarly investigation of Luigi Nono's compositions. He tells us not only what Nono composed and how he composed, but also why and for whom he wrote his works.

It has been a pleasure discussing Nono's life and interests with Jonathan and on every one of his stays in Venice I was more and more convinced that the resulting book would be an important contribution towards the understanding of Luigi Nono's life and works.

I would like to thank him for 'doing such a great job', but that would be banal and reductive. I know that for Jonathan it has been an exciting musical and human journey, and I am happy for him and for the readers of his book.

Nuria Schoenberg Nono
Giudecca, 2018

INTRODUCTION

Of the post-war, post-serialist generation of European composers, it was Luigi Nono who succeeded not only in identifying and addressing aesthetic and technical questions of his time but in showing a way ahead to a new condition of music in the twenty-first century. His music has found a listenership beyond the aging constituency of 'contemporary music'. In Nono's work, the audiences of sound art, improvisation, electronic, experimental and radical musics of many kinds find common cause with those concerned with the renewal of Western art music. His work explores the individually and socially transformative role of music; its relationship with history and with language; the nature of the musical work as distributed through text, time, technology and individuals; the nature and performativity of the act of composition; and, above all, the role and nature of listening as a cultural activity. In many respects his music anticipates the new technological state of culture of the twenty-first century while radically reconnecting with our past. His work is itself a case study in the evolution of musical activity and the musical object: from the period of an apparently stable place for art music in Western culture to its manifold new states in our century.

Almost all Nono's music is available on commercial recordings. Indeed, he is the most recorded composer of his generation; the recent recordings of Nono's later works are particularly fine. The fluid state of the commercial recording industry, the expanding number of such recordings and their wide availability in many formats would make a conventional discography immediately obsolete. Thanks to a laudable commitment on the part of his publisher Ricordi, scores of most works are now available in critical or authoritative editions – a particular challenge in the case of his later music. Fundamental to any research is the *Archivio Luigi Nono* in Venice, which houses the large collection of Nono's manuscripts, sketches, correspondence and library. Led by Nuria Schoenberg Nono, it is a paragon in its balance of openness and care for the materials, of generosity and responsibility, fully in the spirit of Nono's work itself. In a world where access to knowledge has become an instrument of power, the Archivio is a rare beacon.

A large body of research into Nono's music has accumulated over the nearly three decades since his death. His compositional, cultural, political and personal activity connected with so many areas of life, so many communities of different kinds, that there is room for many views from particular perspectives. Studies of individual works have also proliferated, and important bodies of documentation have been published: from De Benedictis and Rizzardi's invaluable

Introduction

collection of Nono's writings to his correspondence with Ungaretti, Mila, Lachenmann and various political figures. With some notable exceptions, the majority of this work is in Italian or German, although that situation is beginning to change and a selection of Nono's writings is soon to be published in English.[1] His autobiographical interview with Enzo Restagno of 1987, translated in that volume, is an invaluable companion to any study of Nono's work. Unravelling Italian politics is not straightforward; Italian political history and journalism tends to assume a body of accumulated knowledge and is rarely non-partisan. A sense of Nono's political–historical context is crucial to understanding his thought, however. Excellent starting points are the English translations of the memoirs of two of Nono's comrades in the Italian Communist Party – Lucio Magri and Rossana Rossanda – as well as the docu-fiction of Nanni Balestrini.

What is lacking, particularly in English, is a broader picture in which to situate this body of excellent, highly focused research. The present book attempts such a task. It is important to acknowledge the vital research of the many experts in particular areas, but particularly of those whose broad and deep knowledge of the music, texts and materials is foundational to any work on Nono: Angela Ida De Benedictis, André Richard, Veniero Rizzardi, Erika Schaller, Jürg Stenzl, Claudia Vincis. Together with these, I would like to thank Nono's collaborators Roberto Fabricciani, André Richard, Giancarlo Schiaffini and Alvise Vidolin for their invaluable input. Any errors or omissions are, of course, my own.

As the title of the book suggests, there is an implicit thesis. At the end of Nono's life, Pietro Ingrao referred to him as 'a great European intellectual'. This is true, but the suggestion here is that the principal mode of his thought is musical – indeed, compositional. Developing the notion of 'musical thought' from Schönberg, Nono would later insist that 'Music is not just composition. It's not artisan work, not a profession. Music is thought.'[2] Nono's views and actions must be seen in this light: the coherent line of development through his thought is musical.

Composition is an inescapably technical matter. If we are to survey the nature and evolution of Nono's musical thought, we have to address technical questions, therefore, and I make no apology for the degree of compositional–technical discussion that follows. There is more emphasis on technical aspects of the earlier works; it is in these that Nono consciously establishes patterns of thought and practice that will subtend and inform future work, even where they seem almost untraceable from the musical surface. Such a survey reveals some consistent tendencies in Nono's compositional reasoning – tropes and threads that will emerge with some regularity: spatial, numerical, graphical, perspectival, polyphonic. While this is not a cognitive study, it would be interesting to explore further the spatial nature of Nono's thought, on the basis of ideas such as those of Peter Gärdenfors (2004) or David Danks (2014). Mirrors and echoes abound, across the full range of time and space from the rhythmic to the historical. Polyphony, the essential property of Western art music, is at the core of Nono's musical thought: simultaneity of directions, perspectives, times and possibilities. To these we must add the geography and urban landscape of Venice itself. Nono is a materialist also in his practice; however evolved his theory, he deals directly with the stuff in question, be it paper, performers, electronics or the sound in a room. In particular, we must point to his development of a space in which symbolic, representational, sonic and processual modes of thinking about and manipulating music are entirely congruent. There is, for example, nothing 'hybrid' about the late works combining score, electronics and intensive performer interaction. Nono's thought works across a canvas united by space and memory. His is a continuous, iterative process of inscription, reflection and remediation of which we are fortunate to have many of the traces.

'Was this the angriest composer who ever lived?' asked a headline in *The Daily Telegraph* a few years ago. While justly taking exception to this appalling banalisation, we must recognise

xxi

Introduction

that anger at inhumanity and injustice is indeed a major driving force in Nono's art. But it is rooted in a love for humanity – a faith, we have to call it – that is stronger still. There is no nihilism. Nono's engagement with politics is not for its own sake; politics is the socially constructed framework for confronting injustice. His faith in humanity is balanced by a faith in the transformative power of art. This he will rationalise from various theoretical perspectives – he constantly feels the need to do so, as he reflects uncompromisingly on his own role and practice – but it is rooted in personal experience. Similarly, his commitment to the Italian Communist Party is grounded in a particular historical moment of vision and resistance; Nono's adult life is coterminous with the post-war Italian Communist Party, the PCI. As an uncompromising materialist, however, his responses evolve with the situation in which he finds himself. His fundamental questions are straightforward: what are the conditions and materials of art music in our time, and what work should it do? In addressing them, Nono confronts doubt and paradox not as weakness but as part of common human experience.

There are some excellent films featuring Nono, largely made for television and hence available only sporadically, although excerpts are to be found online. Some contain documentary footage of performances or rehearsals, others incorporate interviews or, more rarely, talks by Nono. Particularly beautiful and instructive is Olivier Mille's *Luigi Nono Archipelago* (*Archipel Luigi Nono*) of 1988, in which the composer is interviewed as he walks around Venice. We hear both the intensity of this highly creative late phase and the wisdom of decades of experience, combined in love for his city and environment. An important preparatory exercise before reading any of his texts – including the translations offered here – is to listen to Nono's voice, irrespective of any language differences. The gentle urgency, the complex, fragmented, often polyphonic syntax, should be in the mind of any reader as they approach his thought. Sound – listening – is key to understanding Nono.

From Nono's instructions to performers in *Fragmente-Stille, an Diotima*, but perhaps to all who would listen:

> but many other moments, thoughts, silences 'songs'
> of other spaces, other skies
> to otherwise rediscover the possible, do not 'say farewell to hope'.

Notes

1   De Benedictis and Rizzardi, 2018.
2   'Altre possibilità di ascolto', 1987. LNI, p. 531.

1

PROLEGOMENA
A Venetian pre-biography

Many of the complex sources of Nono's musical thought are rooted in the musical history of his city, as will emerge from the chapters that follow. A brief survey of Nono's family background makes clear the extent to which important components of his thought relate to wider areas of Venetian artistic, intellectual and cultural history. There are two commemorative plaques on a facade on the Zattere, on the western edge of the main group of islands forming central Venice. The house looks out over the canal of Giudecca, where cruise ships now follow the path of earlier Venetian traders. It looks out across the island of Giudecca itself, across the lagoon and the Adriatic towards toward what were the liminal regions of European culture. Both plaques carry the name Luigi Nono.

At the end of the nineteenth century, a cultured Venetian would have had no difficulty in identifying Luigi Nono, the composer's grandfather, as one of the city's foremost representatives of Italian *verismo* painting, as a widely appreciated painter of the landscape and people of the Veneto, and a pillar of the Venetian cultural establishment. The family name derives from their feudal landownership in Santa Maria di Non, a small rural parish in the diocese of Padova. Luigi senior's father, Francesco, was born in Bergamo, nearer Milan than Venice. He followed in the steps of his own father, a customs collector on the western border of the ex-Venetian republic, which had been an Austrian possession since the downfall of Napoleon. As Bergamo was incorporated into the new Cisalpina, the family moved back to Venice in 1849, eventually to Fusina, the small port on the mainland from where the newly constructed railway bridge first connected the city to the mainland. Urbano, the seventh of thirteen children, was born on San Giorgio Maggiore in 1849 and would become a renowned sculptor.[1] Luigi, the eighth, was born in Fusina the next year.[2] As a keen observer of natural phenomena, Francesco would set down his meditations in the form of dialogues. He would also share his experiences with his children; the sensitivity of the young Luigi to the dynamics of natural phenomena was already in evidence on these excursions:

> But one of them [Luigi], more serious and by nature meditative, made me observe how the water of the sea threw waves up onto the beach; as they receded they did not merge back into the resurging water but slid underneath, sticking to the seabed.[3]

In 1865, Luigi went to study at the 'Imperial and Royal' *Accademia di Belli Arti* in Venice, where his peers included Giacomo Favretti and Guglielmo Ciardi, likewise to achieve

Prolegomena: a Venetian pre-biography

prominence in Venetian painting of the late nineteenth century. One of the leading critics and spokesmen for the cultural identity of the new Italy was Camillo Boito (1836–1914), brother of Arrigo, the librettist for Verdi's late Shakespearean works. In reviewing the graduation exhibition of the Accademia in 1871, Boito described a painting by Nono:

> Something about that little work suggested that this architectonic scene – serious, dry, painted and repainted a hundred times – was not only copied by the artist but really felt; something bespoke an uncommon inventiveness in this novice Luigi Nono.[4]

Continuing Austrian domination meant that artistic education in Venice was somewhat isolated from developments elsewhere in Italy, particularly the *verismo* or realism developing in Tuscany and Naples as a reaction to earlier neoclassicism.[5] The emergent ideas of its principal exponents the *macchiaioli* combined a concern with Italian reality and history with a quasi-scientific approach to understanding light, colour and spatial relationships.[6] The rapid unification of Italy through the 1850s provided a conduit for the rapid spread of such discussions, but the Veneto would not join until ceded by Austria after the Austro-Prussian war of 1866. Luigi Nono adopted such modern ideas immediately upon leaving the Accademia. The stippled light and colour of *La sorgente del Gorgazzo* (1872) represent a mature assimilation of macchiaioli technique; here he comes closest to the innovations of his French contemporaries. In 1872 he returned to the family home, now in the town of Salice between sea and mountain in the Venetian hinterland. His younger brother Igenio, a talented musician, drowned in the river running below the walls of the house. The experiences of these years provided subject matter for much of his subsequent work: the landscape and people of the Veneto, the intimate sorrow of family suffering. We can again turn to Boito for a contemporary impression of Nono's mature style; he described Nono's *Convalescenza* in a review of an exhibition at the Brera in Milan in 1874:

> it seems that he wants to embrace figures, perspectives, landscapes, everything that is true, because he feels that to represent the pews of a church, the trees of a field, the faces of men and a family scene, it is necessary only to see truly and to reproduce exactly.
>
> But in order to see truly his vision is dry; and in order to reproduce exactly his painting is often hard. [. . .] his paintings are like a verbal process, an inventory; in Nono there is something of the instructing judge or the notary. [. . .] and while imitation can only produce pretentious, empty painting, from this rigorous study of nature may perhaps be born a modern painting, a source of new life.[7]

Such a contemporary voice is important in understanding the earlier Luigi Nono's painting in its cultural and historical context; modernist critics of the turn of the century would cease to distinguish finely observed sentiment from banal sentimentality in their rejection of both. Boito's analysis identifies properties which, from a modern critic, could only remain projection or conjecture. His comments point to the aesthetic detachment that allows human and natural phenomena to be portrayed in their complexity. In this mediation of fine observation and profound reflection through refined technique, with human and natural dynamics subjected to the same critical analysis, we see crucial characteristics of the later composer. In the work of both artists an understanding of the irresolvable tensions of humanity, unafraid of the cruel, is transcended by the precision of its mapping to the aesthetic. Boito also notes the didactic, polemical potential of this rigorous unsentimental observation of human states. Throughout the

Prolegomena: a Venetian pre-biography

painter's life commentators would refer to the moral properties of his work; this is perhaps the quality that allowed him to resist fashion but also advances in artistic thought. While its nineteenth-century connotations exclude the term from the various discourses with which Nono the composer would later be associated, morality in its broader sense is a central thread of his art. For both grandfather and grandson, historical, social and technical factors inform their responsibility to search for artistic integrity.

Luigi Nono senior's career blossomed in the new Italy as his work enjoyed both critical and commercial success. That he was not unaware of the political implications of his work is suggested by the fact that his *Fanfara dei granatieri* (1875) – a virtual scene compounded of military parades witnessed at Milan in 1874, his brother's uniform and his native pre-Alpine landscape – remained hidden in a chest until his death despite its subsequent popularity.[8] In 1888, Luigi married the Contessina Rina Pruili Bon (1865–1920) whose portrait he had painted two years earlier, thereby entering the circle of Venetian patrician aristocracy; her family had provided the city with three doges.[9] They moved into the new house on the Zattere, where, according to his son Mario, 'he listened to the bells across the waves from Sant'Eufemia della Giudecca'.[10]

Nono's wider reputation was founded on *Refugium peccatorum* (1883),[11] one of a long-term series of paintings of a woman praying before the Madonna on the quayside at Chioggia. In the others she holds a baby and we see the full statue. In this work she is alone, kneeling in front of a statue of which we see only the base. The name of the painting is the only hint as to the source of her grief, but more importantly the object of her supplication is not visible. In the unwilled act of imagining this object, the viewer is made complicit not only in her grief but in her faith and its uncertainties. The figure of Maria is likewise out of sight in *Ave Maria* (1892). Admirers of *Refugium peccatorum* included a young D'Annunzio and the new King Umberto. Its impact was such that it inspired a novella and even a melodrama by the historical dramatist Luigi Sugana and composer Ausonio De Lorenzi-Fabris, both Venetian.[12]

In 1899 Luigi was himself appointed to the Accademia as professor of painting, moving his teaching to Bologna while Venice became a front-line city during the First World War. Part of the generation that instigated the Biennale di Venezia, his *Il funerale di un bambino*, three years in the painting, was exhibited there in 1897 and later bought by the representative of Czar Nicholas. The fourth Biennale of 1901 dedicated an entire room to twenty-five of his paintings, but perhaps his later development was inhibited by being identified so explicitly with Venetian style of a certain period and with 'exhibition' painting. His subsequent fame was such that there are streets named for him in Venice, Salice and Milan.[13] Remarks made in a memorial speech the year after his death in 1918 by his friend the politician Pompeo Molmenti are telling:

> In art as in life, Nono always demonstrated the direction of his thought: he didn't strike deals, never descended to vulgar compromise [. . .] His vision of art was certainly hard-wrought; but facility is often synonymous with lightness, and you barely needed to know him or see him to understand the composure and unity of his life.[14]

The interconnectedness of Venetian cultural life is illustrated by the fact that the central figure in one of Nono's most popular and sunniest paintings – the young man relaxing in a boat in *La sorgente del Gorgazzo* – is his fellow student Luigi Rosa, to become the father-in-law of the future composer's mentor Gian Francesco Malipiero. His circle also included Giovanni Tabaldini, director of the *Capella Marciana* (the choir of San Marco), and Ermanino Wolf Ferrari, composer and director of the *Liceo Musicale* (later the conservatory). However unfashionable his painting would become in the context of innovations elsewhere, Nono's

Prolegomena: a Venetian pre-biography

place at the centre of Venetian cultural life was assured. He was president of the *Circolo Artistico Veneziano*, the most prestigious group of amateur painters who exhibited annually. More significantly, he was a member of the city's *Consiglio Accademico*, the committee responsible for decisions concerning planning and conservation. As such, he was party to the decision to rebuild the collapsed campanile of San Marco 'dov'era e com'era' ('where it was and as it was') in 1902.[15] He must therefore have been very aware of the discussions that had been central to Venetian civic life since the time of Ruskin and the arrival of modern tourism with the railway – the tension between a view of the city as the repository of its historical values and the need for continual self-renewal. These are at the heart of the aesthetic discourse within which the ideas of the younger Luigi would develop. In his music the twin obligations to past and future do not compete; their possible realities define a space in which he seeks to identify a present.

Mario, the composer's father, was born to Luigi and Rina in 1890. In 1921 he married Maria Manetti – again from a historic noble family, this time Florentine. Trained as an engineer, Mario was to become chief surveyor for the *Cassa di Risparmio di Venezia*, the city's major bank. Like his father, he took his civic responsibilities very seriously. He became chairman of the city's environment committee, redistributing the original lighting from St Mark's Square around the city and personally refitting the ubiquitous transparent lamps with their original coloured glasses. He had trees planted to obscure the new social housing on the island of Sacca Fisola, in front of the family home, which he considered alien to the architecture of Venice. These acts bespeak a certain conservatism to which the composer's own recollections of his father attest. Continuing to live in the home in which he had grown up, still surrounded by the late nineteenth-century art which was his father's world, Mario's life – that of the high bourgeois cultured professional – seems to have been something of an attempt to resist the passage of time.[16]

Much of the above detail comes from a memoire of his father written by Mario for his children Rina and Luigi after his own retirement in 1963.[17] This text conveys a deep and affectionate understanding of the painter and his milieu, but also an awareness that such understanding may be disappearing and a profound nostalgia for the cultural world of fin-de-siècle Venice. As well as eulogising the older Luigi and his work and describing in lively detail the place and moment he loved – the artists gathering in the Caffé degli Artisti or Caffé Giacomuzzi, now ice-cream parlour and gift shop respectively, he laments – it is impossible not to read into this text a litany of barely coded messages to his own artist son. Mario emphasises his father's 'participation in a life that was artistic and intellectual, but never political.'[18] Discussions with his peers were often heated, but 'avoided all traces of resentment, were never rancorous.'[19] His religious observance was sufficient to be noted for its lack of rigidity, although he sadly died 'without the supreme comfort of an Italy victorious and saved.'[20] The wise nobleman who had bought Luigi's painting for the Russian court, on the other hand, was 'murdered by the Bolsheviks along with the Royal family', the death of the Czarevich echoing the painting's very subject. His work was 'always fed by a breath of poetry and a wave of feeling.'[21] Above all, the art of Mario's father was 'characterised by a candid sincerity, without hermetic abstruseness.'[22] In this last observation we sense perhaps not only loss but something of the pain of alienation for a father who cannot find a way to his son's art. Faced with the evidence of professional success, Mario would later come to accept his son as a composer, but as a music lover steeped in the nineteenth century it is doubtful that he ever heard Luigi's music as other than difficult.

In many ways, Boito's contemporary interpretation of Luigi Nono's painting is more modern than that of Mario, and reveals more parallels with the work of the later composer. Boito himself was an architect and artist of both aspiration and accomplishment. The understanding

Prolegomena: a Venetian pre-biography

of beauty through the artist's *process* is an idea that runs throughout the practice and theory of Venetian art. Vasari noted Giorgione's exploitation of the drying-time of oil paint as a new dimension of creativity. Among Venetian painters of Luigi Nono's generation, the artist's studio, palette and paintbox were popular self-reflective subjects. The term *pittoresco*, later devalued as signifying the decorous or superficial, was introduced by the theorist Boschini in 1660 to describe the painterly qualities specifically of Venetian art: the presence of the artist's hand, the traces of his interaction with his materials.[23]

In Venetian music, the practical relationship between composer and work similarly becomes part of its theoretical context. Banchieri, a younger contemporary of Zarlino – the towering figure of late sixteenth-century Venetian theory – discusses aspects of composition beyond the rules of counterpoint.[24] His book is called *La Cartella Musicale* – the erasable tablet for music, the two-dimensional space within which musical calculations are made – and he considers the implications of printing for the practice and role of the composer. Indeed, Banchieri and his comic masterpieces would become important for Nono at the very moment when his compositional practice seemed farthest from tradition. A century and a half later, Tartini's rationalisation of tonal harmony is based not on abstract laws of nature, like that of Rameau, but on his own cognitive experience. He derives tonal principles from the *third sound*, the resultant tone he hears in his own head as a product of each interval.[25] Zarlino's sense of music theory as a historical construct, Banchieri's awareness of the spatial nature of musical reasoning, Tartini's close critical listening to the very phenomenon of musical sound and even Vivaldi's flickering between the vulgar and the sublime are instances of a transcendental pragmatism peculiar to Venetian culture. Criticism of the Biennale is still today polarised between the charge of indulgent aesthetic abstraction and that of being a glorified shop front. Nono's leading role in protests against the Biennale in 1968 is characteristic of his ambivalent relationship with the cultural life of the city. That enlightenment thought had relatively little transforming power in Venice reflects less a lack of intellectual activity – despite having reached a state of post-decadent torpor in the late eighteenth century – than its already being in an advanced state of high bourgeois free-market mercantilism, of cosmopolitanism and vested interest. She has always accepted many faiths but taken instructions from none, as her indifference to repeated excommunication demonstrated. A radical independence of thought in Venice and the Veneto rings through to the present, to thinkers such as Massimo Cacciari and Antonio Negri. A complex relationship with German-speaking culture is also characteristically Venetian. It would inform Nono's trajectory in many respects, above all through Schönberg, from whom Nono said he learned to 'think musically'.[26]

Pensiero musicale – musical thought – is a term much easier to use in Italian than in English. Nono's frequent use of the term is no linguistic glibness, however; he uses it with profound respect when referring to Schönberg, to Dallapiccola and to Maderna. His work could be seen as a meditation on the very nature of musical thought: a project inherent in his first relationships with music, which finds voice in his work with Maderna and which continues as a research project of visionary courage and rigorous honesty. His own mind and experience constitute its locus and material. Such a project is on one hand an intensely practical undertaking; on the other, it embodies a notion of the artist as hero, with all the pitfalls and paradoxes thus implied. This book will argue that a vital property of Nono's musical thought is precisely that it takes place within an entirely musical domain, largely free from arbitrary mappings or extraneous conceits. The vast network of associations is mediated by an essentially composerly activity. The intense and historically theoretically grounded formal structures at the heart of his work generally guard against the need for formalism and free his imagination. Nono's sketches show a continuous alertness to the risks, however – a self-monitoring that for him is clearly one with

Prolegomena: a Venetian pre-biography

a conscious resistance to dogma of all kinds. As in political thought, the coherent implementation of principle without resorting to dogma or betraying history is a heroic challenge; this is perhaps the key to Nono's poetics and practice.

Other domains facilitate representation and experimentation, but the time-based architecture of music does not allow for the scaling or sketching possible in visual arts. Despite the central role of graphical representation and textual analysis in his practice, Nono resists the mapping of reasoning from other domains on to music. Decisions are musical decisions, not graphical, theoretical, architectural or metaphorical. At the same time, this autonomy is what allows his work to resonate richly with other modes of meaning: political, cultural, musical or personal. His practice is, above all, the active instrument of a warm and intense humanism, with all its social and personal implications. As in politics, the striving for integrity is fraught with difficulties, frictions and paradoxes; coherent long-term concepts have to be reconciled with responses to events and circumstances. This activity is itself a physiological process, however. Part of the process of mediation is its own embodiment. The cyclic, iterative process of externalisation and remediation is one of mental prosthesis, of technology, whether the technology is wax, paper, magnetic tape or computer. The mode of inscription of musical material – to call it notation would be too reductive – determines the operations that can subsequently be performed. Inscription–notation–manipulation–reasoning–imagining are different metaphors for an indivisible process. The act of inscription is also one of labelling. Material becomes material, it develops a degree of autonomy, at the moment it is externalised and detaches itself physically from the composer. Nono will refer to the workshop environment of the early Venetian masters; craft and community are continuous threads through his own creative process.

In Nono's case, the activity of composition has a major graphical–spatial component from the outset. Space is important to his understanding of sound, as will become clear later, but also to the process of construction. Given the above account, one might be tempted to relate the pages of spontaneous invention to his grandfather, those of painstaking draughtsmanship to his father. To describe the thousands of pages of work as *sketches* suggests something rough, approximate, as yet undefined. Rather, they are both the locus and the instruments of thought. From the beginning, multiple colours increase the dimensionality of the working space, which usually evolves simultaneously on large sheets of paper of two kinds: in diagrams, tables and words, and in music notation. Initial ideas, pre-compositional workings, drafts and fair copy exist for most works. At the conclusion of each project he would bundle the materials together. Broad, marker-pen handwriting suggests that much later in life Nono went through materials that had escaped this process, associating them with particular projects. He later brings operations from the recording studio to his desk, cutting and splicing paper like magnetic tape. Early on, he establishes a sequence of relationships with his material – designing and spinning, weaving, cutting, assembling and finishing – which will provide a technical sureness at moments when compositional or personal circumstances lead him into difficulties.

It is not surprising that the wider environment in which Nono grew up was also rich with connections to the visual and spatial arts. In his last and fullest autobiographical interview, for instance, he refers to his youthful experiences at the gallery *Il Cavallino*.[27] Two individuals in particular must be identified as having a major influence not only on Nono's thought but on his working practice, its spatiality and his sense of the significance of the act of inscription: the painter Emilio Vedova (1919–2006) and the architect Carlo Scarpa (1906–78). Both were products of the Accademia, where Nono's grandfather had studied and taught, and where Vedova would himself become professor.[28] These spaces of inscription and construction are quite contiguous with Zarlino's musico–cosmological space, Gabrieli's space of sound and

Prolegomena: a Venetian pre-biography

Banchieri's lively depiction of social spaces. To this many-dimensional spatiality, Nono's grandfather contributes the spaces of human activity and sensibility, of nature and of their city. Importantly, there is no contradiction between the last two: there is nothing futurist in Nono's use of technology, nothing automated about his compositional process. Given his apprenticeship in pre-classical polyphony, Nono naturally generates and approaches material in terms of polyphonic proliferation in a space not only of pitch and time but also of colour, movement and meaning. He weaves *tessuti* – fabrics – which retain the traces of this work, however sophisticated and removed from their origins they become. The weaving of rich fabrics is one of the foundations of Venetian wealth and culture, and Fortuny's new factory faced the Nono home directly across the canal. Meanwhile, through the same pre-war years the area of Porto Marghera, clearly visible on the southern horizon from Zattere, was being developed into one of Italy's largest industrial centres. Its petro-chemical works would be the focus of much of Nono's later political activity.

Place is everywhere in Nono's music. Still, in the late *La lontananza* we hear the sounds of the recording studio itself. Of Venice we hear not only the theatres and churches and their music, but appearance and disappearance, the disorienting topography of the city, sound as it travels across water and reflects from buildings in ..... *sofferte onde serene ...* or even as it is diffused through the Adriatic fog (masquerading as the Danube) in *Post-prae-ludium n. 1 per Donau*. Nono's very home occupies a liminal position between cultural sophistication and implacable nature, between water and a city that is itself an interface between east and west. Venice is a city where 'soundwalking' has sense, where one can navigate by sound alone; a polyphony of intersecting alleys, cross-cut acoustics, sudden state changes of piazza, canal or sea, punctuated by soundmarks of church, café or ship. Echo, resonance and reverberation will become important structuring metaphors in Nono's later technique.[29]

Time, the natural complement to space, is the other parameter along which Nono's work can be uniquely characterised. There is a contiguity between the awareness of history that informs all of the elements that nourish the evolution of his thought, and his sense of *musical* development, the way in which one musical idea or event succeeds or coincides with another. Even the most complex structures are dramatic, never symphonic. In Italian, and particularly Venetian culture, music was (and to a great extent remains) primarily a theatrical experience. Italy was left largely untouched by the wave of concert hall building that swept Europe in the later nineteenth century, and they remain the exception. The theatre is therefore the natural arena and model for musical thought. Indeed Baars' view of a theatre of consciousness, with its actors, lights, scripts, scenery and audience, would invite a full theoretical development.[30] The implicit suggestion of Jürg Stenzl's early monograph is that Nono's work all relates to his music theatre, explicitly or not.[31] Nono's *azione scenica* – a concept which evolves throughout his work – is a space for the disposition of musical and extra-musical ideas (political, aesthetic), a locus for their interaction or simultaneity and for their encounter with society. Despite his Marxist affiliations, a non-dialectical understanding of progress runs through his thought – radical, courageous and prophetic in a pre-postmodern world. This is the property that produced such transformative resonance in his encounter with the thought of Massimo Cacciari in the 1970s and beyond. It can be traced on multiple levels. It has roots in the pre-classical music theory in which Nono's work is grounded. It relates to the non-aligned narrative of Venetian cultural history, in particular the phase-shifted relationship to enlightenment thought and historical events. It embraces Jewish, East European and Russian thought. Finally, on a personal level it is the inevitable result of a youth lived in denial of the present, under fascism. This non-dialectical sense of progress generates a productive friction when it encounters the standard line

Prolegomena: a Venetian pre-biography

of communism. The relatively short shrift given to his father and grandfather in Nono's later autobiographical reflections likewise reflects personal and political frictions and contradictions, and perhaps his acute awareness of their central place in his own artistic process.

Notes

1　His work included a statue of Manin in Florence and one of Calvi in Pieve di Cadore, destroyed by the Austrians in the First World War. Like his brother, he eventually taught at the Accademia in Venice. He died in 1925.

2　An authoritative concise biography and thorough bibliography are contained in Pavanello and Stringa, 2004, pp. 410–12. They also reproduce several of his major paintings.

3　Nono M., 1990, p. 13.

4　Nono M., 1990, p. 18.

5　The most recent attempted insurrection was that led by Manin in 1848. A powerful image from the history of the Veneto is that of the posters listing interdictions of the Austrian occupation in the 1840s and those of the German occupation a century later; they are almost identical. Today, however, a casual conversation in any café in the Veneto as to whether the region would prefer to be linked administratively to Rome or Austria will not produce the unequivocal opinion one might imagine. This political ambivalence reflects the profound pragmatism that runs through Venetian culture.

6　The name derives from *macchia* or stain, a term proudly appropriated from early disparaging descriptions of their painterly technique.

7　Nono M., 1990, pp. 21–2.

8　Having been rediscovered, it was seen by King Vittorio Emmanuele III, who questioned the accuracy of the weapons depicted.

9　The family also built the Palazzo Priuli-Bon – later known as Palazzo Dandolo – a Gothic palace of the fifteenth century on the Grand Canal near San Stae.

10　Nono M., 1990, p. 47.

11　Displayed in the Galleria Nazionale d'Arte Moderna, Rome.

12　Mario Nono tells us that the melodrama failed to convey an appropriate gravitas. An unfortunate instance of overacting during a love duet left the audience at the Teatro Malibran helpless with laughter (Nono M., 1990, p. 36).

13　The small town of Sacile, on the edge of the Venetian plain at the foot of the Dolomites, still has an active *Circolo Artistico Luigi Nono*.

14　Nono M., 1990, pp. 80–1.

15　In inspecting the works, he lamented the cultural and technical poverty of modern builders and pointed out errors in the reconstruction of the steps of the campanile that reduced the available sitting-place for Venetians.

16　Indeed, as Nuria Schoenberg-Nono has pointed out in conversation, his buying back of his father's work may have inhibited its wider appreciation.

17　Published privately by Rina and Luigi in 1990, fifteen years after their father's death.

18　Nono M., 1990, p. 31.

19　Nono M., 1990, p. 32.

20　Nono M., 1990, p. 80.

21　Nono M., 1990, p. 93.

22　Nono M., 1990, p. 93.

23　Boschini, 1660. Discussed in detail in Sohm, 1991.

24　Banchieri, 1601.

25　Tartini, 1767.

26　Nono, 1980.

27　*Il Cavallino* continued to be influential. It was the first gallery to mount an exhibition of video art.

28　Having studied *belle arti* rather than architecture and despite his reputation and output, Scarpa was only accepted as an architect in professional terms reluctantly and late in life.

29　Geiger and Janke, 2015, explore the notion of Venice as 'the composed city' in Nono's music.

30　Baars, 1997.

31　Stenzl, 1998.

2

ACCELERATED LEARNING
Years of study, 1942–50

A classical education

Every time I hear music, whether in my imagination or through my senses, I begin anew to question all that I know, all that I am.[1] These are the first words that Nono underlined in his copy of Leibowitz's *Schoenberg and his School*, the book that also contains the material for his first mature work, *Variazioni canoniche sulla serie dell'op. 41 di Arnold Schönberg*. This small action typifies the acuity with which he identified and assimilated key ideas and techniques and used them to give form and fuel to his own emerging identity as a musician. Nono's mature working practice, his views of the role of the composer and his ceaseless questioning have their roots in the relationships formed in this process. His works are snapshots of a continuous personal and musical evolution. Nono would often speak of *musical thought* as a distinct mode of human activity, one that he was happy to describe but never define. This chapter will attempt to locate the origins of some of the components of this ethos.

Nono later described his study of music as having begun with his purchase of Rimsky-Korsakov's *Treatise on Harmony* during his time as a law student at the University of Padova.[2] Emerging from Zanibon's music shop in its prominent location on the *Piazza dei Signori* (under fascism the *Piazza Unità d'Italia*), he would have been immediately confronted with the lion of St Mark and the Palazzo del Capitano, the symbols of that Venetian cultural and political authority that would ground and condition his own musical evolution. His development from that moment to the composition of his first major work, performed at Darmstadt in 1950, traces an exponential trajectory; three years or so to his first discussions of composition with Bruno Maderna, and barely another four to the individual and assured technique of *Variazioni canoniche*, major components of which would remain central to his compositional process for forty years. The very efficiency of this path is remarkable, the result of his own clarity of thought and purpose, but also the product of a series of circumstances and encounters with ideas and individuals – with political and musical theory and with artists such as Malipiero, Dallapiccola, Maderna, Ungaretti and Scherchen. Personal relationships and social reality are woven into the fabric of Nono's music at a fundamental level. The loss of Malipiero, Dallapiccola, and Maderna would later be a major factor in the transformation of the very ontology of Nono's music from the mid-1970s.

There is a degree of revisionism in Nono's self retelling, however. On both personal and cultural planes, the advantages of high bourgeois existence became difficult to reconcile with

Accelerated learning: years of study, 1942–50

his mature ideas about art, artist and society. Only in later interviews is there a sense of acknowledgement of the important roles of family and society in his development. In this, there is perhaps a mirror of his father's reluctance to acknowledge the future.

Luigi was born to Mario and Maria on 29 January 1924. His sister Rina had been born two years earlier. Early piano lessons seem to have been the practice of a highly cultured household rather than a response to precocious musical talent. His teacher was a family friend who moved away after a couple of years, at which point young Luigi – Gigi to all who knew him then and after – was already bored with the exercises. He seems to have preferred football, an undertaking with its own technical challenges whether avoiding the water on the Zattere or windows in the campi behind.[3] As well as paintings, Mario also brought a constant flow of new books into the home, the foundation of Nono's own enormous library. This was the moment when Italian editors such as Giulio Einaudi began their project of internationalising Italian culture by translating foreign literature and thought. Nono's lifelong continuing of his father's accumulation of books began already in his teenage years. Russian authors were a particular fascination, particularly those of the time of the revolution, and Russian writing, cinema and theatre remained central interests. In the light of his later work, it is not difficult to see how their balance of social reality and detachment, direct emotion and abstract construction would have instinctively appealed to him. Ivanov and Zoshenko were in the house, and Nono seems to have bought Russian writers extensively, including Gogol's *Dead Souls* and poets such as Mayakovsky and Pasternak. He would later mention the Serapion brothers, Lev Lunc and Sergei Esenin.[4] The former are particularly significant; Nono bought Yevgeny Zamyatin's *Islanders*, in which the protagonist finds himself caught between the false seduction of individual expression and the totalitarian standardisation and mechanisation of society and culture.[5] Russian thought and approaches to the making of art would play a major role through Nono's work; visionary avant-gardism and the politicisation of the personal play their part, but Venice has also long been the Western outpost of Orthodox Christianity.

Nono's father was also an avid collector of gramophone records, the sound of which filled the house. Nono would remember particularly Mussorgsky, Wagner, Toscanini's recordings of Beethoven and Mengelberg's of Mahler's *Adagietto*.[6] His parents performed at their musical evenings; Mario played the piano, his wife was a fine soprano. Their rendition of *Boris Godunov* was an early memory for Nono, and his mother's copy of songs by Wolf would find its way back on to his desk much later in his life. They were regular visitors to *La Fenice*. As Pierluigi Petrobelli has pointed out, theatre and music are to a significant extent synonymous in Italian culture of the nineteenth and early twentieth centuries.[7] The dramatic *space* of music, its stretching out into wider social issues and behaviours, and the notion of music as intrinsically theatrical may have appeared radical in the context of avant-garde absolutism. In terms of Nono's personal experience and cultural background, they are perfectly natural.

Contemporary accounts depict Nono's father as being a man of the nineteenth century; this would be brought into relief by the friction of Mario's incomprehension of his son's chosen path. The stern severity of Nono's father was balanced by the warm indulgence of his mother. Summers – uncomfortable in Venice – were spent under a quite different regime at the Manetti family villa in Limena, in the flat agricultural area just north of Padova.[8] Here Gigi, Rina, their friends and cousins could play with the local children, walk and ride bicycles in the country and listen to popular dance music. In this climate of relaxation and rurality Nono could also listen to the socialist opinions of the Manetti family – anti-fascist views perhaps more easily expressed away from the city in this period of increasing repression.

Secondary education at the *Liceo Marco Polo*, a classical grammar school, was a diet of Latin, Greek, Italian, literature and history, as well as mathematics and science. It brought Nono into

Accelerated learning: years of study, 1942–50

contact with a wider social and cultural circle that would sustain him through the years of war and his study at university. The home of his school companions Luigi and Giovanni Vespignani provided another alternative domestic environment. Their father Arcangelo, a leading radiologist, was also a socialist – a dangerous path at the time – and keenly interested in cultural life. The Vespignani household was therefore a stimulating venue for political and artistic discussion, for listening to a wide range of music and meeting artists. Listening included an early recording of Monteverdi's *Orfeo*; after the war the company went to hear Schönberg's *A Survivor from Warsaw* in the Venice Festival of 1950. An increasing number of artists were gravitating to the strange confusion of wartime Venice, and Vespignani's house became something of a gathering place. There, Nono encountered artists of a previous generation including the sculptor Arturo Martini (1889–1947), once a student of Nono's uncle Urbano at the Accademia. Martini had recently turned to painting having decided that sculpture was a dead art.[9] He also met writer and some-time composer Massimo Bontempelli (1878–1960), an associate of Pirandello, who was writing a book on Malipiero.[10]

Other members of the circle included another of Nono's nearby friends, Carlo Berghinz, who introduced him to architect Carlo Scarpa, a lifelong source of inspiration. Scarpa redefined the relationship between architect, materials, artisan and design process. A close relationship between the texture and tactility of materials and large-scale form reflects his early work in design. The discontinuities of his own style allowed Scarpa to incorporate historic elements in his restorations; his work with exhibitions, museums and monuments represents a challenge to conventional architectural intervention. He used paper thick enough to retain the traces of all the work done on a particular drawing; indeed, Scarpa would reject out of hand students' graduation projects presented on the wrong paper. The artist is thus constantly aware that the result is a surface trace of a dynamical, multidimensional process and of the constant interaction between thought and materials. Nono's own design process has much in common. From *Variazioni canoniche* to the final works, Nono's development and organisation of materials is such that they remain transparent to him throughout the compositional process, allowing him to take architectonic decisions at multiple levels. Painter Emilio Vedova, five years Nono's senior, already had an established reputation when they met in 1942. His early work took as its starting point the spatial dynamics of Venetian churches and painting. By the 1940s, figure was transformed into abstract, neo-baroque forms of energy, personal and natural. His paintings had become improvised explorations of space, light and the act and gesture of inscription. Vedova and Nono developed a close and occasionally intense relationship. Their collaboration on various projects over the next forty years is well documented, but their awareness of each other's working practice represents a more fundamental exchange of ideas.[11] By the time of their work on *Prometeo*, forty years later, both space and colour would become part of Nono's compositional material, mapped directly from his own working process.

An emerging interest in music was also facilitated by the second husband of Nono's paternal grandmother, Rina. Luigi Marangoni, as the architect responsible for the fabric of the basilica of San Marco, introduced him to the choirmaster and gave him access to the music library. Even in a religious context music was closely associated with theatrical occasions, whether the Christmas masses at San Marco or the rites of the Armenian Church. Nono returned to piano lessons and began to practise avidly, as all those who remember this period attest, though there are no traces of compositional activity at this early stage. Other diversions included sailing in the lagoon with Marangoni, Berghinz or Francesco Rossi, the teacher of Greek at the Liceo. Greek appealed to Nono much more than Latin or Dante, partly because of Rossi's socialism and charismatic teaching, but perhaps also because of a natural reaction to the Fascist annexing of Italian culture and history.

Accelerated learning: years of study, 1942–50

Nono's decision to read Law at the University of Padova was the result of paternal pressure, an extraordinary resistance to the possibility of making a living as an artist, given Mario's own father's background and preoccupations. Horror in the face of contemporary reality and incomprehension when confronted with contemporary art led Mario to insist on a path of social, economic and professional solidity for his son. The study of Law must also be understood as the continuation of a classical education within a particular social milieu, rather than the expression of any professional intention. From the autumn of 1942 – through the last year of fascism, occupation, near civil war, liberation and reconstruction – Nono pursued a very full legal curriculum,[12] making the short journey from Venice by train when necessary, despite increasingly regular interruptions from allied bombing.[13] In order to satisfy his father and return his full concentration to music as soon as possible, he clearly made a decision to conclude his studies in the most rapid, energy-efficient way, taking full advantage of wartime academic confusion. *Cultura militare* was a temporary addition to the list of obligatory subjects both at the Liceo and during his first year at university. The university itself was responsible for ensuring that students were registered for military service. A medical crisis in later teenage precluded the physical tests that were part of the fascist *maturità* on leaving school. The support of Vespignani was probably instrumental in the acknowledgement of this by a military doctor when Nono reached the conscription age of 20, and he was allowed to continue with his studies as medically unfit for service.[14] The university authorities required full declaration of family background every year. The evolution of Nono's description of his grandfather from 'member of the Commission of Fine Arts of the City of Venice' to 'painter' – as ambiguous in Italian as it is in English – perhaps reflects an emerging discomfort with the bourgeois connotations of his own chosen path.[15]

The ethos and atmosphere of intellectual independence and responsibility at the University of Padova in those years were largely the product of the leadership of the Rector Concetto Marchesi (1878–1957) and Prorector Egidio Meneghetti (1892–1961). Marchesi's works on Tacitus and Seneca had become handbooks of non-conformism.[16] He refused to cooperate with the fascists on behalf of the university and eventually had to go into hiding, remaining a leading organiser of resistance activities until the end of the war. Nono, at the beginning of his second year, was doubtless aware of Marchesi's departing appeal to the students which they themselves distributed, and it is unthinkable that he would have been unaffected.[17] With his friend Carlo Berghinz, he was assisting with the clandestine distribution of resistance newspaper, a task not without risk. *Fedeltà d'Italia* was produced by a resistance group of which his later brother-in-law Albano Pivato was part. It was printed on an illegal duplicating machine in the office of Berghinz's father in the top floor of the *Adriatica* building on the Zattere, the remainder of which was occupied by the Germans. They had their friend Ennio Gallo bring a copy of Marchesi's speech from Padova to be published in the paper. Marchesi's successor, poet and pharmacologist Meneghetti, was decorated hero of the First World War who dedicated himself wholly to fighting fascism after losing his family in the Second World War.[18] He was arrested in January 1945 while planning a public broadcast of university resistance to fascism, and survived months in a concentration camp. Uniquely, the university itself was awarded the gold medal for military valour.[19]

Discussion in the Faculty of Law centred on the need to create a new legal structure rooted in historical principles to guarantee individual, social and democratic freedoms. Nono's teacher of the Philosophy of Law was Norberto Bobbio (1909–2004), active in anti-fascist circles and himself arrested in 1943. Bobbio describes the impact of this moment at the beginning of his autobiography:

Accelerated learning: years of study, 1942–50

The twenty months between 8 September 1943 and 25 April 1945 formed a period in our lives that involved us in events far bigger then ourselves. Fascism had forced us to disregard politics, and then suddenly we found ourselves compelled to take part in politics in the exceptional circumstances provided by German occupation and the War of Liberation, for what might be called moral reasons. Our lives were turned upside down. We all encountered painful incidents: fear, flight, arrest, imprisonment and the loss of people dear to us. Afterwards we were no longer what we had been before. Our lives had been cut into two parts: a 'before' and an 'after'. . .[20]

Bobbio, a charismatic and influential participant in Italian public life to the end of the century,[21] seems to have made a lasting impression on his student.[22] Many of his ideas run through Italian socialist intellectual and political discourse for the next half-century. In Nono's case, they informed his development as an artist from the very moment when he began to consider such a path. Views of the fundamental relationship of liberty and responsibility, the role of intellectual labour and a faith in internationalism were expressed fearlessly in Bobbio's lectures, and subtend Nono's own intellectual activity from the outset. 'Only those of us who were present can understand how great was Bobbio's courage. [. . .] . It would have taken just one informant for him to have been liquidated', recalled a fellow student. [23] Bobbio was released with the fall of Mussolini, and during Nono's studies he was both a member of the resistance in the *Partito d'Azione*[24] and working on his first major book,[25] his only foray into existentialism and a critique of 'academic and irrational philosophy'.[26] He organised resistance activities from the Faculty of Law itself, which he described as a 'free zone'.[27] A significant contributor to the debate that produced the new Italian constitution in 1946, Bobbio saw resistance not just as a circumstantial necessity but as a vital and continuing part of a healthy civic and cultural life – a mode of cultural behaviour which would safeguard the distribution of power: 'unfinished or interrupted resistance serves to indicate an ideal goal, not to prescribe a result'.[28]

His ideas remain at the centre of public discourses in which Nono would increasingly participate, particularly in the political turbulence of the 1970s.[29] Bobbio's much-quoted observation that the responsibility of culture is to seek questions not answers and his description of intellectuals as 'clerics of doubt'[30] inform Nono's thinking through to his explicit involvement with the question-based philosophy and poetry of Edmond Jabès forty years later. In both their cases, social and ethical first principles and an acute sense of historical context motivate every opinion.

Other students of Bobbio were certainly involved more actively in resistance activities;[31] Nono's own subsequent account of the time presents a somewhat marginal engagement.[32] While to posit a sense of guilt would be to overstate the situation, it seems possible that the vocality of his later political motivation may be partly rooted in an awareness of the implications of *not* engaging fully with political events. This very point was later made by Maderna, who spent the last two years of the war fighting with the partisans, in a gentle rebuke in response to a letter from Nono questioning his friend's political commitment.[33] The difference in age between Nono and Maderna, Vedova or Pivato is significant, however. Reports of his contemporaries show that his youth was an asset in supporting the activities of those who had to remain more invisible, while Nono and his friends could still indulge in diversions such as swimming from a sunken German MTB in the basin of San Marco. On one occasion Nono and Berghinz found themselves at La Fenice listening to Beethoven's *Triple Concerto*, carrying false papers and surrounded by an audience of SS. As liberation approached and the horrors of civil war intensified, more direct action became inevitable. Even liberation became a theatrical

Accelerated learning: years of study, 1942–50

activity in Venice; in March 1945 partisans staged an insurrection in the Teatro Goldoni, swinging down from the circle into the stalls full of German officers. All those connected to the resistance prepared for the final insurrection a month later, as allied forces approached. Nono was no exception. He armed himself with the rifle which, together with an illegal radio, had been hidden in the family home. While he and his comrades awaited the signal to attack behind the pillars in Piazza San Marco, the German command marched out and surrendered. This is not to suggest that the liberation of Venice was peaceful. Particularly intense was the battle with the fascist *Decima MAS* brigade in the naval college of Sant'Elena.

Given the urgent work on which Bobbio was engaged, his refusal to supervise Nono's dissertation on Nicolai Berdiaev (1874–1948) may have been pragmatic rather than ideological; or possibly such metaphysical ideas were of little interest to one dealing with the most life-or-death implications of political philosophy. Berdiaev, professor of philosophy in Moscow until his expulsion in 1922, had a wide following in a Europe hungry for humanist alternatives to communism, fascism and materialist atheism. The first general introduction to his thought in Italian was published in 1944 and was bought immediately by Nono, whose interest in Russian revolutionary thought and in the cultural modes of non-Catholic Western religion would persist and become instrumental in his work.[34] One might trace Nono's own union of spirituality and communism to Berdiaev's existential Christianity and theistic revolutionary socialism. While never shying away from the polemical, Nono is wary of manifestos; a rare exception from 1959 embodies both Berdiaev's concept of creativity as a transcendental human activity and obligation and Bobbio's humanist, culture-driven revolution in summarising the role of the artist:

> Spiritual order, artistic discipline, and a clarity of insight [. . .] a revolutionary with a clear idea of the situation in which he finds himself who is thus able to bring down existing structures to make way for existing structures that are growing up in their place.[35]

More concretely, Berdiaev's theories as to the place of the creative act relative to historical time could be seen to have a direct bearing on *Prometeo*, forty years later.

Culture and cultural values are produced by man's creative act: in this, man's genius is revealed. Man has invested enormous values in culture. But here is also revealed the tragedy of man's creativity. There is a difference between the creative idea and the creative act on one hand and the product on the other. Creativity is fire; culture is the cooling of the flame.[36] And God awaits from man an anthropological revelation of creativity; in the name of man's god-like freedom, God has hidden from him the ways of creativeness and the justification of creativeness.[37]

It is certain that Nono was personally engaged with music rather than Law; that he should do anything lightly is unthinkable, however. Despite his impatience, he would later recall the university as a stimulating intellectual environment.[38] Family anecdote recalls one particular law examination in which he was unable to answer the questions. Declaring himself more interested in Beethoven than a legal career, the examiners agreed that Beethoven was indeed a more interesting topic for discussion. Nono passed his examinations with speed and efficiency. The title of the thesis that was finally submitted, discussed and approved in autumn 1947 was *Concetto e natura giuridia dell'exceptio veritatis* (*Concept and legal nature of the defense of truth*). Two years after the end of his courses, this extended period of writing was presumably due to the extent to which Nono's attention had turned to music in 1946. On the surface, a more technical legal subject than that originally considered, this thesis nevertheless deals with an issue that crucially informs his first serious encounters with musical thought: the relationship between the truth of abstract structuring principles and that of an individual context, the priority of truth before law. In his musical studies he marked every reference to Artusi's dispute with Monteverdi – a confrontation between historical absolutes and individual expression. Here, he considers three approaches to the legal position of an individual who would speak the truth when doing so contravenes the law: absolute prohibition (the instrument of fascism), absolute freedom, and a mixed position based on a measure of relevance to public life. He decides in favour of the latter, as embodied in the legal code of 1944. This thesis contains early expressions of concepts that remain central to Nono's thought and that are clearly informed by the motto of the *Partito d'azione*: 'freedom and justice'. 'In a democracy. . . the freedom of the citizen is one of the fundamental principles, its only limits the result of the necessity of social existence; the affirmation of the institution of the proof of truth is a logical consequence.'[39]

Encounters

Gian Francesco Malipiero

That Nono worked through his copy of Rimsky-Korsakov's *Treatise on Harmony* conscientiously and in detail is clear from the annotations with which it is covered. From his childhood musical experiences and sporadic piano lessons, it seems unlikely that he was unacquainted with the difference between major and minor triads, for instance. Even this has been thoroughly considered, however, such that we must assume that he decided to immerse himself in music theory from first principles to gain a solid grounding. Through his father he sought the guidance of Gian Francesco Malipiero, Director of the Venice Conservatory since 1939, who had to some degree escaped the taint of fascism.[40] A Venetian of the same generation as Nono's father, Malipiero likewise came from the high bourgeois elite that governed the city's cultural life at the turn of the century.[41] Malipiero's reputation was based equally on his work as a composer and his advocacy of earlier music, especially Monteverdi – the first modern edition of whose works he had completed in 1942[42] – and later Vivaldi. It is relevant to recall the observation of Bach's first biographer Forkel, that it was from Vivaldi that Bach learned how to *think musically*. Thus, a view of composition as a historically informed, continuous cultural process creates the context in which Nono first seriously engages with its workings.

Rather than admit his friend's son directly into the then, as now, rather bureaucratic Conservatory structure, Malipiero proposed that he should attend courses initially as an observer, as well as personally overseeing his first contact with the theory of composition as a mode of thought.[43] In 1947, Nono took the courses and examinations of the first level of composition, achieving 9/10 for tests of harmony and classical pastiche. He worked through the early chapters of Hindemith's *A Concentrated Course in Traditional Harmony*, presumably at Malipiero's behest. In the middle level, two years later while already working on his own language, Malipiero awarded him only 7. Here the tests were of another order: a four-part fugue on a given subject, a double chorus over a bass line, an analysis of the *Kyrie* from Palestrina's *Missa Papae Marcelli* (the first score Nono had seen some years previously in the library of the choir of San Marco), and the completion of a movement for piano. In the latter, one can see the traces of an emerging individualism, to which Malipiero presumably took exception. In the context of a 3/4 classical pastiche, Nono creates an additional level of structural rhyme with the regular insertion of a bar of 2/4. Trivial as these details might be, they illustrate an extraordinary speed of development, from complete absorption in the established techniques of music to their assimilation and transcending.

Accelerated learning: years of study, 1942–50

During his final years as a Law student, Nono was therefore simultaneously pursuing two courses of study. On finishing his Law degree, however, he clearly decided that his engagement with music had to be complete and that the Conservatory was not an appropriate environment; 'eight years of Conservatory, fairly "useless" and still more inadequate' was how he later described his time there.[44] In such subsequent rejections Nono is careful to distinguish between the conservatory as an institution – and his continued criticism of that system as a member of the left-wing musical establishment – and the role of Malipiero. His later claim to have lost time in this period recalls a sense of impatient urgency; in practical terms it could not be further from the truth.[45] Whatever his own subsequent judgement, Nono's contemporaries recall the most intense engagement with music through his teenage years. It may be that such a paternally mediated line felt too close to home in every respect. As a figure, Malipiero stood for much that Nono, in his developing self-image, wanted to detach himself from. He would later describe Malipiero as *holding court*; Nono seems to have been a good listener, never a courtier. Recollections of Malipiero's teaching by other students corroborate Nono's description. Gatti talks of him giving his lessons in the cafes of Venice, always surrounded by a dozen or so 'disciples' and other hangers-on. Bontempelli recalls the constant stream of Venetian dialect as the master dissected a student's work, rarely leaving space for others to speak until challenging them for remaining silent: '*Nisun galo niente da dir?* ('Has no-one got anything to say?')[46] As a character, Malipiero's pessimism could not have been the match Nono's enthusiasm was seeking, and as a composer his apparent informalism was perhaps unable to provide satisfactory responses to Nono's increasingly specific technical questions. In 1945, Malipiero entered a period of profound distress as his political credentials were questioned and what he felt was his saving of the Conservatory for Venice went unrecognised.[47] With the end of the war, from which both perhaps sought escape in their own way, Nono must have been keen to confront his emerging identity with a new real world.

There are components of Nono's mature approach that relate directly to Malipiero's relationship with his own work, however. The two share a lifelong fascination with the possible relationships between music, text and stage that informs much of their other work. Nono was close to Malipiero through the period of composition of *Vergilii Aeneis* (1943–4), a non-staged dramatic *sinfonia eroica* which the composer placed at the centre of his achievement.[48] At moments of difficulty, both find solace in the sounds of their own city, Venice; Malipiero in his third symphony *delle campane* (1944–5) and Nono in ..... *sofferte onde serene* ... (1975). Much as he felt mistreated by the city, Malipiero felt himself '*veneziano prima e italiano poi*' ('Venetian first and then Italian.').[49] A sense of Venice as an idealised cradle of modern Western musical thought emerges from his study of the development of Italian music theory from Zarlino to Padre Martini, *l'armonioso labirinto*. Published in 1946, it gives a picture of Malipiero's thought during the period of Nono's study with him, and which he was presumably discussing during their 'ritual meetings'. In his own copy, Nono underlined Malipiero's assertion that: 'Certain rules cannot be broken – rules not dictated by nature or by God but by philosophers, by mathematicians, and by reflection by the theorists of music.'[50] Nono would recall this book when working on *Prometeo*, nearly four decades later.[51]

Malipiero certainly transmitted to both Nono and Maderna an idea of the development of music theory and practice as being peculiarly *Venetian* achievements, and of Venice as a place outside – a place of cultural, intellectual and religious independence. This sense of history and responsibility would often be expressed in their correspondence. It unites them as they find a place in the wider musical world in the 1950s, corresponding in ever-deeper Venetian dialect as a mark of their common identity (letters that are part Socratic dialogue, part-comic double-act, part-Maderna's own later *Satyricon*, which almost seems to take up moments described in

Accelerated learning: years of study, 1942–50

their letters). More specifically, the grounding of his technical understanding in pre-classical musical thought will later allow Nono to propose historically consistent solutions that sidestep the contemporary consequences of enlightenment thinking.[52] Malipiero's engagement with earlier composers and theorists ran much deeper than a rediscovery of more distant repertoire. The sixteenth-century texts of Vicentino and Zarlino were fundamental to his own self-reconstruction in the 1920s.[53] They remained central to his thought, to his teaching of Maderna and Nono and to their own work together. An observation made by Malipiero to a board of inquiry into the teaching of composition in 1942 is particularly relevant to the subsequent development of Nono's approach: "While they [Zarlino *et al.*] concentrated on counterpoint, they were less concerned with harmony which was incidental, as it should be today [. . .]. A true evolution will come about automatically if we should recover our great sense of counterpoint . . . " [54]

It was Nono's assimilation of a musical discourse through his contact with Malipiero and the Conservatory that prepared the ground for his contact with Maderna, that primed him for their mutual catalysis. Furthermore, through Malipiero Nono had come into contact with enough recent work to have germinated an incipient sense of his own musical concerns that would enable him immediately to find common cause with his new friend.

Malipiero remained sceptical as to the role of dodecaphony.[55] Nono became acquainted with twelve-note technique through his counterpoint teacher Raffaele Cumar, one of Malipiero's students. At the end of the decade, after Maderna had replaced Malipiero as Nono's mentor and the two had fully embarked on their common journey, their teacher's dismissal of their researches became more scornful. This was perhaps not without some jealousy, and a sense that having sent them to study with Scherchen the pair had somehow ungratefully abandoned him. In a letter to Dallapiccola, Malipiero described Maderna as *'figlio mio snaturatissimo'* ('my most denaturalised son'). He had a more direct route to Nono, through his friend Mario. On hearing his son denounced as a charlatan, someone with no hope of success as a composer, Nono's father cut his allowance in the hope of convincing him to take up a more promising career. Nono was thus obliged to manage on hand-outs passed from his mother, from her already tightly controlled housekeeping budget.[56] Only a letter from Malipiero on hearing of Nono's engagement to Schönberg's daughter would relieve this paternal disapproval, some five years later, its tone a mixture of congratulation and self-justification.[57] As their relationship became increasingly one of equals, Malipiero was more circumspect in his direct communication with Nono. In one letter he even suggested that 'If the 12-note movement should lose ground, music, as an art, would cease to exist.'[58] Despite the difficulty his first teacher had procured him, Nono continued to offer Malipiero an invaluable friendship through his later years. The older man acknowledged this explicitly in his letters; their meetings in Venice or, more usually, at his home in Asolo were a source of delight and of continued contact with the newest debates in music. For his part, Nono would maintain a studied ambivalence. When talking of his own development, Malipiero provided *'un smosso'*, a shove, and brought him together with Maderna and Scherchen.[59] In a wider context, Nono invariably speaks of his sensitivity and intelligence, and it was Malipiero 'who initiated and determined [. . .] the renewal of Italian music.'[60]

Bruno Maderna

It was Malipiero who proposed that Nono should contact Bruno Maderna. Maderna had returned to Venice from Verona early in 1946 after his wartime experiences, was studying composition with Malipiero and newly married. Malipiero helped him find work at the

Accelerated learning: years of study, 1942–50

Conservatory as his assistant, nominally teaching *solfeggio*. Nono was keen to study Hindemith's *Unterweisung in Tonsatz*, and Maderna had a copy.[61]

> I consider that the meeting with Maderna was fundamental. With him I left the Conservatory, I recommenced all my studies, everything in a completely different way; historicised studies, not only of the European past but also that of other countries.[62]
> With him I recommenced harmony all over again and restarted my studies from the beginning! It was Maderna who gave me technique.[63]

Maderna's own recollection suggests that Nono approached Hindemith's manual with the same avid, painstaking meticulousness seen in his earlier working through Rimsky-Korsakov. His self-awareness and sense of purpose come across clearly:

> Nono has always been radical in his choices: he realised that he had studied music badly, and started all over again, right back with common chords. But he applied himself with such violence (I knew him at the time, in 1946), that in a few years he had done the whole of counterpoint with me, and he is the possessor of a fabulous technique, a technique he uses how and when he wishes . . . [64]

It is not clear whether he had reached this conscious decision prior to his meeting Maderna for the first time, at La Fenice during the Festival of Contemporary Music, on 21 September 1946.[65] The labelling of that concert – *la giovane scuola italiana* (*the young Italian school*) – must itself have been a challenge, a glimpse of the real possibility of a similar role. Maderna himself conducted the concert, although his *Serenata* is now lost.[66] In an essay for the Biennale of the same year, Maderna sets out his own manifesto and indicates an awareness of the stylistic distance yet to cover. These are presumably the thoughts with which he was occupied at the moment when Nono became his pupil and, almost immediately, closest friend:

> There is a need for research rather than for construction and, all too often, for inventory, for statistics.
> [. . .] I don't have scientific convictions, but as far as music is concerned I believe that it's not a question of discovering but of creating. [. . .] it is enough to think of the voluntary subordination to aesthetic and formal canons accepted by artists in the most fertile periods of art history to realise that in realising his own work the artist, like the scientist, follows a process which one could reasonably describe as rationally constructive.
> [. . .] One can certainly not talk of a return '*ab imis*' as a remedy for the excessive particularism of the individualist stance which is fashionable among the majority of contemporary musicians and musicologists, but there's no doubt that a serious obstacle will be removed when we approach being a musician with the same modesty and desire for simplicity, commonness, as anonymous as possible, which gave birth to 'tropes' and 'antiphonies' from those monks who despised fame and who wrote their music to the exclusive and greater glory of God.[67]

This short text incorporates several important themes of Maderna's subsequent teaching – or rather of the project of common study he led, a social structure that was the product of cultural idealism and personal insecurity. Technical solutions, personal role, common endeavour and historical context are inseparable, guided by a humble transcendental humanism that echoes aspects of Berdiaev and would shortly find political expression in the published texts of Gramsci.

Accelerated learning: years of study, 1942–50

Although Messinis is justly cautious about the numerous easy comparisons that have been made between the subsequent work of Nono and Maderna, for both composers the significance of these few years of close and intense co-exploration is unquestionable.[68] Indeed, it assumes such proportions as a unitary event in their subsequent descriptions that unfolding a narrative is sometimes difficult. The nature of their initial contact was such that Maderna had natural authority as a teacher, although several reports testify to the fact that as soon as soon as a composition student became a friend – the only circumstances under which Maderna would teach – he would no longer accept payment. Maderna's experience in his father's provincial dance band (the *Grossato Happy Company),* as a child prodigy, as a performer of classical and contemporary music and with various teachers of composition was relatively vast; born in 1920, the difference in years from his students was little. Nono's experience, though more limited, had been assimilated in a more reflective mode, free from the practical concerns of both concert giving and income earning. The stability of Nono's family and material background, however tested at various moments, allowed him to develop with a greater sense of distance and self-assuredness. It must have been clear to him that Maderna's sheer musical fluency – the fluency that allowed him to produce his despised film music to order in these early years – would never be accessible to Nono. Indeed, as their relationship developed over the following decade, it was Nono who became indispensable to Maderna, both practically and emotionally, as their constant correspondence describes. Nono became the sounding-board for Maderna's own ideas, for his creative and personal insecurity. He acted as Maderna's assistant, organising payments or scores, as an ear on the politico–musical establishment, smoother of private affairs and as deputy leader of the group of fellow student composers: his *luogotenente* in every sense.[69]

The care with which Nono set about weaving his material and evaluating its fitness for purpose can be seen as a mechanism for compensation. While Maderna's ease of production may not have been available to him, Nono did share his friend's disinterest in blind formalism. Malipiero's sense of craft and Maderna's workshop-based practice instilled in Nono a composerly pragmatism from the outset. As Maderna's imagination was to become ever more extravagant, Nono would constantly refine his focus, become more rigorous in his self-questioning. Their common role at Darmstadt was to form a resistance to reductionism and empty formalism.[70] Nono was more disposed than Maderna to allow discussion to penetrate the metaphysical roots of his craft, but both then and later he was scrupulous in avoiding the common fallacy of slipping from metaphor to simulacrum. He refused to talk about 'how I compose' and was disparaging of note-counting exercises applied to his music.[71] *Musical thought* is how he would later repeatedly describe the mode of activity that he developed during these few years of work with Maderna.

> Maderna taught me to think in music [. . .] Thus, he didn't teach me to compose – I repeat, it's not possible – he taught me much more: "What is thought?", in this case: "What is it to think in music?"[72] Bruno Maderna taught me to think. Thought, musical thought, needs time.[73]

Questioning and time: two key components of Nono's musical thought. He refers to the time of composition – a temporal trace of thought and decision inscribed in the score – but also to the acrostic nature of musical time itself. This dynamical tension between the architectural, multidimensional times of musical reason and the inevitable unidirectionality of musical experience (*outside* and *inside* time in Xenakis' terms) is fundamental to Nono's art and has its roots in these discussions. It is what makes it, as Cacciari would later suggest, a genuine philosophy *in* music. It underlies the challengingly classical nature of his music; this tension is never occluded by local temporal teleologies for the sake of comfort or resolved in favour of

Accelerated learning: years of study, 1942–50

atemporal abstraction. It is also the structural property that allows Nono to embody a relationship between personal experience and music theory, giving his work its poetic strength. In Maderna's 'school', observed Nono, time was not thought of as progressing from left to right but in multiple perspectives, fluid and elastic.[74] This is not post-factual rationalisation; rather, it indicates his deepening understanding of the workings of both renaissance polyphony and twelve-tone music, the understanding that will allow Nono to meticulously weave materials robustly over an extraordinary range of time-scales.

This understanding was grounded in a thorough study of compositional theory and technique, particularly of pre-classical music. The very mode of this thoroughness recalls earlier approaches to the study of composition, painstakingly copying out entire chapters of books or movements of works: Padre Martini's *breve compendio* in its entirety, long passages of Fux, Coussemaker, Artusi, motets by Dufay, Ockeghem and Zarlino. The writings of Zacconi and Vicentino they studied from the original editions, having been introduced to the Biblioteca Marciana through Maderna's editing work for Malipiero. The self-contextualising historicism of Vicentino and Zarlino provided a model for the painstaking, auto-analytical construction of a valid identity in a changing world.[75] Vicentino's microtonal proposals would resurface in Nono's later work, particularly when he consciously returns to trains of thought of this earlier time in *Fragmente*. Padre Martini was central to Maderna's teaching; Nono worked through every example, he summarised his *History*. In a letter after Maderna's increased conducting activity had begun to leave Nono with much of the responsibility for teaching, Maderna advised him always to return to Martini. Nono returned thirty years later to Martini's *saggi fondamentali* after working on the loosest of his mature works, *A floresta*; he noted the famous passages on the compositional importance of the cantus fermus, the dangers of the unreflective application of rules and the stylistic impoverishment of following fashion.

Copies of movements are covered with technical detail: notes on proportional notation, analyses of contrapuntal and formal devices. Elsewhere he poses himself the musical problem before copying and analysing the original. A version of Josquin's *Victimae Paschali* is based on serial manipulation of the figures. Modes from theoretical works or compositions are transcribed and enumerated, analysed for their interval content, and then combined at different transpositions. Maderna and Nono would exchange enigmatic canons like other friends might play with crossword clues or chess problems. Later writers on music are also present: Eitner, Ambros, Fétis, Haba. His notes from Haba's *Sulla Psicologia dell'aspetto musicale* begin: 'I am not a musical artist – music is my mode of expression.'

> Bruno had an intelligence, an extraordinary need to know and study and experiment. With him, when I began to study music after eight useless and inadequate years of the Conservatory, I really dedicated myself. It was a comparative study: the various Masses of the Flemish composers, the different ways of treating the tenor relative to the other voices in various composers of the time, the development of variation form from Beethoven to Schönberg, the use of text and of the human voice in various composers, the choruses in Dallapiccola in relation to the solo parts, pitches and timbre in Schönberg. The method was to pursue a question, not to its exhaustion, enclosing it in a museum, or within the historical grid of a given period, but always opening our interests to the developments of a composer, of a form, of a period, of a style, of a technique and then making comparisons and analysing the differences. Not to find influences or historical traces but to discover the diversity of process: not to find formulas but to try to arrive at the richness of imagination of a particular consciousness. The more there is a scientific awareness, the more there develops a capacity for fantasy, for invention. With Bruno, I carried out a sort of methodological

Accelerated learning: years of study, 1942–50

training that helped me to continuously widen my fields of study. And it was with this system of analysis that I first approached the scores of Schönberg and Webern, the ones that one could find at the time.[76]

So the concept isn't fixed once and for all, but changes dynamically in its variants through different periods. The continuous mutation of rhythmic values that is found in the *Missa Di dadi*[77] continued to be generated in other music of other times: I could find its reflection in Schumann's *Fantasia in C*, in the Variations of Beethoven, Brahms and Schönberg. At other times our study turned to song: we started with Francesco Landini and his rhetoric, continued to the tenor of the *Homme armé* in the Odhecaton and the Masses of Ockeghem, and thence to the Lieder of Schubert, Schumann, Wolf, Webern and Dallapiccola.[78]

The very detail of his subsequent memory of this period testifies to the salience of each new idea, of their occurrence at the right moment in the right order. From variation to canon to Schönberg; despite the panhistorical scope of their study, the trajectory towards Nono's *Variazioni canoniche* could not be more direct. The company around Maderna included Renzo Dall'Oglio, Gastone Fabris,[79] Franco Prato and Romolo Grano. Their routine involved working together in Maderna's attic, eating and attending concerts together, working in the Biblioteca Marciana and trips to the beach. Nono consciously saw this as *Venetian* activity, recalling Zarlino's reports of his conversations with Willaert, della Viola and Merulo in Piazza San Marco. Their work on the *Odhecaton* in particular was a group activity. Malipiero had found a copy of Petrucci's 1501 edition in Treviso, and asked Maderna to help him prepare a performing edition.[80] Maderna, in the spirit of group endeavour, subcontracted his band of students. It fell to Nono to coordinate the selection and allocation of work – transcription and orchestration – and the passing round of the precious volume. Maderna himself orchestrated Ockeghem's chanson *Malor me bat*, which would reappear in Nono's *Fragmente* after his friend's death.[81] Their comparative mode of seeking out parallels in music history cannot have failed to observe that *Odhecaton*, the first printed collection of music, represents a moment in which Venetian practice led a technology-driven transformation of the very state of music.

Following the end of his studies at Padova, Nono had made a visit to the poet Giuseppe Ungaretti in Rome.[82] He set about planning a set of five *Liriche d'Ungaretti*: *Eterno*, *Sono una creatura*, *Dannazione*, *Fase* and *Casa mia*, five of the tersest from Ungaretti's first collection *Allegria*. Despite Ungaretti's own distinctly cosmopolitan origins and his status by this time as a national figure, these poems have a local, north-east Italian resonance. They were written during the poet's time as a private soldier in the mountain campaigns of the Great War, participating in the very battles the fires of which had so traumatised Malipiero at Asolo. The first and last have notes as to instrumentation: *vibrofono*, and *viola, sax, oboe*. Otherwise, only a single sketch from the first remains. It is enough, however, to encapsulate central threads of his work with Maderna (Figure 2.1): the place of text at the most structural level, care in word-setting, an insistence on achieving absolute poetic and abstract formal clarity, and an acute sense of historical continuity. On the basis of a preliminary rhythmicisation of the first of Ungaretti's two lines using a symmetrical diminution of metre (3213123), Nono constructs a metrical and rhythmic palindrome, the fifth bar of which is still to be fully resolved. To this he adds intonation, the nascent melodic cells expanding against the formal reflection. Here we already see the archetype of Nono's mature conception of musical material – the shape of a musical thought, to use Schönberg's term.[83] A symmetrical outward and return movement is set against a line of continuous development. While Nono's concern with number sequence and structural symmetry anticipates his later practice, the proportional tempo changes recall their studies of the Gabrielis, an element that would also resurface in later works.[84]

Accelerated learning: years of study, 1942–50

Figure 2.1 Liriche d'Ungaretti: sketch for *Eterno*

Hermann Scherchen

Hermann Scherchen was born in Berlin in 1891, playing with the Blüthner Orchestra in Berlin at the age of 16 and conducting it at 24. He was Schönberg's assistant for the first performances of *Pierrot Lunaire*, and gave the Berlin premiere of the *Kammersymphonie*. Having spent the war years interned in Russia, where he turned to composing, music directorships followed in Leipzig, Frankfurt, Königsberg and Zürich. He continued to be involved with the most advanced innovators, including the first performances of Berg's *Violin Concerto*, parts of *Wozzeck* and Webern's *Variations*, as well as performing earlier music including a much-performed orchestration of *The Art of Fugue*. Haba, Krenek and – significantly for his own teaching – Hindemith were among his regular collaborators. He played an important part in the activities of the International Society for Contemporary Music (ISCM) through the twenties and thirties, founded the journal *Melos* as a mouthpiece for radical ideas, and the *Ars Viva Verlag* to publish 'old and new music'. In 1929, he published what remains a standard work on conducting.[85] Such a thorough kapellmeisterly background became an increasingly rare phenomenon after the Second World War, which he spent in Switzerland conducting, lecturing and writing. During this enforced break from international touring, Scherchen had time to develop his ideas about the relationships between music, society and technology.[86] He also continued an annual conducting course where he enthusiastically shared his technique, experience and vision. As a champion of new music with impeccable artistic and political pedigrees, Scherchen had been associated with the new *Ferienkürse für neue Musik* at Darmstadt since 1947. He re-established his activities in Italy, promoting the work of Dallapiccola in particular, and in 1948 was invited to hold his course in conjunction with the International Music Festival in Venice. Malipiero, as president of the organising body, suggested to both Nono and Maderna that they should attend the course, which took place from 20 August to 30 September 1948. He presumably had a hand in its description:

> Scherchen's teaching will range from an analytical study of the work (form and language) to the realisation of the musical composition according to its essential properties of civilisation, taste and culture. [. . .] He will select the examples for this

Accelerated learning: years of study, 1942–50

performative analysis from preclassical, classical, romantic and contemporary art: up to the development of the dodecaphonic system.[87]

The same document hints at Scherchen's ascetic approach to music-making; for him, the radio provided a model of pure musical communication, free from superfluous visual interference.[88] Much later, Nono would pare down the visual components of *Prometeo* until they were eliminated entirely.

As Dallapiccola later pointed out, Scherchen's relevance was based as much on his advocacy of earlier music as that of serialism, and his urge to understand the innermost workings of every style and piece was driven by his own largely sublimated desire to compose.[89] His approach was contiguous with the comparative research that Maderna and Nono had established for themselves. As ever, Nono kept copious notes. The technique of conducting as such was incidental to the seminars on particular works or analytical themes; if not advertised as composition lessons, Scherchen's seminars were certainly received by Nono as such. The breadth of Nono and Maderna's technical view of twelve-note music to date was severely restricted by historical circumstances and practical accessibility; Scherchen's, by contrast, was in some respects wider than *any* of the individual composers of whose music he had become the advocate. Already in the second seminar Nono writes out the *scala dodecafonica* (a chromatic scale), the series from Schönberg's *Suite* op. 25 with its BACH motif, a symmetrical series, another 'with all the intervals' – a form he would adopt exclusively at a later stage – and a combination of the two. Nono's note to himself 'write series' presumably applies to the day's homework, not a lifetime project. Work then proceeds in multiple strands: music analysis (from Bach and Rameau to Ravel and Honegger), instrumentation, compositional technique (structure of Gregorian chant, harmonic clarity and closure, melodic and rhythmic elasticity) and serial technique. Melody and form are related in considering the role of the *Höhepunkt*, the high-point of musical tension. Following a transcription of Scherchen's analysis of an extended Gregorian chant, Nono constructs another page-long melody with a similar rhetorical architecture but using serial devices. Later, perhaps for the conservatory, he writes an entire motet movement by treating the initial phrases of *Veni creator spiritus* in serial fashion.

The complete armoury of serial devices is here: all-interval series, permutation, canon, the hexachordal reordering of Schönberg's last quartet, the permutation of the *Lyric Suite*. They are applied to all types of material; the *lack* of obsession with the number twelve is crucial. To record Scherchen's analysis of the *Ave Maria* from Verdi's *Quattro Pezzi Sacri*, Nono transcribes the entire piece. He notes the composer's age at the time, 85, and writes out the *scala enigmatica*, the interval series on which the piece is based. This will later become the primary material for *Fragmente*. Nono notates analysis of the horizontal and vertical properties of tetrachords using interval matrices; these also become a stable element of his technique, allowing him to see interval relationships in all directions, plot multiplications and permutations and generate Latin squares. Nothing arises which does not become material to Nono's thought.

Scherchen gave his students exercises to realise with just 2, 3 or 5 notes. Nono himself noted the resurfacing of this practice in *España en el corazón* and *Liebeslied*. It is already evident in *Composizione per orchestra n. 1* of 1951, and underlies several of the later works as his capacity for technical and poetic focus is refined still further. Musical examples from plainchant to Schönberg are analysed in terms of melodic and harmonic tension. The placing of tritones in melody, in harmony and in abstract structures arises in several contexts, including many examples from Schönberg. This thought also persists, resurfacing notably throughout the string quartet *Fragmente* thirty years later, together with its explicit recollections of Maderna. The tables of intervals, analysis of melodic and harmonic tension and careful observation of the role

Accelerated learning: years of study, 1942–50

of the augmented fourth were familiar to Nono and Maderna from their study of Hindemith's *Unterweisung in Tonsatz*. It is not clear to what extent Scherchen had adopted this principle directly from the same source; it may have been common currency in the Berlin of the early 1930s which he and Hindemith inhabited. Other writers pointing to the structural importance of the interval include Webern, who in his lectures in the same decade identified the augmented fourth as the main structural interval after the octave.[90] Hindemith's book, the product of his own teaching, incorporates an attempt to rationalise and integrate harmonic and melodic characteristics. On the basis of the harmonic series and resultant or 'combination' tones, he arranges pitches in order of their relation to a central note and intervals in terms of their relative tension:[91]

> Series 1 provided us with the principal members of the structure; Series 2 will furnish the smaller materials [. . .]. Even if the larger members are made out of the smaller ones, the properties of each of the latter are of importance only until the next similar unit is reached.[92]

This principle is evident in Nono's early works as the guarantor of coherence of material on one hand and efficiency of large-scale decision-making on the other. The last in each of these basic series is a tritone, 'a foreign body and a ferment among the intervals',[93] which serves to articulate all possible chords into two groups.[94] The 'tension' noted by Nono corresponds to the 'harmonic fluctuation' (*harmonisches Gefälle*) of Hindemith's book, which there becomes a parameter by which to plot the harmonic evolution of a passage. It appears frequently in Nono's notes from Scherchen's course, and continues to be an essential component of both Nono's and Maderna's technique through the early 1950s, as Rizzardi has shown.[95]

As with Maderna, the trans-historical integration of musical thought informed Scherchen's teaching. Scherchen's long experience was matched by his political maturity. Having grown up in imperial Berlin, witnessed the Russian Revolution, taken part in workers' music organisations throughout Europe, travelled to China, Russia and South America, given concerts with the Palestine Orchestra in the Middle East and spent the war assisting refugees from his hotel room in Zürich, he had not only a well-developed sense of social justice and the urgent need for social change, but specifically a vision of what place music and the musician might have in such a programme. Furthermore, his work and writing seek to pursue the implications of such principles for the activity of music itself. His 1944 talk on music and radio, for example, brings together two central points: the democratisation of culture and the purity and autonomy of music.[96] The vision of these twin goals as a unity is rare in cultural politics of the time; it certainly plays no part in Soviet-inspired communism. Gramsci's writings were only just beginning to appear in print, and those of the Frankfurt School would have little impact in Italy until the 1960s. In Scherchen's opinion, the responsibility of the composer is precisely to advance musical thought as a vital component of social progress. In an essay entitled *The present situation of modern music* he reports from the First International Congress of Dodecaphonic Music congress in 1949 (which 'at the end declared itself superfluous'), and notes that the composers fall into three categories: the political-belligerent, the opportunist-individualist, and the *absolute* musician – the most important, according to Scherchen.

> The truth is that the truly modern music – today as always – encounters only rejection. The reasons for this are less important in the first place than the fact that nevertheless no first-rate composer would ever be turned back to a 'natural', more easily understood mode of expression.

Accelerated learning: years of study, 1942–50

To put it precisely: without the engagement of Marxist theorists no excellent musician would have made the attempt, as it were, that his work should reach back towards earlier stages of music.

Art should be a 'superstructure' that expresses society. But every society is a becoming, a form of life, which for certain characteristic reasons – themselves being further developed – constantly develops ever finer organs. The life of the true artist was always to remain a champion of these finer new organs of society, despite personal-material opposition.[97]

Scherchen's vision is never abstract, however. A practising musician to his core, his examples include those we know from Nono's notes taken at the course in Venice: Bach's *The Art of Fugue*, Beethoven's late quartets and Verdi's *Ave Maria*. In the writings of Scherchen from the time of his first encounters with Nono we see a highly developed vision of the unity of aesthetic and social change, integrity and responsibility. New music and social transformation go hand in hand, driven by technological advance. He demonstrates and explains this process in great detail and in purely musical technical terms.[98] He does so in a way that is completely style-independent. The critical detail of Scherchen's vision is ultimately musical; for him, there is nothing socially abstract about 'autonomous' music. The importance of this encounter in the development of Nono's own self-image as a musician, to his understanding of what a composer might be in relation to his own work and to the world within which he acts, is incalculable. For all his vision, Scherchen came from another world, one in which great conductors had as much in common with generals as poets. He expected to command, as TV recordings of his rehearsals in the 1950s clearly show. As Nono grew in self-confidence, it seems to have become clear that their relationship could not become a dialogue between equals.

The question of Scherchen's overt political involvement is interesting, given the explicit and committed nature of Nono's later activity. We find indications in his correspondence with Schönberg from two years later. In 1950, Schönberg was living in Los Angeles from where he was supervising arrangements for European performances of works including *Der Jakobsleiter* and extracts from *Moses und Aron*. Given his precarious status and the anti-communist political climate, Schönberg was very concerned to know exactly where Scherchen stood. Scherchen's answer was unequivocal:

I was since my early youth a convinced socialist. Every convinced socialist recognises only communism as a true socialist social structure. [. . .] Dilettantism, with which human life has been brought to a long heavy torment both physiologically and spiritually, has made me so impatient that I no longer had the will or ability to live had I not had the will and certainty that the WORLD can be transformed, and not too soon [. . .]

Here you have me without reflection or cosmetics – I have NEVER been political, NEVER belonged to a party / I am not political and belong to no party.[99]

Eunice Katunda

The course attracted an international studentship, including a large contingent of Brazilians. A concern with the music and politics of Latin America continued through Nono's life. The two Venetians befriended particularly the pianist/composer Eunice Katunda.[100] Born Eunice de Monte Lima in Rio de Janeiro in 1915, she had been a piano prodigy.[101] She was encouraged to compose by Villa-Lobos and Joachim Koellreutter, an ex-pupil of Scherchen who having

Accelerated learning: years of study, 1942–50

escaped from Germany was working as a flautist with the Brazil Symphony Orchestra. He had founded the organisation *Música Viva* in 1938 to promote contemporary music. Following Scherchen's South American tour the previous year, Koelreutter brought a group of eleven of his protégés to the conducting course in Venice. Katunda especially remembered the opening concert at La Fenice, in which she sang Verdi's *Ave Maria* with Maderna and others, conducted by Scherchen. Katunda, Maderna and Nono were soon an inseparable band:

> This was the best time of my life. I went to attend a course of two months and stayed for a year! We worked intensively, studied, ate, breathed music. I got to know Bruno Maderna, Luigi Nono, Scherchen, Dallapiccola, Ungaretti, Aliás; Maderna was the most complete musician I have ever known. He, me and Nono formed a group which worked regularly together, from serialism to *The Art of Fugue*. Scherchen treated us in a special way. He always called on us for various jobs – teaching, rehearsing sections – and there we were, together, us three![102]
>
> With Maderna and Luigi Nono we discussed problems of aesthetics, we tried to resolve technical problems, we played and listened to music; in fact, I to owe them most of what I learned there that was beautiful and new in the field of music.[103]

Among the enthusiastic descriptions of Venice and her new band of friends, Katunda's memoir of her journey contains insights into the activities of Scherchen's course and the atmosphere he generated:

> Imagine we were making music in the air. We have to conduct the score by heart, without the orchestra, in front of the students. It is the most wonderful thing, almost painful, the struggle to achieve concentration and the joy of victory. Again today we stay from 9 to 11 in a room watching the exercises. We study the score so much that we could write it out again from memory with all its details. Then S[cherchen] whistles the melodic part and people create the musical space with an incredible force of expression, of rhythmic and melodic gesture, indicating all the entrances of the instruments, everything. Only on Thursday will we realise the musical ideas physically (with the orchestra). It is wonderful to observe the struggle of those who comprehend the real value of this. Because even understanding or feeling this does not lead to the exteriorizing of the gesture in music. Of all of us, until now, only L[uigi[N[ono] has been successful in conquering this victory which transforms creation![104]

They worked for an entire week, five hours a day, on Scherchen's orchestration of *The Art of Fugue*.[105] Nono assisted Katunda with a translation of her *Negrinho do Pastoreio*, a chamber cantata for female voices based on traditional Brazilian melodies.[106] Moments of Venetian dialect serve to retain the Brazilian Portuguese rhythms. Scherchen took up Katunda's cause; he conducted her *Quatro Cantos à Morte* for Swiss radio in December 1948 and arranged Nono's conducting debut with *Negrinho* for Radio Zürich on 10 May the next year. Nono introduced Katunda to the poetry of Ungaretti; she in turn introduced him to that of Federico Garcia Lorca. Lorca remained central to Nono's music over the next decade – not just the poems themselves, but his personal and political struggle and the ideal of an Andalusian spirit. Katunda's membership of the Communist Party must also have been a challenge to Nono's own emerging sense of political identity.

The intensity of Katunda's activity gives some sense of the urgency with which Italian composers were addressing the new challenges. As well as well as giving recitals and workshops

Accelerated learning: years of study, 1942–50

on Brazilian music, she attended the *First International Congress of Dodecaphonic Composers* in Locarno in 1948, together with Nono. In December the whole band – Nono, Maderna, Togni, Katunda and Koellreutter – followed another of Scherchen's courses in Milan. In a letter to his parents, Nono mentions Scherchen's teaching of Bach and dodecaphony. At the subsequent *First International Congress of Dodecaphonic Music* in Milan the following year, Katunda performed a work by Maderna.[107] For health reasons, she returned to Brazil unexpectedly in May 1950, where an impassioned debate would soon break out about the nature and role of Brazilian art and music, conducted on aesthetic, cultural and political planes.[108] She moved to Bahia to be part of a community of socially engaged artists and continue her research into Afro-Brazilian music. The intensity of her experience in Italy prepared her for the discovery of her own Brazilian identity, she said, but her own subsequent refutation of the abstract nature of modernist European music was absolute and specific: the Brazilian people want rhythm to dance, melody to sing and repetition to enjoy, and who else should music be for?

> Is it possible to compose atonal or dodecaphonic music of a national character? [. . .]. The answer is NO! [. . .] what can we do with this obsession with novelty, which prohibits repetition, dissonant, fragmentary, problematic and incomprehensible? [109]

After an initial flurry of exchanges of news and reviews, her correspondence with Nono ebbs.[110] She seems to have left him with a specific and crucial challenge, however: how to incorporate meaningfully non-serial material into a project of compositional research? Despite the fact that they would develop divergent answers, Katunda suggested to Nono clues and material for its solution. Not only was her own use of Brazilian material an inspiration, she also left Nono with the indigenous Brazilian melody *Jumanja* which would be richly mined as a resource in *Polifonica-Monodia-Ritmica*. Katunda describes another revelatory common experience which it would be surprising if Nono had not shared and discussed: Visconti's 1948 film *La terra trema*, which the band went to see on 2 September. Improvised and acted by Sicilian fishermen, this provided a model for the emergence of uncompromising aesthetic work from the lives and activity of working people, a model that would inform Katunda's work in Bahia in a more populist spirit. Such ideas would resurface in Nono's music as his political engagement developed, and remained central to his ethos.

René Leibowitz

Annotations referring to Katunda in his copy suggest that Nono began to study Rene Leibowitz's *Schoenberg et son école*, published the year before, in the wake of Scherchen's course. He worked through the text and examples with the same conscientious thoroughness that he had brought to bear on earlier historical and theoretical writings. Spangemacher suggests that Nono may have met Leibowitz at the Milan congress in 1949.[111] Despite his later reservations concerning Leibowitz's approach, a hungry Nono clearly devoured the most authoritative text of its time.[112] His underlinings of Leibowitz's words continue:

> It is in this way that Schoenberg, Berg and Webern have taught me to consider the past of the art of music: [. . .] as the succession of generations of musicians who were men like us, <u>who strove and struggled, who had to take into account the same problems which confront us, and who carried out their resolves with the means at their disposal, that is to say with those furnished by the language of their time</u> [. . .][113]
>   ★'GOOD' [Nono's annotation]

Accelerated learning: years of study, 1942–50

In my opinion the true artist is who not only recognises and becomes <u>completely aware of the deepest problems of his art</u>, but who also proceeds to their solution with the utmost integrity and with uncompromising moral strength.[114]

It was not only the revelatory tone of Leibowitz's book that resonated with Nono. Part of its authority resided in the fact that it rehearses the same historical narrative as the historical pillars of music theory that Nono knew intimately. It reaffirms a polyphonic lineage through Notre Dame, Zarlino and Fux; Schönberg's project is presented as 'the reactivation of polyphonic evolution'.[115] Leibowitz's themes of historical inevitability and synthesis, the role of the man of genius and the evolution of polyphony as a crucial property of Western music are wound together. Nono's annotations of Leibowitz's text indicate the central roles of polyphony and the horizontal/vertical relationship in his understanding of compositional technique:

Basically different in this respect from all other forms of musical expression, the Occidental art of sound has been polyphonic for about a thousand years. This polyphony may be considered as the very key to its existence [. . .][116]

we may consider polyphony not only as a progress from one acquisition to the next, but also as a <u>continual synthesis,</u> in the midst of which all the preceding acquisitions continue to exist and form a whole [. . .][117]

we have seen that, because of the necessary <u>equilibrium between voice-leading and the vertical aggregations which result from it,</u> counterpoint has never had a chance to be realised in its pure form.[118] [Nono's underlining]

This is the direct result of the teaching of Malipiero, Maderna and Scherchen, to be sure, but also perhaps a resonance with the musical workings of his own mind. Polyphonic working will remain at the heart of his production of material. Even when writing a monophonic piece, Nono continues to think polyphonically; the resultant line is a trace within networks of possible or implicit activity. Multiplicity, simultaneity and the exploration of worlds of parallel possibilities extend from the complex canons that generate the surface of Nono's earliest work to his subsequent thinking about kinds of material or activity, physical spaces, meanings and modes of existence.

Luigi Dallapiccola

Leonardo Pinzauti later described Nono as mentioning only two names 'almost with a sense of devotion': Malipiero and Luigi Dallapiccola.[119] The one work Nono completed under Malipiero's indirect tutelage was the lost *La discesa di Cristo agli inferni*, an attempt to use the language of Monteverdi. Given his teacher's recent completion of the Monteverdi edition, there may have been a sense of trumping the neoclassicists. On Malipiero's suggestion, he sent it to the newly re-formed Italian section of the ISCM.[120] Nothing was heard until by chance he encountered Dallapiccola walking in Piazza San Marco with Malipiero:

Then one day Malipiero presented me to Dallapiccola and he said: 'I have seen your score and I understand that you have much to express in your heart, but you have to study much to be able to express it.' It gave me a push to begin my musical studies again from scratch, so I began my apprenticeship with Maderna.[121]

Accelerated learning: years of study, 1942–50

Having renewed their acquaintance after a performance of Dallapiccola's *Due Pezzi* for orchestra in 1947, Nono wrote to the older composer about his own hopes and asked after the score of Dallapiccola's *Liriche greche* which he had presumably heard in the performance of that July.[122] Dallapiccola's reply gives a sense of the exceptional nature of Nono's vision in the cultural context of the time:

> You are right to consider yourself fortunate to be a pupil of Malipiero, the man we might regard as the only one who doesn't close the door in the face of the most burning problems. [. . .] Study hard and rigorously, and for the rest it seems to me that in your letter there is a tone of faith which cannot fail to lead to worthwhile artistic results. In essence it is just a question of faith. You should know that your letter pleased me for this reason above all. In this world in which the last twenty years and the war have taught only *arrivismo* (I know young composers who have written two or three hundred bars, who would like to hear them performed all over the world and who complain about their fate because everybody doesn't bow down before their unformed and presumptuous attempts), I consider your letter a rare document. So: courage. You know that the path is difficult and that with the years it becomes more difficult. The first steps are the hardest 'towards the others'; the following steps most difficult 'towards yourself'. I hope that, whatever the cost, you may realise this one day.[123]

Nono and Maderna seem to have obtained scores of the *Liriche greche* with some speed. In response to Maderna's submission of their findings and questions a few months later, Dallapiccola described his application of techniques from Bach's *Musical Offering* to twelve-note music in what he considered his major work.[124] Their brief summary describes the tension and textual relevance of Dallapiccola's use of intervals, his fragmentation of the series and the roots of his technique in historical counterpoint.[125] What would seem to have left a deep impression at this stage is the fundamental role of *canon* in Dallapiccola's music.[126]

'Due liriche greche'

Scherchen was tacitly elected godfather of the group. Nono began to work with him at his home in Rapallo, attended his concerts – especially premieres such as Dallapiccola's *Il Prigioniero* – and even hatched a plan that they should all go and live there to work on their great project. This involved the rather dubious purchase of a second-hand bus and never came to fruition. Scherchen suggested that they should test their ideas in some vocal pieces. Nono and Maderna having unpicked the canons of Dallapiccola's *Liriche greche* in 1947, Scherchen revealed to them more of the inner workings: 'he revealed to me the extreme music-specific intelligence (not just technical difficulty) of com-positional knowledge, of conflicting contemporaneities of signs and thoughts.'[127]

Nono seems to conflate Katunda's introducing him to the poetry of Lorca and the subsequent gestation of the *Epitaffii* with this particular work:[128]

> Scherchen suggested we set poems: Bruno chose Greek lyrics in Quasimodo's translation, Katunda chose Garcia Lorca and I took some of one and some of the other. What most drew our attention was not so much Lorca the gypsy as the metaphysical and surreal; it was a voice that put us in touch with other worlds.[129]

Accelerated learning: years of study, 1942–50

In fact, Katunda also set two of three *Liriche greche* she had planned: *Dormono* and *E il sonno*. Her own recollection was written rather closer to the time:

> At the request of Scherchen, who was in Florence to conduct a concert of works by Dallapiccola, we three – Maderna, Nono and me – went to meet him and together we spent three days during which we showed him a series of Greek lyrics for voices and instruments. Each of us wrote three. They were all dedicated to him as a tribute of gratitude for everything Scherchen was for each one of us: teacher, friend and guide.[130]

The wider publication of Salvatore Quasimodo's translations of Greek fragments in 1944 spurred several composers who in seeking to rediscover the lyric roots of an Italian musical identity were looking for texts both contemporary and pan-historical – alternatives to futurist violence and politically loaded epic or sentiment.[131] Quasimodo's versions of lyrics by Sapho, Alceo, Anacreonte and others – new poems in their own right – peel back the accumulated baggage of the intervening centuries to find pre-Roman human and social truths. Luciano Berio, a student at the conservatory in Milan where Quasimodo had been appointed professor of Italian literature in 1941, also produced *Tre liriche greche* in the same years. Given the environment described by Nono, it seems likely that he and Maderna were working on their *Liriche greche* not only simultaneously but side-by-side. This is supported by their instrumentation; both require chamber choir, two pairs of woodwind (flutes and clarinets or saxophones), piano and similar arrays of percussion (timpani, various drums and cymbals). In addition, Maderna requires a bass clarinet, Nono a viola and vibraphone. The use of percussion anticipates Nono's works of the early 1950s; it occupies a liminal space that allows mobility between pitch and rhythmic reasoning, and acts as the carrier of external material. Both of these roles continue to resurface, especially in *Con Luigi Dallapiccola* (1979). Perhaps the later piece, the product of a period of introspection in Nono's work, is in a way a reflection on the difference between the very social context of his compositional apprenticeship – the sense of common purpose encouraged by Scherchen – and Dallapiccola's own approach to teaching at the time. Inspired by his beloved Proust, Dallapiccola refers to *the first delicate reading of the interior book* and suggests: 'It would be good that a young artist should know that among the many possibilities of life there is also that of solitude, which absolutely does not mean absence of contact with the soul of men.'[132]

In constructing his material, Nono treats rhythm and pitch separately but in analogous ways, such that they converge on poetic and formal intentions. In both cases his use of traditional notational units conditions his manipulation of the material. Rhythm develops in the context of phrase or bar structures, generating new artefacts as it is accommodated; pitch is reckoned in diatonic intervals rather than semitones, a practice he would retain until after the *Variazioni canoniche*. The essentialist approach to defining his material which can be seen through all his subsequent work is already in evidence here; having identified the material which will suit his purposes, it is designated *base* and the processes of polyphonic weaving and architectonic cutting can begin.

Rhythmic material springs entirely from the text. Once established, it is notated as multiples of several different basic values. He can thus pilot different strands of canon and permutation through various time bases, creating the elasticity of time they had discussed. By *Con Luigi Dallapiccola* this process is extended to a range of irrational values; here he restricts himself to divisions of two and three.

Figure 2.2 Due liriche greche: pitch material

The pitch structures likewise evolve from a single idea, a symmetrically expanding shape archetypal of Nono's later material (Figure 2.2a). Having selected a pattern, transposed and retrograded, he remembers Scherchen's lesson on the augmented fourth and tries proceeding without one, to find himself in a classic structural stalemate (Figure 2.2b – the diatonically-based interval notation is Nono's own). He then invents a new all-interval 11-note series which retains the patterns of mirror and permutation developed in the previous stage (Figure 2.2c). From this he filters his first thought, generating two new structures that form the basis of the two pieces (Figures 2.2d, 2.2e). As later, what is missing from the pitch material is significant in the generating of longer term structure. In *La stella mattutina*, the absent note – B – is restored on the word *tenebre* ('darkness') (Figure 2.2f). This chromatic completion at the Höhepunkt allows for the revealing, the release of Nono's original idea. Following the permutations, elisions and canons of the first piece, the second establishes clear harmonic fields. Each section presents a permutation

Accelerated learning: years of study, 1942–50

of the *Base*, transposed in turn to E♭, C♯ and E (Figure 2.2g). The timpani outline a bass which is exactly that of *Con Luigi Dallapiccola* – there sustained by large metal plates – which in that case Nono relates to the *fratello* motif from *Il Prigioniero*, the leitmotiv of brotherhood and freedom.[133] Even before arriving at Darmstadt, therefore, Nono had developed an additional compositional parameter: a coherent technical means of handling figure, external material and self-reference; the construction of asymmetrical spaces that allow for shifting perspective and horizon.

It would appear that Nono had the experience of composing these pieces in mind when imagining *Con Luigi Dallapiccola* twenty-five years later. The later piece is *with* Dallapiccola in more than the sense of being a homage, or by virtue of its three-note reference to *Il Prigoniero*. The emergence of modes from filtered series, the canons and cross-cutting between rhythmic augmentations and diminutions in different time bases, the use of motivic material as formal and harmonic pitch centres, and the emergence of exquisite lyricism from unlikely sources, all recall how close he felt to Dallapiccola. Uniquely among his peers when he arrived at Darmstadt in 1950, Nono had developed a mode of musical thought – a unity of theory, practice, history, revolution and identity – which already assimilated and transcended conventional serialism. Within the expanding musical environment he had developed, a sort of hyperspatial dynamic allowed him to access multiple forms of thought and material – his own and others – and locate them in his own present.

Notes

1 Leibowitz, 1949, p. x.
2 Interview with Enzo Restagno, 1987. LNII, p. 482.
3 His childhood friend Ennio Gallo cites Nono's wanting to take the blame for such a breakage at the house of the parish priest as an early instance of his urge to confront ethical situations (Gennaro, 2004).
4 Interview with Enzo Restagno, 1987. LNII, p. 482.
5 *Islanders*, written in Newcastle during the First World War, is a biting satire of English bourgeois repression. Zamyatin's later *We* (1920), itself the model for Orwell's *1984*, puts a development of the same story in a futurist, constructivist setting. A musician figures in *Islanders*, in the next experiment *Fishermen* and in *We*, his role permuted between establishment, seducer and seduced.
6 A curious pre-resonance of Visconti's use of the piece in his film of *Death in Venice*, given Nono's vicarious connection with Thomas Mann through the Schönberg family.
7 *Italian music from fin-de-siècle to fascism*, conference at St Johns College Oxford, June 2004.
8 Now an undistinguished component of the industrial hinterland of Padova.
9 *La scultura lingua morta* (Venice, 1945). Martini also supplied the clay for faking official stamps.
10 G.F. *Malipiero* (Milano, 1942). Bontempelli developed an aesthetic theory of *magical realism* in his own work.
11 See, for instance, Cecchetto and Mastinu, 2005, pp. 27–8.
12 In the first year alone, for example, he took courses in: history of Italian law, institutions of private law, history of Roman law, institutions of Roman law, constitutional law, political economy, military culture, colonial law, medical law, common law, international law, philosophy of law and economics.
13 For this information I am indebted to my late mother-in-law, Elvira Brusaferro, who lived through the war next to the station at Padova.
14 The certificate, dated 17 January 1944 and a photograph of which was submitted by Nono to the university, gives the cause as 'pulmonary infiltration on the right, with signs of pleurisy'. Nono's brother-in-law Albano Pivato recalls a bicycle journey they made together to Udine to carry false X-rays for Vespignani.
15 Nono's student records are in the archive of the University of Padova.
16 Bobbio, 2002, p. 43.
17 Marchesi, 2003, p. 15–16.
18 A full account is given in Bonuzzi, 2003.
19 The full citation is in Marchesi, 2003, p. 43.
20 Bobbio, 2002, p. 11.

Accelerated learning: years of study, 1942–50

21 Bobbio was made life senator in 1984. As a teenager in Torino, his intellectual circle included publisher Giulio Einaudi, Cesare Pavese and Massimo Mila – a resistance fighter, the most influential left-wing musicologist of post-war Italy and an early supporter of Nono. Nono mentions first meeting Mila in 1954 (LNII, p. 506).

22 Nono was later invited to speak with Bobbio at a conference on 'Cultura e Partiti' organised by the PSI and the Club Turati on 28–9 October 1977 in Milan (letter from the Direzione Nazionale of the PSI in ALN).

23 Carlo Chevallard on Bobbio's teaching in Torino in 1944, quoted in Roccia and Vaccarino, 1995, p. 512.

24 The *Partito d'Azione* (action party) was the political rallying point of liberal intellectuals and resistance fighters, bringing together nearly all the non-communist anti-fascist elements within a single democratic-socialist organization (De Luna, 1982, p. 17). In a recent resurgence of interest, its manifesto and search for a 'third way' have been described as a continuing model for Italian liberal socialism (Favretto, 2002), and Bobbio's last major work *Destra e sinistra* (Bobbio, 1995) became a best-seller.

25 Bobbio, 1948.

26 Bobbio, 1997, p. 71. Bobbio's own description of this approach as 'the philosophy of crisis' (Bobbio, 1948, p. vii) anticipates a major theme in the early work of Nono's future collaborator, philosopher Massimo Cacciari (Cacciari, 1976).

27 Bobbio, 1997, pp. 45–6.

28 Bobbio, quoted in Bianco, 1973, p.XI.

29 See particularly Bobbio, 1975, 1976.

30 Bobbio, 1955.

31 A fellow student of Nono's, Gianfranco De Bosio (b. 1924), to become an important theatre and film director, made a film of his experiences with the resistance groups around the Partito d'Azione in Venice, *Il terrorista* (1963). This film, which achieved cult status in the politicized environment of 1960s Italy, also gives an invaluable impression of the non-tourist post-war Venice.

32 Interview with Enzo Restagno, 1987. LN II, p. 484.

33 Letter from Bruno Maderna, 1 June 1952, ALN. Maderna's own elaboration of the events of this period must be born in mind (Mila, 1999, p. 116; Fearn, 1990, p. 332).

34 Del Bo, 1944.

35 'Presenza storica nella music d'oggi', 1959. LNI, p. 53.

36 Berdiaev, *Slavery and freedom*, 1939, translated in Lowrie, 1965, p. 315.

37 Berdiaev, 1955, p. 99.

38 Interview with Enzo Restagno, 1987. LNII, p. 484.

39 Nono, 1947, p. 2.

40 In fact both he and Bobbio had sought the approval of Mussolini (Waterhouse, 1999 pp. 44–7; Bobbio, 1997, pp. 54–5); in both cases context suggests that this should be understood as necessary survival strategy for holders of state teaching positions. There was a move to unseat Malipiero from his position at the Conservatory, but he survived as director until his retirement at the age of 70 in 1952. A contemporary assessment of the damage sustained by Italian musical institutions over the period of fascism can be found in *Rivista Musicale Italiana* 48/I: pp. 67–87 (1946).

41 Malipiero's ancestors included two doges of Venice. His grandfather, a composer of opera, had been seen as a rival to Verdi (Waterhouse, 1999, p. 7).

42 He completed the edition in the villa on Lake Garda given to D'Annunzio by Mussolini, a somewhat compromising circumstance.

43 The syllabus had been unchanged since 1930. The examinations taken by Nono were: composition (lower) 9/10 (1947), subsidiary pianoforte 6.2/10, Italian literature, poetry and drama 8/10, subsidiary organ and Gregorian chant 6.5/10, composition (middle) 7/10 (1949). A new national syllabus for composition was not discussed until 1951 (*Rivista Musicale Italiana* 53/IV, pp. 388–94).

44 Interview with Renato Garavaglia, 1979–80. LNII, p. 242.

45 Michele L. Straniero: 'Colloquio con Luigi Nono su musica e impegno politico', 1969. LNII, p. 50.

46 Gatti: 'Una lezione di Malipiero' in Scarpa, 1952, pp. 76–80. Bontempelli, 1942, pp. 167–70.

47 Malipiero makes this clear in a letter to Guido Gatti of 14 October 1945 (Palandri, 1997, pp. 408–9). He refers in his letter to a document demonstrating his resistance, which was finally published in 1992 (*Il sole 24 Ore*, 25 October 1992).

48 Scarpa, 1952, p. 152.

49 Palandri, 1997, p. 409.

Accelerated learning: years of study, 1942–50

50 Malipiero, 1946, p. 72.
51 Interview with Ágnes Hetényi, 1986. LNII, p. 387. In particular, he talks of Vicentino's use of microtones.
52 Interview with Ágnes Hetényi, 1986. LNII, p. 385.
53 Nicola Vicentini *L'antica musica ridotta alla moderna prattica* (Rome, 1555). Gioseffo Zarlino *Le istitutioni harmoniche* (Venice, 1558), *Dimostrationi harmoniche* (Venice 1578). Malipiero bought these books in their original editions in 1922 at considerable personal cost, as he pointed out in his later, self-consciously Venetian autobiographical note (Malipiero, 1966, p. 82).
54 Malipiero in 'Del contrappunto e della composizione', *Rassegna Musicale* XV, 6: pp. 189–193. Quoted in Sanguinetti, 2003, p. 46.
55 Roman Vlad pointed out dodecaphonic tendencies in Malipiero's later work, particularly the *Fantasie concertanti* (1954) (Vlad, 1957, pp. 48–51).
56 Personal communication from Nuria Schoenberg-Nono.
57 Letter from Malipiero to Mario Nono, 1954, ALN.
58 Letter from Malipiero to Nono, 8 August 1951, ALN.
59 'Colloquio con Luigi Nono su musica e impegno politico', 1969. LNII, p. 49.
60 'La battaglia del musicista per una nuova società', 1964. LNI, p. 170.
61 Published just before the war, the book's reputation was more widespread than its distribution.
62 Michele L. Straniero: Colloquio con Luigi Nono su musica e impegno politico, 1969. LNII, p. 49.
63 Interview with Martine Cadieu, 1961. LNII, p. 3.
64 Maderna, quoted in Fearn, 1990, p. 319.
65 The programme comprised: Maderna *Serenata per undici strumenti*, Riccardo Malipiero *Piccolo concerto*, Valentino Bucci *"La dolce pena", cinque rispetti di Agnolo Poliziano*, Guido Turchi *Trio*, Camillo Togni *Variazioni* (LNII, p. 564).
66 Maderna's conducting experience had already included Webern's *Variations* in 1942.
67 From the programme book of the IX Festival Internazionale di Musica Contemporanea, in Mila, 1999, pp. 119–20.
68 Mario Messinis in Baroni and Dalmonte, 1985, p. 170.
69 See, for example, Nono's note to himself in Figure 3.6, otherwise a vital page of compositional working.
70 Interview with Carlo Peddis, 1981. LNII, p. 266. Interview with Enzo Restagno, 1987. LNII, p. 492.
71 Interview with Klaus Kropfinger, 1988. LNII, p. 459.
72 Interview with Klaus Kropfinger, 1988. LNII, p. 459.
73 Interview with Lothar Knessel, 1988. LNII, p. 471.
74 Interview with Enzo Restagno, 1987. LNII, p. 489.
75 Zacconi, 1596 and Vicentino, 1555.
76 Interview with Renato Garavaglia, 1979–80. LNII, pp. 241–2.
77 The Mass by Josquin in which (in Petrucci's Venetian edition) the proportions of the tenor are indicated by dice faces.
78 Interview with Enzo Restagno, 1987. LNII, pp. 488–9.
79 Both subsequently of the Italian state broadcaster RAI. Dall'Oglio's *Cinque espressioni* was performed at Darmstadt in 1952.
80 Maderna in Barone and Dalmonte, 1985, p. 92.
81 A collection of orchestrations from *Odhecaton* was later published by Scherchen's Ars Viva Verlag.
82 Ungaretti signed a copy of his newly published *Sentimento del tempo* for Nono.
83 Schönberg, 1995.
84 Interview with Enzo Restagno, 1987. LNII, p. 507.
85 Scherchen, 1929.
86 Scherchen, 1946.
87 Programme of the *XII Festival di Musica Contemporanea* (1948), p. 143.
88 Scherchen conducted the first performance of Hindemith and Brecht's radio work *Lindberghflug* in 1929.
89 Dallapiccola, 1970, p. 84.
90 Webern, 1963.
91 Hindemith, 1942, pp. 56–81.
92 Hindemith, 1942, p. 58.
93 Hindemith, 1942, p. 82.
94 Hindemith, 1942, p. 137.

Accelerated learning: years of study, 1942–50

95 Rizzardi, 2004.

96 Pauli and Wünsche, 1986, pp. 74–8.

97 Scherchen, 1991, p. 143.

98 Scherchen, 1991, p. 144.

99 Letter from Scherchen to Schönberg, Zürich, 30 September 1950, in Pauli and Wünsche, 1986, p. 63.

100 Married to Omar Catunda in 1934, she changed the spelling of her name after their separation. Nono uses the earlier form.

101 Katunda died in São José dos Campos, São Paulo, in 1990, the same year as Nono.

102 Kater, 2001, p. 20.

103 Katunda, 1949 *A minha viagem para a Europa*. In Kater, 2001, p. 59.

104 Kater, 2001, pp. 49–50.

105 Kater, 2001, p. 52.

106 The copy given to Nono is in ALN. The work is reproduced in Kater, 2001.

107 The organising committee included Riccardo Malipiero, Dallapiccola, Karl Amadeus Hartmann, Koelreutter and Katunda herself.

108 Kater, 2001, p. 24 gives the date as April 1949, Katunda on p. 60 as May 1950.

109 Katunda, 1952 *Atonalismo, dodecafonia e música nacional*. In Kater, 2001, pp. 63–71.

110 Part of Katunda's 1952 refutation of serialism seems to refer specifically to her Italian colleagues: Who would embark on the mermaid's song, making national music using atonality and dodecaphonic techniques, will fall into the same error as the present author: that of sinning by lack of consciousness and excess of ingenuity, which is likewise a form of ignorance. Katunda, 1952, Atonalismo, dodecafonia e música nacional. In Kater, 2001, p. 71.

111 Spangemacher, 1999, p. 35.

112 'Nowadays, in 1969, to limit ourselves to numerical analysis of the series – the technique of Leibowitz, which he himself now mocks – is ridiculous.' LNII, p. 67.

113 Leibowitz, 1949, p. xiii.

114 Leibowitz, 1949, p. xvi.

115 Leibowitz, 1949, p. 18.

116 Leibowitz, 1949, p. xix.

117 Leibowitz, 1949, p. xxi.

118 Leibowitz, 1949, p. 72.

119 Pinzauti, 1970, p. 81.

120 The Italian ISCM was re-formed in 1946. Its patrons included Malipiero and Casella; Dallapiccola, Petrassi and Gatti were among the directors, and Dallapiccola was secretary (*Rivista Musicale Italiana* 48/III: 407–8). Malipiero wrote to Dallapiccola to encourage the ISCM to consider Nono's work. (Letter from Dallapiccola to Nono, 15 January 1948, ALN).

121 Interview with Renato Garavaglia, 1979–80. LNII, p. 242.

122 RAI Torino, 7 July 1947.

123 Letter from Dallapiccola to Nono, 16 November 1947, ALN.

124 Letter from Dallapiccola to Maderna, 27 June 1948, Paul Sacher Stiftung. Notes on the script are in Nono's hand, but given their working practice and Dallapiccola's reply to Maderna it seems unlikely that he and Nono produced two independent analyses.

125 'Luigi Dallapiccola e i "Sex Carmina Alcei"', c. 1948. LNI, pp. 3–5.

126 Dallapiccola himself made clear the role of canon in post-tonal polyphony: *We must underline that the canon [. . .] is not a form but part of the principle of polyphony*. (Dallapiccola, 1970, p. 165)

127 'Con Luigi Dallapiccola', 1979. LNI, pp. 483–4.

128 She gave him two volumes of Lorca's poetry in translation, one of which contains a dedication in Venetian dialect.

129 Interview with Enzo Restagno, 1987. LNII, p. 501.

130 Katunda, 1949, *A minha viagem para a Europa*. In Kater, 2001, p. 60.

131 They had been published with a more limited distribution in 1940. Apart from academic pedantry as to the accuracy of the translations, his earlier hermetic style and subsequent focus on reinterpretation allowed Quasimodo's work to escape fascist censorship.

132 Dallapiccola, 1970, p. 129.

133 That Berio's *Cinque Variazioni* for piano (1952–3) also makes use of the 'fratello' motif (Restagno, 1995, p. 7) may suggest a wider currency of its symbolic role; whether of individual discipleship of Dallapiccola or a sense of common cause is not clear.

3

CONFRONTING MODERNISM

Darmstadt

The emergence of a language

Tall, long, infinitely slim, he carried on his straight narrow shoulders a head likewise all length, which irresistibly made one think of that of some painting, still primitive, of the pre-renaissance, perhaps one of the familiar saints. The gentleness of a vague expression, which seemed to come from very far and to be going very far, towards some mysterious inner vision, a whispering voice, airy, dying on final syllables which one never understood, an apparition, transparent in the air which seemed to vibrate around him, without thinking twice I would have thought him to be Francis of Assisi. [. . .]

These Variations in the form of a canon gave rise to an enormous scandal, [. . .] a scandal provoked, above all, by the sonic consistency of this music, which seemed to call in sound just as a vacuum calls in the air, irresistibly. [. . .] Little by little, these soft short sounds organised themselves like a procession of signals moving slowly forwards, with long spaces between them, spaces inhabited by a disturbing silence.[1]

Antoine Goléa's florid description conveys the impact Nono made at the Darmstadt *Internationalen Ferienkurse für neue Musik* in August 1950.[2] Scherchen had first taught conducting at Darmstadt in 1947; on this occasion he proposed that both his Venetian apprentices should submit works for the concerts he was to conduct. Nono worked on the orchestral *Variazioni canoniche sulla serie dell'op. 41 di Arnold Schönberg* from autumn 1949. In May 1950 he sent his score to Wolfgang Steinecke, founder, director and guiding light of the Darmstadt Summer School.[3] A month later, Steinecke replied that 'The score met with the high approval of the jury, and I think that the work will be programmed if the considerable performance difficulties can be overcome.'[4] He immediately offered Nono a scholarship to attend the course.

As Maderna's conducting career began to flourish, Nono found himself in the role of assistant to both Maderna and, increasingly, Scherchen. He attended Scherchen's concerts, as far as means allowed, visited him at his home at Rapallo in Liguria, and carried out research to support Scherchen's increasing interest in performing pre-classical music.[5] He was party to the rapid, avaricious evolution of Maderna's compositional thought; for Maderna, study, research and teaching were a single process of shared intensity. Maderna's early serial experiments embody much of Dallapiccola's influence – contrapuntal development through canons and mirrors, total chromatic harmony consolidating about quasi-tonal centres – but maintain a reflective distance: 'Personally, I thought that serialism offered musicians more possibilities than the, lets say, "traditional" technique. But I never really felt like poor old Leibowitz [. . .] nor yet like Dallapiccola, enclosed within his rock-crystal.'[6]

Maderna's work retains a synthetic quality; he confronts the listener with a multiplicity of connections reflecting the diversity of his musical experience. From the outset, the interweaving of structural and referential elements is more mediated in Nono's music. In *Variazioni canoniche* he consciously sets out the elements of a coherent, self-assured and individual language and the foundations of his subsequent practice. Many of the fundamental components of his technique are here, particularly the weaving of densely worked material from polyphonic strands – even if the result is to be a single line – and the initial spinning of its warp and woof from miraculously fine resources. These resources have a crucial lack of mimetic or semantic burden. Nono's essentialist approach to material allows him to carefully manage its evolving structural properties through an iterative compositional process. At the same time, a self-awareness of composition as an ethical activity subtends the poetic integrity of the musical surface. That Nono developed this approach before becoming embroiled in the wider discourses of compositional modernism and politics is crucial to the independence and poetry of his work.

> For me it has always been clear that a man can realise himself only in his relationships with his equals and with society. In my first pieces individual sounds are not so important; for example pitches do not count so much as intervals, the relationships between resulting musical figures; and these relationships cannot be explained away in terms of the vertical or the horizontal but embrace every level of composition – like a net that extends in all directions. [. . .]
>
> I always worked in three stages. First I chose the material, intervallic, timbral, rhythmic. Then I experimented with this material, subjected it to various procedures just to see in what directions it could evolve. And then I composed, deduced an appropriate form from the material and from its inherent possibilities. Thus for me composition was never the making concrete of preformed structures.[7]

Nono's concise description of his process holds for much of his career. This chapter will consider his early procedures in some detail; we see the emergence of paradigms and practices that will evolve and resurface throughout his work.

'*Variazioni canoniche sulla serie dell'op. 41 di Arnold Schönberg*'

The idea of basing such a significant work on material from Schönberg was with Nono from the outset. He writes out the twelve-note rows from the *Suite* op. 29, *Quartet* op. 30, *Piano Piece* op. 33a and *Piano Concerto* op. 42 as well as the op. 41 *Ode to Napoleon Buonaparte* itself. The op. 41 row stands out in its reflective symmetry and concentration on two intervals: semitone and major 3rd (Figure 3.1). As in his notes from Scherchen's lectures, each is notated as a series of intervals as well as pitches. Schönberg sets Byron's poem against tyranny for *Sprechgesang*, strings and piano. The *Ode* is the embodiment of his own ethical stance and serves as reference for Nono in many respects.

Figure 3.1 *Variazioni canoniche*: series from Schönberg op. 41 as notated by Nono

From the beginning Nono planned four 'episodes'. He already displays an acute sense of the *scope* of compositional structures, of the time and degree of manipulation they can sustain. The *Due liriche greche* could be built as single spans; here a more complex architecture is necessary to sustain his aesthetic vision. As he maps the terrain of his new work, models and procedures emerge that allow a glimpse of Nono's conceptual musical space – archetypes of thought that will persist and evolve. For example, he uses an iterative, narrowing spiral remapping to generate three new series. He takes every seventh note of the original, every seventh of the result, and subsequently every third, eliminating pitches already used. He maps the interval content of each series against an axis of 'calma – tensione' derived from Hindemith's *Unterweisung* (5 4 6+ 3+ 6– 3– 7– 2+ 4+ 7+ 2– in Nono's diatonic notation). This practice would persist; Guerrero makes a convincing argument for the fundamental importance of Hindemith's approach to Nono's early works, but its traces remain throughout the next forty years.[8] He marks the series' characteristic intervals and works over the material in its every manifestation using multiple colours. Analysis in colour seems to derive from conducting practice as taught by Scherchen. Such multilayered graphical filtering will become increasingly central to Nono's compositional process.

The third variant, rich in perfect fourths, is marked *serie iniziale* at one point (Figure 3.2). The E he considers eliminating; in fact, it will become a structural pivot. In the midst of this serial exploration appear verses 9 and 10 from the Gregorian *Dies Irae*. Nono notes that, like Schönberg's row, it consists almost entirely of seconds and thirds. The interval analysis of Gregorian chant was a staple in Scherchen's classes. The *Dies Irae* is central to Dallapiccola's *Canti di Prigionia*, his own statement against repression, which Nono presumably had in mind. On the same sheet he sets out the rhythmic base of the work – a characteristically essentialist sequence of values reducing from eight semiquavers to one, the last three grouped together to make six elements in all (Figure 3.3). A variant replaces each value with two of half its length; retaining ties between note values introduces an asymmetry that makes the new variant more than an elaboration of the original by creating distinct retrogrades. This property is retained in a sequence of canons and permutations. The role played by the conventions of notation is significant. In later work, such durations become abstract values; here their development is conditioned by the metrical structure.

Figure 3.2 Variazioni canoniche: third derived row

Figure 3.3 Variazioni canoniche: rhythm base and variant

Another area for exploration is opened out through a process of permutation and remapping, a graphical technique that allows him both to perform distant manipulations of the material and to see potential structure in the results. Schönberg's row is transformed by remapping space rather than series. The first begins with a 'salto a 1' ('jump by 1'). Instead of 12 . . . 1 down the vertical axis, we now have 11 9 7 5 3 1 2 4 6 8 10 12. The pitches of the original series are projected onto this new space. By mapping the transformed pitch space back onto a conventional ordering, a new series is derived; 9 10 5 6 becomes 11 2 4 9 (Figure 3.4). Below, Nono plots the interval succession thus generated, noting symmetries, periodicities and similarities. Variants of this process are grouped into four sections in which he performs such permutations on reducing subgroups of 12, 6, 4 or 3 notes, such that the numbers of possibilities increase. The folding and stretching of space will remain characteristic of Nono's musical thought. In working with contrapuntal models it permits him to manipulate abstract structures while retaining a sense of their compositional role.

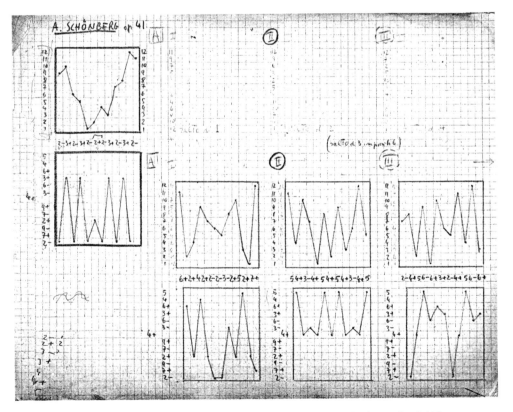

Figure 3.4 Variazioni canoniche: remapping of series. (ALN 01.01/05. © The heirs of Luigi Nono. Reproduced by kind permission.)

Four episodes do indeed emerge, characterised not by row form, but by their different polyphonic weave. The first, *Largo vagamente*, sets the sonic scene described by Goléa and establishes key elements of Nono's palette: low woodwind at a dynamic such that they barely speak; high, muted string harmonics; a tempo (♩ = 30) below the range of human physicality that leaves space for hearing to explore detail; the whole punctuated by isolated, ringing harp notes. The listener is unsure whether perceived melodic fragments are actually written into the musical surface or are a product of their own search for structure in this shifting space. This property will become the very stuff of Nono's music in the later works.

A 10-bar passage of two-part counterpoint forms the basis of the whole section (Figure 3.5). It appears to be a product of the process of reordering described above, and the rhythm cell is clearly presented in the last four bars. Nono's use of this material demonstrates his technique for weaving a musical fabric irrespective of the number of voices it ultimately contains. His indications 'a 2', 'a 3' etc., redolent of earlier polyphony, refer to the simultaneous number of such textures; the number of individual voices may be much greater. Rooted in Venetian polyphonic, polychoral writing, this will remain fundamental to Nono's practice. This material is developed as a double mirror-canon according to a scheme described in full in terms of inversion and direction, transposition and relative delay (Figure 3.6). 'Per Bruno' refers to a list of errands for his absent friend.

Figure 3.5 Variazioni canoniche: Largo vagamente, contrapuntal basis

The resulting four-voice polyphony is subjected to painstaking analysis in four colours. Nono looks for harmonic augmented fourths, unisons, semitones and emergent motivic relationships. Below, he constructs a new polyphony of five voices from the aggregate of the double mirror-canon. The notes of the original are freely selected, recombined and octave-shifted. This is subject to further analysis to derive a second set of new voices, now four. In both cases a bass part is written first, perhaps an artefact of his continuing study of conventional counterpoint. An additional voice is constructed of the notes *not* used in the second four-part construct. This concept of negative material will become important, a reminder of the broader space of potentiality through which a work navigates. Finally, the four voices are retranscribed in conventional order, marked as section I and annotated with ideas for orchestration and tempo (Figure 3.7). This passage, its durations doubled, will become the first fifty bars of the *Largo vagamente*.

A canonic structure distributed among multiple voices of percussion elides into the *Andante moderato*. Sustained rolls at extreme dynamics will become another stable Nono trope. Waves of *muovendo* and *rallentando* are laid across a patchwork of canons – canons in their origin and

Confronting modernism: Darmstadt

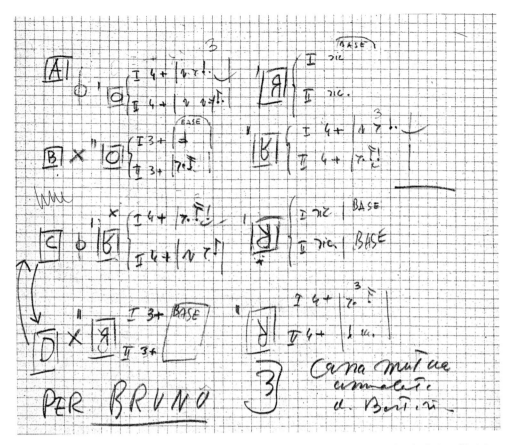

Figure 3.6 Variazioni canoniche: combination scheme. (ALN 01.03.01/02 (detail). © The heirs of Luigi Nono. Reproduced by kind permission.)

in their strength as musical fabric, but without a transparently imitative surface. They begin as rhythmic structures. The six elements of the *ritmo base* and their mirrors are rearrranged in four permutations. Each of these is also mapped as a sequence of pairs of pitches from the original row, retaining traces of Schönberg's melodic succession in their rearrangement. In another process of remediation, Nono then constructs a thirty-two bar three-part rhythm canon in 6/8 using the sequence of permutations of rhythm elements. The gap between voices is progressively increased by an additional quaver between each group of six elements. From this Nono derives a sparser five-part rhythmic texture, ignoring ties in the original where additional attacks are needed (Figure 3.8).

He is careful to give the new voices quite distinct characteristics, introducing asymmetries and additional imitation. He then maps out a series of mirror-canons based on these five voices, and a process of substitution by which the rests are to be gradually reduced. The first three of these are the basis of the *Andante*, the last (marked *base*) of the third episode *Allegro violento*. The second voice appears in the double mirror canon 2–2R–3R from bar 95 (Figure 3.9).

The original three-part canon provides the rhythm of the *Allegro violento*, its durations doubled to make sixty-four bars. Pitches appear precisely as in the plan of rhythm-pitch correlation made prior to the canon. Schönberg's row is thus the first to appear, the presentation

Figure 3.7 Variazioni canoniche: mirror-canon, filtering and retranscription. (ALN 01.03.01/03r. © The heirs of Luigi Nono. Reproduced by kind permission.)

Figure 3.8 Variazioni canoniche: derivation of new voices from canon on *ritmo base*

Figure 3.9 Variazioni canoniche: second voice from Figure 3.8, in bars 95–8

of each pitch by two instruments preparing the pairwise permutations that map out the subsequent pitch space of this section. Nono exploits rhythmic and imitative continuity to draw broad, dramatic waves of crescendo and diminuendo punctuated by single attacks, repeated notes or brief passages of sustained *fff*. Extreme registers and colours characterise the orchestration; piano, harp and timpani link the remaining percussion into the structure. As often in Nono's later work, clearly pitched sounds are the mid-point on a timbral continuum from the spectral complexity of percussion to the perceptual ambiguity of extreme registers and dynamics.

The final *Lento* seems to have been taking shape in Nono's mind from early on. He had experimented with the fourth-rich third variant of the row at various stages. He writes out all twelve transpositions of Schönberg's row, each followed by its mirror. Below, he notates two ascending circles of fourths – one beginning on E, the other ending on E. The twin circles of fourths and map of mirrored rows reflect Nono's initial conception of the work as an enveloping mirror form. His sequences of permutations use patterns of forwards and return, often illustrated graphically. Nono regularly seems to imagine a structure simultaneously with its mirror, and there is a further simultaneity in his exploration of this space both as sequence (out followed by back) and as bifurcation (two parallel possibilities of development). This is a lesson learned from his study of early polyphony. Herein lies the origin of the 'wedge' shape of expansion and contraction, ascent and descent, which writers would observe in Nono's work. It is evident in his very first sketches for the opening of this final section and will determine its entire serial structure (Figure 3.10).

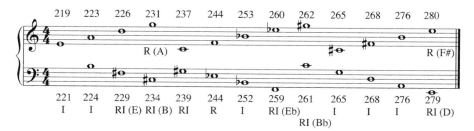

Figure 3.10 Variazioni canoniche: pitch structure of *Lento* (bars 217–83)

Two circles of fourths – one rising E–E, one falling E–E – form the skeleton around which Nono hangs all twelve transposition of Schönberg's row, in their various mirrors and inversions, but otherwise unchanged. With two exceptions, the ascending cycle presents original forms of the row while the descending cycle explores its variants. The original row is introduced by the harp over the fourth-chord F♯–B–E–A–D sustained from the opening, and balanced by an inversion in the piano. Its complement at the end of the work, a retrograde starting on F♯, is likewise presented by the harp at bar 280, now over a chord of fourths built on B♭. The centrepiece of this symmetrical journey is the soprano saxophone solo in bars 244–53, presenting the original row on F – the sixth member of the ascending cycle – followed by its mirror, with rhythms permuted from the original six-element cell. Accompanying this uniquely sustained lyrical passage, the retrograde row on E♭ – the sixth member of the descending cycle – moves up through the entire string section. This sustained texture sustain dissolves into individual pizzicato attacks following the mirror of the same series at precisely the moment when the saxophone begins its return in bar 249. Either side of this solo, Nono manages serial transparency with great invention. There are melodic loops, elisions, echoes and compression into harmonic aggregates – especially in the piano. He plays with the degree of continuity – timbral, temporal and rhythmic. A series might continue after a gap and with an entirely different gesture. Whole series in single voices are rare; the complete violin 1 statement at bar 226 is mirrored near the end by the viola at bar 276. Once again, Nono approaches the problem graphically, drawing interlocking shapes to show the distribution of different versions of the row among the multiple strings – four violins, violas and cellos, two double-basses. Apart from the saxophone, the wind remain silent to the end of the work. Each presentation of a row-form is characterised by its degree of polyphonic complexity, the number of real voices across which it is distributed (as distinct from the number of instruments for which it is scored). The initial expansion into the cycles of fourths illustrates this process (Figure 3.11).

The remaining pitch material derives from the modulation of the various row forms with the cycles of fourths which occasionally emerge explicitly, as in the harp at bar 264. This process – the resonance given to certain pitches because of their relation to a wider harmonic context – both shows traces of modality and anticipates the 'spectralist' composers of thirty years later. Figure condenses into ever smaller units through the final section. The romantic gestures of string solos are focused down into pinpoint outlines of piano and harp, a last clear image emerging from rolled cymbals. They rehearse the four-note shape with which Schönberg's row begins and ends, like fragments of song-memory in a Mahlerian coda.

The moral, supra-political engagement of Schönberg's *Ode* clearly stood as a landmark for Nono, but the resonances are also structural. Nono certainly knew Leibowitz's analysis, in which he points to the importance of fourths and fifths, the freedom or opacity of Schönberg's use of the series (it never appears straightforwardly), and the way in which Schönberg constructs

Figure 3.11 Variazioni canoniche: Lento bars 223–27, showing distribution of rows Oa and Ib. (Reproduced by kind permission of Ricordi.)

a language that moves freely between chromatic and triadic patterns. All of these are important properties of Nono's *Variazioni*. In addition, Schönberg's explicit references to the *Marseillaise* and Beethoven (the Fifth Symphony at the entrance of the reciter and the heroic key of E♭ in the final cadence) anticipate Nono's own incorporation of other material. Schönberg's radical recasting of the relationship between word and musical figure, his reimagining of song, will have a fundamental and enduring impact on Nono's thought.

Nono later described the performance on 27 August as 'an incredible scandal', a situation that may have been exacerbated by Scherchen silencing the audience; he described them as 'a band of pigs', Nono recalled.[9] Hans Heinz Stuckenschmidt reported the scene described by Goléa, but his conclusion was less generous; he found the music 'incomprehensible to the unprepared'.[10] Developments at festivals such as Darmstadt were discussed in detail in newspapers across Germany – a situation difficult to picture in our own century. While several critics found no music in Nono's work, others reflected in more detail. The *Darmstädter Echo* found that:

> The Italian composers demonstrate a felicitous connection between structure and sonority: Bruno Maderna in his *Composizione II* for chamber orchestra, and Luigi Nono in an even more concentrated, esoteric way in his *Variazioni canoniche* which puts sections of exceptional development against long-winded passages which thus slowly maltreat his tone-row to death.[11]

For the *Göttinger Tageblatt*, Nono's 'economical variations on a theme of Schönberg bespeak a very subtle sensitivity to sound, but also an uneven focus [. . .]'.[12] There was also partisan

Confronting modernism: Darmstadt

reaction: Hans-Werner Henze, another of Scherchen's protégés, found that 'This music unites past and future [. . .] Nothing is known, neither the borders nor the paths that lead to them.'[13] This last observation will prove prescient in terms of the motto of Nono's last years. The variations would have to wait thirty-five years for another performance; the only score was lost and Nono would reconstruct it from the parts for a performance conducted by Michael Gielen in 1985.

As well as the self-confidence gained from a first encounter with the international atmosphere of Darmstadt, Nono's development was fuelled by contact with extraordinary individuals. Three lectures on 'The Sound-World of Electronic Music' were given by composer and sound editor Robert Beyer and scientist Werner Meyer-Eppler. Meyer-Eppler, on the faculty of the Phonetic Institute of the University of Bonn, had set out a view of purely electronic composition and its relationship with speech in a book in 1949.[14] His work with communication related to the new science of information theory. At Darmstadt he gave a lecture on 'The Problem of Timbre in Electronic Music' in which he demonstrated not only filtering techniques but also the vocoder, developed for the analysis and resynthesis of speech.[15] Sound is thereby understood in terms of its energy in different frequency bands, a radically new mode of conception for musicians that Meyer-Eppler illustrated graphically, projecting 'the score of the future'. Nono thus encountered ideas on information theory, psychoacoustics, models of sound, graphical representation, and the role of technology that were entirely outside his experience and were to become fundamental to his work.

Most dramatic was Nono's encounter with Edgard Varèse, whose presence at Darmstadt marked his rehabilitation in Europe and the acknowledgement of the visionary nature of his earlier work.

> The day after the performance I went to his class and he asked me for the score. He analysed it for some hours and then instead of giving me his opinion, he posed problems, he made me understand what questions that score gave rise to, informing me in that way what I had done without realising. As you see it's always a question of that famous mystery of composition.[16]

Varèse's *Ionisation* for percussion was performed the week before *Variazioni canoniche*. As we have seen, Nono was already exploring the liminal space between pitched and unpitched sounds in the opening of his own work. Here he is establishing a continuum between sound and not-sound – an active silence of many possible colours – which will become a principal structuring feature of his later works. Already in these early pieces the use of extreme registers and dynamics begins to blur the distinction. There are other Varèsian features in Nono's work which pre-date their meeting: the use of pitch to articulate rhythm, the dimensional shifting of pitch material from horizontal, linear energy to a vertical gravitational force and the use of clear attractors in both pitch and rhythm. Varèse's fascination with the energy of figural rhythm also resonated with Nono; in his work premiered at Darmstadt the following year, he would likewise turn to Latin-American sources. Nono was particularly struck by Varèse's 'projection of harmonic space',[17] an image that tells us much about his own modes of thought. The most important product of meeting Varèse appears to have been a sense that Nono was not alone or eccentric in his intuitions and concerns, that the thoughts taking shape – formulated quite differently to those of his peers – constituted a coherent response to the historical and technical state of music.

Dodecaphonic variations

Venice, 2 June 1951

Dearest Maestro,

I have sent a copy of my music for Darmstadt to Zürich: 'Polifonica-monodia-ritmica', together with the score on transparencies.

In this work I have tried to express three successive relationships with nature: **polifonica**, based on an original Brazilian rhythm shown me by Catunda in Venice during your course, is a gradual coming alongside to nature to find myself, in the **monodia**, listening directly to silences, to songs, to echoes that she seems to suggest and which draw me into her primordial life, making the indestructible force even clearer to me – **ritmo**, which is life itself.

You will sense the presence of Catunda in my work: with Eunice particularly I felt nature – in Fučík the force of nature is identified with the serene resolution of man –

I have finished the first episode: it characterises the limits which would constrain man, almost destroy him – arrest, interrogation, violence and the consequent state of semi-agony –

In the second episode the memory of the reality of struggle allows the overcoming of the dangers of isolation; and in the third episode the man, despite his impending execution, is strong and serene in the certainty that 'life is cut down in one and grows in a hundred, life is stronger than death', that 'the duty of man does not end with this struggle: being a man will continue to require a courageous heart, until men are finally completely men.'[18]

This characteristically non-linear letter summarises Nono's work since the previous summer – two major compositional projects: *Fučík*, never to be finished, and *Polifonica – Monodia – Ritmica* for wind, piano and percussion, finished but radically edited before its performance at the Darmstadt Summer School in 1951. It suggests a close relationship between them; two parallel three-part narratives, one concerned with the experience of music, the other with that of humanity. The letter also points to the emergence of longer term concerns: silences, songs and echoes, and a sense of the fundamental relationship between creativity, individual struggle and human progress. It is surely no coincidence that Maderna had been working on another literary project, a treatment of Kafka's *Trial*, likewise not to be completed.

'Fučík'

Julius Fučík's *Notes from the Gallows* is an account of his imprisonment as a resistance organiser in occupied Czechoslovakia and subsequent condemnation to death in Berlin in 1943.[19] Assembled from notes smuggled out of the prison, it details the basest and finest of human behaviour. Fučík's journalistic skills are evident even in this distressing document, and the book

Confronting modernism: Darmstadt

went through many editions. Particularly poignant and significant for Nono's later dramatic work are the moments when the prisoners sing together, united in their resistance to inhumanity despite their different languages. Buoyed by the experience of *Variazioni canoniche*, Nono now confronted head-on both the ethical and technical aspects of his view of composition.

Fučík – no more polished title emerges – is conceived as a cantata for chorus and orchestra with both singing and speaking soloists. A model may have been Schönberg's *A Survivor from Warsaw* which Nono had heard Scherchen conduct at least twice: at the 1948 Venice Biennale and at Darmstadt a week before his own *Variazioni canoniche*. Three episodes are planned from the start, as Nono experiments with three-sided acrostic permutations of forces (Fučík, Nazis, chorus), material and compositional approaches (melody, rhythm, harmony). He begins by distilling a dialogue from crucial scenes: Fučík's arrest and brutal interrogation, separation from his wife and his final meditations before his execution. From this, Nono derives quasi-natural speech rhythms in a framework suggested by the Nazis' first instruction: *Marsch!* He works with nested permutations of the anapest rhythm *Hände Auf!* to construct a *canone atomica a 4* by shifting and augmenting the delay between entries. In this he plans a microcosm of the whole and of the parallel work: voices (melody) – percussion (rhythm) – harmony.

Nono's starting point is an expanding all-interval series of the kind demonstrated by Scherchen in his course, arranged such that its inherent symmetry is partially obscured (Figure 3.12).

Figure 3.12 Fučík: pitch series

Writers would later point to the importance of an expanding all-interval series in works from *Il canto sospeso* onwards. Here Nono already explores the role of the series as a pitch mine, a dynamic generator of intervallic material. The series had lost any trace of thematicism with the permutation techniques of *Variazioni canoniche*. In *Fučík*, Nono still prefers to characterise dramatic elements at this level, however. He evolves separate series for Fučík himself – 'melodic', an outward-facing undulating series of major and minor ninths and major sixths – and the Nazis – 'harmonic', major and minor sevenths and minor sixths descending across seven octaves. Individual and social structures orthogonally define a conceptual space to be explored in music. From these he plans to derive two versions for each of the three episodes, the intended sequence of which is the mirror of Nono's subsequent *Polifonica – Monodia – Ritmica*:

1   episode: harmonic – rhythmic;
2   episode: monody;
3   episode: contrapuntal and harmonic construction.

Nono experiments with applying permutation to dynamics, anticipating a more integrated serialism. He also begins to cut pages of sketches into strips of one, two or three staves, reassembling them into extended lines. The physicality of his material is becoming important.

The first episode is complete apart from some of the vocal parts. Again, a slow introduction seems to bring music into existence from nothing, presaging Nono's later obsession with liminal sounds at the boundaries of audibility or stability. He shares with the listener the emergence and self-construction of the music from space, silence and the slightest of gestures. Pianissimo percussion are joined by pitched sounds in extreme registers, energy increasing as the texture is disturbed by extreme crescendos of unpredictable speed. An *allegro violente* follows, built around the 'nazi canon'. The shout 'Hände auf!' initiates the process in an array of percussion, the entries of wind and strings intensifying the drama and providing distorting mirrors for the canon. This rhythmic complexity evolves in dialogue through Fučík's interrogation in the third part, an *ostinato ritmico*, between the unbending *ritmo nazi* and Fučík's freer human prose rhythm. Fučík is alone in the final *adagio*, his speech rhythm derived from Nono's initial annotation of the text. His line dissolves as the composer seems to wrestle with the question of how to give it appropriate dramatic prominence against the background of closely woven orchestral texture.

Why was Nono unable to finish a project so close to his heart? The political currency of Fučík's book is illustrated by Burjakowski's 1951–2 production at the Deutsches Theater in East Berlin, which Nono saw during his first visit. It may be that after this experience he felt either that his own work was no longer necessary or that it was dramatically irresolvable. The compositional process itself presented a technical challenge: the construction of a complex orchestral texture, albeit on the basis of rhythm derived from the text, on which Nono lays the solos and choral parts carrying the words themselves. In effect, therefore, the music was structurally and poetically complete before the addition of the text. Stenzl suggests that Nono had recognised that a work based on a text by a communist was unperformable in the current climate.[20] The powerful melodrama of the existing episode suggests a more personal reason, however: that Nono was resisting the temptation to treat the material in any way that could possibly be regarded as indulgent. The suddenness of his discontinuing of *Fučík* suggests that he had surprised himself with the ease with which his technical fluency could generate a musical narrative with its own emotional momentum. Still decades later, working with live electronics, he would describe the risks of sound becoming lost in its own beauty.[21] The voice of Fučík will resurface in *Intolleranza 1960*, which in many ways is the realisation of musical-dramatic, political and technical ideas developed in the earlier project.

'Polifonica – Monodia – Ritmica'

The more abstract nature of *Polifonica – Monodia – Ritmica* would seem to confirm its inception as a series of technical studies for *Fučík*. Even here, however, the work is bound up with external narratives. The fair copy of the score is dedicated to Eunice Katunda. The process of its composition manifests a desire to explore the personal and social power of music, motivated by Nono's understanding of the common, transforming ownership of a simple piece of musical material – the Brazilian popular song *Jumanja* shared with him by Katunda.[22] He does so forensically, experimenting with the primacy of various parameters in the compositional process, approaches Nono had refined in his work on *Variazioni canoniche*. In *Fučík*, these types afforded a dramatic function. Here, their sequence constitutes a perfectly classical scheme: structural and developmental weight in the first movement, clearer, more spacious melodic focus in the second, and a finale driven by rhythmic energy.

Polifonica, the most complex, consists of four episodes based on the same pitch material but structured quite autonomously. In the opening *Adagio* Nono adopts a technique developed by Maderna over the previous months.[23] The original series is analysed by interval content, as was by now conventional in their work. New sequences of diminishing length are then generated as each pair in one iteration is replaced by a single pitch in the next. The new pitch is

Figure 3.13 Polifonica: series substitution process. (ALN 02.03/02rsx. © The heirs of Luigi Nono. Reproduced by kind permission.)

determined by the difference between the two it replaces (A–D or 1–6 in this case, a difference of five semitones) counting from A, the note of origin. Hence in this case A and D are replaced by C♯. This progressively reduces the length of the derived series, such that after ten iterations only a single pitch remains. The intermediate stages have intervallic roots in the original material but little audible thematic relationship. This filtering of pitches creates the kind of opportunity for disequilibrium being sought by composers as they confronted the implications of serialism. Nono arranges the results as inverted pyramids, one for each form of the series. Repeated notes are replaced with rests, giving each form its own rhythmic character and decreasing the density of events as the process evolves (Figure 3.13).

Nono lays bare these properties by allocating a full 12 quavers to each stage of the process – two bars of five, one of two. He begins from the most reduced stage of each of the four rowforms in canon, separated by 3 quavers. Some intervening rests and repeated notes are replaced by cymbals – a different pitch associated with each the row form. Cymbals alone mark the start of the otherwise empty twelfth line of the process with which the piece begins, their succession outlining the pitch contour of the initial entries. The wind play *sempre suono d'eco*, the cymbals are touched only with feathers; the music arises from the distant memory of its own outline. Clarinet, bass clarinet, flute and horn then each add a single note to the texture and the subsequent increase of textural, rhythmic, intervallic density follows Nono's plan (Figure 3.14). Pitch centres and characteristic intervals thus emerge to dissolve into a more complex texture as entropy increases, until at bar 34 they are presented in sequence, each distributed through the entire ensemble.

The *Andante* that follows is a remediated, redistributed rhythmic canon of the type used in *Variazioni canoniche*. He begins by generating a set of elemental rhythmic figures from the simple long – short seed (Figure 3.15).

To this he adds additional semiquavers, producing further rhythmic figuration by combining some into quavers. These are recombined according to a plan of permutations to produce the

Figure 3.14 *Polifonica*: opening, bars 1–14

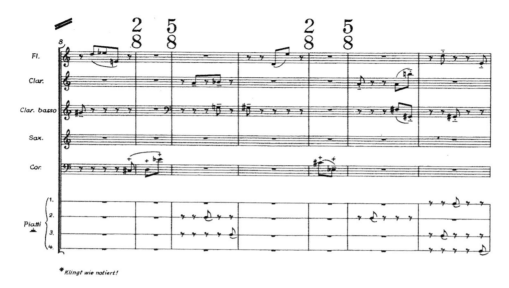

Figure 3.14 continued

Figure 3.15 Polifonica: root rhythm from Andante

upper and lower voices of the rhythmic canon. The middle voice disrupts their symmetry by an incremental process of additional rests. Permutations of inversion, retrograde and retrograde inversion of the opening series match the ten groups of six rhythm cells. They are extended by internal loops, creating local figure, pattern and pitch centre.

Finally, the canon is analysed for interval content and retranscribed, its three-part nature largely obscured in the process (Figure 3.16). Despite references to percussion in the canon – usually the 'tails' of sixteenth notes – the retranscription is for wind only, clouding its rhythmic origins still further.

That Scherchen almost entirely removed this passage from the performing edition – 120 bars between bars 58 and 59 of the published score – may have benefited the drama of the work at its first performance at Darmstadt on 10 July 1951. Indeed, Nono's sense of form in this case was certainly architectural rather than rhetorical, but this *Andante* presents a fine example of Nono's craft at this moment. The folding together of layers of process design, invention and selection is such that every element of the resulting musical surface is the product of multiple modes of decision-making. At each juncture Nono is careful to produce materials that both afford his next intended manipulation and are robust under its transformation: plastic, highly integrated and able to withstand radical composition decisions. If the structural derivation of the musical surface is often opaque in Nono, it is because of this richness of origin and significance. Choice, circumstance and technique are carefully situated in the process.

Scherchen's cut also encompasses the fifty bars of the following *Allegro moderato*. Another redistributed canonic structure, it uses exactly the same pitch material as the previous section. Rhythmic elements now derive from Katunda's song, its main figure divided into three units (Figure 3.17).

Figure 3.16 Polifonica: retranscription of opening of *Andante*. (ALN 02.03/02vsx. © The heirs of Luigi Nono. Reproduced by kind permission.)

Confronting modernism: Darmstadt

Figure 3.17 Polifonica: rhythm from Katunda

An additional quaver rest allows Nono to permute, shift and reconfigure these elements to create six three-beat variants, each with its retrograde. Materials and their mirror by default exist together, whether rhythm or pitch, allowing him to pilot their development through time by the introduction and management of asymmetries. The basic rhythm pattern is finally announced by percussion alone at the start of the *Allegro* (bar 179 = bar 59 in the published edition) and generates the rest of the movement. Density and orchestration give shape to the internal canons as they shift between percussion, piano and wind; sometimes pure rhythm, sometimes in waves of fragmented polyphony, sometimes punctuating the texture with harmonic rhythmic unisons. A progressive reduction of density and rhythmic diversity towards the end of the movement mirrors the opening, reinforcing the bidirectional nature of the underpinning structures and returning to isolated percussion sounds.

The central movement *Monodia* is an orchestrated, elaborated monody, to which Nono adds an almost programmatic narrative in one sketch:

> In the face of nature (sand dunes – sea – serene nocturnal atmosphere) – echoes of natural life are heard from afar
>
> To be able to join in! Very difficult
> They seem less unclear to us: perhaps they're not just echoes
> Still difficult!
> The desire to understand and participate is strengthened by the will to liberate
>   ourselves from the superstructure to which we are conditioned
> [. . .] but is this possible?
> Gradually the echoes reveal themselves as songs of freedom
> Nature begins to join in
> It is already less difficult to understand
> Joy grows within us; we are constantly more aware of the relationship – perhaps
> nature continues to sing
> nature calls us; we hear it, sweetly penetrating us with violence, with loving insistence
> we are sand dunes, sea; serene nocturnal atmosphere[24]

The role of this text is ambiguous: a structuring device, his response to his own work, a personal confirmation of his music's poetic origins, or perhaps for another reader, for Maderna? It appears to be by Nono himself, recalling the concerns of his grandfather and echoing the imagery of Pavese, in whose work Nono would soon be immersed. Most resonant are the references to 'echoes and silences'. 'Suono d'eco' is a performance instruction that appears here, at the opening of *Variazioni canoniche*, and throughout Nono's work. Echoes and silences are not dramatic or colouristic devices; they are essential technical/aesthetic material woven into the whole and will become a vital structuring metaphor. In his late works, the physical response of an acoustic to a single sound will provide enough feedback to seed the compositional process. Here the quietest possible sounds magnify and explore the edge of silence, the edge of the act of performance, just as he often uses percussion to investigate the edge of pitch.

For *Monodia*. Nono selects a sequence of series permutated in pairs and spatially reordered as in *Variazioni canoniche*. They are characterised as being either harmonic or melodic according

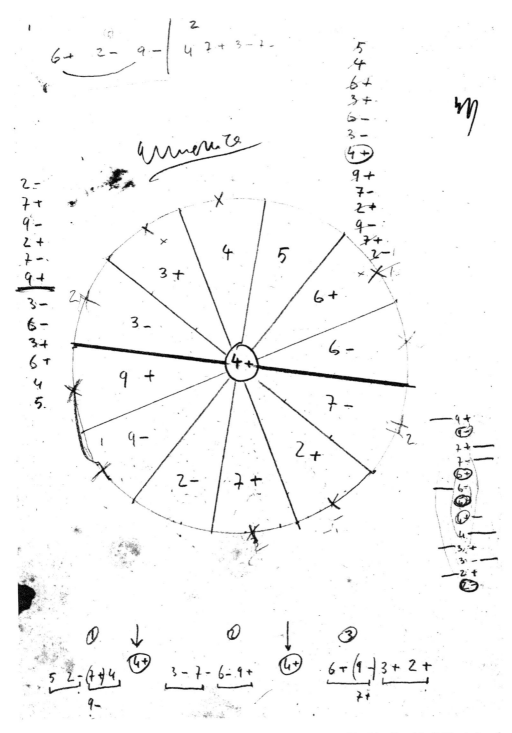

Figure 3.18 Interval circles: 'melodic' and 'harmonic'. (ALN 02.02.01/82r, 81v (details). © The heirs of Luigi Nono. Reproduced by kind permission.)

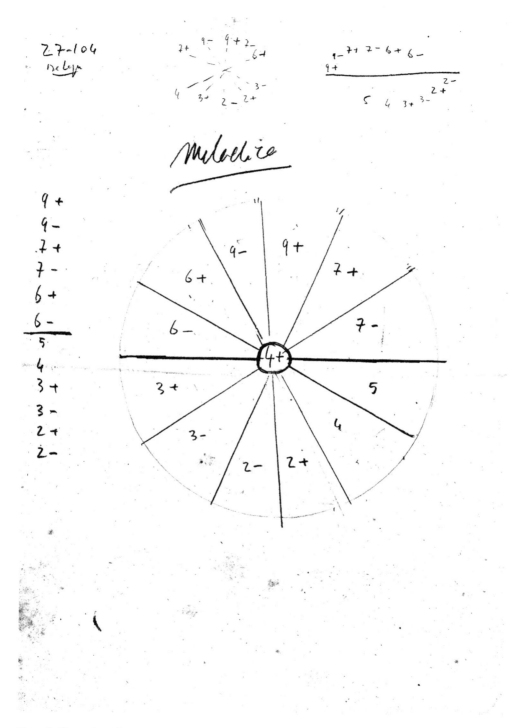

Figure 3.18 continued

to circular diagrams Maderna and Nono derived from Hindemith (Figure 3.18).[25] Probably not by coincidence they resemble one of Schönberg's row-manipulating devices, or the colour wheels of Goethe or Johannes Itten, whose work would inform Nono's late music. The harmonic wheel derives directly from Hindemith's *Unterweisung*, with the addition of ninths.[26] The melodic wheel embodies a principle of complementarity whereby the narrowest intervals are balanced by the widest. In both cases the tritone, the still point, stands at the centre. In Monodia, chains of intervals of different lengths persist, are transformed, disappear and return as in the multiply folded and kneaded forms of chaos theory. Nono arranges them to give the movement a characteristically symmetrical form:

A – 4 harmonic, 2 harmonic/melodic
B – 9 melodic
A – 2 harmonic/melodic, 4 harmonic, original series.

In the first performance and subsequent edition, Scherchen retained the drama and symmetry at the cost of entirely removing the melodic heart of the movement.[27] The monody runs through the entire movement. Nono uses the poem as a guide for its orchestration – distributing the monody, sculpting texture by overlapping and proliferation, and adding his ideas for the percussion. We hear the fine grain of his material as melody is constructed through the first section: first with a single note barely emerging from the sound of cymbals, then two overlapping pairs, phrases of four notes, six notes, and finally an extended nine-note phrase ending with the first repeated pitches of the movement and returning to the percussion in a double echo (Figure 3.19).[28]

Figure 3.19 Monodia, bars 1–6

Confronting modernism: Darmstadt

The monody is a song suspended above the sound of quietly rolling cymbal, as if condensed from its sonic background by breath. No sound is static in Nono's music; attention is constantly drawn to their dynamic equilibrium. The movement proceeds by the progressive elimination of silences until the entire middle section is almost seamless. At the same time the rate and diversity of internal rhythmic figuration increases such that complex melodic constructs become single rhythmic gestures. Repeated demi-semiquavers and isolated tom-tom triplets begin to suggest faster rhythmic grids. In his final draft Nono marks this last section 'più armonica'. Certain pitches are subject to more sustained repetition ('nature continues to sing') as periodicity leads to pure rhythm in the accelerando to the last movement, the piano mediating between pitched instruments and percussion in a mirror of the opening emergence of pitch from noise.

The mirror continues in the opening of the final movement *Ritmica*, now with reference to the opening of the whole piece: unpitched rhythm emerges from the sustained pitch of the horn. The formality of a fugue, replete with subject, countersubject and episodes, is disguised by the essentialist nature of its material (Figure 3.20).

Figure 3.20 Ritmica: rhythmic seed

Once again, there is no figure in this; material does not emerge over-formed but is moulded according to its role. A single beat, the essence of rhythm, is simply repeated at diminishing intervals, as is its negative, a rest. The minimal countersubject plays with different internal divisions while the episodes develop fragmented and permutated subgroups, almost invariably presented with their mirror. The remnants of pitch consist of a series presented by the xylophone, emerging from a sustained horn note and followed immediately by its retrograde as if being folded away. Finally, selective piano resonance is punctuated by a synthesis of percussive piano chords and cymbals; resonance and percussion die back into the space of barely perceptible pitch and time, the rests of the rhythm subject augmented until it dissolves. *Polifonica – Monodia – Ritmica* is a tribute to Varèse as well as Katunda; the percussion-reverberating piano resonance of its final bars is a clear echo of a similar effect at the end of his *Ionisation*, heard at Darmstadt the previous year.

The performance was a resounding success in the hall. Critics largely admired the intensity, coherence and originality of the work, although some were uncertain as to at what point the boundaries of music might be overstepped. Karl H. Wörner wrote: 'in his three movements for 10 soloists, Luigi Nono writes a twelve-tone music of the highest mental concentration, even if it is completely isolated in its uniqueness.'[29] His view was echoed in *Die Zeitschrift für Musik*: 'The Italian Luigi Nono pushes farthest ahead. The extreme economy of his musical language leads to the complete abstraction of composition and ends coherently in rhythmic noise.'[30] Even an unconvinced critic had to acknowledge the clamorous reception:

> Then came a 'work' from the 23-year-old Italian Luigi Nono; it had a priceless advantage: the whole thing lasted only six minutes. [. . .]. What happened then was shocking. For more than ten minutes the hall was in rapturous uproar (mainly young snobs). Again and again Mr Nono appeared on the stage waving both hands as a sign of thanks like a boxer after delivering a knock-out blow.[31]

Herbert Fleischer identified *Polifonica – Monodia – Ritmica* as the most original work of the evening and described it as being a study for a longer work.[32] Perhaps Nono had suggested a

Confronting modernism: Darmstadt

link with the ongoing *Fučík* project. The swingeing cuts made by Scherchen are telling in terms of the relationship between Nono and his mentor. The latter clearly saw his role as vital to the success of the work, as letters make clear. He wrote to his wife after the performance:

> The applause for Nono was rare for a young man – at the end of the piece everything broke out into bravo and praise. The problem with his work is its cerebral nature, which I had moderated a little [. . .]. Thankfully Nono seems to have enough integrity not to draw false conclusions from this success.[33]

Scherchen also put pressure on Nono to publish the work with his own *Ars Viva Verlag* rather than with Schott. In a letter emphasising his role, he ambiguously expresses his certainty that Nono is above the vanity of others.[34] Nono's immediate response illustrates his self-awareness and growing independence. Not only had he immediately acknowledged his mentor's part, he says, but he has also learned from Scherchen not to reflect flattery.[35]

His success in this final concert of the 1951 Summer School seems to have consolidated Nono's position at Darmstadt, although only in 1957 would he become a faculty member. He arranged an invitation for Steinecke to come as a guest to the Biennale in September, for the premiere of Stravinsky's *The Rake's Progress* and a Schönberg memorial concert to be conducted by Scherchen. Steinecke was unable to attend, but over the next few months the relationship reflected in their correspondence evolves from respectful formality to warm friendship; 'Herr' and 'Doktor' become 'Gigi' and 'Lieber Freund.'

'Composizione per orchestra [n. 1]'

Herbert Hübner, producer of *Das Neue Werk* for North-West German Radio, had been in correspondence with Nono since hearing *Variazioni canoniche* at Darmstadt. A year later he proposed a new orchestral work, to be conducted by Maderna. Nono set out his intentions in a letter to his friend:

> I am thinking about a work [. . .] in which I confront the famous melodic/harmonic problem getting right to the bottom of the magic square procedures and reducing my own intervention to the aspect of timbre – a line that progressively gives rise to counterpoint. Two movements: the first a melody using the squares in two different ways, at first alone, rhythm is also derived from the square, then, using simultaneous projections of the squares in a harmonic sense instead of rhythmically, to initiate a harmonic plane that in the second movement develops into polyphony. The second movement will be essentially rhythmic and schematic, naturally without mechanical processes ['soluzione di continuità'].[36]

On one hand, 'reduction of intervention' reflects the search for a more organic integration of parameters that was preoccupying young composers. On the other, the development of the work itself demonstrates his search for a way of relating parameters that runs deeper than numbers or remapping. In particular, the relationship between melody and harmony is mediated by a concept of counterpoint, of proliferation on multiple time-scales that inevitably has rhythmic implications. The idea of simultaneous projections is a clearly spatial mode of thought that allows him to conceive of developments in multiple dimensions. The binary model imagined for both the overall form and the inner structure of the first movement is characteristic of Nono: two different perspectives of the same musical organism, or two possible worlds that

Confronting modernism: Darmstadt

spring from the same underlying premises. It will resurface through Nono's work, but appears also to have been a point of discussion with Maderna, who adopts a similar principle in his 1955 *Quartetto per archi in due tempi*. Finally, at the heart of this work there is still drama, theatre, however far removed it has become from its seed, *Fučík*.

Composizione per orchestra [n. 1] lasts 283 bars, precisely the same number as *Variazioni canoniche*. Given his architectural plotting of balance and proportion – always early in the process – a coincidence seems unlikely. As in that work there are four episodes, here framed by an introduction and *finale tripartito*. For the most part Nono uses a series of only nine pitches, developing Scherchen's discipline of choice limitation. In place of variation or proliferation we see emerging a sense of process as inherent in the material, as material itself. The introduction and first episode are the most literal in their non-intervention in such processes. A table in Maderna's hand now relates duration to intervallic tension (Figure 3.21). As Guerrero has pointed out, in this Hindemith-derived continuum of intervallic tension, the tritone has moved from its earlier position of neutrality at the centre of their interval wheels to that of extreme tension.[37]

This determines the rhythm of the slow introduction, the pitches a sequence of permutations of a nine-note series (Figure 3.22a) distributed among a group of high-pitched percussion – the

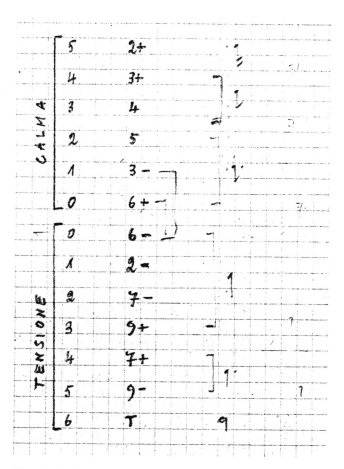

Figure 3.21 Composizione per orchestra [n. 1]: interval/duration mappings. (ALN 03.01.03/01 (detail). © The heirs of Luigi Nono. Reproduced by kind permission.)

Confronting modernism: Darmstadt

instruments of Maderna's 'fixed sounds' (*suoni fissi*), as Rizzardi has observed.[38] The same instruments continue to punctuate the first episode as a monody works its way across the entire range of the large string orchestra. Here Nono begins to use a technique developed with Maderna, a solution to the integration of melody, harmony and rhythm that had so exercised him in previous works – the 'magic square' of his letter.[39] A Latin square, a square in which every horizontal and vertical line contains the same elements in a different order, is constructed of the same dimensions as the pitch series – here 9×9. It consists initially of letters rather than numbers so that the composer can experiment with different values, including duplications – here (3, 4, 6, 9, 11, 15). One line of values is then read from the square for each element of the series (Figure 3.22b). The pitch series is mapped onto a grid of the same dimensions, the values from the Latin square determining the intervals between the recurrence of each pitch such that after a full cycle of nine the original series is restored (Figure 3.22c). Thus, in Figure 3.22c, initial repetitions of successive members of the series are separated by 3(F), 4(F♯), 4(C) and 15(B) silences, followed by different permutations of the number series. The sequence for each pitch adds up to 90: the sum of the number series (72), nine instances of the notes and the nine initial offsets. The grids thus produced are mapped on to the musical surface by selecting a basic duration; Nono uses a quaver. Organisation of pitch and rhythm is unified in a series of displacement matrices; Nono and Maderna refer to this as their 'tecnica dei spostamenti' ('displacement technique'). Here, Nono plots the first episode from the first repeated pitch, F, reducing his intervention in this passage to 'the aspect of timbre' (Figure 3.22d – note that in the first square he uses only the bracketed elements).

Figure 3.22 Composizione per orchestra [n. 1]: derivation of episode 1, bars 17–21. (ALN 03.01.02/05r (detail). © The heirs of Luigi Nono. Reproduced by kind permission.)

Confronting modernism: Darmstadt

In this way repetitions, patterns and simultaneities can emerge from a serial procedure. Through this symbolic–graphical technique, the same structure of relationships can produce quite different musical surfaces by changing the offset values, time-base or pitch series. In his 1957 Darmstadt lecture on the development of serial techniques, Nono would point to this innovation as having freed dodecaphony from its one-dimensionality: 'the series is projected into a wider space. [. . .]. The results of the permutations produce the sonic material [. . .] from which the composer creates his own music.'[40]

From this two-dimensional matrix emerges an integrated pattern of melody, harmony, density and rhythm. Nono leaves himself free to concentrate on colour, register and dynamics, with which he constructs a rich space for the monody to move through. Annotations in his displacement matrices indicate how he had considered reading them in two directions and generating counterpoint by working through them at multiple tempi. Material is proliferating into different spaces. Units of material and their associated polyphonic and serial processes become mobile, bidirectional objects from within which he can project onto 'real' musical space. Halfway through the first episode these projections begin to multiply; an accelerated time-base generates a greater variety of rhythmic figuration against a sustained aura of violins (con sordina, sul tasto, sempre *ppppp*) and suspended cymbals.

The remaining sections avoid any suggestion of mechanical process. Chains of internal, external and retrograde permutations grow from three rhythm cells with distinctive characteristics: three different short/long pairs, a sequence of diminishing note values, and a pattern of two, three and four attacks separated by rests. They are presented in sequence at the opening of the second episode (bar 71) in a fragmented monody to which an additional rhythmic voice is added with each new cycle (Figure 3.23). Here Nono's line follows the displacement matrix of Figure 3.22c from the beginning, selecting single pitches from dyads and triads that occur.

Figure 3.23 Composizione per orchestra *[n. 1]: II episodio*, monody bars 71–78

The finale, for percussion only, is introduced by the three missing pitches – E♭, E, D – in the timpani. After a series of multiple canons they restate the motto at the end of a final accelerando. The three notes Es (E♭), E, D – Nono's sketches are annotated increasingly in German through this period – appear on an early page 'for Hamburg', suggesting that the motif might have some wider relevance. SED may well be a subversive reference to the *Sozialistische Einheitspartei Deutschlands* (German Socialist Unity Party), the state party of the DDR since 1949. Shortly before the Hamburg premiere of *Composizione* Nono had met composer Paul Dessau in Frankfurt, where Scherchen was conducting the controversial first Western performances of his and Brecht's *Die Verhöhr des Lukullus*.[41] Dessau, to become the leading establishment musician of the DDR and with whom Nono later had extensive contact, used the musical notes D E Es (Des) as his signature.

Engagement

The efficiency with which Nono was able to respond to this important commission reflects the level of his technical fluency, and with this came the confidence to confront other issues. He already had a sense of the importance of this moment; as he arrived in Hamburg, he wrote to his parents: 'You can imagine how happy I am – I know well that all these opportunities are offered by people who have faith in me – now it's up to me to turn them into something positive'.[42] His work was taken seriously when Maderna and the North-West German Radio Symphony Orchestra gave the premiere on 18 February 1952, in a programme called 'Young Italy'. *Die Welt* described it as 'An impressionistic playing with extreme colours, sounds and rhythms, almost confusingly naturalistic in its effect and yet at the same time strictly stylised like Byzantine mosaics.'[43] Such reception contrasted with what he perceived as the corrupt conservative provincialism of his own country. A month later he wrote to Hübner: 'I feel myself ever closer to the musical life of Germany, that the brotherhood with people[Mensch]-musicians like you grows ever stronger and more powerful, and that our hope to work in your sweet and lively country is ever greater.'[44]

The trip to Hamburg seems to have been transformative. In Frankfurt Nono had also met Karl Amadeus Hartmann – composer, producer of the Musica Viva series in Munich and previously a student of Scherchen. In Hamburg he encountered the radical theatre director Erwin Piscator, recently returned to Germany, and spent the days in excited discussion with Maderna. After the project, on the way to Zürich to take conducting lessons with Scherchen, he accompanied Hübner to Hannover, to hear a new piece by Henze. A successful premiere outside the protected environment of Darmstadt and being accepted as a fellow artist by major figures in German cultural life such as Piscator and Hartmann engendered a clear sense of opportunity and responsibility, as Nono makes clear in conciliatory letters to his parents:

> We will always remember these days in Hamburg – in four days we have slept perhaps seven hours – and all because of the intensity of the work, the limited time. At a certain point Bruno and I said: maybe we'll suddenly just collapse, or perhaps we will actually live forever [. . .] we have understood even more clearly the intensity and concentration with which we should live.
>
> Hübner and other musicians have told me that they were surprised at the violence and tension in my music – given my appearance, or demeanour, of being calm and almost in a dream – and that my inner strength is most violent [. . .] [45]

Discussion of future plans with Maderna had evidently proceeded apace at Hamburg, reanimated by a new sense of place in the wider world. Nono wrote to his friend:

> I have a great yearning for the incredible plans of Hamburg. I think that's what life is. In fact I'm sure.
>
> You could say that it's the first time that we have shown ourselves together to the others, openly and directly. Now our work and our life in common is stronger and more certain than ever, also our responsibility. Scherchen told me: your talent brings obligation and a heavy responsibility. [. . .] He wants that our work should be intense and total. I think we will never die.[46]

Confronting modernism: Darmstadt

While his friends were touring Europe pursuing their conducting careers, Nono spent much of 1951 and 1952 in Venice taking care of Maderna's composition class and copying scores onto transparency for Scherchen's publishing venture, while running errands for both. He visited Zürich to assist Scherchen, who suggested he should take over the running of Ars Viva and encouraged him to study conducting. 'It's a dog's life,' he wrote to Maderna in June 1952.[47] Nationality – or, perhaps regionality, given Nono's developing internationalism – was evidently beginning to exercise him in terms of both career and politics. After the Hamburg concert, when Maderna had returned to the south of Italy for concerts, Nono wrote to his friend: 'Don't let yourself be influenced by the south. The north is for us.'[48] A month later he would write to Stockhausen that both he and Maderna hoped to live in Germany.[49] And yet in November of the same year he would write to Maderna concerned about the dominant influence of Germany in their work.

The differences in tone between the impassioned, committed declarations of the two friends become most notable in the area of politics. In the almost entirely state-funded cultural world of post-war Europe, musical and political influence were inextricable. 'Where the Italians arrive, there's trouble for us,' wrote Maderna of the closed circle of broadcasting and festivals.[50] Composer-turned-power-brokers such as Mario Labroca and Mario Peragallo were regarded as particularly unsupportive – perhaps both protective of their power within Italy and envious of the Venetians' reputation in the wider world.[51] Of the powerful Italian critics, Nono identified only Massimo Mila as 'a rare man, for his simplicity, his seriousness, his human openness – gold!'[52]

Mila – anti-fascist, partisan leader, mountaineer, public intellectual and music critic – was a generation older than Nono. His radical politics, rooted in the Italian liberalism of Croce and *Giustizia e Libertà*, were not aligned with those of the PCI (*Partito Comunista Italiano*, the Italian Communist Party), and he maintained a scepticism in respect of any perceived musical formalism. Such crucial differences of perspective fuel the rich exchange of ideas that would later run through thirty-five years of correspondence – a relationship of deepening mutual respect and affection.[53] They had met in Venice some months earlier. Nono had arranged for Mila to be invited to Darmstadt and they discussed the possibility of a new music journal. Their idea of such a journal being progressive both musically and politically represented significant risks in the context of mid-century left-wing orthodoxy, as Mila pointed out in a letter. On one hand, this would entail contradicting the party line; on the other, such explicit political declaration could be seen as 'artistic heresy' and would 'make life difficult for both of us in a Europe that is increasingly demo-Christian and compliant.'[54]

While beginning to engage with the manoeuvrings of cultural power, both Nono and Maderna had also decided to make clear their party-political affiliations in the new Italy, to become members of the PCI. The PCI had strong links with the resistance movement in what Pavone has described as the civil war of 1943–5. Mila spoke of that time as a 'self-revelation', a sense of new possibility for the Italian people.[55] Pavone documents a spirit of vision, liberation and common struggle at the beginning of the resistance, a humanism both joyful and tragic that echoes Nono's later references to 'a sense of the possible'.[56] When Nono talks of 'continuous resistance' it should perhaps be understood in the light of these events that informed his own coming of age. The PCI took part in the initial post-war government of 1946 and under Palmiro Togliatti became a mass party, the second largest in the country. Nevertheless the right-wing Christian Democrats, with US support, would govern Italy for the next four decades. By 1952, therefore, the political optimism of the new Italian Republic had evolved into a new, much longer struggle that external powers from both sides successfully manipulated as a proxy cold war.

Confronting modernism: Darmstadt

His sister Rina has suggested that Nono was introduced to communism by Katunda; however, taking a political stance must have been unavoidable for an increasingly public figure in the febrile political atmosphere of post-war Italy, and Gramsci-informed Italian communism gave a particular role to the artist-intellectual. The mature writings of Antonio Gramsci were produced in 'exile' – imprisonment by the fascist government from 1926-1937 – from which he was not released until he was too ill to survive. Their publication between 1947 and 1951 was a major contribution to a national re-formation.Gramsci's ideas would influence many aspects of subsequent Italian and European communism as well as cultural theory more generally. His writings address the specific state of evolution of Italian society, rather than assuming a Soviet model; they also pre-date external awareness of the brutality of Stalinism. Their significance to the Italian left was enhanced by their myth-inducing transmission: from his prison in the south of Italy to his sister-in-law in Rome, to his wife in the USSR and thence to Palmiro Togliatti, Gramsci's successor as leader of the PCI, who returned to form part of the new Italian government in 1944.

Nono seems to have acquired these books soon after their publication: the *Letters from Prison* and the volumes of theory distilled from the *Prison Notebooks*. Three strands should be identified as particularly important at this formative point in the evolution of Nono's thought: Gramsci's concept of the organic intellectual – the engaged intellectual who will emerge from the working class to lead social change – his observations on the particular nature of Italian culture, and his views on the political roles of culture and the artist. Gramsci notes the dominant role of the lyric theatre in Italian culture, which encourages the national tendency to melodrama – to sentimentalise and thereby distract from human realities while giving the impression of offering 'higher' feeling; he holds Verdi specifically responsible.[57] His insistence on the responsibility of artists to lead, to present truths and alternatives, is at odds with the Zhdanov doctrine of socialist realism adopted by much post-war communism; in many respects it has more in common with Adorno, even in his consideration of the relationship between material and form. Gramsci's observations on literary criticism seem to encapsulate Nono's emerging ethos:

> It seems clear to me that one can talk of a 'new culture' rather than a 'new art'. [. . .] One has to speak of a fight for a new culture, that is, for a new moral life that cannot but be intimately tied to a new conception of life, such that it becomes a new way of sensing and seeing reality and, therefore, a world which is connatural with the artist and his works.[58]

The *Letters from Prison* were the first to be published, the most personal – reflections on his own situation and intellectual development, on his family and the education of his children. The notes on Nono's copy have the air of a biblical concordance. Nono seems more interested in matters of personal development than political theory; inside the back cover he lists Gramsci's observations on love, old age, solitude, happiness, moral reform and the church. He marks a line that will resurface in one of Maderna's letters: 'It is not difficult to find splendid formulas for life; living it is difficult, however.'[59] Gramsci's humanism and his views on the role of the artist–intellectual stand at the root of Nono's musical and political development; the two lines are fused inseparably from this early point. Nono seems to have expressed some doubt as to the political motivation of Maderna, who replied with some admonishment: 'My joining is a conscious and deeply-rooted act. I have done it in a moment of fundamental importance. [. . .] I have done what I can. But practically, not reading nice texts or following great examples.'[60]

This seems to have struck a chord with Nono. Two months later he confessed: 'I really need direct, practical contact with reality. [. . .] MORE SOLID, REAL MUSIC. Even here he [Scherchen] is right.'[61]

Lorca: drama, struggle and reference – 'Epitaffio n. 1–3 per Federico Garcia Lorca'

Brecht's Berliner Ensemble had been invited to the Venice International Theatre Festival in the autumn of 1951, but were declined entry visas. Protest was led by film director Luchino Visconti and would certainly not have gone unnoticed by Nono. Scherchen had introduced Nono and Maderna to the thought of radical Weimar culture with which he had been closely connected. Brecht himself had been a protégé of Erwin Piscator, who, after his expulsion from the USA, had returned to Germany in 1951.[62] Piscator's return was much discussed in the socialist press; as a senior German artist free of Nazi association the new cultural establishment gave every opportunity for his radical productions. Nono was most likely absorbing the ideas from Piscator's 1929 *Political Theatre* while he was working on *Fučík*.[63] Its intellectually coherent mix of political, aesthetic and technological elements must have resonated with Nono's current preoccupations. Piscator's use of architectural and theatrical space, of other media such as film, and his distribution of narrative across multiple threads and time-scales would all contribute to Nono's concept of *azione scenica* ('staged action'), not only in the stage works, but at the root of his approach to composition in general. From the early 1950s onwards, the making of theatre works becomes perhaps the most appropriate analogy for Nono's perception of his own activity as a composer.

Nono met Piscator in Hamburg in February 1952. He would later recall the moment when 'I suddenly found myself in the presence of one of the people who would most inspire my imagination.'[64] In their subsequent exchange of letters, Nono displays his keen sense of sociocultural responsibility. He volunteers to facilitate publication of an Italian translation of *Politische Theater* – a project eventually realised in 1960 – and stresses the importance to Italian culture of organising a production by Piscator, possibly in Venice. He describes his current project, a setting of Myakovsky's *Lenin*, and his desire to discuss a new form of music theatre with Piscator. His request for advice on the selection of a further text gives an insight into his pre-compositional formal thinking and the primacy of drama in his imagination:

> I would like a German text, in which women speak, tell, sing of the contemporary feelings of contemporary women, a piece of contemporary life. It must be a general, simple human text, in which everyone thinks about and reflects on contemporary life. The text must be [both] individual and common, so that I can build a dialectical musical construction between solo and choir. The choir can also function as commentator. [. . .] And they will speak, recount, sing – also with Sprechgesang. The text must not be explicitly political, otherwise it will certainly not be performed, but human in terms of our political opinion.[65]

'Epitaffio n. 1: España en el corazón'

In the event it was the poetry of Lorca that provided the stimulus and text for the next group of works, to become *Epitaffio 1–3 per Federico Garcia Lorca*. Katunda had given Nono copies of Lorca's poetry in 1949. Thirteen years after Lorca's assassination by Spanish falangists, his reputation was spreading rapidly as awareness of the extent of his achievement grew. From Manzoni's *I promessi sposi* to Dallapiccola's *Il Prigioniero*, Spanish oppression in Italy and elsewhere had served as a metaphor for dark political forces in Italy. Through the post-war years, opposition to communism in Italy was still centred around the Church. The continuing fascist regime in Spain provided Italian commentators and artists with parallels to their own recent past and the hazards that they still faced.[66] Even in 1961, the year of Maderna's Lorca setting *Don Perlimplin* and of Nono's own *Intolleranza*, a right-wing coup was a real possibility. Political instability, corruption and intrigue may have averted civil war in Italy, but they afforded little nobility of cause with which to identify. There is perhaps also a yearning for a vital folk culture to which Nono could subscribe, that could provide the authentic basis for his compositional and cultural vision. Many of the more vital musics of Italy, such as the Sicilian songs later explored by Berio, have roots in the Spanish-influenced culture of Bourbon rule.

For Nono the resonances of Lorca's poetry were manifold: the combining of modernism and a deep sense of history, of political charge and individual humanity, of the popular and the radical, of cruelty and love, even of consonance and dissonance, and not least the personal significance it held for Katunda. He was attracted by the metaphysical, surreal qualities of Lorca, not just the poet of the *gitani* and *cante jondo*.[67] As Nono selects poems, he marks aspects of their structure, including Höhepunkt – a remnant of Scherchen's melodic analysis – rhyme patterns and ideas for orchestration or dynamics. Structural thought and instinctive poetic response are indivisible in the germination of the work. A simple architecture emerges for what will become *España en el corazón* (*Spain in the heart*), the first of the series of three *Epitaffii* dedicated to Lorca. For soprano and baritone soloists, speaking chorus and woodwind, strings and percussion, it sets two poems by Lorca – *Tarde* and *Casida de la rosa* – which were to surround the more complex treatment of Myakovsky's *Lenin*.

Nono's correspondence with Maderna and, since Darmstadt in 1951, with Stockhausen suggests the urgency of the common search for a post-dodecaphonic way forward. Nono's previous works already contained indicators of possible paths. In *Tarde* he divides the series into three four-note groups, expanding and contracting in range (fourth, fifth, augmented fourth) and subjected to a two-dimensional permutation (Figures 3.24a, b).

> I was still under the influence of those studies that Scherchen had me do using three or four notes. If you take the pieces of the *Epitaffio* you see that they're based on four or five sounds. These four or five sounds can come from *Bandiera rossa* or that song from Katunda or, in the last part of *Guardia civil*, simply from the sounds of the six strings of the guitar.[68]

Durations are now mapped from intervals in a more sophisticated manner (Figure 3.24c). He selects and hews material before sculpting his design layer by layer. The opening – again a characteristic clarinet *pp*, *suono d'eco* against a suspended cymbal – is filtered from the resulting monody (Figure 3.24d). Shifting the rhythm to avoid beats is typical of Nono's close attention to the detail of sound, performance and reception; it helps the player maintain a sense of tension and temporal suspension.

Again, we hear the material forming itself from almost nothing. This habit seems almost a matter of integrity, of validation. It demonstrates that the work and the stuff from which it is made have a necessary, essential relationship. Both arise in the act of their performance. Pitch and rhythm emerge self-organising from silence and noise. The obsessive circling around a few pitches recalls the melos of the Andalusian music that Lorca himself had sought to preserve. Two phrases of soprano vocalise reinforce this image and relate the instrumental material to the speech patterns of the poem, spoken by a baritone. Moments of madrigalian word-painting emerge: 'ha florecido en círculos concéntricos' is accompanied by the longest uninterrupted phrase in the piece, the clarinet cycling through permutations of its four notes.

For the concluding Lorca poem – *Casida de la rosa* – Nono divides the series asymmetrically to articulate colour, materials and musical roles. Flute and vibraphone carry the melodic

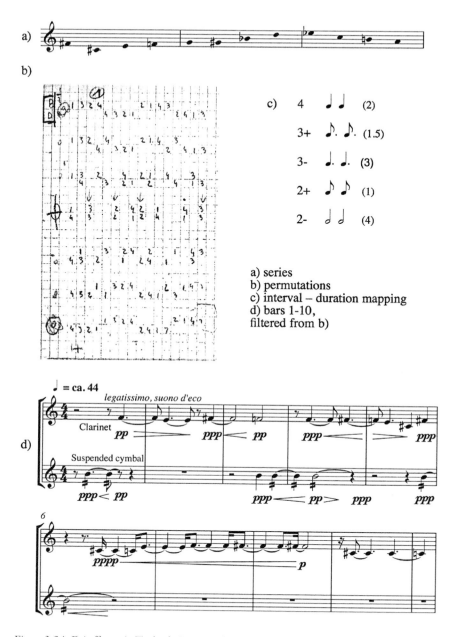

Figure 3.24 Epitaffio n. 1: Tarde: derivation of opening. (ALN 04.02.02/02r (detail). © The heirs of Luigi Nono. Reproduced by kind permission.)

development of an eight-note set, against a backdrop painted with the colours, dynamics and registral disposition of the rest of the ensemble (harp, celeste, piano, strings, flutes and clarinets) using the remaining four notes – G, A♭, A, B. He constructs displacement matrices for both pitch sets as before, using Latin squares of offset values to produce cycles of permutations. That of the four-note group is read straightforwardly in crotchets, that for the melodic line in quavers. Foreground and background thus evolve at different speeds. Simultaneities become chains of semiquavers and long notes are extended to enhance melodic differentiation. He then selects passages from the result to create a melodic architecture and rhetoric that embody his conception of the poem. The natural speech rhythms of the poem and the autonomous rhythmic process of the background are tailored to complement each other without compromising their internal coherence. The occurrence of three-note chords frames the opening lines of the poem, that of longest durations shapes the scope of flute phrases. At bars 10, 19 and 30 the entire background structure is shifted by a semiquaver, changing the relative phase of melody, poem and background, and disrupting any emergent sense of over-stable pulse to maintain the floating atmosphere of the whole. As in *Tarde*, the relationship and overlapping between melodic intervention and spoken poem continuously shifts. The distribution of the melodic line between flute and vibraphone likewise marks its relationship with the poem. The vibraphone becomes the shadow of the flute, maintaining the ghostly presence of the line between the flute's phrases and entering the sound world of the background group; sometimes it echoes or pre-echoes, adding additional beats. The range of the line itself expands continuously from the closest possible form, reminiscent of *Tarde*, to two and a half octaves.

What was to be the central piece, the first-imagined setting of extracts from Mayakovsky's *Lenin*, is more complex structurally and dramatically. Mayakovsky had worked with the revolutionary theatre director Meyerhold; both would afford lifelong inspiration for Nono. The heroic vision of Russian constructivism appealed to Nono more than the shaky theoretical foundations and fascist overtones of Italian futurism. There is a brazenness to Mayakovsky's poetry that Nono seems to emulate in his choice and use of musical source material; it derives entirely from two phrases adapted from inner voices of *Bandiera rossa*, the anthem of Italian socialism, such that the total pitch material amounts to a scale of Bb (Figure 3.25).

Figure 3.25 Epitaffio n. 1: *Lenin*: extracts from *Bandiera rossa*

The first is divided into seven units in three groups, their permutations nested, alternated and cross-cut before being combined into canons. Scored for large percussion section, a group of xylophone, harp and piano, speaking chorus and reciter, *Lenin* consists of four episodes. All but the third are based only on the first of the two phrases. In the opening canon for unpitched percussion, the distribution of rhythms among instruments is determined by their pitch in the original phrase, such that a vestigial melodic structure emerges. Timpani and xylophone introduce the pitches directly in the section that follows. The entry of the reciter, 'Compagni! Basta!', is the interruptive rhetorical gesture of Beethoven's 'O Freunde, nicht diese Töne!' – surely, a conscious reference to Schiller's revolutionary summons. A moment of dramatic quietness ('qui venendo senza rumore [...] passo Lenin') begins a crescendo to the climax in the third section, after which the secondary material is introduced. The first phrase is asserted clearly by the timpani at the opening of this section (bar 66) and at the end of the piece after a percussion coda – a transformed mirroring of the opening.

As Nono explained to Maderna, he knew that *Lenin* was unperformable in the political climate of the time,[69] although he would return to Mayakovsky in *Intolleranza 1960*.[70] He chose to replace it with a setting of a poem by Pablo Neruda, *La Guerra*, which develops some of the same themes in a more distanced context: the brutal destruction of Inca civilisation, an allegory of the suffering in Spain. The eventual title of the whole group – *España en el corazón* – is that

Confronting modernism: Darmstadt

of Neruda's collection begun following Lorca's death and printed in the midst of the Spanish civil war.[71] Neruda – communist, internationalist and close friend of Lorca – had lived in Italy since 1950, in much-publicised exile from his native Chile. The authorities had made attempts to expel him, fearing he might become a focus of political activity. His presence was thus a matter of public debate during the composition of *España en el corazón*.[72] By joyful coincidence, Neruda's arrest warrant in Chile was dropped in June 1952, and Neruda returned home to support the candidature of Allende on 26 July, five days after Nono's premiere in Darmstadt.

The five stanzas of Neruda's poem are set as seven episodes; Nono adds an interlude after the third and a coda for percussion, mirroring that of *Lenin*. Flute, clarinet, bass clarinet and low strings are added to the hard-edged instrumentation of *Lenin*. The musical material for *La Guerra* is likewise taken from *Bandiera rossa*, but, as with the political themes of the text, these melodic roots are less blatant, subjected to more sophisticated development. The first phrase is now also used in inversion a semitone lower, to give a combined set of B♭, C, C♯, D, E♭, F. This provides the pitch material for the first section of the piece, which, like every piece of the first *Epitaffio*, begins from nothing with *ppp* woodwind and suspended cymbals. A Latin square generates three polyphonic textures; sections are differentiated by orchestration, density of voices, the rate at which rhythms are read and the degree of substitution by rests. For the opening, he derives three voices by reading in different directions: for clarinet (omitting F), harp (using all six pitches) and flute (omitting B♭), the latter in a rhythmic diminution of 3:2. To these are added a voice constituted of four suspended cymbals outlining the melodic contour of *Bandiera rossa*, the repeated note dotted figure of the second and third notes omitted to allow more explicit reference to emerge in the course of the piece (Figure 3.26).

In the second stanza (from bar 34), the introduction of the second phrase from *Bandiera rossa* with its inversion expands the pitch set nearly to a full chromatic (no E or B) as well as intensifying rhythmic figuration and complexity. Given an emerging dynamic whereby single pitches constantly expand to chromatic completion, the use of negative pitch bands, of discontinuities in the chromatic continuum, is becoming increasingly important. The strings provide an additional polyphonic unit with which to explore this expanded palette. A group of four drums relates perceptually to the speech rhythms of the chorus and baritone reciter while sharing the rhythm and pitch material of the other instruments. A second group of drums is added for the third stanza, which is entirely without pitched instruments. Its final outburst – 'aguijoneado en agonia' – heralds the *Violento* instrumental interlude, the last four pitches of which are sustained *pp* in harmonics by the strings. This static halo of sound – a reminiscence of the first section of *Composizione* – illustrates the hushed tension of the text. It is a technique borrowed from the scherzo of Beethoven's Seventh Symphony by means of which two musical discourses can exist simultaneously; the time of one is suspended while we examine the development of another. The flute and clarinet return to the limited pitch range of the opening flute line, in the low register, *pp*, and with the rhythmic units distributed equally between rests and notes. In the last stanza the unison speech rhythms of the chorus, united and defiant as they reach 'y sereunan los frutos dividos en la tierra', are accompanied by four groups of four percussionists. Permutations of the source material are distributed among them sparsely and with metrical simplicity, such that recognisable figures emerge. In the fourteen bars of the percussion coda the initial four-bar phrase is announced in full three times. Mapped across the relative pitches of the drums, each statement is more assertive until there is nothing more to say.

For all its raw emotion, *La Guerra* is a polished centrepiece to the group. The swiftly changing moods and sounds of Neruda's poem become the framework of a complex dramatic miniature. At the same time, Nono's use of material is less episodic, more economical than hitherto. He has developed a technique best described by Boulez's later term *polyphony of*

Figure 3.26 Epitaffio n. 1: La Guerra: opening. (Reproduced by kind permission of Schott Music.)

polyphonies, that allow him to manage the density, rate of development and perceptual clarity of coherent, but ever-changing textures in which pitch and rhythm derive from the same sources. Nono has found a way to mould the rhythms of crowd dynamics, balancing the intensity of individual expression. This will be clearly evident in the dramatic works, but the relationship between subject and group is now a fundamental driving force; composition and idea are inseparable. *La Guerra* also brings together much of the repertoire of rhetorical devices developed in previous works; from a technical points of view it constitutes an elegant self-portrait.

Among the other premieres at the *Music of the Young Generation* concert at Darmstadt on 21 July 1952 were Maderna's *Musica su due dimensioni* and *Kreuzspiel* by Stockhausen, with whom Nono had developed a warm correspondence since their meeting at Darmstadt the year before. This comprehensive picture of the state of new music led to the mythologizing of the evening as the 'Wunderkonzert', and it looms large in various reports.[73] 'In this way we made the leap', recalled the flute soloist Severino Gazzelloni dramatically. 'No more Stravinsky, no more Hindemith, no more of anyone but the young the Darmstadt team ready for conquest.'[74] To Stockhausen's chagrin, Steinecke had proposed a money-saving scheme whereby the composer, Nono and Maderna would all play percussion in *Kreuzspiel*. At the end, only the irrepressible Maderna took part. Nono's work is certainly vastly different from Stockhausen's absolutist architecture. His relationship with his material is more intimate – by no means less coherent, but less brittle, more plastic. Maderna's *Musica su due dimensioni* is one of the earliest instances of a new genre that would become central to Nono's later work: the combination of live performer and electronic sounds. On this evening, Nono's *España en el corazón* ended the concert and was applauded until it was encored. Critics also praised his work, finding it less incomprehensible than those of Stockhausen and Maderna, although, as Iddon describes, they tended to conflate the styles of all three as 'punktuelle Musik', despite the clear stylistic and technical differences.[75] As a term to describe what was perceived as a discontinuous, post-Webern style, 'punktuelle Musik' had gained currency despite its very specific technical connotations for the inventor of the neologism, Stockhausen.[76]

During the Summer School, Nono attended the seminars on rhythm led by Olivier Messiaen. Messiaen's *Modes de valeurs et d'intensité*, often seen as the first attempt at multi-parameter serialism, had coincidentally been written at Darmstadt in 1949.[77] Boulez and Goeyvaerts had been his students in Paris, and Stockhausen had joined Messiaen's class there following a lecture by Goléa at Darmstadt in 1951 at which he had played a recording of the *Quatre etudes de rhythme*. Indeed, Boulez's *Structures* uses the material from Messiaen's earlier piece, and Stockhausen acknowledged its influence on *Kreuzspiel*. The explicit coherence and individuality of Messiaen's technique as set out publicly in his 1944 book clearly attracted Nono.[78] He painstakingly worked through the musical examples. He annotated the text, especially the more metaphysical passages – replacing 'human imagination' with 'my imagination', for example – and paid particular attention to Messiaen's observations on the properties of popular song. Indeed, while *Modes de valeurs et d'intensité* is iconic for its structural innovation, it may be that the two *Iles de feu* movements may have been of more significance for Nono, with their rhythmic energy, permutation patterns and explicit reference to the sounds of Papua New Guinea. Assimilating the clear, recognisable figure of significant material within a more mobile musical space was emerging as an important preoccupation. However, to consider the stuff of Nono's own compositional thought as 'material' is perhaps misleading. The elemental units of Nono's invention are rather the seeds of behaviours, dynamics and emergent structure that articulate and give life to broader canvases of pitch, rhythm and colour.

'*Epitaffio n. 2: Y su sangre ya viene cantando*'

A newly confident grasp of form is clear in Nono's work on the second *Epitaffio* – *Y su sangre ya viene cantando*, for solo flute with large string orchestra, suspended cymbals and the group of *suoni fissi* (celesta, xylophone, vibraphone and harp). He worked rapidly on this, a commission from South-West German Radio for Heinrich Strobel's prestigious *Ars Viva* series in Baden Baden to be conducted by Hans Rosbaud with flautist Severino Gazzelloni. Nono had acted as translator for Gazzelloni when he taught at Darmstadt in July, and heard his performance of Maderna's *Musica su due dimensioni*.[79] Strobel had heard a tape of *Composizione* and proposed a work for the recently revived festival in Donaueschingen. This would not happen until the

Confronting modernism: Darmstadt

following year with *Due espressioni*; in the meantime, Nono worked through the summer to prepare the new piece for a studio concert in Baden Baden on 17 December 1952.

The title *Y su sangre* is taken from Lorca's *Llanto por Ignacio Sanchez Mejias*, an impassioned description and lament on the death of his friend, the famous bullfighter, writer and champion of the culture of the people. Nono uses the line to refer to the blood of Lorca himself. The poem *Memento* is a poignant but more accepting view of death:

> When I die, bury me with my guitar beneath the sand.
> When I die among the orange trees and mint plants.
> When I die, bury me, if you would, inside a weathervane.
> When I die!

Images of nature such as these resonate through Nono's subsequent work. His use of the poem in *Y su sangre* – printing one stanza under the solo flute part in each of the three sections – pre-echoes the silent role of lines from Hölderlin in *Fragmente* twenty-eight years later.

His bold graphical plan for a five-part architecture was rapidly resolved into three sections to match those of the poem – I–II, III, IV–V – but its formal complementarity persists (Figure 3.27).

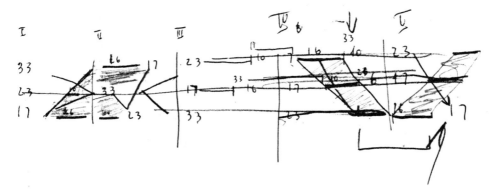

Figure 3.27 *Y su sangre*: formal plan. (ALN 05.02/02v (detail). © The heirs of Luigi Nono. Reproduced by kind permission.)

Initial ideas included the use of brass and drums, perhaps to conjure up the atmosphere of the bullring as a celebratory finale to the series. He intended from the outset that three Spanish dances – one for each image – should provide the rhythm. The dances are used for their capacity to generate continuous energy rather than as reference. Pitch and rhythm are derived separately in this case; the origins of both remain farther below the surface than in *La Guerra*. Nono returns to the use of a 12-note series: three groups of four notes, the first chromatic, the second with the addition of a whole tone, the third two semitones and a minor third. This interval pattern anticipates his segmentation of the scala enigmatica, introduced in Scherchen's course of 1948, which will become central resource for the works of Nono's last decade. Here, he characterises the versions for each of the three sections by their *absent* intervals. Like the backwards and forwards of his directional structures, positive and negative coexist.

The sound world of *Y su sangre* emerges seamlessly from that of the first *Epitaffio*. The solo flute continues its role established in *Casida de la rosa*, but begins again from the minimal, obsessive melos of *Tarde*. Its quasi-poetic pattern of phrases, accents and rests is produced by dividing the continuous line generated by Nono's established polyphony-reducing process between flute and harp. The accompaniment – three groups of suspended cymbal, *suoni fissi* (here celesta, xylophone, vibraphone and harp) and strings – is like a magnification of the detail of the first *Epitaffio*. Permutations of the series and readings of an displacement matrix produce three sequences of rests, notes, bi- and trichords projected into a three-dimensional instrumental space through which the sustained flute line with its harp shadow can move freely. Rhythms derive from augmentations, reorderings and retrogrades of the simplest of figures and its altered diminution – a *Sarabanda*, as Nono begins to look to Spain also for musical source material (Figure 3.28).

Figure 3.28 Y su sangre: Sarabanda rhythms A and B

The manipulation of polyphonic space – not just the number of voices but the perceived complexity and correlation of material – is the parameter by means of which Nono shapes the piece. Instrumental colours bounce between the three instrumental surfaces, used to distinguish or conflate them; strings *arco, pizz, arco battuto* and *col legno battuto* provide continuity across the timbral space. The whole first section is united in a great sweep of accelerando; continuous crescendi and diminuendi mark changes of density across the whole orchestra.

The brief central section, labelled *armonico* as Nono began work, again develops what has become a trope: high violin harmonics and suspended cymbal sustained throughout, against which the *suoni fissi* bring together the strands of accompanying material of the first section and concentrate them into a single sound-space. This suspended harmony of the spheres provides the background for a more free, rapidly developing flute line – a *canto sospeso*, a suspended song. The latent energy built up in the process bursts into the final section, in the event the only part that makes explicit use of a found Spanish rhythm. The fandango, almost as elemental as the initial cell, is subjected to the same processes (Figure 3.29).

Figure 3.29 Y su sangre: fandango

'Epitaffio n. 3: Memento – Romance de la Guardia Civil Española'

As soon as continued funding was assured for the *Neue Werk* series, Hübner offered Nono a new commission. His enthusiasm for Nono's music was clearly genuine, but the regionalised structure of West German support for new music may also have engendered a spirit of competition for the most exciting projects. Certainly, Nono's own country afforded fewer opportunities; in June 1952 he wrote to Hübner: 'for Bruno and me it gets worse and worse here (RAI and the festivals are taboo for us and always fighting); but we always work with strength and joy.'[80] In November, Scherchen conducted *Polifonica – Monodia – Ritmica* at La Fenice in Venice. It was not the moment of recognition that Nono must have hoped for. Both audience and press, there to hear Haydn and Beethoven, responded uncomprehendingly. The local newspaper wrote of 'absurd, disconnected processes [. . .] squalid, formless laments,

Confronting modernism: Darmstadt

a receptacle of all the most corrupt, extreme consequences of dodecaphony.'[81] Nono wrote to Maderna:

> *Polifonica* opened a wasps' nest! Of course from the outset we knew that the only serious and intelligent reactions would come from our circle. [. . .] I have understood certain errors, or rather the dangers of some of our situations; for example that Germany is monopolising our musical life. Dangerous, because it takes us away from life in Italy, or rather we are distracted from considering reality. And yet we are well placed relative to the others (Henze, Stock., Boulez etc.), closer to clarification.[82]

Nono started work on the final *Epitaffio* as soon as its predecessor was complete. It would be too late to be the opening work of the new season, as Hübner had hoped, but Nono was able to set out his needs for the new piece when they met at Donaueschingen in December, days before the première of *Y su sangre*. Most of the new work was written between November 1952 and January 1953 at the seaside villa rented by Scherchen at Rapallo, on the Ligurian coast – a villa owned by a relative of Nono's mother, it transpired. Nono wrote to his parents full of enthusiasm for the place and for the mentorship of Scherchen: 'we have made an interesting new plan of study – analysis and study of historical and modern Italian songs, special melodic studies (using five notes at most) – all never done before – together with my own work, of course.'[83] His physical environment is important to him: 'I'm in a room on the first floor, quite nice, small and quiet; the sea comes right under my window, against the rocks, it is beautiful.' He also writes to them about the political situation, tentatively but firmly, as if testing a new relationship. The premiere was to take place in Hamburg on 16 February, as part of a programme dedicated to settings of Lorca. Maderna was engaged to conduct and the *Sprechstimme* part was to be performed by Christa Ludwig, who had participated at Darmstadt as early as 1949.

For the final *Epitaffio – Memento*, Nono chose one of Lorca's longer and most dramatic poems. *Romance de le Guardia Civil Española* tells the story of a nocturnal gathering of Andalusian *gitanos*, massacred in their city by the fascist paramilitary police.[84] Having analysed the poem, Nono envisages a four-part structure: a Prelude, two *tempi* (*festa gitana* and *sacco della città*) separated by an interlude, and a Finale. He reduces the text by about half, principally and tellingly by eliminating passages with religious references. Saints Mary and Joseph, around whom the victims gather for protection, disappear. Religion and superstition play no part in Nono's Gramscian understanding of an ideal state of popular culture, but perhaps the paradoxes and complexities of Lorca's poem also have to be somewhat simplified for the sake of clear music drama.

Following Messiaen's example, Nono finds source material in an encyclopaedic collection of Spanish popular song and dance: *La musique et la danse populaire en Espagne*.[85] He groups the rhythmic patterns of some fifteen dances by region and metre. He experiments with juxtapositions, relationships and subdivisions, selecting those that afford properties of interest: contrast and asymmetry. From these simple materials Nono will spin and weave the entire work. *Memento* is constituted almost entirely of three- or four-part polyphony. Some or all voices may be unpitched, or one may take the foreground as a monody, in which case either rhythm or pitch material is derived differently from the other voices. Such contrast between different types and densities of polyphony is the principal architectural device. He plots the dramatic structure in terms of these rhythms, sometimes dividing material between the two groups of protagonists (Figure 3.30).

Figure 3.30 *Memento*: form and dances

The first section – the original Prelude – is a four-part canonical texture derived entirely from the Rueda rhythm, against which the chorus speak the opening scene-setting lines to adapted speech rhythms. Clarity of text is never compromised; changes in type or number of voices shape colour and accent. There is no precise pitch, only speech and drums. The ordering of the four bars of the rhythm is subject to continuous permutation. A process of complementary deletion means that quavers sounded in bar 1 become rests in bar 2. While the retrograde is used as equivalent to the original, a single non-retrogradable rhythm in bar 3 functions as a rhyme in the polyphonic ebb and flow. Tension between rhythm bases of quaver and crotchet

Confronting modernism: Darmstadt

generates forward momentum until a process of erasure and alignment dissolves the polyphony into a unison punctuated by *ff* rolls.

The second section – bars 102–62 – corresponds to the *festa* of Nono's first plan. Its three distinct parts illustrate well his use of different polyphonic textures, reminiscent of the Venetian patchwork of Gabrieli's motets; they develop from a monody to pure rhythmic polyphony. A twenty-six bar melody was first intended to be sung by solo alto, accompanied by two harps. In a characteristically graphical process, Nono interleaves Sarabanda and Fandango rhythms to construct an oscillating, expanding quasi-Andalusian cantilena recalling the earlier *Epitaffii*. The text is now spoken by the alto, while the unison wind melody loops its way through the first nine notes of the main series, outlining a modal region that relates directly to the 'modes of limited transposition' of Messiaen's *Technique*. The accompanying harp lines are each distributed among a group of three *suoni fissi* in a form of compressed isorhythmic heterophony (Figure 3.31a). Nono will develop this principle to clarify polyphonies within polyphonies in subsequent works. Wind monody and text form a tightly constructed song in rhythmic heterophony. Words begin to emerge as the monody leaves its initial E♭ modality, pivoting about G♯/A♭ at 'ciudad de los gitanos', low harp C♯ reinforcing its new C♯ minor modality (Figure 3.31b). The start points of the *suoni fissi* voices are organised such that they coincide at the Höhepunkt 'ciudad de dolor', forming a C major triad with the Monteverdian lamenting monody (Figure 3.31c).

By generating pages of sequenced pitch material containing dyads, rests and local loops and repetitions, Nono is free to experiment with different start points and time-bases to cut the fabric he requires to assemble his design for the next section. Now the pitches constitute an

Figure 3.31 Memento: bars 102–7, 110–12, 118–21

Figure 3.31 continued

Ionian mode on A with an additional C♯. Mode and rhythmic proportions are derived from a popular song from Polesine, an area of the Veneto. Rhythms are mapped on to a set of six reducing durations in versions based on both quavers and semiquavers. Its own text 'Guarda la luna' ('look at the moon') relates to the lines of Lorca in this section, 'cuando llegaba la noche' ('when night fell'). Against this, three small percussion – nackers, triangle and tambourine – sound like folk instruments after the massed drums of the opening. As the lines develop, their own rhythmic origins become clearer – Malagueña, Charrade and Bolero – and the three dances remain alone as the *festa* emerges.

Pitch and figure re-enter dramatically at the height of the crescendo, with a switch to four new dances: Zortzico, Ezpata, Jota Castillana and Baille, arranged by Nono as two pairs of polyphonic voices, then distributed across the entire orchestra. The basic rhythms are divided into separate components which with their retrogrades are reordered by non-repeating permutation. The final texture is created by selecting and overlaying passages from pages of painstakingly prepared potential material. An examination of the provenance of a single strand of this texture demonstrates the weaving and folding, the inner polyphony of an individual line (Figure 3.32). The Baille rhythm is divided into nine segments, ordered by reading a Latin square forwards and backwards (the permutations numbered in the figure), subject to a process of erasure, then interwoven into contrary sequences that are folded together and divided by rests which expand every time voices come into alignment. Pitches come from a continuous permutation of the series, ordered according to displacement matrices.

This section is the dramatic centrepiece of the work; a surreal, swirling, impossible dance, in its conception as much *La Valse* as Darmstadt. The robustness of Nono's material leaves him free to pay great attention to orchestration, articulation and dynamics. The essentially orchestral movement in 6/8 is punctuated by returns of the previous percussion coda under Lorca's description of the dance. These two interruptions divide the section into three parts; the second Nono gives to strings only, the third to wind and harps. By erasing elements of his fundamental

Figure 3.32 Memento: bars 163–75, first four sequences of Baille

polyphony during a sustained diminuendo, he increases the tension until with a fortissimo interruption the arrival of the Guardia Civil is announced.

The menace of the opening is now realised and the sack of the city begins. Nono had intended to use the Ezpata and Zortzico rhythms here, experimenting with layers of multiple 5/8 material. Instead, his concentration on that of the Rueda produces a straitjacketed, totalitarian conduit for the violence of the scene. The rhythmic structure derives from the same fabric of sequenced permutations as previously, spread over multiple time-bases. As in the Prelude, the chorus narrates the terrible events in unison speech-derived rhythms, intonation and accent enhanced by changes in voice and number. Against them the drums continue their inexorable searching. Pitch begins to play a greater part here, however, introduced first in low double basses – almost the sound of the drums – and then sustained low clarinets: rhythmicised sequences of notes from the same series as before. After a central passage of unison string and drum rhythms as the gypsies congregate to face their attackers, a three-note figure signals their resistance to inhumanity. Like a series of shouted exchanges using one bar of the Rueda rhythm, this figure uses diatonic sequences from the series stretched across wide intervals. As it resolves into a two-note figure of fourths or fifths, the strings begin to accumulate a sustained chord *ppp*; the resonant halo another evolving Nono trope. Here the pitches are those of the open strings of the guitar, the instrument of the people and the natural vehicle for the rhythmic material that has generated the entire work.

Melody triumphs, therefore, and with it the spirit and voice of the oppressed. From this virtual guitar resonance springs a pentatonic, unison, unaccompanied choral melody – the first time the chorus actually sing, their voices freed. In the simplicity of this coda Nono may have had in mind Katunda's chosen path, or the devotional modality of Messiaen. Something between a hymn and a spiritual, the careful melodic balance of this final lament bears the traces of Scherchen's lessons on Gregorian chant. Indeed, the final draft of *Memento* is dedicated to 'Hermann Scherchen, Maestro – Father – Friend.' Another is dedicated 'to the glorious fighters for liberty'. The score was finished at Scherchen's home at Rapallo, and comments in German through the sketches suggest that the two discussed the progress of the work.

Azione scenica is the term Nono will shortly use to refer to his own concept of socially, culturally, politically aware music theatre. To refer to *Memento* as an *azione scenica* is, of course,

Confronting modernism: Darmstadt

a stretch of the imagination. However, it represents an important stretching of Nono's own imagination in the direction of a new music–text–drama relationship, integrating ideas and aspirations from *Fučík*, *Lenin* and *La Guerra*. The very scope of Nono's thought has broadened and matured, and with it a keen sense of how to support such structures. Melodic and rhythmic figure are used confidently in an architecturally moulded flow of polyphony. Local periodicities and modalities emerge in keeping with his poetic vision. The action is carried essentially by the chorus, the people, from whose own musical material Nono generates his fabric in a completely coherent, consonant process. In technical terms, he is confident in being able to provide himself with decisions and choices appropriate to his poetic vision. Together with Maderna, he has developed a synthesis of polyphonic and serial techniques that will underpin the rest of his work. He has established a practice, a repertoire of strategies – intellectual, graphical and physical. The use of resonance, space, silence and the suspending or folding of musical time have found place at the centre of his thought. The resonances of performance and the act of listening are written in to the musical surface; they are given space and a structural role. Above all, he has confronted the central question of meaning, central to the musical understanding of his mentors – Dallapiccola, Scherchen, Varèse, Messiaen and, vicariously, Schönberg – and to Nono's mind avoided by his own contemporaries.

Scherchen conducted subsequent performances, including the first full sequence of *Epitaffi* with the Berlin Philharmonic in 1957. Following the success of *Il canto sospeso* the previous year, Nono's international reputation was confirmed. *Le Monde* wrote:

> For many listeners it was a moment of rare and intense emotion. But the beauty of this work lies not only in how it is made. It is a deeply moving work in which we find, transfigured to the plane of sound, the lyrical, sometimes tender, sometimes cruel tension that characterizes the genius of Garcia Lorca. [. . .] A work that confirms Nono's place at the highest level of contemporary music.[86]

Nono's own text for that event makes his purpose clear:

> The music of us young people is the core of our humanity in human society. In this fundamental truth exists the reality of our work. This is the only possible way to exist for us and only in this sense can we be musicians today. Unfortunately this is not clear to all of us. Today there is too much talk of technical problems and of the ordering of material, as if this was our only goal. Or we put music on the operating table, as if it were an object of curiosity, and at the end proudly announce that we have expressed something valid. But we talk and write too little of the heart of our music; that is, of our own heart. [. . .] The song of free Spain is around us and within us [. . .] [87]

Notes

1 Goléa, 1962, vol. I, pp. 191–2.
2 The courses initially took place at Schloss Kranichstein, on the edge of the city. From 1949 to 1957 the courses were held at Seminar Marienhöhe (Borio and Danuser, 1997, vol. 1, p. 61).
3 Iddon, 2013, pp. 1–32, provides a concise picture of the origins of Darmstadt and the role of Steinecke.
4 Letter from Steinecke, 26 June 1950. ALN.
5 Legrenzi's opera *Totile*, for example.
6 Maderna, quoted in Fearn, 1990, p. 26.

Confronting modernism: Darmstadt

7 Interview with Hansjörg Pauli, 1969. LNII, pp. 23–4.

8 Guerrero, 2009.

9 Interview with Enzo Restango, 1987. LNII, p. 495.

10 Hans Heinz Stuckenschmidt, 'Speilerei, Pathos und Verinnerlichung.' *Neue Zeitung*, 30 August 1950. Quoted in Iddon, 2013, p. 37.

11 *Darmstädter Echo*, 29 August 1950. Uncredited press cutting. ALN.

12 *Göttinger Tageblatt*, 30 August 1950. Uncredited press cutting. ALN.

13 Stenzl, 1998, p. 19.

14 Meyer-Eppler, 1949.

15 Ungeheuer, 1992, pp. 104–5.

16 Interview with Enzo Restango, 1987. LNII, p. 495.

17 Interview with Massimo Cacciari, 1980. LNII, p. 253.

18 Letter to Hermann Scherchen, 2 June 1951. ALN.

19 Fučík, 1948.

20 Stenzl, 1998, p. 23.

21 André Richard, interviewed in Ehrhardt, 2001.

22 Interview with Enzo Restagno, 1987. LNII, p. 501.

23 It appears in the sketches for Maderna's *Studi per Il Processo di Kafka* (Rizzardi, 2004, p. 19).

24 ALN 02.04/17–18.

25 Next to the diagrams there is a reference to Pietro Cerone's *El melopeo y maestro* of 1613, a 22-volume compendium of music theory renowned for its extensive and obsessive treatment of subjects including the nature of intervals.

26 Guerrero, 2009, pp. 489–91.

27 34 bars are cut at bar 10 in the earlier edition. The central section ('nature joins in') comprises bars 20–43 of the complete version.

28 Scherchen's cut, presumably agreed with Nono, occurs at this point.

29 *Das Musikleben*, September 1951, vol. 4, no. 9.

30 *Die Zeitschrift für Musik*, September 1951, vol. 112, no. 9.

31 Hans Mayer, in Iddon, 2013, pp. 47–8.

32 Herbert Fleischer in an unnamed Italian press agency cutting. The other works on the programme were: Michel Ciry *Troisiéme symphonie*; Peter Racine Fricker *Concerto No. 1 for Violin*; Serge Nigg *Pour un poète captive*; Armin Schibler *Sinfonische Variationen*.

33 Scherchen, quoted in Stenzl, 1998, p. 20.

34 Letter from Hermann Scherchen, 22 July 1951, ALN.

35 Letter to Scherchen, 22 July 1951 [*sic*]. ALN.

36 Letter to Maderna, August 1951, ALN. The number squares developed by Nono and Maderna are usually referred to as Latin squares. Each side produces the same constant when summed. Webern's SATOR – ROTAS word square is an analogous example. A magic square also produces the same constant along both diagonals.

37 Guerrero, 2009.

38 Rizzardi, 2004, 49. Nono uses the term in his sketches for later works.

39 Rizzardi gives a detailed account of the evolution of this technique in Maderna's *Improvvisazione n. 1* of the same year and its use in *Composizione* (Rizzardi, 2004).

40 'Lo sviluppo della tecnica seriale', 1957. LNI, p. 34.

41 The Dessau performances began on 30 January 1952. Nono's premiere in Hamburg took place on 18 February.

42 Letter to Mario and Maria Nono, 14 February 1952. ALN.

43 *Die Welt*, 21 February 1952. Other works on the programme were Maderna *Improvvisazione N.1 per orchestra* and Petrassi *Coro di morti*.

44 Letter to Hübner, 14 March 52. ALN.

45 Letter to Mario and Maria Nono, 19 February 1952. ALN.

46 Letter to Maderna, February 1952, in Baroni and Dalmonte, 1989, p. 60.

47 Letter to Maderna, June 1952. Sacher Stiftung, Basel.

48 Letter to Maderna, February 1952, in Baroni and Dalmonte, 1989, p. 60.

49 Letter to Stockhausen, 13 March 1952, in Stockhausen, 2001, pp. 39–40.

50 Letter from Maderna, 13 May 1952. ALN.

Confronting modernism: Darmstadt

51 Mario Labroca (1896–1973), pupil of Malipiero, manager of the Teatro Communale, Florence 1936–44, artistic director of La Scala 1947–9, director of music for Italian Radio 1949–58, and subsequently involved in the Venice Biennale and festivals. Mario Peragallo (1910–96), pupil of Casella, Artistic Director of the Accademia Filarmonica, Rome, 1950–4.

52 Letter to Maderna, June 1952. Sacher Stifting, Basel.

53 Benedictis, Ida and Rizzardi, 2010.

54 Letter from Mila, 16 July 1952, in Benedictis, Ida and Rizzardi, 2010, p. 3.

55 Mila, 1945.

56 Pavone, 2013, Chapter 2.

57 Gramsci, 1977, vol. 2, p. 969.

58 Gramsci, 1977, vol. 3, p. 2192.

59 Gramsci, 1947, p. 124.

60 Letter from Maderna, 1 April 1952. ALN.

61 Letter to Maderna, June 1952. Sacher Stiftung, Basel.

62 Piscator (1893–1966), theatre director and theorist, had pursued a radical rethinking of German theatre through the 1920s, worked in the USSR from 1931–6 and subsequently in the USA until he was obliged to leave in 1951. De Benedictis and Schomerus, 1999/2000, provide a survey of his relationship with Nono.

63 The socialist martyr Karl Liebknecht, who figures in Nono's original thoughts on Fučik, appears in Piscator's *Trotz alledem* of 1925.

64 Interview with Enzo Restagno, 1987. LNII, p. 518.

65 Letter to Piscator, 14 March 1952. ALN.

66 Pestalozza, 1989, describes the significance of Lorca's poetry and the struggle in Spain for Italian composers.

67 Interview with Enzo Restagno, 1987. LNII, p. 556.

68 Interview with Enzo Restagno, 1987. LNII, p. 502.

69 Undated letter. ALN.

70 Following his theatrical suicide in 1930, Mayakovsky had been praised by Stalin as a national hero, his work disseminated as state propaganda.

71 Lines quoted in Feinstein, 2004, p. 125, are characteristic of Neruda's opinion of Lorca: 'we, the poets of Spanish America and the poets of Spain, cannot forget or ever forgive the murder of the one who we know to be the greatest among us, the guiding spirit of this moment in our language.'

72 In fact, Neruda visited Venice on 5 June 1952, but there is no indication that he and Nono met.

73 Also on the programme were Camillo Togni *Omaggio a Bach* and Jacques Wildberger *Quartett*.

74 Gazzelloni and Granzotto, 1984, p. 86.

75 Iddon, 2013, pp. 85–8.

76 Stockhausen, 1989, p. 35.

77 Messiaen's *Quatre etudes de rhythme* for solo piano also include *Neumes rythmiques*, composed at Tanglewood in 1949, and *Ile de feu I* and *II*, written a year later (Deliège, 2003, p. 101).

78 Messiaen, 1944.

79 Letter from Steinecke, 22 April 1952.

80 Letter to Hübner, 1 June 1952. ALN.

81 *Il Gazzetino*, 16 November 1952.

82 Letter to Maderna, November 1952, in Baroni and Dalmonte, 1989, p. 60.

83 Letter to Mario and Maria Nono, 25 November 1952. ALN.

84 A short extract was used for the popular civil war song *Noche Nochero*.

85 Lavignac, Albert 1920. *Encyclopèdie de la musique et Dictionnaire du Conservatoire*. Paris, Librairie Delagrave. Première Partie. Nono's transcriptions are to be found in the Paul Sacher Stiftung and ALN.

86 *Le Monde*, quoted in *Il giorno*, 15 October 1959.

87 Programme note for Berlin performance, 1957. LNI, p. 421.

4

TAKING POSITIONS

Song

Traveller . . .

In 1952 [. . .] there was a very important concert at Darmstadt: there was Stockhausen's *Kreuzspiel*, Boulez's *Structures* for two pianos and my *España en el corazón*. How is it possible that the critics united these three compositions under the same technique? How can these three compositions be analysed in the same stylistic or technical terms? It was a falsification due to the interests of a German cultural hegemony.[1]

Nono's *mis*-remembering of this event – *Structures* had been heard in Paris that year but would not be performed at Darmstadt until 1955 – illustrates the degree to which he considered his own work part of a wider common project. Steinecke made the same error in his own memoir, describing the works of Stockhausen, Maderna, Nono *and* Boulez as having set the agenda for a generation.[2] Like Nono's later identification of a 'Darmstadt School' (of which he would subsequently deny being a representative just like all its other putative members), this points to a significant personal paradox.[3] On one hand, a sense of internationalist common cause is emerging from shared technical, cultural and political challenges; on the other, as he enters an international professional stage he has to confront rivalries, cultural politicking and individual and national differences of emphasis. After a visit to Cologne in early 1952 he wrote to Stockhausen:

With Dr. Eimert, Maderna and I have talked a lot about how it would be possible to create a connection between us young [composers] [. . .]. A real association such that we could all work together, live together often and really work together on the musical problems of today, to share a genuine and free and open-hearted criticism, [4]

For Nono, the friendship and support of Wolfgang Steinecke were crucial. Nono attended Darmstadt annually through the decade, teaching in 1957 and 1959, with major performances almost every year and no fewer than seven commissions. In Germany, the regeneration of musical infrastructure was particularly linked to state support and foreign aid. As well as Steinecke, radio producers such as Herbert Eimert (NWDR Cologne), Herbert Hübner (NWDR Hamburg) and Heinrich Strobel (SWF Baden-Baden) took their responsibility to the future of music very seriously. Concert series such as Strobel's *Donaueschinger Musiktage*, Hartmann's *Musica Viva* in Munich[5] and Hübner's *Das Neue Werk* in Hamburg were funded

Taking positions: song

by radio stations as organs of high-level performance of new music. Henze described the situation thus: 'The directors of regional radio systems began to play one composer against another. They behaved like 18th century princes [. . .]'.[6]

In other countries, different cultural dynamics obtained. From 1954, Boulez's *Domaine Musical* addressed an urbane Parisian constituency, as IRCAM would later.[7] For personal as well as professional reasons, Maderna had almost entirely abandoned Venice from 1951. His time was now divided between Germany, where he would become musical director of the Darmstadt Landestheater, and new initiatives elsewhere in Italy. Geographically and in his work Nono retains an outsider's distance. As we have seen, his correspondence with Maderna shows an ambivalence in respect of Germany. At the same time, even before establishing himself definitively in Venice in 1955, he expresses little faith in the openness or fairness of the Italian music establishment. Of the Biennale he says: 'The festival here is a festival against new music'.[8] For the rest of the decade he would continue to feel shunned by his Italian peers in their encounters at international events.[9]

Schönberg was due to teach composition at Darmstadt in 1951. 'This is not only enough reason to go, it makes it a necessity, to go and learn directly from him', Nono wrote to Bussotti.[10] To mark this highly symbolic return to Europe, the summer school incorporated the Second International Twelve-Tone Congress, with the première of the *Dance of the Golden Calf* from his as yet unperformed opera *Moses und Aron* as its centrepiece. Sadly, Schönberg was too ill to travel and in his place Steinecke invited Theodor Wiesengrund Adorno. Adorno's *Philosophy of Modern Music* of 1949 was an account of the importance of Schönberg's thought not only in compositional terms (the 'asphyxiating academicism' of Leibowitz[11] had been the principal European source of such understanding during Schönberg's exile), but also as an aesthetic, cultural and ultimately social project – an *ethical* response to the situation of music. Adorno's godfatherly role as critic and conscience of the avant-garde would evolve through the decade. Despite their apparent political common ground, Nono later expressed disagreement with Adorno's understanding of the cultural implications of Marxism; he saw him as a personally ambitious icon of German cultural hegemony.[12] Nono also disagreed with Adorno's views on the development of music:

> Adorno ended really by denying the presence, the significance of Webern [. . .] Adorno, that is, failed to pick up in Schönberg both the relationships with tradition and the fact that the moments of formulation of new compositional principles would not have a predetermined, unique, linear trajectory.[13]

A photograph from Darmstadt in 1951 shows a conversation between Nono, Stockhausen and Karel Goeyvaerts, a student of Messiaen.[14] The conversation depicted in this image was significant in Goeyvaerts' memory. Twenty years after the event he recalled that 'Stockhausen and I put forward the view that a word can only be used musically when its sonic substance can be integrated into the musical structure. Nono, on the other hand, saw the emotional content of the text as a compositional stimulus.'[15] Years later still, he described their discussion of the just-premiered *Polifonica – Monodia – Ritmica*:

> Luigi would not continue with the experiment of "Polifonica" [. . .]. He was already too concerned with the way text works, with its semantic meaning; in short, with the extra-musical elements that a text presents. This was the main topic of our conversation in the meadow.[16]

Taking positions: song

This conversation would come to a head in 1957. The apparent intensity of this exchange belies the diffidence with which Stockhausen later asks whether Nono might remember their meeting.[17] One of the pieces discussed in Adorno's composition class was Goeyvaerts' *Sonata for Two Pianos*. The isolated notes of the second movement reflect the complete surface independence of events; their coherence inheres entirely in an underlying formalism. Adorno was bemused and Stockhausen described his attempt at analysis as like 'looking for a chicken in an abstract painting'.[18] Goeyvaerts had proposed that the dynamic relationship between pitch, duration, timbre and dynamics could be seen as a fundamental and quantifiable property of a particular work, and developed his concept of the *synthetic number*: a constant value reflecting numerical relationships within the set of parameters. As change takes place on one parameter, the others adapt to maintain the constant, hence Goeyvaerts' term *static music*. Such a view must have resonated with the ideas of Meyer-Eppler – at Darmstadt in 1951 to talk about 'The possibilities of electronic sound production' – who was an early proponent of information theory. Stockhausen grasped the significance of this idea immediately and developed the idea in composing his first significant work *Kreuzspiel*, which he says was sketched shortly after meeting Goeyvaerts.[19] An early sketch for Nono's *Polifonica – Monodia – Ritmica*, performed during the same days, suggests that conversations with Nono also influenced Stockhausen's new work. Nono's diagram is divided into inversely symmetrical quadrants of wind and piano/percussion, between which the material moves diagonally over the course of the piece.[20]

Meyer-Eppler was at Darmstadt for a two-day workshop on 'Music and Technology'.[21] Debate centred on the polarised positions of Pierre Schaeffer and the more engineering-focused Germans such as Meyer-Eppler, Eimert and Friedrich Trautwein. Schaeffer's work with musique concrète was now reaching a more mature stage: his *Toute la Lyre* had been premiered in Paris just days earlier. Meyer-Eppler demonstrated the additive synthesis of complex timbres from electronic sounds using the *Melochord*. When he was finally able to enter the studio later in the decade, Nono would combine elements of both approaches. Also prescient was Robert Beyer's introductory talk. The electroacoustic medium would make possible a revolution in hearing, he said, introducing 'the sounding space as tonality-forming moment'.[22]

Stockhausen explained the technical basis of *Kreuzspiel* to Nono in full while studying in Paris in March 1952.[23] Their accelerating correspondence reveals the intensity of their respective researches and a mutual warmth and respect. It also bespeaks a common desire for community, for common purpose, together with a delight in passionately defended difference. Nono makes this clear in a letter to Stockhausen after the summer, thanking him for some photographs:

> pictures of our discussions and war!!! Especially for this reason I am very happy to have these pictures, and really because we are always in discussion together. I am sure that we are genuinely friends and brothers, and that our brotherhood is very active.[24]

At one stage Nono had negotiated a role for Stockhausen with Scherchen at Rapallo, an offer that marriage obliged him to decline.[25] Their friendship evolved through the exchange of ideas and ideals, shared musical experiences and holidays taken together with their young families. It cooled later in the decade as their paths diverged. For Nono, the relationship of the collective and the individual are as central an issue in compositional life as in compositional technique. In his correspondence with Stockhausen he resists the reduction of musical debate to dogma and counter-dogma:

> For me our humanity is the principal foundation for everything: life, being, work, love, music (which is nothing other than LIFE). Within me there is a part of collectivity, I come from collectivity, and I live and work on this foundation.[26]

Taking positions: song

In Cologne in February 1952, Maderna and Nono had met with Herbert Eimert at the new *Studio für elektronische Musik* of North West German Radio, where Eimert also played them the recent recording of *Kreuzspiel*.[27] It is not clear when Nono first encountered Eimert's *Lehrbuch der Zwölftontechnik*, published in 1950. They presumably met at Darmstadt in 1950, where Eimert, then a NWDR producer, first discussed the possibility of a new studio in Cologne with Meyer-Eppler and Beyer.[28] Nono eventually had copies of the Italian edition from 1952 and 1954, but there are remarkable resonances of Eimert's approach in his early serial technique. Perhaps there was discussion of Eimert's work at the *Primo congresso internazionale di musica dodecafonica* in 1949. In his book, Eimert presents a view of twelve-tone music radically different to that of Leibowitz. Indeed, as a theorist one might consider him together with Schönberg and Hauer, given that his approach was developed in the 1920s. There is no trace of the post-thematicism of the former or the modality of the latter. Eimert presents the new language as a continuous, combinatorial twelve-tone space for exploration. He considers circularities, symmetries, tensions and statistical probabilities, operations of permutation and rotation; the 'classical' serial techniques of transposition, inversion and retrograde seem to be of secondary importance. If Nono did indeed encounter these ideas in 1949, then Eimert's discussion of series built on fourths may have had some bearing on *Variazioni canoniche*.[29] Eimert investigates different types of series, notably the all-interval series in various arrangements, including the symmetrically expanding chromatic form that would be Nono's primary material for much of the 1950s: 'All of these rows lead back to a single one, the chromatic basic form of the all-interval row. Among the countless twelve-note rows its precise equivalent is the chromatic scale.'[30] Eimert's graphical way of exploring the properties and potential of series also appears to inform Nono's practice: he lays out matrices of values 1–12, annotating patterns of symmetry, sequence or recurrence of intervals. These ideas can already be seen in plans for *Due espressioni*; they soon would be explored fully in *Canti*, *Incontri* and *Il canto sospeso*. Certainly, the conversations of early 1952 motivated the younger composers to reinvigorate their investigation of musical space: 'Dr. Eimert has become more than a friend to us; now we will send him our new studies in twelve-tone technique, and he will give his opinion and criticism.'[31]

Stockhausen summarised his concept of *punktuelle Musik* (music of points) in an essay written during his study with Messiaen in Paris in early 1952:

> the rhetorical devices of repetition, development, variation and contrast cease to obtain even between adjacent sounds. The craft of music – musical thought as opposed to thinking about music – proceeds by considering its material rather than by realising intentions. [. . .]. The organisation of sound therefore means the organising of sounds under a unifying principle. [. . .] Consequently, for a particular work X there are only sounds of organisational character X, which have sense only as such and in this work.[32]

These precepts underlie Stockhausen's subsequent criticism of *Y su sangre* and *Memento* – that their formal, dynamic and dramatic gestures do not spring directly from the material, that rhythmic detail and longer durations are not related, and particularly that 'octave-register proportions, so important for clarity of hearing, are hardly considered. I have had to make similar criticisms to Boulez [. . .]'.[33]

Clearly, these are observations made in the light of Stockhausen's own current preoccupations, rather than Nono's concerns with architecture and drama, for example. In particular, Stockhausen's comments reflect his developing compositional technique of *groups*[34] and his theories of the relationships between pitch and rhythm, experiential and structural time,

Taking positions: song

subsequently set out in *How time passes*.[35] The question of register was taken on board fully by Nono and would become an integral part of his thinking in *Due espressioni*.

Nono's travels as Scherchen's assistant had included his first journey to Paris in late 1952. 'Here is so beautiful and so simple, and so human that I really didn't believe it. One can really live here. Here everything is very good,' he wrote to Steinecke. [36] This is more than tourist hyperbole. From his many communications to a widening circle of friends, there emerges not only an avaricious enthusiasm for new experience, other places and ways of being, but also an instinctive analysis of what they might suggest for his own work. Above all, he wants to generate an internationalist group effort to share the excitement of grappling with the future of music.

This visit gave Nono the opportunity to develop his acquaintance with Pierre Boulez, whom he had met briefly at Darmstadt in July. Boulez had recently concluded a remarkable period of theoretical and technical development, working through the implications of his understanding of serialism – a moment he would later describe as 'a reduction of style to the degree zero'.[37] Having reached an impasse in *Polyphonie X*, Boulez was searching for ways of reintroducing compositional decision-making without compromising the structural integrity of the whole, of reinventing properties of ambiguity and multiplicity. He wanted access to local imbalance, to the sonorities or pitch-complexes described by Cage and to the compression and expansion of pitch and time of Pierre Schaeffer's experiments with musique concrete.[38] In an article of some months before, *Possibly . . .*, Boulez had set out his understanding of the challenges and responsibilities confronting the composer, as well as his technical responses. Neither undirected superficial creative liberty nor the academic dogma of dodecaphonists ('fat idiots') are sufficient; rather:

> A consciously organizing logic is not something independent of the work, it contributes to its making, it is connected to it in a two-way circuit; for it is the need to pin down what one wants to express that directs the evolution of technique; technique reinforces the imagination, which can then project itself towards the previously unperceived; and in this way, in an endless play of mirrors, creativity pursues its course; a living and lived organization, allowing every discovery, enriched by every new experience, self-completing, self-modifying [. . .] [39]

Boulez's concept of 'encoding' is resonant with Nono's evolving practice. He suggests that an algebraic representation of abstract 'sound figures' allows more flexible manipulation than conventional notation. A month before meeting Nono in Paris, Boulez had finished the first draft of the core movement of the work in which he would address these issues: *Le Marteau sans maître*.[40] In a letter to Pousseur in the month of their meeting, Boulez wrote of his crisis of conscience, of having fallen into the greyness of formalism, and of the difficulty of balancing the autonomy of material and process with the ability to 'act musically'.[41] These are therefore likely to have been the issues on his mind, the questions he would have shared with fellow travellers.

Expressions

'Due espressioni'

Nono spent much of February 1953 in Germany – in München with Scherchen for Hartmann's Musica Viva series, and in Hamburg where Maderna conducted the premiere of *Memento*. Christa Ludwig's performance of the *Sprechstimme* made an impression on Nono, who

Taking positions: song

immediately wrote to Strobel asking that an alto soloist should be incorporated in the new commission that they had agreed for the Donaueschingen Festival in October. This was part of his idea for the piece until at least the spring.[42] In the event it was not to be, but Ludwig remained fundamental to the evolution of the work.

For the first time material is identified not just with characters (as in *Fučík*), but with real people. Christa is a seven-note row; the composer himself remains an incipit G–G (Gigi). The relationship between material and individual is neither mimetic nor semiotic. We might rather speak of a *social* model of composing in which, as it develops, not just notes but sounds and actions, not just individuals but groups, ideas and texts interact as agents. Materials, ideas and 'meaning' become commensurable; together they constitute a dynamic society that generates its own drama of which we hear one possible surface trace. The process of composition can begin once Nono has assembled a collection of elements of sufficient richness and balance that he can plot a path to a surface that is self-sufficient, that no longer relies on these associations to be musically meaningful. A mark of Nono's faith in humanity is his conviction that this trace will catalyse a related transforming richness in the listener. Music becomes a vehicle for sharing an understanding of human experience in its inexpressible, irreducible complexity. A four-part structure is planned for the new work, its autobiographical origins clear:

A – Christa. Dolce e piano. Strings and woodwind, with cymbals. I 16, II 32 [bars].
B – Gigi. Forte, violento. With a plastic line.
C – Ex unita. Christa e Gigi.
D – Danza finale.[43]

An initial five-note cell characterised by semitone, fourth and augmented fourth is derived from 'Christa' by German note-spelling (Figure 4.1a). 'never 2–/4/4+' Nono writes, as if to expunge some unrealisable component of his thought; a significant articulation of interval space is emerging.[44] This uncompleted adventure is replaced by a seven-note series (Figure 4.1b), the intervallic complement of its predecessor, and tested through a series of displacement matrices. Its narrow intervals favour the production of unaggressive, singable lines, but immediately Nono begins to analyse his material for its potential to generate a minimal set of six intervals – from semitone to augmented fourth. In exploring the possibilities he considers a series of expanding intervals, semitone to major seventh – another appearance of the *Allintervalreihe*. Starting on G, this might indeed be the series that Nono associates with himself, and not only in the local context of this particular drama; it becomes an element of energy and potential, unconstrained in its surface identity. He selects alternating and intersecting pairs to produce two sets that have much in common with the seven-note series. In their closed form they consist only of minor seconds and thirds (Figure 4.1c).

The series he finally selects can be seen to combine elements of both (Figure 4.1d). Nono derives this from an initial version by removing augmented fourths and limiting semitone movement to the fulcrum point, in accordance with his earlier resolution marked 'I episodio'.[45] It is symmetrical about the central G–F♯ semitone axis, and each seven-note half (including both central notes) contains the entire minimal interval set apart from an augmented fourth. Two perfect fourths/fifths in each become part of the nature of the piece. This series is the basis of the two-movement work that emerges: *Due Studi* through much of its development, and ultimately *Due espressioni per orchestra*, conducted by Hans Rosbaud at Donaueschingen on 11 November 1953. They evolve from the *Christa* and *Gigi* movements as first envisaged, together with the *Furlana* rhythms that Nono had imagined for the final dance.

Taking positions: song

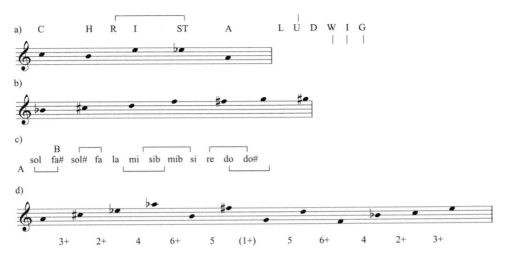

Figure 4.1 Due espressioni: evolution of pitch series

The first *espressione* derives directly from three displacement matrices. Nono selects long passages from each according to the density patterns they produce. Having experimented with sets of twelve prime numbers adding up to 132 (the spaces between note onsets, which together with the twelve notes themselves make a full cycle of 144 units), Nono replaces them with a sequence of integers from 6 to 16, with the pivotal 11 repeated. This mirrors the shape of the *Allintervalreihe*, closely integrating pitch and time. His numerous pages of trial matrices, all analysed for number of coinciding pitches and length of contiguous rest, demonstrate that this solution also generates a more even flow of density. The resulting texture affords the tracing of what Nono describes as a 'plastic line' – an idea central to this work from the outset and which each movement realises in a different way. This mediation of the logical consequences of his initial material is the space Nono creates for his freest compositional intervention. He abstracts a line, choosing between coincident pitches. Register, colour and duration thus become the parameters through which he gives form to the movement. Returning to his original 16-bar modulus, he designs three sections across the first two matrix-derived passages; the fourth section eventually coincides with the third passage:

Matrix		Section (letters in sketches)	
II	bars 1–28	[A]	bars 1–15
		B	bars 16–33
I	bars 29–54		
		C	bars 34–52 (originally 57)
III	bars 55–68	D	bars 53 (originally 58)–68

The slow non-figural opening has become a trope – a process Nono needs to go through to find his way into a new composition, and one that offers the listener the same path into the work. De Assis has pointed to a four-fold structuring paradigm underpinning all the formally complex works of this early period.[46] There is certainly an awareness of conventional formal rhetoric here. Classical models – many of the slow introductions of Haydn or Beethoven, but also of Bach – serve to establish disorientation and prepare the listener. In the context of 1950s modernist expectation, those of Nono allow us to hear his exploration, his establishment of a

Taking positions: song

coherent space within which the work and its understanding will be able to grow. Through the opening section, a line gradually coalesces from single quasi-pitches (*col legno*, *sul tasto*, *pizz.*, harmonics) into two- and three-note phrases. A continuous line traces a broad melodic arch through each of the following sections, both with a classical Scherchenian Höhepunkt, to fragment back into barely pitched sound-points in the coda. As first imagined, strings carry the body of the texture. Faux canons in groups of cymbals and triangles time-shift the rhythm and melodic outline of certain passages such that figure simultaneously emerges and recedes. Only the notes of the melodic line are played *normale*, but the distinction between line and non-line is blurred as the 'spare' notes remain in the strings with other colours. This role is taken up by woodwind and harp as the now continuous line is passed between strings in the central sections. Flutes and clarinets sustain the non-melodic pitches through the third section – a slowly shifting background against which the increasingly complex line stands out in relief and forms new harmonic tensions. Having established the precedent of anticipatory canon, Nono introduces the only rhythmic variant – a pair of semiquavers announced by the jazz cymbal and adopted by the melodic line. His choice of intervals in tracing the line is crucial to the flow of tension. The slowness of its unfolding is such that the listener apprehends each interval individually, with just enough contour and trace of rhythmic figure for it to seem part of a larger, not-quite-graspable song; again Mahler is present. If Nono's 'never 2–/4/4+' was a decision to eliminate an initial idea, he clearly thought again. This very interval shape appears at critical moments; these intervals will define the melodic/harmonic universe of his last decade. As the newly continuous line emerges, this shape assumes an almost motivic role in bars 19 and 21–3. Indeed, the final notes of the movement are B–F–B♭–E in violin harmonics. As melody dissolves upwards into unpitched sound and then silence, the memory of the figure of Christa remains as a fading constellation.

The *Furlana* is a courtship dance from the Friuli – an interface between the Italian- and German-speaking worlds. While in the first *espressione* time and pitch sequence derive from the same source, the rhythm of the second is generated entirely by the *Furlana*. Other parameters are brought into a new close relation, however, such that Borio has described this movement as 'emblematic of the transition to the mature phase of serial technique'.[47]

The basic Furlana rhythm is divided into three cells, into each of which is inserted a one-beat rest in three possible positions: beginning, middle and end – the technique of *Ritmica*, the superimposition of a negative rhythmic layer and an early instance of Nono's micro-fragmentation. This spreading of triple-time figures across units of four ensures that however much momentum develops, the dance itself cannot take over the rhythmic flow. New rhythmic chains are formed from permutations of these variants, and the new material is then compressed on to three shorter time-bases (Figure 4.2a). A vast palette of choices is thus produced from the slightest of interventions in the simplest of material. There are four layers of such chains through much of the movement – 'a 4', in Nono's archaic notation. Each voice of this four-voice polyphony is *spezzato* – broken up between different players – in another 'polyphony of polyphonies'. In general, each three-celled, twelve-unit chain occurs twice in succession; certain sounding elements are erased in the first appearance, and only they appear in the second. The opening eight bars of the lowest voice of percussion are a clear instance, presenting two complementary images of the basic rhythmic material. Two kinds of silence are thus established: rest and 'negative presence' (Figure 4.2b), anticipating the formalising of rhythmic silence in *Incontri*, *Il canto sospeso* and *Varianti*.

Polyphonic density and integration are Nono's main formal tools. Four strands of rhythmic cells are present throughout, the 'unvoiced' elements presented by percussion. Dividing his large orchestra into family groups – percussion, woodwind, brass and strings (eventually in two

Taking positions: song

Figure 4.2 *Due espressioni*, 2: derivation of Furlana rhythms

groups) – he plans a stepped increase through four episodes from a single group of percussion to four orchestral groups (bars 1–59), followed by a corresponding filtering back down to unpitched attacks (bars 60–114) and a tutti coda (bars 116–54). Any sense of regression in the second section is counteracted by a progressive accelerando; linear time has to fight the gravitational pull of symmetry. Pitch is determined by conventional serial techniques from the same symmetrical series as the first movement. All 24 discrete forms are used.[48] In the first two sections they are distributed such that a series in one voice is balanced by its simultaneous inversion in another, while a different series in a further voice is followed by its inversion. The full set of pitch material is thus locked together in a single structure of vertical and horizontal symmetries.

With pitch and rhythm-points determined, Nono experiments with the idea of fully serialised dynamics. This produces a potentially disjointed texture, fragmenting the coherence established on other planes and dislocating his design of a great arch of rhythmic and timbral energy. His decision to abandon this path was perhaps also informed by Boulez's experience with *Polyphonie X* the previous year. Instead, Nono relates the parameters of density, colour, dynamics and octave-doubling in a single device. In the initial episodes, a matrix of four voices by eight rhythmic elements is increasingly filled by layers of pitched instruments, the remainder sounded by percussion until the texture is complete. Successive layers are characterised by increased dynamic levels and correspondingly dense octave doublings, until at the beginning of the second section there is an orchestral perspective five deep, like the layers of a stage set. Octave doublings are added below the central pitch in the first section, above in the second – an additional duality of shade/light, negative/positive. Timbre is used to create perspective in a texture much denser than that of the first *espressione*. Isolated notes form multiple relationships against the perceptual background, while dramatic octave doublings create centres of gravity and foreground objects. Rhythmic energy constantly generates near-melody, the realization of which is thwarted by still more production until the rhythmic energy itself finally implodes. The relating of timbre to volume – in particular, the increase of high-frequency content with increase in volume – is a concept Nono may have encountered in Darmstadt. Herbert Eimert

Taking positions: song

and Werner Meyer-Eppler, the founders of the Cologne studio, had given talks on 'The problems of electronic music' and 'Models of sound production' on the same day as the premiere of *España en el corazón*. Boulez had then introduced a programme of recent musique concrète. The frequency–intensity relationship is an early observed property of many instruments and of the voice; given Meyer-Eppler's advocacy of the vocoder he is very likely to have discussed it. It is also significant for Nono that Meyer-Eppler's work was rooted in communication; his 1949 book was subtitled *Electronic Music and Synthetic Speech*. Early exposure to this association of ideas would have long-lasting resonance for Nono.

The *Due espressioni* are two expressions of the same underlying aesthetic, poetic, personal and technical identity. They are two sonifications of the same abstract object in different dimensions. Here Nono is exploring a musical paradox that will remain central to his thought: the relationship between the time-independence and multiple dimensionality of musical abstraction or reflected experience, the dynamic flow of experiential time in music, and the linear directionality of compositional time. His tendency to binary, complementary structures has evolved into the exploration of parallel possible spaces, of different paths through time. Spatial models play a crucial role in his exploration of the potential of material and structures. One shape in particular stands out from his evolving graphical repertoire (Figure 4.3):

Figure 4.3 Symmetrical/directional figure, common in Nono's early sketches

Various arrows often indicate traversal in multiple directions. Versions appear throughout this period; it occurs through the sketches of *Due espressioni*, and reflects a model that will become dominant in *Varianti*. It embodies both symmetry and directionality, contains turning-points and folds in multiple dimensions. In the time of performance, certain musical thoughts cannot have a single instantiation, therefore. They must be set out simultaneously or, as in this case, sequentially. Objects and structures – in time, pitch-space, sound or silence – coexist with their inverses or negatives. Only the time of performance and the negentropic process of composition have unique directionality, and even these will be challenged to their limits in the later works.

This elegance of thought did not come lightly; Nono wrote to Steinecke that the work was taking him much longer than anticipated.[49] In *Due espressioni* Nono approaches the integration of form and surface, of timbre, register, dynamics and rhythm identified in Stockhausen's letter, but also the symbiosis of technique and imagination sought by Boulez. The works on the programme for a presentation of taped performances with *Y su sangre* on 24 July at the 1953 Darmstadt course embody crucial aspects of the state of serial thought at that moment; Boulez's *Polyphonie X* would be withdrawn, while Stockhausen's *Kontra-Punkte* was a response to a preceding work *Punkte* that the composer felt should not yet be heard. Both had compressed structural 'meaning' into atomised sound-events, to create surface relationships that escape the gravitational pull of classical-romantic rhetoric. While fully engaged with the same issues, the modes of compositional thought that Nono had assimilated and evolved had roots stretching farther and deeper:

> I have never written musica puntualle; this is an invention of the critics. [. . .] In my early works the individual sounds are really not so important; for example the pitches

Taking positions: song

don't count so much but rather the intervals, the relationships between musical figures; and these relationships cannot be reduced to what is called horizontal or vertical, but they embrace every level of composition – like a net extending in all directions.[50]

'La Victoire de Guernica'

Equally telling is a symposium organised by Steinecke the previous day to mark the seventieth anniversary of Webern's birth. Nono's response to Steinecke's invitation was enthusiastic:

> You don't need an answer from me. No answer, because you must know how my heart is bound to Kranichstein. IS THAT CLEAR?!?!?!?! Especially in this case: to say something new about Webern, against the mentality according to which Webern is almost just a highly abstract mathematician and against those who speak about his music with formulae.[51]

Stockhausen, Goeyvaerts and Boulez spoke of Webern as a heroic figure who had freed music from the accumulated weight of its previous rhetoric and who had both opened out and integrated the parameters of musical space.[52] Despite their protestations of radicalism, it should be noted that the unity they envisage – a DNA-like encapsulation of entire structures in single events – stands at the heart of German romanticism, traced by Webern himself to Goethe.[53] In fact Nono's caricature of his colleagues is unfair, but there is certainly a fundamental difference of balance. Their attention is focused firmly on the nature of the material – what Boulez described as 'a new kind of musical being'[54] – rather than Webern's response to his own cultural context. Nono later described the analyses he and Stockhausen presented of the *Concerto* op. 24 as being like the north and south poles.[55] Nono was concerned with Webern's humanity, and saw in his music an intense, compressed lyricism. He saw a new model not of technique but of being a composer. His contribution makes pointed reference to dogmatists who would ignore this essence:

> In Webern I see the new man, who with the qualities of serenity and confidence has been able to imbue contemporary life with inner tension. The tension in Webern's music is the same tension that governs life and nature as dialectic. It would be a great mistake and a profound error to try to grasp Webern's creative force only in technical terms, to understand his technique as a table of calculations. Rather one should try to understand why and how he used this technique. If you only consider the technical moments of the music, you fail to recognise its sense and content. Only on the basis of an understanding of the true sense of the music can you find deep, clear and very simple guidance as to its essence.[56]

Confronting these inescapable differences of approach marked a turning-point for Nono. From Cologne, where he spent most of the autumn, he wrote to Steinecke:

> I think a new period is beginning for me, in every sense. The Webern evening with its violent discussion, deep into the night with Stockhausen, was very important for me, and I think that just as he has given me something, so I have to him, just as it should be between two friends. I am sure that Stockhausen will become an ever more important and livelier musician.

Taking positions: song

Here everything is DEATH and SHIT; people think that Bruno and I come from Mars, but instead I am more and more pure Italian and of this earth.[57]

Nono's isolation was twofold. At home he found musical incomprehension and exclusion from cultural politics, but to this was now added the realization that his understanding of the path of music was fundamentally divergent from that of his peers. This was not just a question of style, although that was becoming increasingly evident. After the November premiere of *Due espressioni* in Donaueschingen, Goléa wrote:

> The *Due espressioni* brilliantly demonstrate that it is possible to accommodate Italian lyricism within the constraints of serial technique and still to incorporate much subtle writing.
> [. . .] Next to Malipiero, Nono and Messiaen the other premiered [composers] appeared no more than dutiful representatives of a time that circles around unified expression without ever in the least achieving it.[58]

The need to revise his vision of a community, of a brotherhood of composers united by common purpose, must at times have been painful. It must also have been compounded by Nono's own political maturing and that of the post-war world; while in Italy the dynamics of reconstruction were manipulated by the interests of capital, wider communist ideals were being challenged by the new political realities of a cold war. The nature of Nono's epiphany following the Webern event is directly reflected in the work he presented to the same community the following year. *La Victoire de Guernica*, conducted by Scherchen at Darmstadt on 25 August 1954, is something of an enigma – perhaps the complement of *Due espressioni*. He would later describe it as 'a letting-go born as a reaction against everything that was happening at Darmstadt: more and more repetitive sterile formulas, the supreme exalting of the products of a unifying rationale'.[59] Technically and expressively, it represents Nono's resistance to the formalism he perceived in the trajectories of other composers, but in its choice of subject – the resistance and triumph of humanity in the face of inhuman, totalitarian oppression – the political statement is unmistakable.

On the surface, Nono's music *expresses* the text in a uniquely unmediated, directly emotive setting. Indeed, Maderna's subsequent judgment was absolute:

> Dear old thing, don't believe in politics and humanity in broad terms. Don't write *Guernica* any more. Forgive me if I say this. For your part, you don't spare me harsh criticism. You must believe absolutely in the *2 Espressioni*, in *Polifonica*, in the *Composizione per Orchestra* 1952.
> These are the compositions that make you a true and genuine composer, the beloved and sincere friend, the precious and courageous companion.
> Dear, dearest Gigi, it's an old story: Scherchen is right when he says that music must be man, but wrong when he says it must be the man of the street. We are not, cannot be men of the street. Objectively, we can't be, when we think what is the man in the street in the USA or the Soviet Union.[60]

This last remark gives a flavour of political context. Was Maderna afraid that his friend had inadvertently produced a piece of cold war propaganda? *La Victoire de Guernica* is certainly an exceptional work, but in an exceptional year: a love song and love itself, the first pieces for the stage and a joyful asserting of identity and independence. Eluard's meditation on the massacre

Taking positions: song

of Guernica, a version of that written to accompany Picasso's painting at the Paris Exposition of 1937, marks a high point in the political engagement of his poetry following his sustained and serous involvement with Dada and the surrealists.[61] Indeed, the Spanish Civil War assumes almost allegorical status in the rest of Western Europe, still close to its own conflict. Eluard was a national cultural–political hero whose poetry Nono had come to know on his first visit to Paris, just a month before the poet's death. As we shall see with other such figures, it was not only the beauty of Eluard's words that drew Nono, nor even his passionate concern with events in Spain; Eluard's vision of the poet as resistance fighter – as voice of the people – and his active use of his art as an instrument of hope and liberation constitute a model for the work of the artist.

Returned to Venice, Nono worked on the piece in late 1953 and the first weeks of 1954. He wrote to Steinecke:

> Already back in Venice. Because I have to work immediately and I can't stay in Cologne any longer. In Cologne I have seen and understood everything: there's a lot of rubbish! in the way it is made and intended. I'll stay there longer next year, calmly: but it's not easy.[62]

On 3 February he could tell Steinecke that it would be with choir but no soloists; on the 15th from Paris (where he was assisting Scherchen) that he had postponed a trip to Düsseldorf because of a 'special development' in the piece, and on the 25th that it was almost finished and would have a 'secret' ending. By 4 May, *La Victoire de Guernica* had received Scherchen's enthusiastic approbation, and Nono was convinced that this was his best work yet.[63]

As Nono would later recall, the material for *Guernica* is derived essentially from '*l'Internationale*: like Josquin used the intervals or the durations of the tenor to invent the other parts of the mass.'[64] In fact, this is not entirely the case; an additional source reflects his evolving political–theatrical awareness. The Spanish Civil War song *Mamita Mia* was in the repertoire of Ernst Busch, an actor who, having fled Nazism to Soviet Russia, had fought with the International Brigades in Spain and was again working with Brecht and Piscator in East Berlin. The figure of Busch fascinated Nono as he worked on Eluard's text. He tried to find out more about Busch through a Darmstadt friend, Berlin pianist Ursula Müller, but the division of Berlin made this impossible.

Nono begins by returning to Scherchen's discipline of working with a limited set of pitches. He analyses the pitch content of both source melodies, initially including their transpositions to the dominant; whether out of habit or historical materialist fidelity to their inherent nature is not clear. The opening bars of *l'Internationale* produce a scale of B♭ major, those of *Mamita Mia* a six-note diatonic mode on G. By cross-pollination he generates two versions of a nine-note series that provide the pitches for the entire work apart from the last twenty-five bars (Figure 4.4).

This is Nono's first mature choral work; the vocal lines are wide-ranging but singable, often triadic. Eluard's fourteen short stanzas form two balanced parts, an architecture carefully followed by Nono. Each begins by praising the strength, beauty and innocence of the people of Guernica, words sung in an extended polyphony that does indeed recall Josquin. Each half then reflects on the inhumanity of the people's enemy – never named – in lines spoken starkly by the chorus such that no word might be misunderstood. The opening choral passage, 'beau monde', is in four-part polyphony. Short, proto-figural phrases of up to four pitches seem to be generated by a boiling rhythmic-dynamic energy, as if a continuation of the second *espressione*. The individual notes and brief phrases are not isolated 'points', as Nono made clear, but form

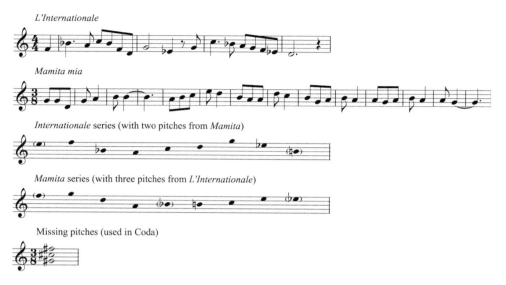

Figure 4.4 La Victoire de Guernica: derivation of series

changing constellations of emergent figure; registration, dynamics and octave doubling provide perspective and temporary centres of gravity. Each listening finds its own trajectory, as will be the case with works such as *Incontri*. Phrases extend in length through this choral passage, finding a *piano* stasis at 'visages bons' and reigniting to a final *ff* 'bons à tout'. 'voici le vide' is spoken in unison against a *subito ppp* bare, high fifth D–A. The sudden change is characteristic of Nono's dualism through this period; suddenly we are examining the other face of the same human situation. 'ils ne sont pas de notre monde' the chorus finally shout in unison; song is the preserve of humanity. As reflection and rhythm evolve together, the musical development condenses into unpitched percussion, its inhuman intensity reminiscent of *Fučík* or *la Guardia Civil*. A timpani duet concludes each half, anticipating that of *Il canto sospeso*; here, both are preceded by a sustained brass unison. The second part begins 'les femmes les enfants' for female voice alone: two parts in octaves, of which the sopranos sing *bocca chiusa* creating an otherworldly, nostalgic sound. Its final timpani duet is more extended than the first, under static, stuttering unison speech: 'ont la couleur monotone de notre nuit'. This decay is more than redressed by the continuous crescendo of a sustained, sung affirmative coda.

In the event, the work derives almost entirely from the *Internationale*-based series. Nono plots the pitch/time consequences of his displacement matrices, as is his practice. He uses a 9×9 square, initially ordered by one of his archetypal shapes – contracting symmetry (1 9 2 8 3 7 4 6 5) – and rotated left for each subsequent row. Now he develops his own approach to what Boulez would later describe as 'local indeterminacy'.[65] Pitches are generally used in sequence. However, instead of following an even time-unit, rhythms, note repetitions and durations are produced from the cells of the two songs mapped onto different time-bases. Notes are omitted and added. Families of rhythm cells are differentiated by dynamic layer and shape. The note B – external to his main material – serves as a pivot; its occurrences are moments at which he might change direction, permutation scheme or canon structure. Pitch structure is asymmetrical relative to the broader bipartite plan; the first part of the second half (bars 93–139) forms a central section in which Nono returns to his early technique of jumping numbers of notes, working to and fro and deleting them from the remainder as he proceeds. For the rest of the piece Nono works backwards through his initial material. The timpani duets are moments of refocus; the first presents the pitch material immediately preceding this central folding-in of material, the second arrives back at the very opening but in retrograde. Once again he insists on the multiplicity of musical time; the directional time of performance and the re-examinable time of memory co-exist with the 'outside time' structures (to borrow Xenakis' concept) of architecture and abstraction. They are not superimposed or reduced to formalisms, but embodied in the same musical surface, the same sequence of compositional thought.

Nono's nine-note series already imparts a modality to the piece. Diatonic intervals with a chromatic neighbour-note are characteristic, and as he traces a line through his pre-compositional plan he uses this property to manage texture and tension, molding the energy flow of pitch and register in a polyphonic relationship with the density, continuity and tension of rhythm. The first choral passage of the second section (bars 108–11) ends in bare fourths shifted chromatically up and down. In colour and shape it pre-echoes the female chorus of much later works such as *Das atmende Klarsein*. The choral opening outlines a C major triad, and Nono chooses to locate the central point just after his pre-compositional plan produces a perfect cadence, stated clearly by the timpani in bars 90–2 (Figure 4.5).

Figure 4.5 *Guernica*: timpani duet, bars 90–2

The last section is the 'secret' mentioned to Steinecke. Eluard's poem changes voice; its dialectical struggle is resolved in the victory of humanity, in the brotherhood of the poem's subject and object. 'Nous en aurons raison' is an affirmation of resistance, optimism and faith. Nono likewise shifts perspective. The entire coda uses only the three pitches absent from the rest of the piece: C♯, F♯, G♯ – the technique of *Composizione per orchestra [n. 1]*. As the voices sustain a consonant line of open intervals the brass announce the opening rhythm of *L'Internationale* in a proportional canon – a brazen challenge to conscience and conventionalism.

Why did Maderna take issue with *Guernica*? It is the least mediated of Nono's early works, in terms of both 'message' and its musical material. The poem is expressed in musical rhetoric and gesture. Nono's articulation of harmonic space produces not only a quasi-modality in certain passages – a bi-modality, even, where voices simultaneously explore different aspects of the material – but in its definition of primary and secondary areas, both with diatonic properties, it suggests a formal tonality. This contributes to the sense of a dangerously conventional rhetoric – an oratorio in the Roman tradition. The conclusion could be heard as an improbable resolution, despite Eluard's clear call for continuous resistance. Therein lies Maderna's own political resistance – not to the sentiment of the poem, but to the challenge that echoes from the end of Nono's setting. On a personal level, it must have served as a reminder of the companions' different relationship with their communism; professionally, it may also have struck him as approaching foolhardiness. The last paragraph of Maderna's letter contains reference to two vital shared concerns; one would remain complex, the other Nono would shortly address head-on. The artist, the bourgeois intellectual, must inevitably remain non-identical with the 'man in the street', however much, following Gramsci, Italian communist

Taking positions: song

theory rationalized the situation, however genuine, true and active the empathy. The same question of detachment underlies the need for objectivity in presenting social and political realities in art, a topic of great concern particularly to Italian cinema of the early 1950s. In this respect, *La Victoire de Guernica* was the catalyst for a rethinking of the relationship between text and music; as the vital role of text in Nono's thought became increasingly clear, he felt that he had not yet reconciled the two aspects of his work.[66] At the same time, *Guernica* presents a glimpse of a personal emotional world; Nono produces a musical surface very close to his own response to the poem and its topics, a drama of great immediacy. Perhaps we should think of the poem not as being expressed but performed. The process by which Nono produced the work, the kinds of thought and action and their sequence, is not radically different from its predecessors. But his choosing not to follow the path of more formalist modes of serialism was also an act of reflection. *La Victoire de Guernica* is a conscious assertion of the importance of the performative nature of Nono's composition. The final stage of selection from precompositional and experimental material ensures that the composer, his context and concerns in that moment, are embodied in the trace of the music itself.

'Liebeslied'

Incontrovertible is the expression of emotion in *Liebeslied*. The long-awaited posthumous premiere of the two completed acts of Schönberg's *Moses und Aron* was an event of huge symbolic importance. In its subject matter, its reconceiving of the nature of opera and its central place in Schönberg's thought, *Moses und Aron* occupies a unique historical position. Scherchen had been a tireless advocate and had undertaken the preparation of the material, to which Nono contributed as a copyist.[67] As soon as it emerged that Hübner might programme a concert performance in Hamburg, Nono wrote to him that Scherchen should naturally be invited to conduct. Despite Nono's protestations, cultural politics eventually determined that Hans Rosbaud should direct the performance, and on 12 March 1954 the new music community gathered in Hamburg for the event.[68] Here Nono met not only Schönberg's wife Gertrud but also their daughter Nuria. She and Nono would be married a year later.

Liebeslied is a setting of Nono's own love poem, dedicated to Nuria. Written at great speed at the end of his work on *La Victoire de Guernica*, it is a condensed version of the same structure, a devotional miniature that springs from the same conceptual and technical space; Borio sees it as a microcosm of the path ahead.[69] Scherchen had asked him for a short piece for Hannover. A month after the Hamburg encounter, Nono announced that it would be a love song, and by early May he could tell Steinecke that the work for choir, harp and percussion was finished.[70] Against the five-part choir, the percussion are the *suoni fissi*, the fixed points in Nono's pitch firmament; with harp and glockenspiel at the centre of the group, suspended cymbals and timpani mark the edges of clear, momentary pitch, vibraphone the attempt to sustain that moment. The poem is both all-encompassing and reduced to the essential: two stanzas of balanced meter and ideas conclude with a final line that mirrors the opening and condenses to the irreducible. It has the archetypal Nono structure of this time – bipartite, at once directional and symmetrical:

Erde bist Du	You are earth
Feuer Himmel	fire heaven
Ich liebe Dich	I love you
mit Dir ist Ruhe	with you is peace
Freude bist Du	you are joy

Taking positions: song

Sturm	Storm
mit mir bist Du	you are with me
Du bist Leben	you are life
Liebe bist Du	you are love

Nono's poem recalls the style of the love poetry of Cesare Pavese from the early 1950s, in particular the poems of *La terra e la morte* from *Verrà la morte e avrà i tuoi occhi* (1951). It combines Pavese's asymmetrical forms and the imagery of poems such as *Sei la terra . . .* and *Sei la vita . . . .* Nono had sent Nuria a copy of *Verrà la morte* after their first meeting.[71] He had revived an early interest in Pavese's poetry on a visit to the poet's home city of Turin earlier the same year.[72] Pavese would become Nono's most constant poetic companion – in his repeated returning to Pavese's texts, but also as a major source of the images and metaphors that run through Nono's work. Turin had made a very favourable impression: an outward- and forward-looking city with a recent history of socialism and resistance, the city of Gramsci and Einaudi. There he had met the editors of Pavese's poetry: Massimo Mila and Italo Calvino, with whom he would develop plans for a music-theatre piece.

In *Guernica*, his reduction of material to a nine-note series allowed Nono an 'other' pitch-space of three. For *Liebeslied* he divides the total chromatic between the two stanzas, each subseries a five-note set with a single opposite pole (Figure 4.6).

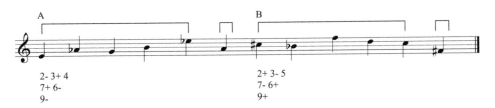

Figure 4.6 Liebeslied: pitch material

He constructs a 5×5 number square and displacement matrix as before, using the same values for each set (1 3 4 5 7) but changing the relative order for the second stanza. He reads these almost literally to determine the succession and simultaneities of pitch alone, omitting sequences at which the five elements are realigned. Each member of each set is then allocated a duration – in duple time for the first stanza, compound for the second. To afford greater rhythmic development in the treatment of simultaneities in the matrices, subdivisions of each duration allow for two or three notes to be separated. Each pitch is assigned a sequence of permutations of these values. The first five instances of E♭, for example, follow values 1–5 in their initial order (Figure 4.7).

Nono can now write the score in a single gesture, from beginning to end. He knows how to imagine, construct and test the space within which his musical thought and his emotional response are free to act together. Density, length of line, the focus on particular intervals, dynamics and tessitura are all sculpted to reveal the work that has grown in his imagination. As often, the balances and symmetries do not coincide; this becomes very clear in such a tight form. The analogy with his subject is also clear: knowledge comes not from the artificial aligning of elements, but through the negotiating of difference. Nono is increasingly aware that this property balances his architectonic thought; it creates forward motion in musical time. Each stanza of Nono's love poem covers an enormous emotional trajectory. Like *Guernica*, the piece is in two analogous halves followed by a short coda. Each half explores its five-note material,

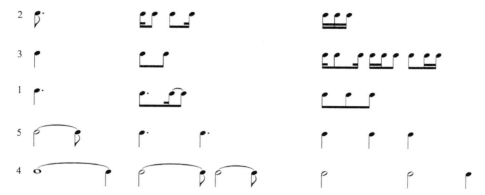

Figure 4.7 Liebeslied: rhythmic material for first stanza

finally 'resolving' on to the missing pitch. Harp and percussion move with a slower harmonic rhythm than the choir; in the first stanza an E major triad outlined by the timpani accompanies the first half, replaced by a high percussion and harp A♭–G oscillation in the second. Each stanza begins tranquilly, its lines lengthening and rhythmic activity intensifying as Nono introduces the alternative duration patterns. They build to imitative climaxes on *Feuer* and *Sturm*, the subsequent calm interrupted by unison resolutions with *Dich* and *Dir*. The second half of the piece does not begin with the second stanza of the poem, however, but with the serene 'mit Dir ist Ruhe'. The coda states not only the final line, but also the conclusion of the second stanza, creating its own internal symmetry. Four notes from the first set are followed by four from the second, the internal part crossing of the two phrases mirroring each other, surrounding a central timpani A; the last five bars are the entire work in microcosm (Figure 4.8). On the day he completed his song, Nono wrote to Stockhausen a letter full of human warmth. *Liebeslied* is a madrigal of love, a gift of Italian poetry and Venetian music. Its structural rhyme with the previous work tells us something very important about *Guernica* – that it is also a work of faith, of optimism, rooted in human love.

Figure 4.8 Liebeslied: coda

Into the theatre: 'Der rote Mantel, Was ihr wollt'

If *Liebeslied* shares structural properties with *La Victoire de Guernica*, its emotional core is developed in the ballet *Der Rote Mantel*.

> In Lorca everything grows from the earth, from life and from love – a people lives in this, from this. On this foundation Lorca loved his people and his time, as man and poet, and my relationship with Lorca is based on just this. [...] love is born and grows in Belisa; she is beauty which is reborn in love.[73]

Taking positions: song

Nono was continuously scanning his world for material with which to explore his developing ideas of music-theatre, as would remain his practice. In letters to his parents, references to world events and possible theatre pieces seem to derive from the same line of thought: the terrible floods of the Po Valley in 1950, for example (to figure in *Intolleranza 1960*), or the Gracchi brothers, martyred leaders of an agrarian revolution in Imperial Rome. He discusses a theatre project with Walter Jokisch of the Hannover Opera (the dramaturg of Henze's *Boulevard Solitude*), another in Munich and a radio drama with NDR Hamburg.[74] In February 1954, a month before the trip to Hamburg, Nono was approached by Gerhart von Westermann, Director of the Berliner Festwochen, to write a piece for an evening of ballets by Tatjana Gsovsky. He wrote immediately to Scherchen: 'I would like to make a ballet, also to get closer to the theatre'.[75] A month later agreement had been reached as to the subject:

> It's all decided for the ballet: the text is The Love of Don Perlimplin and Belisa (F Garcia Lorca), a hymn of love. [. . .] I've had to work hard in every sense – on the people from the Berliner Festwochen as much as on the libretto (they proposed Sodom and Gomorrah!!!!!) and the performance.[76]

To his parents he described discussions with Gsovsky as being 'violent but necessary'.[77] In the same letters he discusses the Hamburg performance of *Moses und Aron*. He praises its 'incredible expressive violence' and Schönberg's development of expressive and formal tradition to address the needs of today. These may well have been the principles he had in mind for the new work when Gsovsky's libretto arrived on 23 April. He replied:

> the libretto is beautiful –
> Our collaboration must be just wonderful –
> In Berlin it is too early for new music – old kings of the day before yesterday live
>   there –
> who are ready and willing to shoot us down – who have already noticed it –
> So our ballet must be a bomb. The most beautiful, cleverest, simplest, most natural,
>   most complex, maddest, purest, boldest there is today –
> Because only thus can one live, especially today.[78]

Born in Moscow in 1901, Tatjana Gsovsky founded a ballet school in Berlin in 1928. In her choreography she succeeded in introducing aspects of modernism and internationalism that in music were being rigorously repressed. Gsovsky managed to remain politically unaligned through the war and had been immediately invited to become ballet mistress of the Deutsche Oper in 1945. Her previous commission for the Berliner Festwochen had been a version of Dostoyevsky's *The Idiot* with music by Hans-Werner Henze, in which she had developed a new form of narrative dramatic dance – 'a synthesis of acted and danced presentation'.[79] Gsovsky's mature understanding of the role of artists and their work suggests a profound resonance with Nono's emerging ethics:

> Politics, religion and social issues are factors in which contemporary man is immersed and which act upon him constantly. The artist cannot do otherwise than to pay these problems their tribute; his participation is distinguished by the choice of means, not in the selection of themes.[80]

Lorca's play *The Love of Don Perlimplin and Belisa in His Garden* – probably written in 1926, repressed by the authorities and finally performed in 1933 – is an erotic, tragic farce.[81] The

Taking positions: song

confirmed bachelor Perlimplin falls in love with young Belisa; he disappoints her on their wedding night and suffers the frustration and humiliation of the cuckold. Only by pretending to be another lover can he assert his manhood and win back the love of Belisa. In the final surreal twist, Perlimplin is thus obliged to murder his wife's new lover – himself – thereby ending the hope of love for both of them. Love and death, reality and the surreal, idealism and self-destruction are inextricable.[82] 'What particularly excited me about Don Perlimplin is the contrast between the lyrical and the grotesque, which can melt into each other at any time', said Lorca.[83] Gsovsky adds five characters, the series of lovers whose seduction of Belisa forms the choreographic centrepiece. Lorca's Christological references would not have gone unnoticed: Perlimplin's red cloak, his self-sacrifice and the direction that the table in Act III should resemble a primitive Last Supper.[84] While the choice of subject was not Nono's, the resonances of this project were long lasting. At the première on 20 September, the reception was mixed:

> From the gallery they called the name of the composer. It was not clear whether they meant 'Nono!' or 'No! No!'. In any case the boos left no doubt. This work certainly has a peculiar fascination. Redolent of Salvador Dalí, Jean-Pierre Ponnelle's sets reinforced the impression of a real-unreal sphere, in which it's all about a piece of wretched humanity. [. . .] One laughs perhaps, mocks, because it is shocking, but is clearly moved.[85]

The popular draw of this programme of Gsovsky's work was a revival of her 1946 choreography of Ravel's *Bolero*. She had told the story of how she had begun to hear Ravel's indefatigable rhythm as she had made her way 'like a homing pigeon' on foot back to a destroyed Berlin, to find her school still standing.[86] *Bolero* had thus become the very embodiment of Berliners' resilience, persistence and common purpose in this initial phase of rebuilding. It is not surprising, therefore, that an audience anticipating an evening of self-confident duende may have been unprepared for Lorca's emotional complexity or Nono's sophistication of musical language. In fact, the relationship with Ravel's work runs much deeper; sublimated as it may be, the Bolero rhythm plays a crucial role.

On receiving Gsovsky's libretto, Nono set about finding appropriate musical forms. Act I is articulated into *esposizione, prima conseguenza, scena centrale, primo risultato*. The maturity of his technical palette frees Nono's imagination to respond to the emotional and gestural range of Gsovsky's plan. Rather than starting immediately to compose the planned series of numbers, Nono establishes sets of materials relating to the two main protagonists – Perlimplin and Belisa – and another representing their union. The complex potential of two individuals united in love is understandably his dominant motif. Nono sets out from a quasi-symmetrical ur-series – designated *Amore* – consisting only of semitones (5), major thirds (4) and perfect fourths (2). Those for Perlimplin and Belisa are derived from this original series by his long-standing permutation technique of using every *n*th note, in different versions for each of the first two acts (Figure 4.9).

The sketches make it clear that considerable initial thought was invested in developing this limited pitch material. At the time (and for some time to come), a piano was a constant presence in Nono's physical composing environment. It seems quite likely, therefore, that he would have heard and reheard these series as melodic material. Parentheses, cuts and shifts of sequences in the raw pitch material suggest substantial rehearsing before it generates more complex structures. In its original form, the *Amore* series rises through two-and-a-half octaves, with just two semitone downward turns. This already highly expressive melodic gesture also traces clear tonal implications. Nono's straightforward use of displacement matrices – one for each act –

Taking positions: song

Figure 4.9 Der rote Mantel: Amore series and derivatives. (ALN 10.03/06r. © The heirs of Luigi Nono. Reproduced by kind permission.)

inhibits the emergence of any motivic qualities; pitches occur in the order and with the simultaneities determined by the matrices. Like the series itself, the matrices all derive from a single source: his plans suggest a Latin square read differently for Perlimplin and Belisa in each of the first two acts, a single unified reading in the third. This structural reconfiguration clouds both the melodic gesture and the harmonic charge of the original material, and yet each number is suffused with the particular constellation of harmonic fields generated by one of the five series.

Rhythmic material is likewise clearly defined at the outset. Perlimplin and Belisa are each allocated a group of related Spanish dance figures: five in quintuple metre for Perlimplin (four Basque dances and the Castillian Rueda), and five in triple time for Belisa (including the Bolero), all taken directly from Lavignac's book.[87] Rather than searching for new technical solutions, Nono seems to have worked rapidly using his familiar processes of segmentation, varying the fundamental unit, mirroring and erasure to construct sequences of permutations. For each number he weaves these into more complex layers, sculpting the flow of rhythmic intensity and textural density. This rhythmic substrate can then be populated by the pitch material, leaving Nono free in his use of register, dynamics and orchestration to respond with spontaneity to the dramatic stimulus. Here we find another association with Ravel – to the underlying rhythmic drive of *Bolero*, certainly, but also to *L'Enfant et les Sortilèges*, to the intimate relationship between the lyrical and the fantasmagorical and to its exquisitely acute sense of sonority. Sensuousness and a heightened emotional state emerge from a language that

Taking positions: song

at times approaches colouristic orientalism. This is manifest immediately in the opening *Introduction*, a sextet of triangles using Perlimplin's Aurresku rhythms. Figure condenses from this surreal firmament through percussion and pizzicato until clear pitch material arrives with Perlimplin himself and is transformed into song by Belisa. At the end of the same act, *Belisa's disappointment* (their wedding night), extraordinary doublings of octave and articulation weave through stuttering melodic fragments like an ensemble of impossible exotic instruments narrating a tale of unrealisable eroticism.

The narrative is carried by dance; Lorca's text appears only in the songs of Belisa in the first and last acts, that of Perlimplin in the second – all three joined by a chorus – and a choral serenade. Distinguished from the layered rhythms of the other dance movements, these stand out as architectonic pillars. They support the otherwise fragmented structure – images of a world in which present and future, sequence and the apparent directionality of time are illusory – in a way that anticipates *Prometeo* thirty years later. As there, the passage from text to non-text is often blurred as the central melodic line moves between voices and instruments, continuously changing colour. The emergence of speech, of text, draws our attention to a central thread of Nono's thought: the complex relationship between words, music and meaning. There is a continuum through instrumental and vocal sound, at one end of which is the human ability to articulate speech. This is what Stockhausen would fail to grasp in his later dispute with Nono. For Nono, words are not the origin but an emergent property of 'meaning', which permeates the entire musical text; labeling his ur-series *love* is neither a private compositional conceit nor Wagnerian symbolism.

In Nono's annotated libretto, Belisa's Act I song is a 'hymn of love'. The wordless high B with which she enters is prepared throughout the previous number by its repetition in flute and glockenspiel.[88] As her melos moves from the instrumental gestures of the previous section to focus if the text itself, the chorus sustains sequences of consecutive pitches in Nono's familiar halo effect. With minor adjustments, Belisa's two songs are rhythmically identical, both derived from the scaling and permutation of cells from the Fandango. Perhaps there is a private reference to the sentiments of *Y su sangre*. Through the remainder of her song, Nono's local rhythmic structures develop nests of dances within dances; each dance of the sequence that follows is more clearly defined. Belisa's final love song effects a move from melody to text analogous to the first, but now in a more developed form as befits the complexity of love that has been explored in the meantime. The *Amore* series is announced in its prime form by instruments and wordless voices, then in retrograde, inversion and retrograde inversion by Belisa – the only direct statement of material in the work. In finding completeness, it denies its own future, like Belisa's love. Narrative text brings a quality of temporal directionality to the multidirectional exploration of structures and materials. Belisa's final love song is a continuous instrumental/vocal unison rising from low chorus and brass to the soprano's highest register, where it reconnects with the opening canopy of triangles. Words emerge from the song, the melos of which is articulated and reverberated by shorter or longer sounds. The rising major sevenths of the song's opening echo across its conclusion, surrounding the whole like temporal parentheses; it is inserted into the flow of time and reality. Again, Nono invokes the half-remembered songs and endless decays of Mahler – not so much nostalgia as an invitation to the listener to search their own memory.

Nono wrote immediately to Steinecke about his experience: the tumult surrounding the premiere, his enthusiasm for Ponelle's surrealist sets and his mixed feelings about the choreography: 'Here I am really quite alone – even more of a Martian.'[89] Perhaps because of the severe practical constraints of this first experience in the theatre, he seems to have discovered new areas of creativity. To his parents his criticism was more explicit: 'The performance was

Taking positions: song

not good. Despite the bad conductor my music imposed itself strongly, after having surprised with its novelty. For a first work for the theatre I am very happy. I have understood much and learned.'[90] If his sense of isolation was more acute in Berlin, the experience consolidated emergent aspects of his thought – the role of experimental theatre, for example. On Scherchen's suggestion he had contacted Bertolt Brecht and the composer Paul Dessau.[91] A deep and lasting friendship would develop with Dessau, sustained through many visits to East Berlin. Maderna wrote to Nono from Venice – partly, it seems, as a brotherly reminder of their common project, a response to his friend's newfound emotional, professional and technical independence: 'I'm glad you've met Brecht [. . .]. It doesn't matter if we have difficulty in realizing our ideas [. . .] the important thing is that they are understood. Give my regards to Dessau [. . .]'[92]

Nono made further contacts in the theatre world of Berlin. While there, he was invited to provide music for a production of Shakespeare's *As You Like It* (*Was ihr wollt*) at the Schlosspark Theater in November. Three songs and some twenty-one short instrumental cues are scored for voice and five instruments.[93] In the interests of both compositional expeditiousness and singability – presumably these songs would have been performed by actors rather than professional singers – Nono uses the reductive pyramid technique that he and Maderna had developed a few years earlier to distill shorter, more straightforwardly patterned sequences of pitches and intervals.

Integration

'Canti'

On Christmas day 1954, Nono wrote to Steinecke:

> Finally I know what to do with the theatre. 4 beautiful scenes of Lorca, almost unknown. Each is something different, with a different sense and form. Together they constitute a new form of theatre. Everything is determined: stage direction, set, scenery, lighting. From May 1955 <u>only</u> this work.[94]

The months between the Berlin visit and the spring of 1955 were a period of intense activity and difficult adjustment to his role as a composer. Following his experiences in Berlin, long-gestating ideas had begun to find form, but a living had to be made and he had responsibilities in his informal role as Scherchen's assistant; letters through this period describe his frustration at the time spent copying transparencies for Ars Viva.

On a visit to Paris with Scherchen for Boulez's Concerts Marigny in October 1954, Boulez had proposed that Nono should compose a new work to be presented there the following March.[95] Steinecke had then written to Nono in Berlin offering a commission for Darmstadt the next year.[96] Shortly after his return to Venice, Nono received a letter from Strobel offering 1,500 marks for an orchestral work ('free from percussion'), probably to be played at Kassel, at the ISCM World Music Days in Baden Baden and at the festival of Aix-en-Provence – but it would have to be delivered by May 1955. The management of his own creativity thus became a burning issue for Nono on every level. An economy of musical thought emerges to inform both his compositional practice and its relationship with the cultural world, a conscious keeping track of the development of his own ideas and their potential role.

Engagement with the business and cultural politics of his art was also unavoidable. A warm friendship had developed with Karl Amadeus Hartmann, director of the *Musica Viva* series in Munich. Hartmann had himself been an early protégé of Scherchen, and Nono was happy to feel part of a wider like-minded family: 'The most important is that we are not alone, this awful

105

Taking positions: song

isolation that destroys so many artists today, but we are people among people, and only thus can we be ourselves; and that, especially is to <u>understand today</u>.'[97] To Hartmann Nono confessed his frustration at being outside the cultural power structures of Italy, particularly the ISCM.[98] On his way back from Berlin, Nono visited Scherchen at his new home in Gravesano in the Swiss Ticino. Scherchen was keen to confirm Nono's arrangement with the publishing company he had established in Zürich.[99] *Ars Viva* was now a serious undertaking, having been incorporated into Schott's catalogue the year before. Nono's faith in his mentor is such that it is difficult to distil an objective picture of Scherchen from their correspondence. Among musicians he had a reputation as authoritarian, and he clearly was not used to negotiating with dissent. Boulez's description of Scherchen at the time of the Marigny concerts gives a sense of the forcefulness of his character:[100]

> I might describe him as a slow proselyte, a solemn promoter: both adventurous and patriarchal in character; persuasion and conviction were both deeply rooted in those recesses of the soul where agitation is clearly ridiculous and superfluous; a groundswell unconcerned with surface eddies. He was certainly not what is called an easy person: the tenacity of his opinions either carried you with him or left you stranded. With him even the unforeseen took on the colour of eternity.[101]

A plan for a new music-theatre work based on Lorca was the fruit of Nono's discussions with Scherchen, who advised him to work on the first part for the following year's Darmstadt commission. Steinecke, however, was still anticipating a set of Italian love songs – presumably the settings of Pavese dedicated to Nuria that Nono had described in November.[102] He had already begun engaging soloists and negotiated a fee of 1,000 marks from the city of Darmstadt; Hans Rosbaud was to conduct the premiere there on 30 May .[103] But Nono's ideas were galloping ahead. By mid-January he had almost finished the piece to be played in Paris in March, to become *Canti per 13*. The process of composition had been smooth from a technical point of view, and yet this seems to have been frustrating his now urgent need to be grappling with other issues. Meanwhile, recognition in Germany made his sense of cultural and professional isolation in Italy more acute. To Steinecke he wrote: 'Now I know nothing about anything. Very poor, in every sense. Very alone. Just work.'[104] A month later: 'Too much work here! Too many transparencies! Too much music to copy!!! SHIT. And not particularly peaceful.'[105] Shortly thereafter, a visit from Henze had cheered him up: 'For me it was good because it was a dark and disturbed period, a shit time.'[106] Confronting the paradoxes and pragmatic realities of the profession of composing was not easy. Despite finding a path through these difficulties, Nono maintained an ambivalent relationship with the role, subsequently reconciled in part by viewing it in sociopolitical terms; it was part of his cultural role as an intellectual, and he would continue to maintain a reflective distance from the 'profession' of composing.

The use of the voice, its relationship with text and their presentation in some kind of theatrical context were the inextricable issues that burned to be addressed. The new technologies much discussed at Darmstadt, and now being explored by his friends in Paris and Cologne, were another outstanding matter. At the same time, another realm of exploration was now becoming a practical possibility: the electronic studio. In August 1954, on the way to Berlin, Nono had attended the opening congress at Scherchen's new research studio in Gravesano, a venture supported by UNESCO. After much tangential exposure to such ideas at Darmstadt, he now felt able to participate in the discussions of scientists and technologists, but his understanding of their implications ran ahead: 'I also contributed to the discussions (on the relationship between score and performer) – they looked at me as if I'd come from Mars.'[107] This relationship would

Taking positions: song

become one of the central concerns in his work through the 1980s, with the advent of live electronics. As the person most likely to accommodate his aspirations, Nono wrote to Steinecke with his revised plans for the Italian love songs: two voices with multiple tapes of sine tones, for the production of which he would accept the offer of help from 'the pope of Cologne' – Stockhausen, now Eimert's assistant at the NWDR studio and working on his two *Studie*.[108] Steinecke was aghast, but agreed to a compromise; he would negotiate with Strobel for the SWF commission to receive its premiere at Darmstadt at the end of May. The commission from the city itself would be postponed for a year, but he still hoped for an orchestral work.[109] Nono's ideas had moved on again; in January 1955 he wrote to Steinecke:

> Damn! Damn! Damn!
>
> Now I can't write 'love songs' [. . .] because now I understand much more than some months ago. Problems and developments have progressed, and now I envisage a new style of song; and that just at the moment that I want to write an opera. And I need to study that calmly [. . .] now my work for 13 instruments is finished I can see the new development and I need to do that immediately. There are new structural possibilities and I need to work on them with larger forces.[110]

Nono was now able to approach the orchestral work for Strobel (to become *Incontri*) with more equanimity, but his letters show him still anxious to get on with developing longer term ideas. This rapid but intense process of reflection on technique and musical language, the trajectory to *Il canto sospeso*, already makes itself felt in *Canti per 13*. It may have been titled after its completion, but subsequent comments by Nono clearly indicate that the work's name (*Songs*) is of great significance:

> In *Canti per 13* I wanted to return to just using instruments and to find new ways to confront technique, language itself. Kraus said that thought develops with language and in this sense I'm talking about a continuous study between language and thought. Sometimes musical language leads me to a sort of distortion of the text. Not only does the text inspire me, it is also acoustic material; it must, it can become pure music. At other times the text superimposes itself on the musical language. In *Guernica* the two elements are in conflict, as they often are.[111]

The dedication of *Canti* 'to Pierre Boulez in his humanity' suggests a personal context, but also perhaps an empathetic awareness of the artistic courage required to fully confront the implications of current musical thought.[112] *Canti per 13* prepares the ground for a new relationship with text and meaning in *Il canto sospeso* the following year. In addressing these technical issues, Nono returned to two of his fundamental points of reference: Webern and Gabrieli. With Maderna he had developed a view of Webern as a hyper-distillation of German song, an essence of romantic expression: 'Thinking of how I understood Webern with Bruno, for me every note was a song, an entire Lied.'[113] The texture of *Canti* is made up largely of single notes: 'the instruments sing and the conductor sings with them'. [114] The ear of the pattern- or connection-seeking listener is thus drawn to form its own polyphony, just as the players are inevitably led to shape each sound individually. Active listening – the discovery of multiple paths through the constellations of *Canti* – becomes integral to Nono's conception of his work. Single or repeated notes are interspersed with rarer phrases of two, three or even four notes that momentarily refocus the texture and concentrate attention on intervals and connections. The texture is almost continuous; brief silences mark its formal architecture.

Taking positions: song

Composer, performer and listener share the emergence of song from sound, of common purpose and understanding from individual activity; that audible, vocal text should rise to the musical surface is only one of the possible states of song in Nono's music.

The Venetian canzona of Gabrieli – itself a polyphonic elaboration of the chanson – provided another model. Nono divides the thirteen instruments, the one-of-each chamber orchestra of Boulez's concert series, into four variably constituted mixed groups of three. The double bass remains a free agent, able to join any of the groups. Conceptually, the forces are those of a large Venetian instrumental work of 1600, the four groups underpinned by an autonomous thorough-bass. Nono thus has available a four-voice texture; the notes of each voice can be distributed among three or four instruments. Once again, he seems to have had a binary form in mind from the outset, analogous to the imitative and dance-like ('Alleluia-like', Nono calls them) sections of a canzona.[115] Both the architecture and the grain of *Canti* emerge from the very stones of Venice. Later pictures of Nono's studio show an environment rich in images, photographs, shapes and colours, among which are photographs of marble facing. Laid symmetrically around their split point, the veins of two slabs converge in opposite directions. Nono selects his material similarly; ur-material rather than thematic or abstract, its characteristics permeate both surface and structure. Like two adjoining pieces of split marble, the two equally proportioned parts of *Canti* (173 and 181 bars) are both symmetrical about their central point (bars 87 and 264). It is as if the space of possibilities needs to be traversed twice, to explore its potential but also to counter any implicit monodirectionality. As in Nono's later work, possible words coexist. This material consists of two essentialised components: an all-interval 'wedge' series expanding from semitone to major seventh (A to E♭) and a Latin square based on a rising and falling quasi-Fibonacci sequence (1, 3, 5, 8, 13, 18). The two parts of *Canti* are characterised by their treatment of these elements. In keeping with the canzona model, the first part presents them in a tightly organised imitative texture that resolves only across the entire span, while the second is based around repetition and rhythmic elaboration.

Nono constructs four displacement matrices, one for each form of the series, using values from the Fibonacci square obtained by reading its rows and columns in four different directions. This material he then retranscribes in musical notation (still using the bass clef – perhaps a remnant of his early training on harmony and counterpoint), subsequently analysed for patterns, repetitions and singularities. The Latin square also generates durations. The sequences of numbers – twelve rows or columns, according to the four directions of reading beginning from the four corners – are mapped on to four different basic rhythmic values: O, I, R and IR are mapped to divisions of the beat of 2, 4, 3 and 6. The passage from abstract form, concepts and material to the final surface is mediated by graphical processes; the work emerges from the stages of its inscription. A pattern of polyphonic density reflects the expanding and contracting nature of the material itself (Figure 4.10).

This shape informs both the outline structure for the first part of *Canti* and the flow of polyphonic density, rhythmic intensity and tempo within each section. Nono thus leaves himself clear parameters of freedom. The quasi-Fibonacci duration series is chosen not for any mystical or numerological reason, but because as its elements are scaled over the different rhythm values, the resulting durations are unambiguous. The association of the voices of pitch material with readings of the square is unchanging; their mapping on to the four rhythm bases changes at structural points, however. The clarity of voices is also assured by their continuity of orchestration within each entry. The 220 possible permutations are not explored systematically, but Nono makes multiple lists of combinations that have different characteristics – degrees of homogeneity of colour, register or articulation – from which he selects in order. A similarly informal scheme is developed for dynamics, designed to enhance the sense of breathing, of

Taking positions: song

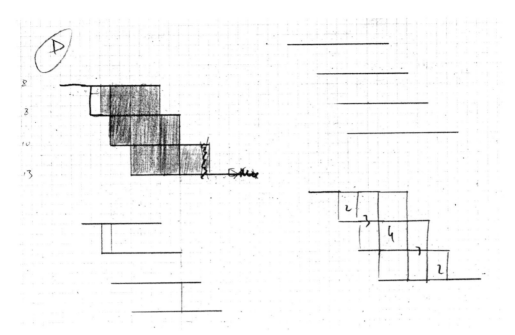

Figure 4.10 Canti per 13: densities. (ALN 12.01/09v (detail). © The heirs of Luigi Nono. Reproduced by kind permission.)

continuous expansion and contraction, that runs through each strand of material. Each duration is associated with a different dynamic; the range increases with polyphonic density (from *ppp–mf* to *ppp–ff*), but also inverts such that with a single voice the shortest and longest sounds are quietest, while with all four the situation is reversed. As the distribution of pitches and rhythms across voices and instruments changes in the mirror from bar 87, the mapping of dynamics and articulation are different – the material resists its own reversal in time.

The adaptations made to the abstract material in laying it across the skeletal structure allow us to observe Nono's decision-making with clarity. The principle of tight imitative polyphony is established at the outset; over the first four bars, each voice is allowed to establish its autonomy by presenting its opening semitone uninterrupted. Voices may be shifted to create aggregate pitch centres (A♯–C♯ in bars 43–50), or to elide in octave doubling. Rests from the matrices may be ignored or used as phrase markers. Additional rests highlight fragments of figure. While shorter values generally aggregate around the crests of waves of intensity, the longest are occasionally sustained through these passages like fragments of cantus firmus: for example, the bass clarinet B♭ followed by clarinet and trumpet Bs through bars 25–30, the line dissolving into a surrounding cluster, or a rare triple-attack in 29.

Figure 4.11 shows how some of these relationships are constructed in a brief four-bar passage concluding the opening section. At this early stage of its development the pitch material produces no rests (or empty cells), so while pitch, duration and dynamics are determined for each voice, the precise placement of sounds is 'free-hand'. The multiple pitch correspondences interwoven between voices often produce the 'halo' effect of separated attack and sustain characteristic of Nono's early work. As well as local pitch relations and rhythmic coincidences, the broader contours of this passage re-present a compressed version of the basic material

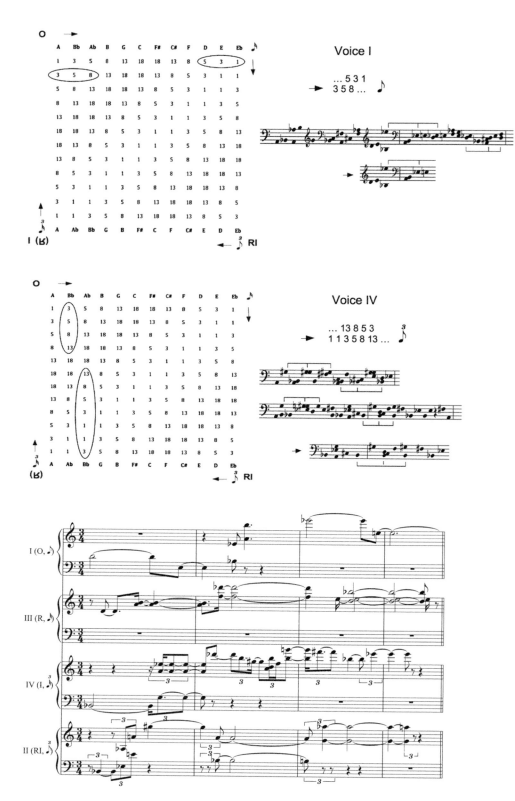

Figure 4.11 Canti per 13: derivation of bars 19–22[116]

Taking positions: song

presented by the individual voices at the opening of the piece. After the assertive B♭ from voices II and IV with which the passage begins, the prominent pitch centres fan out to A then B. An almost pan-chromatic accumulation of pitches then dissolves to leave only the inevitable goal E before the next section can begin.

The second part of *Canti* presents the original series 58 times: in the first half forwards (A–E♭), in the second backwards, with a central mirrored half-series. As in the dance sections of a canzona, this secure pitch world allows the listener to focus on the rhythmic interplay of the voices. Again, the architecture is a function of polyphonic density and alignment. As in the first part, there are four sections either side of the mirror point, and Nono's initial plan is informed by the same overlapping principle: a four-voice opening section reducing to two (bars 174–205, 206–13), a second section of three voices (214–33), a third of four (234–50) and the last reducing incrementally back to a single voice at the point of reflection (251–63). In drafting the score, the second section becomes a homophonic, block-chordal interlude between the rhythmic intricacies that surround it, and Nono reverts to the full four voices to achieve the effect. The four sections successively reduce in length and in the number of presentations of the series. The stable rate of presentation – every two to three bars – generates an even wave-like motion.

Durations are again from the Latin square, but now using only the rhythm bases of triplet and quintuplet. Ambiguities are now possible, therefore; a single beat may constitute a value of either three or five from the sequence. The palette of rhythmic values (the number sequence on its two base values) is expanded on macro- and micro-levels. The pattern of durations for each pitch in each voice follows one direction of reading of the square, creating a long-term coherence within which Nono has great flexibility in distributing and locating individual notes. In this way, the values are no longer contiguous; there is both greater unpredictability and the possibility of multiple simultaneous or sequential instances of the same value. At the same time, the single-note values are subdivided into groups of one to six attacks in all but the chordal second section. The rolling pitch structure shimmers as each note dances from within. This inner vibrance is enhanced by dynamic schemes for each voice that allocate a different dynamic (*ppp–sff*) to pairs of pitches for each duration. The light falls differently on individual sounds, groups or figures, almost too fleeting to assimilate as they detach themselves from the breaking waves. The many colours with which Nono distinguishes dynamics, voices or structures through these sketches suggest the same metaphor – not just the stones of Venice, then, but its lapping waters.

The initial processes, the practice by which Nono's thought found a path to the realization of an abstract compositional idea, are well rehearsed, but in *Canti* the nature and dynamics of the musical entities that emerge are radically different. For Nono, Scherchen's role was now less that of mentor than of conduit – an aerial by which, thanks to Scherchen's unquenchable thirst for the new, Nono could receive an enthusiastic if partisan digest of current thought. Two likely topics of conversation are recognizable in *Canti*. In November 1954 Scherchen was in Paris, preparing for the premiere of Varèse's *Deserts* on 2 December. *Canti* is a classicised embodiment of Varèse's fundamental structuring principle of musical bodies moving at different speeds and directions. While in Paris, Scherchen had met Iannis Xenakis who had shown him the score of *Metastasis*. Presumably, they discussed the stochastic concepts that Xenakis was developing, and his view of the limits of serialism that would be set out in a paper for Scherchen the following year.[117] In *Canti*, Nono works directly with the statistical properties and implications – the shifting focuses, ambiguities and emergent structures – of the techniques that he and Maderna had evolved.

Taking positions: song

'Incontri'

Canti per 13 would be performed in Paris on 26 March 1955, conducted by Boulez in a programme with Stockhausen's *Kontrapunkte*. Meanwhile, Strobel's orchestral commission for Darmstadt had to be addressed with some urgency; Rosbaud wanted the material by mid-April. Still referred to by Strobel as an *Ouvertüre*, to Nono's dismay, this was to become *Incontri*. The commission from Steinecke was postponed for a year while the seeds of *Il canto sospeso* were germinating: 'an orchestral work (large orchestra) or a work for the theatre (1 act or so) – is that possible? Because finally I want to confront the theatre [. . .]. In the last work (for 13 instruments) I have understood and considered many new things.'[118] He was therefore able to set about *Incontri* with renewed enthusiasm. 'THE FUTURE BELONGS TO US,' he wrote to Steinecke a few days later, again mentioning plans for the theatre.[119] He also contemplated a holiday before the Darmstadt summer school, perhaps in the Black Forest. This is the first glimpse of the development in Nono's imagination of another place, another environment: peaceful, natural (paradoxically, given its situation, Venice is the product of intense human exchange and artifice), perhaps utopian, a refuge from the stress he had suffered during the writing of *Canti per 13*. The Black Forest would indeed later become an important and productive refuge.

Nono also explored issues of musical multiplicity in dialogue with Maderna, who had been through a parallel, almost simultaneous process of evolution in writing his *Quartetto per archi in due tempi*. Like his friend, Maderna had arrived at a balance of structural repetition and mirrors across different time-multipliers using their 'magic square' technique. A letter from Darmstadt, where he was now established with his family, conveys a sense of the competitive atmosphere in which these steps were being taken, but also of their common position in the carefully monitored political space of the 1950s:

> My quartet works well [. . .]. For the first time I am writing coherently, objectively. I really believe that this is without doubt my best work [. . .]. Anyway, old thing, I want to tell you that this is our true path, our legitimate path. That which we found together. That which in our years of work and study in Venice – painful for me but now wonderful in my memory – we found patiently and pursued with incorruptible enthusiasm. We can do more and better than Stockhausen. We are Latin, hence Europeans, hence of the world, hence right and true, hence communists.[120]

The friends shared a world of political references: the last line of Maderna's letter is a paraphrase of a famous line from Togliatti's statement to the Constitutional Assembly in 1946.[121]

Early sketches would seem to be contemporaneous with his work on *Canti*; references to the work for Aix place them before Steinecke's letter of 31 January 1955 and Strobel's confirmation of a week later that the performance would be in Darmstadt. A fully symmetrical form was part of the original conception. *Incontri* is a literal mirror, reflected about the middle of the central bar 109. The listener's attention is constantly drawn to its architectonic nature by unmistakable salient signals such as groups of repeated notes in extreme registers or clear timpani figures. The individual strands of polyphonic texture are referred to in sketches as 'canti' – originally eight, soon reduced to a maximum of six. *Incontri* emerges from a web of song. Under the heading 'Tensione a 4 spazi' he lists their parameters: timbre, rhythm, dynamics and pitch (harmonic and melodic). Sound events – sequences, chains, textures of notes – are located in a four-dimensional space in which each point is uniquely characterised, but this is

Taking positions: song

very different from formulaic determinism. In *Incontri*, the truth of each event is the product of layers of compositional mediation and depends entirely on its relationship with all the others. The relative tensions in each parameter are constantly shifting, such that each note is kept in a carefully calibrated suspension.

While the super-condensed expressive Lied of Webern's melos is still at the centre of Nono's thinking, in order to sustain the 'Tensione a 4 spazi' he requires pitch material that does not result in Webern's acrostic motivic polyphony. In the second part of *Canti*, the series had been transformed from a mine, a generator of pitch material, into an indissoluble acoustic whole. Instead of being constantly just beyond the consciousness of the musical surface, the series stands fully at its centre. There it is used only in its original form, without permutation or transposition. For *Incontri*, Nono constructs the only figural series he uses in this way – neither subject to permutation beyond its 12-note scope nor essentialised to the all-interval series. Analysis of the series in the sketches demonstrates its potential as two elements both intertwined (Figure 4.12) and next to each other (Figure 4.14).

Figure 4.12 Incontri: series (Nono's annotation)

While there is a repetition of rising and falling melodic gesture, and each three notes outline a minor third, the series avoids precise symmetries. Each pair of intervals is unique; the stability of pitch sequence functions as a horizon against which he can construct interval complexes and relationships. His view of the total interval potential, the incidence of intervals roughly in proportion to their size, relates his conception of pitch material to the Latin squares and mapping tables of other parameters.

From the outset, Nono projected structural symmetry on two planes: two elements evolving inversely, the whole mirrored about a central point. His programme note from the May performance describes them:

> Each of the two structures is in itself autonomous, and distinguishes itself from the other by its rhythmic construction, timbre (colour and instrumentation) and dynamics of harmonic and melodic projection. But there exists a relationship of constant proportions between the two structures.[122]

He set out the plan in detail in a letter to musicologist Luigi Rognoni (Figure 4.13).[123] The tail of structure A and the beginning of B are repeated and cross-cut; fermata mark the end of the full exposition of A and the opening of that of B. The entire edifice is reversed from the middle of bar 109, quite literally such that the ends of notes become their start points and dynamic shapes are inverted. Nono follows this scheme quite precisely in multiples of bars of 2/4. The non-correspondence with bars in the score is the result of his notating structure B in 3/4, a musicianly strategy to encourage the performers to distinguish between the two elements. Occasional 1/4 bars also serve to mark boundaries, as well as making up the numbers. The last two sections of B (20 and 32 beats respectively) each lose one beat, the latter at the point of reflection, the former as an anticipation.

Taking positions: song

```
A   18    13    8     5     3    1    U
    1-18  19-31 32-39 40-44 -45-48-
B   2     4
    -49-52-
A               8     5
                53-60 61-65
B               6     10
                66-69 70-77
A                           3    1    U

B   2     4     6     10    16
    82-83 84-87 88-91 92-98 99-109
```

Upper numbers from Nono's explanation
Lower numbers show corresponding passages from bars 1-109 in published score

Figure 4.13 Nono's diagram of distribution of materials A and B through the first half of *Incontri*

    The different number sequences reflect how Nono imagined the two structures: odd and even, absolutely essential to and integrated with one another, yet of entirely discrete identities. Structure A is initially associated with a Latin square using the same quasi-Fibonacci sequence as *Canti* (3, 5, 8, 13, 18), B with an analogous even sequence (2, 4, 6, 10, 16, 10). The return inwards, the final 10, confers a different character on the even values. It also reflects the shape of each hexachord of the series. A doodle on a page of pitch material begins as a stick person and is transformed into a version of Nono's early symbol for bidirectional symmetry, his informal icon for the multiple directionality of time and the simultaneous existence of something and its opposite, its reverse, inverse or negative. It finds a new form as two pairs of opposites, meeting at a common point; two discrete but mutually dependent beings with the same destiny – two people united (Figure 4.14).

    The polyphonic density of sections is proportional to their length: A decreases from eighteen bars of six voices to a single bar of one; B increases from four beats of one to thirty-one of six. The architecture of *Incontri* being clear, Nono can begin to render its surface. The unvarying pitch series provides a perspective that connects horizontal and vertical relationships. The

Figure 4.14 From sketches for *Incontri*. (ALN 13.01/06 (detail). © The heirs of Luigi Nono. Reproduced by kind permission.)

Taking positions: song

analogy with tonal space is strengthened by a clear sense of harmonic rhythm. The rate of appearance of the series becomes an important factor. Through the first four sections of structure A it decreases linearly – 12, 6, 3, 1 – with a single series shared by the final two (bars 45–8). The register and voice allocation of each sound event is free – each facet of the surface is applied by hand. Sequences of durations come from the columns and rows of a single 12×12 matrix combining the two number sets. Nono develops a new device for maintaining control of texture: reading values from the matrix as rests:

> it wasn't a matter of a series, rather of a procedure, of a catalogue of intervals which in *Incontri* are continually reordered by a procedure which then I called positive and negative. The positive was the duration and the negative a rest equal to that duration.[124]

He allows himself freedom in selecting the most appropriate element from which to start reading. Every note is uniquely characterised by means of a more complete, complex version of the mapping system developed for *Canti*. Dynamics and rhythmic substitutions are derived from a sequence of mapping charts for each kind of voice (divisions of the beat by 3, 4 and 5 in original and augmented versions) and for structures A and B ('odd' and 'even') – i.e. twelve in all. The substitute rhythms are often uneven subdivisions, introducing an element of figure available as the composer requires. The repetition of notes also produces new melodic and harmonic artifacts that create local tension against the flow of the series. Six dynamic levels (*fff*–*ppp*) are each associated with two pitches. Their initial sequence is largely contiguous, rotated for each row. The chart is thus read down from the duration value and along from the pitch to provide a dynamic. The series rotates through an n-dimensional dynamic space as it passes between voices, anticipating the geometric models of Xenakis.

Figure 4.15 illustrates this process in the four-voice polyphony of the third section of structure A, bars 32–9. Beginning with the B♭ of bar 32, the series is presented three times. Durations are read from the third, fourth and fifth columns of the number square, downwards from successive elements of the quasi-Fibonacci sequence (1, 3, 5). Two voices of semiquavers and two of quintuplets each maintain a continuous line, taking the next available pitch from the series and duration multiple from the number square as a note ends. Each voice is a new construct, incorporating only occasional patterns from either source, and is further dispersed and refracted by the various instruments and registers of its associated group.

The microcompositional process consists of managing the degrees of compositional freedom and exploiting the potential that emerges on every level. The passage begins with the multiple *fff* attacks that accumulate at the end of the previous section. It is opened and closed by the same repeated-note rhythm in the 1st timpani (voice 2), giving the move from F to E a sense of structural voice-leading. The initial F soon reappears in voice 2, establishing a tension against the low E of voice 3. This tension underpins the whole passage as the 2nd timpani introduce a fast repeated E (itself part of an imitative exchange passing from voice 2 to 1 to 3), and then an echo of the initial F against the 1st timpani final E, again in voice 3. New melodic relationships emerge as rhythmic substitutions generate additional attacks, with the additional C in voice 4, bar 33, for example. Without his usual displacement matrices, Nono has only single pitches available; their polyphonic distribution and additional attacks produce new harmonic constructs. The anomalous rest in bar 34 is a product of Nono's identifying of emergent voices; it allows the cello line to move directly from the C♯ of voice 1 to D♯ in voice 4. Register is vital to the colour and tension of pitch space. The final high B of bar 39 signals a shift into the new atmosphere of the next section, such that its predecessor in bar 34 becomes a pre-echo.

Taking positions: song

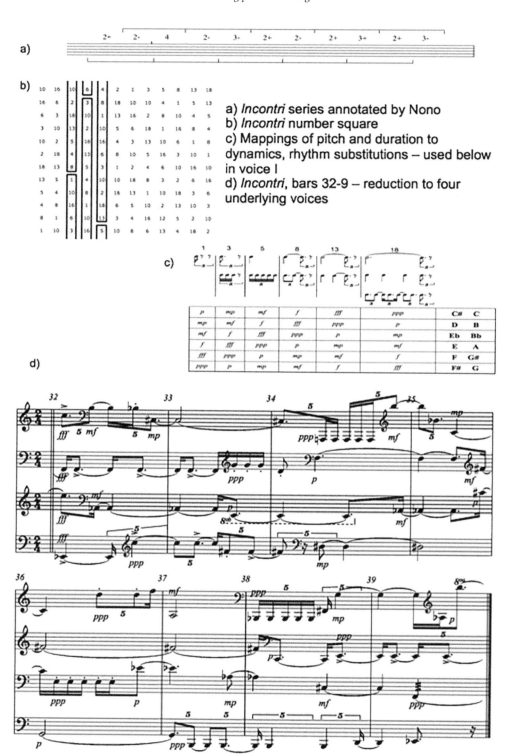

Figure 4.15 *Incontri*: derivation of bars 32–9

Taking positions: song

The composer as subject could not be more present than in the poignant first encounter of the end of structure A – distilled to a single voice, distributed *ppp* through extreme registers – with the start of structure B, around the fermata of bar 48. There is a hint of D phrygian modality, as well as of the all-interval series as the new structure begins to form itself. Instead of rhythmic substitution, the texture of structure B is given direction and momentum by constant dynamic change. The rich rotating spectra of the last B section form an opposite pole to the fragmented nervous energy of the opening. Balancing the stillness of the four fermata as the structures meet is the keystone of the architecture; the symmetry of bar 109 announces itself *fff* as the only incontrovertibly figural event of the work; for one brief moment it approaches being an absolute statement. Either side of this watershed the texture is in a constant motion of speed, density, register and detail.

Incontri was given pride of place in a concert by Rosbaud and the SWF Symphony Orchestra to mark the tenth Darmstadt Summer School, in the company of Berg's *Kammerkonzert* and Schönberg's *Variationen für Orchester* op. 31 – pillars of the new canon. Once again the audience demanded that Nono's new work be repeated. Iddon points to the remarkable divide between the enthusiasm of aficionados at Darmstadt and the incomprehension of many critics beyond.[125] Everett Helm – previously Music Officer for the US administration and himself a composer and critic – wrote of a 'cult' around the young composers. Like many critics, in describing the new music to a broader readership he made little attempt to differentiate between their different approaches, reinforcing an impression of a 'school': 'it breaks so completely with the past that neither the vocabulary nor the concepts are clearly enough defined or disseminated to make discussion possible – except in the very small circle of the "initiated".'[126] As part of his policy of integrating the discourses of composition and criticism, Steinecke invited critics to respond immediately to new works. Rognoni was present at the first performance of *Incontri*, as were Stuckenschmidt, who heard traces of sonata form in its duality, and Goléa.[127] Nono's final comment on the structures of *Incontri* leaves little doubt as to their autobiographical relevance: 'Thus like two beings, distinct and autonomous, they encounter each other and in their encounter becomes not so much a 'unity', but a reciprocal correspondence, a coexistence, a symbiosis.'[128] For Durazzi, this symbiosis will be dramatised in *Intolleranza 1960* in the relationship between the emigrant and his companion, but it is already present in the poetry of Pavese in *La terra e la compagna* (1957).[129] The archetypes of Nono's dialectical, social models of musical relationships (or vice versa) can be traced though the three instrumental works of the mid-1950s: *Canti per 13*, in which all sound-events depend non-hierarchically upon each other, the dual symbiosis of *Incontri*, and *Varianti* (1957), which explores the relationship of a particular individual with the group.

Stenzl mentions a letter to Nuria in which Nono includes a drawing of their encounter as realised compositionally in *Incontri*.[130] Shortly after its first performance, Nuria Schoenberg and Luigi Nono announced their engagement, writing to their respective parents from Darmstadt; they would be married in Venice on 8 August 1955. The symbolism of *Incontri* was not lost on the Darmstadt community, as its ever-florid chronicler Goléa observed:

> they formed a magic, legendary couple, like Richard Wagner and Cosima Liszt in the last century. *Incontri* – a work of exceptional lyrical intensity, where a powerful, clamorous, serious fundamental structure in the masculine, triumphant timbres of the brass seeks ceaselessly to encounter an aerial, diaphanous, smooth structure of strings and woodwind – is the epithalamium composed by Luigi Nono for his marriage, for his own encounter with Nouria Schoenberg.[131]

Taking positions: song

While Strobel was less impressed with what he heard in rehearsal – 'it considerably maltreated my ears' – and cancelled the Swiss performance – 'as I don't think the work appropriate for the Basler Musikfreunde'[132] – he soon changed his opinion. Nono wrote to his parents: '[Strobel] told me that a new Nono is beginning – IT'S TRUE – but this is my natural development, logical and coherent'.[133] The concerts in Baden Baden and Aix proceeded as planned. The couple travelled to Provence together, visiting the home of painter André Masson, who would provide the cover art for an LP release of *Incontri* recorded in Paris the following year. In a stream of letters to his parents, Nono seems to be in a state of heightened awareness; he expresses his appreciation of their love, his love for Nuria and his ecstasy at entering a new stage.

Notes

1 Interview with Leonardo Pinzauti, 1970. LNII, p. 90. The significance of this constructed memory is confirmed elsewhere – for example, LNII, p. 24.
2 Steinecke, 1961, p. 15.
3 *Lo sviluppo della tecnica seriale*, Darmstadt, 23 July 1957. LNI, p. 34.
4 Letter to Stockhausen, 13 March 1952, in Stockhausen, 2001, pp. 40–1.
5 Rothe, 2007, gives a full picture of Hartmann's directorship.
6 Peyser, 1995, p. 266.
7 The importance of the German cultural infrastructure for new music is made clear in a letter from Boulez to Cage in 1953: *. . .in concerts here: Nothing. It's desperate. Everything, from that point of view, is going on in Germany* (Nattiez, 1993, p. 145).
8 Letter to Stockhausen, 12 September 1953, ALN.
9 Personal communication from Nuria Schoenberg-Nono.
10 Letter to Bussotti, 15 May 1951. ALN.
11 The term is from Boulez (Nattiez, 1993, p. 24).
12 'Emigranti a Berlino', 1969. LNI 256. Interview with Hartmut Lück, 1970. LNII p. 67. Interview with Leonardo Pinzauti, 1970. LNII p. 86. Interview with Wolfgang Becker-Carsten, 1972. LNII p. 97. 'La funzione della musica oggi', 1972. LNII p. 115.
13 Conversation with Massimo Cacciari, 1980. LNII, 253.
14 Stockhausen, 1963, opposite p. 33.
15 Goeyvaerts, 2010, p. 201 (1972).
16 Goeyvaerts, 2010, p. 69 (1988).
17 Letter from Stockhausen, 10 March 1952, in Stockhausen, 2001, pp. 39–40. Maconie reads a difference of personality into their modes of dress and physical attitude – Stockhausen reclining on the grass in shorts and open-necked shirt, Nono tense and intense in suit and tie (Maconie, 2005, p. 40).
18 Stockhausen, 1989, p. 36.
19 Kurtz, 1988, p. 61. Sabbe, 1981, documents the close relationship between Stockhausen and Goeyvaerts and the co-evolution of their ideas through their correspondence.
20 ALN 02.01/06r.
21 Ungeheuer, 1992, pp. 112–17.
22 Ungeheuer, 1992, p. 116.
23 Letter from Stockhausen, 20 March 1952, in Stockhausen, 2001, pp. 44–5.
24 Letter to Stockhausen, 4 September 1952. Stockhausen-Stiftung für Musik.
25 Letter from Stockhausen, 12 November 1952. ALN.
26 Letter to Stockhausen, 4 September 1952. ALN.
27 Eimert worked for Cologne Radio before the war, as well as writing for journals such as *Melos* and *Neue Zeitschrift für Musik*. Following the war, he was the first producer of the reformed NWDR and founded the Studio for Electronic Music with Meyer-Eppler in 1951. He also edited *Die Reihe* with Stockhausen from 1955. Grant, 2001, pp. 228–36, provides an excellent account of his theoretical approach.
28 Deliège, 2003, p. 153.
29 Eimert, 1950, p. 21. He refers to *Quartverwandlung* and *Quintverwandlung*.

Taking positions: song

30 Eimert, 1950, p. 25.
31 Letter to Stockhausen, 13 March 1952, in Stockhausen, 2001, pp. 40–1.
32 Stockhausen, 1963, pp. 17–23.
33 Letter from Stockhausen, 9 May 1953. ALN.
34 'By group I mean the number of notes that can be separately distinguished at any one time, which is up to seven or eight. And they have to have at least one characteristic in common' (Stockhausen, 1989, p. 40).
35 Stockhausen, 1963 (first published in *Die Reihe* in 1957)
36 Letter to Steinecke, 25 October 1952, ALN.
37 Boulez, 1975, p. 55.
38 Boulez had worked in Schaeffer's *Studio d'Essai*, participating in his project of cataloguing *objets sonores* and producing two studies. He and Cage had been corresponding since Cage's visit to Paris in 1949 (Nattiez, 1993, p. 3).
39 Boulez, 1991a, p. 139.
40 The draft of *L'artisanat furieux* is dated 23 September 1952, in Decroupet, 2005.
41 Letter from Boulez to Pousseur, October 1952. Paul Sacher Stiftung, Basel. Quoted by Decroupet in Borio and Danuser, 1997, vol. I, p. 319.
42 Letter from Christa Ludwig, 4 May 1953, ALN.
43 ALN 07.01.01/02r.
44 ALN 07.01.01/06r.
45 ALN 07.01.03/1vdx.
46 De Assis, 2009.
47 Borio, 2004, p. 90.
48 Borio, 2004, p. 91, sets out the full distribution.
49 Letter to Steinecke, 8 August 1953. ALN.
50 Interview with Hansjörg Pauli, 1969. LNII, pp. 23–4.
51 Letter to Steinecke, 19 June 1953. ALN.
52 Eimert in Borio and Danuser, 1997, vol. III, pp. 58–65. Boulez's paper was read by Eimert.
53 Webern, 1963.
54 Eimert in Borio and Danuser, 1997, vol. III, p. 60.
55 Interview with Carlo Peddis, 1981. LNII, p. 265. Stockhausen also uses the term 'polyphony of polyphonies' (Stockhausen, 1953).
56 Borio and Danuser, 1997, vol. III, pp. 63–4 (German). LNI, p. 7 (Italian).
57 Letter to Steinecke, 8 August 1953. ALN.
58 Unattributed press cutting, 14 November 1953. ALN.
59 Interview with Enzo Restagno, 1987. LNII, p. 514.
60 Letter from Maderna, 11 March 1955. ALN.
61 *La Victoire de Guernica* appeared in Eluard's 1938 collection *Cours Naturel* (Paris: Sagittaire). He extended the poem to become the text for Alan Resnais' 1949 film *Guernica*, with music by Guy Bernard.
62 Letter to Steinecke, 11 November 1953. ALN.
63 Letter to Steinecke, 4 May 1954. ALN.
64 Interview with Enzo Restagno, 1987. LNII, p. 503.
65 Boulez, 1963, p. 38.
66 Interview with Enzo Restagno, 1987. LNII, p. 506.
67 Schönberg-Nono and Spangemacher, 1995, p. 266.
68 Letters to Hübner, 20 March 1953, 22 May 1953, ALN.
69 Borio, 2002.
70 Letter to Scherchen, 23 April 1954, ALN. Letter to Steinecke, 4 May 1954, ALN.
71 Breuning, 1999, p. 86.
72 Interview with Enzo Restagno, 1987. LNII, p. 506. In the same interview, Nono recalls having encountered the poetry of Pavese while still at school (LNII, p. 482).
73 Interview with Philippe Albèra, 1987. LN II, p. 425.
74 Letter to Mario and Maria Nono, 18 October 1953. ALN.
75 Letter to Scherchen, 14 February 1954. ALN.
76 Letter to Scherchen, 21 March 1954. ALN.

Taking positions: song

77 Letter to Mario and Maria Nono, 11 March 1954. ALN.
78 Letter to Gsovsky, in Busch, 2005, p. 132.
79 Gsovsky, quoted in Busch, 2005, p. 111.
80 From the notebooks of Tatjana Gsovsky, in Busch, 2005, p. 57.
81 Gibson, 1989, p. 156.
82 Dalí was a close friend of Lorca at the time of his work on Don Perlimplin. Dalí suggested to Buñuel that he should film the play (Gibson, 1989, p. 157).
83 Lorca, quoted in Walsdorf, 2003, p. 7.
84 Gibson, 1989, p. 157.
85 Friedrich Herzfeld, *Berliner Morgenpost*, 22 September 1954, in Busch, 2005, p. 125.
86 Gsovsky interviewed in 1966, quoted in Busch, 2005, p. 26.
87 Neidhöfer, 2009, surveys the distribution of rhythmic materials through the drama.
88 Nono wrote to Christa Ludwig, hoping that she might sing in the concert version. As a mezzo soprano, it was too high.
89 Letter to Steinecke, 22 October 1954. ALN.
90 Letter to Mario and Maria Nono, 22 September 1954. ALN.
91 Letter to Scherchen, 21 April 1954. ALN.
92 Letter from Maderna, 9 October 1954. ALN. *Don Perlimplin* would stay with Maderna; he made a 'radiophonic opera' in 1962.
93 *O Schatz! Auf welchen Wegen irrt ihr?, Komm herbei Tod* and *Und als ich ein winzig Bübchen war*.
94 Letter to Steinecke, 25 December 1954. ALN.
95 Letter to Steinecke, 15 January 1955. ALN.
96 Letter from Steinecke, 2 November 1954. ALN.
97 Letter to Hartmann, 12 December 1953, in Wagner, 1980, p. 207.
98 Letter to Hartmann, 15 November 1954. ALN.
99 Scherchen had tried to persuade Nono to allow Schott to handle negotiations for *Was ihr Wollt* (letter from Scherchen, 28 October 1954. ALN).
100 Maderna had already begun to escape Scherchen's force-field; in Scherchen's letters to Nono he repeatedly expresses his frustration at the difficulty of communicating with their friend. Nono seems to act as intermediary in matters professional, artistic and personal.
101 Boulez, 1986, p. 499.
102 Letter to Steinecke, 22 November 1954. ALN.
103 Letter from Steinecke, 28 December 1954. ALN.
104 Letter to Steinecke, 15 January 1955. ALN.
105 Letter to Steinecke, 14 February 1955. ALN.
106 Letter to Hartmann, February 1955, in Wagner, 1980, p. 210.
107 Letter to Mario and Maria Nono, 15 August 1954. ALN.
108 Letter to Steinecke, 15 January 1955. ALN.
109 Letter from Steinecke, 21 January 1955. ALN.
110 Letter to Steinecke, 24 January 1955. ALN. The opening does presumably not refer to Lerner and Loewe's stage work of the following year.
111 Interview with Enzo Restagno, 1987. LNII, p. 505.
112 The dedication was subsequently withdrawn, but bridges had been rebuilt by the time of *A Pierre*, thirty years later.
113 Interview with Enzo Restagno, 1987. LNII, p. 506.
114 Interview with Enzo Restagno, 1987. LN II, p. 507.
115 Interview with Enzo Restagno, 1987. LNII, p. 507.
116 From ALN 12.01/01–7.
117 Xenakis, 1956.
118 Letter to Steinecke 14 Febua ry 1955. ALN.
119 Letter to Steinecke, late February 1955. ALN.
120 Letter from Maderna, 11 March 1955. ALN.
121 Available at: www.futuraumanita.it/palmiro-togliatti-discorsi-allassemblea-costituente-sul-progetto-di-costituzione/ (accessed 10 October 2017).
122 *Incontri*. LNI, p. 426.
123 Rizzardi, 2002.
124 Interview with Enzo Restagno, 1987. LNII, p. 510.

Taking positions: song

125 Iddon, 2013, pp. 124–6.
126 Helm, 1955.
127 Borio and Danuser, 1997, vol. I, p. 431.
128 *Incontri*. LNI, p. 426.
129 Durazzi, 2009.
130 Stenzl, 1998, p. 39.
131 Goléa, 1962, pp. 129–30.
132 Letter from Strobel, 11 May 1955. ALN.
133 Letter to Mario and Maria Nono, 27 May 1955. ALN.

5

'DOCERE E MOVERE'

Il canto sospeso

Genesis

Nono subsequently dated the beginning of work on *Il canto sospeso* to October 1955.[1] The young couple were taking a delayed honeymoon at La Mortella, the villa of William and Susana Walton on the island of Ischia, where Henze was also a guest. Two letters to Steinecke from Ischia in the last months of 1955 document the progress of his postponed Darmstadt commission. After two weeks on the island the concept had evolved into a setting of two poems by Pavese for soloists, choir and orchestra, but then:

> at last my preparatory work for the opera: at last I have found a wonderful opera text, another theatre piece by Lorca, never performed or at least only once because it is considered experimental, but it is wonderful theatre. So the way is there! [. . .] 'asi que pasen cinco anos' [. . .] . The Darmstadt work will be in five parts, and follow directly from 'canti per 13' and 'incontri'.[2]

As he threw away rejected ideas and sketches, Nuria collected them. By the end of their stay Nono was able to inform Steinecke that he was at work on the third section. In a further letter he seems to have told his commissioner that the work would now be entirely orchestral, provoking measured frustration. He had returned from Ischia with only the first two orchestral movements complete. At the end of January Nono finally announced that the piece would be *Il canto sospeso*, with choir and soloists reinstated and a full provisional outline of twelve movements. The ever-patient Steinecke now sought a possibility for the performance of a work the forces and preparation for which were beyond the means of Darmstadt. The premiere was scheduled for July, for Frankfurt Radio under the direction of Otto Matzerath. Such a major project implied clear deadlines for the delivery of material and was important for the relationship between the two institutions. Nevertheless, Steinecke was unstinting in his encouragement when, despite a major push by Nono through the spring of 1956, it was decided at the beginning of June that the score had arrived too late and was too difficult for the choir to prepare.[3] Steinecke and Scherchen – Nono's strongest supporters – met with Eigel Kruttke of Cologne Radio and agreed a premiere in Cologne for October.[4] Schott, administering Scherchen's Ars Viva Verlag, managed to convince Kruttke of Nono's precarious situation and the need for an increased fee.[5]

'Docere e movere': Il canto sospeso

Il canto sospeso, for three soloists, choir and large orchestra, was finally performed in Cologne on 24 October 1956, conducted by Hermann Scherchen. It was a public and critical triumph; according to Eimert, the performance 'left the most significant impression of any concert work by the young generation to date.'[6] Reports give a clear sense of the commitment of the performance, and that the work was immediately seen as a milestone in two respects: as the expressive maturing of an avant-garde language, and as a cultural confronting of the scarcely confrontable. Eimert saw it as a timely intervention in the context of Germany's satisfaction with its own restoration. On all counts, *Il canto sospeso* seems to have been received as the fruit of a supreme effort – of courage, technique and imagination. *Die Welt* reported the sustained rapturous applause of the audience, Heinz Joachim in the *Neue Zeitschrift für Musik* that 'The work is so at the limit not only of what can be realised in performance but of what is linguistically or musically conceivable, of human expression, that it stirs up the deepest questions of artistic form.'[7] In the *Darmstädter Tageblatt*, Wolf-Eberhard von Lewinski explained that 'It shows [. . .] the way to the future of music, which nobody now need fear. [. . .] In fact, the public, rightly attached to masterworks, now has the prospect of more. Nono has given us new proof.'[8] Acutely sensitive as he was to the cultural mores of his own city, one can only imagine that this gloss of 'masterwork' may have caused Nono some ambivalence when *Il canto sospeso* was finally performed in Venice four years later:

> There were three seconds of silence. But what broke out afterwards was the most beautiful delirium of enthusiasm, of gratitude, of recognition, of adoration that I have ever seen. [. . .] Aristocratic Venice had finally found a maestro of its stature, of its breadth.[9]

Perhaps Nono's later incorporation of some of *Il Canto sospeso* in *Intolleranza 1960* would be to some extent a way of obliging the Venetian audience to engage more directly with its substance.

The subsequent history of *Il canto sospeso* provides a fascinating narrative of the evolving role and understanding of musical modernism over the past half-century. Its iconic reputation and vast body of analysis colour the work's position. Despite being one of the most discussed works of its generation, it was not commercially recorded until 1992. Even that event was motivated by a confluence of political statement on the part of a newly united Berlin and the initiative of Nono's friend Claudio Abbado.[10] Nicolaus Huber has suggested that the work's story is itself one of a *canto sospeso*, a suspended song.[11] Its musicological history is at least as extraordinary; perhaps only *Le Marteau sans maître* can rival *Il canto sospeso* in terms of years of analytical life expended. Even among the major studies, Motz worked on the piece for a decade before being able to hear it, and, after a long period of concentrated analysis, Bailey was still unable to decide whether it is actually music.[12] Its reputation in an anglophone world disposed to cynicism in the face of perceived political or intellectualising tendencies was founded on reports such as that of Reginald Smith-Brindle from the 1960 performance in Venice. Well intentioned as that report is – 'Nono's work stands supreme amongst the European avant-garde for its great humanitarian expression' – the writer promulgates a view of *Il canto sospeso* that entirely detaches what he describes as the 'mechanics' of the work from the 'spiritual'.[13] On the basis of his analysis of the second movement, Smith-Brindle asserts that:

> it will be relatively easy to show how his music is an admirable unity of pre-determined elements. [. . .] Construction is in the essence of Nono's nature. He distrusts 'divine inspiration', for mysticism is foreign to his temperament. Composition means for him

'Docere e movere': Il canto sospeso

the controlling and placing of every smallest element in a musical design according to a pre-conceived plan.[14]

This is to utterly misread Nono's relationship with the stuff of his art. In later publications, Smith-Brindle authoritatively reiterated his view of Nono's 'constructivist' aesthetic and his 'pointillist' style ('the maximum isolation of sounds').[15] Even Eimert – enthusiastic and perceptive as he was – had fallen into this trap. He described *Il canto sospeso* as 'the first purely structural music that Nono has written', implicitly confusing his appropriate description of 'uncompromisingly radical' with an entirely inappropriate implication of formal abstraction.[16] It clearly became tiresome for Nono to continually have to refute such simplistic misinterpretations:

> Often I thought it seems for many that I had died after and not written anything else. Worse for them. Perhaps the superficial effect of *Il canto sospeso* was determined, at least in part, typically by an ideological reading. Not so much from listening to the music. The texts, those fragments of letters, have favoured the 'easy ideology', the 'impossibility of analysis'.[17]

Recent decades have seen more informed interpretation. To list only the major studies, Motz, Feneyrou and Nielinger-Vakil each present a thorough technical analysis.[18] The various studies fall naturally into two groups: those before Nono's sketches were made available, and those after. The first group tend naturally to seek to uncover the work's structural mysteries; the second have many of the compositional facts before them. This by no means invalidates previous readings of the work, however. Forensic investigation of the process is clearly instructive, but earlier analysts had to deal directly with the surface – the score and the sound that Nono had determined were the true result of that process. An interesting case in point is to be found in the analysis of Motz.[19] In the first movement he finds structural voice-leading which is crucial to the melodic outline and harmonic tension of the whole. There is no trace of this in the pre-compositional material. It is the product of the most vital final stage of compositional mediation; it confirms the importance of the act of inscription in Nono's work.

Text

In January 1952, Einaudi had published a book of *Lettere di condannati a morte della Resistenza italiana* (*Letters from the condemned of the Italian Resistance*) by Piero Malvezzi and Giovanni Pirelli, both literary figures with significant credentials as resistance fighters. This was acknowledged widely as an important act of documenting and coming to terms with the recent past. In the climate of post-war political repositioning and cold war CIA intervention, it also contained a clear political warning: recognition of the sacrifices and ideals of the resistance was a crucial reminder to the country's political conscience. In 1954, Malvezzi and Pirelli broadened their scope in a further volume *Lettere di condannati a morte della Resistenza europea*, the final communications of resistance workers about to be executed, to family, friends and comrades.[20]

Nono had started on the new work with the idea that it should be a setting of poems by Pavese – presumably the love poems anticipated by Steinecke. The orchestral movements therefore seem to have been intended for quite another work. As his thinking developed, Nono decided instead to set words from the second collection of Malvezzi and Pirelli. There is some continuity; an early draft of extracts from the letters is headed *Canti di vita*, a title that would return in relation to a setting of Pavese, and one that perhaps reflects the understanding at the root of his use of these texts – songs not of death but of life. From the enormous body of letters Nono initially selected sixteen fragments, some to be set simultaneously.

Music

Following *Canti per 13* and *Incontri*, Scherchen had written to Nono reminding him of the responsibility involved in undertaking a work for the theatre and of the 'creative dangers of continuous symmetry'.[21] In *Il canto sospeso*, song is suspended in a dynamic network of multiple mirrors: structures run forwards and backwards in time, sounds are balanced by their non-presence as rests, components of words are reflected through time and pitch space. The careful, constant balancing of architecture and detail, design and handcraft, is Palladian. Developing the innovations of *Incontri*, Nono finds a response to Stockhausen's theorising of the relationship between pitch and time. The result is not the top–down working-out imagined by his less reflective critics, but rather a many-limbed emergent structure in which every detail is related to every other in ways that are determined at the moment of their inscription; more analogous to a Mass by Ockeghem or Josquin than Boulez's *Structures*.

> In *Incontri* I also used the mirror procedure quite schematically, because I was interested in the process of retrograde, often present not only in Flemish music but in their painting, in certain broken perspectives of Tintoretto, in Pollock, in Vedova, in Burri. It is not so much a technical question as one of thoughts of different simultaneous perspectives, disunited, which continue in waves through history. From a musical point of view I was interested in trying other modes of attacks, of endings, of the sound quality of different superimpositions, including being silenced, which change trivial implications. There are the same problems – a divertimento of various modes of compositional thought, if you like – in *Il canto sospeso*.[22]

In the presence of reflections and refractions at every structural level, it is the fundamental invariance of the series that signifies the passing of time. The all-interval series is the only pitch material used, appearing in retrograde, inversion or permutation only where that serves an architectural purpose. In his analysis of Webern's op. 30 *Variations*, Nono emphasises the 'ambivalent' properties of the series, its capacity to move in all directions free from the weight of figure.[23] His own series for *Il canto sospeso* is a perpetually self-redefining space of possibilities, within which new configurations constantly form. He reinvents and extends his own technical repertoire for each movement, constantly finding new ways of achieving balance by modifying symmetries.[24] Writers tend to present his all-interval series – expanding symmetrically by semitones from A to E♭ – in the closed form used in his earliest sketches. Shortly after completing his work, Nono chose to present it in a more melodically suggestive form (Figure 5.1).

The all-interval series is a background, a musical–linguistic environment or perpetual generator, not a starting-point. Its role is more akin to that of tonality than theme; it generates local horizon or perspective, its interval relationships permeate every surface and its internal dynamics propel the music to constant forward motion. Eimert's view of the series as a

Figure 5.1 Il canto sospeso: all-interval series as notated by Nono[25]

generative dynamical model finds its clearest realisation in Nono's work.[26] Mila noted the dynamic balance between direct presentations of the series and its indirect expression through various permutations and rotations, and that Nono's use of the series creates anticipation in the ear of the listener.[27] Pestalozza would later point to its broader implications, describing the series as having:

> a circularity of intervals, in the sense of a directionality that strives towards the octave. It thus becomes the negation of the conventional method, as immediately becomes clear if instead of method we talk about ideology. Because it is with the negation of *that* that we are dealing. In fact something musical is negated in this series – the minor second, the chromatic interval, the structural idea of dissonance, which turns against itself: it functions as the motor of the circle [. . .]. If it ended with the octave, this would paradoxically constitute no opposition: consonance and dissonance are annulled and negated in the course of the series, the succession of intervals. That is why, above all and essentially, there is no dialectic in that structure. Its end has no beginning, that is: no themes, or better: no synthesis. [. . .] It was his way to be anti-ideological, beginning from his row. [28]

Nono refers to the *projection* of the series; it is the light that brings the forms to life, an illuminating material not a sound-object. The title is no metaphor, it relates the musical substance to its textual material. We have considered the suspension of time. The song is also held in suspension; we, as listening subjects, are moved around it with different speeds, angles and filters. The apparent fragmentation of the score is necessary for song to emerge from the performed sounds as an immanent reality for the listener. The score allows no opportunity for its *mis*representation, for reduction or sentimentality. To impose figure – above all, to 'express' these texts – would not be aesthetically credible, and yet song underlies this entire work. This is not a metaphysical position but a technical compositional challenge. Nono's remaining materials – the odd and even Fibonacci sequences and a number series 1–12 – are also essentialized from his previous practice, as is the repertoire of techniques. The radical departure is in their common focus on the suspension of song, particularly evident in the fragmentation and dispersal of text.

The balance of structural tensions is evident architecturally. Having made a first selection of texts, Nono planned a sequence of eleven movements, grouped 4–3–4. Orchestral movements were to begin and end the first and third parts, soprano and tenor solos to surround the central two-part choral movement of the second. This symmetry was then recalibrated such that two of his structural archetypes pull in opposite directions to sustain the whole. A more subtle, nested nine-part architecture, now centred about the fifth movement – the most intimate text of all – is set against an incremental reduction of movements through the three parts (Figure 5.2).

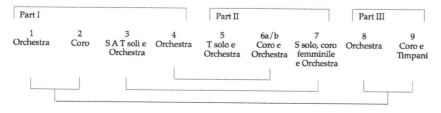

Figure 5.2 Il canto sospeso: formal balance

'Docere e movere': Il canto sospeso

Instrumental movements 1, 4 and 8

The first and fourth movements, written before the work took shape as *Il canto sospeso*, still frame the first part. They bear traces of *Incontri* and complement each other in several ways. Both use a 12×12 displacement matrix to order pitch, a number sequence 1–12 with rotational permutations. Both movements are built on a mediated symmetry, an arch from which the view on the ascent is different to that on the return; Nono seems to have heeded Scherchen's observations. Both are the product of an evolving relationship between two bodies of sound, and of that between the material and its negative.

The sketches suggest that the fourth movement was written first; it is the most straightforward projection of the material onto compositional space. The pitch structure generated by the matrix is worked through in sequence, such that each pitch appears 13 times and returns to its initial position. The polyphonic texture is at its clearest; serialised use of the wind and percussion presents a kaleidoscopic surface of a single rhythmic voice, tightly compressed into the middle register. Using durations from the same matrix, the rhythm base shortens incrementally from triplets to semiquavers, quintuplets and septuplets over the first four 12-element sequences, and back over the next four, followed by a short coda as the pitch material resolves and the textures dissolve. The range of dynamics shifts up and down at the same steps. Blank locations in Nono's initial working-out of the pitch structure are represented by unpitched percussion. The wind and pitched percussion he arranges serially, reordering the sounds by permutation for each appearance of a pitch. Against this, solo strings render a negative image in an entirely algorithmic relationship. They map out the spaces between recurring pitches – their memory, their anticipation and the evolving chromatic world that produces them – by alternately sustaining pitches between their occurrence. The result is a timbral zoetrope, speeding up and slowing down. The residual traces of its sequence of different coloured points within a restricted range of hearing produce a moving line, its dynamic envelope rising and falling as it speeds up and slows down.

If the fourth movement functions as a kind of delayed exposition, the first represents a Beethovenian opening strategy. Not only is the fundamental order of the elemental material quite opaque, the work begins by marking its very absence, its negative. Formally, this movement is the direct descendant of *Canti per 13* and *Incontri*, but it also represents a transition from the discourse of the previous instrumental works to a new expressive space. Each half of the movement presents a different kind of mirror. Up to the movement's mid-point (bar 53), two cross-cut sound-worlds develop along opposing trajectories: wind and timpani, their timbral focus shifting from brass to woodwind, alternate with a string texture that evolves from a single line to a fabric woven of ten parts. As the former is reduced in length and complexity the latter expands, each across four occurrences, following which an echo of the opening section heralds the turning point. Nono now imagines his polyphonic elements as choirs rather than voices, the individual voices in each choir characterised by their rhythm base: the crotchet and its divisions by 2, 3, 4, 5 and 7. In his drafts, he maps out the number of groups and their internal polyphonic density. The wind move from a single five-voice choir ('1 a 5') to four of two voices ('4 a 2'); the number of rhythmic subdivisions reduces accordingly until the reprise that ends the first half (bars 49–52). The voices of the strings remain independent – from '1 a 1' to '4 a 1' – each with a different rhythm base. In both cases, voices are distributed among a larger group of instruments; the string material naturally generates more contiguous lines. Nono exercises freedom in the placing, ordering and register of note-complexes to weave relationships across the surface: melodic, harmonic, rhythmic and formal. The unitary voice of the strings generally remains continuous, such that long lines and positive harmonic relationships contrast

'Docere e movere': Il canto sospeso

with the kaleidoscopic texture of the wind. Nono's brushstrokes, the marks of his note-to-note decision-making, are much more in evidence here than in the fourth movement. It displays an acute sense of architecture – balances, symmetries and rhymes appear on every level – but also of the performed sound. The major decisions are made in the short-score draft, but as shapes emerge Nono adjusts detail to allow them to be heard.

The pitch material of the first movement is that of the fourth, worked through nearly three times. Durations – multiples of the different rhythm bases – are taken from the same matrix. The ordering of pitches in the wind and timpani is obfuscated by elements from the sequence being grouped into complexes, allocated to choirs and reordered by virtue of the different rhythm bases. This is further complicated by a system of negative durations – rests of values derived from the same material as the note-lengths, calculated from the start-point of the complexes as Nono distributed them across the proportions of his subsections. The very opening exemplifies the process: the five voices each sound a note lasting five times their basic unit (divisions of 2, 3, 4, 5 and 7). They enter after rests of 1, 4, 2, 5 and 3 units respectively, using the principle of negative values developed in *Incontri*. These bars establish the inner life of the material of *Il canto sospeso*; the *forte* trombone A forms a nucleus the energy of which is redistributed dynamically and registrally before the timpani echo reinforces it as a horizon (Figure 5.3).

Figure 5.3 Il canto sospeso No.1: opening

The timpani A is mirrored with a crescendo to introduce the tripartite second half of the movement. Wind and string materials develop simultaneously through bars 53–67. The middle of this half (bars 68–88) is itself an arch; two great brass climaxes are articulated at its centre by the strings. The final section has its own symmetry; the high chromatic cluster with which it opens anticipates the very last sound of the movement. The number of unitary voices reduces until for the last twelve bars a single unbroken song based on semiquavers – the longest of the movement by far – sweeps up through the entire range of the orchestra, sporadically interwoven with another on the same base, shifted by a semiquaver, and a third in triplets (Figure 5.4).

In all three instrumental movements, dynamic mappings – shifting ranges and degrees of homogeneity – are used to reinforce both formal and polyphonic architectures. They illuminate textural complexity as well as structural sections. This is most clear in the eighth movement. Indeed, in his otherwise sympathetic review Joachim found this movement disturbingly stark. In his first extended essay on Nono, following the Venetian premiere of *Il canto sospeso* in 1960, Mila understood the architectural role of this movement as a return to the sound-fields of the first, a conclusion to the emotional intensity of the centre of the work and a preparation for

'*Docere e movere*': Il canto sospeso

Figure 5.4 Il canto sospeso No.1: final melody, bars 96–107

the final chorus: 'a shadow zone similar to that from which the composition emerged'.[29] Motz sees its absolute nature as a confirmation of the transcendental state to which the preceding soprano solo has brought us.[30] In that sense, and in its echoing of the opening movement, we might see this as the structural conclusion of the whole work, followed by a choral reflection that looks beyond the present tragedy.

It is perhaps this sense of the supra-emotive that Nono had in mind when later he recalled how this movement most reflects the influence of Varèse.[31] The palette is also redolent of Varèse, or perhaps 1950s performances of Gabrieli: only the direct, energy-rich sounds of brass, flutes, clarinets and timpani. It takes on a thoroughly Venetian form. Rapid bursts of repetition, echoes of Monteverdi's toccata to *L'Orfeo*, are set against sustained blocks and interwoven crescendos and diminuendos. The polyphonic texture is directly related to structural proportions. He takes the aggregate density of possible textures from one to four groups, each of one to three parts. This set is then redistributed across three sections of four each, determining both polyphonic density and numbers of bars: 4(4 a 1), 2(1 a 2), 6(2 a 3), 3(3 a 1) – 9(3 a 3), 2(2 a 1), 8(4 a 2), 3(1 a 3) – 4(2 a 2), 1(1 a 1), 6(3 a 2), 12(4 a 3). The brass are divided into four groups of three. Clarinets and flutes substitute in quieter passages and the timpani function as a free agent or continuo, like the double bass in *Canti per 13*. The last two sections were elided as Nono worked on their realization, emphasizing the clear dramatic structure of the movement. The pitch series is presented baldly by the brass *fff* in the first two bars and again in the last two. In a moment of stasis at the very centre of the movement (bars 514–15), the bass clarinet sustains an A *mp*, re-establishing the horizon. The final dramatic swell grows from a single voice *ppp* to the full brass *fff*; again a range a dynamics of shifting focus and homogeneity is associated with different degrees of density.

Negative values again separate and sculpt individual complexes. Longer notes are replaced by repetition, such that pitches form new melodic sequences rather than being assimilated harmonically. At the start, the repetition of alternate pitches from the series creates a tension appropriate to such an extended structure. Repetitions at the opening of the long last section add to the sense of recapitulation, returning in a final defiant fanfare, a triumph of the human spirit that transcends anguish, a gesture closer to Beethoven or Mahler than Bach or Schönberg.

Solo vocal movements 3, 5 and 7

The intensely personal leave-taking of the fifth movement is the emotional centre of *Il canto sospeso*. The tenor is the first solo voice of the work, the first unmediated subject: 'If the sky were paper, and all the seas of the world were ink, I could not describe my suffering and all that I see around me. I say goodbye to all of you and weep.'

After the tragic drama of the third movement, there is a stillness to this keystone of *Il canto sospeso*. The texture is of the utmost clarity. The tenor line with its instrumental echoes is a song, an aria, suspended at the centre of the work. Three continuous layers are based on divisions of 4, 5 and 6 – the former being the longest, the others are nested almost symmetrically within its 100 beats. The central quintuplet layer is carried by the tenor, continued during rests by marimba and vibraphone; the voice of the subject is suspended, it persists as a shadow. Solo strings and woodwind with a reduced brass choir colour the other lines. Two harps play only pitches of the shortest durations, like an intimate lute or guitar accompaniment; pizzicato strings blend their sound with the remaining fabric. Each layer presents a different arrangement of Nono's basic series together with four variants derived through a process of shifting and folding that introduces new tritones. The central role of the tritone is confirmed by his marking their positions in each series. These series have innumerable internal reflections, echoes and transpositions, rather as Nono had observed in his analyses of Webern. They are projected on to four duration series, each consisting of four versions of a basic cell (1, 2, 7). As each sequence adds up to 40, every repetition on the semiquaver and quintuplet layers coincides with the underlying beat. This maintains rhythmic complexity while minimising rhythmic tension in performance, enhancing the clarity of the movement.

The central quintuplet layer is planned first and has the clearest structure: the four new pitch series worked through in sequence, then in reverse and retrograde, and finally the retrograde and original of the basic series. The four duration series are repeated in their original sequence two and a half times. This voice carries the tenor both vocally and structurally. The semiquaver layer follows the same sequence of pitch series, but beginning from the original retrograde. Nono finds an arrangement of rhythm series such that the semiquaver introduction and coda are symmetrical. The overall melodic trajectory of the layer, from E♭ to A, is the reverse of the original series. It is as if the basic material has been explored in magnification to reveal a new song suspended within. This canon in augmentation is mirrored by its own diminution in the sextuplet layer. It follows an identical duration sequence and is an exact canon in inversion until, in the middle of bar 305, Nono shifts it down by a tone, presumably because of the emergent pitch relationships. Another shift to a transposition a tone higher than the original at the end of bar 311 balances the account. The choice of duration values, polarised between short

Figure 5.5 Il canto sospeso No. 5: bars 288–98, quintuplet layer

'Docere e movere': Il canto sospeso

and long, allows him to set the text to maximum effect, with a clear, almost operatic distinction between consonants and vowels (Figure 5.5).

The fifth movement is balanced symmetrically by the vocal trio of the third and the soprano solo of the seventh. The third is a motet in the manner of those Nono and Maderna had studied together years earlier; three voices relating to the same fundamental material present three different texts together, each casting a different light on the others. In his 1960 paper *Text – Musik – Gesang*, Nono explains how this practice runs through the history of Western music; not by coincidence are his examples from Bach's *Mass in B Minor* and Mozart's *Requiem*.[32] Here the three texts from Greek martyrs all have an active voice, all refer to the perpetrators of evil: *They are taking me [. . .], Today they will shoot us [. . .], They are hanging me [. . .]*:

> In the third movement of my *canto sospeso* we find an example of how a new text results by interpolation from the musically distinct superposition of three different texts. [. . .] the superposition of the three texts, which deal with analogous situations, the moment preceding the execution of that very victim, has given rise to a new text in which that which all three situations have in common is formulated with increased intensity.[33]

The materials for this three-layered structure are minimal: the basic series and a sequence of odd numbers 1–9. From the latter, Nono constructs displacement matrices for each of the three voices, with a preponderance of shorter or longer initial values in proportion to their tessitura:

Soprano: 1 7 1 3 5 3 3 5 3 1 7 1
Alto: 5 3 1 9 5 7 7 5 9 1 3 5
Tenor: 3 7 1 5 7 9 9 7 5 1 7 3

These produce pitch sequences for each voice by simply shifting them one place to the left for each successive member of the series. The tighter arrangement of the soprano layer naturally produces the densest texture – up to five pitches at a single location. They also produce associated duration tables by a succession of five palindromic permutations. All three use a single rhythm base – the semiquaver. The notation of the whole in 4+3/8 and its fast tempo give the movement an uneasy urgency. Again, the soprano layer is shortest and is worked through almost twice against the single complete presentations of the alto and tenor. Despite their origins as soprano, alto and tenor material, these three layers are distributed through the changing palette of the orchestra, while the solo voices generally each follow a single strand. Vowels from the different texts are sustained between voices, drawing the listener into the rich semantic web they jointly constitute.

Nono uses echoes and analogies between the layers of material to weave the motet. At bar 179, for example, the F and F♯ in the flutes form part of the soprano layer, but also serve to reintroduce the next stage of the tenor – a bifurcation point. Empty locations in the material may become rests or be skipped entirely. In the brass introduction, Nono largely allocates the different layers to instruments in the same register, creating a phasing effect of anticipation and delay – a device that will figure vitally in his later works with electronics. For Mila, the soprano's wide intervals at 'mi portano a Kessariani' express a final agony and are the embodiment of one of Nono's initial motivations and the source of the title.[34] A poem by Ethel Rosenberg, written during her imprisonment before she and her husband Julius were executed by the US government as communist spies in 1953, begins: 'You shall know, my sons, shall know why we leave the song unsung'.[35] Motz sees the entry of violins with the voices as analogous to the first movement. This entry likewise approaches a tonal quality – here E♭ major. A brief hiatus precisely at the mid-point in bar 199 allows a moment's reflection on the decaying 'perché' ('why'), suggesting

'Docere e movere': Il canto sospeso

a question mark not present in its original context, immediately following which the tenor continues 'sono patriota' ('I am a patriot'). The E on the second syllable of 'sono' – here from the tenor material – is immediately echoed by another E in the soprano layer, which Nono doubles with a crescendo in the cellos to give a rush of emotion. The four syllables of 'patriota' are placed to coincide with a rare succession of four equal duration values (7), and pitches that outline a clear D♭ tonality, briefly giving the word the qualities of a patriotic song. It is echoed by 'patria', with which both the other texts conclude. The instrumental introduction is balanced by a brief interlude, now reduced to a single layer, for trumpets alone – an unmistakably referential final signal. This leaves the last line of the third text to form a coda: 'Tuo figlio se ne va, non sentirà le campane della libertà' ('Your son departs, he will not hear the bells of liberty'). Surely, the careful framing of 'tuo figlio', the first unaccompanied phrase in the movement, reflects its resonance for Nono and would have assured its recognition in an audience still well acquainted with Bach. They prepare an identity for the subject of the fifth movement, the solo tenor – a Christus figure, perhaps. The only sustained unison of the movement follows: 'non sentirà le campane' is contradicted by clear monody; song becomes immovable resistance. The final instrumental gesture brings all three layers together in the densest moment of the work. The full brass and divisi strings present their combined pitches simultaneously; time is compressed to an instant. To pursue Mila's analogy, this movement is a *Crucifixus*, an eloquent piece of liberation theology.

The seventh movement sets a girl's farewell to her mother: 'Goodbye, mother. Your daughter, Liubka, is going into the moist earth [. . .].' It is a response to the sixth: 'How hard it is to say goodbye forever to life which is so beautiful!' The text is set with great clarity for solo soprano, wordless female chorus, two flutes, tuned percussion, harp, celesta and reduced strings – a light, high, transparent texture. At the same time its inexpressibility, the very difficulty of saying the words, is integral to its structure and sound world. Both soprano and chorus sing with a range of colours from *bocca chiusa* (even on high Cs) to *normale*, although only the soloist goes further to enunciate the words. This provides a continuous spectrum of colours from bright percussive or plucked sounds to speech. In an early sketch Nono enumerates the vocal gradations, exploring their structural potential. The two flutes connect instruments to voices: one with the soprano, the other with the chorus. Mila justly described this seventh movement, counterpart to the third and echo of the fifth, as the work's lyrical highpoint, as an *Agnus Dei* following the *Benedictus* of the fifth movement.[36] Indeed, it is of an intense and – one hesitates to use the word – Italianate lyricism that will remain a vital element of Nono's palette. Solo soprano, female chorus and flute are also characters that will reappear at the most critical moments in his later work.

As in the third movement, Nono plans a maximum of three layers, all on the same semiquaver base. Here there are only two strands of pitch material, however: the same twelve series read forwards and backwards. The former he imagines for the soprano, the latter for the chorus, both distributed between voice and instruments. They and their associated twelve duration series are derived from a quasi-Fibonacci sequence, ordered from opposite ends to obtain a pattern analogous to the all-interval series itself. For subsequent duration series Nono uses his common technique of pairwise rotating permutation ('salto a 2'). The same sequence generates the pitch series (Figure 5.6).

The remaining eleven series are produced by a non-mechanical combination of permutation and folding, often shifting or reordering three-note groups to create motivic relationships. Nono analyses the interval content of each; they are now clearly distinguished. The first has the closest shape, only thirds and seconds; the last is the only one to contain two augmented fourths. He marks tonal triads as they occur. The twelve pitch and duration series, each lasting thirty-one quavers, are mapped out for the soprano. Having set out a range of six dynamics,

'*Docere e movere*': Il canto sospeso

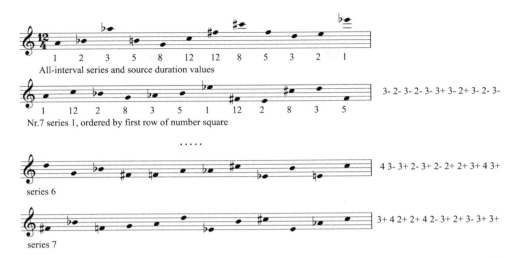

Figure 5.6 *Il canto sospeso* No. 7: derivation of series

Nono opts for only three – *ppp*, *p* and *mf* – which he adds to the table of durations, distributed differently but always in the proportions 3–4–5. A pattern of densities – equal numbers of 1, 2 and 3 – distributes the retrograde material for the chorus, asymmetrically balanced about the centre point at which they cross (Figure 5.7).

The most explicit musical relationship between soprano and chorus is arranged around the fulcrum in bar 451. Throughout, the expressive flow of vocal lines is managed through the careful use of open and closed intervals; sixths become the most emotionally charged. They figure importantly though the fifth section (bars 438–44), echoing the intonation of the soprano's repeated 'addio' (Figure 5.8). The soprano follows suit on her last two syllables, at the beginning of the next section. Through sections six and seven, soprano and chorus work through the same material in opposite directions. The end of the sixth series and the beginning of the seventh present an entire E major scale, followed by one of B♭; only the C arrives out of sequence. This and rhythmic reflection allow the chorus to answer the soprano's 'mamma'

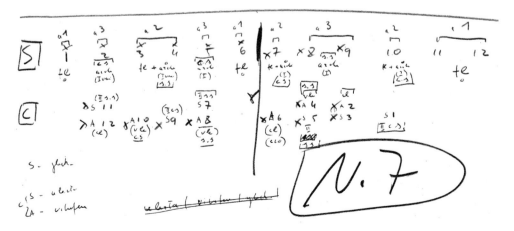

Figure 5.7 *Il canto sospeso* No. 7: form scheme. (ALN 14.02.07/01 (detail). © The heirs of Luigi Nono. Reproduced by kind permission.)

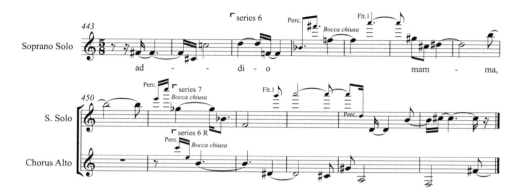

Figure 5.8 Il canto sospeso No. 7: bars 443–55

with a reciprocal gesture. Together, the two outline the E modality, including their second echoing exchange. The central point itself is marked by a high, arpeggiated C–E dyad accompanying the soprano's silenced sigh, a rhetorical device worthy of Gesualdo or Monteverdi. The near-silent chorus alto here surely assumes the voice of the absent mother. This intensity of expression is no indulgence; there is no risk of sentimentality; it is organic to the nature of the material, textual and musical.

In distributing the lines between voices and instruments, Nono sets up anticipations, echoes and delays between soprano and chorus. In their first entry, the chorus high B modulates the colour of the same note in the soprano; their sustained E♭ generates the halo effect we know from earlier work. Immediately after, the soprano follows the chorus in the incremental change from *bocca chiusa* to *normale*, in a timbral canon. The use of the chorus to develop tight blocks of density around individual pitches or to open up localised harmonic fields establishes practices that will endure to Nono's late work.

Choral movements 2, 6 and 9

The choral movements elicited the strongest reaction from contemporaries. Technically and aesthetically they presented the strongest challenge to performers and listeners. They also embody some of the most important concepts for Nono's later work, as he would subsequently acknowledge: 'Only later, at the electronic studio in Milan and especially with the live electronics of Freiburg, did I realise what I had been hoping to obtain in certain choral parts of *Il canto sospeso*.'[37] We have already mentioned the self-justifying analysis of Stockhausen and the misguided reductionism of Smith-Brindle; both refer to the second movement, for eight-part chorus alone. Mila dismisses as formalist a programme note that also explains the fragmentation and distribution of text as the serialisation of vocal timbre.[38] Instead, he saw this movement as a *Credo* to follow the 'grey unclarity' of the orchestral *Kyrie*.[39] Joachim heard it as: 'an extreme compression of musical structure which thereby reaches a concentration of form and expression that one feels to be absolutely identical with the boundary state of the author of the letter [. . .]'.[40]

The letter, the first statement if *Il canto sospeso*, is indeed an affirmation of life and faith:

> I am dying for a world which will shine with light of such strength and beauty that my own sacrifice is nothing. Millions of men have died for this on barricades and in war. I am dying for justice. Our ideas will triumph [. . .]

'*Docere e movere*': *Il canto sospeso*

Technically, the movement is certainly highly compact; this makes Nono's compositional decisions all the more critical. The all-interval series appears nineteen times, always complete and in its original form. It is distributed across four rhythmic layers, based on quaver, triplet, semiquaver and quintuplet. Duration values follow an actual Fibonacci series (1, 2, 3, 5, 8, 13) arranged in ascending and descending order to derive a twelve-element duration series. This provides eleven further permutations in a simple one-step rotation; repetition of the first three provides durations for the initial fifteen pitch series, the first part of the movement. These are followed continuously in the four layers; each takes the next pitch and duration available, applying it to its own rhythm base. Dynamics are likewise determined serially. A series of twelve dynamics, predominantly low with isolated bursts – (*ppp, p, mp, mf, f, ppp, ppp<f, f>ppp, ppp<mf, mf>ppp, p<f, f>p*) – undergoes single shifts for each pitch on the downward slope of the all-interval series (A♭, G etc.), triple shifts for the ascending pitches. The text is distributed between the rhythmic layers and voices. Every word (apart from *per*) is presented fully at least once in a single voice, and they appear in order until the final section. Against this, words, fragments of words and individual vowels anticipate, reinforce, blur or echo the emergence of individual voices. Over a decade later, Nono explained his intention and his frustration at its misinterpretation:

> I had developed a new choral style; to begin with I had subdivided the words into syllables, often into single phonemes and allowed them to live through the entire chorus. Critics and performers were so used to pointilliste composition that they saw my treatment of text as another step in isolating acoustic elements. [. . .]. Instead it was a matter of something quite different. I wanted a horizontal melodic construction that embraced all the registers; a fluctuating from phoneme to phoneme, from syllable to syllable: a line that sometimes consists of a succession of single notes or pitches, sometimes condenses into sonic bands.[41]

The technique and poetry of this movement have as much to do with Josquin, Gesualdo and Monteverdi as with serialism; construction, expression and representation are inseparable. A meaningful analysis would have to trace the attention of a listener through an infinitely complex map of possible routes. It would look like Nono's own map of possible paths between the various kinds of material in *Post-prae-ludium per Donau*, some thirty years later. The tight structure of this movement accommodates its expressive detail and creates the space for the rich discourse of *Il canto sospeso*; it avoids the work being immediately overwhelmed by the enormity of its subject. The opening wide intervals of 'muoio' ('I die') and 'mondo' are cries to which the rest of the movement responds. The motivic stretto on 'splenderà', the only word to be repeated in this way, is a clear statement of resistance. In *Text – Musik – Gesang*, Nono shows how Gesualdo sets the word 'splende' – a clear model, a 'pluridimensional whole formed of constellations of words and phonemes'.[42] 'Luce' rises in sustained notes from the bass, to a soprano high C on 'forte', a light passing across the whole texture. The four voices that join a sustained 'non' in bar 121 are unified in resistance, while a solo 'io' four bars later is actually not part of the text, but the subject ('I') emerging from echoes of 'muoio' and 'sacrificio'. 'Millioni' and 'guerra' are rare four- and five-bar words, both rising to a *forte* high C – the voices of the people united. The final section (bars 142–57) solves the architectural problem of finding a non-arbitrary conclusion to a potentially infinite structure. The four rhythmic layers are nested about the beginning of bar 150, their durations arranged symmetrically in decreasing and increasing order as they work through the four remaining pitch series. The alto begins and ends the passage; a sustained crescendo A 'muoio' is mirrored by an equal decrescendo E♭ single

'*Docere e movere*': Il canto sospeso

vowel 'o', tracing the ambit of the original series. This entire coda is a condensed meditation on one word and one interval. About the central rhythmic hiatus, multiple voices join the lone subject with elements of 'le nostre idee vinceranno', against which is counterpointed a single cry of 'le nostre idee vinceranno' ('our ideas will prevail'), against which is counterpointed a single cry of 'giustizia' ('justice').

The proportions of movements 6a and 6b reflect the internal division of the second. Nono sets the text in two separate parts of action and reflection:

6a
The doors open.
Here are our murderers.
Dressed in black.
They drive us from the synagogue
6b
How hard it is to say goodbye forever to life, which is so beautiful!

Nono's student Nicolaus Huber has suggested that this allows the composer to focus fully on the emotional content of each; the murderers have no role in the second. However, as Huber points out, this does not mean that Nono is referring to an abstract utopia: 'The good life, as a concrete goal, requires commitment and struggle, it is no gift from above. This is also a Marxist corrective to the view of life as pure physical existence.'[43] Here, Nono thinks initially in terms of colour and polyphonic density. For 6a, he lists the densities, 'a 1' to 'a 6' in ascending order of complexity, with soprano and bass soloists. For 6b, he develops a new way of visualising such architecture: a time-oriented bar graph of blocks of different height and colour. The same voice is heard in two registers, through two filters: in 6a, an eight-part chorus, low strings, low wind and brass, timpani; in 6b, a four-part chorus with high strings and two notes from a single trumpet. With the appearance of the murderers, this is the dramatic centre of the work; Mila describes it as a *Dies Irae*.[44] Each line of text is a brutal attack led remorselessly by low brass and timpani. The movement shares its emotional and musical core with *La Guerra* and with the later stage works *Intolleranza 1960* and *Al gran sole carico d'amore*, but here the malign intention has greater clarity; this is a representation of totalitarian purposefulness.

The careful separation of the four lines of 6a allows them to be heard with clarity, urgency and drama through a complex rhythmic polyphony. Having counted the syllables in each, Nono sets them on varying combinations of triplet, sixteenth and quintuplet, to incrementally increasing sets of pitches (1, 2, 3, 4) from an all-interval series on Eb. Durations are taken in order from a table using a quasi-Fibonacci series (2 3 5 8 12 17 and back) with a 'salto a 2'. Twelve dynamics are arranged in descending order of single levels (*fff* – *ppp*) followed by ascending crescendos and diminuendos, all rotated to produce further series. These are associated with different voices in order and read according to the duration value. Having composed these brief passages of polyphony, Nono decides on the proportions and character of the four sections they will inhabit. He shifts the voices relative to each other within these longer sections, emphasising the particular architecture of each (and confounding the analyst, as Huber, Bailey and Motz attest). The four sections now have lengths of 9, 17, 7 and 12 bars; the starts and ends of the vocal passages are organised in a simple sequence of independent (<, >) and unison (|) gestures that ends with the chorus united: <|, < >, | |, <|. The shaping of sound complexes – musical constructs in the space between horizontal and vertical – would come under higher level control with Nono's use of 'negative' values. Here his taxonomy of such shapes begins a trajectory that will lead to their fundamental role in *Varianti*.

'Docere e movere': Il canto sospeso

The orchestra follows the same structure in reflection (Figure 5.9). Section lengths, density and rhythm – with some variation from the disaligning process – are the mirror of the chorus. Their pitch material would also appear initially to be the retrograde: the first four notes of an all-interval series starting on A rather than the chorus' single E♭. In the third orchestral section the relationship changes, however. The orchestral material is unable to complete itself; it gets drawn back to its own obsessive behaviour, to attempt the same path. This A and its subsequent B♭ are the very notes implied by the chorus series:

Figure 5.9 Il canto sospeso No. 6a: pitch structure

Huber sees the orchestra as the murderers, dehumanised in their voicelessness, but perhaps the relationship is more subtle. The timpani answer to the tenor's 'eccoli, i nostri assassini' ('here they are, our killers'), the same figural rhythm mirrored about the movement's pivot point in bar 341, would certainly seem to be a reply, a representation. The symbolism of the E♭ timpani dialogue – Es Es (SS) – and its tritone with the strings' low A (SA) is unmistakable. They create a constrained, limited pitch space with no way out for victim or murderer. The interval is that of the death of Monteverdi's Euridice, the unyielding gesture and low harshness those of Caronte, its indifferent vehicle. This is no coincidence; *L'Orfeo* is itself a story of the suspension of song and life, a redefining of the relationship between music and text to which a Venetian could lay some claim. The 12-bar sustained low A, decaying only under the entry of the last chorus tetrad, and the more rapidly dying final B♭ appear to be defeated by the defiance of the chorus. The fact that A and B♭ are the very pitches implied by the final chorus section suggests a more symbiotic possibility. By the same token, the next pitches the victims would provide in bar 345 are precisely those that their murderers were unable to reach in the passage from bar 331, before their return to their own tritone prison.

In contrast, the flow and plasticity of 6b are seen by Huber as the very embodiment of the beauty of life. It moves smoothly, with no sharp edges, no menacing repetition, only static dynamic levels limited to *forte*. It is a four-part song, each part shared between a vocal line and a corresponding string voice. The text is stretched rather than fragmented. Words are divided between voices, echoed, their vowels sustained by other voices, but only at a single point is there simultaneity of text: 'vita così bella' ('such beautiful life'). The use of only two rhythmic bases – triplets for alto and tenor, quintuplets in soprano and bass – produces a continuous wave-like motion. The voices present the all-interval series eleven times with no variation, followed by a final high A that moves seamlessly into that of the seventh movement; Nono notes the segue in an early sketch. Durations and dynamics derive from similar Latin squares – one descending 17–2, the other increasing *ppp-f*. Nono invents a new way of relating pitch and dynamics: he writes rotating pitch series into the table. The soprano presents nearly the entire text, others anticipate and echo words and vowels. The use of *bocca chiusa* and sustained vowels provides a continuous spectrum between words and instruments, establishing the sound world of the seventh movement. He distributes the voices (with their instrumental alter egos) and the number of layers according to a bar chart that illustrates this plasticity (Figure 5.10).

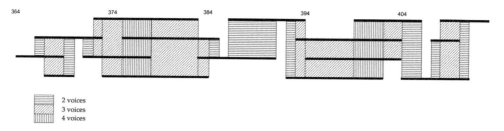

Figure 5.10 Il canto sospeso No.6b: density scheme[45]

Within this framework, the expressive potential of register and of the placing of individual voices are exploited to the full. The two most charged words, 'addio' and 'bella', are particularly worthy of attention. The soprano augmented octave C–C♯ 'addio' in bar 378 is answered by the trumpet's high D–C♯ – a Mahlerian farewell, itself echoed by the tenor D as if a hint of poignant hope remains. 'Bella' is the last and most repeated word, a madrigalism reminiscent of 'splenderà' in the second movement. Its rising and falling three-note motif is echoed four times by inversion, compression and extension until only a falling fifth remains, disappearing into the closing, thinning, rising coda.

The last two movements reprise the sequence of the first two. They have echoes of an instrumental canzona and choral motet concluding a major rite at St Marks. The ninth movement is for chorus, varying constantly between four and twelve parts, and timpani. Its sheer compositional virtuosity suggests that it was written last, when Nono felt he had fully assimilated the techniques of the other movements. It combines three fragments of text from victims of different nationalities, significantly including German. As a final declaration of internationalist faith through tragedy it superimposes three parts of a credo:

I am not afraid of death
I will be calm and at peace in the face of the execution squad. Are those who have condemned us equally at peace?
I go with faith in a better life for you

Rhythmic figure derives from a development of Nono's rotational space, a spiralling archetype that has suffused the whole work including the all-interval series. In a two-stage process, each half of his symmetrical set is first treated separately, producing evolving patterns, repetitions and symmetries (Figure 5.11).

Figure 5.11 Il canto sospeso No. 9: rhythmic process

'Docere e movere': Il canto sospeso

Nono's method in this final pillar confirms his concern with architectural symmetry. He composes the body of the movement (the first fifty bars) backwards. Pitches are determined in reverse: fifteen series, as in the analogous part of the second movement. This is no conventional retrograde, however. Durations are also used straightforwardly in order, distributed across three layers based on triplet, semiquaver and quintuplet. But here it is the ends of the notes that are in sequence. Dynamics are read from another table using the same subdued range as movement 6b, derived from twelve rotational permutations of a rising and falling sequence.

The entire last movement is a fabric of latent imitation and counterpoint. If they were exact or explicit the dynamical balance would be upset; instead, the listener's ear is drawn to search constantly for new potential. The careful placing of each entry, its timbre and register, anticipates the phase of choral works to come. Words are distributed among voices, crucial sequential threads of text and melody indicated by arrows in the score. Nono's replacing of one of the three original extracts points to his having arranged the text across the musical fabric at a late stage. Individual syllables blur the edges of clearer statements, rarely more than two words, both rhythmically and by using close intervals. The last words before the *bocca chiusa* coda are clear, and complete the core assertion of *Il canto sospeso* begun in the second movement with its very opening word: 'Muoio [. . .] per voi' ('I die [. . .] for you'). Wider intervals are used to open up melodic and harmonic spaces. Nono gives particular prominence to the descending semitone, a signifier of pain, and to the sixth: the opening interval of the sopranos and which dominates the melos of the wordless coda. The last eleven bars plainly restate the original series three times, perhaps another theological reference. The work is reabsorbed into the musical matter within which it is suspended. In anticipation of Nono's later fascination with Giordano Bruno, its historical events take place within a broader cosmology.

Song

At Darmstadt in 1957, Stockhausen presented his analysis of the contemporary use of text in lectures on *Le Marteau sans maître*, *Il canto sospeso* and his own *Gesang der Jünglinge*. Of Nono's work he observed:

> In certain passages of the 'Canto', Nono composes with the text as if it should be withdrawn from view, where it doesn't belong. [. . .] he doesn't interpret, he doesn't comment; he reduces language to its sounds and makes music with them.[46]

Stockhausen goes on to find serial structures in Nono's use of vocal sounds. His talk provoked an immediate outburst from the composer and probably sealed the end of their friendship. The central issue is not merely technical or aesthetic, but ethical. The vehemence with which Nono refuted Stockhausen's analysis demonstrates the absolute priority of the texts in *Il canto sospeso*, their material relevance to the whole process of its composition. His response was immediate, but the challenge triggered a more considered answer in his own seminar at Darmstadt in 1960, *Text – Musik – Gesang*.[47] Through a series of examples, he shows how the phenomenological reality of sung texts and their musical setting – including their polyphonic fragmentation, proliferation and multiplication – is integral to Western vocal music. His thesis is that *canto* is more than the sum of text and music; he anticipates Tim Ingold's argument that a 'single register' of human expression in song pre-dated a modern separation of language and notes.[48] He shows how in the third movement of *Il canto sospeso* a new compound text emerges from the careful superposition of three extracts. Nono's studied reflection on Gabrieli, Gesualdo,

'Docere e movere': Il canto sospeso

Monteverdi, Bach, Mozart, Beethoven and Schönberg concludes with an impassioned acknowledgement of its initial impulse:

> Did we learn nothing but shame from the passion of Christ? And did this latest passion of millions who were not gods but men teach us nothing but to be ashamed? Did they die for this? I don't want to judge who it is who should really be ashamed. The spiritual testament of these letters has become the expression of my composition. And all my subsequent choral works are to be understood on the basis of this relationship between language as a phonetic-semantic entity and music as the composed expression of language. It is completely absurd to want to deduce from a structural analysis of the text that in this way the semantic content has been expelled. The question of why this text rather than that has been chosen for a composition is no more intelligent than the question why to pronounce the word stupid one uses the letters s-t-u-p-i-d.[49]

With hindsight, we might make two important points with respect to Nono's relationship with text. First, 'meaning' (for want of a less unsatisfactory word) is paramount. However, it extends beyond a single particular textual formulation. A specific text is an emergent property of a wider set of events, concepts and concerns – one possible view of a constellation. Words and music are both instantiations of this deeper sense. Second, the distribution, extension and apparent fragmentation of text is not a destructive process but one of consolidation, of coalescing. The music develops a textual surface, it gives birth to words, at moments when the deeper sense takes specific form, and this is a continuous process not a binary state. The music is not 'about' its text in any literal or descriptive sense, as Nono's subsequent comments attest; there is no such division.[50] Indeed, a cultural reception that associated any perceived dissonance or fragmentation with suffering would be grossly ill founded. What, then, is the key to this relationship, the material relationship between textual subject and musical surface? At the heart of the work is the suspension of time, such that a moment can be explored and reflected in multiple directions. Nono's technical, theoretical and aesthetic investigations converged on this point, one to which they would find their way again two decades later. The texts he selected concern the awful moment when death is inevitable – an arbitrary death, not inscribed in the trajectory of the individual. They are each an irrevocable leave-taking, but humanity-asserting in the very expression of that farewell. This is as close as life can come to time ceasing to pass; brief yet infinite, excruciatingly present in their announcing of absolute absence. They are intensely of this world, loving of this world, yet transcend it; the moment before death is one of clear-seeing. The suspension and exploration of this moment is not merely a metaphor but a structuring principle. Through the Lorca settings and *Guernica* it had emerged as the focus of Nono's aesthetic. To the 'deliverance from the obsession with death' of *Prometeo* and the fascination with the otherworldly time of Tarkovsky's films, this would remain the portal through which Nono accesses his compositional space.

This is the moment of suspension, therefore, when being and not-being exist simultaneously, when time is both felt most acutely and arrested. *Il canto sospeso* is song in the 'single register' that Ingold describes, a state prior to the separation of language and sound, meaning and feeling. It is song as Nono understood every note of Webern to be. On finishing his composition in April, he wrote to Stockhausen, joyful that the young couple had finally moved to their own house in the workers' quarter of Giudecca and keen to invite his friend. He responds to Stockhausen's analysis of Webern's String Quartet and finds weakness in its classical form:

'Docere e movere': Il canto sospeso

> Tradition??? Or compromise??? Or formalism???
> Just as in his songs.
> song, just song, and Viennese song
> Now I am at the end (third part) of a work for three soloists [. . .], choir and orchestra,
>   now it is clear to me that today one sings as today one writes for an instrument.
> even in Webern it wasn't like this.
> but always song.[51]

The mention of 'Viennese song' may well be an oblique reference to Schönberg's 'The relationship to the text', his 1912 essay from *Der Blaue Reiter* to which Nono refers on several occasions. There, Schönberg says he 'understood the Schubert songs, together with their poems, from the music alone, and the poems of Stefan George from their sound alone'.[52] Not only is clarity of text not the sole criterion, but 'the outward correspondence between music and text [. . .] belongs to the same stage of primitive imitation of nature as the copying of a model. Apparent superficial divergences can be necessary because of parallelism on a higher level.'

In *Il canto sospeso*, every note and its every relationship hold the potential for song; song is suspended in time, listened to and explored in every direction, at every speed, through different filters. Nono's enduring technical concern with the directions, rates and complexity of time here finds focus. The existence and directionality of both song and time are constantly kept in question. Both the fragility and the robustness of the work are guaranteed not by pre-compositional calculation but by Nono's final stage of inscription, the detailed decisions concerning the placing of each sound as it enters the draft score.[53] A mundane issue highlights the crucial importance of this stage in Nono's compositional process:

> As for the piano reduction, the situation is this: I can only make one from the hand-written score which is now with Schott: it is only possible from the manuscript. Because I determined everything directly in the manuscript; that is, I made changes directly in the score such that it isn't possible to make a piano reduction from the draft sketches I have here.[54]

In 1954, Adorno had first presented his *The Aging of the New Music*, a comprehensive, perceptive and coruscating critique of tendencies in the music of the early 1950s avant-garde. Adorno criticises young composers for attempting to eliminate compositional freedom, to replace it with rigid determinacy, a rationalisation of art that 'tips over into chaos'.[55] He points to an infatuation with material at the expense of its forming, the subjugation of the compositional subject to a mechanical intellectualising, the absence of historical awareness and the loss of the critical impulse of new music – the 'danger of the danger-less', as Metzger would later put it. Presciently, in respect of *Il canto sospeso*, he observes:

> The only authentic artworks produced today are those that in their inner organization measure themselves by the fullest experience of horror, and there is scarcely anyone, except Schoenberg or Picasso, who can depend on himself to have the power to do this.[56]

He gives some indications of the path needed:

> It is time for a concentration of energy in another direction; not towards the mere organization of material, but towards the composition of truly coherent music out of a material however shorn of every quality. [. . .] It is not expression as such that must be exorcised from music – otherwise nothing would be left except the designs of

resounding forms in motion – rather the element of transfiguration, the ideological element of expression, has grown threadbare. [. . .] What is needed is for expression to win back the density of experience [. . .] [57]

Adorno reasserted this view when after a lengthy gestation his talk appeared in a major book in 1956.[58] In a further article of 1955 he explicitly included Nono in the group of young composers for whom 'objective construction must encompass all elements mathematically'.[59] In a heated response, Metzger pointed out that the roots of Adorno's arguments could be traced back to the Darmstadt seminar of 1951 when Goeyvaerts had presented his ideas of objectifying composition and material.[60] While there was doubtless no shortage of what Adorno called 'music festival music', we should understand his article not as a review but rather as a reflection on the implications of compositional developments. His arguments were validated in that he identified precisely the issues that would exercise the main protagonists as they confronted that tipping point. It is clear from subsequent discussions that central to his concern was the inadequacy of radical serialism as a response to the 'Schönberg paradox': a historical situation wherein musical material had evolved ahead of its forming.[61] *Il canto sospeso* is clearly a paradigmatic counter-example to Adorno's arguments in almost every respect, but it is by no means a response. While not mentioning Nono, Metzger points out that composers were addressing Adorno's very concerns. His article effectively accuses Adorno of tilting at windmills, of ignoring the body of music that had emerged since 1951 and especially recent masterpieces: Boulez's *Le Marteau sans maître* of 1955 and Stockhausen's tape work *Gesang der Jünglinge*, premiered in May 1956. With hindsight, it is clear that these two works and *Il canto sospeso* together constitute the first pinnacle of aesthetic and technical achievement of the avant-garde, united – as Stockhausen's analysis would explore and Nono had long advocated – by their use of text (Figure 5.12).

Figure 5.12 From a letter to Stockhausen, 4 September 1952. (Reproduced by kind permission of the heirs of Luigi Nono and Stockhausen-Stiftung für Musik, Kürten.)

Why, then, is there such little mention of *Il canto sospeso*? There is a grudging acknowledgement of its power by Metzger, but only to condemn the work as an example of radical constructivism.[62] Metzger's later explanation of his criticism of other works (in an essay in which he appears, having made his peace, to try to outdo Adorno) is illuminating. Given the central concern with the nature of material among avant-garde 'purists' he was presumably not alone in being uneasy with Nono's use of popular song and dance and his increasing political engagement. Indeed, he accuses Nono of exploiting the unquestionable humanity of his texts to give life to lifeless notes: 'the trick, as Kagel has pointed out, is that Nono presents the humanity of these texts as his own, directing their prestige to himself'.[63] This develops Metzger's previous criticism, that Nono's use of popular melody and rhythm was a sop to socialist realism as proposed by the 'Prague Manifesto'.[64] Patently unjust as such criticism is, it challenges us to

'*Docere e movere*': *Il canto sospeso*

explore the nature of the relationship, to try to understand how the work embodies its 'meaning'. Adorno's opinion is less clear. One clue lies in a report on an ISM round-table discussion on the question 'Is that still music?' following a further Cologne performance of *Il canto sospeso* in 1958. The writer reports Adorno's argument that music must express its own time:

> Nono's *Canto sospeso* is valid, healthy music, despite its "expression" of the terrible, of the massacre of resistance fighters. Furthermore, it is humane music. Adorno first hinted at this in his conclusion, where he spoke of the delight and felicity of [its] musical form.[65]

Perhaps the most revolutionary aspect of *Il canto sospeso* is the nature of the work as a whole. From its earliest indications to Steinecke to a letter to Hartmann on its completion, Nono refers to *Il canto sospeso* in terms of the theatre. In initial sketches Nono referred to the work as a cantata, although there is no reason to see this as anything more than a generic appellation. In his 1960 article, Massimo Mila described it as a 'Freedom Mass'.[66] That Mila judged the work to be a valid response to the texts would have been highly significant for Nono: 'the highest praise that one can give is that the music proves itself worthy of the texts'.[67] In compositional terms, Mila saw *Il canto sospeso* as an act of authentic human expression that transcended the dialectical relationship between total determinism and chance: 'Precisely because it comes from this context, the significance of *Il canto sospeso* goes beyond the usual joy at a successful work of art. It denies the historical pessimism of Adorno.'[68] Mila's reference to the Mass is quite specific; universal redemption through individual sacrifice is at its centre.

Other models present themselves. Dallapiccola's *Canti di prigionia*, *Il prigioniero* and *Canti di liberazione* deal with similar themes. More immediately, Maderna had set a letter from Malvezzi and Pirelli's earlier collection in his *Kranichsteiner Kammerkantate* of 1953, along with letters from Gramsci and Kafka. As musical material he had used the Russian song Katyusha, popular in the Italian resistance as Fischia il vento. By neither representing the struggle nor importing referential material Nono achieves an altogether more reflective, universal pathos. As we have seen, the text-based works of Schönberg were an important object of study, and increasingly so over the next few years. *A Survivor from Warsaw* was a significant example, as was *Moses und Aron* – in the questions it raises, its difficulties, as much as by example – but the voice of *Il canto sospeso* is quite different.

What kind of aesthetic construct is *Il canto sospeso*? In his review, Heinz Joachim described the work in terms of Bach's Passions. Nono was too circumspect to declare such a model, but as well as referring to Christ in his response to Stockhausen, he cites Arnold Schmitz on the nature of the Passions in *Text – Musik – Gesang*. Nono was engaged in intensive study of the relationship between music and text, and of the notion that with the right aesthetic and ideological understanding they might together produce something greater than the sum of their parts but authentic to both. His collection of Bach scores included Katunda's copy of *The Musical Offering*, presumably studied with Scherchen, as well as several volumes of cantatas from the *Neue Bach-Ausgabe*. A copy of the first *Brandenburg Concerto* may have been worked on with Maderna; it has conductor's marks, but also indications of symmetries, imitations, retrogrades. Cantata 4 *Christ lag in Todesbanden* has the chorale analysed and annotated intensively in its polyphonic use 'like the Flemish'. Most telling of all are notes in his early copies of the *St Matthew Passion*. There are frequent references to Schönberg's *Moses und Aron*, especially at moments when the chorus enter the narrative. Particularly relevant is his marking the chorus' line 'dass er für uns geopfert wird' ('that he was sacrificed for us') in the chorale *O Mensch, bewein dein Sünde gross*, and their taunting of Christ *Weissage uns, Christe*. Musically, dramatically and ideologically such moments provide models for the reflective and active voices of the chorus in *Il canto sospeso*. According to Nuria, his LP copy of the *St Matthew Passion* was nearly worn out with repeated listening.

Through the 1950s Nono collected several texts on Bach. In a volume from 1955 he marks an article by Heinrich Besseler, *Bach the Pathfinder*.[69] Always concerned with the social nature of music as an activity, Besseler develops a concept of 'inner singing' as the basis of Bach's mature polyphony, the path by which instrumental music was able to become an authentic voice of the subject. He finds a crucial relationship between formal architecture and the character of a particular sequence of notes. The most fully annotated of these texts is Arnold Schmitz's 1950 book *The Depictive Nature of the Text-Based Music of Johann Sebastian Bach*. Schmitz's premise is as follows: 'Bach's oratorio style is characterised by that fact that of the three possible aims of rhetoric – docere [to teach], delectare [to delight] and movere [to move] – it aspires especially to docere and movere [. . .]'.[70] He suggests that the depictive qualities of Bach's choral music must be understood in terms of the musical oratory of the time, that text and music both work according to rhetorical principles. He bases his analysis largely on the treatises of Matthias Flacius (1520–75) and Johann David Heinichen (1683–1729); it will not have escaped Nono's attention that both spent their formative years in Venice. In Schmitz's lengthy exposition of the figures of rhetoric as understood in Bach's time, Nono marks the observation that in music they are structured hierarchically: 'again in Schönberg', he notes. He notes Bach's use of numerology – very relevant to a composer acutely aware of the tendency to number-fetishism identified by Adorno and Boulez. He seems to have been particularly interested in the uses of rhetoric in early Lutheran theory and preaching, in the capacity of *oratio figurata* to teach and move and in its role in Bach's choral music. Following the Florentine Camerata, the theatre becomes a place for oratory, says Schmitz. Nono studies the detail of rhetorical figures closely, noting that Webern reduces them to three types. He follows the analysis of figures in the *St Matthew Passion* and underlines description of the use of the rising minor sixth for the *exclamatio*, surely with the end of *Il canto sospeso* in mind. He notes elements of Schmitz's conclusion:

> The goal is in fact one of musical hermeneutics. This hermeneutics must reckon with the fact in his text-based music, Bach uses depictive and affective figure not only in relation to the sense of certain words or strophes, but to the scopus of the entire text, indeed to a scopus that may be quite other to the text being sung, as the example of the aria *Können Tränen meiner Wangen* shows, a composition that runs contrary to its madrigalian-pietistic text. In such cases Bach's oratory is particularly powerful, in its Docere with Movere.[71]

The contention here is therefore that the choral music of Bach, and specifically the *St Matthew Passion*, provided Nono with the closest model for *Il canto sospeso*, a teaching, moving, virtual music theatre – indeed, a theatre that must ultimately be virtual, as *Prometeo* would later become after its long journey. It provided a model for the multiple roles of the chorus, in its aggregate *canto* – a function of music and text, voices and instruments – in the relationship between subject, artist and contemporary world, and even in its very melos. Indeed, the relationship between the *Kyrie* fugue subjects of Bach's *Mass in B Minor* and his own all-interval series must have been clear to Nono. Having understood the materials and processes with which Nono equipped himself for its composing, the decisions he made in producing the score of *Il canto sospeso* may well be best understood in terms of rhetoric, of sequences and counterpoints of melodic, harmonic, rhythmic and dramatic figure.

'Docere e movere': Il canto sospeso

Like Bach's choral music, *Il canto sospeso* is a moral work for the present, however; Nono would have had little interest in writing an abstract tragedy, a memorial or a documentary. He may have associated Schmitz and Besseler's socio-historically contextualising approaches to Bach with another important area of his reading at this time, the literary criticism of Marxist theorist György Lukács. One essay marked by Nono is particularly apposite. In *Narrate or Describe* (1936) Lukács explores the relationship between the artist, the events he portrays, their time and his own time. His view, grounded in historical materialism, is clear: 'No "artistry" can exist independently of and in isolation from social, historical and subjective conditions which are unpropitious to a rich, comprehensive, many-sided and dynamic artistic reflection of objective reality.'[72] As description becomes increasingly obsessive, the epic power to move and teach diminishes, says Lukács; there is a clear analogy with Adorno's criticism of the objectification of musical material.[73] Narration establishes proportions, description merely levels. Lukács' assertion that epic narration requires a complex, non-linear relationship with time and events is already reflected in *Il canto sospeso*; the complexity of time becomes a major structuring principle in the later works. Again we find a resonance with the contemporaneous investigations of Calvino. Far from proposing a manifesto of socialist realism, Lukács praises the humanism of certain formalists, a sophisticated understanding of the role of the artist that also runs through the work of his early colleague Gramsci and thus becomes part of the unique character of Italian communism. Most crucially, the artist must have his own standpoint:

> But the writer himself must possess a firmly established and vital ideology; he must see the world in its contradictory dynamics [. . .]. The deeper, the more differentiated, and the more steeped in vital experience the ideology, the more variegated and multifaceted its compositional expression.

And without ideology there is no composition.[74]

Notes

1 Letter to Eigel Kruttke, 13 October 1956, in Flamm, 1995, p. v.
2 Letter to Steinecke, late 1955. ALN.
3 Letter from Steinecke, 2 May 1956. ALN.
4 Letter from Steinecke, 12 May 1956. ALN.
5 Custodis, 2004, p. 95.
6 Eimert, 1956.
7 Joachim, 1957.
8 Wolf-Eberhard von Lewinski, *Darmstädter Tageblatt*, 24 October 1956.
9 Goléa, 1960.
10 *The Gramophone*, October 1993, p. 110.
11 Huber, 1981, p. 59.
12 Motz, 1996, p. 9; Bailey, 1992, p. 329.
13 Smith-Brindle, 1961, p. 247.
14 Smith-Brindle, 1961, p. 248.
15 Smith-Brindle, 1975, p. 164; Smith-Brindle, 1966, p. 130.
16 Eimert, 1956.
17 Interview with Enzo Restango, 1987. LNII, p. 511.
18 Motz, 1996; Feneyrou, 2002; Nielinger, 2006.
19 Motz, 1996, p. 32.
20 Malvezzi and Pirelli, 1954.
21 Letter from Scherchen, 5 May 1955. ALN.
22 Interview with Enzo Restagno, 1987. LNII, pp. 510–11.
23 'Lo sviluppo della tecnica seriale', 1957. LNI, p. 28.

24 Guerrero, 2006, proposes an exhaustive taxonomy of Nono's serial procedures in *Il canto sospeso*.
25 'Sullo sviluppo della tecnica seriale', 1956. LNI, 14.
26 Eimert, 1950.
27 De Benedictis and Rizzardi, 2010, p. 271.
28 Pestalozza, 1981, p. 3.
29 De Benedictis and Rizzardi, 2010, p. 270.
30 Motz, 1996, p. 123.
31 Interview with Enzo Restagno, 1987. LNII, p. 512.
32 Translated as 'Testo – musica – canto', 1960. LNI, pp. 57–83.
33 'Testo – musica – canto'. LNI, p. 73.
34 De Benedicits and Rizzardi, 2010, p. 268.
35 Julius and Ethel Rosenberg, 1994, p. 566.
36 De Benedictis and Rizzardi, 2010, p. 262.
37 Interview with Enzo Restagno, 1987. LNII, p. 511.
'There are choral parts that remind one of distant choirs, echoes, intuitions [. . .] which I can now say are 'suspended' choirs waiting for *Caminantes [. . .] Ayatucho*, 1987 [. . .]'. (LNII, 512).
38 De Benedictis and Rizzardi, 2010, p. 264.
39 De Benedictis and Rizzardi, 2010, p. 262.
40 Joachim, 1957, p. 103.
41 Interview with Hansjörg Pauli, 1969. LNII, p. 24.
42 'Testo – musica – canto'. LNI, pp. 76–9.
43 Huber, 1981, p. 79.
44 De Benedictis and Rizzardi, 2010, p. 269.
45 From ALN 14.02.05/06.
46 Stockhausen, 1964, p. 159.
47 'Testo – musica – canto'. LNI, pp. 57–83.
48 Ingold, 2007, p. 18.
49 'Testo – musica – canto'. LNI, pp. 81–2.
50 Motz, 1996, p. 34.
51 Letter to Stockhausen, 4 April 1956, ALN.
52 Schönberg, 1975, pp. 4–5.
53 It is almost irresistible for the analyst not to point out 'mistakes' in the detail of the score. Printing errors can, of course, be identified by reference to Nono's autograph. In other cases, some apparent errors of reckoning or transcription may equally be hard-wrought decisions taken for reasons of taste, effect or practicality.
54 Letter to Steinecke, 15 May 1956. ALN.
55 Adorno, 2002, p. 192.
56 Adorno, 2002, p. 200.
57 Adorno, 2002, p. 191.
58 First given as a radio talk during the Stuttgarter Woche für Neue Musik in 1954, the article appeared in *Der Monat* the following year and then in the 1956 collection *Dissonanzen*.
59 Adorno, 1984, p. 132.
60 Metzger, 1980a. Metzger also recalls that Adorno saw Messiaen's *Modes de valeurs et d'intensités* as an archetypical example in which the material is presented mechanically at the expense of any compositional mediation.
61 Metzger, 1980a.
62 Metzger, 1980b.
63 Metzger, 1980c, p. 120.
64 The Second International Congress of Composers and Music Critics was held in Prague in May 1948.
65 *Kölner Stadt-Anzeiger*, 27 June 1958.
66 De Benedictis and Rizzardi, 2010, p. 262.
67 De Benedictis and Rizzardi, 2010, p. 274.
68 De Benedictis and Rizzardi, 2010, p. 261.
69 Besseler, 1955.
70 Schmitz, 1950, p. 12.
71 Schmitz, 1950, p. 86. Nono's underlining.
72 Lukács, 1970, p. 121.
73 The concept of reification was one of Lukács' main themes in *History and Class Consciousness*.
74 Lukács, 1970, p. 142.

6

POETRY AND DRAMA

'Varianti'

There are no dogmatic truths, no handbooks of formulae, no keys, nobody has the divine truth.

But the basis is strict study, rigorous discipline in work, a conscience which rules thought and reason, and sensitivity.

It is necessary to use reason – above all and always, and to understand the how and why of the development of music and of every experience, concretely, in its cause and origins and tendencies.

It is necessary to recognise oneself, to have clear and absolute responsibility for one's own action: one doesn't live or act arbitrarily, but always in a determined and determining situation.

It is necessary above all to awake a new consciousness, which alone can give life to a new music.[1]

These words from Nono's introduction to his composition seminars at Darmstadt in 1958 give a concise picture of his mature, resolute compositional ethos, of his continuous questioning. The refusal of dogma or formulae makes coherence of thought all the more vital. Nono's sense of responsibility on personal, social and musical planes is manifested in new relationships with material, performance and performers through the last years of the decade.

Collaboration

Immediately after finishing *Il canto sospeso*, Nono wrote to Steinecke that 'right now a work for violin, soprano and orchestra is flying around in my head'.[2] The work had initially been discussed with the Hungarian virtuoso André Gertler, whom Nono had first met at Darmstadt in 1952. Gertler had arranged the commission with Strobel for performances in April 1957. Since 1953, the professor of violin at Darmstadt had been Rudolf Kolisch, who also gave a series of chamber music courses which Nono had followed with interest. Moreover, Kolisch was the brother-in-law of Schönberg, with whom he had studied composition; his quartet had given premieres of Schönberg's last two string quartets, Webern's op. 28 and Berg's Lyric Suite. He was also a friend of Adorno and well acquainted with the socio-aesthetic context

147

of Nono's music.[3] There was now a family connection in every respect, therefore, and it was with Kolisch that the project went forward. Then living and teaching in Wisconsin, Kolisch's visits to Europe were precious and carefully planned. In August 1956, he came to Venice to see the new branch of his family and work with Nono on the new piece. Kolisch was then able to study the first part of the 'concerto' through the autumn. Strobel confirmed his role in December but then rescheduled the premiere for Donaueschingen in the following autumn. This was fortunate; despite rapid initial progress, Kolisch had still not received the remainder by May.

This uneven compositional sequence is explained by the particular shape of *Varianti*, the work for violin and orchestra performed at the Donaueschingen Festival in October 1957. As Nono worked with Kolisch on technical possibilities, he seems to have had two movements in mind, but also two voices within the solo violin part itself; even here his thought is immediately polyphonic. He considers two threads of sound – *normale* and *sul ponticello* – and looks at how these might be combined by the angle of the bow to produce a simultaneous *suono d'eco*. Echo is already a structural, melodic, rhythmic and timbral device. His diagram of bow positions and string-crossing may have reminded him of his own mirror forms; it persists in the gestural archetypes of Nono's string quartet, two decades later (Figure 6.1):

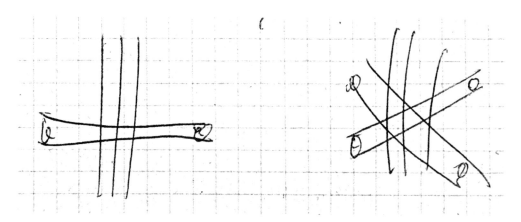

Figure 6.1 *Varianti*: diagrams from preparatory sketch. (ALN 15.01.01/02r (detail). © The heirs of Luigi Nono. Reproduced by kind permission.)

The eventual architectural concept develops that of *Incontri*; two formal elements are each mirrored in succession: 'A B A *ritroso* B *ritroso*', in Nono's notation. In *Varianti* the levels of dialectical opposition and mirroring are even more pervasive, however. The two are related at a fundamental structural and conceptual level, but remain distinct on the musical surface; their relationship is both dialectical and parallel. As Schaller has pointed out, there are traces of sonata form in their opposition and of classical concerto in the role of the soloist, and yet form and material deny conventional development or rhetoric.[4]

Reflection

While planning *Varianti*, Nono was working on an exhaustive analysis of Schönberg's Op. 31 *Variationen für Orchester*, which became part of a paper he presented at Darmstadt the following

Poetry and drama

year: *Die Entwicklung der Reihentechnik* (*The development of serial technique*).[5] Steinecke had proposed to Nono that he might contribute to a new series of publications – eventually the *Darmstädter Beiträge zur neuen Musik* – as well as the possibility of a new wind quintet. Nono clearly found the idea challenging; his mind was elsewhere:

> because now I'm working on the piece for Rudi [. . .] and so difficult! for 4 months I have worked and worked and always thrown away everything! it was not good and I am unsettled. because there are new ideas in the air and one needs time.
> [. . .] for the book, that is mosssssssst difficult!!! you know, I've never written anything! so that should also begin sometime. obviously I'll do it for you.[6]

Nono's difficulty in writing is perhaps reflected in the somewhat systematizing tone of his article. His analyses are informative in terms of what Nono sees as important in his examples. In its more formal analysis of the work of other composers – Schönberg, Webern, Boulez, Maderna and Stockhausen – this paper provides insight into Nono's ways of conceiving of the elements of contemporary technique, of their roles and relationships, and of the music–historical narrative they embody. He articulates three phases of this history: Schönberg's quasi-thematic use of the series; the reduction and subdivision of forms, and the place of symmetry and multiple set-membership in Webern; and the current phase in which the serial principle permeates every aspect and the chromatic series can undergo perpetual permutation and reconfiguration. This narrative presumably reflects Nono's own sense of place:

> These [compositions] are the result of the historical evolution of music, conditioned by the musical and human needs of our time. They are also conditioned by the most recent research, above all the greater possibility of using single sounds according to [. . .] their own nature.[7]

His analysis of the *Theme* from Schönberg's op. 31 is particularly detailed, perceptive and relevant to his own thought processes. Indeed, looking at his beautifully annotated copy of Schönberg's score, analysed in multiple colours like his own sketches, one must talk of love for the music and the thought that produced it.[8] That this very close reading informed Nono's own *Varianti* would hardly be surprising. He examines the relationship between interval content and transposition of the series, micro- and macro-structure. He demonstrates the characterisation and permutation of rhythmic cells, their grouping according to segments of the series and the insertion of rests or 'negative values'. Most tellingly, he explores the shape and use of Schönberg's theme itself: the symmetries, mirrors and carefully balanced asymmetries of interval content, formal duration, row form and horizontal or vertical 'projections' of the series. The theme divides clearly into two sections, their properties both related and opposing. The multi-modal tightness of this structure is what allows its elasticity through the variations, and what permits Schönberg maximal freedom in a work of classical balance and conciseness. Having traced the evolution of the series from theme to principle, Nono approaches his own *Varianti* accordingly: 'The musical and compositional elements of this work are born of continuous "variations", that is from variations on a single principle that is at the root of everything.'[9] In Webern's *Variations*, op. 30, he finds a more fluid musical space based on the intersection of pitch sets and the development of rhythmic materials from minimal, pre-figural cells.

Poetry and drama

In the third, present stage, the total space of permutations of a given series constitutes what he describes as the 'sonic material' from which the composer creates a work. In rather less detail – understandably, given his expert audience – Nono describes the freedom with which Maderna uses his new permutation technique in the *Due studi per il "Processo" di Kafka* (1950) and the strict procedures of Boulez's *Structures*, the time-frequency relation at the heart of Stockhausen's electronic *Studie 1* and the temporal 'pluridimensionality' of his *Zeitmasse*.

Nono's reference to a 'Darmstadt School' is often mentioned – usually to point out that by the stage, at least, such a unified view cannot be substantiated. However, if we consider Darmstadt as the locus of shared concerns rather than a style-label, then the disagreements that are clearly emerging actually reinforce Nono's notion. He makes this very point:

> Everyone takes part in this development according to their own nature and culture, on the basis of their personal experience. For this reason a multiplicity of distinct forms of musical expression relates to these common compositional principles. In fact individual nature and culture are not dissolved within common evolution, but rather they contribute in large part to determine its characteristics.[10]

Composition

There is an intimation of another new principle of Nono's work early in his paper:

> And the sound is analysed, its generating spectrum studied for the first time, thus making possible its direct composition (electronic music). This new phase of study, logical and coherent, is shaping a new way of conceiving music, of creation and realisation, which will be our tomorrow.[11]

His analysis of Stockhausen's electronic *Studie I* shows how Nono was fully conversant with the construction of complex timbres through the accumulation of sine tones with different pitches, amplitudes and start and end points. This analytic/synthetic approach to the construction of sound objects is what allows him to respond in musical detail to the time indifference of formal symmetry. He now had the conceptual and technical means to handle the evolution of individual sounds and their degree of coincidence in time and pitch, their horizontal and vertical projections.

The initial impulse for this close consideration of the inner life of sounds came directly from his work with Kolisch. Early in their research, Nono notes the possibilities of the same pitch played on more than one string: critical differences of pitch, dynamics, colour and articulation keep the whole constantly in motion as the player shifts weight and pressure. This sound becomes the seed of *Varianti*, its point of departure and object of investigation; Kolisch described *Varianti* as 'the articulation of the unison'.[12] During his stay in Venice, Kolisch and Nono worked through the complete repertoire of violin techniques. Nono's copious and systematic notes show that this encounter established the model for a series of such collaborations. The probing of combinations and permutations, the exploring of taxonomies, groupings and orderings suggest that it was Nono who led the joint research. This is the first time that Nono works through a series of possibilities external to his own imagination, the first time he maps a trajectory through the musical behaviour of a particular performer. This empirical, collaborative process will become a central pillar of his practice and the means by which he takes some of his most important steps. With Kolisch, he looks for continuities of sound, forming spaces within which he might find potential structure: 'Unity: between harmonics > flautando sul

Poetry and drama

ponticello > col legno > two sounds: 1st arco, 2nd legno (simultaneous) > two sounds not simultaneous: 1st arco tenuto, 2nd sul ponticello'.[13] He looks for connections between violin and orchestra: 'unity between pizzi[cato] after lento bow – percussion'. In the event, there was to be no percussion, but the timbral and physical shape of the orchestra was part of Nono's sound picture from the start. He experimented with four subgroups of wind, brass, strings and pitched percussion, distributed symmetrically across the stage about a central shared group of horns and bass clarinet – the physical mirror of the form itself. 'Perhaps' and 'possible' are becoming two of the most common words in his notes to himself. The orchestra would eventually consist principally of strings with the *flautando* extended by triple flutes and clarinets. Despite the scale and homogeneity of forces, each note in the score is played by a single instrument; Nono insisted that this was not a concerto but chamber music.[14]

His investigation moves towards a space defined by polyphonic density and sonic possibilities. Pitch material is clear; the all-interval series is an unquestioned source, now expanding from an initial C. Formal and micro-structural principles evolve together, developing and formalising ideas from *Canti*, *Incontri* and *Il canto sospeso*. In order to begin experimenting with the emerging concept of sound complexes, he needs coherent webs of rhythm and dynamics. The Latin square from which he will take durations embodies the fundamental binary opposition and mirroring that govern the form of *Varianti*. He returns to the odd/even opposition of *Incontri*: two sets of elements that are inextricably interwoven yet remain distinct. They are distributed symmetrically at the centre of the square (rows 6–7), from which mirrored sets of spiralling series are produced by a simple *salto* procedure, each a different refraction of the converging pattern of the all-interval series. As Erika Schaller has pointed out, the fifth and eighth rows are exactly the interval sequence of the all-interval series discussed by Eimert in his *Lehrbuch der Zwölfton-technik*.[15] The graphical path Nono traces to produce the originating number series demonstrates the fundamentally spatial nature of his conception (Figure 6.2).

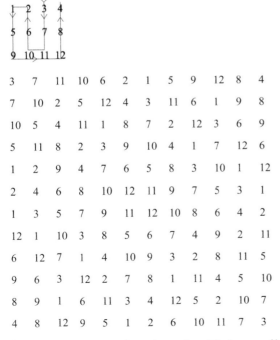

Figure 6.2 *Varianti*: initial number path and Latin square[16]

Poetry and drama

These he applies to his established grid of divisions of the beat by three, four, five, six and seven – five possible layers. He plays obsessively with permutations of the numbers 1 to 5 until shapes begin to consolidate, their relative lengths proportional to their density.[17] Form emerges from patterns of polyphonic density, therefore. The value 1 will represent a single line, the others the homogeneous orchestral textures Nono is imagining. Instead of a 5×5 space, he designs five sequences of values 2 to 5 to determine the bar structure of the first section. Four instances of the value 1 are inserted into the second of these sequences, diminishing incrementally to a single instance at the beginning of the last. Single-bar sections fall to the soloist, who also joins the orchestra in the central three sequences. The first four lines shape the first section of *Varianti* (bars 1–80). Rather than completing the pattern, Nono leaves it open to be mirrored later (bars 155–234) (Figure 6.3).

```
5 4 3 2
1 2 1 3 1 4 1 5
1 1 5 3 2 4 1
4 2 1 1 3 5
(1) 5 4 3 2
```

All 1 apart from (1): solo violin alone.
Underlined: solo violin with orchestra.

Figure 6.3 Varianti: lines 1–4 show pattern of bars 1–80, reversed in bars 155–234

In an early draft, polyphonic density follows the formal structure: five voices of chromatic complexes, each in rhythmic unison, through the first five bars, four voices through the following four bars and so on. Nono then introduces another level of movement. Single pitches are now played by multiple instruments (eventually from the same instrumental group), each on a different rhythm base. The proportions of different densities are the same, but now their distribution is modulated by a series of progressively subsiding waves – perhaps another process inspired by the talks on electronic music at Darmstadt, but certainly an archetype of movement that will resurface significantly in ..... *sofferte onde serene* ... and become an important structural element of *Fragmente-Stille, an Diotima*. The structuring role of the number five also recalls Stockhausen's electronic *Studie II* (1954); that Nono knew Stockhausen's early electronic works in technical detail is clear from his Darmstadt paper.[18]

A new conception of musical objects emerges through this process – or rather, perhaps, a necessary rationalisation. This seems to be driven by three components of his evolving practice: the proliferation and distribution of polyphonic 'voices' through spaces of time, pitch and timbre; the emergence of autonomous structures within polyphonic chains; and ideas from the electronic studio. The same process of permutation and mirroring of the number sequence suggests the number of musical objects to be distributed through the regions thus defined. Nono extrapolates from the soloist–orchestra dialectic to define the axes of this space: single horizontal lines and dense vertical groups, the melodic and harmonic projections of his material. The principle of dynamically changing densities and proportions also applies on a micro-level. Sound complexes reveal their internal texture; single lines become polyphonies of multiple voices. Early in the process Nono sets out a taxonomy of possible sound complex shapes, pursuing ideas developed in *Il canto sospeso* (Figure 6.4). These remain the archetypes, despite early experiments with more complex polyphonies.

Kolisch himself explained the derivation of the initial sound objects of *Varianti*, in an article in Scherchen's *Melos* contemporaneous with the premiere.[19] His technical account presumably

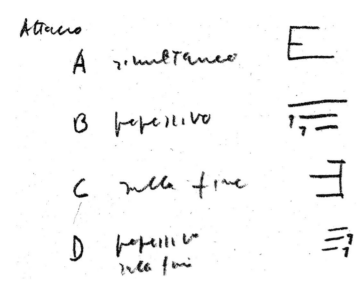

Figure 6.4 Varianti: sound complex shapes from sketches. (ALN 15.01.02/23 (detail). © The heirs of Luigi Nono. Reproduced by kind permission.)

comes directly from Nono. Figure 6.5 reproduces his illustration of the opening, which explains the obscure pitch sequence. In a development of serial permutation technique, the entrance of the first five-element group (C C♯ B D B♭) is measured from the start of the piece according to the initial number sequence (3 7 11 10 6), counted in triplets. Their duration is then measured by the same member of the number sequence, in the rhythm base of each voice. As the number increases, so does the differential and degree of offset. The following group of four four-voice pitches (E♭ A E G♯, offset by 2 1 5 9) is located by the same process, here relative to the fifth beat of the piece and again counted in the longest rhythm base, now semiquavers. However, to transform the aggregate sound shape, the E♭ and A are now counted from before the reference point, by two and one semiquavers respectively. The sound-complex shapes of Figure 6.4 are arranged clearly in sequence and permutation through the opening of the work: A B C D B D C A D A C B. As he distributes them through the score, they become less stark, more organic.

As density diminishes, longer rhythm bases are removed until only sextuplets and septuplets remain. Notes follow contiguously in the longest values, with an additional 'negative value' between two consecutive groups of the same density. An additional level of permutation thus elaborates Nono's opening strategy as values overlap. The positioning of individual notes according to sound shape further complicates their ordering. The rate of movement is increased in subsequent presentations by inverting longer values: 7–12 can become 6–1. These modulating oscillations of density, movement and register give Nono significant freedom to create a rich fabric of finely woven relationships: the four-voice G♯ of the second series (bar 4, beat 2), sustained diminuendo, ends in the next beat with the short, brisée four-voice G♯ of the next series. The series is no longer a 12-element sequence. Rather, it is a continuous unfolding of the chromatic space from which objects, figure and relationships emerge – a source of energy, not just notes. Nono's micro-compositional structures are like moving filters illuminating a constant chromatic background; their relative movement and focus produces perpetually changing spectra of peaks and troughs. The full chromatic space is evenly balanced. Its unfolding

Poetry and drama

Figure 6.5 Varianti: bars 1–3, annotated by Kolisch[20]

Poetry and drama

is not even or linear, however – its waves overlap. The evolving space between the last and first notes of successive series illustrates this clearly: the second series begins just before the last note of the first is sounded; the sequence is reversed in bar 4; the fourth C anticipates the third F♯ by a bar; the fifth C arrives at the centre of the fourth F♯; and the following two pairs coincide completely apart from a single septuplet F♯ symmetrically anticipating and delaying. Other structural resonances surround the formal scheme; an augmented fourth A–E♭ is held across the first double bar (end of bar 5), its transposition B♭–E across the next, and the four pitches together introduce the entrance of the soloist. Dynamics are organised on a six-level scale; a set of twelve values is completed with crescendos and diminuendos between adjacent levels, arranged in twelve permutations by pitch and duration in a different table for each density. This gives each aggregate sound shape a unique and shifting balance, and the evolving texture a constantly changing perspective within an architecturally managed scheme.

As the initial waves of density subside into an entire series of two-voice pitches, the energy of the piece allows for reduction to a single voice and the entry of the soloist with a single note. The violin line extends progressively from pairs of notes to sequences of five, separated by rests equal to the following value, terminating with another single note in bar 39. Kolisch describes this as the 'horizontalising' of the opening material.[21] The line shifts between rhythm bases according to the density of the sound shape formed with voices in the orchestra, following the principles already established. Nono plays with spectral–registral perception using aggregated harmonics in the low strings and the serialised use of playing *am Steg* (on the bridge). The sound space is given depth and perspective as instruments in the orchestra play single pitches against this texture, completing and further permuting the serial unfolding of pitch and duration. The woodwind play only in this section and in the presence of the solo violin, as if to materialise its *flautato*. Schaller sees bars 15–33 as the solo exposition of an implicit concerto form, 34–66 as its development. Certainly, the underlying movement of density changes from bar 34; the full range of 5 to 1 – presented in sequence and mirrored in bars 29–32 – is replaced by a spiralling 5 1 4 2 3. At the heart of this section lies the most continuous passage for the soloist: seven pairs of notes followed by six groups of three, all separated by their following value. The concluding orchestral bars 67–80 return to the overlapping linear density flow, now dissolving to single pitches, and can be read as a recapitulation of the opening.

In contrast to the continuous flow of part A, part B (bars 81–154) is fragmented and static. It functions as an other, a different but non-intersecting view of the same material, in a double bind like the odd and even sequences from which it is structured. The ebb and flow of contiguous phrases is mirrored between violin and orchestra; while orchestral phrases contract and expand through even, then odd numbers of notes, the soloist does the opposite. As the melodic arch of the violin is extended, only at the centre of this section (bar 114) is a full series of pitch, duration and dynamics presented. Nono achieves this textural definition by diminution, remapping the duration sequences on to one half or one quarter of their full range, vastly narrowing the range of difference in individual passages. The contrast between lines and blocks in section B is further enhanced by Nono's keen sense of the effect of notation on performance – time signatures change continuously – and by the superimposition of a grid of twelve pauses. This layer of fermata is a device for increasing the 'pluridimensionality' of time, to use Nono's term, that will persist until his final violin works. In his 1957 paper, Nono attributed the introduction of negative values and rhythmic substitution by subdivision to Maderna's *Quartetto per archi in due tempi*.[22] Here, in addition to the use of negative values between phrases, Nono inserts them into longer values together with note repetitions. As Kolisch points out, repetition now replaces layering in Nono's investigation of the unison.[23]

Poetry and drama

Repetition also becomes part of the complex vocabulary and rhetoric of the solo violin. Throughout the work, single values are played *pizzicato*; short subdivisions are now also played *col legno battuto*. Like language itself, the violin line is a product of superimposed layers of structure and relationship; indeed, it develops a rich repertory of sounds with its own patterns and habits, like the phonemes of an unknown human language. Every note determined by the dynamic tables to be *ppp* is played *flautato*. Half of the soloist's notes are played *am Steg*, distributed according to patterns of odd and even values, as if to demonstrate an infinite regression of polyphony within unity; even the solo line consists of two voices, themselves rearticulated (Figure 6.6).

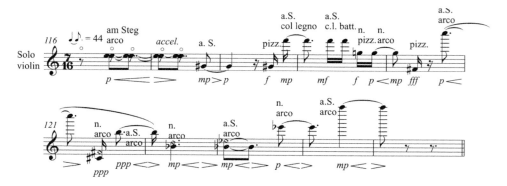

Figure 6.6 Varianti: solo violin, bars 116–25

Where is the ideology in *Varianti*, then? In some ways it is the most consistently radical of Nono's works from the 1950s; the audience at Donaueschingen seem to have heard it as such. Yet it remains in close contact with its roots in Venetian polyphony and, through Schönberg and Kolisch, the Viennese tradition, particularly in moments when the soloist leads his chamber group through waves of tempo change with finely detailed, eminently violinistic gestures; everything is lightness and movement. The mosaic musical surface might call into question Nono's denial of ever having composed 'pointilliste' music, yet the essential perception behind *Varianti* is precisely that no sound is disconnected, no sound is static, singular in number or manifestation. Under any magnification, a musical sound is constantly in movement – even its after-image is transformed in reverberation and as echoic memory is processed and replaced, as Nono's late work would explore. The act of listening itself is recognised as crucial to the way that sounds find form, become music. This infinite world opened through a single sound, multiplied, delayed and pitch-shifted, now begins to co-exist with the total chromatic and its own inner dynamics (such as the all-interval series), as the conceptual ground from which figure, form and work take shape.

The series is fully assimilated as an originating environment – self-reproducing and self-reflecting. Serial structures on all parameters are no longer sequences of objects, let alone themes of any kind, but motivating patterns of movement in both energy and detail. The score is the surface of their intersection, determined as Nono constructs and passes through the space they constitute, giving form to his own view and perspective. The underlying chromatic space itself tends constantly towards entropy; the minor second has a crucial directional role as every note has the imperative to chromatic expansion, an imperative that will drive Nono's harmonic language until the late works. This is never a static cluster-technique, however; a particular cluster does not define a sound object. Rather, they are stages in the ubiquitous potential of

Poetry and drama

notes or lines to reintegrate with their chromatic environment, a continuous passage between vertical and horizontal projections. The incremental chromatic thickening of lines, exploring the space between figure and ground, becomes integral to his technique in works such as *Como una ola di fuerza y luz* – analogous, perhaps, to the relationship between individual and group.

There are technical properties in common with the evolving languages of his peers – they are addressing similar issues – but the space of Nono's musical imagining and reasoning is configured quite differently, made of different fabric. It is both more integrated and more plastic. Technical discussions at Darmstadt in 1957 reflect shared concerns. In *Aléa*, Boulez considered how to achieve greater freedom in a coherent post-serial compositional process without recourse to chance techniques or improvisation. In his 'how time passes'. Stockhausen put forward his theory that rather than being orthogonally related, as Western concepts and notation might suggest, pitch and rhythm are different zones of the same continuous spectrum.[24] In *Varianti*, Nono achieves the managed compositional freedom that Boulez explored in *Le marteau sans maître*. He develops parallel devices – the serial manipulation of reduced groups of elements, the cross- or self-modulating of material, the local emergence of figure – but without the separation of surface from thought. He shares with Stockhausen a new way of conceiving of sound objects derived from the analytic/synthetic principles of electronic music, but without either the 'static music' tendencies of the electronic *Studie* or the need to create zones outside the fundamental architecture as in *Gruppen*.

The question of whether the musical text, the score, is arbitrarily fixed or static and a new awareness of the creative role of the performer were crucial common concerns. Tudor had presented part of Cage's *Music of Changes* the previous year, provoking a public disagreement between Boulez and Stockhausen; there was a race for ownership of the implications of Cage's work.[25] At Darmstadt in July 1957, Boulez's talk on 'Aléa' discussed the possible nature of material that would afford the performer greater structural freedom without compromising compositional integrity, to be partially realised in the *Third Piano Sonata*. In the final concert of the Summer School, Paul Jacobs performed Stockhausen's *Klavierstück XI* in which the performer plots their own trajectory through the material; Boulez's *Sonata* would not be heard until September. Nono eschews such artificial and soon-abandoned freedom, and would present his reasoning in a talk there two years later. His creative partnership with Kolisch, a genuinely open exploration of an individual performer's potential means of expression, is established prior to the development of notated material. The subsequent compositional process is predicated on this relationship which then influences every aspect of the work. This process would subtend Nono's later evolution; his creative relationship with Kolisch was the first in a long line of close collaborations. These would be not just technical or sonic. Many projects were to proceed through dialogue, but a dialogue in which for Nono his interlocutor is perhaps an idealised avatar. Nono enters their persona, musicianship and experience by building common cause on a much broader plane. He imagines a behaviour, a creativity, a deep empathy with the as yet unrealised project and with his evolving ethos, which may stretch and stimulate, and may even run ahead of his collaborator's own imagination.

Herein lies the ideological. Nono's evolving understanding of the role of the artist, of the mode of his contribution to the development of social and individual consciousness, meant that a work did not need to advertise its own ideology; the ideological is inherent in its nature and in the act of its production. *Varianti* is radical in both its conception and its composition. This radical conception is what necessitated a greater degree of formalisation – a coherence to resist the arbitrary and the attractors of past music and practice. He would later write to Mila that the concept of 'total determinierte Musik' was a device for 'crowing popes and anti-popes', but that *Varianti* was the closest he had come, 'for the discipline of study and to analyse the

Poetry and drama

result'.[26] *Varianti* explores what for Nono is an entirely new way of conceiving sound, a model in which what might previously have been considered the single 'note' – fixed in time, pitch and timbre – is now but one point on a dynamic continuum. This is the sense in which *Varianti* represents the very opposite of 'point' music. At the same time, the process of its creation acknowledges the social, situated nature of composition, a non-unique creative ownership. The very body language of the soloist, the movement and fragmentation of masses through the orchestra, are imagined anew. These two aspects are embodied in the technical essence of the work: the single sound played by the many, the single sound tending to its full chromatic environment.

There is a temporary bifurcation. In order to resist the pull of the emotional rhetoric of *Il canto sospeso* – and of those who would have liked him to produce more in that vein – and to be able to continue his investigation freely and coherently, Nono seems to have decided to separate two main strands of development. In *Varianti* he explored the nature of the sound object, its shape and constitution, its variable relation to time and its variable presentation in sequence or simultaneously, horizontally or vertically. He explored the possibility of evolving a new instrumental language through close cooperation with a particular performer. There remained the other side of *Il canto sospeso* to develop: vocal polyphony and the lyrical.

Earth and sea

In February 1956, Nuria and Luigi had moved into their own home, an apartment on the island of Giudecca. Separated from the centre of Venice by a wide canal navigable by large ships, Giudecca had been an area of poor housing and small shipyards. Nono would often observe that this was a 'workers' quarter'; he was happy to feel part of society here after the ambivalent tension of his relationship with the high bourgeois Venetian cultural world. Their upper-floor apartment faced away from the city, looking out across a small park to the open lagoon and the sea beyond. From now on, the dated flourishes with which he finishes his fair copies say not *Venezia* but *Giudecca*. With his back to the church of the *Redentore* and Venice in general, this light and peaceful place was the perfect working environment – separated yet still belonging. As later events would demonstrate, his physical environment was crucial to both Nono's *stato d'animo* and his creativity. Here he inhabited both land and sea, nature and city, poetic themes of two choral works that emerged during 1957–8: *La terra e la compagna*, a setting of poems by Pavese for soprano and tenor soloists, 24-part choir and orchestra, and *Cori di Didone*, extracts from Ungaretti's *La terra promessa* for 32-part choir and percussion.

A part of the audience, perhaps anticipating the raw emotion of *Il canto sospeso* or what the press repeatedly described as the 'Italian lyricism' of the Lorca settings, had found *Varianti* too challenging. Nono perhaps already had a sense that his reception from performers and audience would not be smooth. Following an unsatisfactory visit to Berlin to hear Scherchen conduct his music – he was not impressed by the attitude of the Berlin Philharmonic, the teaching of Blacher, the music of Henze and Stockhausen, the general level of organisation or the petty politics of musical life – he returned to Baden-Baden to await the start of Strobel's rehearsals for *Varianti*. 'I feel ever more isolated!' he wrote to Steinecke. 'Obviously the best thing is to concentrate on one's own work, but it's difficult when the others are so well organised. We'll see, when Strobel arrives tomorrow, but everything's strange in Donaueschingen.'[27] There, Kolisch performed *Varianti* on 20 October 1957, with Rosbaud and the Südwestfunk Symphony Orchestra. Not for the last time, critical response included not indifference but anger. 'True to tradition, this year's festival produced a much-hoped-for *scandale*', reported a less than sympathetic *Musical Times*. 'The murmurings, which began about half-way through the

Poetry and drama

composition, increased in volume and intensity, finally to explode into a bedlam of catcalls, whistles and boos when the final note had been split.'[28] Kolisch wrote to Nono that he had been sent about 60 reviews, all of the same opinion, 'describing the "scandal" with schadenfreude'.[29] Hübner was also at the premiere, describing the 'scandal-mongers' as 'laughable, immature peasants'.[30] Good grace was not in abundance at Donaueschingen that year. Henze's *Nachtstücke und Arien* was generally well received, but his composer peers were less patient with its musical language:

> From my seat I could see that already in the first bars Boulez, Stockhausen and my friend Nono got up together and left the hall quite demonstratively, such that everyone saw and was intended to see. This music begins in a sort of G$\sharp$ minor [. . .] they didn't want to listen.[31]

Having completed *Varianti*, Nono returned to contemplating possible subjects for the opera he was keen to finally work on, still planning a work for Darmstadt. Instead, it was Hübner who presented Nono with the opportunity to complete the long-standing Pavese project, a commission for the anniversary of his series *Das Neue Werk* in Hamburg.

'La terra e la compagna'

Nono seems to have had in mind setting poems from Pavese's 1951 collection *Verrà la morte e avrà i tuoi occhi* since encountering it on his first visit to Turin. He now returned to the poems not only in a spirit of structural and semantic intervention, but with a confident sense of textual polyphony. As in *Varianti*, this polyphony may take the form of multiplication and proliferation, or of a deconstructing exploration of inner complexity. Pavese's collection consists of two sequences of poems: *La terra e la morte* from 1945–6, and *Verrà la morte e avrà i tuoi occhi*, poems collected after the poet's suicide in 1950. Nono's notes show that he concentrated on the former sequence – mature examples of Pavese's poetics of myth. For Pavese, the role of the artist is to bring to light, to actuality, personal and collective mythologies evolved through history and childhood. The poetic event occurs when they are illuminated in a particular consciousness in terms of individual experience and reason.[32] This understanding of the performative action of art in the individual is close to a position stated often by Nono. Pavese's personal mythologies of nature and love, reflecting his childhood and a series of tormented relationships, are united in his own symbolic iconography: earth, hill, cloud, sea. The terse, constantly varying line lengths and a fundamental dualism of imagery must have resonated with Nono's own melos of thought. The political engagement that emerged in Pavese's post-war novels also finds expression in his poetry here, in the shape of the *compagna* – the female comrade companion.[33] In their reflection on love and death, these poems are united by a common unnamed female *tu* whom they all address. Nono's textual arrangement presents this *compagna* as both comrade and lover. He explored the structure and imagery of at least seven poems from the whole collection before deciding to start work with three from the first sequence: *Terra rossa terra nera*, *Tu sei come una terra* and *Tu non sai le colline*, all written in late October, early November 1945 following the end of Pavese's love affair with fellow author Bianca Garufi.[34]

Nono's final versions of these poems show a remarkable willingness to intervene in the text itself, not from disregard but because the poems are so thoroughly assimilated into his own creative process. Typewriter and an early duplicating machine are integral components of his composing environment. He makes changes to the texts that subtly alter their voice and

Poetry and drama

emphasis as he forms the three into a unitary composition of his own conception. As well as omitting some semantically redundant single-vowel words, he chooses not to set the final four lines of the first poem and the penultimate of the second. In omitting the lines that speak of the eternity of love, Nono puts Pavese's imagery directly into the present. The third poem loses its references to an unnamed woman, leaving a more material narrative of partisan martyrdom. The *compagna* of Nono's title replaces death in Pavese's; traces of mythologising are removed. There are also structural, compositional reasons for these changes. Nono seems aware of his tendency to binary vision and dialectical process: forwards/backwards, temporal/outside time, individual/group (whether sounds or people), external proliferation/internal complexity, positive and negative sound. This is evident in his successive analyses of the poems. The opening duality of *Terra rossa terra nera* establishes the fundamental behaviour of the poem. Nono's two analyses relate the poetic to structural, contrapuntal and rhythmic compositional elements (Figure 6.7a, b). In observing the patterns of binary images he considers their grouping and density, their relative weight and length. An architecture emerges, a flow of tension that finds a central still point at 'il tuo fiato riposa' ('your breath rests'). A third analysis, still prior to reducing the text, adds a possible distribution of soloists and chorus. It also incorporates a sketch of possible distributions of elements of the first two words – Te-rra ro-ssa – that connects the genesis of this work to other aspects of his thought: the textual fragmentation of *Il canto sospeso* and the repertory of aggregate sound shapes in *Varianti* (Figure 6.7c). Another finds a binary internal structure for the first section, allocating symmetrical sound shapes and internally mirroring patterns of permutation (Figure 6.7d).

Annotations indicate more degrees of vocal openness than just *bocca chiusa*, and hence a continuum of comprehensibility. An initial plan to set *Tu sei come una terra* for soloists against a choral version of *Terra rossa* was abandoned in favour of a more homogeneous, flexible palette.

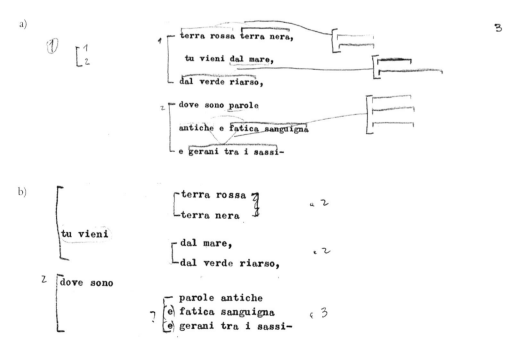

Figure 6.7 La terra e la compagna: successive text analyses. (ALN 16.01.02/1r /2/4/7 (details). © The heirs of Luigi Nono. Reproduced by kind permission.)

Poetry and drama

c)

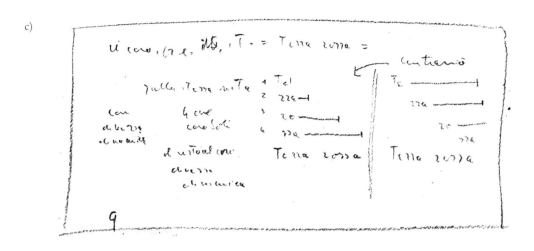

d)

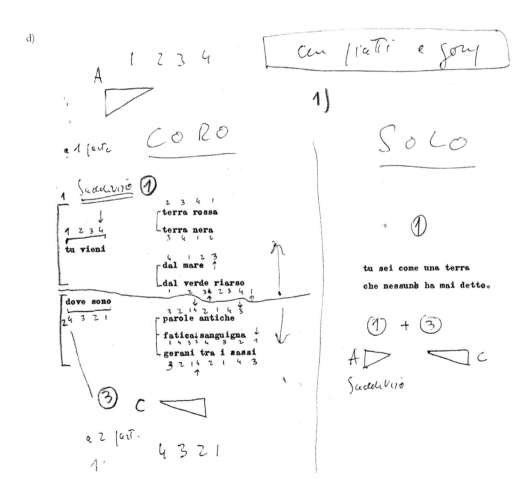

Figure 6.7 continued

Poetry and drama

Nono experimented with parallel timbral parameters in voices and instruments, degrees of *bocca chiusa* and *flautato*, but it soon became clear that the poetry itself gives shape and rhythm to colour. The spatial disposition of performers was also an early consideration – expanding concentric semicircles of soloists placed within the chorus, wind and strings, and percussion.

In the event, the final four lines of *Terra rossa* are lost not only for reasons of relative emphasis but because they fall outside the parallel four-part structure that Nono builds between the first two poems. The balanced binary architecture of *La terra e la compagna* is sufficiently self-contained that its projected continuation would have been problematic. Its total length – 160 bars – is fixed early in the sketches and divides almost exactly into the two sections of the finished work.[35] In the first, the poems *Terra rossa terra nera* and *Tu sei come una terra* are set simultaneously for chorus with percussion; in the second, *Tu non sai le colline* (soloists, chorus and orchestra) is followed by an instrumental postlude for flutes, brass and percussion. In spatial terms, the first half divides in two horizontally, the second vertically; a sketch shows three blocks of diminishing size.[36] An unrealised further part was to set the third poem of Pavese's sequence, *Anche tu sei collina*, using a pattern of echoes, a fundamental principle of his later work. Its last stanza 'Sará dolce tacere' is the point in Pavese's poetry to which Nono would shortly return.

As the work forms in his imagination, Nono is able to manage the sculpting of such a complex abstraction by a meticulous recording of his evolving thought. He creates critical distance from his own musical logic:

> <u>RULE</u> you always subdivide the longest value in a group
> Just one square – for the groups – for dynamics
> A square is necessary for the sounds
> To use –
> whole values (lento)
> subdivided values (più mosso)
> In the groups: dynamics remain fixed for the whole group, <u>according to the first note</u>
> according to the square
> So: the rhythm base, in the subdivision of values, remains simple from H > h.[37]

As is his recent practice, pitch and rhythm are related by being derived from the same abstract archetypes. The initial line of a number square (12 1 11 2 10 3 9 4 8 5 7 6) reverses the expanding pattern of the all-interval series; successive lines rotate by one place. He returns to generating pitch material by using this 'carré' as a displacement matrix. Nono no longer needs to carefully rule out patterns on squared paper; he maps out the note sequences directly on manuscript. His technical means are substantially those of his recent works; however, new properties emerge as they are refined, reflected, brought into new relationships and used to address new challenges. The tightly interwoven parallel texts of the first section are a case in point: how to successfully articulate both the simultaneous unfolding of the two poems and the inner dualities of the first? The sequence of decisions makes clear his requirements: an initial trial using the square in order from the top results in too polarised a texture – largely single notes or groups of four or five. He recommences, starting from below to generate a more satisfactory distribution, as his own analysis shows: 36 single pitches, 29 dyads, 15 triads, a tetrachord and two pentachords.[38] *Terra rossa terra nera* moves sequentially forwards and backwards through this sequence, its empty positions marked by percussion.

Schaller has proposed the Bachian cantata as a model for *La terra e la compagna*, in terms of its form, forces and polytextuality.[39] For the first part of the work (bars 1–78) a madrigal motet

Poetry and drama

is a more precise analogy, or perhaps a chorale-based opening chorus. Until the last three lines of the poem, *Tu sei come una terra* is sung only by the tenors. Against the convoluted serial permutation of *Terra rossa terra nera* in the other voices, the tenors set out the all-interval series in sequence and only in single notes before embarking on their own process of permutation, a cantus firmus requiring a clear exposition to be understood against its contrapuntal derivatives. Only the penultimate two lines, set contiguously, spread into the altos. The aggregate pitch material thus reflects Nono's fundamental binary archetype: as one layer balances its forward and backward motion – constantly in movement but never prioritising a single direction – the other pursues a continuous evolution. The text is dispersed by syllable throughout; the performers become a single subject through which Pavese's images can proliferate and be expressed simultaneously. Nono explained the relationship in his lecture *Text – Musik – Gesang* at Darmstadt in 1960; through the syllabic fragmentation of the texts he seeks to create additional semantic-aesthetic dimensions.[40] This commences immediately with the parallel statements of 'terra rossa' and 'terra nera', their respective syllables distinguished only by their different patterns of rhythm base. An analogous presentation of 'tu vieni' and 'tu sei' in bar 3 allows the second poem to merge with the second line of the first. The constant flux of density amplifies the constantly changing colour of the voice itself. Only at 'tu tremi nell'estat'' (bars 62–4) does the poem take over the entire choir. Vocal and chromatic density describe an informal spectrogram of the text, opening and closing through 'tu tremi nell'', to explode on the second syllable of 'estate' – Monteverdi and Meyer-Eppler in equal measure. This 15-voice chord uniquely occupies the full chromatic space, to dissolve into '. . .te, . . .e' through the final elements of the all-interval series to its last note, a single tenor F♯.

The subtle flexibility of poetic rhythm presents a significant challenge, and leads Nono to add a new level of mediation to his technical repertory. Early in the process he experiments with expanding and contracting rhythmic sequences. The question seems to be how to retain the momentum and proportion of poetic foot without resorting to pulse or figure: 'avoid the sense of the 'gruppetto' or the decorative [. . .] no equal values in the rhythmic subdivision'.[41] His solution is to reduce the number of duration values to different sets of four, on to which the values read from the number square are mapped by a sequence of matrices. Perhaps a product of the four-part common structure Nono saw in the poems, the number four becomes a governing element; 'SERIE 1 2 3 4 !!!!' he writes above possible rhythmic sequences.[42] Permutations of these numbers then determine the length of note sequences: the threads from which sound complexes, setting individual passages of poetry, are woven. The initial 'base ritmica > 4 5 6 7' provides the subdivisions of the quaver beat for the second and third parts;[43] the finer grained rhythmic palette of 5, 6, 7 and 8 is contiguous with the sequence lengths in the first. Dynamics for the whole work are also determined by a double-mediated serial process. Ten twelve-element sequences of dynamics each have their own internal symmetries and repetition patterns. Crescendos and diminuendos are introduced after the initial series. Levels remain generally within the range *ppp-mf*, with occasional instances of *f*, until two instances each of *ff* and *fff* appear in the penultimate series. Each sequence is then subject to Nono's habitual rotational permutation and indexed by pitch to generate a perpetually evolving dynamic profile with non-repeating traces of its internal patterning and a broad dynamic architecture.

A passage from the centre of this first part illustrates the construction of Nono's own musical–poetic response to Pavese (Figure 6.8). 'Parola' ('word') links the two overlapping poems. *Terra rossa* here has a characteristic dualism – 'tu dura e dolcissima parola' – the components of which are set simultaneously. The initial 'tu', a single F in bar 31, echoes the same note that begins 'Tu sei come una terra' in bar 4. The syllables of that poem are set sequentially to continuous permutations of the all-interval series. Durations are read sequentially

Poetry and drama

from the number square and mapped to values of 1, 3, 6 and 10, which are then used in further permutations of the rhythm bases 1/5, 1/6, 1/7 and 1/8. Within each phrase of text, notes overlap by the minimum possible to create a continuous line.[44] As these melodic chains link together to form larger constructs, their varying length is the horizontal image of their continuously changing density. They contrast with the more fragmented and reordered syllables of the previous poem. The three substantive words of the phrase – 'Dura', 'DOLcissima', 'PArola' – appear almost simultaneously at the end of bar 32. The same minimally overlapping principle is used to construct the four lines that constitute the whole sound complex to which 'tu dura e dolcissima parola' is set, but their variable density (single pitches to triads), the simultaneous fragmentation of words and the distribution of consecutive syllables between lines makes this brief passage an indivisible entity. Nono no longer calls these sequences 'voices' in his sketches, although he still uses the archaic 'a 4' to describe polyphonic density. Their entry is determined using a technique developed from the sound-complex shapes of *Varianti*, now formalised, that relates the vertical to the horizontal, polyphonic complexity to melodic succession. At this point, the pitch material from the displacement matrix has been presented forwards and is now being worked through in retrograde. Four such lines, each of four elements, work backwards from positions 22, 18, 14 and 9. Empty positions in the pitch material are represented by cymbal strokes of appropriate length. The minimally overlapping durations are now mapped onto values of 3, 4, 8 and 10 in the same rhythmic divisions of 5, 6, 7 and 8. The successive entrances of the four lines are calibrated to shape the passage as a whole: after the second element of the initial sequence (element 21 in the pitch material: dyad A–E♭)

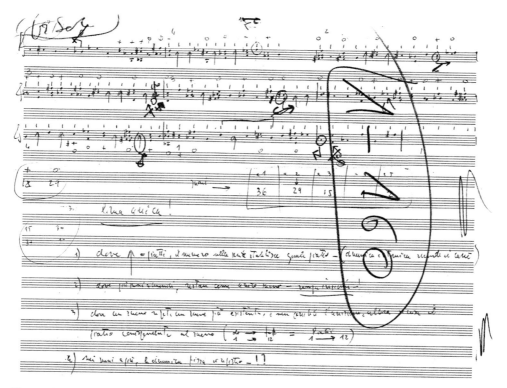

Figure 6.8a La terra e la compagna: offset pattern (ALN 16.03.02/03vsxa (detail). © The heirs of Luigi Nono. Reproduced by kind permission.)

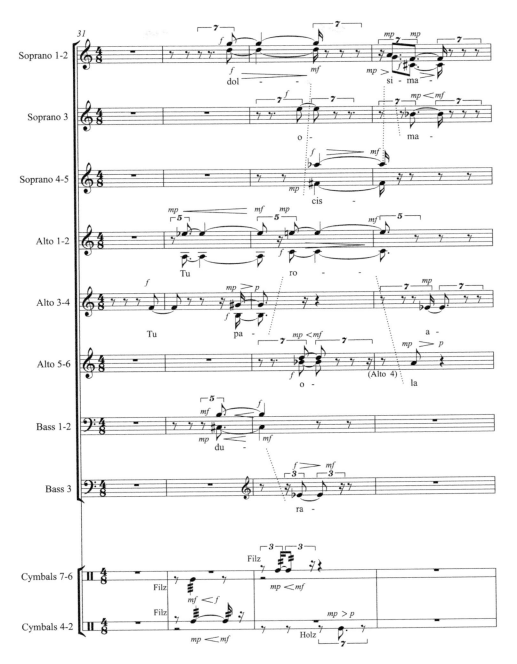

Figure 6.8b La terra e la compagna: bars 31–4. (ALN 16.03.02/03vsxa (detail). © The heirs of Luigi Nono. Reproduced by kind permission.)

Poetry and drama

enters by the principle of minimal overlap, the next two sequences (elements 18 and 14, both empty hence represented by cymbal rolls) enter together precisely at the end of element 22, on the second quaver of bar 32. The fourth sequence (element 9: dyad G♯–B) enters at the end of 14, on the last semiquaver of the same bar.

After his careful early analysis of the poems, Nono knows how the number of individual sounds in a particular complex will relate to the passage of text; his architecture is multimodal as well as multidimensional, a polyphonic–phonetic–semantic network of relationships and densities. Precise phoneme placement is determined in the process of drafting the score, together with register. Note combinations are kept largely within the same tessitura to retain the harmonic properties of the pitch material; consecutive elements of a line may stay in the same register to enhance the comprehensibility of a compound word. Thus 'dura' and 'dolcissima' are placed in opposite registers, for example – an explicit word-painting to embody Pavese's binary opposition. The melos of 'dolcissima', with its expressive chromatic accent on the second syllable, short third and descending exit, follows the Italian precisely.

The architecture of the second part of the work, *Tu non sai le colline*, is generated by the unfolding of the all-interval series itself in another four-part structure. Durations and dynamics are governed by the same devices as previously, the rhythm bases now geared down a step to 1/4, 1/5, 1/6 and 1/7. Elements are again overlapped in threads of 1–4 elements, some doubled or replaced by percussion. Nono extends and rationalises the pitch doubling of *Varianti*, extending it into a horizontal dimension through a dynamic pattern of repetition and echoes. He plots the unfolding pitch contour and aggregate rhythm against the draft score to have broad control of the rate of change or expansion. This new sculptural layer mediates the inherent wave motion of the series; it allows the kind of focus on single pitches or small changes that will characterise some of the late works. Here, pitches are added roughly every twelve beats; the number of echoes is determined by the rhythm patterns on to which the duration sequences are mapped. The placement of text and dynamics is such that the first in a series of repeated pitches is not necessarily heard as the prime; the listener perceives anticipations and pre-echoes as well as reflections. The shaping of form is therefore crucial; each of the four sections concludes with a clear cadential gesture.

Through the first 16 bar section, solo and chorus tenors present the first part of the poem to a single exposition of the first half of the all-interval series. The clearest text, 'e il nome' ('and the name') is announced on the final repeated E♭ – a point of arrival. Echoes and anticipations disperse the sound of the poem across time. Against this, the solo soprano echoes vowels from the text, and with the flutes and trumpet sets out the second half of the series through bars 90–4. Replacing the female figure removed from the text by Nono, a soprano vocalise leads the wind and percussion through four complete series in the next seven bars, their overlapping permutations retaining traces of the underlying expanding patterns such that the final notes outline a clear cadential gesture.[45] This substitution of sound for poetry allows a retrospective re-evaluation of the work to this point: if text can disappear into pure vocal sound or be fragmented into its constituent elements, then its transformation into instrumental sound is no less part of the poetry. Vocal and instrumental elements are part of the same acoustic–semantic space.[46] The choral tenors, joined by the soloist, recommence the series at the beginning of a third section in bar 102, note by note, syllable by syllable, moving through the series followed by its retrograde twice. They are initially accompanied by a complex 18-part string texture using only the first half of the series. This setting of 'uno solo di noi' again recalls Monteverdi's use of the tenor voice, here 'et in tre unum sunt' in the motet *Duo Seraphim*; the word-painting is unapologetic. The solo tenor stops at 'fermò' ('stopped'). At 'vide il cielo' ('saw the sky') the strings stop and a peal of four cymbals introduces the phrase from tenors alone, a four-voice

Poetry and drama

descending tetrachord. A sudden switch of colour is characteristic of the work; 'chinò il capo e morì' ('bowed his head and died') returns to the solo tenor, now accompanied by the wordless chorus with repeated echoes. That they sing only the second half of the series, now in retrograde, makes it clear that these two sounds, these two phrases, are complementary views of the same essence. In a brief coda (bars 123–30) four presentations of the series are incrementally realigned, restoring the clarity of the opening of this part of the work. As the solo and choral sopranos outline elements of the series, it becomes clear that the twelve different cymbals and tam-tams represent its pitches, confirmed by their two final 12-note peals.

'Pitched' and 'unpitched' have ceased to be polarised concepts in Nono's increasingly sophisticated understanding of his sound world. Analogously, 'meaning' is not restricted to the presence of text. The fragmentation of text, the use of wordless voices and the distribution of musical material between clearly pitched and what the listener now hears as complexly pitched instruments all serve to mark out a space for the exploration of poetic ideas in which word-carrying voices are one reference point. Voices pass their semantic tokens seamlessly into a zone of more subtle development. An early note in the sketches shows how the technical–conceptual means derive directly from the early electronic studio and Meyer-Eppler's phonetics: 'so Klangartikulation from 1 and possible variations ALL ACCORDING TO THE VOICE! Absolutely reversible – voices as instruments – that is, it is possible that the soloists become Klangartikulations of the instruments.'[47]

Words do not emerge from the surface of a non-semantic ocean; neither is there any artificial mapping of ideas or symbols to sound. The complex polyphony of Nono's response to Pavese's work is woven across this entire space; there is therefore no sense that it has ceased with the absence of voices in the short concluding third part of the work. Having been drawn in to attend to the subtle gradations of timbre, articulation and dynamics of the percussion, the listener follows an interplay of ideas and emotions as they recommence their permutations, the rhythmic material now moving through a faster-changing sequence of mappings to sets of four duration values. This is thrown into relief by a layer of harsh, direct wind, insistently echoing elements of a total, unordered chromatic series in closed position: four notes each for trombones, flutes and trumpets. Stenzl interprets this a symbol of war; certainly, it recalls the references to unyielding brutality of *Il canto sospeso*. Perhaps for this reason there is no assimilation; the intrusion dissolves into pitched percussion and gives way to the subtle disourse of cymbals and tam-tams as they re-establish their natural serial order. Their final realigning peals seem to return to nature and its cycles, the originating references of the poems themselves.

This formal wholeness may partially explain why Nono did not pursue the setting of *Anche tu sei collina* commenced in the sketches and to which he would return. The number '161' at the head of his typed copy of the poem leaves little doubt as to his intention: *La terra e la compagna* lasts 160 bars. Certainly, this was the basis of his dealings with Hübner at the NDR. In December 1957, a month before the premiere, Hübner wrote:

> If you don't think you will be able to finish 'La terra e la compagna', and if you have come to the conclusion that your work must have a broader cyclic form, then with a heavy heart we must make do with the first part. We must at all costs avoid the impression that this is an unfinished work. [. . .] In the meantime, the choir have worked very intensively on your piece, and I now have the impression that they have overcome the difficulties and that we are assured a good performance.[48]

This hope was to be fully realised. *La terra e la compagna* was premiered in Hamburg on 13 January 1958, conducted by Rosbaud in an extraordinary programme that also included the

Poetry and drama

first performance of two of Boulez's *Improvisations sur Mallarmé* – to become part of *Pli selon pli* – and followed that of Schönberg's *Die Jakobsleiter* the day before. Such an event attracted wide international attention; in a grey world, it was inevitable that references would abound to the music's lyricism, its 'southern' qualities. However, Nono's work achieved not only praise but critical comprehension. Josef Haüsler wrote:

> A new relationship between word and sound is presented here; surprising references to half-forgotten musical forms of the middle ages arise behind its patchwork of sound shapes, as if from under a thin skin. No doubt – Nono's was the most unusual work of the evening.[49]

Heinz Joachim echoed: 'Luigi Nono pushed ahead farthest into the new musical world with his choral work'.[50]

Following such success, why did Nono not immediately continue with the Pavese project? An opportunity was already scheduled: the postponed commission from the city of Darmstadt brokered by Steinecke. He now had half a year clear to concentrate on such a symbolic undertaking, interrupted only by an occasional work to celebrate Strobel's sixtieth birthday. *Piccola gala notturna veneziana in onore dei 60 anni di Heinrich Strobel* consists of five series in five layers with five sets of durations, orchestrated for a chamber group of two clarinets, pitched percussion and strings: a note for each of Strobel's years.

Nono's Pavese settings are not poetic, they are poetry. The madrigalisms are not illustrations bolted on to an emotionally appropriate but otherwise autonomous musical entity. Like Pavese's symbols, they are points of entry, emergent figures on the surface of a network of association, meaning and structure that draw the listener in to engage with the artist and allow them to explore their own experience and response. The multiple directionality of time is a vital property; *reflection* is no mere metaphor, it requires the construction of a temporal and referential environment in which it can move freely. In this sense, *La terra e la compagna* is precisely not dramatic; its temporal mode is reflective and Pavese's broader social–political stance, while well understood by one as well acquainted with his work as Nono, is opaque to an unprepared listener. The possibility of a new kind of music theatre remained the imperative focus of Nono's imagination.

'Cori di Didone'

Nono declined an invitation to celebrate the new year at Gravesano with Scherchen, Steinecke and their families in order to discuss a new opera text with Alfred Andersch.[51] Andersch occupied a unique position in the post-war re-establishment of German literature. An ex-socialist who had lived through Nazism in Germany and deserted from the army in Italy, he had explored the conflicts and self-questioning of the German experience in his 1952 autobiographical novel *Die Kirschen der Freiheit*, of which Nono had a copy. Nono and Andersch were acquainted through Nono's work with South-West German Radio, where Andersch was responsible for cultural programming.[52] While their opera project was not to be realised, Nono would acknowledge the role of Andersch in the evolution of his concept of 'azione scenica', leading to *Intolleranza 1960*.[53]

Contact with Ungaretti had resumed with a more regular rhythm since the idea of a work for the theatre had consolidated as a major goal during the composition of *Il canto sospeso*. Nono had courted the poet through a protracted correspondence in the hope of persuading him to collaborate on such a project. Ungaretti sent his *La Terra Promessa* in March 1956 along with

Poetry and drama

a tantalisingly ambiguous response: 'I have never tried writing for the theatre, and I wonder whether perhaps I don't have the necessary attitude. But maybe I could also do something in this area, so new for me, something really of the moment.'[54] *La Terra Promessa* made the prospect even more beguiling for Nono; it is a fragmented, hypertextual gloss on the tragic states of Dido and Palinurus from Virgil's *Aeneid*, in musically highly suggestive forms: canzone, choruses, recitative, variations, finale. *Canzone* had its origins during 1932–5, before Ungaretti's return from Brazil, and evolved through personal loss, the national tragedy of fascism and what the poet perceived as the autumn of his own creative powers.[55] The *Cori di Didone* 'dramatically describe the separation of the last glimmers of youth from a person, or from a civilization'[56] *Finale*, also set by Nono, finds consolation in the repeated wave-like refrain 'the sea, the sea'. The 'reappearances of moments of happiness [. . .] of the delirium of love 'are vital to the poetry and, we must imagine, to Nono's empathy with it; they are the truth that validates the pain, the evidence of faith and perpetual resistance to the inevitability of loss.

Subsequent correspondence suggests that while Ungaretti, a very public literary figure, did not want to give up on the possibility of collaboration, either it was difficult for him to find the time for such a major undertaking or he found technical difficulties in its poetic conception. In one letter he mentions that Cesare Zavattini, the screenwriter of neo-realist films, including *Ladri di biciclette* and *Umberto D.*, had come up with a possible idea; in another he enthuses about the unlimited expressive potential of electronic music.[57] It seems to have been yet another suggestion from Ungaretti in October 1957 that someone else might take on the project that convinced Nono to go ahead with existing texts by his elusive friend – either in the absence of any alternative in the near future, or perhaps in the hope of finally convincing Ungaretti.[58] A possible long-term operatic subject seems to have arisen soon thereafter: *The Diary of Anne Frank*, the publication of which in Italy in 1955 had aroused as much emotion as in the rest of the world.

While Nono was working with the texts of the *Cori di Didone* from *La Terra Promessa*, Ungaretti wrote with more detailed ideas for an opera based on Anne Frank's diary. He still intended to delegate the detailed work, now to his assistant Mario Diacono. The approach he outlines suggests some structural analogy with the *Cori di Didone*:

> everything will take place within the last 24 hours of the diary. It will be the task of the chorus to convey the events that happened before, with commentary on the state of mind of Anne and the states of mind of the historic moment. We have thought that the whole performance should last no more than 45 minutes, and we should not exceed 200 lines of text. I thought of the essentiality and linearity of Greek tragedy, in the spirit [. . .] and dramatic complexity and intensity of today.[59]

Nono replied immediately:

VIVA VIVA
[. . .]
No limits on the time [. . .] as you think fit.
Your news helps me enormously.
In fact it's a difficult period for me:
It seems to me that everything is getting ever more difficult! New technical and
    expressive problems emerge continuously.
[. . .]

Poetry and drama

> your idea, the last 24 hours, is just right – with the choruses – one problem: how to represent the figure of Anne on stage – perhaps hearing her <u>but not seeing her</u> – but we'll see –
>
> IN THE MEANTIME: I am working on your choruses from 'La Terra Promessa'!
> A composition for:
> – 2 soprano soloists
> – chorus
> – percussion
> [. . .]
> there would be just ten choruses – <u>with your permission</u> –
> I am studying the composition of each chorus in terms of your use of vowels and consonants: often and marvellous!!!
> [. . .] Because then in the choir I will use the consonants and vowels as phonetic elements in themselves, constitutive of the word – today Prof. WINKEL [*sic*] from the Technical University of Berlin arrived to discuss the possible musical use of consonants (and pieces of consonants) and vowels – [60]

Nono included examples of how he planned to use the sonic patterns of Ungaretti's verses – the rhythms of repetition of particular vowels, for example – in building a material relationship between poetry and music. In June, as well as expressing his gratitude for Nono's new undertaking, Ungaretti was able to report that Diacono had made a first draft of the text; Nono was already in Cologne, staying with Stockhausen, to attend initial rehearsals of *Cori di Didone*.[61]

Were Nono's difficulties with the development of his music–theatre concept, or with the task now in hand, the composition of *Cori di Didone*? His initial conception had included the sopranos Ilse Hollweg, soloist in the premiere of *La terra e la compagna*, and the American Gloria Davy, whom he had heard at Donaueschingen the year before. From the twenty-one *Choruses descriptive of the state of mind of Dido* in Ungaretti's *La Terra Promessa*, Nono considered twelve, reduced them to nine plus the final poem of the collection *Finale*, then eventually to numbers II, III, VII, XII, X and *Finale*, set for thirty-two part chorus and percussion. Again, he monitors the emergence of the work, its language and form, through a process of careful textual and musical triangulation. The poems are analysed in even greater detail than before; his experience with Pavese, the encouragement of Ungaretti himself and the technical concepts from Winckel and Meyer-Eppler give Nono renewed confidence. His increasingly essentialist musical material is tirelessly explored for potential, as are the possible permutations and distributions of his performing forces: extravagant (32 professional voices) yet elemental (human voices and percussion); in the most absolute binary opposition, and yet a single palette within which Nono can construct relationships and networks. Nono's sketches bespeak the influence of scientific and technological models, the discourses of linguistics and the electronic studio. At the same time, the text is physically present, a performed reality. Thirty years later, Nono would still recall the poet's voice, his considered consonants and rapid vowels.[62]

The kind of materials at his disposition are incrementally rather than radically different to previous compositions, but as he adds layers to his own practice the graphical evidence suggests that the conceptual models within which he understands and manipulates the materials, turns them to his expressive needs, are informed by these new discussions. If his textual analyses, as exemplified by those he sent to Ungaretti, derive from acoustic aspects of linguistics, his patterns of waves and blocks of musical material are those of early synthesis techniques.[63] These are informal devices – instruments for the development of his own musical ideas rather than symbolic structures to be mapped directly on to a composition – and yet in their increasing

Poetry and drama

precision are beginning to acquire a more formal nature. Could this be one of his technical-expressive problems? To someone as unafraid of the consequences of his own thought as Nono, the pull of formalism must have been clear: a science and technology-derived objectivity, a new repertoire of historically and socially topical models that address the most pressing musical issues. And yet this very coherence of thought is motivated by a deep emotional attachment, an expressive need to which formalism could represent a fundamental threat. The reconciliation of these imperatives may have been the difficulty he described to Ungaretti.

Perhaps for this reason the global architecture of *Cori di Didone* does not need to have the tight fractal structure of *La terra e la compagna*. The poems are already a gloss of meditations on an unseen drama, so even with their further filtering and reordering the underlying dramatic thread remains intact; formal proportions reflect those of the texts. The virtual drama of the poems becomes a virtual sound-theatre of even more dimensions in its encounter with Nono's evolving understanding of music and language. Not only syllables but consonants and vowels are now considered separately, their sonic properties distributed beyond the voices into cymbals and tam-tams. As Nono would point out in *Text – Musik – Gesang*, the phonetic and the semantic are inseparable; musical poetry transcends the explicit linear presentation of text. Such a mobile treatment of the poems required firm control of musical substance. Ligeti cited *Cori di Didone* in an article discussing the post-serial handling of form and material and the recent focus on more global aspects:

> Nono has chosen the chromatic scale itself for his raw material; this is really no longer a series but simply a regulator to ensure an even distribution of the 12 notes. The vertical disposition of this material no longer results in a piling up of neighbouring tones. It is no longer primarily the intervals that constitute the structure but relations of density, distribution of registers and various displacements in the building up and breaking down of the vertical complexes. [...] Nono's attention is concentrated mainly on the construction and dismantling of piles of layers (which represent in a way a macroscopic projection of attack and decay processes that are not usually analysable by the human ear), and in this context a pitch-series, however artfully constructed, would have been no use to him at all – it would have gone astray and succumbed in a network of structures such as these.[64]

Looking at the sketches one might take issue with some points, but Ligeti's analysis must reflect discussion and perception at Darmstadt. Nono returns to the all-interval series – in Ligeti's words, 'an interpolation of two sequences of semitones in contrary motion' – from which he constructs the complexes described by Ligeti: vertical blocks sometimes tilted almost to the horizontal, or masses of short polyphonic chains formed as in the previous work, passed between voices one or occasionally heard two sounds at a time. The series flows through the six movements almost uninterrupted, a generator of layers and intervals in constant motion. This motion provides a vital middle level of musical movement that had been missing in the music of high serialism – something akin to harmonic rhythm in tonal music – as Nono controls the rate and shape of its waves: an ever-changing play of gravitational pulls, the same forces constantly re-expressed in new contexts. The ears of composer and listener are thus inevitably drawn to interval, to simultaneity and sequence.

As in *La terra e la compagna*, durations are drawn from a single carré. There the generating sequence represented the all-interval series in retrograde; here we have its retrograde inversion (1, 12, 2, 11 etc.), again remapped on to more focused sets of 4, 5 (part 3) or 6 (part 4) values within individual complexes. This enumeration of possible combinations of forces is a pre-compositional process through which Nono enters into the new work. Series of multiples of his usual rhythm bases (divisions of 3, 4, 5, 7) are plotted against a single beat; not a Carter-like scheme of metrical modulation but rather a means to observe the constant tempo oscillations of individual micro-structures relative to a stable grid. This is confirmed in a drawing that takes its cue from the studio: a duration-value sequence is aligned with the fragmented attack and decay of a sound complex and the positive segment of a sine wave (Figure 6.9).

Alongside his musical imagination, Nono is always studying his own process, the workings of his invention, to sharpen its focus and to create new affordances for his own thought. His polyphonic concept is developing new dimensions. As he begins to experiment with separating not just syllables but phonemes, Nono now draws whole passages of lines and blocks. His attention is moving to a broader perspective, a more formal view of detail, as Ligeti pointed out. More consistent use of a rhythmic guideline technique allows this greater mobility of focus in the process of composition. The rhythmic detail of individual complexes is sketched in different versions such that Nono can rehearse the implications of particular decisions and their relationship with the poems. As these structures are transferred into a working draft score, he notates the harmonic implications of the unfolding series in short score, identifying intervals to highlight or avoid. A guideline, a central skeleton of voice-leading, emerges, from which the sound complexes proliferate their individual intervallic material. Formal and local detail spring from the same sources, but Nono's practice has developed the openings for compositional intervention his creativity requires.

Figure 6.9 Cori di Didone: rhythm base and sound complex patterns from sketches. (ALN 18.03/04r (detail). © The heirs of Luigi Nono. Reproduced by kind permission.)

Poetry and drama

Figure 6.10 shows the guideline for the opening of *Cori di Didone*, with the secondary voices below. Both forward and retrograde readings of the number square are mapped on to the possible set of durations (2 5 7 9) such that both patterns initially produce alternations of 2 and 9 on rhythm bases from semiquaver to septuplet. As the pitch aggregate completes its expansion from single semitone to full chromatic, durations switch to 5 and 7 and the aggregate thins from the middle. Stasis is almost reached at 'sospeso', surely a conscious self-reference to his earlier work, suspended in a major seventh oscillating at the opposite pole to the opening of the piece. Nono matches the first twelve syllables of text to the guide rhythm such that their culmination in 'fuoco' (bar 8) marks a new rhythmic episode, placed on a new bar after

Figure 6.10 Cori di Didone: bars 1–9, reduction of rhythm and pitch

Poetry and drama

preparatory rests. Thirty voices present the entire series within the single word, compressed to the range of a single octave. 'fuoco' is fragmented into five different entries that carefully follow the spectral and amplitude envelopes of the spoken word, from the opening fricative 'f' to the final hollowed 'o'.

Such forensic treatment of words extends to their emotional weight. The elements of 'declinio' (suicide) in the fifth poem, for example, are widely separated in register, time and dynamics to poignant effect. Here is what for Nono is the centre of gravity of the work. As well as the printed dedication to Wolfgang and Hella Steinecke, there was another: to artists who had taken their own lives. 'The particular historical reference – the love between woman and man – of the myth (or reality) of Dido, is intended here in the broader sense of relationships between people, also tragically contemporary'.[65] Nono's use of the choir embodies this very principle: the collective as an interdependent set of individuals.

In general, Nono selects much more constrained sets of dynamic mappings than in the previous work, giving a greater sense of both continuity and emotional architecture. The percussion – cymbals and tamtams – become extensions of the voice. They substitute fricatives and plosives from the text and pitches from the series until in the fourth and fifth movements choir and percussion become equal partners. There, the percussion constitute a mirror: parallel with the voices in the fourth, following them in the fifth. In every sense the musical poem has an existence beyond its direct reciting. The painstaking poetic craft of the inner life of the succession of sound complexes distinguishes Nono's continuous flow of chromatic expansion from the clusters of Lutoslawski, the clouds of Ligeti or the stochastic fields of Xenakis. The additional stages of mediation, filtering and remapping retain the essential behavioural properties of the background serial flow while reducing the combinatorial complexity of its foreground implications. The material becomes tractable to compositional craft; 'structural' and 'poetic' decisions can inform each other continuously.

In the sixth section, for example, each line of Ungaretti's *Finale* ends 'il mare, il mare' ('the sea, the sea'), their lengths varying like the wavelengths of the sea itself. Nono's response is produced by the modulation of the text by several further layers of waves: the pitch series, the reduced set of durations, the flow of densities and the intervals that result directly from his structural decisions. A new concentration on intervals is now emerging. On the draft score he arranges the chromatic scale as a sequence of six augmented fourths. From this, he appears to select the pitches for the single-voice sounds; these become the symmetrical, salient structural moments of the movement, a role reinforced by their rhythmic placement and by their being sung in unison by the entire choir: F♯, C, B, F, F, B (represented by a tamtam), C, F♯. Nono even manages a pun; the unison B is sung to the word 'Fa'. The dyads are likewise prominent to the ear: perfect fourths or major seconds. These pitch attractors mark the ebb and flow of intervallic tension. A forward rolling motion is generated by the changing phase relation between this pattern of interval and density, and the refrain 'il mare, il mare', often fragmented, compressed or shared with the percussion. Two more flows or oscillations are superimposed. The wave motion of 'mare' is reflected in a pattern of echoes – the repetition of certain voices within a sound complex – like incoming waves at a point of stasis as the tide turns, their forward energy reduced. Prompted by the substitution of short values by bells, the choral texture is almost absorbed into the cymbals on three occasions. Consonants are taken by cymbals and tamtams, other sounds sustained in the choir *bocca chiusa*. The refrain at the end of the penultimate line illustrates these effects (bars 225–6). Both the unison 'Il' and the four-voice 'mare' are echoed wordlessly, extending the words to three rallentando bars; the repeat of the former comes inside the latter, like waves overlapping at the edge of the ocean.

Poetry and drama

Bernard Zimmerman and the Kölner Rundfunkchor had to perform *Cori di Didone* twice at its premiere in Darmstadt on 7 September 1958, to a rapturous reception. Von Lewinski was convinced: 'Nono made manifest the words of the poem as sound, colour and function [. . .], their semantic aspect – what the words "mean" – he likewise brought into the purely musical sphere and there he led [the words] to a heightened validity in a new, objectivised form.'[66] 'Nono's most mature work yet' was Joachim's opinion.[67] A week later, in an article contemplating the twin dangers of chance and formalism, Joachim identified this work as one 'which, despite the strictest construction, achieves the most intense spirituality and most moving expressive power'.[68]

Despite the widespread appreciation of the new work, 'maturity' may not have been the quality of greatest concern to the newest members of the Darmstadt community, now in its second decade. Artists of a new kind such as Mauricio Kagel and Nam June Paik were searching beyond the issues of post-serial composition and looked to Cage as having opened a new world, one that Boulez and Stockhausen were also tentatively exploring. Iddon suggests that the division over Cage was a proxy for that between 'the rising star of Stockhausen and the established force of Nono'.[69]

Diary and design: 'Composizione per orchestra n. 2: Diario polacco '58'

Inception

The composition of *Cori di Didone* had been followed by frustrated attempts to persuade Ungaretti to come to Darmstadt for the summer course – even the proposal of a conference with René Char, author of *Le Marteau sans maître* – all of which came to nothing. The success of *Cori di Didone*, the need for appropriate translations and Nono's continuous entreating had clearly maintained Ungaretti's interest, however. A year after their initial discussions, amid countless references to the difficulties of ageing – an issue that had preoccupied Ungaretti since the 1930s and partly shaped his subsequent poetry – he was still hoping that their Anne Frank project might be realised.[70] He sent Nono recent poems, including the final choruses from *La Terra Promessa* and two more in manuscript that would appear the following year in his *Il Taccuino del Vecchio*. Nono remained convinced that his venerable friend could help him imagine a new mode of music theatre:

> Once more – reading your latest 'choruses' I am convinced that only YOU can write
>   me the text for a new musical theatre –
> because of your humanity and your essence of the vital in life and nature –
> and it would be a new theatre –
> Dearest Ungaretti, do it!
> write me the text! (Anne Frank or something else)
> it is necessary for me!
> you can resolve everything –
> I will continue to bombard you with letters![71]

The weeks surrounding the premiere of *Cori di Didone* brought important new experiences. Nono and Maderna jointly led a workshop for young composers at Darmstadt, following the withdrawal of Boulez a month before the course. After an unsuccessful request to Stockhausen, Steinecke also recruited John Cage, already on tour in Europe.[72] A few days before *Cori di*

Poetry and drama

Didone, Stockhausen came to give *Music in Space*, a talk based on his experiences in the studio and with *Gruppen*, his major work for three orchestras premiered the previous March. The following day, John Cage and David Tudor presented *Indeterminacy*, 'a lecture on composition which is indeterminate with respect to its performance', the centrepiece of *Composition as Process* and of their residency.[73] European composers were already acquainted with the music of Cage and his circle – the correspondence between Cage and Boulez, the role of Tudor as a highly praised performer and the involvement of Maderna in presenting works such as Earle Brown's *Available Forms II* all attest to this – but his visit to Darmstadt represented a symbolic confrontation with mature serialism. As has often been observed, Cage was perceived to resist the idea of performer improvisation as much as Boulez had in *Aléa*. Here his concern was with formal indeterminacy: its vital role in the music of Wolff and Brown and its ineffective use in Stockhausen's *Klavierstuck XI*. The third lecture, *Communication*, makes pointed reference to Boulez's absence; Nono and Maderna escaped his gaze, but nobody in the room could have remained unaffected. Nono's considered response would come in a talk at Darmstadt two years later, *Geschichte und Gegenwart in der Musik von Heute* (*History and presence in the music of today*).[74]

Steinecke asked Nono to edit an issue of the *Darmstädter Beiträge*, and Nono proposed that it should be dedicated to the issues raised by Cage's interventions. In October he had asked Stockhausen, Ligeti, Tudor and Brown to contribute, and planned to contact Boulez.[75] Later that year, after beginning work with Calvino, he told Steinecke that this was becoming impossible. He had hoped to assemble the responses of fellow composers, but Cage was more interested in the views of critics such as Metzger: 'mit allem Metzgerei geht es nicht' ('with all that butchery it doesn't work').[76] As an alternative, he proposed inviting contributions from composers in different countries, to assemble an international view of the state of new music. In the event, the volume would publish the texts of that year's Darmstadt presentations. Nono's relationship with Cage was certainly not negative. Cage visited the Nonos in Venice in February 1959, and a subsequent letter from Nono mentions a possible project for Rome with Maderna, Berio, Burri and Vedova, as well as the hope that he might work with Cage and Cunningham in the US.[77]

In October 1958, Nono headed to Poland, to the second *Warsaw Autumn* festival of contemporary music. The first festival had emerged two years earlier in the cultural momentum of the 'Polish October', as Władysław Gomułka led the communist state to some autonomy from the Soviet Union, restoring – however temporarily – a measure of national optimism and cultural independence. After the tragedy of the Hungarian uprising, Poland presented a positive alternative to Soviet communism. This first contact with Eastern Europe and some of the realities of a communist state clearly left a lasting impression on Nono. Such enthusiasm infused his meetings with Patkowski, the director of a new electronic studio, and Lutoslawski, whose *Funeral Music* he heard at the festival. It heightened already emotional encounters: visits to Krakow, the Warsaw ghetto and Auschwitz. On his return he wrote immediately to Hartmann:

> Just back from Poland!
> My most beautiful experience to date, as man-musician.
> Very important there: enormous hope!!!!!!!!!!!!!!!!!!
> Musical situation: verrrrrrrry beautiful
> Real friends there, mad-romantic-alive friends!
> On a human basis, no clique, no snobbery: one is as one works.
> The audience, 2000 people, enthusiastic for Schoenberg and Webern: *A Survivor from Warsaw* repeated three times [. . .]
> [. . .]

Poetry and drama

Now perhaps a plan for theatre-opera!!!!!!!!!!
Necessary for me: finally!!!!
Nothing else![78]

The most promising prospect for a music–theatre work to date arrived shortly thereafter. Replying to Nono's approach at the beginning of October, Italo Calvino expressed his interest in a joint project: a positive response facilitated by their mutual friend Mila. In January 1959, he sent a complete treatment, *Monica*. This story of a woman resistance fighter, love and life in post-war Italy must have had immediate resonance for Nono after the months spent with the writing of Pavese; in fact, its nearest successor is the dramatic setting of Pavese's poems in Nono's unfinished *Deolo e Masino* of 1965. Other preoccupations would intervene, but their plan to work together persisted. A further unrealised proposal, *La bomba addormentata nel bosco* (the sleeping bomb in the wood – a clear reference to *Sleeping Beauty*), anticipates the subject of his *Canti di vita e d'amore: Sul ponte di Hiroshima*. With Calvino's characteristic balance of formalism and fairy story, it examines reactions to an H-bomb that falls in a forest without exploding, until the only conclusion is that either the bomb or the contemporary world of human folly does not exist. This would have made a fascinating precursor to Berio's later work with Calvino, or Ligeti's *Le Grand Macabre*. Given the strength of Nono's imperative to write for the stage and Calvino's positive and detailed proposal, it is interesting to reflect on why there was no musical development. Perhaps even in the context of Nono's wider evolving ideas about music theatre, his creative response at this stage is lyrical, to the word. This is what allows his imagination to connect with the presence of music, with the act of performance. Calvino's subsequent observation on his circle of writers at this moment might apply equally to Nono: 'We were all content-driven, yet there were never such obsessive formalists as ourselves; we claimed to be a school of objective writers, but there were never such effusive lyricists as us.'[79]

The intensity of these experiences contributed to a growing self-confidence, a greater willingness to state his position without dogma but with penetrating clarity. Resistance to dogma, a sense of personal artistic freedom and responsibility, is a constant in Nono's ethos, but it seems to be at the front of his mind from the manifesto for the composition workshop in 1958 (quoted at the start of this chapter) to his text on *Diario polacco* a year later. It was this sense of an ethical imperative for the composer's presence to be continually embodied in the work, in the score, that came to a head in his talk on Cage and his public disagreement with Stockhausen. While Nono had not yet used the words of Mayakovsky in music, the poet was already an important reference point in his unceasing commitment to communism, the intensity of his emotional life and his tireless probing of the possibilities of poetic communication: 'I wanted to unite nascent thoughts with a language that could renew feelings, expression itself.'[80] The dissolving sense of common project at Darmstadt may also have fed into Nono's growing feelings of isolation. Nono had agreed a new commission with Strobel for 1959: a work for solo flute and orchestra. Initially for Donaueschingen, the premiere was rescheduled for Boulez's *Domaine musical* in Paris and Gazelloni was engaged. Sketches for a work for solo flute, tapes and orchestra are marked 'Musica per Donaueschingen'. Through Schott, Strobel heard of Nono's plan – now two flutes and tapes – and instantly wrote to dissuade him. 'Obviously you can write what you want,' he generously observed, 'but I have to withdraw the commission and ask that the advance be returned.' Nono did just that, to Strobel's evident discomfort: 'I would rather have deferred the commission [. . .] it's just that electronic things are not possible for us currently'.[81] Soon afterwards, Nono mentions discussions with the Venice Biennale – presumably with Mario Labroca, who was about to return as director of the Contemporary

Poetry and drama

Music Festival and would shortly commission Nono's first stage work.[82] The faithful Steinecke lost no time in renegotiating the commission with the Hessische Rundfunk, for performance at Darmstadt.[83] Maderna conducted the premiere of *Composizione per orchestra n. 2: Diario polacco '58* in Darmstadt on 2 September 1959.

Space and movement

Since hearing the first performance of part of Schönberg's *Die Jakobsleiter* in Hamburg a year earlier, Nono had been studying a copy of the manuscript of his late father-in-law's unfinished oratorio.[84] As both work and idea, *Die Jakobsleiter* embodies concepts that are vital to Nono; as with *Moses und Aron*, its incompleteness must have contributed to its idealisation. Interrupted by the First World War, revisited towards the end of the Second, the work marks an important stage in the evolution of Schönberg's technique, but its vision involved challenges that remained intractable. In a 1912 outline of his plan, Schönberg wrote of the metaphysical nature of his project, the search for a post-religious spirituality, and of 'the modern composer who observes his duty'.[85] Returning to the work in a new technological climate he suggested cinematographic solutions, 'renouncing the "unity of space and time"'.[86] More materially, *Die Jakobsleiter* requires groups of performers to be distributed through the performing space and beyond, for which Schönberg later suggested using microphones and amplification.

The constitution of the large orchestra made possible by Nono's commission – quadruple woodwind and brass, large percussion group – immediately afforded polychoral and symmetrical structures. Its disposition on stage seems to have been the initial vehicle for his imagination. 'Doppio coro' appears on many drawings, all with different forms of horizontal symmetry; he subdivides them to produce groupings 'a 13' or even 'a 16 cori'.[87] Some retain the plan to use 'electronic tapes on 4 channels', the loudspeakers placed in the corners of the room.[88] Extensive listings of percussion are grouped into 'fixed' and 'non-fixed'; *suoni fissi* will continue to mark a constant point in Nono's increasingly rich timbral universe. As the tape component disappears, two vital new elements are transposed from the electronic world into the orchestra: a vertical symmetry and indications of direction of movement. In an initial experiment, this additional, opposing arc of instruments incorporates a transition (from trumpets to horns to trombones) subsequently absorbed into the wider symmetry, but the intersection of these curves is to remain crucial to the final plan. Figure 6.11 shows how the last stage of this evolution retains such inner structure. Its architectural polyphony is the product of the superimposition of superimposed symmetrical shapes. Rather than static 'choirs', the different instrumental groups can be dynamically reconfigured as material proliferates, reflects, consolidates, dissolves and moves through space.

The drawings in Nono's sketches develop a new spatiality – concepts that spring from consideration of the physical space but have resonance in the ways he conceives of the material itself. Not by coincidence the graphical exploration of space recalls his research into the envelopes of sound complexes. Percussion are now listed in groups of sixteen each of metal, skins and wood, each group mapped to the chromatic scale. The number of percussionists required was such that Nono had to find additional players from Cologne.[89] At the end of his sequence of drawings, a brief note describes three kinds of musical material:

A   fixed more or less
B   mobile . . . less
C   fixed . . . more[90]

Poetry and drama

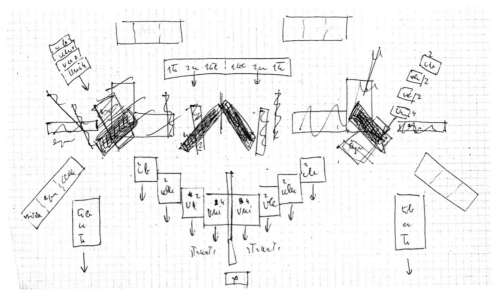

Figure 6.11 Composizione per orchestra n. 2: Diario polacco '58 – spatial concept. (ALN 19.02/13. © The heirs of Luigi Nono. Reproduced by kind permission.)

In an article to accompany an early performance, Nono explained the origins and formal role of these categories:

> The three different states of being of sound and their different compositional use correspond to the three states of mind I explained above: dismay, admiring amazement, enthusiasm.
>
> The rapid succession of different 'diary' scenes corresponds to the rapidity of succession, simultaneity even, of the different situations that struck me: rapid sudden changes where the unexpected happens and its variety surprises.
>
> [. . .] the techniques and quality of sound always have an expressive function.
>
> never a formal game for its own sake.
>
> it should also be very clear that the concept of *l'art pour l'art* is completely foreign to me.[91]

We can identify four conceptual origins of the form of *Diario polacco '58*, therefore: the sonic manipulation of tape editing in the electronic studio, Venetian polychoralism, *Die Jakobsleiter* and the memory of Nono's Polish experience. The latter is imagined through Schönberg's renouncing of the unities and the cross cut narrative of film. The early Soviet film director Sergei Eisenstein, who had previously worked with Meyerhold, had become an important model for Nono – in his political motivation and the human empathy of his films, his theory, and his manipulation of form and materials. The construction of *Diario polacco '58* will resurface, most notably in the string quartet *Fragmente-Stille, an Diotima*. He divides the orchestra into four equal groups (inconveniently also labelled A–D), with a reminder to 'leave space free for the solo flute'. The tape element has been eliminated by this stage; in February he wrote to Hübner and Steinecke explaining that he had been unable to get permission to work at the Studio di Fonologia of the RAI in Milan.[92] The studio had been founded under the direction of Berio and Maderna in 1955

Poetry and drama

and had already produced significant works.[93] One can only surmise as to political reasons for Nono's difficulty, but a similar situation obtained when Scherchen tried to have the RAI hire Nono as his assistant.[94] That Nono already knew and trusted the engineer at Milan, Marino Zuccheri, is clear from a further letter to Steinecke explaining why the tape part could not be realised at Scherchen's studio in Gravesano.[95] They had presumably met during Nono's visits to Maderna. Zuccheri, a fellow Veneto-speaker and member of the *resistenza*, would become Nono's collaborator in the studio for two decades. Nono's sustained interest in the electronic forays of his peers had been further piqued by a meeting with Varèse after the elderly visionary's frustrating experience with his *Poéme Electronique* at the Brussels World Fair.[96]

As will become increasingly his practice, Nono reflects on lessons from previous works: the relationship between tenor and chorus in *La terra e la compagna*, and in *Varianti* 'the vibrations of the sound of the soloist with other instruments (different dynamics and rhythms)'.[97] The latter is particularly telling; it appears as type B as he begins to consider in detail how to define four different compositional techniques:

> A – Multiple sounds (blocks and layers)
> B – Single sounds with vibrations (individual pitches with multiple attacks, timbres, rhythms)
> C – Single sounds with values 1/4 1/5 1/6 1/7 (the 'chain', constellational counterpoint technique of complex-construction, as introduced in *La terra e la compagna*)
> D – Counterpoint of multiple groups (ABC)[98]

He also identifies the parameters that each technique must address:

> – rhythm
> – dynamics
> – sound (single – many) [pitch]
> – octave
> – attack, duration, end of the sound
> – formal (bars)
> – movement of sound in space!!! (fixed in stereo, fixed at a point, mobile, maximally mobile)[99]

Prior to any drafting, Nono works through the mechanisms and implications of each technique in exact detail. He tests the workings of sound complexes, of echoes and spatial movement. He also establishes a maximum of four layers for each type of material, denoted in his sketches by roman numerals (hence Biii represents a three-layer texture of materials of type B). Such salient numbers (5 in *Varianti*, 4 here) afford conceptual flexibility, not numerology. They facilitate the remapping and manipulation of abstract structures. Nono still has a solo flute in mind as he begins to map the space of possible combinations and subdivisions of four orchestral groups, four compositional techniques and four levels of density; it largely disappears before drafting begins. As he considers their sequence and distribution, a new element is introduced: ordering 'by chance, extraction by lotto', anticipating his later use of dice and frequent references to Josquin's *Missa Di dadi*.[100] With such forces, his idea here is presumably not that of 'indeterminacy with respect to performance' as in Boulez's *Third Sonata* or Stockhausen's *Klavierstück XI* – in his later works Nono would develop a much more sophisticated role for the performer – but rather the use of chance techniques in composition, more akin to Cage's own *Music of Changes*. As Schaller has pointed out, the sequential logic of pitch and

Poetry and drama

rhythm structures through the final work suggests that this path was abandoned before the musical surface began to take shape.[101]

The thirty-two sections range from one to fifty-three bars in length. They fall into three main parts (in the final score bars 1–107, 108–239, 240–82), with a short, intense coda Div, itself of seven sections (283–306). '!Viva!', he writes as he is finally satisfied with a hierarchical scheme of section length and distribution – 'BASE – BASISSIMA' as he sees how internal durations, dynamics, pitches, 'vibrations' and subdivisions can all be related to the source material:[102]

> Everything in relation to the square 1 > 12
> a) values of each group
> b) dynamics
> c) sounds: unified (on the chromatic series)
> multiple (from 1 to 12 according to the square)
> d) vibrations of sounds (according to the number from the square)
> e) subdivisions! according to the part!
> when the subdivisions reach the end of a pattern of bars, go back[103]

'Vibrations' are note repetitions, and the scheme of reflection at the ends of sections generates greater intensity at the boundaries. Proportions and subdivisions are organised using the same reasoning as durations; form and rhythm are contiguous. In practice, D sections consist only of A and B material, except in the compound coda. Sections of type C become the other to A and B, as confirmed in the coda where A and B are always heard simultaneously. The time effects of memory – multiple pasts, the ambiguity of past and present, the simultaneity of asynchronous events – find formal expression in a conceptual space that is thoroughly polyphonic. Here we see an anticipation of Nono's later fragment-based technique. Rather than being renounced, unities of time and material are viewed from multiple and simultaneous perspectives as their bounding spaces are threaded together in new polyphonies, to be retraversed in the linear time of performance. Such threads may figure as single notes, as layers or complexes of sound, or as richly characterised musical material, but they are always subject to longer term dynamics and processes. Discussion of the emergence of form from fragments seems to have been current. In a letter shortly after the premiere of *Diario polacco '58*, Alexander Goehr explains his own technique to Nono, mirroring his friend's sources: based on fragments of 8–10 bars, each with its own 'circuit', Goehr sees this approach as deriving from Bach ('blocs à la Bach') and from the montage technique of Eisenstein.[104]

Nono's design for the second part illustrates this; the four compositional strands each have their own rhythm, their own pattern of change (Figure 6.12).

Having determined techniques and form, Nono is free to construct the score sequentially. The use of the all-interval series, always in its original form, gives an indication of his understanding of the shape of the work. Only the series on F♯ is used through the first part. In the second it rises chromatically from G to C♯ before falling back to B♭. The D–E♭–E–E♭–D pattern in the third part mirrors its symmetrical sequence of technique-types: Ci Aii Biv Aii Ci. In the coda, the sequence itself begins to outline an all-interval series on F before ending on the F♯ of the beginning. Durations come from the same square as for *Cori di Didone*, now read vertically from below or right to left. Durations and subdivisions are again mapped from their twelve-element generators on to reduced sets, mostly of six values. These are now much more closely designed to meet the needs of a particular section. As the final work emerges, Nono increasingly uses the values on two planes: original and double. Dynamics are still read

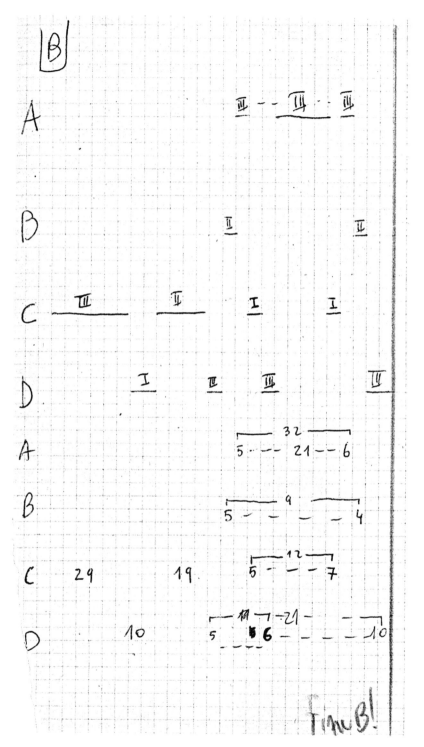

Figure 6.12 Composizione per orchestra n. 2: Diario polacco '58 – arrangement of materials in bars 108–239. (ALN 19.06/06. © The heirs of Luigi Nono. Reproduced by kind permission.)

Poetry and drama

according to pitch, but the set of possibilities for each section is more individually focused and characterised. If the techniques themselves are developments of his recent practice, their disposition in space and time is entirely new. Nono's opinion of certain trends in the spatialisation of electronic music is clear:

> This spatial conception of music refers to the Venetian school of Andrea and Govanni Gabrieli.
>
> But it is completely different in its compositional and sonic conception. The ping-pong idea, basing everything on the passing from right to left like a ping-pong ball, is quite foreign to my music. Here it is the sound that is composed spatially, using distinct and spatially separate sonic origins.
>
> This concept will be the basis of the new music theatre I have in mind.[105]

These comments, written immediately following the composition of *Diario Polacco '58*, make clear the fundamental roles of space and drama in his conception of the work. The material, its development and form are not merely programmatic of the autobiographical motivation, he now sees them as essentially dramatic in their nature; the music is not spatialised, it is spatial. This is not simply a matter of location; the acoustic artefacts of space are integral to the construction of material. The 'vibration' technique of the B sections is a form of modulated early reflection. Single pitches return at unpredictable and overlapping intervals from another orchestra, their timbre and dynamics transformed. The single choir of the opening Bi section allows this process to be heard clearly as it passes through all four groups, as if to map out the space for the listener. The initial F♯–G dyad is sounded in two different rhythms, orders and inversions by groups 1 and 2 to the left, 3 and 4 to the right. The following three pitches (F A♭, E) are articulated differently in all four groups, reducing to three layers (groups 1, 2 and 3, 4) for the C♯–F♯ dyad that concludes the opening brass paragraph in bar 6. Nono uses what the sketches describe as 'echo' rather differently; it applies to entire sound complexes or extended passages. In his plan for section Ciii (bars 108–35), the first and last passages are marked 'con eco'. The strings in group 4 present a delayed reconstitution of the string material in group 1. The flutes and clarinets of the two central groups have further modulated echoes, acting as a single timbral body. The cymbals of all four groups add another layer of echo, gently punctuating a complex texture that remains within the dynamic range *ppp-mf*. The echoes of a single layer of material thus articulate the space in three ways. After a non-echoed passage for the combined forces of the two central groups, now constantly moving between *p* and *f* (bars 114–18), the process is reversed.

The multiple strands of narrative and time prepare the way for maturing dramatic ideas. Through all Nono's work there are traces of music theatre awaiting the appropriate catalysts and an environment he judges propitious, stimulating and supportive. Just as the text is absorbed and extended in his musico–poetic responses to Pavese and Ungaretti, Nono's experience of real-world events suffuses the music it provokes; the work is fundamentally dramatic irrespective of the presence of text.[106] In *Diario polacco '58*, Stenzl, Stenzl identifies specific associations with Nono's experience in Poland, developed from *Il canto sospeso* and reappearing in *Intolleranza 1960*. He relates the fourth section (bars 20–38), with its extreme dynamics and the sound of whips from all directions, to Nono's impression of the horror of Auschwitz, and the following brief, subdued passage for four flutes to his own response. The long seventh section (54–107) Stenzl sees as a dramatisation of the ghetto uprising, its percussive outbreaks subdued by the full weight of the orchestra.[107]

Poetry and drama

The meticulous compositional process is the result of Nono's constant reflection on the nature of his own practice. The construction of *Diario polacco '58* is a carefully managed design process, a mature instance of the practices he has evolved over a decade. He considers the brief, the challenge, from every angle: the commission, the problem of writing for a large orchestra, but also the demands of his own particular compositional impulse, the state of development of his technical repertoire and his historical view of musical language. From these he evolves a detailed set of materials and techniques in parallel with a set of formal principles, each researched and tested in detail in prose, graphics and musical examples. These are selected to define exactly the creative space he has in mind, such that when he begins the drafting process the spirit is of freedom rather than constraint. Layers are added, structures transferred from elsewhere, in different colours; emerging shapes take new graphical form until further elaborated in notation. The printed score of *Diario polacco '58* is itself a remarkable graphical object. The four orchestral groups are laid out to mirror each other, their instrumentation marked in different colours, as in Nono's sketches, on the end papers. This process is architectural in its behaviour as well

Figure 6.13 Nono's studio, late 1950s. (Photograph © The heirs of Luigi Nono. Reproduced by kind permission.)

Poetry and drama

as its result. It is the full fruit of his father's training as a civil engineer. Nono's very composing environment had architectural associations. As a wedding present, the son of Carlo Scarpa, Tobias, had built Nono a desk to his own specifications (Figure 6.13). He could now work in his studio surrounded on two sides by a long, deep desk at the back of which vertical supports allowed a clear view of yet more material. Later images show every possible surface hung with sketches: Nono is surrounded by graphical and symbolic representations of aspects of an evolving composition. The increasingly numerous sketches are not sequential, they coexist like the different structural, technical and contextual layers of architects' drawings. In the continuous, iterative process of inscription and reflection, his physical and graphical environment map out the many interdependent dimensions of the musical problem, of the emerging object. A typewriter is an indispensable element in his composing eco-system, as are scissors and tape. His physical environment will remain crucial not only to his practice but to his very ability to compose. In some respects, the composition of *Diario polacco '58* is an exemplar in its management of creative impulse, the distribution of ideas, material and their development through different modes of representation. As his imagination and intellect constantly add dimensions to those reflected back to him by these materials, the design process will often become less smooth.

Historical presence and present tensions

For all its radical richness of conception, invention and process, *Diario polacco '58* was not a great success at Darmstadt, where both Nono and Stockhausen were now formally members of faculty. To the new generation, such intensity of compositional thought may have been bewildering. By Nono's peers, the investment of such resources in one performance may have been resented. *Diario polacco '58* requires intensive and sustained listening. It neither offers the 'Italianate charm' of which critics had patronisingly spoken, nor does it scream novelty; no explicit technical or theoretical innovations had been presented for the Darmstadt community to debate, to take possession of. A newly self-confident Germany had tired of hearing about Nazi atrocity, and cold war demonisation limited interest in Polish attempts to regain some autonomy and freedom. Nono would return to Darmstadt in 1960 to deliver his talk *Text – Musik – Gesang*, but this would be his last Darmstadt commission. As if to put the seal on his relationship with Germany, the German Social Democrat Party (SPD) explicitly denounced communism at their November 1959 convention in Bad Godesberg. It is ironic that the critical success that marked the beginning of Nono's last decade – the premiere of his string quartet *Fragmente-Stille, an Diotima* in 1980 – would take place in that very city.

The warmth of reception of *Diario polacco '58* was certainly not enhanced by the talk given by Nono the day before, on 1 September 1959: *Geschichte und Gegenwart in der Musik von Heute* (*History and presence in the music of today*). It is above all a call for composers to take personal and historical responsibility:

> Today there is a prevalent tendency, in both the creative and critical-analytical fields, not to want to integrate an artistic–cultural phenomenon in its historical context, that is, not to want to consider it in relation to its origins and the elements that formed it, not in relation to its place in present reality and its effect on that reality, nor in relation to its capacity to project into the future, but exclusively in and of itself, as an end in itself, and only in relation to that precise instant in which it is realised. [108]

Nono begins by dismissing, in the person of Antonin Artaud, 'those who would illude themselves that they can begin a new era *ex abrupto*', and the notion of 'so-called "free

Poetry and drama

spontaneity" in human creation'. He proceeds to criticise those who would systematise such illusory freedom through 'the tendency to seek abstract refuge in a scientific principle or mathematical relationship', now citing Joseph Schillinger. There are other thinly veiled personal attacks. Indifferent new works rescued and brought to life by great performers such as Gazelloni and Tudor 'grow like funghi' – a reference to Cage's answering questions on mushrooms on the game show of Mike Buongiorno, the lowest common denominator of mass entertainment. 'Those who would absolutise the "concept of time"' presumably points to Stockhausen.

Cage's 'method' he relates to the attempts of imperial China to deny historical evolution. The youth of Europe are being offered 'the resigned apathy of "it's all the same anyway" in the complacent form of "I am space, I am time". [. . .] This is capitulation in the face of time, the flight from responsibility'.[109] That this anticipates Pestalozza's criticism of Nono himself, twenty years later, is an indicator of the sensitivity of this argument.[110] In other cultures, improvisation is used on defined parameters, and always in the service of some higher essence. The principle of collage is ancient and derives from colonialist forms of thought, although he cites the cathedrals of Ravenna and Venice, as if to claim an Italian precedence nonetheless. He rails against the artificial dualism of freedom and constraint as a social concept 'now in its sunset'. 'Without that reciprocal compenetration of concept and technique – which cannot be realised if the spirit does not likewise have a clear idea – any expression of the material is restricted to the decorative.'[111] His judgement is that 'The rhetorical use of concepts of liberty and non-liberty in an artistic-creative process is nothing other than an umpteenth propaganda trick, and a very cheap one, to attempt to influence the future.'[112]

Nono's argument against chance continued in response to Stockhausen's lecture *Musik und Graphik* four days later.[113] Tudor reported to Cage that everyone except the critics knew that Nono's talk was directed against Stockhausen,[114] but critics seem to have taken it more at face value. Ernst Thomas and von Lewinski both reported the controversy and the challenge to Darmstadt collegiality, but in the light of disagreement over the ideas of Cage.[115] The emollient Steinecke was clear as to the intended targets – for publication he suggested removing references to Gazelloni and Tudor – and to analogies of certain compositional processes with totalitarianism.[116] He was initially nervous about publishing the text, and an edited version appeared in *Melos* before being eventually published in the *Darmstädter Beiträge*. In a letter to Hartmann in the intervening months, Nono mentions that he has now understood why composers have looked for sanctuary in the neoclassical. His response to Cage was by no means dismissive, however:

> I had proposed dedicating the second issue [of the *Darmstädter Beiträge*] to Cage, because I had understood that there was an issue that needed addressing. From that stemmed my total isolation, caused by my denouncing an analytical incapacity to deal with Cage and his world, reducing it to an easy-to-copy formula. The Darmstadt circle was incapable of penetrating the significance of Cage and his ideas, and was thus responsible for their being misunderstood. I remember that when I finished reading, Stockhausen was violently against me because he felt attacked personally, and he was right. In fact I said clearly that John Cage represented a culture coming from California, a culture that displays clear connections with the East, in painting and in music; think of Tobey, of Rothko, of other schools from that country that have relationships with certain mentalities, thoughts, Chinese, Buddhist, Indian and Zen practices.[117]

Nono's is a historical materialist stance; a more historicist view might have seen this undesirable situation as itself a product of context. Perhaps the real addressee of this concentrated outpouring is Nono himself – a multiple 'no, not that!' as he also searches for a new practice,

Poetry and drama

a new mode of existence for the work. The undeniably negative tenor of Nono's talk would tend to obfuscate its motivating force, but it ends with an expression of faith, a call to courage:

> Music will always remain a historical present, a testimony of those who consciously confront the process of history, and who in every instant of that process make decisions in the full clarity of their intuition and reason, and act to uncover new possibilities in the vital need for new structures. And there is still much marvellous work to be done.[118]

Helmut Lachenmann

One of the students at Nono's course on Schönberg and serial technique at Darmstadt in July 1957 had been 21-year-old Helmut Lachenmann. Nono had given him a signed copy of the newly printed *Il canto sospeso*, and two months later Lachenmann wrote Nono a long letter setting out the questions confronting him as a young composer and the ways in which Nono's seminars had opened paths. He wrote again having heard the premiere of *Varianti* in October:

> It was the first time I let go of all the critical, dialectical speculation that normally attends a first performance; for the first time with a new work I completely forgot that I am 'also a musician' and want to compose; it was as if I was in a dream, but this dream was quite real, it was a reality of such purity and clarity that is nowhere else to be found in the music of today. Concepts like beauty or purity are far too crass for what one experiences with such music.
>
> [. . .]
>
> The whole problematic of composing today – that has to explain itself in respect of the power of the classical musical art with old and worn-out means, this problematic I found <u>re</u>solved and <u>dis</u>solved.[119]

Nono replied immediately with advice on the study of composition: to study the past, how composers have used and renewed the material of their own time 'and how they composed, always precisely according to the material and always on the material – and as always the spirit governs everything!'.[120] 'You are already thinking with your head', he says, 'others come to Darmstadt just to steal something.'

Lachenmann expounds his views and aspirations in several long letters culminating in a series of incisive technical questions about *Varianti*. Nono responded with an invitation to study in Venice. 'Perhaps he just wanted to discover whether he could teach', Lachenmann later suggested.[121] It cannot be overstated how exceptional this was. Nono had little respect for the institutions of music education, as these letters make clear, and later encounters with such institutions would remain fractious. He enjoyed talking with groups of students but would rarely accept individuals as long-term students; David Bedford in 1961–2 and Nicolaus A. Huber in 1967–8 were other exceptions, but the relationship with Lachenmann would remain uniquely intense and important to both student and teacher. Replying to the questions about *Varianti*, in a characteristically non-linear mixture of German and Italian, Nono sets out his position – a statement that remains valid through to the final works:

> Fundamentally, this is my principle:
>
> There is a mentality (though – compositional technique) which is grounded on a particular and precise basis, <u>but</u> which is always realised in the moment in life: so it

Poetry and drama

always determines itself in the moment, according to the reality of the moment: that is, it's necessary to recognise and see where when how and what is happening, to act–interpret–intervene with precision, as we are all capable: never rigid dogmas that always result in wanting to <u>impose</u> from outside or above [. . .][122]

Lachenmann worked with Nono in Venice from November 1958 to May 1959, and again from October 1959 to May 1960. He lived in the same Giudecca apartment building and joined Nono's circle of friends at the Trattoria Altanella. Meetings were irregular, determined by Nono's rhythm of composing and travelling. The various anecdotal reports of Lachenmann and those he encountered at the time suggest an openness in Nono's teaching, combined with an absolute resistance to perceived traces of 'bourgeois' figuration (Stockhausen) or ornamentation (Boulez) on one hand and formalism on the other.[123]

Their early correspondence develops a balance of compositional and aesthetic questions, politics, professional detail and easy banter in dialect. Letters document Nono's distancing himself from the debates and people of Darmstadt: his diminishing respect for Stockhausen ('Bismarck', 'St Ockhausen', the 'Kölner Klan') and for composers who abdicate the responsibility of determination. They also describe his travels through Germany, France and England: Nono prefers the English Gothic (Exeter and Salisbury) to the French. As Lachenmann's mentor, Nono recommends his work through his network in Germany – Steinecke, Strobel, Schott – as well as at home; on Nono's suggestion, Labroca programmed Lachenmann's *Fünf Strophen* for the 1962 Biennale. A letter of August 1960 gives a snapshot of the cultural–professional context in Germany that Nono would soon reject. Lachenmann had proposed a substantial orchestral work to Schott, and reports the reply to Nono:

> Listen to what intelligent stuff he writes:
> First lots of compliments, because I attempted to formulate my ideas in the article; this is very good – he says – because all the great composers do this. Henze is a real maestro, Nono is making progress, also in German!, and Boulez is formulating his ideas neatly in German. (Because the German language is the language of the musical world – Heil! Heil!) this is not what he says but what he thinks.[124]

Lachenmann's reports to his funder, the *Studienstiftung des deutschen Volkes*, are detailed, reflective, almost confessional. He describes Nono's environment:

> Giudecca is a part of Venice between the harbour and the Lido, largely occupied by communists. I have been accepted quite readily by people of a quite different social background – port and factory workers, the crews of transport boats, vegetable traders, fishermen – and have had the kind of contact that would never have been possible with such social groups on Germany.[125]

He describes the topics being addressed in initial study with Nono: 'the evolution of sound, of space, of vibrations, the abstraction of tone-colour'.[126] His final report suggests a greater independence from Nono through Lachenmann's second stay: 'But contact with him remains an essential stimulus, and I will never deny this contact, even if I come back to work in Germany.'[127]

In an unpublished article from 1961, shortly after his study, Lachenmann explains the strength of Nono's work:

Poetry and drama

The uncompromising nature of Nono's language arises because it never gives up human-centred communication, to the annoyance of both reactionaries and modernists. While the others engaged in an acoustic variety show with serial, anti-serial and aleatoric gags, Nono stuck to a stubbornly serious communicativeness, and a wonderful free pathos.[128]

Just a few years later their intense artistic intimacy would effectively be interrupted for almost two decades, partly by diverging paths but especially through Nono's refusal of Lachenmann. As often in human dealings, the most absolute personal denial conceals the deepest attachment; one might surmise that this was rooted precisely in the depth of their mutual understanding, which crucially involves questions and doubts. The seeds of division were inherent in their early relationship. Lachenmann's recollection also gives us the most concise picture of Nono's trajectory: 'Nono permitted no stirrings of inner life that were in some way depressive or agitated by crisis [. . .]. There was no doubt of this kind, he didn't recognise it. And that then transformed itself into fundamentally the opposite.'[129] As Nono embarked on a new journey through the 1960s, perhaps his friend's tireless, forensic questioning of art and its role represented potential challenges that would have been too close to his own heart to risk acknowledging. It would take a long path of artistic labour to arrive at the point of not only confronting doubt, but of transducing it into his essential compositional material.

Some confusion was caused by Lachenmann's inclusion of the text of *Geschichte und Gegenwart in der Musik von Heute* in his collected writings as 'in the name of Nono'.[130] It is clear from pages sent to Lachenmann in the summer of 1959 that the content and much of the prose were entirely Nono's.[131] He asked Lachenmann to help with translation prior to presenting his talk at Darmstadt – doubtless aware of the need for clarity, given the storm that would inevitably ensue. On his way to Darmstadt at the end of August, Nono stayed with Lachenmann in Leonberg, where they worked on the German text. Lachenmann later described the process: 'I let loose my whole polemical passion and said things that I would never have said myself. And I did it in my best academic German. Nono's language was more halting and disjointed.'[132] The collaboration was sufficiently satisfactory for Nono that he invited Lachenmann to Venice again the following summer, to help with his text for the 1960 summer school: *Text – Musik – Gesang*.

Melos reborn

Melody should not be understood in terms of the typical succession of tonal music. Here, the rhythm-pitch relation ends with the following rhythm-pitch relation. (Incomprehensibly, this is a residue of tonal music that still characterises almost all music today and thus constitutes a limit, a confusion, a possibility of reactionary regression in present evolution.) We are dealing with a melody of simultaneity in the differentiation of rhythmic values that are unitary in their duration and their relationships.[133]

Nono's understanding of melody in the recently finished *Diario polacco '58* establishes a basis for a new phase of development. His periods of travel were likewise activities of intense research and stimulus. *Diario polacco '58* had taken half a year to complete. It was finished in mid-July 1959, after the birth of their first daughter, Silvia, in May. Following his momentous contribution to Darmstadt the couple drove to England for the Dartington Summer School, where Nono would teach annually until 1962. This was the first of a number of important invitations from the founder and director of Dartington, William Glock, who had recently become Controller of Music at the BBC. In November there was another visit to Poland for

Poetry and drama

a performance of *La Victoire de Guernica*; *Diario polacco '58* had been presented at the *Warsaw Autumn* in September. Nono stopped in Prague to see Radok and Svoboda's *Lanterna Magika*, recently installed following its Brussels World Fair debut. Their multi-screen productions of movement, light, film and sound provided the catalyst Nono's emerging theatrical concepts needed. He wrote to Mila 'finally a new theatrical concept that develops the theatrical experiences of Berlin (Piscato–Toller–Brecht) very important!'[134] Helmut Lachenmann describes the months that followed as 'a pause for thought':[135]

> Nono was insisting on a renewal of his musical resource with a degree of determination and clarity of vision which rejected as retrograde or escapist all avenues which promised to lead to a harmless structural paradise and involved a tacit return, hiding behind blind organisational, serial or aleatory procedures, to the old bourgeois spirit in the guise of science-fiction idyll or of a pseudo-anarchical, playful eclecticism.
>
> [. . .]
>
> Nono's ideas on composition at the time admitted no figurative – and basically no melodic elements. He replaced the linear gesture with a constellation of acoustically defined sounds. Music as the tension between individual points in time.
>
> [. . .]
>
> In those days Nono did not move further on – he went deeper. And while all the other composers, in these times of upheaval, at some stage decided to settle down for the rest of their creative lives in the terrain in which they had ended up, Nono the structuralist constantly forced Nono the expressively-oriented visionary to forge his way ahead.[136]

A prestigious commission from the Elizabeth Sprague Coolidge Foundation in the Library of Congress represented welcome recognition from outside the West European new music establishment. A vocal chamber work, for two four-part groups of soloists, was an opportunity to refocus his relationship with practice, material, text and expression. With *Sarà dolce tacere* Nono returned to his untiring exploration of Pavese, to the project started with *La terra e la compagna*. He would often use Pavese's poetry until *Al gran sole* of 1974. He set, or considered setting almost every poem from Pavese's last collection *Verrà la morte e avrà i tuoi occhi*, as if the final body of work before the poet's death crystallized for Nono a crucial historical and emotional moment. In addition to the completed works that incorporate texts from Pavese – seven in all – there are at least four other distinct Pavese-based projects, both lyrical and dramatic. It seems that Pavese's writing held such a deep personal resonance for Nono that in returning to it time and again Nono could re-engage with the emotional centre of his own inner life. These projects did not need to be completed to bear fruit. One might more hesitantly relate Pavese's fascination with text – not just poetry, drama and oratory but also everyday speech given weight by its historical context – to Nono's own use of language. His verbal expression is often fragmentary, enriched by multiple ideas and connections; he resists conventional argumentation. Above all, his ideas brook no reduction, caricature or misrepresentation. The line from Pavese's *Anche tu sei collina* he now selected as a title, 'sarà dolce tacere' ('it will be sweet to be silent'), presages later work as he listens ever more closely to inner and outer worlds. The expressive power of the four vocal works from these years springs from their balance of intense intimacy and forensic detachment:

> It is particularly difficult for me to talk about these choral works because each of them has a very particular, very intimate motivation, which concerns not just the secrets of

Poetry and drama

composition but the secrets of life. *Sarà dolce tacere* is dedicated to Bruno Maderna for his fortieth birthday, and Pavese who talks of life, vine, wine, of the peace of the countryside in which at a certain moment 'it will be sweet to be silent'. [. . .] The silence of nature leads you to listen to sounds, the voices of nature, that are often or forgotten. [. . .] *Sarà dolce tacere* with its eight voices (four against four) recalls Andrea and Giovanni Gabrieli, studied so much with Bruno. [. . .] it echoes the two choirs of San Marco.[137]

Nono began work on the Pavese piece as a direct continuation of *La terra e la compagna*, planning for the same forces and returning to his analyses of *Anche tu sei collina* and *Di salmastro e di terra*, to which he adds *Sei la terra e la morte*, also from the 1945 collection *La terra e la morte*. They remain in their sequence from the collection, creating a diminishing stanza structure: 4–3–2 (the two stanzas of the last consolidated as a single section of Nono's plan). 'Sarà dolce tacere', the thirtieth of thirty-four lines in *Anche tu sei collina*, acts as the central moment of the projected work and its place is marked as such by Nono. In the event, *Sarà dolce tacere* sets only this first poem.

The poetry of Antonio Machado had also been important to Nono for some time; its concise, wise balance of personal despair and ecstatic faith in humanity would continue to accompany him. He had been thinking about Machado while working on *La terra e la compagna*, quoting him in a note on that work:

> it is not logic that sings in poetry
> but life,
> even if it is not life that gives structure to poetry,
> but logic.[138]

Discussions were continuing with Steinecke about the possibility of a Darmstadt commission for the long-planned stage work.[139] In the meantime, Steinecke proposed that Maderna should conduct *España en al corazón* in July. Instead, Nono took the opportunity to plan a new work to celebrate his daughter Silvia's first birthday, a setting of four poems by Machado that affirm the miracle of life in the fewest words possible: the two haiku-like miniatures both beginning *La primavera ha venido* (*Spring has come*), *Canta, canta* (*Sing, sing*), and *Si vivir es bueno* (*If living is good*). Work on *"Ha venido". Canciones para Silvia* thus proceeded but a step behind that on the Pavese project. The forces Nono chooses for the two works represent a characteristic conceptual duality. In *Sarà dolce tacere* he writes for two groups of solo SATB voices, in *"Ha venido". Canciones para Silvia* a soprano soloist with a chorus of six more sopranos. They are vertically and horizontally extended images of the same subject, the voice, each with their own internal symmetries. This duality is all the more evident because of the common technical roots of the two pieces. They would be finished within a month of each other in April and May 1960.

'*Sarà dolce tacere*'

For *Sarà dolce tacere*, structural ideas emerge from Nono's analysis of Pavese: 'analyse and fix relationships between syllables and pitches, also from 1–(12)8 chromatically?'[140] The number 8 becomes significant, another modulus of conceptual mobility. The whole is planned in eight sections, for eight voices, and there are several early references to sets of eight sounds or values. As ideas develop we see the tireless self-re-examination described by Lachenmann. Nono's relationship with his own evolving practice, his own experience, is analogous to his view of

Poetry and drama

music history; it is neither to be ignored nor repeated. He now formalises the sound complexes of recent works, bringing them into new relationships on all parameters: 'Groups of notes, from 2 to 8! – basis – which are then articulated in various ways according to the moment.'[141] The *group* is now the fundamental unit, the materialisation at a single point of several virtual parameters further mediated by the composer's response to text, surrounding groups and the flow of the work. The poem is the seed, however. He considers a balance of sung and spoken word 'for clarity of text', although the final score is entirely sung.[142] He moves from associating syllables with pitches to considering each word as a group. He tries out group-shapes by word, creating a polyphony of syllables starting together, ending together or staggered. These shapes, their inversions and retrogrades provide the lexicon of forms for the note-groups of the eventual work; the graphical symbols he uses recall his serial shorthand, a development of the technique introduced in *Varianti*. Early notes contrast groups of 1–8 voices with 'canto libero' or 'canto lineare', a distinction that resurfaces as the work emerges.

Nono has to find a new way of relating parameters. A number square still generates the sequences of values. That Nono uses the same square for both vocal works and then returns to it for *Intolleranza 1960* is an indication of how he sees its role; akin to that of the all-interval series, it no longer a serial mechanism uniquely characteristic of a particular work but rather a means for statistical generation with a precision of twelve. This is the number of differentiable elements that Nono is used to working with, remapped on to specific sets of values (usually four) for each parameter. For each section of each work – four in both cases – he designs a new structure with twelve values of group density, seed duration and intervals; the source sets are different for each section. Elements from this constellation of associations are then read according to the sequence from the number square. He sets out the principles for the use of durations and rhythm bases within groups: all durations the same, or following the duration set for the section; all on the same rhythm base, or cycling the divisions of the beat by 3, 4, 5 or 6. In *"Ha venido"*. durations are also subdivided, unevenly, offering even greater plasticity of time. An entire group might constitute a single duration value. These techniques ensure the coherence and characterisation of sound objects while retaining their resistance to conventional melodic gesture. The source material is projected through groups onto the many planes of the musical surface; in Nono's projection the spatial concepts of Varèse are realised by means of technical developments inspired by Schönberg.

Having been decoupled from the serial dynamics of the musical language, pitch can explore new structural potential; over half a decade the flow of the all-interval series had washed away any residual unreflected melodic gesture. The interval – the atom of his study, earliest works and analyses of Schönberg – had re-emerged as a focus of attention in the event sequences of *Diario polacco '58*. The pitch series can take on a more plastic form, also defined differently for each section but always constructed on the basis of its interval content. His architecture of pitch has a clear hierarchy – intervals inside groups work within the framework of intervals in the series – but each group has its own charge and direction. The musical surface is the product of a network of vectors generating evolving harmonic fields. The rate of this evolution is determined as Nono imagines and plans the schemes for each section, as he builds the succession of groups using contiguous, overlapping, interrupted or subdivided rhythms, and again in the construction of a draft score. He sculpts its density as groups overlap, work their way through the scheme in opposite directions, or have different material, as is occasionally the case between solo and chorus in *"Ha venido"*.

Within groups, Nono builds this interval structure in two ways. Where he determines a set of intervals in the section scheme, these are used to construct the group, based on the pitch from the series. Elsewhere he writes 'according to the basic [row]'. In these cases, the group

Poetry and drama

follows the interval content (not the pitches) of the next elements of the series. The resultant rotating fractal interval shapes anticipate the harmonic–melodic fields of Berio. Figure 6.14 shows Nono's setting of 'ritroverai', beginning the last section of the same work. From his sketches he selects a group shape in which the central pitch persists throughout. The interval pattern from which the groups proliferate (E D A G) is mirrored in that of the first group. In their arrangement for eight voices, the four groups are fused into a single complex that reflects the sonic trajectory of the word itself; the E of *ri* is echoed in the final vowel.

Register, rests, the size and elision or otherwise of groups are all adapted to expressive needs and poetic flow as Nono constructs the draft score. The underlying group architecture is smoothed into its musical surface. The care of his voicing rings on from the last line of poetry, 'un acceso silenzio brucerà la campagna come i falò la sera' ('a bright silence will burn the

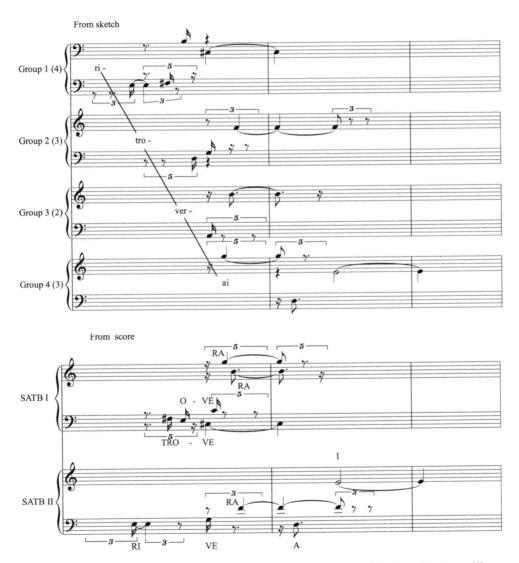

Figure 6.14 Sarà dolce tacere: group structure of bars 89–91 – transcription of sketch and final score[143]

Poetry and drama

countryside like bonfires in the evening'), a characteristic Pavese Ligurian image. Extension of the rhythm sequence and repetition of the note groups as the final line of text recedes into *bocca chiusa* allow a resonant harmonic field to establish – effectively an open mixolydian chord on E and D pedals. Nono's tendency to expand each note chromatically persists; F and E♭ serve to emphasise the root pitch, flickering about it as the bonfires of Pavese's poem surround the perpetual recession into silence. The latent potential of each note to expand as an all-interval series dissolves any residual orthogonal relationship between the vertical and the horizontal.

'"Ha venido". Canciones para Silvia'

The Machado settings of *"Ha venido". Canciones para Silvia* were to be accompanied by flute, guitar and percussion. *Canta, canta* replaced Nono's original selection, *La fuente y las cuatras*. The four poems were to be interspersed with the four verses of Angelo Maria Ripellino's *Vivere è stare svegli*, a powerful (and still popular) credo that would return as the opening chorus of *Intolleranza 1960*. After this second layer of poetry was left to one side, a series of instrumental interludes also became unnecessary, likewise to be used later. In both the new vocal works, reducing his forces to homogeneous groups of voices alone allows Nono to keep his material in clear focus. Expression and technique are inseparable, and in the text-bearing voice their relationship is at its most transparent. With one exception, the voice is a central element in all Nono's music until the cathartic instrumental works of the later 1970s, in which text merely submerges temporarily.

In *"Ha venido". Canciones para Silvia* he achieves an antiphonal relationship between soprano soloist and the six sopranos of the chorus by a greater polarising of the same technique to produce blocks and lines. The soloist may be incorporated into a block, or her line may be shared, echoed or expanded by the chorus. The homogeneity of forces, the projection of a single voice on to multiple planes, suggests techniques from the studio, particularly the spatialisation that has become fundamental to Nono's conception of material: 'the sounds move, they chase each other, they are reconstituted in space as if they come from different acoustic sources, from separate loudspeakers far from each other.'[144] Here the sketches clearly show the planning of numbers of groups of different sizes and their intervallic characteristics prior to their arrangement in the scheme for a particular section. The characterisation of sections by interval picks up the dramatic threads of *Fučík* and relates to Nono's current study of Schönberg. It allows him to create longer lines, to find a new melos, by completely horizontalising the group. Groups can generate blocks of absolute density or lines of infinite length, always encapsulating the pitch, rhythm, dynamic and density properties of local material.

Figure 6.15 shows the derivation of the continuous line at the opening of the last section, 'si vivir es bueno'. The pitch series alternates augmented and perfect fourths. The number of elements in each group (4 3 4 2 3 2 2 3 3 4) is read from the section scheme using the number square; intervals are taken from the following intervals of the series. Nono concatenates the elements of each group into a single line, marking the first of each – the series – as shown.[145] No notes are added, but the direction and sequence of intervals produces striking anticipations, echoes and elisions. As he transcribes the sketch into a draft score, two pitches are omitted: a passing C in bar 91 returns immediately as part of the following group; the E of bar 94 is anticipated at 'mejor', and the sole gap in the line thus created gives poignancy to 'soñar'. The line is amplified vertically, timbrally and spatially in its division with the chorus; the choral reverberation of the solo at 'si' and 'soñar' expand into three parts, in explicit madrigalisms. The augmented fourth /minor second pattern at 'soñar' anticipates the pitch universe of *Prometeo* There is the subtlest modulation of the sustained chorus E♭ preceding the rest in bar

Poetry and drama

Figure 6.15 "Ha venido". *Canciones para Silvia* – bars 88–97

94; the opening of the vowel in one group is balanced by a crescendo in the other. Sounds are in constant motion. This antiphony takes on its own rhythm, and the verbal melos of the fragmented solo part becomes more natural in the process.

Nono had hoped to travel to the USA, but visa problems proved insurmountable. Steinecke's plan to programme *"Ha venido"* came to nothing. Nono clearly had an increasing sense that the radio, Hessische Rundfunk, was boycotting his music. In an interesting exchange, Nono asks why Steinecke had not programmed Cornelius Cardew: 'Cardew is a MUSICIAN above the others; no doubt.'[146]

"Ha venido" was eventually premiered not at Darmstadt, but on 3 November in London, conducted by Maderna for the BBC. Nono's sole but momentous contribution to the 1960 Summer School was the talk *Text–Musik–Gesang*, given a few days before Stockhausen's paper on 'vieldeutige Form' ('ambiguous form'), which was actually presented by Metzger as an extraordinary performance. Nono and Stockhausen did not meet therefore at the 1960 Summer School, and would have no contact for some years. Nono's 1960 talk is effectively a long-considered response to Stockhausen's views on Nono's use of text in *Il canto sospeso*, expressed in his lecture of 1957. We have already considered some of his examples from recent works and the damning condemnation of Stockhausen's analysis. Nono's argument traces a picture of his thinking about text as he prepares for his radical conceptions of the new decade. There is a need for an *ars dicendi*, an oratory mode, for the present, he says, setting out from Schönberg's 1912 observation that in the Lieder of Schubert, text and music 'form a new and autonomous whole'.[147] He ends the first part of his lecture by playing *A Survivor from Warsaw*: 'This masterpiece is, in its creative necessity, in its relationships between music and text, music and listener, the aesthetic–musical manifesto for our time.'[148] In discussing *La terra e la compagna* he draws together all the elements of his new spatial–musical–semantic vision:

> Just as contrapuntal and harmonic elements no longer have a function in a music in which simple melodic and harmonic linearity has developed into a new pluridimensionality of relationships in all directions, so also for text a compositional world has opened up of new combinatorial possibilities of its phonetic and semantic elements.[149]

Analogies with Berio's thought at the same moment are, of course, unavoidable; his *Circles* was premiered just weeks later. This talk was Nono's last contribution in a decade-long involvement with Darmstadt. After Steinecke's untimely death in 1961, his successor, Ernst Thomas, made various attempts to persuade Nono to return, but to no avail. The crucial personal relationships had evaporated as careers had replaced common cause, Darmstadt had become part of the establishment and Germany itself was at one with being robustly bourgeois. Meanwhile, professional barriers were dissolving in Italy, where there was an urgency to the political–cultural situation that afforded Nono a more appropriate field of action.

Into the studio: 'Omaggio a Emilio Vedova'

Technology had a crucial enabling role in the radical theatrical concepts of pre-war Russia and in the *Lanterna Magika*. Its discourse had suffused that of new music through the last decade, including Nono's own models of thought, as we have seen. His peers had already made significant progress in the electronic studio, produced early masterpieces of the genre, and the musicians he most respected – Maderna, Scherchen, Varèse – had all engaged fully in such research. Nono found Scherchen's experiments with mobile sound sources particularly fascinating.[150] Searching for techniques to avoid the static nature of loudspeaker diffusion became an important part of Scherchen's project in the studio.[151] It was at Scherchen's studio in Gravesano that Nono encountered Xenakis, constructing *Analogique B* from grains of sine wave. After Nono's frustrated attempt to explore such means in *Diario Polacco '58*, it was essential that this world should form part of the enormous experiment now in train.

The RAI Studio di Fonologia in Milan was well appointed: wave and noise generators, filters, modulators, envelope and pitch followers, mixers and multiple tape recorders.[152] Since Berio and Maderna's joint *Ritratto di Città* in 1955 it had produced works such as Berio's *Thema – omaggio a Joyce*, using recordings of Cathy Berberian reading from *Ulysses*, and his *Momenti* completed earlier in 1960, an altogether more abstract work. Having pioneered the use of taped concrete sounds with live performers in *Musica su due dimensioni*, Maderna had explored the purely synthetic potential of the Milan studio in *Notturno*. In 1959, Zuccheri had assisted Cage in the production of *Fontana Mix*; Mila said that Cage passed through the studio 'like a lively cyclone'. Its recent acquisition of a four-channel tape recorder was especially relevant to Nono's spatial ambitions. His expectations must have been based largely on Maderna's experiences; Nono was surely present at Darmstadt in 1957 when, two days after his own *Developments in Serial Technique*, Maderna introduced work from the studio in Milan:

> The encounter with electronics led to a complete overturning of my relationship with musical material. At that point I had to completely reorganise my composer's intellectual metabolism. While instrumental composition is usually preceded by a linear development of thought – precisely because that development has had no direct contact with the material – the fact that in the electronic studio it's possible to try various possible ways of realising sound structures directly, that by continuous manipulation you can infinitely renew and mutate these sound pictures, and finally

Poetry and drama

the fact that you can store up a whole stock of partial material, confronts the musician with an entirely new situation. [. . .]

When I began to compose with electronics I was afraid of using them inappropriately, and to get over this fear I decide to give myself over to my musical intuition rather than let myself be guided by rationality.[153]

Nono's long-awaited invitation was the result of a new policy of widening access to the studio; he was among a batch of a dozen composers invited to work there for the first time.[154] At the same time, Berio was loosening the reins. He was increasingly active in America and interested in working in other studios more willing to invest in newer technology. Nono arrived in Milan at the beginning of October 1960, planning to work for a couple of weeks.[155] In fact, it was 31 October before he could write to Mila that after a 'final sprint', *Omaggio a Emilio Vedova*, a four-channel piece lasting 4'45", was finished. Zuccheri described Nono's arrival in the studio:

On his first appearance in the studio Gigi brought a fairly abstract project he had worked on at home; a project that reproduced his idea of a sound achieved by the superimposition of sine waves [. . .]. The moment arrives: I had to synchronise the tape recorders, I had six to start at the same moment, with all Gigi's frequencies. Finally we listen to the result: a whistle! Gigi was so disappointed [. . .]. So he went back to Venice and developed his ideas: after that he returned some days later and did what he did [. . .]. He worked for about a month, always on the basis of other schemes, but in a different way. He thought more about 'colours' – it's no accident that *Omaggio* is dedicated to a painter![156]

Zuccheri's description reminds us of the physical nature of the early analogue studio: walls of dials to adjust parameters; units plugged into each other like a machine model of compositional process; the synchronising of tape recorders, adjusting their speed by hand, copying, combining and remediating material; the cutting and montage of tape. These presented Nono with an alternative map of his own thought, a new model for his own practice, that would persist. If this was his first official appearance, Nono's notes on the equipment and techniques of the studio must be subsequent to his initial disappointment. Although he was long acquainted with the principles and terms of electronic music, Nono took detailed notes on various forms of modulation (ring, frequency, amplitude) and filtering. His drawings of waves and envelopes already seem familiar from the sketches of recent years; the more technical diagrams are presumably explanations in Zuccheri's hand.

At the heart of Alfredo Lietti's design for the studio was a bank of nine oscillators, more stable and finely controlled than the master generator of the Cologne studio. This sine-wave based approach is heard clearly in Maderna's *Notturno* of 1956, but is also the basis of Berio's *Momenti*, produced in Milan shortly before Nono's arrival. Berio's work uses ninety-three sine waves, related by intervals of fifth and seventh. Nono's plan was therefore entirely in keeping with practice in the studio.

'Gigi's frequencies' remained fundamental to the work. His subsequent introduction to the piece presents a list of nine closely spaced low frequencies – the number of oscillators. Sketches include three more such lists and indicate a total of seven bands of sine waves, all recorded on to the first of four reels marked A–D.[157] Nono's subsequent text makes it clear that these have no harmonic relationship.[158] Each band contains a frequency marked 'A' – presumably the

Poetry and drama

'aleatoric' component mentioned in his text, a way to make the whole less static. Combinations of these bands are then mixed on to reel B, and from there on to reel C, producing dense but highly characterised sounds.[159] Arrows seem to refer to changes of pitch, of tape-recorder speed. A list of sounds on reel D mentions further 'acceleration'.[160] As in his studio on Giudecca, Nono is constantly reordering, re-expressing the state of his materials to find an appropriate environment for his imagination. He lists the 'snakes' (lengths of cut tape) from each reel: 12 from A, 6, 4, and 3 from B–D. This allows him to see what to add: 'timbres in motion, long low sounds – not mixed – unique, high (also ring modulated)'.[161] His notes indicate how to produce shorter sounds from these sustained textures: envelope shaping, 'hits' and 'slabs' – presumably short sections of tape giving fast transients.[162] As often, there seems to be a modulus to Nono's thought: four reels, channels, groups of material. He lists processes to be applied to elements A–D high and low band-pass filters, speed change (acceleration) and echo.[163] A further idea – 'low, rich blocks (with hits) – for the second part after the pause' – reinforces a structural interpretation of the fact that both quadraphonic tape copies of the work have a join at the exact mid-point.[164]

At what stage did the new work become a homage to his painter friend? There may, of course, be a more or less ironic refrence to Berio's *Thema (Omaggio a Joyce)*, produced two years earlier ein the same studio. Vedova was a friend since Nono's youth. He was a resistance fighter, somebody who had made his way as an artist without educational or social privilege, a revolutionary artist who had explicitly put his work at the service of social change. Vedova was a communist who, with Nono, had vocally defended abstraction against the dogma of socialist realism.[165] Their collaboration on *Intolleranza 1960* was already underway by October. In this very year, recognition of Vedova came from the Biennale itself in the form of the *Gran premio per la pittura*, enhancing the institutional weight of the theatre project. Vedova's bold, muscular form of abstract expressionism would expand from the planar into the multidimensional structures of his *Plurimi* – a development influenced by his work with Nono, as he later acknowledged.[166] Above all, working in the Studio di Fonologia allowed Nono to experience the physicality and immediacy of Vedova's work; for him the analogue studio was a plastic creative environment:

> the result for me: an immediate experience with no limits, in fact I felt able to express myself, especially a particular dramatic violence, even more freely _
>
> and I now see the possibility for a work I've been thinking about for some time, for chorus, live, partly recorded, and electronic sounds _
>
> the text: extracts from Mayakovsky's *Lenin* _
>
> but can you imagine the RAI allowing me the studio time to work on this????
> [. . .]
>
> Marino Zuccheri, the marvellous studio technician, gifted with a rare sensibility and musical intelligence, and a strong character – he was a partisan in Yugoslavia with Tito – is ready for this new work [. . .][167]

The rich spatial counterpoint of streams of events is the result of a continuous interactive process of listening, selecting and manipulating, but certain architectural events emerge from their alignment. The central pause mentioned by Nono is clear. Sonogram analysis confirms a synchrony of all four tracks at the loud structural events (2'22.7", 3'32.6" of the stereo CD version) that could only result from an edit of the assembled montage at a late stage. This gives a three-part form, or rather – given Nono's binary propensities – a two part form of which the second is also divided in two. This vertical division of the second half suggests that we might

Poetry and drama

listen for a horizontal structuring of the first; streams of events like brushstrokes 'of dramatic violence' are set against layers of constantly shifting filtered frequency bands. In the first part of the second half, more widely distributed events are reverberated to create a broader, more spacious sound-image; Caprioli's forensic analysis shows how Nono uses permutation to revolve four *timbri in moto* in space in the second.[168] The final part consists of two sustained contrapuntal developments of previous material, followed by a more fragmented coda in which the outbursts lose energy and become more distant.

Nono's explanatory note, for a radio audience, conveys his sense of this experience:

> This material, chosen by instinctive expressive intuition, contains within it a provocative compositional strength. The musical concept and the affordances of the material result in a state of continuous osmosis.
>
> And the instinctive improvisation is complemented by a compositional logic in structuring the material, no longer for its own sake.
>
> This position of principle, and not an impossible translation – or worse, description – in sound is the reason for the title of this study, dedicated to my friend Emilio Vedova.[169]

An earlier draft makes it clear that it was Vedova's practice, his expressive spontaneity, that Nono had in mind. Like Vedova he saw this as relating directly to socio-historical context, but in the case of music it was new technologies that afforded the appropriate means of expression:

> there is no reference to the painting of my friend Emilio Vedova, but rather to the fundamental necessity of his way of working.
>
> not to naturalistic ends, however pleasing or fascinating – material in and of itself, almost visual or sonic exhibitionism – but expression determined by the desire for human relationships that in using the new means of our times, whenever there should be human need, finds an increased capacity.[170]

As events unfolded, it becomes clear that this experience – the constant recasting of plans, the immediacy of interaction and decision-making – was a vital preparation for the final production of a score for *Intolleranza 1960*.

Notes

1 Introduzione al Kompositions-Studio di Kranichstein 1958. LNI, p. 44.
2 Letter to Steinecke, 14 May 1956. ALN.
3 Müller-Dohm, 2005, p. 393.
4 Schaller, 1997, p. 81.
5 LNI, pp. 19–42 is the article in its published form from 1958, translated as 'Lo sviluppo della tecnica seriale'. The analysis was intended for Berio's journal *Incontri Musicali*, but Nono found the editorial cuts unacceptable.
6 Letter to Steinecke, 12 February 1957. ALN.
7 Lo sviluppo della tecnica seriale, 1957. LNI, p. 33.
8 Arnold Schönberg: *Variationen für Orchester*. Partitura analizzata da Luigi Nono. Edizioni Collophon, Belluno/Venezia, 2011.
9 '*Varianti*'. LNI, p. 428.
10 'Lo sviluppo della tecnica seriale', 1957. LNI, p. 33.
11 'Lo sviluppo della tecnica seriale', 1957. LNI, p. 20.
12 Kolisch, 1957, p. 293.

Poetry and drama

13 ALN 15.01.01/04v.
14 '*Varianti*'. LNI, p. 427.
15 Schaller, 1997, p. 52.
16 From ALN 15.01.01/08v.
17 See, for example, ALN 15.01.01/15.
18 'Lo sviluppo della tecnica seriale', 1957. LNI, p. 36.
19 Kolisch, 1957.
20 Kolisch, 1957, p. 294.
21 Kolisch, 1957, p. 293.
22 'Lo sviluppo della tecnica seriale', 1957. LNI, p. 36. Nono also identifies Maderna's *Due studi per il "Processo" di Kafka* of 1950 as the first use of their technique of permutation by displacement.
23 Kolisch 1957, p. 296.
24 Schatz, 1957. Source texts in Boulez, 1991 ('Aléa'), Stockhausen, 1963 ('wie die Zeit vergeht').
25 Peyser, 1976, p. 121; Peyser, 2008, pp. 190–1.
26 Letter to Mila, 1 November 1960, in De Benedictis and Rizzardi, 2010, p. 48.
27 Letter to Steinecke, 12 October 1957. ALN.
28 Smith-Brindle, 1956.
29 Letter from Kolisch, 23 November 1957. ALN.
30 Letter from Hübner, 29 October 1957. ALN.
31 Henze, quoted in Krones, 2001, p. 270.
32 Some of the clearest statements of his theory are in *Feria d'agosto* (1946), and his subsequent essays for *Cultura e realtà*. Breuning (1999) gives an excellent account of Nono's relationship with Pavese's poetry.
33 Having been exiled by the fascist regime (for his associations rather than his actions) and lost several friends in the struggle for liberation, Pavese joined the PCI in 1945 He described his novel *Il compagno* (1947) as a political Bildungsroman.
34 Stenzl 1975, p. 412; Pavese 2000, p. 304.
35 ALN 16.02.01/3.
36 ALN 6.02.01/1.
37 ALN 16.02.01/12.
38 ALN 16.03.02/03vsx.
39 Schaller, 1997. p. 239.
40 'Testo – musica – canto', 1960. LNI, p. 75.
41 ALN 16.02.02/01vsx.
42 ALN 16.02.01/13.
43 ALN 16.02.01/21.
44 The overlapping principle was pointed out by Spies (1984).
45 Stenzl, 1975, p. 426, points out the substitution of melisma for text, Breuning, 1999, p. 113, that the number of notes matches the number of syllables.
46 Indeed, Stenzl sees a corresponding symbolism of instruments (Stenzl, 1975a, p. 426).
47 ALN 16.02.01/29.
48 Letter from Hübner, 10 December 1957, ALN.
49 Press agency extract from *Badische Tagblatt*, January 1958, in ALN.
50 *Die Welt*, 15 January 1958.
51 Letter to Steinecke, 19 December 1957, ALN.
52 Andersch had been part of Gruppe 47, a group of writers seeking an identity for the literature of a new Germany free from both Soviet and American pressures. Among their number was also another of Nono's poetic points of reference, poet Ingeborg Bachmann, then living in Rome and working on opera libretti for Hans-Werner Henze. The pattern of Andersch's own life and work gives some texture to the frequent, almost longing references to Italian warmth and colour in German reviews of Nono's music. In 1957, he moved to the Ticino, the southern-oriented face of a German-speaking state, where he was part of a wider German-speaking artistic community. Italy then figured importantly in his subsequent work, especially *Die Rote* of 1960. His second autobiographical novel, *Sansibar oder der letzte Grund* (1957), was to become the subject of an opera by Ekkehard Mayer in 1994.
53 'Alcune preciazioni su "Intolleranza 1960"' (1969). LNI, p. 100. Andersch would also be responsible for the German text of Intolleranza.
54 Letter from Ungaretti, 1 March 1956, in Nono and Ungaretti, 2016, p. 61.

Poetry and drama

55 Piccioni, 2011.

56 Ungaretti, 2011, p. 625.

57 Letters from Ungaretti, 9 August 1956, 23 February 1957, in Nono and Ungaretti, 2016, p. 66, p. 69.

58 Letter from Ungaretti, 6 October 1957, in Nono and Ungaretti, 2016, p. 73: 'Write to ROMANÒ – RAI – MILANO [...] He is a dear friend, a good poet and critic, and I think that knowing everybody and their capabilities he could easily find you the right poet to write the dramatic poetry you want to set to music.' Romanò was director of radio at the RAI in Milan 1955–9, and then very influential as director of television in the early sixties. A detailed obituary appeared in *La Repubblica*, 6 May 1984, p. 35.

59 Letter from Ungaretti, 11 March 1958, in Nono and Ungaretti, 2016, p. 77.

60 Letter to Ungaretti, 14 March 1958, in Nono and Ungaretti, 2016, pp. 80–2. Fritz Winckel (1907–2000) was a physicist and acoustician who had been involved in the musical applications of technological advances since the 1930, including the neo-Bechstein electronically controlled grand piano. He was part of the Arbeitskreis für Elektronische Musik at the Technical University Berlin and contributed to Scherchen's *Gravesaner Blätter*, including a recent article on 'The ear as a time-measurement organ' (Winckel, 1957).

61 Letter from Ungaretti, 24 June 58, in Nono and Ungaretti, 2016, p. 88.

62 Interview with Enzo Restagno, 1987. LNII, p. 513.

63 See, for example, sketch 18.03/04. ALN.

64 Ligeti, 1965, p. 6.

65 'Cori di Didone'. LNI, p. 432.

66 *Darmstädter Tagblatt*, 9 September 1958.

67 *Die Welt*, 9 September 1958.

68 *Die Welt*, 19 September 1958.

69 Iddon, 2013, pp. 224–5.

70 Letter from Ungaretti, 19 July 1959, in Nono and Ungaretti, 2016, p. 117.

71 Letter to Ungaretti, 13 June 1959, in Nono and Ungaretti, 2016, pp. 111–12.

72 Letter from Steinecke to Maderna, 10 August 1958, (Dalmonte, 2001, p. 168). Iddon dismisses Shultis' suggestion that the idea to invite Cage had come from Maderna and Nono (Iddon, 2007, pp. 93–4).

73 Cage, 1961, p. 35.

74 'Presenza storica nella musica d'oggi'. LNI, 46–53. The article appeared in five versions in 1960: in German in *Melos* and *Darmstädter Beiträge zur Neuen Musik*, in Italian in *Il Verri* and *La rassegna musicale*, and in English in *The Score* (27, pp. 41–5, July 1960), as 'The Historical Reality of Music Today'.

75 Letter to Steinecke, 28 October 1958. ALN.

76 Undated letter to Steinecke, late 1958. ALN.

77 Iddon, 2013, p. 262.

78 Letter to Hartmann, 21 October 1958, in Wagner, 1980, p. 211.

79 Calvino, 2009, p. 9 (1964).

80 Interview with Philippe Albèra, 1987. LNII, p. 420.

81 Letters from Strobel, 20 December 1958, 18 February 1959, ALN.

82 Letter to Hübner, 15 February 1959, ALN.

83 Letter from Steinecke, 15 February 1959, ALN.

84 Personal communication from Nuria Schoenberg-Nono.

85 Berry, 2008, p. 5.

86 Berry, 2008, p. 4.

87 ALN 19.02/04, 07r.

88 ALN 19.02/03.

89 Letters from Steinecke, 24 May 1959; to Steinecke, 11 July 1959, ALN.

90 ALN 19.02/14v.

91 'Composizione per orchestra n. 2: Diario polacco '58'. LNI, p. 435.

92 Permission was denied by Guilio Razzi, Director of radio programming. Letter from Razzi, 3 January 1959, ALN.

93 Mila's radio account of the studio's early history is transcribed in Donati and Pacetti, 2002, pp. 160–8.

94 Letter to Hartmann, 3 December 1958, in Albèra, 1987, pp. 49–50.

95 Letters to Steinecke, 15 February 1959, 2 April 1959, ALN.

Poetry and drama

96 Interview with Enzo Restagno, 1987. LNII, p. 516.
97 ALN 19.04.01/04.
98 ALN 19.04.06/03.
99 ALN 19.04.06/01.
100 ALN 19.04.02/13r.
101 Schaller, 1997, p. 144.
102 ALN 19.10.01/02.
103 ALN 19.07/05.
104 Letter from Alexander Goehr, 25 November 1959, ALN.
105 'Composizione per orchestra n. 2: Diario polacco '58'. LNI, p. 435.
106 Rizzardi, 1999, plots the full narrative of theatrical works that nearly emerge.
107 Stenzl, 1998, p. 51.
108 Translated as 'Presenza storica nella musica d'oggi', 1960. LNI, p. 46
109 'Presenza storica nella musica d'oggi'. LNI, p. 49.
110 Pestalozza, 1981.
111 'Presenza storica nella musica d'oggi'. LNI, p. 50.
112 'Presenza storica nella musica d'oggi'. LNI, pp. 52–3.
113 A photograph depicts the moment: Stockhausen, 2001, Plate 23.
114 Iddon, 2013, p. 271.
115 Von Lewinski in *Darmstädter Tagblatt*, 3 March 1959: 'Von der Verantwortung der Komponisten: Nonos aggressiver Vortrag/Ergebnisse der ersten Kranichsteiner Woche'. Ernst Thomas in *Frankfurter Allgemeine Zeiting*, 8 September 1959: 'Kontroverse und Konzert: Darmstädter Ferienkurse und Hessischer Rundfunk'.
116 Letter from Steinecke, 9 November 1959. ALN.
117 Interview with Enzo Restagno, 1987. LNII, 492.
118 'Presenza storica nella musica d'oggi'. LNI, p. 53.
119 Letter from Lachenmann, 22 October 1957, in De Benedictis and Morsch 2012, pp. 7–8.
120 Letter to Lachenmann, 22 October 1957, in De Benedictis and Morsch 2012, pp. 9–10.
121 Nonnenmann, 2013, p. 84.
122 Letter to Lachenmann, July 1958, in De Benedictis and Morsch 2012, p. 32.
123 For example, Lachenmann in Nonnenmann 2013, p. 103; Schwertsik in Nonnenmann 2013, p. 133.
124 Letter from Lachenmann, 6 August 1960, in De Benedictis and Morsch, 2012, p. 61.
125 Lachenmann, semester report 19 February 1959, in Nonnenmann, 2013, p. 111.
126 Lachenmann, semester report 11 August 1959, in Nonnenmann, 2013, p. 119.
127 Lachenmann, semester report 9 March 1959, in Nonnenmann, 2013, p. 143.
128 Nonnenmann, 2013, p. 200.
129 Nonnenmann, 2013, p. 104.
130 Lachenmann, 2004, pp. 311–16.
131 Letter to Lachenmann, July or August 1959, in De Benedictis and Morsch 2012, pp. 44–6.
132 Lachenmann, quoted in Nonnenmann, 2013, p. 129.
133 'Composizione per orchestra n. 2, Diario polacco '58'. LNI, p. 436.
134 Letter to Mila, 27 November 1959, in De Benedictis and Rizzardi, 2010, p. 21.
135 Lachenmann, 1999, p. 23.
136 Lachenmann, 1999, pp. 19–21.
137 Interview with Enzo Restagno, 1987. LNII, pp. 512–13.
138 'La terra e la compagna'. LNI, p. 430.
139 Letter from Steinecke 17 January 1960; letter to Steinecke 21 January 1960, ALN.
140 ALN 20.01.02/01.
141 ALN 20.02/04.
142 ALN 20.02/08.
143 ALN 20.05.02/01r.
144 Interview with Enzo Restagno, 1987. LNII, p. 514.
145 ALN 21.07/01r.
146 Letter to Steinecke, 3 March 1960. ALN.
147 'Testo – musica – canto'. LNI, p. 58.
148 'Testo – musica – canto'. LNI, p. 64.
149 'Testo – musica – canto'. LNI, p. 67.

Poetry and drama

150 Interview with Enzo Restagno, 1987. LNII, p. 515.
151 Interview with Leonardo Pinzauti, 1970. LNII, p. 85.
152 An article from 1956 describing the studio's equipment is reproduced on the CD-ROM accompanying Donati and Pacetti, 2002.
153 Baroni and Dalmonte, 1985, pp. 83–4.
154 De Benedictis and Rizzardi, 2000, pp. 191 and 287.
155 Letter to Mila, 3 October 1960, in De Benedictis and Rizzardi, 2010, p. 31.
156 Zuccheri, quoted in De Benedictis, 2000, p. 193.
157 ALN 22.01/05.
158 'Omaggio a Emilio Vedova'. LNI, pp. 438–9.
159 ALN 22.01/06.
160 ALN 22.01/07.
161 ALN 22.01/09r.
162 ALN 22.01/04.
163 ALN 22.01/09v.
164 ALN 22.01/10.
165 Rossanda, 2010, p. 140.
166 Zuccheri composed an electronic soundtrack *Parete* for an exhibition of Vedova's work in the Italian pavilion at the Montreal Expo in 1967, when Nono was too busy to accept the commission.
167 Letter to Mila, 31 October 1960, in De Benedictis and Rizzardi, 2010, p. 45.
168 Caprioli, 2007, p. 59.
169 'Omaggio a Emilio Vedova'. LNI, p. 439.
170 'Omaggio a Emilio Vedova'. LNI, p. 438.

7

INTOLLERANZA 1960

Gestation

And if I am given this world with its injustices, it is not so that I might contemplate them coldly, but that I might animate them with my indignation, that I might disclose them and create them with their nature as injustices, that is, as abuses to be suppressed. Thus, the writer's universe will only reveal itself in all its depth to the examination, the admiration, and the indignation of the reader; and the generous love is a promise to maintain, and the generous indignation is a promise to change, and the admiration a promise to imitate; although literature is one thing and morality a quite different one, at the heart of the aesthetic imperative we discern the moral imperative. For, since the one who writes recognises, by the very fact that he takes the trouble to write, the freedom of his readers, and since the one who reads, by the mere fact of his opening the book, recognises the freedom of the writer, the work of art, from whichever side you approach it, is an act of confidence in the freedom of men. And since readers, like the author, recognize this freedom only to demand that it manifest itself, the work can be defined as an imaginary presentation of the world insofar as it demands human freedom.[1]

Sartre's *What is Literature?* was published in Italian in 1960 and immediately became a vital reference for Nono. He quoted the words above in *Text – Musik – Gesang* at Darmstadt, and on several occasions over the next few years.[2] Still in 1966, at the farthest point of his political orbit, he would return to the questions that Sartre poses in this text: What is writing? Why write? Who does one write for?[3] Sartre provided the most visible model of the public intellectual who had theorised the role of his art. His philosophy was of less interest to Nono than his political stance as a writer. He was critical of the Soviet Union, a supporter of the independence struggle in Algeria and of the communist experiment in Cuba, all resonant for Nono as his own political engagement – particularly with the emerging Third World – became more active and more public. Nono was confronting difficult questions of subject and narrative in his own emerging concept of a new music theatre: how to explore the relationship between individual choice and social and political dynamics? How to make the work current, relevant to a wide audience such that they would reflect on their own situation? Sartre's concept of a 'theatre of situations' became an important guide:

But we have our own problems: the problem of means and ends, of the legitimacy of violence, the problem of the consequences of action, the problem of the relationships between the person and the collectivity, between the individual undertaking and historical constants, and a hundred more. It seems to me that the dramatist's task is to choose from among these limit situations the one that best expresses his concerns, and to present it to the public as the question certain free individuals are confronted with. It is only in this way that the theater will recover its lost resonance, only in this way that it will succeed in unifying the diversified audiences who are going to it in our time.[4]

In his exchanges with Andersch in September 1957, Nono had put forward an idea inspired directly by David Wark Griffith's 1916 film *Intolerance*. Griffith presents four historically separate episodes that demonstrate different aspects of human intolerance, in a film often regarded as a response to the criticism of his previous *The Birth of a Nation* as racist. Nono proposed '3 episodes of intolerance/3 of '"love-understanding" simultaneity – *together*'.[5] In a subsequent letter he bemoans the returning of the political forces of oppression, citing the case of the poor of the Po delta, south of Venice, annually subjected to severe and often disastrous flooding. The most recent case had taken place just a week earlier, devastating the commune of Porto Tolle.

Nono probably saw *Intolerance* at the Circolo di cinema 'Francesco Pasinetti' in Venice, where he also saw films such as *Strike* and *The Battleship Potemkin* by Meyerhold's student Eisenstein.[6] The circolo was formative in Nono's lifelong interest in cinema: in its contemporary relevance, its political power, its exploration of new technologies and its implications for his own musical thought. Formed in 1948, the club screened historical, classic, foreign, radical and new films but also promoted discussion. Massimo Cacciari remembered it as 'a place of meeting, of debate, of challenge, even polemics, a place of cultural and civil "education".'[7] Venetian historian Giovanni Scarabello describes its 'politically aware, left-leaning membership, debating whether to give priority to form (Croce) or content (Lukács)'.[8] This pattern of the shared experience of artistic work giving rise to debate would become a fundamental component of Nono's practice as a composer. Several directors would play an important part in the evolution of his thought – Visconti, Antonioni, Fellini, Godard and Tarkovsky, to name only the best known – but Eisenstein and Vertov remained touchstones.

Another cinematic model presents itself: Antonioni's *Il grido* had just been released, a study of the misery and uncertainty of life in the Po valley in which the pivotal protagonist is an absent husband, obliged to emigrate to find work. Antonioni's previous film *Le amiche* must also have been of interest to Nono, being based on a short novel by Pavese and much feted at the Venice Film Festival of 1955. Its existential tone and tragic conclusion are presented through a series of tangentially related human situations.

A page of notes, presumably from the time of his exchanges with Andersch, summarises important implications of Nono's evolving approach to music theatre:

> simultaneity of actions – or characters – of complex situations, <u>for</u> their simultaneity, and unique situations
> use of microphones – and loudspeakers, not just for the voices (chorus and soloists) but also for the instruments [. . .]
> PERHAPS ENOUGH of the orchestra pit! instruments all behind the stage [. . .]
> PERHAPS eliminate actor-singers on stage! But singers with the instruments behind the stage.

on the stage
only 'azione scenica' – lights – masses –
<u>IMPORTANT – TECHNICIAN – 'MAESTRO DEL SUONO'</u>!
action on stage <u>SILENT</u>!
very few words on stage –
words spoken and written –![9]

In the same notebook he considers the role of intervallic motif in opera, a crucial aspect of the work to come. In Bach, he notes, this allows the composer to construct clearly recognisable musical-dramatic structures; in Berg's *Lulu*, on the other hand, such characterisation is largely lost to the listener. 'Situations' (he uses Sartre's term) may be simultaneous or follow each other non-linearly, and actions are no longer to be identified with particular performers – Nono studies combinations of live and recorded voices, mimes and dancers. Loudspeakers and light have structural roles, uniting space and drama. Abstract complementary scenarios emerge from Nono's notes – situations rather than narratives: a youth confronting nature, political struggle and love, for example. One such idea pairs factory and forest, anticipating two of Nono's major works of the 1960s: *La fabbrica illuminata* (1964) and *A floresta é jovem e cheja de vida* (1966). Such a richness of thought was more than a single work could accommodate; *Intolleranza 1960* must be seen as a stage in a broader evolution of ideas, many of which would be explored more theoretically in Nono's 1962 paper *Possibilità e necessità di un nuovo teatro musicale*. Perhaps this fertility also created a burden of expectation at the limits of what was realizable in the circumstances.

Nono's avid reading of literature on visionary, politically engaged pre-war Russian and German theatre – Mayakovsky, Meyerhold, Toller, Brecht, Piscator – had shaped his conception of a new music theatre, a development of the line brutally arrested in the 1930s. From Giulio Carlo Argan's 1951 study of the Bauhaus Nono made detailed notes on Walter Gropius' *Total Theatre*, designed for Piscator in 1927, and the stage designs of Oskar Schlemmer. He notes Schlemmer's observation that theatrical space is the product of rhythmical movement, and his vision that 'the theatre will no longer be a moralising institution or a school of sentiment', echoing Gramsci's criticism of Italian lyric theatre.[10] The experience of the Lanterna Magika was a concrete example of what had since become technologically possible. Nono had now accumulated a complex network of references, a critical pressure of creative energy: the virtual drama of *Diario polacco '58*, seeing Brecht's company in *Mutter Courage*, his discussions with Andersch and Calvino, his courting of Ungaretti and approaches to Piscator. Nono was searching urgently for the catalyst for its release.

In 1959, poet and slavist Angelo Maria Ripellino published an exhaustive, sympathetic and penetrating survey of Mayakovsky and Russian avant-garde drama.[11] Nono was already fascinated with the Russian poet: 'My great model in the 1950s was Myakovsky: I wanted to combine thoughts that were developing with a language that could renew feelings, expression itself. It was the time of our resistance to socialist realism.'[12] He made extensive notes on Myakovsky's poems, seemingly with a view to staging several simultaneously.[13] Ripellino's book emphasises Mayakovsky's links with visual art – the futurists and constructivists – the influence of Meyerhold and the cinema of Eisenstein, and his central role in experimental theatre. It presents Myakovsky's work as a nexus of poetry, theatre, artistic and linguistic theory, technology, agitprop and society, all tuned to the historical moment: 'The theatre often serves as a pretext for talking about other arts, that flow together there as in a torrential estuary.'[14] Nono consumed the book immediately. He had encountered friends of Ripellino on his trip to Eastern Europe. As a fellow socially aware artist with an intimate knowledge of such ideas, Ripellino seemed an ideal

Intolleranza 1960

person to enlist in Nono's search for a new kind of music theatre. Nono wrote to him at the very beginning of 1960, hoping that they might meet to discuss his 'musical-operatic theatre project', and asking for advice on a journal that might publish an article by Radok and Svoboda.[15] Ripellino, well acquainted with contemporary Czech culture and the Lanterna Magika, responded to the proposal warmly and positively. This was the start of a fifteen-month collaboration that began with unbounded enthusiasm and ended, despite being a vital step on the path to *Intolleranza 1960*, in frustration. With hindsight, one can see the seeds of misunderstanding early in their correspondence: different aspirations, different assumptions as to the nature of their project and roles, different responses to the practical requirements that emerged. Nono was clear:

> I am sending my ideas for the theatre ahead of hopefully discussing them with you in Rome.
>
> not just to ask for advice or information, but directly for your complete collaboration: that is, in the fixing of the text.
>
> I believe only in collaboration over time, not before or after but at the same time as writing the music.[16]

The immediate impulse for such an approach, he explained in the same letter, was the likely invitation to write a work for the inauguration of the new theatre in Darmstadt in 1964. Nono takes Griffith's model of four parallel but historically distinct instances of intolerance, substituting episodes from the Middle Ages, the Renaissance (Brecht's *Galileo*), recent history (Nazism) and current events (French repression in Algeria as represented by the case of Henri Alleg, to whose account Sartre had written a much discussed preface). Describing a process analogous to his polyphony of choral elements or of the simultaneous development of materials, Nono imagines a structure in which these strands would be interwoven and combined in changing densities. Against these, he planned to counterpoint a fifth thread representing 'life and human conduct overcoming and eliminating all Nazi violence (Nazism as the synthesis and symbol and reality of all that is antihuman).' Further letters would make it clear that Nono regarded current West European regimes as barely more enlightened. His ideas for staging such a spectacle develop themes from earlier Russian and German theatre, as well as the Lanterna Magika: the dissolution of unity of space as well as time, of barriers between audience and stage, between live and recorded material, and the use of technology to distribute sound and image. In short, 'the maximum expansion now possible of the human capacity to transmit-speak-act-show-move-shake, for the maximum now possible for human reception'.

While Ripellino replied with practical ideas for the production, Nono's plan had evolved: 'three or four episodes, all contemporary: thus perhaps harder and more direct. and engaged (especially with the equivocating Jesuit indifference around at the moment – look at Fellini).'[17] In April, Ripellino sent Nono a copy of his new collection of poetry, including *Vivere è stare svegli* (*To live is to remain alert*); its sentiments resonated immediately with Nono, who asked for more to use for a new work. Another common venture emerged: a journal to resist 'anti-artism' from all quarters, to be organised with Calvino and, at Nono's suggestion, Mila. Nono, perhaps still smarting from a dispute over the drastic editing of an article for *Incontri Musicali*, was less enthusiastic about Ripellino's proposal to involve Berio. This project would come to nothing but was a first glimpse of subsequent cultural initiatives; it was also another issue to contribute to the mounting lack of clarity as they exchanged ideas. Little material progress had been made, therefore, when in April Nono announced the possibility of a commission from the Venice Biennale for May 1961, three years ahead of their imagined schedule. Specific plans were

Intolleranza 1960

already under discussion with the Director, Mario Labroca, and Emilio Vedova. In the same letter, Nono declared *Sarà dolce tacere* finished and *"Ha venido"*. *Canciones para Silvia* underway: 'songs – a single line_ and everything for our opera!'[18]

In the midst of ideas and enthusiasm for all their potential projects, it was Nono who sent the first piece of text to Ripellino, an extract from Alleg's *La tortura*. He was keen that they should meet with Vedova: 'come on come on come on!!!! not one day but now!!!!!!!!!!'[19] A clearer vision of the space and design seem to have been as vital to Nono's evolving musical concept as the text. He confirmed Labroca's commission in May, for the following July – notably, in terms of Nono's vision and subsequent events, as the Italian contribution to a festival of music theatre. Institutional understandings of the project, different again, now entered the mix; within a week, Schott's wrote that they were awaiting the libretto impatiently. Just as he was starting work at the studio in Milan, Nono received the news that Ripellino had hit 'choppy waters' with the libretto, buried among updates on other cultural ventures. In November, a letter from Schott's provided a cold summary of the situation: the premiere will be on 17 April 1961, there is no title and no libretto, you will realise the electronic element at the RAI, and the remaining requirements must be modest enough that you can provide orchestral and choral material in little more than two months.

Spurred by urgency, Nono sent Ripellino a detailed plan of ten scenes, key to the structure of the final work. It is an archetypal Nono architecture, a polyphony of musico-dramatic threads balancing interlocking patterns of oppression and resistance (Figure 7.1).

An emigrant worker's attempt to return home provides a narrative thread; more importantly, it constitutes an emotional horizon against which to weigh the human significance of the situations through which he passes. Each scene has its own permutation of soloists, chorus, live and recorded voices, acoustic and amplified instruments. The emigrant (tenor) is present throughout until his death in scene IX; his companion (soprano), appears in scene VI and survives him as the voice of hope. Balance is maintained on other planes: scenes III and VI are ballets, electronics are to be used on scenes III, VI, IX and X, and the Höhepunkte occur in scenes III and IX. Nono's musical plans are organised as spatially as those for the drama, stage and scenography; 'in fact, the stage is above all an architectonic-spatial organism', he notes.[20] Nono's sketches for Vedova propose constantly shifting patterns of photograph, colour and film; he contemplated using sections of Eisenstein's *October*. In a later proposal to Piscator, Nono suggests extracts from Storck and Ivens' 1933 film *Misère au Borinage*, a documentary

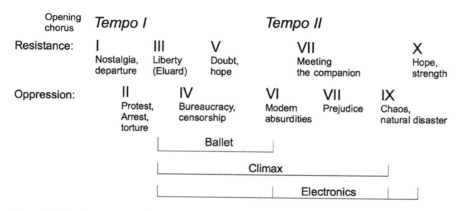

Figure 7.1 Intolleranza 1960: plan, October 1960 (aggregate of several sketches)

study of industrial depression in 1930s' Belgium that had gained new currency with miners' strikes in the 1950s. This was not the first time he had considered using film: in 1954 he had written to Luchino Visconti proposing a film component for the first performances of Schönberg's *Moses und Aron*.[21]

Nono's various layouts of the plan demonstrate his tendency to combinatorial patterns: soloists, emotions, structures and materials. Ripellino's poem in the opening chorus – *Vivere è stare svegli* – announces the perspective of the entire work; it is the story of the emigrant's emerging consciousness as he witnesses the social and human realities around him. Nono's understanding of 'situation' derives directly from Sartre:

> what we have to show in the theatre are simple and human situations and free individuals in these situations choosing what they will be. [. . .] It is through particular situations that each age grasps the human situation and the enigmas human freedom must confront.[22]

The dramatic references are now absolutely of the present: emigrant workers in Belgian coal mines, where 262 (mostly Italian and many anonymous) had died in the 1956 disaster of Marcinelle;[23] the brutal repression of industrial unrest in Italy in 1960, the first explosions of the 'economic miracle' (particularly the use of cheap labour from the south in the industrial north of Italy) and the start of two decades of social unrest; the French colonial war in Algeria; racism and the civil rights movement in the USA, and the plight of the poor of the Po delta, subject to annual devastation – the subject of Antonioni's film. That the work would now be presented in Venice was highly significant for Nono in this respect. His concern with the conditions of local people would become manifest in his direct involvement in the political struggles of the next two decades as the PCI confronted the right-wing state backing of private corporations, particularly in the petro-chemical works of the Venetian mainland. Already in a letter to his parents from a decade earlier he laments the inaction leading to the natural disasters of the Po, as if to prick their conservative conscience. The term 'emigrant' was itself resonant in Italy, where hundreds of thousands of workers from the poorer regions lived in poor conditions in the industrialised north or in Germany, to send money back to their families. The word used by Andersch in his German translation – *Flüchtling* (refugee) – conveys this sense more accurately in the contemporary world.

De Benedictis has shown how the scene-by-scene dramatic and emotional plan and the catalogue of associated texts correspond in large part to the final work.[24] Nono's ideas had evolved ahead of those of his librettist, so any major departure would have been difficult to assimilate at this stage. Ripellino's texts – *quadri* – began to arrive in instalments. An allegory of an emigrant worker, Piero, the piece is fully in the manner of Myakovsky's 1929 satire *The Bathhouse*. Among the descriptions of torture and catastrophe, clowns appear in a scene of bureaucratic absurdity, a high priest conducts esoteric rituals in synthetic near-nonsense language of homophones, and surreal headlines announce seven-headed Martians disembarking at Giudecca, a revolt by elephants and accidental atomic explosions. Detailed descriptions of film, image, lighting and movement include actors placed among the audience.[25] More *Die Zauberflöte* or *Le Grand Macabre* than Brecht, Ripellino's verbose, fantastical text also lacked the discipline necessary for a libretto. Nono in turn reached an agreement with Schott's to send the score piecemeal, as each section was completed; this process partly accounts for the apparent structural asymmetry of the final score. As he struggled to bring the text into usable form, Nono's frustration and urgency clearly increased. He incorporated less than half of Ripellino's first quadro into the first two scenes; for the remainder, Nono's selected sources are interspersed

Intolleranza 1960

Act 1
Opening chorus:
Vivere è stare svegli (Ripellino)

Scene I/II - *in a mining community*
emigrant (T), woman (A) chorus of miners
(an alto, the emigrant's lover, interrupts in Sc. II)

Scene III - *in a city -*
the emigrant participates in a large
popular demonstration
chorus of demonstrators

Scene IV - *in a police station*
interrogation of arrested demonstrators
4 policemen (speaking), emigrant,
woman, voice of Alleg

Scene V - *the torture*
chorus of tortured prisoners, voice of Sartre

Scene VI - *in a concentration camp*
chorus of prisoners, policemen,
victim of torture (voice of Fučík – B),
emigrant, Algerian (Bar.)

Scene VII - *after the escape from the camp*
emigrant, Algerian, chorus of refugees

Act 2
Scene I - *absurdities from modern life*
taped sounds

Scene II - *the meeting of the emigrant*
and his companion
companion (S), emigrant

Scene III - *projections of episodes of*
violence and fanaticism
emigrant, woman, companion,
chorus of refugees and companions

Scene IV - *near a village along a river*
in full flood
emigrant, companion,
chorus of country people, speaker

Final chorus:
A coloro che verranno (Brecht)

Figure 7.2 Intolleranza 1960: final form

with lines from Ripellino as a unifying narrative gloss. *Intolleranza 1960* finally consists of eleven scenes, the texts largely taken from those that had inspired the work in its various stages of evolution (Figure 7.2). Labroca's eventual idea to present the work as being 'based on an idea by Angelo Maria Ripellino' was somewhat ironic; the idea, of all things, was Nono's.

Besides the emigrant (tenor), his lover in Act 1 (alto) and companion in Act 2 (soprano), there are six other anonymous solo voices: an Algerian (baritone), a victim of torture (bass) and four policemen (speaking parts). In addition to the poems by Ripellino and Brecht and lines by Eluard (*Liberté*) and Myakovsky (*La nostra marcia*), texts are taken from Ripellino's libretto, Raniero Panzieri's translation of *La Gangrène* (accounts of the torture of Algerians in Paris in 1958), Henri Alleg's *La Question* (his account of torture in Algeria in 1957) and Fučík's *Notes from the Gallows*.

Nono set out his subject while writing *Intolleranza 1960*:

> The subject is that of *Il canto sospeso*. Intolerance in the contemporary world. We see an emigrant who, out of longing, decides to undertake the path back to his country and encounters all the atrocious realities of today. The camps, torture, the absurdity of bureaucracy, the long suicide of the spirits. I speak clearly and loudly.[26]

Nono's conception of time is quite consistent. He understands historical development, like musical development, in both continuous-sequential and simultaneous terms. Like most conceptual spaces of his musical thought, time divides in (at least) two orthogonally related ways. Just as we could understand his previous ten-scene plan, with its interweaving of oppression and resistance, as formally analogous to the musical dialectic of *Incontri*, so in the final version we have a parallel with *Canti per 13*. The two acts deal with time in different ways; while the first retains narrative sequence, the scenes of the second could almost exist in parallel. In this respect he does not distinguish between 'musical' and 'textual' ideas. The new technological means allow for 'a pluridimensional imagery, in both the unity of a [single] fact and in the simultaneity of several facts, permitting a multi-levelled reading in the conceiving and drafting of a text'.[27]

He articulates the dramatic space in similar fashion; the dialectic of repression and resistance is balanced by the emergence of the emigrant who also has two roles: as individual and as representative of the group:

The two ideas, intolerance and the opposition to it, are not embodied in two characters, but in the varying succession of ways in which they are manifested – capitalist exploitation, fascism, colonialism on one side, and on the other an emigrant miner who rebels, a people who resist and the anticolonialist struggle – revealing new aspects and continuously integrating them, [they] contribute to the polyhedric composition of two situations, the real protagonists, in the prism that results from their contrasting roles.[28]

In its syntax, this sentence conveys the irreducible nature of Nono's thought. His geometric metaphor is well chosen. While the core process is fundamentally dialectical, the shapes it generates take multiple directions; their relationship may not be linear or transparent. We should bear this in mind when considering his materials and processes. They are not static, not abstract points of reference relative to which we can orient or reassure ourselves as to our current position in a wider development – dramatic, musical or compositional. This is a vital resistant property of Nono's music, embodied above all in the three great *azioni sceniche*: *Intolleranza 1960*, *Al gran sole* and – if we might include it – *Prometeo*. In the necessary complexity of his vision, Nono challenges his own creative, emotional and intellectual capacities, his very endurance, to find new provocations and solutions and to broaden his consciousness.

Composition

Nono makes multiple analyses of his text as it is assembled, finding internal structures, balances and affinities; deleting and refining; marking allocation to soloists and texts to be projected. Notes of 'Höhepunkt' or 'punto culminante' mark climaxes within passages or entire acts, recalling the musical-emotional analyses of Scherchen. His articulation of the emerging text is mapped onto the musical space developed in *"Ha venido"*. *Canciones para Silvia*; work on the now-concrete theatre piece had begun as he was finishing the two previous choral works. The flexibility of technique developed over the previous year was thoroughly tested as Nono confronted the magnitude and time-scale of his long envisioned project. In January 1961, Nuria wrote to Lachenmann asking whether he might prepare the piano reduction of *Intolleranza*: 'Gigi works day and night, as you can imagine. [. . .] nobody else could really do it, as you can hardly make a normal piano reduction.'[29] Lachenmann agreed, but needed the material: 'I look forward to working with your score, but also I look forward to it being finished.'[30]

The final score was completed in barely three months, between early December 1960 and 7 March 1961. In contrast, the relatively long gestation period – the second half of 1960 – allowed Nono to conceive a close relationship between the current state of his raw musical materials and the dramatic dynamics of the new work. The number square he uses to determine readings from the group-matrices (duration, group-size, intervals) is the same as in the previous work: an abstract distribution-engine. The interval had been the focus of his recent vocal works, and is his starting point in composing *Intolleranza 1960*. Nono sets out from the same group of pitch series he developed for *"Ha venido"*. *Canciones para Silvia*. That he is able to project the dynamics of an emotional drama on to the intervallic world defined by these materials is an indication of the robustness of the interval as a musical atom, but also of the comprehensive nature of the space Nono had constructed. Figure 7.3 shows Nono's series for four solo voices (the bass material will serve both bass and baritone parts).

In this plan, tenor and soprano both have a main series and one of complementary intervals, alto and bass/baritone just a single series ('fixed'). The chorus should follow the intervals of

Figure 7.3 Intolleranza 1960: initial series for the soloists, with Nono's interval notation

the soloist in question. For the scenes of oppression, Nono plans to use the all-interval series ('to be varied'). As we have seen, this series is a generator, the opposite of a theme; its use suggests that the more figural series be understood similarly, despite the references to 'Leitmotiv' in Nono's notes. The intervals of soprano, alto and bass/baritone are subsets of those of the tenor, apart from the soprano's minor third. The emigrant, the central and most complex character, is thus able to embody the full range of intervallic expressive properties with the exception of one, the absence of which is dramatically structural. The role of the companion, soprano, in offering hope, in providing both emotion and musical completeness, is clearly perceptible. The early lessons of Maderna and Hindemith ring through an unusually technical article on *Intolleranza 1960*. Here, Nono is quite specific as to the connection between interval and character in what he terms the 'integration' of these materials:

> the relationship between tenor and alto develops through various uses of four basic intervals: minor 2nd – major 2nd – fourth – tritone. [. . .] the song of the alto moves, in distinction from that of the tenor, exclusively by minor 2nd (and major 7th and minor 9th) and by tritone, such that the expression of the woman is aggressive and manipulative towards the emigrant. [. . .] the insertion of the minor 3rd, characteristic of the song of the soprano, is an anticipation, in the desire [of the tenor] for the companion he will encounter.[31]

This lexicon of intervals gains strength not merely through their inherent properties, but because of what they signify to Nono as the work is emerging, bar by bar. Nono's article gives examples of his integration of characters by interval. Equally telling are the ways in which he manipulates his draft materials to enhance such properties. The emigrant's impassioned cry of 'Quanti di noi s'inabissono' ('How many of us go down into the abyss') in the first scene is an example of such careful lyricism. Figure 7.4 shows the soprano and tenor lines from the final

Intolleranza 1960

Figure 7.4 Intolleranza 1960: bars 173–5

score, together with a draft version of the soprano part. The tenor line follows the 2– 2+ series (marked with asterisks in the figure), each member of which initiates a horizontal group formed from the aggregate interval potential of the two tenor series, their number determined by the mapping scheme for this scene. In his choice of interval, register and rhythmic subdivision Nono weaves a lyrical line with a clear and powerful emotional trajectory. Without compromising the interval-group principle, he allows minor thirds to form later in the passage (bars 183–4) – a suggestion of optimism colouring the emigrant's despair. Against this, Nono places the retrograde of the same material in a wordless line for the soprano, a further hint of another emotional voice; the soprano will not come into her own character and material until the second act. Initially, this line was to begin at the same moment as the tenor, but Nono sees other expressive potential. He deletes the initial three bars in the soprano, and shifts the line forwards by a beat. Instead of a unison beginning, the soprano now emerges as a continuation of the rising minor seventh F-E♭ in the tenor. Judicious deletion of two pitches of the series (A♭ A) in the tenor at bar 180 creates a dramatic vocal gesture on 'caverne': a wide descending shape resonating through a following silence and echoed by a still higher entry. This deletion, a melodic cavern, establishes a clear centre to the architecture and allows the tenor to seamlessly continue the soprano's final B − echo and echo. The same omission in the soprano allows the two expressive highpoints of the vocalise (C−B, C−B♭; a repeated, extended madrigalian sigh) to be heard in relief over the closing descent of the first tenor phrase, mirroring the rising semitones of the tenor line and outlining an inversion of the tenor series shape. The single whole-tone in the soprano, whose own series contain none, suggests an empathy with the tenor. Other instances potentially generated by the material are erased (bar 177) or octave-shifted (179).

In constraining his freedom while avoiding formalism, Nono constructs for himself 'situations' analogous to those of his protagonist. He confronts himself with a reality within which his choices become a process of self-realisation. The orchestral accompaniment of this passage is typical for the first part of *Intolleranza*. In his sketches, Nono refers to 'bands of sound' (bands rather than layers − their boundedness is important), constructed using his techniques of echo (i.e. also of the attack), mirror and resonance. He identifies two types of band: those limited to the intervals of the soloists, and those constructed by filling intervals chromatically. The former is used here, in strings, woodwind and then brass; the distinction is blurred by anticipating as well as echoing pitches. Two intervals emerge as points of stability throughout the work: perfect and augmented fourth. Their superimposition naturally creates a tension for chromatic expansion.

The extremes of compositional control are represented by the beginnings of the two acts. The opening chorus, Ripellino's *Vivere è stare svegli*, follows Nono's pre-compositional scheme quite formally. Its four stanzas work through the four groups of pitch material, perhaps to suggest that an awakened consciousness embraces the full range of human experience. The chorus parts are all recorded and diffused throughout the hall, for which Nono gives detailed spatialisation directions − a scheme entirely consistent with his earliest plans, but also quite practical, given the circumstances of the premiere. Act Two begins with what his plans term a 'ballet', a formal reference to operatic convention but also a trace of Ripellino's Myakovskian proposal. A scene of movement is accompanied by the sound and projections of the most absurd headlines of the day, a satire with its origins in his letter to Andersch about the nonsense of discussing Sputnik while the poor still live in the past. This took the shape of a nine-minute tape montage, assembled in Milan by Maderna and replaced in subsequent productions by various other forms of topical material. Mayakovsky's *La nostra marcia* concludes Act One and is reprised in Act Two, Scene III. Nono's four-part choral setting is a powerful hymn of resistance. It demonstrates his technique of moving between individual and group, monody and polyphony. Text setting is unanimous, but as lines move between different combinations of voices, certain pitches are sustained while others blossom into harmony.

In his article, Nono shows how he uses techniques from *Incontri* for the internal rhythmic articulation of the sound-bands of Scene III, the demonstration. Rhythms are derived from slogans of protest in multiple languages. This was part of the third instalment to be sent to the publisher, in February 1961. As time progressed he was obliged to develop a much looser approach, repurposing techniques, material and whole passages from within and outside the work. The fourth part of *Il canto sospeso* appropriately appears in the interrogation scene; segments from *Incontri* and *Due espressioni* were incorporated in scenes II and III of the second act. In terms of compositional practice, therefore, the miracle of *Intolleranza 1960* is its coherence, its integrity. Nono's craftsmanship, his interval-based technique, his knowledge of his own material and language were such that he could assemble largely through-composed music and text at high speed whilst retaining a consistent musical core. There are traces of urgency, of course. The units of reference become more literal, but by the same token clearer; Nono points to the fourth/augmented fourth /second pattern of 'qui bisogna restare' ('we must stay here') that returns in the wind as a 'memento' in the final scene.[32] The differences that emerge are one with the developing drama and architecture, leading to the catastrophic bursting of the riverbanks. Nono's departing from initial technical models, already seen in the two preceding choral works, is not only a question of urgency. It is also symptomatic of his ethos of continuous resistance, an integral part of his practice. Still, nearly thirty years later he would often write across an intricately planned sketch 'break mechanical procedures!'

While his Gramscian understanding of the role of the artist is still evolving, it is clear from Nono's technical description that he sees musical relationships not as illustrative of human relationships but as a material intervention:

> each scene is differentiated by its formal-compositional technique, each of which in turn characterises the diversity of the human-musical situation. [. . .]
>
> critical awareness and invention in determining a particular relationship is fundamental for me, whether that between others or especially that of an interval, between two sounds or between groups of sounds, inside them or inside continuous bands of sound.[33]

Nono's 'speaking clearly and loudly' is clearly not intended to reassure the bourgeois opera-goer. Taibon, for example, is of the opinion that there is no beauty, rhetoric, ornament or pathos in the music.[34] However, the above example shows how all are present in the musical surface. The nature of beauty, love or longing does not change; what is radical here is the context within which they are experienced and understood. Nono does not permit their abstraction, idealising or cheapening; other realities cannot be dismissed to another movement or number. Longing is expressed in the shadow of the tenor's despair; the soprano finds the potential for resistance. At the same time, Nono's techniques of interval combination and of the rhythmic articulation of the dynamic- and complexity-envelopes of compound events represent a refining of the aesthetics of sound-events that does indeed advance concepts of beauty.

The tragedy of Vajont, just two years later, must have seemed a terrible vindication of Nono's drama. A state-supported private monopoly power supplier constructed a dam above the village of Longarone, some 100km north of Venice, despite local warnings about geological instability; indeed, the Italian government sued journalists reporting such earth movements. In 1963, a landslide provoked a tsunami that overtopped the dam and caused some 2000 deaths.

Production

Late in 1960, Labroca had officially invited Alfréd Radok, director of the Lanterna Magika, to direct Nono's new work. Radok immediately answered with enthusiasm, but on 31 December wrote that he would not be able to come to Italy.[35] A further letter from the Ministry of Culture in Prague, citing an an unspecified illness, made it clear that this was the result of political intervention. In Radok's place they proposed sending Václav Kašlík, an erstwhile composer and currently a director at the National Theatre – a thoroughly establishment figure. Nono responded with two strategies. He invited Piscator to direct, a long-standing wish, and sent him a detailed description of his vision. This came to nothing as Labroca had to seal an agreement with the Czech authorities, although Piscator expressed the hope that he might collaborate on a German production. At the same time, Nono sought a political route to Radok, soliciting the help of Palmiro Togliatti, leader of the PCI.[36] With little time to spare, Labroca and Nono had to accept the offer of Kašlík.

Carla Henius, the alto soloist, describes in her diary the two weeks of rehearsal, from the end of March to the premiere on 13 April 1961. She arrived from Germany to work with Swiss bass/baritone Heinz Rehfuss, who Nono knew from Darmstadt, and the young American soprano Catherine Gayer. Of the tenor soloist, the central character, there was as yet no sign. The very experienced Romanian tenor Petre Munteanu arrived some days later, and after an uncertain start grew into the role. Vedova seems to have created a storm around himself, urgently revising his coloured slides to project more clearly under theatre lights and negotiating the realisation of his designs with costume-makers. The complex loudspeaker system was installed by Philips who, like Svoboda, were bringing a technology from the Brussels World Fair. Kašlík, used to long and authoritarian rehearsal periods at the Prague National Theatre, was impatient with cast and crew. Maderna, in contrast, was practical and constructive. He arrived on 5 April from London, where he had been rehearsing the BBC Symphony Orchestra, likewise engaged for the Biennale's Music Festival. The orchestra itself arrived only in time for the general rehearsal, its flight delayed by fog. The production narrowly escaped falling victim to a strike by Italian theatre employees, already postponed to permit the Italian premiere of Britten's *Noye's Fludde* to take place. Nono's next *azione scenica*, some thirteen years later, would also be presented in the shadow of industrial strife in the theatre.

Maderna steered the work to a premiere that was spectacular in several respects: as theatre, in terms of its audience reception and media attention, and because of a theatrical political intervention. Members of the neo-fascist group *Nuovo ordine* interrupted at the end of the second scene, shouting support for the police, whistling and throwing leaflets and stink bombs. Interpretations of the facts vary: Henius recalls that some protesters were arrested by the police, while *l'Unità* reported that the authorities chose not to intervene. Henius describes the conclusion:

> At the end of the premiere, the whistlers in the public were drowned by bravos.
>
> Finally all two hundred extras stormed the stage and defended our work, or rather Nono's art, against the fascist mob. They carried Nono and Maderna on their shoulders to the front of the stage. Vedova with his full beard charged onto the stage and challenged the whistlers to a duel! It is half a miracle, half a popular festival. We all howl with joy.
>
> Schlee [Director of Universal-Edition Vienna], who had been at the premiere of *Wozzeck* and who was not Nono's publisher, said that this was the most significant work and operatic event that he had experienced since then.[37]

According to Steinecke, the dispute between the enthusiastic majority and the minority bent on disruption continued long after the final curtain fell.[38] The production was repeated without incident two days later.

Intolleranza 1960

Resonance

Critics were unanimous in their appreciation of the spectacle and the performers. The Venetian *Il Gazzettino* was unequivocal:

> We must say immediately, so that nobody can be in two minds as the to importance of yesterday evening's performance at La Fenice, that was are dealing with the most complex, original, interesting [work] that we have seen in the post-war.[39]

The music was more challenging for some, although most remarked on its expressive power. Typical of the style-focused criticism in the right-wing press was Abbiati in *Corriere della Sera*. He was impressed by the production, especially Vedova's design and Svoboda's projections, and by the performers; he reports the disturbances as differences of opinion as to the quality of the work – despite mentioning its clamorous reception – and finds rare moments of beauty in the music. However, he finds the music 'disjointed, split up among the unlikely notes of the cruel platform of the twelve notes of the series [. . .] to which the composer remains faithful.'[40] A rare simultaneous live broadcast by the BBC focused attention in London. *The Times* wrote the next day that 'Nono's opera is a fine, eloquent work' and that 'The spirit of Mussolini [. . .] is still a living embarrassment to Italy's health.'[41] In a profile a week later, the same paper predicted Nono to be 'the major figure in Italian music for the next quarter century or so'.[42]

A debate emerged in the pages of the communist daily *l'Unità* – then a mass circulation paper – about the appropriateness of Nono's musical language to his apparent intention. Giacomo Manzoni was unstinting in his appreciation:

> For the first time in decades, yesterday evening an artistic event transformed the theatre into a place of encounter of all the forces of democracy, marked the defeat of a carefully prepared provocation that had no effect in the face of the clear reaction of the audience. [. . .] The music leads the listener through every moment, clarifies, intensifies, dramatises and extends itself appeased in a melos that is the innate gift of a musician who is often accused, against all the evidence, of formalist sterility; it is a music that sculpts situation after situation with plasticity, or reaches heights of incomparable poetry whether in the pages for chorus, as in the moments of most vivid agitation, or in others of extended, intimate lyricism; more than ever it constitutes the foundation, the guide, the dramatic prime mover of the whole spectacle.[43]

Piero Santi responded to Ugo Duse's accusation that the work was 'cosmopolitan' – that is, appealing to the intellectual aspirations of an international high bourgeoisie, rather than the audience it would appear to address. Santi insisted that Nono's means of expression were those 'appropriate to reflect the human and social relationships formed by bourgeois society'. Furthermore, the theatrical aspect introduced 'that positive affirmation, that dialectical quality that serialism would tend to ignore'.[44] Their irreconcilable differences of opinion encapsulate discussions of communist musical aesthetics through the preceding decade. In the communist cultural journal *Avanti*, Pestalozza took an overview, finding such polarisation artificial; the evolution of tonal music precisely follows that of international capitalism.[45] Nonetheless, the debate raged on: Scabia declared *Intolleranza 1960* a 'popular' opera, in that it addresses issues common to the people.[46] Mila responded, dismissing the entire discussion as a futile game, but did feel that the work was less successful than *Il canto sospeso*. Fully aware of Nono's time constraints, Mila had explored *Intolleranza 1960* more fully in *L'Espresso*: it was a work of violence and beauty, unprecedented in its realization but rich in its roots in Schönberg, a synthesis of theatrical elements that illuminates the *hic et nunc* of the individual.[47] He was one of the few to deal with the substance of the music. As well as praising the polyphony of the choruses, the lyricism of the soprano solos and the expressive power of the instrumental writing, he notes the increasingly episodic nature of the work as a whole; he describes *Intolleranza 1960* as 'a sequence of cantatas'. Without wishing to deny the problems arising from Nono's running out of time, there are positive aspects to this view: the work is more complex both emotionally and dramatically than *Il canto sospeso* – the scenes it presents could not be received as historical – and ultimately its effect is an emergent, aggregate property of the pattern of situations. Steinecke found similar virtues in Nono's music and extolled his vision, but found weaknesses in the libretto and direction.[48]

Intolleranza 1960 was not heard again in Italy for half a century. This is particularly remarkable given the extraordinary attention the work attracted at the time and its vital role in Italian cultural history. Apart from a production in the USA, fraught with difficulties, and another in France, the remaining productions were all in Germany – the first in Cologne the following year. Following the erection of the Berlin Wall in August 1961, Lachenmann wrote with concerns about the Cologne premiere of *Intolleranza* in April 1962. He suggested adding symbols of communist totalitarianism to balance those of fascism: 'Seeing that disgraceful wall in Berlin I can understand and forgive the allergy to communism among my compatriots.'[49] Nono's reply was unyielding:

I was in Cologne about *Intolleranza* –
much to fight
BUT it will be ONLY how I meant it – wrote it!
as for wall-border in Berlin
too sentimental_
DDR and BRD are 2 states, with their own governments[50]

In a subsequent letter he continued: 'Greetings to the Nazis who are still FREE in the government and the country of the BRD and still dream of such filth. This is your freedom →
not my freedom.'[51]

The use in the printed score of a German translation by Andersch, however sensitive, creates an additional layer of distance from Nono's conception.[52] The only recording is also in German. A series of productions a decade later – recast as *Intolleranza 1970* – kept the work current, particularly in the topical nonsense chosen for the Act II ballet. One might have anticipated a more cultural–historical quality in the significant number of post-2000 productions, but the emotional strength of Nono's music and the increasingly topical plight of the economic migrant have if anything enhanced its potency.

The story of *Intolleranza 1960* begs important questions about the work as we have it. Did Nono's rushed score really address the project he had in mind? If the theatrical aspects were so crucial, how can any production – including the compromised premiere – genuinely realise Nono's vision? As we saw in Nono's sketches for *Varianti*, this project had been accumulating detail in his imagination since at least 1957. The compositional techniques he had been exploring since *Diario polacco '58* allowed him increasing freedom in creating the musical surface from his more abstract material – an expressive freedom that allowed him to get closer to the poetic idea in its realisation. His material had developed a great plasticity and was rich with personal reference. Its reuse in *Intolleranza 1960* is akin to instances in Bach: material that retains its 'meaningful' properties in an entirely different context. Nono's long and obsessive reflection on the nature of his music theatre meant that he could trust his instinct; the score embodies his music theatre conception, and this is what gives it robustness under reproduction. In a sense, the story of his last quasi-theatrical work, *Prometeo*, provides an answer. In this, the most complicated, trans-medial, integrated of these works, the extra-musical elements of its scenography, crucial to its conception, were gradually eliminated through performance. In enlisting the participation of others, active or passive, Nono builds for himself a context for musical action, for its presentation but also for its invention. This context is at once poetic, political, technical, technological and social. He assembles a virtual theatre of the mind, within which a new music can be imagined – increasingly so for non-stage works as well as the azioni sceniche. This shapes and informs the act of composition such that the music inevitably bears the traces of the extra-musical, distributed creative process.

For the most part, *Intolleranza 1960* is not a political work in the same mode as Nono's works of a decade later. The situations it presents are unmistakably challenges to consciousness and society in the strongest possible terms, but even Brecht's words in the final chorus retain a narrative quality, afford an aesthetic distance: 'We went forth, changing country more often than shoes, through class wars, in despair that there was only injustice.' Polarised discussion of the accessibility of the musical language, such as that of *l'Unità*, is not helpful; Nono assumes the responsibilities of an engaged artist, not a musical propagandist. More relevant are the parameters of the debate set out by Adorno in his article of the following year, *Commitment*. There, Adorno takes issue with the politically engaged work of both Sartre and Brecht, arguing that both the explicitly committed and the blindly autonomous ('pre-artistic') work become ideological: 'The moment of true volition, however, is mediated through nothing other than the form of the work itself, whose crystallisation becomes an analogy of that other condition which should be.'[53] True reality is reflected in the autonomous work, in which 'uncompromising radicalism' can aspire to 'a terrifying power, absent from 'helpless poems to the victims of our time'. Adorno numbers 'even Schönberg's Survivor of Warsaw' among the latter, which 'wound our shame before the victims'.[54] But in his dedication of *Intolleranza 1960* to Schönberg, Nono makes it clear that *Die Glückliche Hand* is his model: Schönberg's 1913 music drama composed in the intensity of his collaboration with Kandinsky and *Die Blaue Reiter*, his discussions of theatre, text and colour.[55] There, a single unnamed soloist confronts love, society and his art through a non-linear dream-narrative staged by means of coloured lighting. The score contains detail of lighting, sound and image that affords a cinematographic treatment, and Schönberg outlined the requirements for such a project in a contemporary letter to Emil Hertzka of Universal Edition.[56] Adorno also questions Sartre's concept of individual free choice. Nono presents not so much a series of choices as a pattern of oppression and hope through which the emigrant – the lens of the listener's own subjectivity – evolves. For Nono, the action in the theatre and the musical fabric of the work constitute an indivisible locus of a vision of awakening consciousness. He makes this clear in a letter lamenting the frustrations of a German translation: 'the comprehensibility of the text depends entirely on the comprehensibility of the <u>music</u>'.[57]

Notes

1 Sartre, 1949, pp. 62–3. Quoted by Nono in 'Testo – musica – canto', 1960. LNI, p. 65.
2 'Appunti per un teatro musical attuale', 1961. LNI, p. 92. 'Possibilità e necessità di un nuova teatro musicale', 1962. LNI, p. 131. 'Simplicius simplicissimus e Concerto funebre', 1963. LNI, p. 148.
3 'Risposte a 7 domande di Martine Cadieu', 1966. LNI, p. 198. 'Il musicista nella fabbrica' 1966. LNI, p. 207
4 Sartre, 1976, p. 5.
5 Letter to Andersch, 25 September 1957. ALN.

Intolleranza 1960

6   Interview with Sigrid Neef, 1974. LNII, p. 199.
7   Cacciari, quoted in Calabretto, 2017, p. 12.
8   Scarabello, 2008, p. 51.
9   P09.01/01, ALN.
10 Argan, 1951, pp. 68, 116.
11 Ripellino, 1959.
12 Interview with Philippe Albèra, 1987. LNII, p. 420.
13 Driesen, 2016, pp. 78–9.
14 Ripellino, 1959, p. 15.
15 Letter to Ripellino, 4 January 1960, in Sani, 1992, p. 117.
16 Letter to Ripellino, 11 November 1960, in Sani, 1992, pp. 120–2.
17 Letter to Ripellino, 21 February 1960, in Sani, 1992, p. 124.
18 Letter to Ripellino, 6 April 1960, in Sani, 1992, p. 125.
19 Letter to Ripellino, 5 May 1960, in Sani, 1992, p. 126.
20 23.05/15r, ALN.
21 Calabretto, 2017, p. 95.
22 Sartre, 1976, pp. 4–5.
23 Trials and appeals continued until January 1961. There was only one conviction and nobody was imprisoned.
24 De Benedictis, 2013.
25 Ripellino's full text is reproduced in the programme booklet to the 2011 production at La Fenice, Venice.
26 Interview with Martine Cadieu, 1961. LNII, p. 5.
27 'Alcune precisazioni su "Intolleranza 1960"', 1962. LNI, p. 100.
28 'Alcune precisazioni su "Intolleranza 1960"', 1962. LNI, p. 101
29 Letter to Lachenmann, 3 January 1961, in De Benedictis and Morsch, 2012, p. 76.
30 Letter from Lachenmann, 16 January 1961, in De Benedictis and Morsch, 2012, p. 78.
31 'Alcune precisazioni su "Intolleranza 1960". LNI, pp. 106–8. Nono's examples are from the alto, bars 220–3 and 285–92, tenor 106–9 and alto 241–9, all in Act 1.
32 'Alcune precisazioni su "Intolleranza 1960"'. LNI, p. 109.
33 'Alcune precisazioni su "Intolleranza 1960"'. LNI, p. 105.
34 Taibon, 1993, p. 78.
35 Letter from Alfréd Radok, 6 December 1960. ALN.
36 Letter to Togliatti, in Trudu, 2008, pp. 9–10.
37 Henius, 1995, p. 100.
38 'Die Zwölftonmusik als politischen Instrument', Süddeutsche Zeitung, 19 April 1961.
39 Il Gazzettino, 14 April 1961.
40 Corriere della Sera, 14 April 1961, p. 6.
41 The Times, 14 March 1961.
42 The Times, 21 March 1961.
43 Giacomo Manzoni, l'Unità, 15 April 1961.
44 'La musica e la crisi della borghesia', l'Unità, 17 May 1961.
45 'Luigi Nono e l"Intolleranza"', Avanti, 7 May 1961.
46 "Il dibattito su "Intolleranza 1960" o i compositori moderni: Musica popolare e realismo', l'Unità, 9 June 1961.
47 Massimo Mila, 'Anatomia del nostro tempo', L'Espresso, 23 April 1961, in De Benedictis and Rizzardi, 2010, pp. 275–8.
48 'Die Zwölftonmusik als politischen Instrument', Süddeutsche Zeitung, 19 April 1961.
49 Letter from Lachenmann, 25 September 1961, in De Benedictis and Morsch 2012, p. 85.
50 Letter to Lachenmann, autumn 1961, in De Benedictis and Morsch, 2012, pp. 86–7.
51 Letter to Lachenmann, late 1961, in De Benedictis and Morsch, 2012, p. 89.
52 De Benedictis, 2013b, discusses in detail the process and issues surrounding the German translation by Andersch.
53 Adorno, 1980, p. 180.
54 Adorno, 1980, p. 189.
55 'Intolleranza 1960'. LNI, p. 440.
56 Schoenberg, 1964, pp. 43–5.
57 Letter to Klaus Thiel (Director of Erfurt Opera), 1 June 1963, in De Benedictis, 2013b, p. 648.

8

NEW SPACES

Studio, street, factory

'Canti di vita e d'amore: Sul ponte di Hiroshima'

In 1962, Maderna was to direct a new production of *Intolleranza 1960* in Cologne. Various letters make clear that Nono had little desire to be deeply involved – an early example of the tension between his own full immersion in the current state of a continuous process and the cultural establishment's requirements for repertoire, for schedules of works and appearances. Nono had moved on. Early in the year, he wrote to Hartmann:

> for the first time two pieces are moving forwards together!
>
> 1) "SUL PONTE DI HIROSHIMA"
> for soprano, – tenor – orchestra
> text from the book by G. Anders: 'Der Mann auf der Brücke'
>
> 2) a cycle just for soprano solo + guitar and piano; the first piece is already finished,
> for soprano solo
> [. . .] at last pieces for voice alone
> Monodies – the two works go together, one informs the other.
> The texts of the cycle: up to now, J.L. Pacheco, a young Spaniard who has often been in prison in Madrid. – the others: contemporary poets. on love – the hope of tomorrow – the hope of today –[1]

Günther Anders' book, just published in Italian, is his journal from the 1958 *Fourth World Conference against Atomic and Hydrogen Bombs*, a philosophical–poetic reflection. Anders' thought has several resonances with that of Nono though this period. In particular, his identification of a negative technocracy reflects Nono's view of musical formalism. No copy of Anders' major 1956 work *Die Antiquiertheit des Menschen* appears in Nono's library, yet it clearly pre-echoes his own *Prometeo*: 'Today's Prometheus asks: "Who am I anyway?"'[2] The 'cycle' probably refers to the planned settings of Brecht, Pacheco and Pavese that are elsewhere referred to as *Canti di vita*, a title that had been in Nono's mind since early work on *Il canto sospeso* and encapsulates a fundamental idea of hope through tragedy. The eventual cantata concept of *Canti di vita e d'amore: Sul ponte di Hiroshima* was a response to an approach from the Edinburgh

New spaces: studio, street, factory

Festival, probably at the end of 1961, where George Lascelles, the seventh Earl of Harewood and an opera expert with a missionary zeal for the transforming of British musical culture, had just taken over as Director. The apparent link to Monteverdi – his *Madrigali dei guerrieri et amorosi* – is confirmed by references in Nono's sketches. A soprano monody (dated 23–2–62 in its initial version) was a setting of Jesús López Pacheco's *esta noche*. Nono had met the young anti-fascist poet on his first visit to Spain the previous year. The monody was retitled as a tribute to a celebrated victim of French colonialist torture during the war in Algeria, Djamila Boupachà, who was finally released from prison with the cease-fire of March 1962. As both projects evolved and deadlines approached, *Canti di vita e d'amore* emerged from their confluence, its architecture completed by another stage of Nono's Pavese project, a setting of *Passerò per la Piazza di Spagna* from *Verrà la morte e avrà i tuoi occhi*, here titled *Tu*. The final work thus consists of three parts: *Sul ponte di Hiroshima* and *Tu*, both for soprano, tenor and orchestra, surround the solo soprano monody *Djamila Boupachà*. Once the sequence is clear, dramatic and musical form proceed together through Nono's sketches.

Perhaps as a result of the time pressures of *Intolleranza 1960*, Nono's conscious monitoring of the development of ideas is becoming more acute. There is a maturing of the relationship with his own technique and with language that will develop into the continuous questioning of self and music of his later practice; dogma and formalism are anathema. The emergence of a work is the product of two processes: the evolving and taking form of potential lines of musical thought (materials, techniques, metaphors), and the consolidation and identifying of an appropriate vehicle for a given project. Here there is also a relish at returning to a contemplation of music uncluttered by other concerns; Nono takes the opportunity to review his lexicon and to develop ideas seeded in the vocal works of 1960. His habit of continuously externalising thought on paper allows us to examine this process. This is the articulation of an evolving context for thought, not the working-out of a theory. His notes are an invaluable resource, but they inevitably present apparent contradictions and inconsistencies as he responds to his own ideas and explores possibilities. Such a process of self-subverting requires self-knowledge. In early plans Nono lists sound complexes ('suoni composti'), sound fields ('campi sonori') and sound bands ('fascie'), as well as the interplay of instruments and voices. These have evolved separately in previous works: the sound shapes of *Varianti*, frequency layers of *Omaggio a Emilo Vedova*, groups of *Sarà dolce tacere*, episodes of *Diario polacco '58*. The use of such terms continues to develop through the new process, but they are now combined within a broader, more plastic and dynamic notion of the fundamental compositional unit described in his notes as a 'structure'. In general, he builds the multidimensional instrumental structures independently of the linear vocal parts. As with other terms (group, field), Nono's understanding of structure arises from the exploration of concerns largely shared with other composers. Clearly, there is no attempt singly or jointly to create a common, static repertoire of terms or concepts, but in each case their use and technical implications reveal important characteristics.

A modulus again appears through Nono's pre-compositional thinking; for the three texts he contemplates three 'moments like the evangelist who narrates', three 'ways of singing', three 'uses of rhythm: as sound', and three intervallic 'bases for layers – sound-fields – groups'.[3] Durations and their subdivisions are derived from three quasi-Fibonacci sequences that by addition afford modularity in the proportions 2–3–6: <1, 3, 6, 10>, <2, 5, 9, 14> and <5, 11, 18, 26>. The longer values may be subdivided into values from the same set, and any may be replaced by 'negative' values (rests). They are used on seven different rhythmic planes: the beat and its divisions by 2 to 7.

Nono's thinking in structures consolidates many aspects and implications of his recent practice. Number squares and pitch series are fully reconceived as generators, as characterising a dynamical musical space, and any possibility of the mechanical is eliminated; 'no more complete series', his notes say.[4] His process of technical evolution is steered not so much by the techniques themselves as by the kind of decision he wants to be making at each stage, by the spaces, the degrees to which the techniques do *not* determine musical events. Formed from a palette of relationships, proportions and sequences, each structure has unique architecture, colour, texture and internal dynamics, crafted according to its formal and expressive role. The interval is the fundamental property of the sound field from which each structure is built. Nono experiments with fields built on few intervals; in the event, he rarely uses more than two or three. A set of pitches is constructed by building the intervals (between minor second and tritone) above a base note. He tries sets with just one instance of each interval, and others with more notes using the intervals in rotation; in each case he makes additional sets by permuting the intervals. He then considers how many discrete transpositions each affords, alla Messiaen, or derives additional sets by transposing the whole by the intervals in question, a process analogous to Boulez's 'multiplication'. One complete series is generated by using the semitone–minor third pattern alternately in inversion transposed by fourths; this shape is the 'fratello' motif from Dallapiccola's *Il Prigioniero* that will return in Nono's later works. The intervals have an additional role in bounding the range of a layer within a structure, or in the relationship between simultaneous structures. The pitch ranges of simultaneous or successive structures tend towards complementarity, towards completion of the total chromatic. Quarter tones are used in the strings: to fill a pitch space more densely, to provide an alternative pitch grid on to which intervals can be mapped or to add beating and movement to particular pitches.

As if to have a complete picture of his musical space, Nono enumerates the possible combinations of his orchestra divided into woodwind, brass, two groups of strings and percussion. He lists permutations and combinations ('voices: [. . .] different rhythm or the same, different timbre or the same, different values or the same') to map the spaces of possibilities. He refines the sound shapes ('formi di suono composto') he has used since *Varianti* – envelopes of compound sounds recalling additive synthesis – and adds negative forms analogous to those of rhythm (Figure 8.1).

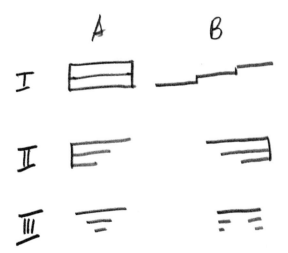

Figure 8.1 Canti di vita e d'amore: Sul ponte di Hiroshima: sound shapes. (ALN 24.03.02/03r (detail). © The heirs of Luigi Nono. Reproduced by kind permission.)

New spaces: studio, street, factory

There are constant reminders to 'differentiate structures' or 'vary the succession'. Certain structures should return, varied, as 'pillars'. The traces of serial thinking are less in the materials themselves than in the way Nono establishes a conceptual space for composing. His lists of possible materials, parameters and processes are grids that allow him to plot movement across the field of action that affords the work. Having established this, he is free to think architecturally and poetically. Early graphical sketches of form demonstrate the need for Nono to work in terms of structures. Objects work within the same kind of constrained modular world as his sets of numbers or pitches. The arrangements of blocks, triangles, lines and space likewise exhibit balance, complementarity and changes of orientation. The more complex outer movements are largely designed graphically, with sections then plotted on squared paper, before he builds the components in detail. Already we can see the movement towards the graph-paper score of *Per Bastiana* and Nono's abandoning of conventional notation for half a decade. He seems to be striving for a continuity of thought across structural levels, from the note-to-note to the architectural; Schönberg remains a vital reference:

> Form is that moment in which, with the maximum of inventive freedom, the creative heightened consciousness of the composer manifests itself from the material as the expressive means of the content.
>
> Here again, the teaching of Arnold Schönberg is fundamental.[5]

Sul ponte di Hiroshima is the most complex movement, and determines the architecture of the whole work. An early plan for the use of Anders' text clearly shows the dramatic roots of Nono's concept, its continuity with *Intolleranza 1960* and the process of transformation it is intended to convey:

1	4 moments	A (1+2) destruction [. . .]	I attempt
		B (3+4) [. . .] : flight [. . .] journey	<u>reaction</u>
		C (5) delusion	
		D – 6 decision – action	
		– 7 cry of action	II attempt
		– 8 No – struggle – action	resolute

in effect 3 parts:
A-B, C, D
2 think of Dowland
epic song – ballad Brecht

	in 4 parts:	A	communication, announcement
		B	denouncing
		C	the beginning of commitment
		D	commitment

3 Epitaph[6]

This form is rearranged in the final version of the first movement – part one is not completed, part two becomes the voiceless body of the movement and part three the sung opening – but the plan informs the architecture of the entire work, moving from commemoration to resolve and hope. From his repeated recopying and analysis of sections of Anders' book, Nono selects an extended passage: 57 lines of imagery-rich lament. In his multicoloured analyses of the text, Nono forms matrices of meaning and sound, of symmetries, reflections and balances; De Benedictis describes 'loops' between the 'language system' and the 'music system'.[7] Articulated by Nono into the eight parts of the above plan, it ends with a characteristically humanist, resolute invocation – 'Each one of you is part of a single great family' – followed by an assertion as to the importance of this tragedy – 'They should not just lie there. Theirs is not a usual death but an admonition, a warning.' In early sketches, Nono also associates this less context-specific passage with the poem of Pacheco; he plans that it should return three times as a ritornello. Again, in his notes he invokes the role of the Evangelist in Bach's Passions.

In the event, only this last passage is sung (bars 1–39), as an introduction to an otherwise orchestral first movement in which a longer extract from Anders' text is printed above the score. Text and music are one; the work grows from sound and idea, not recitation. As the introduction begins, lines moving slowly by semitone or quarter tone are punctuated by tutti string chords and by faster, disjointed rhythmic figuration adding major sevenths and minor ninths. The patterns of successive structures are made clear by their sharp contrasts of colour, texture, movement and sound shape. This dialectic achieves synthesis in a near-palindromic structure, a pattern of minor ninths across four octaves, each pitch surrounded by bands of quarter tones. Inner movement almost reaches stasis, but Nono generates forward motion by shifting rests (the balance of 'positive' and 'negative' values) within the otherwise symmetrical distribution of values of 2 and 5. They are applied to subdivisions of 6, 5, 4 and 3, descending through the layers; Figure 8.2 shows four of the 22 voices.

Figure 8.2 Sul ponte di Hiroshima: rhythm layers from bars 11–13

This quasi-symmetry adds to the sense of strumming, only subsequently explained in the silent text at bar 47. Such associations arise without any explicit illustration, creating a sonic–poetic semantic web the logical architecture of which is independent from that of the text – a lesson from the madrigal, from Monteverdi. After the soprano emerges *bocca chiusa* from a timpani cluster, words are shared between the two voices, maintaining comprehensibility. Instrumental material proliferates from the vocal lines, the brief orchestral figures echoed, reverberated and pitch-shifted as if the singer is accompanying himself.

Language then disappears into the instrumental texture. In their being one, the music can sing of the silencing of voice; the textual clarity of the opening exordium highlights this submerging. The three orchestral sections that follow outline the structure of another passage from Anders printed above the score:

New spaces: studio, street, factory

on a bridge in Hiroshima, a man plucks the strings of an instrument and sings [. . .] (bars 40–70)

where you expect to find a face, you don't find a face but a veil [. . .] (bars 71–117)

until we have exorcised that danger [. . .] he will be on all the bridges that lead to our common future as an accusation, as a messenger. Let us do what is necessary to be able to say to him: you are no longer necessary, you can leave your post.' (bars 118–64)

There are three main types of orchestral texture: fluid, melodic, micropolyphonic textures in 3/4 (A); overlapping sequences of more or less complex structures, notated in 4/4 (B); and more static, sustained layers in 5/8 (C). The three sections present the material in the sequence ACA, BCB, C. Nono refers to *Incontri* in his sketches and in his programme note; the dialectical process of that work is present here both formally and in the interplay of structures within sections.

The change to wider ranging, flowing lines in bar 40 marks the movement of text and song into the orchestra itself. Each of the 36 string parts cycles one of the two whole-tone scales or their quarter-tone transpositions upwards or downwards; the four discrete pitch grids fill the frequency space. Their rhythms all derive from values of 1, 3, 6 and 10 on different subdivisions of the beat. Frequency space is saturated by all 24 quarter-tone divisions, and all 24 permutations of the duration set are used. The entire passage bars 40–6 is a palindrome, as is the development of that material at 58–70. Both reflections change colour and transform the phase of their constituent waves. In between, as the silent poem 'plucks the strings' (bars 47–57), the texture changes to layers of sustained pitches in continuous dynamic change, each surrounded by quarter- and semitones with different dynamic envelopes to keep them in movement. Nono's notes contain references to reverberation. These sustained sounds are the reverberation of the plucked instrument; Nono's sound poetry explores his lessons from the studio. Every note lasts 30 quavers, its internal attacks separated by permutations of 2, 5, 9 and 14 quavers, coming to rest on timpani fourths B–E. The bare fourth now assumes a role as a signal, as a mark of resolve.

The clear differentiation of the next section (bars 71–117) adds an additional layer of distance to the song-within-a poem. A kaleidoscopic fabric of isolated crescendos and diminuendos of between two and twelve voices is built of quarter-tones interlocking by semitones, semitones by whole tones, complementary chromatic blocks of a fourth or quarter-tone clusters a fifth apart. 'Where you expect to find a hand, you will not find a hand but a claw of steel' is the text printed above bars 80–110. In the 5/8 framework, high strings cluster around C–D–E, moving from sul ponticello to sul tasto to pizzicato – static, but full of movement. They are answered by low muted brass and strings, around a B♭ three octaves lower, fragmenting into the mirrored reprise. This central passage is introduced by phase-shifted crescendos and diminuendos crescendos of wind, brass and strings. To close the section, this extraordinary sound is mirrored in compressed form like a tape played backwards – a rare indication of temporal direction – and followed by a series of reverberations. The final section (118–64) returns to the sustained 5/8 pattern. The entire orchestra in 38 parts surrounds in quarter-tones a tight diatonic field – minor seventh G–F in the middle register – each step of which has a different envelope such that unison accents and reattacks emerge from the mass. These appear to consolidate as the texture thins and quarter-tones disappear to leave the bare fourths G–C–F, replaced by their chromatic centres A-B♭–D–E♭ and then the total chromatic, which proves to be the centre of another compressed mirror. Timpani fourths B–E provide a final cross-reference, their crescendo a newly resolute mirror of the cluster that first introduced the soprano.

Again, the soprano emerges *bocca chiusa* from the timpani; her voice cannot remain silent. The central monody *Djamila Boupachà* provides a clear instance of Nono's intervallic architecture; pitch and rhythmic materials are completely horizontalised, as if their orientation were in transition between the states of the outer movements. In his initial analysis of the poem, Nono characterises each pair of lines with a set of intervals. These sets are then transposed to their own initial members to produce distinctive pitch grids. The opening lines use minor second and minor third (2– and 3– in Nono's notation), producing the sequence C C♯ E F A♭ A, then transposed to C♯ and E. He builds local groups around these main pitches (marked with arrows in the lower line of Figure 8.3) using the same intervals – a kind of fractal subsidiarity.

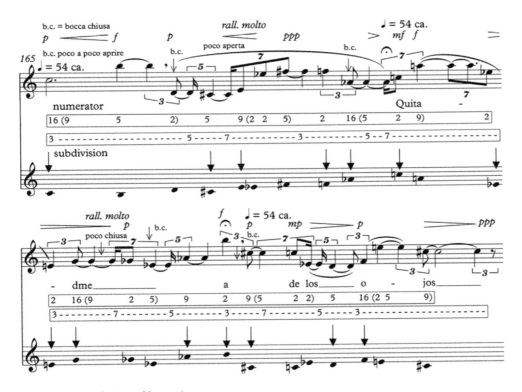

Figure 8.3 *Djamila Boupachà*: opening

The pitch material available for each pair of lines is thus different in quantity as well as kind. Each stanza has clear intervallic characteristics, without any sense of the mechanical: the remaining two lines of the first and the whole of the third stanza are built from tone, fourth and augmented fourth, the second from semitone, tone and fourth. Nono traverses the note sequences in different ways to create local melodic modes (the opening line), harmonic fields ('Quiero mirar las cosas como un niño') or motivic imitation ('Es triste' and its preceding *bocca chiusa*). These last two instances – references to childlike simplicity and sadness respectively – are fully in the Monteverdian expressive tradition. Locally, phrases are shaped by pivotal pitches, chromatic expansion and symmetries; the whole is built into an organic architecture by the use of register and placement of the text. The three stanzas exhibit the trajectory characteristic of *Canti di vita e d'amore*: from lamenting the lack of sight, to identifying the obstacle ('Esta noche di sangre, este fango infinito' – Franco's Spain), to a vision of clarity and

New spaces: studio, street, factory

light. Their high points are the central two-octave descent on 'mismo' ('everything is still the same'), balanced by the ascent to a brief *forte* high C left hanging at the end of the penultimate line at 'luz' ('the light must come'). The third movement will emerge from the reverberation of hope.

Rhythm is the product of layers of modulation, presaging the wave interference patterns of Nono's works from the 1970s. For each line of the poem he allocates a number of subdivisions equal to the number of syllables, cycling one of two sets of three values: <2, 4, 6> or <3, 5, 7>, and their doubles. There are seven syllables in the first line ('Quitadme de los ojos'), producing the sequence <3, 5, 7, 3, 5, 7, 3>. Figure 8.3 shows how this pattern of subdivisions is mirrored around the two triplets quavers of the central low E. Two quasi-Fibonacci sequences provide duration values: <1, 3, 6, 10> and <2, 5, 9, 16> (14 is replaced to enhance modularity). The latter is permutated across these subdivisions – <16, 5, 9, 2, 9, 16, 2> – with some values subdivided into members of the same set. This pattern determines the number of units for each note. To provide a wordless introduction to the line, these values are mirrored around the major seventh E♭–E in the middle of the first word 'Quitadme' (a *bocca chiusa* A of value five is removed in his draft before the first word). Fluctuations of tempo provide the final layer of rhythmic modulation, creating further patterns of interaction with the rising and falling of melody, the stepped or gradual dynamic changes and the cycles of movement between *bocca chiusa* and clear text.

An early page of Nono's notes gives a precise summary of the last movement *Tu*:

4 episodes
interludes
—
song (intervals)
instruments (timbres, rhythms . . .)
—
Tenor
and Soprano: free![8]

As is his practice, he makes successive copies of the poem, searching for sonic–semantic–symbolic structure and the affordance of musical architecture. In his first such gloss on Pavese's poem, he articulates it with three colours (four, if we include the initial black), shown here with the addition of his subsequent formal plan and bar numbers from the final score (Figure 8.4).[9]

This schematic translation shows how Pavese's semantic architecture, articulated in Nono's initial analysis of the poem, is mapped onto his subsequent plan for the structure of *Tu*. De Benedictis sees this process as key to Nono's musical thought:

> Modeling the literary source along his own musical purposes highlights even further the presence of a definitive 'sound thought'. This 'sound thought', coming also after the initial textual 'provocation' quickly acquires its own autonomy. In the definitive typescript [. . .] it is clear that the composer is organizing a musical material. [. . .] they acquire logic and structural coherence within a form as the means 'to represent musical thought', in accordance with Schönberg's teachings.[10]

He divides the poem into three stanzas, each beginning with an opening: 'S'apriranno' or 'S'aprirà'. Each has clear structural links with the other two, marked in his copy in different

New spaces: studio, street, factory

bar nos.	Nono's structure	colour
1.		
166-173	R[itornello]	(black)
174-178	It will be a bright sky.	red
179-184	The roads will open to the hills of pine and stone.	
185-189	E[pisodio]	
190-197	The tumult of the streets will not change	green
198-203	that still air. [The flowers, blossoming with colour at the fountains, will echo like giggling women.] (omitted)	green
204-212	The steps the terraces the swallows will sing in the sun.	purple
213	R	
2.		
214-221	That road will open, the stones will sing,	red
222	R	
223-237	the heart will beat jumping like the water in fountains –	green
238-245	this will be the voice that will climb your steps. [The windows will know the smell of the stones and of the air at dawn.] (omitted)	purple?
3.		
245-248	A door will open.	red
	E [The tumult of the streets] (orchestral)	green
255-262	E [will be the tumult of the heart in the lost light.] (orchestral)	green
263-269	It will be you – still and bright.	purple
270	R	

Figure 8.4 Tu: Nono's structural plan

colours: moments of opening in red, of tumult or beating in green, of hope in purple. Much of the structural strength of Pavese's poem lies in the way resonances of word and image – sky, road, heart, stone, voice – work across the regions identified by Nono. These colours anticipate the kinds of musical material generated by his structures.

The text is carried principally by the tenor; the soprano sings only unaccompanied ('libero!') – an additional, reflective dimension of the tenor, an inner voice audible only when the tumult ceases. These moments arrive at the purple-red transitions. She shares the line 'le scale e le

New spaces: studio, street, factory

terrazze' in order to be able to sing 'le rondine [. . .] nel sole' ('the swallows [. . .] in the sun') in an illustrative swoop, as well its echo as the first line of Nono's second stanza 'le pietre canteranno' ('the stones will sing'), itself echoed by the tenor's still wider melodic elaboration of 'voce'. Her last vocalise replaces 'le finestre' ('the windows'); the opening in the text is itself a window. The vocal lines are constructed much as in the previous movements, although the vibrant sensory images afford a much more transparent relationship with the text. The opening and closing lines are built around major second, fourth and tritone, the second stanza begins with minor second and fourth; major and minor thirds are added in the first and second stanzas respectively.

The sections are marked by clear changes of colour and movement. With the exception of the opening section – single bars punctuated, like the final section, by fermata – the ritornelli (213, 222, 270) are single-bar interventions. Cymbals, bells and tamtams are coloured by *col legno* and percussive double-stops from the strings. Drums replace bells in the green material. As in the previous green passage, the pitch content of the strings and wind through this episode remains static, coloured by shifts of pizzicato position in the lower voices and highlighting pitched sounds from the percussion. The fibrillating rhythms of the green sections are generated by the number sequences, their subdivisions and different rhythm bases accumulating through mirrored structures. They are articulated by striking multiple strings such that they, like the percussion, become semi-pitched instruments. The first is arrested suddenly to produce a dramatic contrast with the words 'quell'aria ferma', unaccompanied and terminated by sustained, still *pp* rolls from cymbals, bell and bass drum. The sections marked 'episodio' in the sketches are more extended passages. Language submerges once more in those of bars 249–62, where the text ('Il tumulto delle strade sarà il tumulto del cuore nella luce smarrita') is printed above the orchestral score. There is a clear change in movement as the tumult of the streets gives way to that of the heart. Through passages marked red, brief interventions supporting the vocal line are from pitched and semi-pitched percussion (cymbals, bells, tamtams) with strings *col legno battuto*. Purple sections (among which we should surely count 'sarà questa la voce che salirà le tue scale', bars 238–45), are purely vocal, although the final words alternate with the clarity-representing percussion. Pitched and semi-pitched percussion, Nono's *suoni fissi*, accompany images of vision, of hope, as often in his work; optimism condenses into bright sound.

Clarity of textual and musical logic and of their relationship is fundamental to *Canti di vita e d'amore*. Words are either clearly understandable or sublimated entirely, establishing a continuity of language and sonic meaningfulness. Communication is not only an important component of Nono's theorising at this time, it is fundamental to the transformational capacity of his work. The title itself has resonances with Monteverdi, with the foundations of Italian music-drama. The subtitle *Sul Ponte di Hiroshima* was retained at the suggestion of Lord Harewood, but it also points to the unity of the work. The first unspoken lines of Anders' text – 'on a bridge in Hiroshima a man plucks the strings of an instrument and sings' – provide the overarching meta-image. These lines of Anders are unspeakable, accessible only to musical reflection. While the sustained lines and isolated chords of the first movement incorporate only rare pizzicato attacks, the sound world of the third is largely an exploration of the percussive potential of the string group, effectively treated as a single complex instrument. If we consider the singers – the tenor and his inner voice – as a single protagonist through the work, the first movement becomes his inhalation, his motivation and reflection on the past, prior to the vision of hope in the third. *Tu* is the movement in which 'a man plucks the strings of an instrument and sings'. It is Nono's response to the apocalyptic situation of Anders' text; Pavese's reflective lines become a call. *Canti di vita e d'amore* is no song-cycle but a process of transformation, of awakening.

This is an important development in Nono's stance as an engaged artist. *Intolleranza 1960* presents recent events and encourages resistance; in *Canti di vita e d'amore* the listener is called

New spaces: studio, street, factory

upon directly to respond to present dangers. Durazzi describes it as 'Nono's first future-oriented work'.[11] There is as yet no explicit political reference, however; consciousness is engendered through compassion, through love of humanity and nature. While the overriding challenge is that of nuclear war, the continuing fascist regime in Spain, the reluctant concession of independence to Algeria in July and – through *Passerò per Piazza di Spagna* – the increasingly repressive Christian Democrat government of Italy are also all represented. Construction of the Berlin Wall began in August 1961; Soviet and American tanks faced each other across checkpoints a few months later. Three weeks after Nono finished *Djamila Boupachà* in February 1962, the USA announced the economic embargo of Cuba, and in May, as Nono was finishing his work, Soviet leader Kruschev informed the Politburo of his plan to site nuclear missiles there. Two months to the day after John Pritchard and the London Symphony Orchestra presented *Canti di vita e d'amore* at the Edinburgh Festival on 22 August, President Kennedy announced the presence of nuclear weapons and put American forces on alert. *Canti di vita e d'amore* is sonically beautiful and carries an ever-relevant capacity for transformation, but the enthusiastic audience and critical response must also be understood in the light of this febrile atmosphere. Indeed, the materialist nature of Nono's own ethos demands that such work be understood in its historical context. The next day, *The Times* wrote that *Djamila Boupachà* was 'the most beautiful piece of sustained vocal writing that Nono has yet given us', and of the work as a whole: 'The effect is fundamental and physical; you would have to be deaf or witless to ignore its fervor or its commonsense.'[12]

In terms of Nono's personal politics, these major world events confronted members of the PCI with difficult questions, opening further divisive debates within the Party.[13] In a talk given in Venice a month after the premiere – *Possibility and necessity of a new music theatre* – Nono was clear as to the task: 'The decisive need is: communication. New situations urgently press for expression.'[14] In his programme note for Edinburgh, Nono emphasises the continuity between *Intolleranza 1960*, *Canti di vita e d'amore* and its successor, *Canciones a Guiomar*. The present work develops the individual search of the opera to explore 'the possibility of love in the consciousness of the reality of today [. . .] as a necessary outcome of the struggle for the life of today', which becomes 'a real dream of love' in the next.[15] Further themes, he says, are being developed in another work, presumably his continuing theatrical project. Nono's assertion of continuity points to a broader conception of theatricality that does not exclude concert works such as this. Notions of collaboration, commitment, social relevance and situated performativity all remain at the heart of his ethos.

When Nono conducted a repeat performance at the Proms the following summer, the audience must have had an acutely heightened awareness of the possible implications of nuclear weapons and of the global political context. The critic of *The Times* suggested as much, and gave a sketch of Nono's performance:

> There were noises of discontent and protest when Luigi Nono's *On the Bridge at Hiroshima* was given its premiere a year ago at the Edinburgh Festival, whose society had commissioned it. But, at the same time, these three linked movements for two singers and orchestra clearly constituted a powerful, nobly lyrical tract of our times, and this year it has made its way to the Proms where, last night, it was heard in complete, intent silence and vociferously applauded. [. . .]
>
> Chiefly, though, one wished to thank Nono himself, who had come to conduct his work (as a conductor he could be said to have steered hopefully rather than arrived), and was thus on show as the creator of a wild, passionate composition with a positive, thoughtful theme strongly in everyone's mind.[16]

New spaces: studio, street, factory

'Canciones a Guiomar'

The success of the Edinburgh premiere and Nono's warm relationship with William Glock – Director of the Dartington International Summer School, where Nono had taught since 1959, Controller of Music at the BBC and Director of the Proms – led to a commission from the Koussevitzky Foundation, to be presented by the BBC. Nono returned to Machado, selecting lines from his *Otras canciones a Guiomar*.[17] *Canciones a Guiomar* is written for soprano, celesta, guitar, a large percussion group (12 chromatic crotales, suspended cymbal and tam-tam), viola, cello and double bass. A version was played at Dartington in August 1962, but the definitive score, dated 21–12–62, was premiered by the BBC on 28 February 1963. A shorter second part, setting a single line for 12-voice female choir, percussion and celesta, was then added in March.[18]

The fair copy of *Canti di vita e d'amore* was finished on 30 June, and a draft of *Canciones a Guiomar* was ready to perform at Dartington in August. In many respects this continues the spirit of *Tu*. Machado's imagery of love and nature wound together, his economical lyricism and the voice of the poem – addressing a non-present beloved – all recall Pavese. In these meditations on Machado's impossible, mythologised love, the role of Guiomar recalls that of Dante's Beatrice, but also of Hölderlin's Diotima, central to Nono's later string quartet. As often in Nono, we might look to Pavese for a link. Machado and Hölderlin name the objects of their love; in Pavese's poetry, the beloved presence is often unnamed, affording the reader a more mobile interpretation. The dynamics of this three-way relationship are similar to those offered by Marx or Gramsci, however. The ideal is at once abstract and requires a personal, practical response. The sea is an important image from the iconographies of Pavese and Nono. The central instrumental section was first intended to represent another passage from the second of Nono's source poems: 'for you the sea tries out new waves and foam'. As well as being an indication of the origins of his sound image for that section, this will become a structuring metaphor in works such as ..... *sofferte onde serene* ... and *Fragmente-Stille, an Diotima*. The work eventually consists of the first two stanzas of the first of Machado's *Otras canciones a Guiomar* sung by soprano, the third and fourth represented by a central instrumental section, and the fifth sung until 'where the sea of a dream is breaking'. The disturbing couplet that Nono omits from his last stanza – 'and under the frowning arch of my sleeplessness, surreptitiously'– would have introduced an element more difficult to assimilate. The words of the choral coda 'I dreamed of you, Guiomar' are taken from two lines of another of Machado's *Canciones*. The sonic character of the new work also develops that of *Tu* – constellations of percussive and plucked sounds within which the perception of pitch has become a compositional parameter.

The guitar features prominently both in the abandoned *Canti d'amore* and throughout early notes for *Guiomar*. Nono's understanding of the instrument evolved through his acquaintance with Julian Bream, also teaching at Dartington in 1961 and 1962. This is now explicitly a reference to Spain. The entire sound world of *Canciones a Guiomar* is an exploration of voice and guitar. There are references to Dowland in the sketches of *Canti di vita e d'amore*, but the influence of the lute songs is felt more clearly here; Bream had performed them with Peter Pears at Dartington in 1961.[19] It is thus an intensely intimate work – the complement, perhaps, of the preceding cantata – and in its vision of sound materials a direct precursor of the late works with live electronics, particularly *Risonanze erranti*. Text, voice and guitar are projected on to new spaces, expanded in frequency and time.

This intimacy is reflected in the central structural role of the poem. Nono's analysis abstracts both the syllabic rhythm of the text and its sequence of vowels and consonants. Such ideas are

New spaces: studio, street, factory

well developed. Patterns of vowels are organised according to syllabic rhythm; consonants are described as 'free', extending Nono's taxonomy of 'fixed' sounds and others, and he proposes 'fields' of both. Initial plans imagined a wider percussion palette of wood, skins and metal to extend vocal phonemes, as in earlier experiments. Instead, extension of the soprano-guitar sound world is condensed to *suoni fissi* and solo lower strings, with the celesta mediating between pitched and unpitched sounds. Nono's planned phonetic structures disappear; perhaps this was too close to Berio's use of text in works such as *Circles*. The only traces of phonetic construction are in echoes of the vowels of 'Guiomar' in the brief vocalises.

The construction is tighter and more transparent than in *Canti di vita e d'amore*, as befits the intimate intensity of this chamber piece. Vocal and instrumental parts derive from the same material, and it wears its constituent reflective and reverberating structures clearly on the surface. The emergence of text from wordless voice and its submergence into instrumental texture are again indicators of the identity of poem and music. The line-scheme of Machado's poem – 3 4 4 4 9 – could be a characteristic Nono sequence. The presence or absence of language follows a dialectical pattern; the words of the first two stanzas are sung, those of the third and fourth silent and of the last surfacing twice from its 'sea of a dream'. There is a confidence, an efficiency, to Nono's rationalisation of his own technical palette. Clarity of thought and process allows the composer freedom to respond and the listener to apprehend. It might also be seen as part of the evolution of his practice towards the clearly defined processes of the studio.

The main body of the work falls into three sections. In the first (bars 1–39), the soprano presentation of stanzas 1 and 2 (bars 5–23) is surrounded by a wordless exordium and its compressed echo, and followed by an instrumental coda (bars 26–39). The second section is predominantly rhythmic, articulated by timbre, in two equal parts: in bars 40–55 the soprano wordlessly stands for 'sólo tu voz y el viento' ('only your voice and the wind') from stanza 3, while 56–71 is without voice. From bar 71 the soprano sings alone until the choral coda, apart from a brief echo from the percussion. With characteristic bi-directionality, Nono is ambivalent as to the role of this third section, the fifth stanza. He describes the form as A B A', but elsewhere as A B C ('C = A + B', 'dream, like the synthesis of A and B'). Symmetrical patterns of tempo frame each section – overarching waves of energy and momentum.

Nono works from pitch sequences produced by combinations of two or three intervals, from the syllable count of Machado's poem and from three sets of duration values: quasi-Fibonacci series based on 2, 3 or 4. As ever, he sets out his space of potential material in its entirety before tracing his trajectory through the process of composition. Pitch is effectively the domain of the voice. All structurally pitched material derives from her line: substantially the monodies of the first 23 bars (announcement, stanzas 1 and 2) and the last fourteen before the choral coda (lines from stanza 5). The work proliferates from the vocal line to become a construction of mirrors, reverberations, anticipations and echoes, which, on the level of local structure, become a pattern of introductions and codas.

An opening cry sets out the initial interval pattern starkly, but the gesture is full of detail. The soprano gesture of augmented fourth and semitone (2–, 4+) becomes a signal, a leitmotiv unusual in Nono's music, always presented at its initial pitch (Figure 8.5). Its association with the name 'Guiomar' is made clear at the end of the second stanza, and these pitches suffused the entire work. They return in the soprano's wordless role in the third stanza, and at the end of the last. Even through the otherwise unpitched instrumental section, the 'Guiomar' notes are present in the celesta. The ear is constantly reminded of their role, as if the work had been processed by three resonant filters in the clearest region of human hearing. The opening encompasses the full timbral range of the voice – soft to loud, open to closed – and its

233

New spaces: studio, street, factory

Figure 8.5 Canciones a Guiomar: soprano, bars 1–4

instrumental expansion. The beginning of her high B♭ is marked by a celesta chord the high, brittle frequencies of which sound more like a construction from the analogue studio than a chord of thirds. The chord is repeated at the end of her note, now shattering into a symmetrical, echoing peal by the crotales.

The vocal line is spun from Nono's intervallic seeds, knitted together with overlapping reflections and extended across time and timbre space by the instruments. In the first line of the second stanza, for example, the interval pattern (3–, 2–) generates two interlocking mirrors that outline a modal melodic wave form about D (Figure 8.6). It is projected by the guitar as a single chord, while contrabass and cello harmonics sustain the outline of the second phrase and a cymbal marks the points of reflection in bars 13 and 15. The whole is introduced by a string harmonic cluster about D that both reverberates the end of the previous vocal phrase and prepares the new focus. At the same time, the guitar echoes the sopranos last two notes (E♭ D♭).

Nono's bidirectionality is displayed in the passage at the centre of the instrumental fourth stanza (bars 59–64, Figure 8.7). Apart from the celesta insistently exploring different expansions of the 'Guiomar' notes, there is no clear pitch. Guitar and strings are playing *tambora*, striking the strings percussively at fingerboard, centre or bridge and 'changing pitches at will, avoiding tonal chords'. Crotales are in triplets, planned as six parts, each with a density of 1 or 2. Viola and double bass move in semiquavers, guitar and cello in quintuplets. It would seem clear that

Figure 8.6 Canciones a Guiomar: reduction of bars 12–16

there is a structure mirrored about its centre (bar 61, beat 4) in some way, and yet the notation suggests a very approximate symmetry. The reflection is doubly obscured. In all the parts, Nono makes a pragmatic decision to notate each attack to the end of the beat. This simplifies reading and avoids players damping sounds; each sound effectively has the same duration, regardless of its notated length. Counting each attack of the viola and double bass level as a semiquaver, it becomes clear that each group of 1, 2, 3 or 4 is separated from the next by four semiquavers. In constructing the retrograde, however, Nono returns to his earlier practice of considering the end of a reversed sound to be its new beginning; by referring to the notated rhythms he produces a new rhythmic sequence not possible under his initial conditions. Guitar and cello mirror each other using the same principle, but now the number of possible consecutive attacks increases to six, and the gaps are three and two. Practical asymmetry gives direction to an abstract symmetry, an effect enhanced by the addition of cymbal and tam-tam in the second half.

Figure 8.7 Canciones a Guiomar: reduction of bars 59–64

New spaces: studio, street, factory

A choral coda had been planned from early on. It evokes the dream in that figure remains just beyond the limits of graspability; its many voices speak in the voice of the subject but are not identical with the now-silent soprano. Nono develops the dense textures of *Canti di vita e d'amore*; here he comes his closest to the micropolyphony of Ligeti's 1961 *Atmosphères*. The coda consists of three monolithic choral blocks, distinguished by shape, timbre and pitch field. The first encompasses the six steps of a whole tone scale between D and C. The whole scale is continuously present, but a wave of motion passes through the voices, moving circularly downwards in the altos, upwards in the sopranos: 'Te he soñado'. Quiet cymbal strokes mark the decay of this shape and the start of the next: 'Guiomar!' Again, the voices move in opposite directions, but now within the chromatic space of a fourth, A–D. The two groups of voices use exactly the same rhythmic patterns; all six voices begin together but their phrase lengths range from four to ten beats, such that the block gradually dissolves. However, the voice-blocks are staggered by two beats; sopranos follow the altos in canon and inversion. The whole process is then reversed, but starting together *bocca chiusa*: six homophonic pairs of voices in contrary motion, all ending together. The final block begins as a bare twelfth E♭–B♭, the twelve voices converging by whole tone on to the fifth A–E. They outline the 'Guiomar' figure, exploring its intervallic shape in minute detail. The open 'U' to which this final passage is sung mirrors the 'A' of the opening – the vowels of Guiomar in reflection.

Canciones a Guiomar provides a study of Nono's evolving technology-informed understanding of his own technique. In comparison with the later *Risonanze erranti*, for example, we see clearly which structures and processes can be understood in technological terms – reverberation and echo, delay, reversal, transposition, filtering, spatialisation and, later, sampling – and which rely on the symbolic manipulation of materials. There is a clear difference between reversing the resonance of a complex sequence, such as the instrumental echoes of the soprano at bars 11 and 26, and structures based on rhythmic mirrors of events. The rich detail and bold structures of the musical surface have been achieved by reducing his materials to the minimum and then subjecting these basic elements to expansion and exploration in various sonic and temporal domains. Already in the context of *Incontri* Nono talked of projecting musical material on more dimensions than polarised vertical/horizontal axes. Now this acoustic transformation of the voice is preparation for the experiments with electronics soon to come, particularly *La fabbrica illuminata*, his next major work.

Machado developed two literary alter egos – heteronyms, as Pessoa described his various identities: poet–philosopher Abel Martin and his student Juan de Mairena. The *Otras canciones a Guiomar* chosen by Nono had appeared in a 1935 article under the latter name as examples of the importance of forgetting in creation. Writers often point to the role of loss in Nono's texts; de Mairena's summary of Martin's thoughts on the vital role of forgetting suggest an interpretation fully consonant with Nono's underlying spirit of resistance:

> Thanks to the capacity for forgetting, the poet [. . .] can pull the roots of his spirit, buried in the soil of the anecdotal and trivial, in order to sink them deeper down in the subsoil or live rock of feeling, which ceases to be the evoker and becomes – at least in appearance – the illuminator of new forms. Because only impassioned creation wins out over forgetting.[20]

The later traces of reference, the structural role of fragment, the perpetual re-searching of an evolving personal space of sound and experience should be seen in this light. Machado's triple mediation of his ideas remind us of their context: the Civil War in Spain that made seeing Guiomar again an impossibility and would contribute to his isolation and death. This sharpens the edge of the poems. For Nono in 1962, the continued fascist regime in Spain constituted a

New spaces: studio, street, factory

present and urgent European political struggle. Human love, nature, liberty and justice are brought together in the Leonora figure of Guiomar; this is as political as any of Nono's works. At the same time, the enthusiastic reception of *Canciones a Guiomar* and *Canti di vita e d'amore* may paradoxically have unsettled the composer. The dedication to Boupachà aside, the only explicit political topic in these works is Hiroshima, and – as the ban-the-bomb campaign itself found – this was a topic so vast that it tended to abstraction, to a sense of individual powerlessness. While comments on the 'immediate sensuous appeal' of his music must have been gratifying,[21] Nono clearly had no intention of becoming the charming Latin conscience of the cultural elite – an avant-garde Domenico Modugno – and still less of appearing to flatter their political intelligence. To engage listeners effectively while resisting assimilation by bourgeois good taste or self-serving cultural institutions remained a challenge.

Possibility of a new theatre

Evolving projects

That the anti-fascist struggle in Spain was at the front of Nono's mind is clear from a project he had developed with Giuliano Scabia. They had met months earlier on the steps of La Fenice at the premiere of *Intolleranza 1960*; Scabia, just recently graduated, was at the beginning of a long career of innovation in action, engaged and situated theatre.[22] Temporarily living in Venice, he was involved with groups promoting socio-cultural initiatives. Together with Emilio Vedova and others, Scabia and Nono planned a multi-media event in Campo Sant'Angelo for May 1962, in support of Spanish strikers. This was no longer to be a work of social comment, but of intervention, of action. Instead, the event was prohibited by the police – the first in a decade of such encounters. The government was increasingly nervous about social unrest; two months later, the largest post-war protest would take place in Piazza Statuto, Turin. Striking Fiat workers, largely immigrants from the south of Italy, were joined in their demonstration by an incipient student movement. Over three days their protest turned into a battle with police, causing many injuries, a thousand arrests and accusations of brutality and agents provocateurs. The official PCI line was to be critical of all violence, but this event marked a turning point in the Party's history. In 1961, a group from within the PCI had launched *Quaderni rossi*, a publication taking a more critical stance in respect of party policies. Edited principally by Mario Tronti and Raniero Panzieri, *Quaderni rossi* proposed new analysis of Marx and of social structures. It put forward an agenda of 'con-ricerca' ('co-research'): the development of new ideas and structures in the workplace, whereby workers are no longer objects of research but co-researchers. Following the revolt of Piazza Statuto, a new tendency emerged, less inclined to reflection and patience; their publication *Classe operaia* commenced in 1964. The group included Toni Negri, Mario Tronti, Romano Alquati and the young Massimo Cacciari. The subsequent *Potere operaio* (*Workers' power*) movement can be seen to have its roots in this event and would have important implications for Nono's future.[23]

Nono outlined the Sant'Angelo plan in an article based on his 1962 talk *Possibility and necessity of a new musical theatre*.[24] Here he looks forward to a synthesis of arts, not mapped on to each other but in a dynamic interdependence. There would be no hierarchy of text, music and stage. Instead, the work would be the product of a collective of different skills and voices, responding together to the singularity of situations. The emergence of new aesthetic and social patterns is indivisible. This 'theatre of ideas, of struggle, closely tied to the certain march towards of new human and social condition' will be 'totally *engagé*, both on the structural–linguistic level and on the social: from the musician, the writer, the painter, the director to the last electrician or stage-hand'.[25] Characteristically, Nono searches for the historical roots of a radical theatre, through to

New spaces: studio, street, factory

Meyerhold, Piscator, Busoni and Schönberg – he sees *A Survivor from Warsaw* as the completion of *Moses und Aron*.[26] The model of Myakovsky is clearly still at play, but that of Eisenstein is also evident in plans for the compositional use of documentary material. The notion of mobility rings through this text: mobility of materials and resources, but also of relationships. An important goal is the freedom of the listener to inhabit the work in different ways – lost, he says, when religious public enactment (*azione scenica* is also his expression for this) was replaced by static representation. Following Sartre, this should be a theatre not of psychology but of situations.

The Campo Sant'Angelo group was to work as a cooperative. Their visual materials included images of Picasso's *Guernica*, documentary films such as Buñuel's *Espagne 37* and Resnais' *Guernica*, photographs from the Civil War and the present, and coloured slides with the words of the songs. Poems, historic texts and songs of the Spanish resistance would be projected through four groups of loudspeakers. The physical situation afforded the spatial treatment of sound and image, as well as an open, non-exclusive, engaged relationship with the audience. Nono had already given practical, composerly thought to the implications of his more abstract ideas, evolving principles that will re-emerge:

1. The director plans in detail the relationships between different elements, leaving the realisation to technicians.
II. To fix certain moments of synchronisation, leaving others open to improvisation 'such that everyone is obliged to direct their own part and respond immediately to each other'.
III. To fix start times and durations of materials. The resulting coincidences are the product of the interaction of the collaborators, not of a single perspective.
IV. To use these techniques 'not as an end in themselves, as current theorists of the open work would propose, but as preliminary and introductory moments, as moments of study, research and rehearsal; and choosing between the technical–expressive results, to fix them in a precise form.'[27]

This was to be no happening or open work, then. Creative tensions – differences of approach or opinion – are embraced, but they must lead to a clearly defined result. While one might wonder how likely these principles were to have been successfully realised in that particular context, they resonate through his composing process in theatre and studio alike.

Such a focus on the precise definition of an individual work is not fully consonant with the continuous nature of the evolution of Nono's ideas on music theatre, which occupy him exclusively for four years from early 1963. Theory, plans and material for specific works develop together in a series of projects, the relationship of which to finished works is partially circumstantial.[28] Nono seems to have met the poet, songwriter and political journalist Nanni Balestrini in 1960, and to have proposed a theatrical collaboration. Balestrini was enthusiastic; words and music should be on the same plane, like a *Theseus* for the present, he wrote. Then an editor for Feltrinelli, he arranged publication of Nono's essay *Possibilità e necessità di un nuovo teatro musicale* in 1963. The full set of texts Balestrini prepared never found their way into a work, although Nono would return to his poetry in 1968. Two ideas found an important role in the development of Nono's long-term music theatre project, however: a structure of short, autonomous scenes, and that the work should focus on the role of women.[29]

An undeveloped project based on Anna Seghers' *Revolt of the Fishermen of Santa Barbara* is mentioned in a letter to Hartmann, perhaps also inspired by Piscator's film version (1932–4).[30] Seen at the Venice Film Festival in 1963, this also has resonances with Visconti's *La Terra Trema*. In the various projects, realised and otherwise, Nono would remain essentially his own dramaturg, selecting texts and events, and recruiting writers, scenographers and directors to help him realise his vision. An interlocutor is vital to his process – only in one case does he take full responsibility for the text – but finding a collaborator whose intellect, perspective and understanding Nono can trust is important.

The tenuous narrative continuity of *Intolleranza* is loosened in favour of assemblages of texts. Nono proposed material to Emilio Jona, one of the first leaders of the Italian popular singer–songwriter movement, but also the librettist for Manzoni's operas *La sentenza* (1960) and *Atemtod* (1964).[31] Through 1963 they worked on an uncompleted project provisionally titled *Technically Sweet* – a comment by Robert Oppenheimer on his pursuit of the atomic bomb, coincidentally also adopted by Antonioni for an unrealised film.[32] The relationship between man and science, as embodied in the lives of Oppenheimer and Max Born, was to be balanced with scenes from the struggle of ordinary people against exploitation and alienation. Nono's notes summarise the project: 'I) Hiroshima – atomic bomb – war and NO II) various oppressions (countries, individuals) and <u>REVOLT</u> III) love which develops and overturns the conditions of <u>non-love</u>'.[33] This is articulated further: 'Love – for woman, for life, for nature'. He clearly intends this work to be as relevant, as close to home as possible; the condition of workers on Giudecca and the sound of the market at Rialto (later developed in *Contrappunto dialettico alla mente*) are considered as material, as is a strike of the employees of the theatre itself, to confront the audience directly. References range wide, especially for the non-trivial challenge of the final scene; here they include *Fidelio, Falstaff* and Fellini's recent *8 1/2*, itself a study of the impossibility of making work leading to the confronting of the author by his own subjects. In his notes, Nono wonders 'relationship Intolerance-Griffith / Intolleranza 1960 8 1/2 and today?'[34] In plans for the scenography he considers in detail the arrangement of characters, movement, events and light. Labyrinths, multiple divisions of the stage and rotating platforms appear in two-dimensional designs that anticipate his work with Lyubimov a decade later. The similarity of these to his sketches of form and sound objects suggest that the theatre had also become a conceptual space as much as a physical reality, a space for the imagining and inter-relating of materials and ideas that other models – score or text – cannot accommodate.

Jona had discussed the project with Cesare Pianciola, associated with *Quaderni rossi* and Panzieri. Pianciola was sceptical as to the link between nuclear science and the workplace technology of common experience. Nono in turn suggested that the writers of *Quaderni rossi* should stick to their own trade.[35]

'Un diario italiano'

Above all, the theatre affords movement; the movement of sound was one of the main topics of discussion with Scabia. Now living in Milan, Scabia had been working on material sent by Nono: poems by Pavese, investigations into the conditions of FIAT workers in Turin and their involvement in the historic strike of 1943,[36] quotations from workers in Palermo, extracts from Castro's 1962 *Second Declaration of Havana* and documents relating to the overflowing of the dam of Vajont in 1963, which killed 2,000 people. Parallels with *Intolleranza 1960* are clear, but these are issues still closer to home. Castro's rhetoric had just regalvanised world politics, and the disaster at Vajont, in the mountains north of Venice, was seen as the result of establishment interests ignoring both engineering advice and local concerns. The conditions of industrial workers were being debated heatedly amid increasing industrial strife, fuelled by a sense that the working class was being excluded from Italy's 'economic miracle' and that the unions no longer represented workers' interests. Giovanni Carocci's 1958 study of class conflict in the context of Fiat at Turin, *Inchiesta alla FIAT*, was an early example of 'con-ricerca'.[37] Nono's copy is annotated with ideas for a music-theatrical setting; his instinctive response to such a situation is compositional. The use of historical material from Turin, however recent,

New spaces: studio, street, factory

may have been a way of avoiding further prohibition. The 1962 riots there had been followed by bitter strikes at Fiat, Lancia and Michelin, documented in Carla and Paolo Gobetti's film *Scioperi a Torino* (*Strikes at Turin*), the script of which Nono likewise later annotated with a view to compositional treatment. Mario Monicelli's 1963 Oscar-nominated *I compagni* (*The Organizer*) also had to use an historical setting for its allegory of contemporary workers' organisation and strikes in Turin. These issues were therefore very alive in the public and political imagination.

All this amounted to another vast venture that threatened to be overwhelming; a new mode of collaboration was needed. At the beginning of 1964, Nono's ideas consolidated into a clearer vision, and he proposed a specific project to Scabia, hopefully for that September's Biennale festival:

> listen: remember how we talked about the possibility of bringing those blessed choruses to the stage
>
> that is: the choruses with texts from Palermo – Fiat – Vajont – as contexts for bringing-transfiguring with a degree of subjectivity women – Brechtian love – present-day Marias – .
>
> a possible staging: chorus in the orchestra + some instruments/on the stage only various devices with words writings photos pictures lights shapes phonemes objects on various planes and with various projection techniques + various surfaces on which the Marias move – mad, resigned, violent, in love, striking – .
>
> so to intervene on three documentary planes (Palermo/Fiat/Vajont) inventing various human irrational explosive moments of the Marias, with various montages (various poetic texts of the twentieth century).[38]

This letter provides a fascinating picture of Nono's sense of the context of his work. The description of his new creative project emerges seamlessly from proposals concerning their political activities. He talks of meetings planned by the Party in Venice to be addressed on topics such as Algeria, Cuba and Yugoslavia by Luigi Longo, Paolo Ingrao and Giorgio Napoletano. He proposes sessions on literature and poetry by Sanguinetti and Scabia, perhaps with Rossana Rossanda – ex-partisan, cultural secretary of the PCI, recently elected to the Chamber of Deputies, a highly independent thinker and an important figure in Nono's later dispute with the Party. One paragraph provides the link between the two parts of his letter; it states the ethos underlying both aspects of his work: 'we must continuously intervene and push harder. everyone with their own ideas, naturally!'

Again, despite Nono's stated and sincere ethos of collaboration and his need for a literary interlocutor it is clear whose idea was the motivating force; the choruses were already in development. Scabia points to Nono's concern with language. Venetian dialect plays an important role in Nono's collaboration; by exploiting its informality and plasticity, Nono can be more precise in conveying his thoughts and feelings. This is a sustained thread: with Maderna, Vedova, Zuccheri and Cacciari he finds the same intimacy of communication. With Scabia, also a Veneto-speaker, they begin to investigate the musico-dramatic properties of regional dialects in the documentary texts from Palermo, Turin and the Friuli. They begin to identify individual characters with particular dialects, wisely dropping the idea as it approaches comic stereotyping. The nature of the Italian language, and particularly its use in literature, was a very topical issue. Later the same year, Pier Paolo Pasolini published his *Nuove questioni linguistiche*, in which he questioned the validity of a literature in a standardized, bourgeois language developed through the economic miracle.[39] Nono would set the male-voice choruses of Pasolini's Friuliano *I Turcs tal Friul* in November 1976.

Scabia responded swiftly in January 1964. In his letter he proposes a single male role – brother, lover and comrade – and a group of five women representing the range of characteristics suggested by Nono: schizophrenic, in love, resigned, violent and self-aware.[40] Scabia describes the characters in novelist's detail. Together they pass through a series of six situations, described in terms of their emotional dynamics and the range of regional dialects. These situations ('figures') are arranged within the confines of the four choruses already planned; the work becomes 'a reading of recent Italian history'.[41] As well as the documentary material, there are poems by Pavese and Hernandez, prose by Eluard. Scabia's drawings of forms and the multicoloured interplay of characters through a scene suggest that he was acquainted with Nono's working method. This is even more evident in the material that then arrives: long strips of paper, pasted together with cut-out fragments of copies of typescript arranged in a polyphony of text (Figure 8.8). The sources are now more focused: documentary text (Palermo, Turin, Havana) for the choruses, poems of Pavese, and dramatic dialogue by Scabia. As it moves through subsequent drafts – now arranged on large sheets of paper – the quantity of text is reduced; it becomes more fragmented and acquires musical rhythm and architecture.

Figure 8.8 Nono working on *Un diario italiano*, mid-1960s. (Photograph © Adelmann.)

New spaces: studio, street, factory

Still more than *Intolleranza 1960*, this now approaches Sartre's concept of a theatre of situations rather than characters. Discussion centres about the relationship between chorus and soloists, polyphony and monody. At issue is the everyman problem. This is not a continuum; an audience will naturally relate differently to an individual than to a large group. Dramatically, the women function as a group of classical muses, each embodying different qualities but together constituting a full picture of human potential. The notion of salvation through love exists in parallel with that of political resistance, as it does in Pavese. To reconcile these we have to see particular political struggles as instances of a deeper human behavior; Gramsci's correspondence provides another model.[42] In his notes, Nono described the solo tenor as 'comrade, fighter, evangelist'; to Scabia he is more specific: 'don't think of the Italian tenor but of Dowland – the evangelist of Bach, not as a narrator!'[43] Nono's solution is for both male and female to be represented by several voices, some of which may be instrumental; text does not need to be continuously audible. In the absence of continuous individual narrative, the chorus becomes the central figure; Scabia reports that the choruses of Bach were Nono's most frequent reference.[44] In both carrying and forming the context for the drama, in their balance of spirituality, humanity and aesthetic form, Bach's vocal works again provide Nono with a model of communication.

By May 1964 the project, now titled *Un diario italiano*, had developed its definitive form of six scenes. A form emerges that anticipates the multiply-layered non-linearity of *Prometeo*: the six scenes are to be interspersed within the four choruses, which in turn may appear as fragments or be cross-cut with other interventions. Svoboda had been enlisted, as had director Virginio Puecher, who five months later would collaborate on the first instantiation of Maderna's *Hyperion* at the Biennale – likewise a collaborative, pluridimensional work that resists reduction to a single score.[45] La Scala invited a concrete proposal, the text of which summarises the work, while carefully avoiding references to specific events:

> Five women and a few men pass through a series of experiences and situations which they have to confront with their presence and their will, otherwise they will be overcome.
>
> The first scene opens with a description of human oppression [. . .] This scene could be taken as an exposition of materials and theme.
>
> The second is a scene of nightmare and delirium. [. . .] It is the scene of inner catastrophe, how in the modern world it closes in on people through the effort and misery of work in industry, with its harsh rules. [. . .]
>
> The third is a scene of violence and despair. As in the first scene, the choir takes the main role as the carrier of Italian history. [. . .]
>
> Fourth scene: the children. [. . .] The scene of all the possibilities of joy and life. [. . .]
>
> Fifth scene: external catastrophe. [. . .] a collective death [. . .] a catastrophe that could have been avoided by collective will (as is the case with war, for example).
>
> Sixth scene: life gradually returns [. . .] a great coming-together of rediscovered humanity . . .[46]

Films, coloured projections and animated images are described in some detail: 'We anticipate the use of various kinds of visual material and graphical processes, and various projection techniques, for which reason there is no scenography in the traditional sense.' To this end, Scabia and Nono were now in contact with the studio of Giulio Cingoli (1927–2017), whose animations for the RAI would become part of contemporary Italian folklore.[47]

New spaces: studio, street, factory

Close text analysis, the basis of everything, developed new directions in preparations for the monodies, especially the settings of Pavese. At Nono's request, Scabia parses the linear text into parallel streams of syllables through which the composer plots trajectories of resonance and movement. This is very different from the semantic and sonic proliferation in Berio's use of text at this time, for example. Nono is rather finding the movement *within* an apparently unitary source of sound and meaning, a path that will lead to the intense inner focus of the later works, to the revealing of different forms of musical life at every level of magnification.

The scale of the choruses necessitates a different approach. While Nono continued to develop ideas for the monodies, he had completed two of the projected choruses in January and March; in May a third was nearly ready and a fourth was to incorporate a choir of children. As in *Intolleranza 1960*, they were to be recorded in advance and spatialised in performance. The first, to texts prepared by Jona, was performed posthumously as *Da un diario italiano*.[48] For 72-voice choir, it represents the zenith of Nono's sound-field approach and of his polyphonic technique. His key references are clearly evident: Venetian spatiality, madrigalian semantic resonances and isorhythmic principles from historical models, and a Schönberg-derived approach to sound and word, speaking and singing. Above all, the example of Bach is clear in the confluence of intense technical refinement and powerful, intuitive expressiveness. Indeed, he initially conceives of the movement as a fugue – its six sections labelled *Expositio, I Divertimento, Expositio, II Divertimento, Pedale* and *Stretta* – although the eventual counterpoint does not correspond directly. Nono's technical preparation is so comprehensive that he is free to invent new solutions to each situation while remaining within strict overall constraints. There are two texts and two choirs, each of nine parts in each voice; they are not divided or opposed, rather the texts move between choirs in fragmentations, simultaneities and coincidences. One, from workers in Palermo, speaks of resignation: 'I am illiterate, that is why we are slaves'. The other, from Fiat workers in Torino, of resistance: 'I was a partisan'. They balance at certain key points – 'you learn everything in prison | I was in prison', 'you know evil | you know good' – and come together at others – references to the insurrection of 1943 and especially the final 'one listens and learns,' anticipating the 'ascolta!' of *Prometeo*. The opening line – 'sono analfabeta' – is a clear statement at the beginning of Nono and Scabia's 'reading' of Italian history. It echoes the refusal to be silenced of the *bocca chiusa* of *Canti di vita e d'amore*.

The shape of the piece derives from Nono's text analysis at different levels. The six *fuga* sections with the coda of this final line match the syllabic proportions of the text. The distribution of text is first arranged graphically, with scissors and tape in a polyphonic collage. He builds two-dimensional sound shapes, especially from the initial word 'sono' – 'I am' but also 'sound' in dialect.[49] Duration values for the two texts begin from the same set of atoms – <1, 2, 4, 7> – but follow divergent patterns of expansion: for Palermo the first value increases – <2, 4, 8, 14> and upwards, and for Fiat the second – <1, 3, 7, 13>.[50] These values are used to build structures as in recent works, but now of greater complexity and subtlety in their inner polyphony, layering and interaction. Different interval-based pitch fields also characterise the two text sources: chromatic fields expand and contract by glissando around unisons or bare intervals, whole-tone fields interlock, minor thirds and fourths offer moments of orientation, repose or expectation. On the last word – 'impara' –two interlocking near-diatonic fields in sopranos and altos fill a high octave C♯–C, gradually thinned to leave only its outer boundaries, at once static and shimmeringly mobile. Fields of two intervals can create timbre or be extruded into figure. Such a moment occurs at 'organizzatori' (bar 36), a knowing gesture; the 'organisers' present the sound field of this section, based on fourths and minor seconds, as a 24-part canon counterpoised with a single E♭ struggling to escape its unison. These events lead to a powerful tutti attack on 'sciopero' ('strike'). The chorus is rich with technical–expressive–dramatic devices. The combined singing and shouting of 'schiavi' ('slaves') (bar 9) is a dramatic gesture that also becomes architectural as it returns to interrupt the next phrase. A complex of insistent rhythms at the chorus' climax, 'Il giorno dell'insurrezione' ('the day of the insurrection'), recalls the earlier crowds of *Fučík* or *Memento*. It resolves into a steely quiet, sustained soprano unison 'di coraggio' ('of courage'), expanded into a tightly rotating cluster, its phonemes whispered below.

If the relationship between sonic detail and mass has something in common with Ligeti's works of this time, its broader formal control is closer to Xenakis' research. A unique quality of Nono's work here is his fine control over comprehensibility, the degree of clarity of the logic of music and text and their combining in a new entity. This requires intensely close listening on the parts of composer, performers and listener. As always in Nono's works for multiple voices, the relationship between the individual and the group is central; solo voices emerge, subgroups form and disperse dynamically, moments of unanimity articulate the wider evolution of the music. Social and political analogies are clear. This presents technical and dramatic challenges when combining such choral writing with soloists, as was becoming clear to Nono early in this project.[51] The emergence of figure is also bound up with Nono's ongoing interest in the role of motif, already clear in *Text – Musik – Gesang* and developed in various notes through the following years; Nono is always concerned that his imagining should afford understanding. As Noller observes, the choruses of early 1964 are the workshop in which Nono develops the new melos of *La fabbrica illuminata*.[52]

Da un diario italiano represents a highpoint in synthesising the full armoury of Nono's score-based technique, concepts derived from the studio and the sure use of both to dramatic ends. Only at the beginning of the next decade would he return to this mode of composing. Whether the entire music-theatre project could have been fully realised with the same intensity is a moot point. Aspects of his notes and letters suggest that this work was moving ever farther away from the institutional theatre. While the theatre remains a vital conceptual space for developing and investigating ideas, in its realisation Nono's thought is fundamentally musical. This assimilation of the conceptual theatre in the musical stuff itself gives it dramatic strength and presence whatever its apparent genre, just as its assimilation of social–historical reality lends it immediacy and relevance irrespective of explicit reference. However, the embodiment of many subtle layers of drama in the music can lead to irresolvably complicated relations with the more absolute and sometimes incompatible realities of the stage. In practical terms, the currency of Marxist discourse in Italy at that moment may have allowed such a work to connect constructively with its audience. In that context, the breadth of its subject matter may also have brought the risk of its becoming aestheticised to the point of political disconnection, or of being politicised to such a degree that Nono and Scabia's intense aesthetic investment would have been lost. *Intolleranza 1960* allows for the abstraction, the generalisation of situations of oppression and resistance. In *Canti di vita e d'amore*, the issues are global but the expression intensely personal, and in *La fabbrica illuminata* the subject will be clear and specific.

Un diario italiano was one near-emergent state of a continuous process. Stenzl refutes the idea of an unconcluded work-in-progress in Boulez's sense.[53] Perhaps we should take a more historical materialist approach: what we see here is rather a continuous process of research and creation at the core of Nono's practice, with specific finished works responding to external circumstances. Textual and musical material would find their way into *La fabbrica illuminata* (1964*)*, *Voci destroying muros* (1970), *Ein Gespenst geht um in der Welt* (1971) and *Al gran sole carico d'amore* (1972–4), as well as other uncompleted projects.[54] *Un diario italiano* thus provided conceptual and technical fuel for a decade.

New spaces: studio, street, factory

'La fabbrica illuminata'

Locating the work

Movements in experimental theatre were gathering pace as writers and directors sought to reduce, focus and contextualise the dramatic event, to explore language, to build a new relationship with their audience. Nono had become interested in the work of Peter Weiss and studied his *Marat/Sade*, to be directed by Peter Brook in 1964. Scabia was becoming a major voice in the Italian debate, and Nono already had in mind a new music theatre project: 'no collage – a text completely invented by you – text – action – everything'.[55] In May, while working on the Vajont chorus of *Un diario italiano*, he was invited by the RAI to write a piece for the September 1964 Prix Italia, still the most prestigious international competition for radio and television work. The festival was to be held in Genoa, home of the enormous Italsider steelworks. At the beginning of the month Nono and Scabia were planning the second scene, the nightmare; five text extracts were to be fragmented by the chorus and sung clearly by the five female soloists.[56] Two weeks later, Nono had a clear view of how a new piece could emerge from that material 'to finish afterwards with the five soloists'.[57] A solo soprano would sing documentary texts while a tape of chorus and recorded sounds 'creates hallucinations', followed by poems by Pavese for soprano with instruments. On the same day he invited Carla Henius to sing 'a fragment of my new theatre work – for you, instruments and tape with choir and sounds'.[58] With the exception of the instruments, this would become *La fabbrica illuminata – The illuminated factory*, with all the connotations of illumination. By 27 May, he was able to describe the work to Henius. It was to be for her and four loudspeakers; in the first three parts she would be accompanied by a tape consisting of a choir and other sounds, in the fourth she would sing alone.[59]

Cornigliano, outside Genoa, was the administrative home and largest steelworks of the Italsider company. Its 40,000 steelworkers were engaged in a series of bitter strikes through 1964. Two particular issues dominated the disputes: the non-introduction of productivity agreements established to balance the ever more tightly regulated workflow, and the privatisation of parts of the docks, allowing companies such as Italsider to bypass union agreements. This was part of a wider picture. Unrest was most widespread among the large workforces of heavy industry, power and transport, but erupted everywhere. As if in fulfilment of Nono and Jona's theatrical vision, theatre workers held a strike in June. From the pages of *l'Unità* emerges a sense that what had been fought for at such a high price was being handed over to caricature capitalists, along with a work force now treated as disposable labour. As the Italian economic miracle accelerated, it seemed that while their government was helping near-monopoly companies – 'companies with state participation' – create unprecedented wealth, Italian workers saw no rise in their living standards but ever-harsher working conditions. They felt treated by their employers with state-sponsored contempt; German steelworkers earned twice as much, for example.[60] The PCI saw the fragmentation of opposition as a dangerous tactic, and sought to build a wider consciousness of the situation among working communities. The chemical works and shipyards at Porto Marghera, opposite Venice, were sites of similar struggles in which Nono took a keen interest.[61]

This project was therefore an opportunity for Nono to engage directly with current political events. In April 1963 he had been on the electoral list of PCI candidates to the Chamber of Deputies. He published a clear position statement, a Gramscian view of the role of cultural–intellectual activity in which he also develops ideas on the collaborative nature of art. 'How come a composer of dodecaphonic origins is in the electoral list of the PCI?' he asks. The characteristic syntax of his answer reflects the inextricability of his ideas:

New spaces: studio, street, factory

In the cultural and political engagement of the communist intellectual there is a dialectical continuity between the two aspects of his presence, never separate: whether in the solitude of the studio, in experimental research and in the invention of a new music, or in the technical–human collaboration of the electronic studio, the testimony of the communist musician and his active participation in the raising of consciousness, of feelings, of collective reality, enriches his activity – hence his natural and logical intervention in the great strikes of Fiat and the metalworkers, in the popular demonstrations of 1960 against the fascist government of Tambroni, those of 1962 for Cuba and in the present elections – [This continuity is] manifested in new modes of relationship between performance and public – thus engaged with continuous and new responsibilities for expression.[62]

Nono's increasing political involvement had reached an important stage in October 1963 when he visited the USSR in response to an invitation from the Union of Soviet Composers. Ironically, *Canti di vita e d'amore* was withdrawn from performance by the DDR; Nono's music was banned as 'most decadent and capitalist', although the ban was rescinded the following year.[63] Nono had even sent a copy of the score to Togliatti, Gramsci's successor as leader; through the vicissitudes of the PCI, he would maintain warm communication with senior figures such as Enrico Berlinguer, Pietro Ingrao and Giorgio Napoletano, to become Italy's president from 2006 to 2015. Nono's balanced report in *l'Unità* expresses warm support for the younger generation (that of Schnittke, Denisov and Pärt) and the sincerity of their research, but concludes 'I have not met the Mayakovsky of Soviet music of today'.[64] Roberta Reader brings together various reports of the visit to give a more rounded picture of Nono's encounter with the Union of Composers.[65] He was indeed allowed to meet the younger composers, but not to speak publicly at length. At the Scriabin Museum, Nono was introduced to the new ANS photoelectronic synthesiser and its inventor, Evgeny Murzin.[66] The ANS would be central to the Moscow studio of electronic music, founded in 1967. It features in the soundtracks of several of the early films of Andrei Tarkovsky, to become an important reference for Nono. He was obliged to listen to recordings of state-authorised music: 'in my opinion the "official" position of the Union is entirely based on the [Zhdanov] resolution of 1948 (the administration dates back to then) with almost no development of critical or analytical method'.[67] Nono's questioning of the very idea of 'socialist realism' in music was removed by the editors of *l'Unità* as they published his report.[68] His companion on this visit was Luigi Pestalozza – partisan, political theorist, musicologist and music critic for *l'Unità*. Pestalozza would become Nono's close friend, collaborator on various projects, and critical mentor. In a letter soon after their return, Pestalozza analyses their situation:

We need to intervene, to develop leadership on a plane other than that of politics and Rome; rather on the level of an authentic revolutionary culture and politics, which in my opinion has to manifest itself in action to raise awareness among the masses [. . .] and thus a raising of awareness, of hegemony, on the cultural level.[69]

The sonic factory

The first issue of *Classe operaia* in February 1964 developed the notion of co-research through Romano Alquati's workplace studies in the factories of Fiat and Alfa Romeo.[70] A new mode of participation thus presented itself. Nono spent three days with Scabia and Marino Zuccheri in the Cornigliano steelworks, recording the sounds of the entire production process – 'from the furnace to the laminating (1.5 km)'[71] – and discussions with workers.[72]

New spaces: studio, street, factory

> But once I was in the tumultuous and incandescent reality of Cornigliano, I was shocked not just by the seemingly fantastic acoustic and visual spectacle [...], or by the implacable rituality of the laminating furnaces, not just fascinated in the abstract, but really by the violence with which I was struck by the reality of the complex conditions of the workers in those places.[73]

The title *La fabbrica illuminata* is taken from Scabia's existing text. A tripartite structure was agreed soon after their visit, although adjustments continued up to the premiere. Nono's score would have four parts, with Scabia's central section divided into Parts II and III. The verses of the first, *Corale I–IV* (together *Coro iniziale* in the sketches) use words from the interviews in a litany of the dangers and miseries suffered by workers, chorale-like in its directness. Each stanza of text begins 'esposizone operaia' ('exposure of workers'). The bulk of the text is sung by the choir on tape; the soloist sings the first line 'fabbrica dei morti la chiamavono' ('they called it the factory of death'), then the last line of the subsequent three stanzas, each as a continuous phrase of monody. The formal, almost ritual pattern of this opening contrasts with the visceral expression of the middle sections. In Part II, *il giro del letto* and *tutta la città* use fragments of the second *nightmare* scene of *Un diario italiano*, mixed with workers' comments in a less structured stream of impassioned anguish. The name of Part III (*swapping beds*) derives from the worker's expression for the night shift, the dehumanising effects of which it explores. Here the soloist picks out isolated words and phrases, sung and spoken, between wordless vocalises, as if internalisation were the only response to such intensity of expression. The final solo monody sets four lines of hope from Pavese's *Le piante del lago* (1946) that had also been intended for the larger work.

At the beginning of June 1964 Nono and Zuccheri were at the Studio di Fonologia in Milan, assembling fragments of the recordings from Cornigliano and adding electronic noise and sine waves. In mid-June the eleven short choral sections were ready to be recorded by the choir of the RAI in Milan, mostly for two choirs of twelve parts each. Projected divisions show that 72 voices were again required. Each of the four stanzas of *Corale I–IV*, apart from the lines sung by the soloist, is spoken by the choir in a dense rhythmic polyphony. Structures of density and intensity, derived from the choruses of *Un diario italiano*, are made of the syllabic rhythms of detached words. Nono plots movement around the circular space, of words and of transitions between whispering, speaking and singing. The chorus also sings the soloist's opening and closing lines and echoes the consonants of the last word of the second stanza – 'intasca' ('earns') – under the third. These three passages are also taken from *Un diario italiano*. In the seven bars of the opening words, the two choirs move in opposite directions through a pitch canon in each of eight three-voice groups – the material of 'organizzatori' in the chorus discussed above. Fourths and minor seconds outline a harmonic field of alternating minor seconds and major thirds, bounded by fourths. The consonants "N–S–TA–I" work through the same field in a slowly expanding chord (Figure 8.9):

Figure 8.9 La fabbrica illuminata: choral fragment 1, pitch field

New spaces: studio, street, factory

There are also four choral fragments in *Giro del letto*, more figured in pitch and rhythm as this more distressed, unpredictable second section balances the clear structure of the first. In this spirit, the singers take different phonemes of the particular text such that sequences and words half-emerge, reorder, overlap and disappear – a barely comprehensible nightmare that the ear is nevertheless drawn to try to decipher, frustrated and exhausted in the process. Only in the second fragment is the text set clearly. The highpoint of the choral component, 'incandescente fabbrica illuminata', mixes sung and spoken text in a dramatic crescendo from *pp* to *fff*.

In the studio, Nono expanded the nature of the choral fragments of each section, cutting, editing and re-recording. Those of the first are shifted, interrupted and spatialised, while those of the second are fragmented still further. The third element to be recorded was Henius herself. She describes the working environment of Nono and Zuccheri when she arrived at the studio in June:

> They had already done a lot, edited and recopied. What they had discarded lay in knee-high heaps in every corner, colourful nests of snakes. [. . .] The disorder in those two tiny studios was such that you could hardly understand how they worked and managed to go straight to the right ten-centimetre piece of tape. They *can* do it, because what they had already recorded and prepared in that short time of experimentation couldn't be done with a magic wand.[74]

The tape is a trace of Nono's actions. For four days they worked from morning to midnight, the first in a 25-year pattern of such intensive studio-based collaborations with individual performers. Henius reports in detail how they worked on isolated words or phrases, how Nono asked her to sing, scream, speak, improvise, explore the text, her own voice, emotions and self-image as a performer: 'It is remarkable to produce sounds with your own voice that you've never heard from yourself – someone unknown to me sighs, slurs, sings, squeaks or roars.'[75] By mid-July the tape for the first two sections was ready, and at the beginning of August Henius returned to record material for third: 'just single notes in every register, every kind of production, long, short, with vibrato, straight, with crescendo and diminuendo, all vowels.'[76] This fascination with the expressive range of the female voice also persists through Nono's work. A particular impulse may have been Nono's admiration of the voice of Mina.[77] An exceptionally popular singer, taken to the heart of the Italian public, Mina was possessed of a unique virtuosity, timbral and emotional range and a reflective self-awareness as an artist that was the model for later performers such as Madonna or Lady Gaga.[78] At this very moment Mina also represented a new and very public feminism. As an openly unmarried mother she had effectively been ostracised by the RAI in 1963; her return in mid-1964 was motivated by a very public sense of popular affection and justice.[79] Mina was at the height of her musical and cultural heroism, therefore.

Luca Cossettini's exemplary musicological edition and ingenious research – filming the passage of the original tape – reveal much about the sequence of its construction.[80] The headings in Nono's own sound projection score make clear its essential architecture: five sections, including passages for tape alone following *Corale I–IV* and *giro del letto*.[81] In broad terms, section 1 contains the sung and spoken choruses, section 2 the sounds of the steelworks and sections 3–5 more processed and closely edited material from Henius herself and subsequently from the choir. The tape ends at 14'20" for the soprano to sing the finale alone:

[Parte I: Corale I–IV]
1 = 0–3'31"   esposizione
[Tape alone]
2 = 3'31"–6'46"   colata [laminating – the steel production process]
[Parte II: giro del letto]
3 = 6'46"–9'42"   e non si fermano
[Tape alone]
4 = 9v42–12'14"   tutte le notti
[Parte III: tutta la città]
5 = 12'14"–14'20"   tutta la città

[Parte IV: *Finale* – soprano alone]

The soprano's phrases in the first and fourth *Corale* remain within the pitch field of the choruses. Both marked *duro, non vibrato*, these are the most continuous material until the finale. The vocal gestures of the central sections are pulled rapidly between the twin poles of the underlying structures of pitch and text and the sonic furnace of the tape. Dynamics, song, pitched and unpitched speech, *bocca chiusa*, breath, clear text and isolated phoneme combine such that expression and vocal production are one. Only at the last word of these sections – 'morto' – does the soprano fully reinhabit her own voice. There her rising figure G♯–C♯–D continues the C♯–D–G of 'morir' at the end of *Corale IV*. This sonic, intervallic, semantic framing adds perspective and dimension to the nightmare of the steelworks. In their condensing of musical essence these phrases also point to Nono's emerging pitch universe, navigated primarily by fourths and semitones, its constituent objects of variable density, distance and internal vibration. Aspects of the writing resemble Berio's work for Cathy Berberian, but the role of the voice is entirely different. Here, there is no self-ironising distance; the investment of the soloist in the work is complete. In a letter to Adorno a few days after the Venice premiere on September 14 1964, Henius describes her experience of working with Nono:

> It seems to me that even when he is wrong in something, as a person he is right. When he is difficult he is dearer to me than clever mediocrities. He can work like a mad thing and allows himself nothing. But he also allows the others nothing. I have often observed how people who have to do with him work a bit better than they would naturally – myself included – because you can't escape this compulsion to the absolute.[82]

The final soprano monody seems to have been finished during work with Henius in Venice in mid-August. As if to reflect the balance that is restored in Pavese's poem, Nono returns to serial principle of retaining a balance between the five intervals of semitone to fourth. This completeness presents a new situation in the context of his recent intervallic practice, resolved by returning to a 5×5 square of intervals. He reads freely from this, inserting repetitions of successive intervals to create new sequences (Figure 8.10).

An intense drama emerges from these elements. It communicates the energy of the brief periods of its composition: a free, tangible, collaborative process that nevertheless incorporated all the reflective thought of the previous period. We are at once in the concert venue, the steelworks and the female worker's mental theatre. The relationship between soloist and tape is as mobile as the sounds themselves. Early timeline sketches show how spatiality, polyphony

New spaces: studio, street, factory

Figure 8.10 La fabbrica illuminata: beginning of *Finale* – derivation of pitch material in three stages[83]

and intensity are inextricably related (Figure 8.11). His informal graphical process is becoming increasingly architectural.

At the opening the soprano emerges from the taped choir as if the camera were zooming in from a view of the entire workforce to a single woman; her relationship with the mass is in constant movement. Moments of unanimity emerge from the many voices of suffering and protest through *Corale II*, to shout together in response to the soprano at the beginning of *Corale III* as if she were addressing the crowd. There are brief madrigalisms: her sustained 'tempi' or the collapse back into the crowd of 'morir'. There is some paradox in the noise of the factory, extended by electronic sounds, as its violent envelopes and uncertain silences take on a futurist beauty, but one in which there is no place for the individual. This is inverted in *Giro del letto* when the soloist enters her inner space. The recorded choir arrive at moments of intervallic transparency and become the multiplication of the soprano. Instead of the masses they are now a thousand individuals, united in the single optimistic, resilient figure of the solo soprano of the finale. The overall trajectory is straightforward; in its contrasting formal properties and voice of successive sections the work resembles a Bach cantata. The people's laments are catalogued in the verses of the chorales, followed by a sonic evocation of their world; a soloist, accompanied by choirs of groups and individuals, explores the emotional implications of this state; and a final solo restores directness and simplicity in its assertion of faith.

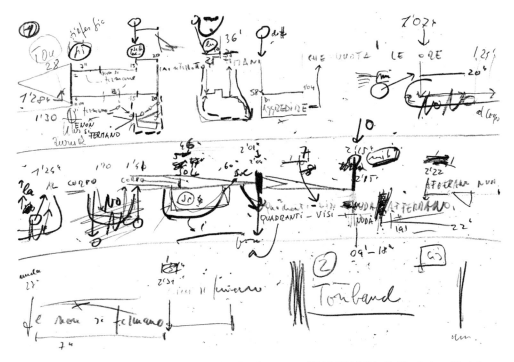

Figure 8.11 La fabbrica illuminata: Timeline sketch of opening. (ALN 27.11/01. © The heirs of Luigi Nono. Reproduced by kind permission.)

La fabbrica illuminata requires presence and engagement on the part of the soloist, a wide timbral range, precise control and a deep sense of drama; Henius refers to it as a *scena*. While the part is intensely challenging to the persona of the performer, it is not technically virtuosic in conventional terms. Nono retains a directness of communication: an expressive, experimental voice but one with which the listener can identify. He is aware of the critical nature of this balance: 'no mimesis [. . .] no populist or popular naturalism'.[84] 'No naturalism' is a note that appears repeatedly through the work on *Un diario italiano*. Scabia would later recall how Nono insisted on the materiality of the piece:

> After I listened to *La fabbrica illuminata* I said to Nono that I felt profoundly moved by a temperature of sound that went beyond the signified (factory, alienation, oppression, nightmare) – it seemed to me a sound that had to do with the tragic, the contemplation of death, the sublime. He did not agree. Today, thinking about his music (sublime) of the eighties I think I can recognise in the excavation of the sixties–seventies (a hard excavation in rare sonic stone, in tremendous ferrous materials, in ideological cages both enchanting and dominating, in enraged hopes) a research towards a substratum and a new light (of sound) emerging with a coherence that is not always recognised, but is profound and visible.[85]

By the same token, and despite its origins, *La fabbrica illuminata* is no radiophonic work. The figure of the soprano is real and personal; she creates a physical–musical space. Just as the work

New spaces: studio, street, factory

has its own autonomy, Nono was clear that the soprano performs a role, as he would explain to Henius: 'you must not have an exclusive right which means that without you "la fabbrica" will disappear.'[86] In its focus the work realises some of his concept of the *azione scenica*; in its very stuff it comes closer to Nono's emerging vision of his own role. This physicality was clear in his performances, in his sound projection – the starting point for a continuing debate concerning an oral tradition of interpretation. Nono would push the sound system to the limits of audio clarity and physical comfort and beyond, as reported by Liliana Poli – often his soloist in performances of *La fabbrica illuminata* – and later by other performers. In his own projection scheme, for example, he marks the end of Corale I–IV *ffffff*, replaced in the score for publication by a more moderate *fff*. This creates conflicting interpretative imperatives for subsequent performers, already reflected in the different approaches to sound projection outlined in the critical edition of this work. Should they seek balance, clarity and fidelity to the text, or to recapture some of the physicality, unpredictability and challenges to listener and performer of Nono's own performances?

While *La fabbrica illuminata* embodies much of Nono's detailed theoretical, political, dramatic and musical thought of the previous two years in its sound, subject and emotion, it springs directly from the works at Cornigliano in mid-1964. Early in August came the news that the RAI would not present *La fabbrica illuminata* at Genoa. Nono had anticipated this possibility from the outset.[87] One might even say he courted it. In a letter to painter and fellow party member Renato Guttoso he expresses his distaste for competitions, for the market and for the initial proposal of the RAI.[88] He lists their reasons in a letter to Pestalozza: this was a betrayal of faith, the RAI have a strict anti-communist stance, the Italsider directors will be at the event.[89] The RAI announced the change of programme 'for technical reasons', but the act of censorship was widely discussed in the press.[90] Instead, it was a group of Italsider employees who led the warm applause at the first performance in the closing concert of the Venice Biennale on September 15; the work is dedicated to the steelworkers at Cornigliano.[91] Calvino and Sartre also arrived for the event. A Biennale premiere might not be considered a political intervention, but Nono would play and discuss this music with workers' associations around Italy and abroad through the rest of the decade. It concluded the PCI Veneto congress in June 1965, for example, at which Nono participated as a delegate.[92] In *Rinascita*, Pestalozza reported on the acceptance of the musical language among such audiences, on the lively discussions that ensued: 'nobody fell into the banalities of modern audiences'.[93] He attributed the success of these events to the communicative properties of Nono's music and the openness of mind of the listeners. Public discussion of the work and the role of the RAI became an embarrassment for the state broadcaster. Shortly after the premiere, they proposed a Rome performance for the 1965/6 season, in the safe context of an orchestral concert conducted by Maderna. Nono wrote to the workers at Cornigliano ahead of a visit in November 1965, now associating their struggle with wider political events and thanking them for their role in his work: 'I consider that the direct relationship with you, workers, labourers and new technicians, is the starting point for the composer–comrade. Obviously that alone doesn't guarantee the validity of music, but it is the fundamental precondition.'[94]

Nono's identification with his direct surroundings was complete. His impatience with German culture – and perhaps a sense of betrayal – had exploded when Lachenmann took part in Stockhausen's new music seminar at the Cologne Hochschule in late 1963: 'he took me for a sort of "spy" for Nono; was always so uncertain, mistrustful [. . .] I wanted to work with him seriously'.[95] Nono answered with contempt for the people involved: 'why do you need more theory???????? Especially when it's all false ?!?!?!'[96] He continued:

New spaces: studio, street, factory

> You need to communicate?? Of course, naturally.
> But why and with whom?
> Each of us has this need and necessity.
> In Venice I communicate with my worker friends from Giudecca
> Certainly not with the various 'failed musicians' or the 'aristoids' here
> [. . .]
> because from these workers I understand a life – my choice, of course – or can the
> environment of La Fenice teach us something????[97]

Nono reported to Lachenmann the withdrawal of *La fabbrica illuminata* by the RAI and his non-acceptance of a DM 20,000 stipend from the Ford Foundation to work in West Berlin for a year: 'that is an attempt at corruption, and worse, right there in Berlin.'[98] In his last such detailed letter for a long time, Lachenmann tried to return their conversation to composition: 'Forgive me the comparison: you work much more *with* sound-structures (ablative), I work more *on* sound-structures (accusative), at least up to now.'[99] Nono would not reply for nearly twenty years.

American journey

Nono's creative and political energies were coming fully into alignment. In 1958, director and conductor Sarah Caldwell had founded The Opera Company of Boston, an independent group with a growing reputation for its innovative repertoire and productions. In February 1965 they planned to produce *Intolleranza 1960*. Svoboda brought his projections and Nono was invited to attend final rehearsals. Despite a 'distinguished person' work permit, his application for a visa at the American Consulate in Trieste fell at the question concerning Communist Party membership. This was widely discussed in both Italy and the USA. *The Boston Globe* reported: 'he was required to fill out the usual form, including questions as to whether he advocated overthrow by force of existing governments (he left that blank) and whether he was a member of the Communist Party. He answered "yes".'[100] Protests from the press and a committee of prominent American musicians persuaded the State Department to intervene,[101] but the visit was not to be altogether constructive. Nono was appalled at the production, the omission of political slogans, the performers' lack of preparedness ('dilettante and primitive'),[102] the translation and by the political apathy of students he met at Harvard. His hosts were similarly unimpressed with what they perceived as ungraciousness; Nono certainly failed to grasp that such a production constituted an act of cultural faith and courage in the climate of the time. Svoboda's impression was quite different.[103] Technologically, this was a step forwards. Video feeds, including the audience themselves and a demonstration in the street, were projected onto large screens on stage, and towers of TV screens presented the texts. It was reviewed widely, critics praising its integrity and courage rather than aesthetic qualities.

The family continued to Los Angeles, Nono's first visit to the Schoenberg home. Already ill-disposed towards the USA, he projected his political anger onto his new surroundings in a letter to *Rinascita*:

> But what is hidden behind all this? Who wants and uses and crushes others with similar power? Yesterday it was made clear to me. While driving through Hollywood, through the lights etc., impressive in the midst of all this snow of security a small barely visible neon sign lighting up an evening paper announcing: Heavy Bombers Landing at Saigon Ready to Bomb North Viet Nam.[104]

New spaces: studio, street, factory

The inferno: 'Die Ermittlung' and 'Ricorda cosa ti hanno fatto in Auschwitz'

Prominent in Scabia's text for *La fabbrica illuminata* are the analogies with fascism: 'the factory of the dead', 'the factory as a concentration camp'. In May 1965, Nono received a long hoped-for invitation from Piscator to collaborate. The project was the production of a new work by Peter Weiss, *Die Ermittlung* (*The Investigation*), a documentary text-based theatre work condensing witness statements from the Auschwitz trials held in Frankfurt from December 1963 to August 1965.[105] *Die Ermittlung* was a unique public theatrical event. On 19 October it was premiered simultaneously in twelve theatres across East and West Germany, as well as being produced by the Royal Shakespeare Company in London, directed by Peter Brook. Piscator's production would be at the Freie Volksbühne in Berlin, a theatre rooted in the workers' movement and with a reputation for defiantly defending directorial freedom.[106] If the trials were intended to be cathartic, they raised as many questions as they addressed: questions of individual and group responsibility, of collaboration, of retribution and forgiveness, of unerasablility and social reconstruction. There is no verdict in Weiss' investigation – he finished the text in the spring and the trials would not end until late summer – so the audience is obliged to draw their own conclusions, to question conscience and responsibilities and to debate with others. In bringing the full horror to individual audiences, *Die Ermittlung* added to the questions; in Piscator's production the bench faced the audience, from which both accused and witnesses came forward. For any artist this was a direct response to Adorno's maxim about the impossibility of poetry after Auschwitz.[107] Steeped in *Moses und Aron*, Nono must also have been fascinated by the challenges to the very limits of law presented by the trials.[108] Weiss' work is subtitled *oratorio in 11 cantos*; each canto consists of three sections. Formally it is a sub-edifice of a larger conception using the architecture of Dante's *Divine Comedy*. In his invitation, Piscator made his view of the music clear: 'To give a special quality to this emotive but static material – the grey of the concentration camps cannot be portrayed – I thought of a choir, so that the music consists only of voices; put roughly: the voices of the six million murdered.'[109]

Various meetings followed: Piscator came to Italy in June, Weiss in the autumn, and Nono made visits to Berlin in August and September. He met with his friend Paul Dessau, commissioned to provide the music for the East Berlin premiere of the same play. Piscator and Weiss both came to Milan, where Nono worked with Zuccheri at the Studio di Fonologia. The Frankfurt trials were only just ending in August – a moment of wide and historical interest. Nono was not impressed with the outcome. He wrote to Piscator 'show them in Berlin who the <u>real Piscator</u> still is today, right there in Berlin, like before '33, and right now in the Bundes-Brandt-Republik!!!'[110] Piscator answered that he had every intention of remaining the 'real Piscator' and that perhaps Nono would like to focus on the music. Through the following months they become firm friends and would indeed discuss the Weimar years with which Nono was fascinated:

> Weiss, Piscator and I became friends and we used to meet in Berlin, often at Piscator's house, for interminable, unforgettable evenings-nights. Piscator shared with me his memories, still vivid and vibrant, of Weimar in the 20s and 30s, one of my foundations. We talked, we discussed, we 'utopia-ized' and we drank incredibly.[111]

On the basis of discussions with Piscator and his own analysis of the barely finished text, Nono was able to make certain decisions rapidly. Formally, the structure of the music would follow that of the play; one cue would preceed each section of Weiss' text – three per canto – with a final passage to balance the opening. This was revised slightly to take account of an

New spaces: studio, street, factory

interval, some silences and overlaps, but the overall pattern remained. His materials were primarily vocal: a recording of soprano Stefania Woytowitcz that appears to have been made in 1959,[112] a recording of the children's choir of the Piccolo Teatro in Milan (probably made as part of *Un diario italiano*) and recorded performances of *Cori di Didone* and *"Ha venido"*. *Canciones para Silvia*. To these were added instrumental fragments from performances of *Diario polacco '58* and *Il canto sospeso* (particularly the dramatic brass, flutes and percussion of no. 8). In addition, his notes suggest recent recordings with soprano Liliana Poli and actress Elena Vicini, as well as clarinettist William O. Smith – all involved in a new project Nono had begun to develop with Giovanni Pirelli during his visits to Milan. To these were added the resources of the studio itself: noise and wave generators, filters, reverberation and the panoply of tape manipulations. The compositional process thus began from two ends: analysis of the text and analysis of his palette of sounds, each annotated for its shape, properties and potential for combining or processing.

In the studio Nono worked directly, physically with sound material, but this was no less a reflective process than his score-based practice. He makes his view clear in an interview from August:

> I find composition in the studio increasingly fundamental, whether in developing material or in the final process of composition. And it is increasingly clear to me that the various improvisations, notated or not, represent the most limited level of research, or experiment, of study and of compositional imagination. If anything they are the initial moments of getting to know some material and its new laws, but in order to compose with it. Their mere presentation is a defect of presumption and incapacity.[113]

In an early text accompanying the tape, Nono wrote:

> This is not intended as incidental music or music illustrative of Peter Weiss' play. The music seeks to express what cannot be said in words or with action on stage. The music – in its autonomous conception and form – is the voice of the six million dead at Auschwitz and in other concentration camps.[114]

Nevertheless, the shape of the drama is evident in these voices. The clear identification of vocal sounds with the victims inevitably leads the listener to hear a drama being played out in sound. The recorded instrumental sound, most notably brass and percussion, recalls Nono's early portrayals of oppressive power. The violence of certain electronic sounds is just that; in context it is difficult not to hear them as shots, blows, doors slamming shut. At other moments the filtered noise and sine waves extend the processed vocal sounds, transcending their earthbound cries. Each canto of Weiss' text has a clear focus; together they plot a trajectory from arrival at the camp and conditions there, through particular individuals and events to the firing squads, gas chambers and ovens.

The 35 cues of Nono's plan range in duration from a few seconds to nearly two minutes (Figure 8.12).[116] The most developed are the opening and its near-recapitulation at the end, which present the reference colour of the whole work: waves of high voices, echoed, reverberated and transposed, in which the distinctions between one and many, figure and texture, are constantly blurred. No. 12 – before the interval in Piscator's production – is a briefer and more processed reprise, a lament of self-arresting grief. Against these stands the most complex exploration of the violent sound world in no. 20. Its dissonant brass signals, sustained, tortured strands of chorus and brutal electronic interjections present a challenge to which the

New spaces: studio, street, factory

Weiss	Nono		Canto 5 – The end of Lili Tofler	
				cue 13
Canto 1 – The loading ramp			I	
	cue 1			cue 14
I			II	
	cue 2			cue 15
II			III	
	Silence			cues 16-18
III			**Canto 6 – Unterscharführer Stark**	
Canto 2 – The camp				cue 19
	cue 3		I	
I				cue 20
	cue 4		II	
II				silence
	cue 5		III	
III			**Canto 7 – The black wall**	
Canto 3 – The swing				cue 21
	cue 6		I	
I				cue 22
	cue 7		II	
II				cue 23
	cue 8		III	
III			**Canto 8 – Phenol**	
Canto 4 – The possibility of survival				cue 24
	cue 9		I	
I				silence
	cue 10		II	
II				cue 25
	cue 11		III	
III			**Canto 9 – The bunker-block**	
	cue 12			cue 26
			I	
				cue 27
			II	
				cue 28
			III	
			Canto 10 – Zyklon B	
				cue 29
			I	
				cue 30
			II	
				cue 31
			Canto 11 – The fire-ovens	
				cue 32
			I	
				cue 33
			II	
				cue 34
			III	
				cue 35

Figure 8.12 Musica per "Die Ermittlung" di Peter Weiss: correspondence between dramatic structure and Nono's tape cues[115]

only response can be the silence that follows the next dialogue. The only near-text is the frequent 'ma' ('but') in the childrens' choir; the opening and closing of voice is a highly emotional sound, but Nono's notes make clear that 'mamma' is also implicit. Regardless of their sonic sophistication, the shortest cues are often given semantic weight by their textual context: a shot, the slamming of doors, and most notably the rush of gas in no. 29.

As the classical architecture of Weiss' play allows the unspeakable to find voice, Nono's music is balanced between clear abstract form and intensity of emotion. In a manner befitting

Weiss' structured legal exposition, Nono presents most of his materials in the initial three cues: to the vocal material of no. 1, electronic sound is added in 2 and instrumental in 3. Some cues compress a narrative into a few seconds. The different kinds of material can be seen in a spectrogram of no. 10, for example (Figure 8.13). This canto, *The Possibility of Survival*, explores the arbitrariness of death. Here there are three waves of sound: in the first, distorted instrumental music suggests human evil (0–4"); clear high voices emerge at the beginning of the second (6"), to be consumed by electronic noise (7"), malign power in the abstract, which reasserts itself in the third (11"), leaving a single, low electronic pitch.

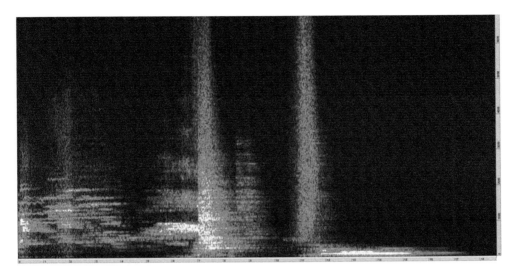

Figure 8.13 Musica per "Die Ermittlung" di Peter Weiss: spectrogram of cue 10

Through Canto V, *The end of Lili Tofler*, a more extended, personal narrative emerges.[117] A wordless soprano monody precedes the Canto – a song suspended in the horror – constructed from interval fields (no. 13, Figure 8.14). Echoes and reverberations reveal themselves as additional voices. It continues under the first section of dialogue such that the audience cannot fail to identify the voice with Lili. In nos. 14 and 15 the continuing monody is subject to greater processing, fragmentation and choral superimposition, until in no. 16 her voice, now nearly a scream, is consumed by electronic and percussive sounds. Weaker in no. 17, the voice disappears into pure resonance; she is more resolute in 18 but now against ominous, low, resonant electronic pulses.

Although the tape is mono, Nono prepared a detailed and dramatic plan of projection through six loudspeakers: at each corner, above the audience and under the floor. 'Using

Figure 8.14 Musica per "Die Ermittlung" di Peter Weiss: transcription of cue 13

dynamics up to the maximum and low frequencies, the floor itself shook and the public likewise. I found an acoustic-musical possibility for emotional involvement beyond imagination.'[118]

In his account of the production, Piscator reports that audience members left during the performance.[119] This was to be his last production – Piscator died a few months later – and it is fitting that it should have become the focus of wide debate. Critics found the music difficult to comprehend. They noted its violence; perhaps they had been hoping for something that would mediate the horror of the drama, or perhaps the drama was already sufficiently challenging that little critical capacity remained to engage with the substance of the music beyond shorthand descriptions. Early the following year, Nono prepared an autonomous concert version. Edited largely from the theatrical material, *Ricorda cosa ti hanno fatto in Auschwitz* is 11 minutes long.[120] The title seems to have been inspired by Alberto Nirenstein's *Ricorda cosa ti ha fatto Amalek* – a study of the fate of Polish Jews under Nazism – which Nono probably acquired on his visit to Poland in 1958. Essentially, the new piece retains the dramatic sequence of the work with Weiss, compressed and more clearly structured; some sounds are cut or reordered, levels and filtering are adjusted. The sonogram (Figure 8.15) shows how Nono has now incrementally increased the level of the first waves of sound (to 2'50"); the last of these brings together cues 3 and 4 of the original. In the following quieter passage (to 3'27"), a reduced cue 6 is extended by cue 9.

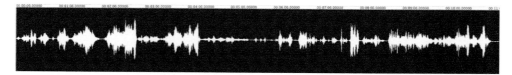

Figure 8.15 Ricorda cosa ti hanno fatto in Auschwitz: sonogram

Nono's initial title *Cori dall'Ermittlung* suggests how he conceived of the work. Its eventual title *Remember what they did to you in Auschwitz* addresses the listener directly as subject, a crucial property of Weiss' play. The sonogram shows the three sections identified by Nono: *Canto del lager* (*Canto of the camp*), *Canto della fine di Lili Tofler* (*Canto of the end of Lili Tofler*), *Canto della possibilità di sopravivere* (*Canto of the possibility of survival*).[121] Spangemacher sees the different voices of *Canti di vita e d'amore* here: inhuman catastrophe, human suffering, human faith.[122] The first part is still framed by cues 1 and 12; *The end of Lili Tofler* constitutes a central section. The final sounds, however, are those from *Zylkon B* and *The fire-ovens*. In eliminating the voices of the final reprise of *Die Ermittlung*, this work elicits a different response. Despite its tighter structure, it is if anything more bleak; humanity is fully consumed by industrialised killing. Nono does not preach or memorialise; he bears witness and challenges the listener to find a way of doing likewise. In a remarkable essay accompanying the 1968 LP release of *La fabbrica illuminata* and *Ricorda cosa ti hanno fatto in Auschwitz*, Konrad Böhmer suggests that 'Nono loudly criticises a bourgeois ideology which would simulate the greatest horror while retreating to a distance from which it has no responsibility for the future'.[123] Both works would find their place in the many recital discussions led by Nono and Pestalozza through the following years, not in the now irrelevant ritual of the formal concert, but in meeting halls, public spaces and places of work.

While working in the Milan studio, Nono also prepared a new version of *Diario polacco '58*, now for orchestra with tape, for the 1965 *Warsaw Autumn*. He incorporated the tape into the original score by adding new pauses of different lengths, further individuating the different

New spaces: studio, street, factory

episodes and connecting his music of the late 1950s to that of twenty years later. As Bassanese points out, a multi-channel tape component was an early part of Nono's idea for the original work.[124] Seven years of intensive reflection on the dramatic, temporal and architectural implications of the 'diary' model have their impact; this the clearest sign yet of the fragment-based approach of later works. In the multiple projections of material and formal disjunction there is a dialectic between the time of perception and that of reflection, between original and echo, between the continuity of musical time and the discrete nature of the event or the unit. We might posit a similar situation in terms of Nono's memory: that the violent impression of his own visit to Auschwitz in 1958 allowed him to return to the work and complete it.[125] Given his work with Weiss, memory, its possibility and its effects become a central aesthetic concern.[126]

The tape consists of twelve extracts from a 1959 recorded performance and some material from the music for *Die Ermittlung*. In a letter to the conductor Nono explained 'the sounds on the tape come just from the score, so that the sound material is subject to many more projections'.[127] Apart from the new extract, the taped cues last between 4 and 22 seconds. The only audible processing is phasing (slight voltage-controlled speed variation of the tape machine) that produces offsets of pitch and timing. These are analogous to the acoustic effects Nono achieves through microtonal inflection and small rhythmic difference, referred to in other sketches of the time as 'vibration' or 'mobility'. Beating and phasing bring otherwise static sounds to life by keeping them in movement. In this way the tape contributes not only spatial projection in the hall but additional perspective in the substance of the sound itself. The combined effects begin to produce the perceptual continuity between time, space and sonic texture that increasingly characterises Nono's musical imagination. As Nanni observes, the interjection of sound from *Die Ermittlung*, particularly the presence of a voice, is a moment at which the aesthetic reality of the work and the historical reality to which it now more explicitly refers are united.[128] Inspired by the form of *Die Ermittlung*, the expanded *Diario polacco '58* reveals its dramatic core.

Nono went on from the Warsaw Autumn performance in September to stay with Piscator for rehearsals of *Die Ermittlung* in Berlin, then to Moscow with Pestalozza, to East Berlin and Prague. Such long journeys were becoming integral to his pattern of life. He sent regular reports back to the Party in Rome, but also, and perhaps more tellingly, to his direct comrades at the local *Federazione* in Venice. His reports are far from uncritical. From Moscow he describes meetings and disagreements, but little change; in East Berlin perhaps things are starting to move, while from Prague, following a meeting at the Ministry of Culture, he is able to report significant developments. At home, the local organisation included people whose company he enjoyed – politically engaged Venetian characters with lives and concerns very different from his own. With them he seems to have found a counterbalance to the isolated existence of the itinerant avant-garde composer. Still, in 1989 he would renew his membership of the Federazione.

In his public political interventions there is an apparent naivety which, over the following years, will become more nuanced as Nono becomes increasingly involved with the various institutions. He was furious when an open letter to the workers at Cornigliano was edited by *l'Unità*.[129] Essentially an invitation to a recorded performance of *La fabbrica illuminata* at a meeting with himself and Pestalozza, his message of encouragement equates global revolutionary movements, current industrial strife and the hard-wrought historical development of music in a way that may frankly have been little consolation to an insecure, exploited, harassed factory worker.[130] And yet this provides an accurate picture of Nono's own intellectual–artistic–ethical universe, fueled by anger at injustice and faith in humanity. Composer and factory worker contribute to the common cause in their own way, through their own organisations, as he often

New spaces: studio, street, factory

points out. Working through the implications and consequences of this worldview becomes his project, which accumulates detail in the process. In various interventions he proposes new kinds of cultural structure to address the needs and develop the creative potential of evolving social structures – in the expanding industrial area of Mestre-Marghera, for example. The increasingly frequent public events with Pestalozza, often based around *La fabbrica illuminata*, were important in developing Nono's own awareness. Communist-administered Reggio Emilia was becoming particularly welcoming for such activities, but the PCI had a wide network of cultural groups in towns and factories. The situation of industrial workers provided a model for his own activity:

> Workers: often almost entirely without any academic cultural 'preparation', but rather subjected to the bombardment of escapist consumption of the radio and [popular] songs. But in their own lives and work they are obliged to be technically in the avant-garde: new technical means of production, of work. Good: then technical rather than aesthetic analysis is the vehicle for their understanding: they easily take on board the process of work and composition in the electronic studio, the phonetic and semantic analysis of text as it becomes music.[131]

In a text written for the 1967 premiere of *Musica per "Die Ermittlung" di Peter Weiss*, Nono describes his new context for composing: 'I find increasingly, especially after my composition *La fabbrica illuminata*, that [working with] only electronic, or only instrumental, or only concrete material remains very limited or just serves the ambitions of purists.'[132] This property of hybridity would characterise his work from now on: hybridity of genre, locus and materials, of historical moment and subject–object relationships, of text, identity and even authorship. He consciously maintains this quality on as many parameters as possible to ensure that personal reflection and renegotiation are constantly necessary – a dynamic instability, a continuous resistance.

Internationalism

The living studio

Work on the unfinished *Un diario italiano* continued. Only at the beginning of 1966 would La Scala definitively decide against a production of such a major work.[133] Antonio Ghiringhelli had been Director of La Scala since supervising the reopening in 1948, and for Nono he was the very embodiment of the conservative 'restoration' project. Before any formal response arrived Nono wrote to Ghiringhelli in his most biting tone: 'I understand it is difficult for you to speak my name [. . .] as well as your just concern and care to keep from away La Scala any theatrical form or subject that [actually] addresses our life (although this is not in the tradition of La Scala – look at the times of Verdi or Puccini)'.[134] Other potential projects were also explored: Henri Alleg and Anne Frank reappear as symbols of cruelty and racism; an outline *Finnegan's Wake* retains the group of female soloists and children's choir of *Un diario italiano*, along with twins Shem the writer and Shaun the postman. Joyce's many-in-one characters, such as Anna Livia Plurabelle, his parallel worlds of events and underlying cosmological structures must have seemed a natural field of potential.

In a sense the evolving, conceptual *azione scenica* of *Un diario italiano* – effectively conceived on the steps of La Fenice at the premiere of *Intolleranza 1960* – is the source of Nono's work from *La fabbrica illuminata* until *Al gran sole carico d'amore* a decade later. It is neither work-in-

New spaces: studio, street, factory

progress nor unfinished work; rather, this is the evolving conceptual space within which projects realised and unrealised gestate. Nono continued to develop the concept and text, eventually under the title *Deola e Masino*. Both are characters from Pavese. Deola is a Turin prostitute who appears in two poems from the late 1930s; she will re-emerge in *Al gran sole carico d'amore*. Masino is the Torinese central figure of the semi-autobiographical poetic narrative of 1931–2 *Ciau Masino*. The theatrical concept remained one of situations, but the figures of the title would bring some cohesion to the diary of events. Nono's plan shows the two figures, each represented by three soloists, as a dialectical frame within which the events could be explored.[135] The Italian documentary material was to remain, with the addition of references to the Lancia strike at Turin in 1962, an event that launched a year of mass strikes and civil unrest.

Following some years of sporadic contact, in May 1965 Nono solicited Giovanni Pirelli's collaboration on *Un diario italiano*.[136] Nono's frequent visits to the studio in Milan allowed a close relationship to develop. Since their earlier work together, Pirelli had been primarily engaged with the effects of post-colonial struggle, especially in Africa. In retrospect, one might see how his humanitarian view might ultimately be incompatible with Nono's increasingly interventionist political stance. Their work would continue until differences of approach became insuperable in 1967, but Nono would later express his appreciation of Pirelli's balanced, undogmatic views and sharp political analysis.[137] Various branches grew from their central project, one of which would evolve into *A floresta é jovem e cheja de vida*, presented at the Biennale in September 1966. For soprano, three actors, clarinet, five percussionists and two four-track tapes, this represents an important stage in Nono's music-theatre concept; the aesthetically abstract and the entirely specific, the acoustic and the dramatic, performer and composer are brought into new relationships. In March 1967 Pirelli would still mention a 'larger work' in relation to their recent *A floresta*.[138] This new project was provisionally entitled *Cronache della Violenza* – like *Un diario italiano* a situation-based music-theatre piece, but now the workers' struggle is presented on a wider political plane. An early letter from Pirelli proposes 'the war of liberation against imperialism' as a subject.[139]

Potential text material was now expanded to incorporate the trauma of the end of colonialism: writings of Patrice Lumumba (first leader of the independent Congo, executed in 1961 with the help of Belgium, the ex-colonial power), of the Martiniquean Aime Césaire and his student Frantz Fanon. Pirelli had met Fanon in Tunisia in 1961 while working on a collection of writings by prisoners in the Algerian War, some of which he would propose to Nono. Fanon's writings had assumed an important place in the theorising of post-colonial unrest. As an African psychiatrist who had fought in the Algerian war, Fanon's writing had an unmatched authority. His most influential book – *The Wretched of the Earth* – was widely translated after is publication in 1961.[140] It was taken by proponents of armed struggle to suggest that there must inevitably be a phase of violence in the passage from colonialism to democratic self-determination; his death in 1961 meant that there was no contradiction. The tenet of internationalism confronted the composer with particular technical-stylistic challenges. In his talks of the time, Nono often refers to a musician using their own 'language' just as any other worker uses their skills to contribute to human development. But he seems to have felt that his earlier materials of post-Viennese serialism, of European resistance songs, had little traction outside a Eurocentric world rooted in its own past culture. To address a wider audience, European or not, and to embody consciousness-raising solidarity with those who had no contact with his own cultural origins, he needed new materials and new ways of working.

Pirelli's encyclopaedic method is clear in the numerous texts he proposed to Nono, carefully organised, numbered and referenced in the original languages and in Italian. Eloquent and

New spaces: studio, street, factory

succinct expressions of struggle, suffering, resistance and liberation were many; the question was how to balance particular issues, struggle and voices. An early artistic problem seems to have been how to represent imperialism in an equally real, present way, without caricaturing or artificially demonising. Pirelli found a solution in an article by Herman Kahn in *Fortune* magazine of April 1965. Kahn's notorious recent book *On Escalation* proposed a game theory-based analysis of the process of escalation of military aggression.[141] It shows how each stage is the consequence of a series of decisions and considers the realities of a post-nuclear war world. Significantly, industrial strike is one of his metaphors for escalation. Public debate was polarised by Kahn's pragmaticism.

Through his wide experience and global network of contacts Pirelli assembled a vast repertoire of texts. In early 1966, he and Nono condensed these into three enormous collages for *Cronache della Violenza*, entitled *Wage labour and capital*, *Old and new colonialism* and *Bad luck or genocide*? The balance between narratives of industrial struggle and those of liberation is important; it was crucial that oppression and exploitation should be understood as present human realities, not culturally or geographically alien. This major work would evolve into a new projected stage work *Ma prima che i boschi si dissechino* (*But before the woods wither*), intended for Florence in 1967, and more radically into a planned work based on Brecht's *The Days of the Commune* for 1968.[142] Neither would be completed before Pirelli and Nono stopped working together, but the latter is the first direct step towards *Al gran sole carico d'amore* of 1974.

The Living Theatre is an experimental company founded in 1947 by Judith Malina and Julian Beck.[143] Malina had been a student in Piscator's Dramatic Workshop in New York and was well acquainted with the experimental music scene there;[144] Beck was an abstract expressionist painter. Their starting point had been Artaud's *Theatre of Cruelty*, but current events — the rallying points of Vietnam and civil rights — had led to more explicit political engagement. Having been deprived of their various venues in New York, The Living Theatre spent most of this decade as an itinerant cooperative in Europe:

> At the moment we are a caravan of exiles, gypsy-like, but free like exiles or gypsies of the responsibilities of place and time, in a certain way; and this makes us just a mite more free, and that freedom is necessary. We need to be free to work, and here we have found some kind of life which makes that possible.[145]

Nono had encountered The Living Theatre at their six-hour production of *Frankenstein* in Venice in late September, and while in Berlin for *Die Ermittlung* he discussed plans with Malina and Beck.[146] Their views on the role of theatre in raising political consciousness seemed very consonant. The company came to the studio in Milan for a week in February 1966, where Nono, Pirelli and Zuccheri recorded some of the improvised exercises and moments from their productions of *The Brig* and *Frankenstein*, and worked with them on developing new ideas. At this stage two projects were being considered: Nono and Pirelli's major theatre piece and a shorter work for Venice, now under discussion with Labroca for September. Recordings of conversations with the group at Pirelli's villa in Varese during the week are revealing.[147] Ideological differences emerged and they had difficulty understanding the nature of Nono's projected work; while his methodology of emergent composition through collaborative research was not foreign to them, the control that he would ultimately have taken may have been. Malina summarises the situation:

> The Living Theatre had worked with Luigi Nono on a piece called *Escalation*, based on a descriptive text by Herman Kahn, in which the acting ensemble, without any

New spaces: studio, street, factory

musical accompaniment, created, under Nono's conducting hand, a sound piece that escalates from limited aggressive warfare to the last gasps of total nuclear destruction. Nono was a dedicated political artist, a Communist, who unlike Piscator never hid or obscured his commitment or his affiliations. The Living Theatre was also preparing a major dramatic work together with Nono and the writer and former partisan leader Giovanni Pirelli, which never came to be because the Living Theatre's pacifism was at risk of being compromised, not by the principles, but by the tactics of Pirelli's armed liberation fighters.[148]

The actors took as a text Kahn's 44–rung 'ladder', a sequence of states that moves from 'subcrisis maneuvering' to 'civilian central wars'.[149] Nono and Pirelli had initially thought to make a work based on *Escalation* in response to the new commission from Labroca for Venice in September. In the event, it would become the central element of the tapes for *A floresta*.

'A floresta é jovem e cheja de vida'

In the spring of 1966 Nono seems to have felt that the material had, once again, become intellectually, artistically and politically unwieldy. The new work for Venice was the spur for a new more streamlined project. It retained their previous idea of combining singers, actors and instrumentalists but in a more compact form; a few texts were to remain, others were added. Eleven texts were selected for the live performers: from Castro, Fanon, Lumumba, industrial workers from Italy and the USA, student protest in California, liberation fighters from Venezuela and Angola, and Nguyen Van Troi. The words of Nguyen Van Troi, the first publicly executed member of the Vietcong, were recounted by his wife in a book published by the PCI in Reggio Emilia, with whom Nono was working increasingly closely. For the tape they chose *Escalation* and other material from The Living Theatre, and one of several calls for peace that Nono had collected: that from the International Days of Protest in Berkeley California on 15–16 October 1965. The title, *A floresta é jovem e cheja de vida*, is taken from the words of Angolan freedom fighter Gabriel: 'They can't burn down the forest because it is young and full of life.'

> I choose documentary texts [. . .] because I believe they have a greater relationship to reality than pure poetry. We still live in the time that Brecht described: it was indeed beautiful to speak of flowers, roses and love, but unfortunately social conditions do not permit it. I am also convinced that as a musician I have a social duty to fulfil. I am convinced that as a musician one lives within a historical situation.[150]

'Documentary' itself conceals many levels of mediation and aesthetic complexity. The artifice in the work of politically engaged writers such as Lorca and Pavese is clear, but even in the case of *Il canto sospeso*, the texts are drawn from an influential collection with its own art and agenda. Documentary, then, might refer rather to the signified – the truth of injustice, of political struggle – than the signifying words themselves. The crucial authenticity seems to be that of the *voice*, the directness of communication whether from artist, hero or victim. There is a crucial relationship between the degree to which words are politically explicit and the nature of the particular historical situation. The urgency of the late 1960s allows little room for mediation, for the voice to be oblique. *A floresta* brooks no misunderstanding.

Vietnam was becoming the major symbolic struggle as America significantly intensified its military campaign. As the 1960s progress, Nono's references are increasingly to resistance

New spaces: studio, street, factory

fighters rather than political philosophers; he was clearly reading Che more than Gramsci, and yet there is continuity. His pattern of activity answers Gramsci's call for the 'organic intellectual':

> The mode of being of the new intellectual can no longer consist in eloquence, which is an exterior and momentary mover of feelings and passions, but in active participation in practical life, as constructor and organiser, "permanent persuader" and not just a simple orator.[151]

When not working on the new piece or talking to cultural groups and festivals, events usually based around recordings of his recent work, Nono's political activism was also becoming increasingly internationalist. He was a member of the Committee for Peace, an umbrella organisation comprising many groups from the left as well as public figures such as Bobbio, Calvino, Dario Fo, Gottuso, Manzù and Pasolini. His involvement was material, including efforts to coordinate international movements and artists such as The Living Theatre.[152] In March he worked in Milan, gave talks in Genoa and L'Aquila,[153] and took part in the massive anti-war demonstrations in Rome coinciding with those across the US, at which the American student movement was prominently represented.[154] Notably, he questioned the text published in *l'Unità* of the call for peace, which omitted the committee's requirement that the US withdraw. A letter from North Vietnamese intellectuals had been specific on this point, and Nono's response makes clear the responsibility he felt to respect their voices.[155] The urgency of action on Vietnam rings through his work on *A floresta*.

After auditioning many actors from Giorgio Strehler's Piccolo Teatro, Nono selected five voices. He recorded them improvising on an Italian translation of the call to end the war, published in the magazine of the communist youth movement. He guided their performances with sketches of pitch shapes, gestures and phonetic fragmentation. Three of their number – Kadigia Bove, Elena Vicini and Berto Troni – were then invited to be part of the performance. In April Nono began recording with soprano Liliani Poli in a similar process. If he had sought sonic properties from the actors, it seems to have been Poli's dramatic skills that were paramount here. The integrated nature of Nono's new practice is clear in his use of sounds and gestures created with performers in the studio – repeatedly relistened to, annotated and organised, to form ideas for the live material. The three actors and Poli were brought together in June, now concentrating on the Vietnamese sounds of Nguyen Van Troi's words. Of particular interest to Nono was the vocal dialectic of the classically trained Poli and Somalian actress Kadigia Bove.[156]

The voice is at the heart of *A floresta*, a fascination that also has internationalist implications. In response to a question shortly after the premiere he said that:

> Fundamental is a comparative study of different uses of the vocal apparatus itself (for example, in Japanese and Italian), in respect of the phonetics of the different languages, in the various physical–acoustic techniques of vocal emission. Similarly fundamental is the comparative study of the use of the voice in different societies, cultures and practices.[157]

He had first intended not to use any amplification, but realized that the microphone afforded additional dimensions of vocality: 'even more than in my previous compositions, I tried to bring together and make use of all possible human sounds, but avoiding any *a posteriori* studio manipulation that might destroy their freshness and truth. I wanted [. . .] to extract the maximum expression from the human voice.'[158]

New spaces: studio, street, factory

Two instrumental elements were to be added to the material. William O. Smith had begun his comprehensive researching and cataloguing of clarinet multiphonics in 1960, and demonstrated his work to Nono the following year. Nono contacted Smith again to spend some time in the Milan studio in the summer of 1965, where they also worked with voices. Some of this work entered *Die Ermittlung*, but Nono had a large recorded repertory of sounds that suggested a new approach to combining instruments and tape; he would now use extended instrumental techniques to approach the electronic sound world. Smith's seamless transitions between pure, modulated and complex sounds were ideal for Nono's integrated sonic palette. Filtering and ring modulation further extended their spectra in the studio. Five large bronze sheets were an inspired addition. Nono and Zuccheri experimented with various combinations of plates, tubes and microphones. Initial recordings were made in the studio with those of Kadigia Bove, others in September with the percussion group for the premiere. The use of recorded percussion in *Die Ermittlung* is sometimes uncomfortable; the sounds almost belong to the electronic world, and yet bring an unmistakable weight of reference. Here the solution is at once sonic, performative and scenographic. Lit from below, the plates constitute frame and chorus as well as the work's sonic horizon. It is also very practical; the percussionists act as a semi-autonomous group with their own conductor and their parts are fully notated. Players could therefore be found locally to any production. As with the clarinet, the processed and natural recorded sounds and those produced in performance act within the same perceptual space; they are indistinguishable to the listener. Smith's part would be developed as he joined the company for the two weeks of rehearsal in Venice before the premiere on 7 September.

In April, Nono invited soprano Liliana Poli to Milan. She remembers her impression of Nono and the beginning of their work on *A floresta*:

> a gentle expression, youthful, sympathetic. He almost always spoke in Venetian, and to my ears the sound of this, almost feminine, made him very pleasant to listen to. At the radio he put me in the studio, in front of a microphone, and told me to invent everything that came into my head, singing, speaking, shouting – everything completely freely.
>
> [. . .]
>
> We all put together our own parts on the basis of Gigi's suggestions, and with my personal choice of sounds that gave me the best possibility of achieving the expression the composer wanted. It wasn't an easy task, but step-by-step research to understand Gigi's thought and bring it to life.[159]

The two four-track tapes thus took shape through the spring of 1966. Letters to Labroca develop the programme idea for September. In May it is referred to as a work for performers and tape; by the end of July its description and title are complete. Other reputations were also well formed by now; Nono beseeches Labroca not to let Stockhausen's rehearsals overrun, as would be the tendency.[160] Once fixed, the tapes provided the formal architecture within which Nono developed individual roles with the performers in the final weeks before the premiere at La Fenice. Smith recalled the process in a later interview: 'The overall planning was his. It's like when you work on a film, you don't really know how it will all fit together but the director does. We didn't have discussions about the overall project.' [161] Nono's view was somewhat different; in Gallehr's beautiful film documenting the development process he describes it as 'a common searching for the end-form'.[162] There we see the physicality and immediacy of their work. The semi-staged production was directed by Virginio Puecher, Strehler's long-standing assistant at the Piccolo Teatro. Known to Nono since his work with

New spaces: studio, street, factory

Maderna, Puecher would also direct Poli in a version of *La fabbrica illuminata* that would often accompany *A floresta*, as well as the Italian production of *Die Ermittlung*. Characteristically, Nono had established the spatial distribution of performers and loudspeakers early on a visit to the theatre in June. The physicality of the spotlit performers and their interaction needed no further intervention. Behind them the percussionists were raised on a scaffolding construction recalling the industrial sets of The Living Theatre. The bronze sheets were suspended from the next level, reflecting the lighting around the theatre as they moved. To replicate the close vocal detail developed in the studio, each of the main performers uses a microphone. The two tapes were operated separately and projected through two independent systems. Apart from amplification and spatialisation, there is no live processing, but *A floresta* approaches the live electronic medium of later works in that the distinction between live and recorded or processed sound dissolves. Performative presence remains vital, however; the direct presentation of the texts presents an immanent challenge to the listener.

A floresta é jovem e cheja de vida bears a dedication to the Vietnamese National Liberation Front – a situation no different to much Western classical music, as Nono pointed out. We might identify five continuous parts.[163]

Part I 0'–12'20"

Historical context. Sound comes from the far distance of space, frequency and dynamics as the plates and then the tape bring sound and words to the room. The first two texts set the scene, announced in clear heterophony by the actors, supported by the clarinet and soprano working as one:

1. 'As Marx said, we are in prehistoric times' (Umberto Bellese, mechanical fitter from Bergamo)
2. 'We know that this is a struggle between past and future' (Fidel Castro)

The third text is more reflective, the female actors in near-hocket further distributed by the sound projection:

3. 'Our mistake was to believe that the enemy had lost his dangerousness, his combativeness' (Frantz Fanon)

They continue a wordless accompaniment to the widely spaced clarinet multiphonics that emerge from their recorded pre-echo. Against this, the male actor's response initiates a soprano descant:

4. 'Don't cry for me, my comrade' (Patrice Lumumba)

Part II 12'20"–21'

The struggle. On the tape, the anti-war appeal and The Living Theatre's act of violence explode, mixed with clarinet sounds. Announced by the percussion, the next statement is constructed like the first two:

5. 'But the struggle will be long, very long' (Pedro Duno, guerrilla commander FALN Venezuela)

New spaces: studio, street, factory

From the decaying recorded clarinet sounds, the live performer begins a long sonic exploration, its gestures too slow or too fast to be perceived as figure. It illustrates the sustaining over time and invites reflection both on the text and on the subject's own listening. The percussion softly take up its resonance, now as a background from which the words of Nguyen Van Troi emerge and recede:

6. 'Quyen, they have taken me
    One day you will understand
    I understood at the moment they took you
    They are about to shoot your comrade
    Learn to live in joy'

Part III 21'–30'35"

Escalation: for tapes alone. The Living Theatre's exercise *Reading the dollar bill* introduces the numbered stages of *Escalation*, intensified by another of the scenes *Jungle*. Against this we hear the appeal for the suspension of war; its being in Italian creates a dialectic, a friction, but also elicits identification from the original performers and listeners. The other texts are in their original language. The climax of *Escalation* collapses into post-nuclear abstract sound and wordless voice, but this moment (27'05") is marked by the first of an increasingly close series of unison percussion strokes, overlapping with their own echoes, that will introduce the final section.

Part IV 30'35"–37'40"

An alternative: resistance. The soprano brings unanimity and the clearest melodic assertion of the work to the statement of Castro:

7. 'in the fields and mountains of America, along the slopes of its sierras, on its plains and in its woods, in solitude or in the city traffic, on the shores of the great oceans and rivers, this world begins quite rightly to show its hot fists'

Then, as the resonance of the plates dissipates, she emerges alone with a strong, stark line (marked *timbrare con violenza*) that barely moves, like Gregorian chant – a song of faith that has remained suspended in its resoluteness:

8. 'They can't burn down the forest because it is young and full of life' (Gabriel, Angolan guerrilla)

The influence of Pavese is clear; at the highest moment of resistance the imagery turns to nature. The following two texts are constituted like those of the opening:

9. 'If the struggle does not begin here in the coal mines, in the auto steel, in the electrical industries, there shall be no freedom' (industrial worker from Detroit, Michegan)
10. 'Someone has betrayed us' (Walter Zanoni, Fiat worker)

New spaces: studio, street, factory

Part V 37'40"–40'.00"

The actors' final statement returns responsibility to the listener – a dismissal, an 'Ite, missa est', a 'Go forth in peace' that carries active obligations:

11. 'Is that all we can do?' (student slogan, Berkeley, California)

Despite the integrated sound world, roles are generally clear. The actors carry most of the text, usually as a group; as in Nono's previous vocal music, degrees of unanimity and independence are primary features. While the material was determined in workshops, there are many traces of the polyphony of his score-based practice: words are passed between voices and intonation patterns are imitated at different rates or in unison with different dynamic envelopes. The final crescendo repetitions of 'Is that all we can do?' follow three different time-bases like voices of a motet. Through the first two sections the soprano works with the clarinet, adding colour to the actors' interjections; in the last she becomes the main dramatic figure. The clarinet's trajectory is similar in retrograde. In general, its role is to mediate between acoustic and electronic sound, between performed present and studio, but at the end of the first section it emerges as an expressive voice beyond words. As well as forming a physical and sonic environment, the percussion also have a mediating status, as a chorus both resonating the words from the stage and bringing voices from elsewhere. This association is established at the very beginning, in the combination of live and recorded plates and multiple distant voices. Unison strokes mark formal, architectural moments.

Such a group-derived, performer-owned work required a different approach to notation. This was no score; a philological edition was prepared only in 1998. For rehearsals the performers worked from part-books – still thoroughly in the Venetian musical tradition – largely prepared by themselves (Figure 8.16). The only score is that for the six percussionists. Overviews are provided by Nono's sound projection plan, with details of the eight recorded tracks and indications of salient elements from the live performers, and a summary guide that Nono seems to have used for the first performance. Two video extracts and a studio recording made with Nono the following year give further insight into the material and performance practice of the work.[164]

Timing was not by stopwatch but relative to sounds and words, both on the tape and cued between the performers. Notions of improvisation are misguided. Smith compared the work to a production of a play:

> It was pretty much set – as much as an actor in a play has his part set. [. . .] The group was like five actors – the pacing of one actor would determine where I would come in. The pacing was free to the extent of a Shakespearean dialogue. [. . .] Nono was like the director of a play and gave us our pacing. [. . .] It is not by any means an improvisational or open piece.[165]

Interviewed by Gallehr during the production, Nono refers to the process of discussion that led to a 'definitive form'. Critic Massimo Mila summarised thus: 'This is as little aleatoric as *Casta diva* or Wotan's farewells.'[166] While authorship remained firmly Nono's, perhaps the most radical aspect of *A floresta* is the way in which the creativity embodied in the work as experienced is distributed through time, people and materials. Rizzardi describes the performers as '"living materials" in whom the work is fixed by means of their own specific oral tradition',[167] although there would be some substitutions in subsequent performances. It would become the

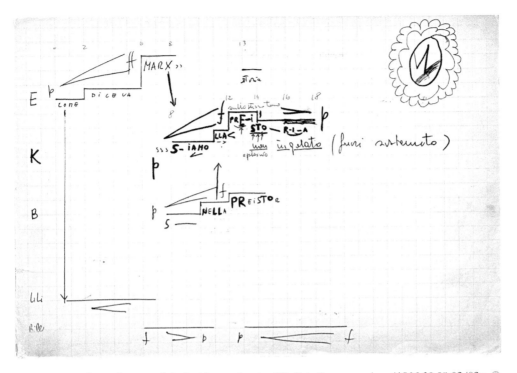

Figure 8.16 A floresta é jovem e cheja de vida: part-book of Kadigia Bove, opening. (ALN 30.09.02/02v. © The heirs of Luigi Nono. Reproduced by kind permission.)

work that Nono himself performed most often, receiving regular performances over the next decade, often with *La fabbrica illuminata* and *Ricorda cosa ti hanno fatto in Auschwitz*. Members of the group also became his regular collaborators over this period – a laboratory of creative research and an early model for that of the 1980s.

Critics were agreed that *A floresta* constituted a major musical event. That their subsequent judgement divides along political lines is perhaps a testament to Nono's success in creating a personal challenge to the listener, in touching a raw nerve – the work is, after all, remarkably free from sloganeering. The critic of *Corriere della Sera*, for example, praised the work as 'formidable, probably a masterpiece. But for us, adherents of a civilisation of art and life, *A floresta* makes unjust spiritual assumptions, ignores too many historical factors, apart from an infinity of truisms. There's an aspect of fanaticism to Nono's position, which we cannot share. As for us, we remain on the right side of the nest of snakes.'[168] With Anglo-Saxon pragmaticism, Smith-Brindle in *The Musical Quarterly* wasted no words on cultural history in stating that 'ideological polution begins to contaminate the works of Luigi Nono.' But even he has to acknowledge that 'Nono builds up a convincing sound structure, which has an undisputable unity and forward movement. This work lasts forty minutes, and the measure of Nono's success in this medium can be summed up in the fact that these forty minutes seem no more than ten.'[169] Such views reflect a contemporary discourse that presented an extreme right-wing view as the norm, as reasonable and as the guardian of civilisation. Only in recent years have the various conspiracy and counter-conspiracy theories been untangled sufficiently to have a view of the degree to which Italian public opinion and political power were manipulated by an unholy alliance of vested interest and foreign intervention, and by violent means where

New spaces: studio, street, factory

necessary. This was the era of P2, Operation Gladio and events that led to the Piazza Fontana bombing, of the wilful creation of fear and confusion by all sides. The US State Department saw the Italian Communist Party as the largest in the Western world, and as being generously funded by the USSR.[170] The PCI and all forms of socialism were to be discredited at all costs.[171]

Asked about the role of politics here, Nono talked of his sense of historical responsibility as a musician, not in the abstract but in terms of its implications for the process of composing. Material and experiment are never ends in themselves, he says, but points of departure that make possible the moment of composition and hence the moment of consciousness for the listener; the meaning of the words is his guide.[172] Pestalozza grasped this in his counter-review:

> an exceptional success, prolonged in insistent, convinced applause from an audience that jammed La Fenice. We should say immediately that Luigi Nono's new work was a triumph not only because of its great musical value that even the critic of Corriere della Sera described as 'formidable.' There is something else: there is Nono's merit in having communicated the text [. . .], and there is the creative force of a music that in its vast and complex formal conception has realized the boldness and newness of its material.[173]

Mila's view is more objective. He dismisses the arguments of those who rail against political engagement as specious, as contradictory: 'it is obvious that the validity of an engaged work does not lie in its capacity to win the war in Vietnam or make the revolution succeed, but simply in the artistic quality of the work that political passion has inspired.'[174] Mila identifies two major technical issues successfully addressed in *A floresta*: the use of technology and Nono's relationship with the voice:

> Now we have to see how and to what extent Nono can mature. It is a painful crisis, with bitter moments, reflected even in his disquiet and irritability. But it seems to me that especially this last work, more than *La fabbrica illuminata*, demonstrates that he is on the way to a happy resolution of his problems. [. . .] the results are more than sufficient guarantee and promise to dispel any remaining doubts about the unresolved issues in Nono's new work.[175]

The work's liminal state – neither notated nor improvised, neither fully determined nor open to reinvention – could be seen as a radical model of the 'conventional' Western work – that is, the deconstruction of the work concept since the 1960s has led us to understand that even the most fully determined work inhabits such a space. In the process of producing a performing edition after Nono's death, such that the work would not be lost or betrayed, Rizzardi concluded that 'it would certainly be wrong and inappropriate to perceive in this practice an antecedent of that aesthetic of "infinite possibilities" which led him, in the Eighties, to question the uniqueness of a work's physiognomy and therefore the idea of a definitive text.'[176] He describes this philological, archaeological, ethnomusicological task as 'a recomposition in score form'.

In material terms, *A floresta* was a new kind of work, unpublishable in the conventional way. A year later, as his publisher continued to request performing scores of *La fabbrica illuminata* and *A floresta*, Nono was still uncertain as to the best mode of graphical representation – he was considering squared paper or transparencies – and *A floresta* would not be made available for thirty years.[177] It was also Nono's first venture with his new publisher, Ricordi. Dissatisfaction with Schott had been accumulating for some time, particularly concerning payments. In Boston

New spaces: studio, street, factory

he had discovered that they had been paid a substantial amount for the production of *Intolleranza 1960*, of which he had only seen a small proportion and in exchange for which they had done little to ensure musical success. An angry letter of March 1965 also points out that there was an unauthorised TV recording and that the only publicly available material was (and still is) a bad study score in German. To compound things, the only score of *Variazioni canoniche* had been lost – Schott suggested he might construct another from the parts. Further letters continue the complaints: promised study scores had not appeared, and despite a reluctant agreement to publish the electronic works there had been no support for his work at the studio in Milan. There are other publishers, reminds Nono, also in Milan. In fact, he had begun negotiating with Ricordi that spring. Ricordi were keen to support his work at the Studio di Fonologia, including the recording of *La fabbrica illuminata* and *A floresta*. The death of Scherchen in June 1966 was perhaps the catalyst; it was through the purchase of Scherchen's Ars Viva Verlag that Nono had joined Schott, and he must have felt some reluctance to break this last connection. Nono finally decided not to renew his contract with Schott in September, buying back the rights to his tape works. They would continue to support him indirectly through the Wergo LP release of *La fabbrica illuminata*, "*Ha venido*". *Canciones para Silvia* and *Ricorda cosa ti hanno fatto in Auschwitz* in 1968. However, the new situation with Ricordi – the publisher of Verdi and Puccini – was important to his self-reimagining, to his sense of leaving behind conventional modes of music-making and aligning himself with the theatre and with Italian culture. It was, after all, in theatre, in the theory and experiments of Meyerhold and Piscator, that a new relationship with the audience had been imagined, and Nono suggested that *A floresta* 'leads to the need for a new capacity and attention in listening'.[178]

Notes

1 Letter to Hartmann, February/March 1962, reproduced in Albèra, 1987, pp. 52–3.
2 Anders, 1961, p. 23.
3 ALN 24.03.02/10r, 09, 97, 06v.
4 ALN 24.03.02/03v.
5 'Musica e Resistanza', 1963. LNI, p. 147.
6 ALN 24.03.02/05r, 05v.
7 De Benedictis, 2006.
8 ALN 24.05.01/01.
9 De Benedictis, 2006 and Durazzi, 2009, discuss this analysis in detail.
10 De Benedictis, 2006.
11 Durazzi, 2009, p. 454.
12 *The Times*, 23 August 1962, p. 4.
13 For a discussion of the PCI response to the Cuban missile crisis, see Campus, 2014, pp. 245–7.
14 'Possibilità e necessità di un nuovo teatro musicale', 1962. LNI, p. 131.
15 '*Canti di vita e d'amore*', 1963. LNI, p. 441.
16 *The Times*, 11 September 1963, p. 7.
17 'Guiomar' is generally agreed to be the poetess Pilar Valderrama, whom Machado met in 1928 and from whom he was terminally separated by the Civil War.
18 The first passage comes from the first part of *Otras canciones a Guiomar*, the choral coda from the second of *Canciones a Guiomar* (CLXXIV, CLXXIII in the collected poems: Machado, 2001, pp. 382–8).
19 Benjamin Britten wrote *Nocturnal after John Dowland*, a set of variations on *Come, heavy sleep*, for Bream in 1963.
20 Machado, 1982, p. 43.
21 *The Times*, 1 March 1963.
22 Scabia, 1990, p. 43.
23 Lanzardo, 1979, p. 205.
24 'Possibilità e necessità di un nuovo teatro musicale'. LNI, pp. 127–30.

New spaces: studio, street, factory

25 'Possibilità e necessità di un nuovo teatro musicale'. LNI, p. 121.
26 Scabia, 1990, p. 44.
27 'Possibilità e necessità di un nuovo teatro musicale'. LNI, pp. 128–9.
28 Breuning, 1998; Rizzardi, 1999, pp. 47–51; Josefowicz, 2012, pp. 13–15 provide surveys of these projects.
29 Letters from Balestrini, 20 December 1962 and 13 August 1963. ALN.
30 Stenzl, 1998, p. 59. This was Piscator's only film and his last visit to the USSR.
31 Jona, 1993.
32 Antonioni, 1998, p. 225.
33 ALN PR7/07v.
34 De Benedictis, 1998, p. 156.
35 Jona, 1993, pp. 152–4.
36 From *Nuovi Argomenti*, a journal founded by Carocci and Moravia on the model of Sartre's *Temps Modernes*.
37 Carocci, 1960.
38 Scabia, 1990, p. 49.
39 Published in *Rinascita* (n. 51, 26 December 1964). Also collected in Orazio Parlangeli, *La nuova questione della lingua* (Paideia Editirice, Brescia, 1971, pp. 79–101), which also contains responses from Calvino.
40 ALN 26.02.01/1–23.
41 ALN 26.02.03/01.
42 This parallel is explored in Buey, 2015.
43 Scabia, 1990, p. 50.
44 Scabia, 1990, p. 44.
45 For a description of the first performance and discussion of the materials, see Casadei, 2014.
46 Noller, 1993, pp. 158–9.
47 Calabretto, 2017, pp. 213–18. Cingoli's work became well known through his animations for *Canzonissima* and *Carosello*, as well as the signature images for the RAI, publicity for Fiat and Pirelli, and collaborations with Dario Fo and Fellini.
48 A copy of the manuscript came to light in the collection of Swiss critic Aloys Mooser.
49 ALN 26.07.02/07.
50 ALN 26.07.04/07–08.
51 Letter to Scabia, 31 January 1964, in Scabia, 1990, p. 50.
52 Noller, 1993, p. 160.
53 Stenzl, 1991b, p. 32.
54 Stenzl, 1991a; Josefowicz, 2012, p. 40.
55 Letter to Scabia, 11 March 1964, in Scabia, 1990, p. 55.
56 Letter to Scabia, 6 May 1964, in Scabia, 1990, p. 55.
57 Letter to Scabia, 15 May 1964, in Scabia, 1990, p. 56.
58 Letter to Henius, 15 May 1964, in Henius, 1995, p. 17.
59 Letter to Henius, 27 May 1964, in Henius, 1995, pp. 21–3.
60 *l'Unità*, 9 June 1964.
61 Chinello, 1996, pp. 297–305.
62 *l'Unità*, 23 April 1962, p. 3 (also LNI, p. 141).
63 Hoffmann, 2016, p. 205.
64 'Viaggio attraverso la musica nell'URSS', 1963. LNI, p. 153.
65 Reader, 2016, pp. 106–10.
66 Calabretto, 2017, p. 63. Smirnov, 2013, pp. 229–36, describes the development and role of the ANS.
67 'Viaggio attraverso la musica nell'URSS', 1963. LNI, p. 151.
68 Reader, 2016, p. 109.
69 Letter from Pestalozza, 9 November 1963, in Trudu, 2008, p. 41.
70 "Lotta alla Fiat. Un aspetto recente: il 'gatto selvaggio' negli scioperi delle fonderie e dell'Aeritalia", in *Classe operaia*, 1, 1964, pp. 6–8. English translation available at: www.viewpointmag.com/2013/09/26/struggle-at-fiat-1964/ (accessed 25 October 2017). "Lotta all'Alfa. La ricerca dell'organizzazione politica negli ultimi scioperi della grande fabbrica milanese – dal 'gatto selvaggio' alla pianificazione operaia delle lotte", in *Classe operaia*, 1, 1964, pp. 11–13.
71 Scabia, 1990, p. 44.

New spaces: studio, street, factory

72 'Musica per la rivoluzione', interview with Herman Lück, 1970. LNII, p. 77.

73 '*La fabbrica illuminata*', 1964. LN I, p. 446.

74 Henius, 1995, pp. 28–9.

75 Henius, 1995, p. 30.

76 Henius, 1995, p. 34.

77 Interview with Nuria Schoenberg-Nono, June 2013. See also Nono in Zehelein *et al.*, 1978.

78 *Brava* (1965) is an exceptional display of Mina's virtuosity, *Se telefonando* (1966) of her sense of drama. Written with Ennio Morricone, the latter is an interesting example of mutual influence; Morricone's cellular intervallic structure comes from a thoroughly contemporary music concern with the nature of material. The place of opera in Italian culture in the mid-twentieth century also engendered an integration and mobility of musical culture unknown in the anglophone world; Italian popular songwriting of the time owes more to Puccini than rock and roll. Mina's rehabilitation TV show included music from *Tosca*.

79 'Mina, la prima feminista'. *Corriere della Sera*, 26 March 2010, p. 36.

80 Cossettini, 2009, 2010.

81 ALN 28.18/02.

82 Henius, 1991, p. 80.

83 From ALN 27.15.04/03, 05.

84 '*La fabbrica illuminata*', 1964. LN I, p. 448.

85 Scabia, 1990, p. 47.

86 Henius, 1995, p. 63.

87 Letter to Scabia 25 May 1964, in Scabia, 1990, p. 58.

88 Letter to Guttoso, 1 July 1964, in Trudu, 2008, pp. 61–4.

89 Letter to Pestalozza 7 August 1964, in Trudu, 2008, pp. 46–8 (where the date is given as 7 April 1964).

90 *l'Unità* 18 September 1964, 7.

91 Letter from Giuseppe Delfino, 8 September 1964. In Trudu, 2008, p. 66. *l'Unità*, 17 September 1964, p. 11.

92 Chinello, 2008, p. 166.

93 *Rinascita* 21 August 1965.

94 'Lettera di Luigi Nono agli operai dell'Italsider di Genova-Cornigliano', 1965. LNI, p. 187.

95 Letter from Lachenmann, 21 December 1963, in De Benedictis and Morsch, 2012, p. 112.

96 Letter to Lachenmann, 2 January 1964, in De Benedictis and Morsch, 2012, p. 113.

97 Letter to Lachenmann, 16 February 1964, in De Benedictis and Morsch, 2012, p. 117.

98 Letter to Lachenmann, 16 August 1964, in De Benedictis and Morsch, 2012, p. 126.

99 Letter from Lachenmann, 27 December 1964, in De Benedictis and Morsch, 2012, p. 129.

100 *The Boston Globe*, 29 January 1965.

101 *Los Angeles Times*, 21 March 1965.

102 Trudu, 2008, p. 71.

103 Svoboda, 2006.

104 Translated in *The Boston Globe*, 26 May 1965.

105 Translated as The Investigation: Oratorio in 11 Cantos (Weiss, 1966).

106 The Freie Volksbühne had begun in 1890 as a cultural initiative of the workers' movement. Piscator had worked with the company in the 1920s. He had returned as Director in 1962, supervising their move to Fritz Bornemann's modernist building and remaining with the theatre until his death in 1966.

107 'The critique of culture is confronted with the last stage in the dialectic of culture and barbarism: to write a poem after Auschwitz is barbaric, and that corrodes also the knowledge which expresses why it has become impossible to write poetry today.' Adorno, 1981, p. 34.

108 Explored in Pendas, 2010.

109 Letter from Piscator, 7 May 1965, in Kontarsky, 2001, p. 69.

110 Letter to Piscator, 20 August 1965, ALN.

111 'Un'autobiografia dell'autore raccontata da Enzo Restagno', 1987. LNII, p. 519.

112 Kontarsky, 2001, p. 56.

113 Interview with Erasmo Valente. *l'Unità*, 1 September 1965, p. 6.

114 Undated letter accompanying the first part of the tape – presumably September 1965. ALN.

115 Based on ALN 28.2/03–13.

New spaces: studio, street, factory

116 Some were cut in rehearsals for Piscator's original production.
117 Lili (Lilly) Tof(f)ler, 23 years old, was executed at Auschwitz in 1943 for writing to a boy in the same camp. Her letter ended: 'I ask myself how I shall be able to live after all that I have seen and known.' Her story emerged at the trial of Adolf Eichmann in 1961. Available at: www.nizkor.org/hweb/people/e/eichmann-adolf/transcripts/Sessions/Session-070–03.html (accessed 10 October 2017).
118 Interview with Enzo Restagno, 1987. LNII, p. 519.
119 Piscator, 1966, p. 101.
120 The booklet accompanying the CD edition of Nono's complete works for solo tape – STR 57001 – contains extensive background information and technical detail as well as Nono's own programme notes.
121 'Ricorda cosa ti hanno fatto in Auschwitz', 1966. LNI, p. 453.
122 Spangemacher, 1983, p. 237.
123 Böhmer, 1968.
124 Bassanese, 1999, p. 96.
125 Interview with Enzo Restagno, 1987. LNII, p. 514.
126 See the discussion in Nanni, 2004, pp. 264–74.
127 Bassanese, 1999, p. 101.
128 Nanni, 2004, p. 276.
129 Trudu, 2008, pp. 76–7.
130 'Lettera di Luigi Nono agli operai dell'Italsider di Genova-Cornigliano', 1965. LNI, pp. 186–8.
131 'Risposte a 7 domande di Martine Cadieu', 1966. LNI, p. 199.
132 'Musica per "Die Ermittlung" di Peter Weiss', 1967. LNI, p. 451.
133 Josefowicz, 2012, p. 89.
134 Trudu, 2008, p. 86.
135 ALN P10.05/19v-20v.
136 Letter to Pirelli, 12 May 1965, ALN.
137 Weill-Ménard, 1994, pp. 144–5.
138 Nono, 1998, p. xxxviii.
139 Letter from Pirelli, 15 August 1965, ALN.
140 Published in Italian by Einaudi as *I dannati della terra* in 1962.
141 Kahn, 1965.
142 Nina Josefowicz gives clear descriptions of these projects on the basis of available materials (Josefowicz, 2012, pp. 124–9 and 169–75).
143 Available at: www.livingtheatre.org (accessed 10 October 2017).
144 See, for example, her mention of Cage, Tudor and Wolpe in Malina, 1984, p. 210.
145 Beck, 1965.
146 The productions of *Frankenstein* and *Mysteries and smaller pieces*, also performed in Venice, are described in Gottlieb, 1966.
147 Josefowicz, 2012, pp. 253–70.
148 Malina, 2012, p. 164.
149 Kahn, 1965, p. 39.
150 Nono, in Gallehr, 1968.
151 Gramsci, 1971, p. 10.
152 Trudu, 2008, pp. 87–9.
153 Trudu, 2008, p. 92. *l'Unità*, 21 March 1966.
154 *l'Unità*, 28 March 1966, p. 1.
155 Trudu, 2008, p. 89.
156 Josefowicz, 2012, p. 155. Bove would become active in the PCI and marry Achille Ochetto, its leader from 1986 to the effective dissolution of the PCI in 1991.
157 'Risposte a 7 domande di Martine Cadieu', 1966. LNI, p. 203.
158 '"Un discorso sonoro" Conversazioni raccolte da Maurice Fleuret', 1966. LNII, p. 9.
159 Poli, 2016, p. 62–3.
160 Letter to Labroca, 29 July 1966, ALN.
161 Smith, 1994.
162 Gallehr, 1966.

New spaces: studio, street, factory

163 In 1966 Nono described the form in four sections, conflating Parts III and IV below (interview with Maurice Fleuret, 1966. LNII, p. 8).

164 Gallehr, 1966; Piccardi, 1977; Arcophon, AC6811.

165 Smith, 1994.

166 Mila, 1966.

167 Rizzardi, 1998, p. xxix.

168 Franco Abbiati in *Corriere della Sera*, 12 September 1966.

169 Smith-Brindle, 1967.

170 Benjamin and Kautsky, 1968.

171 See, for example, Philip Willan's article in *The Guardian*, 24 June 2000, p. 19: 'US supported anti-left terror in Italy: Report claims Washington used a strategy of tension in the cold war to stabilise the centre-right.'

172 Gallehr, 1966.

173 Luigi Pestalozza, 'Successo di Nono a Venezia'. *Rinascita* 37, 17 September 1966.

174 Mila, 1966.

175 Mila, 1966.

176 Rizzardi, 1998, p. xxix.

177 Letter to Ricordi, 9 May 1967, reproduced in Rizzardi, 1998, p. xxix.

178 'A floresta é jovem e cheja de vida', 1966. LNI, p. 455.

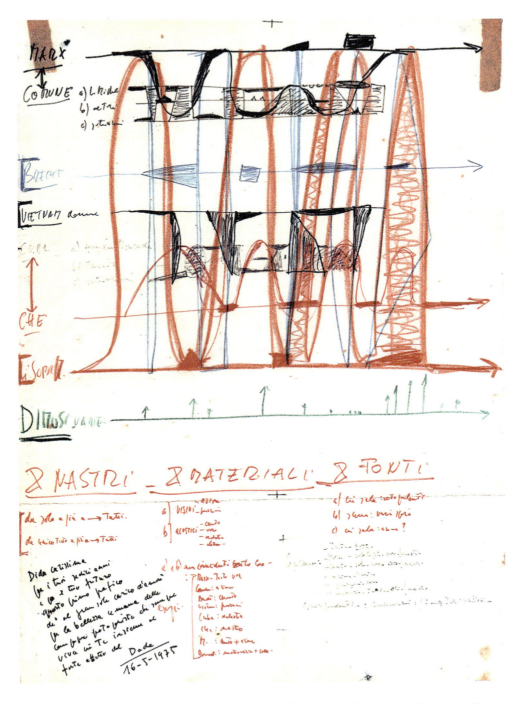

Plate 1 *Al gran sole carico d'amore*: sketch. ALN 40.06/01. © The heirs of Luigi Nono. Reproduced by kind permission.

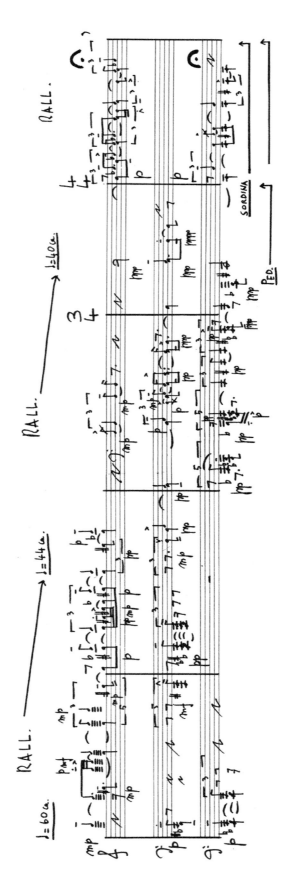

Plate 2 ..... *sofferte onde serene* ...: bars 1–5. (Reproduced by kind permission of Casa Ricordi.)

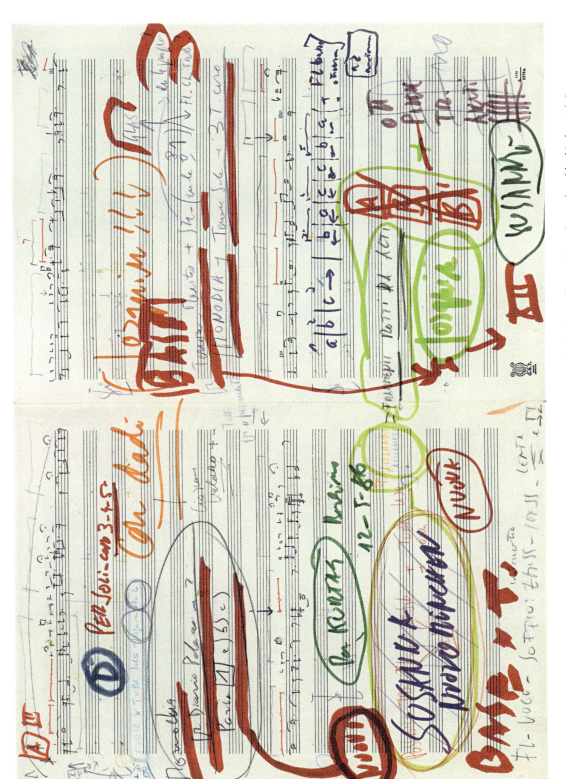

Plate 2 *Quando stanno morendo/Omaggio a György Kurtág*: pitch material. ALN 47.07.01/01. © The heirs of Luigi Nono. Reproduced by kind permission.

Plate 3 Guai ai gelidi mostri: Nono's postcard of Giovanni Bellini *Sacra* Conversazione. ALN 50.02_001_r. © The heirs of Luigi Nono. Reproduced by kind permission.

Plate 4 Photographs by Nono of his working spaces during the composition of Prometeo, 1983–4. © The heirs of Luigi Nono. Reproduced by kind permission.

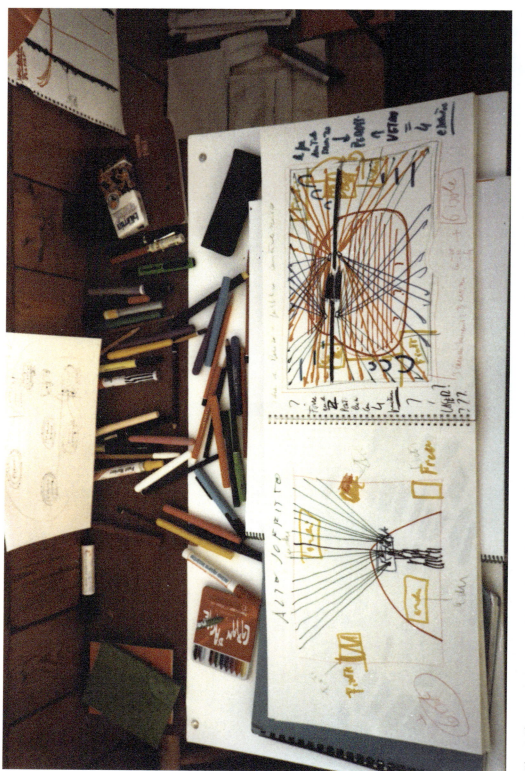

Plate 5 Photographs by Nono of his working spaces during the composition of Prometeo, 1983–4. © The heirs of Luigi Nono. Reproduced by kind permission.

Plate 6 Photographs by Nono of his working spaces during the composition of Prometeo, 1983–4. © The heirs of Luigi Nono. Reproduced by kind permission.

Plate 7 Prometeo: Nono at the mixing desk, showing part of Piano's performance space in San Lorenzo, Venice, 1984. Photograph © Graziano Arici.

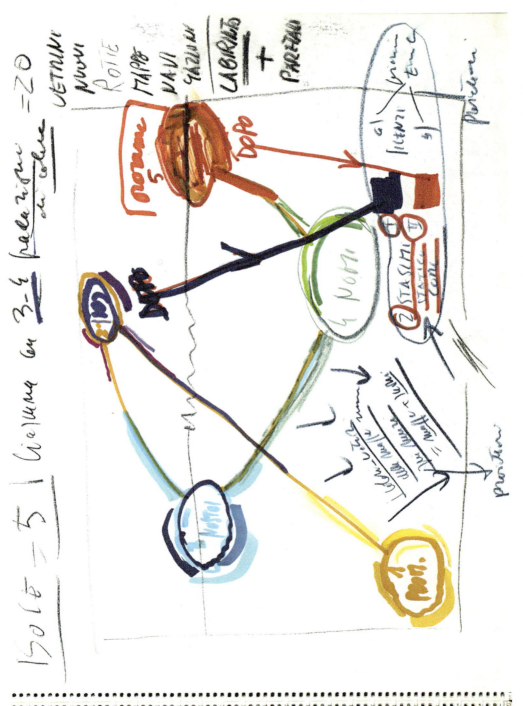

Plate 8 *Prometeo*: sketch of disposition and colours of *isole* in San Lorenzo. ALN 51.38.02/08. © The heirs of Luigi Nono. Reproduced by kind permission.

9

MANIFESTOS

Anti-revisionism: 'Per Bastiana – Tai-Yang Cheng'

I learned to understand the problem of culture in a new way. I've understood that there is no difference if I write a score or organise a strike. They are two aspects of the same thing. For me there is no longer any difference between music and politics. [. . .] Music is an integral part of life.

(Nono, 1969)[1]

This unequivocal statement of Nono's position as a politically engaged composer would come in 1969, at the end of a decade in which his musical, personal and political paths converged ever more explicitly in response to external events.

Following further trips to East Berlin and Prague in the autumn of 1966, Nono joined the Deutsche Akademie der Künste of the DDR – their most prestigious artists' association, of which Dessau had earlier been vice-president. Nono returned to East Berlin the following March for a performance of *Canti di vita e d'amore* and to give a seminar at the Hochschule für Musik Hanns Eisler. In the meantime, Dallapiccola wrote to ask whether Nono would accept nomination for the Berliner Akademie der Künste of *West* Berlin, of which he had been a member since 1958. On 2 February 1967 Nono informed Dessau of his decision to decline this new invitation, and explained more fully to Dallapiccola: 'the Academy of a socialist country should be different to an Academy here: a real working relationship, because the cultural and musical situation urgently demands help with development and active participation, not just a mere membership of "honour".'[2]

Nono's difficult relationship with institutions is unsurprising – since his early contact with the CIA-sponsored Congress for Cultural Freedom he was wary of the use of artists as propaganda tools, as instruments of political validation – but it makes his long-term adherence to the PCI still more significant. The next five years would see his most explicitly political works, as well as events that would severely test his political allegiances. As his internationalist activities broadened, Nono would argue that for him there was no distinction between actions in the worlds of music and politics. This is no facile reconciliation of two domains, however. Rather, it seems to be the inherent friction, their mutual resistance, that drives his invention. Following the experiences of *La fabbrica illuminata* and *A floresta*, each work now responds to a very specific political context.

Manifestos

The next commission would immediately challenge some of the steps he had taken in developing his own consciousness as a composer. It was for The Toronto Symphony Orchestra, to be performed there under Seiji Ozawa on 31 October 1967. Following the advances of *A floresta*, this would be very different in terms of his relationship with both material and performers. This work would require a fully notated score, to be interpretable by performers with whom he had little contact. The result was *Per Bastiana – Tai-Yang Cheng*, a fifteen-minute work for tape and orchestra dedicated to his second daughter, Serena Bastiana, born in 1964. At the centre of its musical material is *The East is Red*, the anthem of the Cultural Revolution in China, from which comes the second part of the title: 'the sun is rising'.

The orchestra is divided into three groups. The orchestra is divided into three groups: 8 violins, flutes, clarinets and trumpets to the left; lower strings, oboes, bassoons and trombones to the right. These high- and low-register groups surround a central ensemble of 16 violins, 6 horns and 2 bassoons, the musical and perceptual focus of the work. The internal arrangement of each group is symmetrical, and the two channels of the tape are projected from between the three groups. The score is notated in seconds, on graph paper. Only the material of the central group uses staff notation, with quarter-tones and microtonal glissandi. The other two groups are notated in terms of register. The range of each instrument is divided into low, middle and high bands, within which the line graphically indicates three further subdivisions and microtonal inflection – a development of the scheme developed in the part-books of *A floresta*. Players select pitches individually; they are instructed to avoid tonal implications and even-tempered divisions, to keep the sound constantly in movement. The tape is represented graphically at the centre of the score. Nono avoided staff notation right up to the point of producing a fair copy, maintaining his distance from his earlier practice. When developing material based on *The East is Red* he uses sol-fa notation and numbers rather than notes. The work is like a single sound in continuous transformation. Even where their gestures are shorter, the orchestra only produces sustained sounds. On the tape there are two kinds of material: bands of synthesised frequencies at 10Hz intervals, kept in movement by their internal beating and modulation, and metallic percussive sounds, the tubes and plates recorded during Nono and Zuccheri's research for *A floresta*, mixed with the voice of Liliana Poli and processed recordings of his own music. There are clear orientalisms: the tape material is characterised by gong sounds, and the heterophony of low horns in the central group recalls Tibetan trumpets. The orchestral sound reaches towards that of the tape: sharp attacks in the midst of slowly evolving inharmonic spectra, reverse envelopes and quiet, noisy, mobile string clusters too high or low to be perceptibly pitched.

The work is a play on perception; when Nicolaus A. Huber came to study with him in 1967, Nono encouraged him to study the psychology of human responses.[3] At no point does *The East is Red* emerge into the aural sunlight; rather, it 'appears and disappears gradually, is constructed in a chromatic basis, resulting and differentiated from that in the harmonic and melodic intervals that characterize it'.[4] The three groups form constantly shifting perspectives on the space framed by the two main sources: the complex sounds and gestures of the tape, and the vestigial traces of *The East is Red*. Pitch and time displacements in the central group are more closely concentrated around material derived from the pitch source; in groups one and three they are less correlated and closer to sounds on tape. Gabrieli and Josquin are strong presences in the derivation, fragmentation and spatialisation of material. The use of the orchestra anticipates the 'musique concrète instrumentale' of Nono's student Lachenmann. Nono controls the degrees of focus in pitch, time, dynamics and space of layers of sound objects.

A strict architecture underpins this continuous, organically evolving sound. The tape lasts exactly 15'00", subdivided differently in the three groups (Figure 9.1).

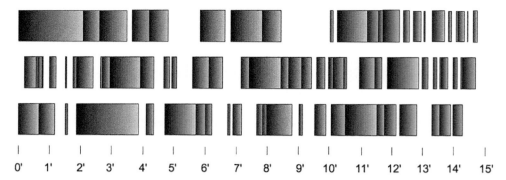

Figure 9.1 Per Bastiana – Tai-Yang Cheng: Pattern of blocks in orchestral groups 1–3

This creates a natural hiatus at about 10'00". Each subsection is further divided into thirteen unequal blocks of vastly differing proportions – from one second to over two minutes – five of which will be silent. As an additional layer of modulation, the thirteen fragments of each section are subject to a further permutation. In Nono's sketches, each subsection is designated A (high) B (low) or A+B. In all three groups, individual blocks are continuous for the instruments selected. Within this continuous sound, internal rhythm is generated by changes in dynamics and pitch, generated by techniques similar to those of *Canti di vita*. The individual rhythm of each voice is marked by sharply polarized dynamic movement: *f–p, ff–pp, fff–ppp*. The shape of pitch change in each voice follows a different sequence of proportions, such that the internal life of each block, its mobility, is the product of the modulation of two patterns: dynamics and pitch. The first block of the first group is the densest and most sustained example. Consisting of twenty-four individual voices sustained for two minutes, it functions as a kind of exposition, its inner complexity contrasting with unison *sffp* impulses from the third group. This texture, in different registers and colours, returns throughout almost as a refrain. At the Höhepunkt of 10'00" it moves across to the third instrumental group.

The fragments of the central group come into focus from 2'00" in the echo of this introductory block, accompanied by a tutti sustained pedal from the third group. Patterns of dynamic change are determined as for the other two groups, but the development of pitch material for this focal, conventionally notated group follows a linear trajectory through the work. Its formal proportions correspond to those of the tape material; they match the arrangement of the primary sound of tubes and plates. From halfway through the piece, this group abandons extremes and plays entirely in the middle register, as if searching for clarity and communication. Having analysed the limited interval content of *The East is Red*, Nono puts it at the centre of a wider pan-chromatic, all-interval interval matrix. The fragments thus produced explore the expanded pitch space step by step, until the pitches and intervals of the melody itself gradually emerge from their chromatic negative through the eight passages of the third section. The final passage contains the opening and closing phrases of *The East is Red*, looped untransposed in bassoons and violins. Their pentatonic profile and proto-rhythmic figures almost emerge from a rich body of horn and violin semitone movement around A–G–F♯: a group of individuals forming a single, lively unit from which optimism arises. The work reveals itself as a narrative, a joyful birth.

The few breaks in the orchestral texture are not silences but a means of directing attention fully to the tape. The first such moment at 6'38"–50" reveals the loudest tape sound thus far, a complex gesture that seems to signal the transition to a new state. The two short breaks during the ninth minute prepare the drama of 10'00". A brief interruption before 13'00" and the ten second tape solo shortly after seem to introduce a coda; the work ends with a tape solo which is interrupted in mid-gesture, as if to invite the continuation of an unending process.

Political engagement at home and abroad

Canadian critics had difficulty parsing the sound-stream of the new work on a single hearing. The orchestral component of *Per Bastiana* represents Nono at his most formalist. Perhaps for him this was the Maoist truth of this particular work: not to fear the consequences of coherent thought. Nono's choice of *The East is Red* is open to multiple interpretations, most of which probably have some grounding in truth. Primary are doubtless the joy in his young daughter and hope for her future expressed in his programme note: 'The title is taken from the words of the Chinese song and means "the day arises". Exactly. For Bastiana "the day arises", life begins tinged with red.'[5] To critics, the immediate motivation seemed to be a desire to provoke, to challenge. This is likely the case, but it is surely not so straightforward. Nono had followed Mao's writings since the 1950s; he had a full collection of those published in Italian. Mao was becoming an icon for those in the West who saw social development being stifled by consumerism; the horrors of the Cultural Revolution, begun in 1966, were not yet fully understood outside China. The ostensible rationale for this new phase of Chinese communism may have been resonant for Nono on two levels: a philosophy of continuous resistance and consciousness-raising allied with a historical materialist view, and a specific recognition of the dangers of revisionism and internal political obstruction. The latter appeared particularly relevant to the Italian situation. The wave of revolutionary energy that seemed to be sweeping through the world beyond the cold war, itself now a frozen conflict, offered an opportunity to re-energise the resistance-based Italian communism that had been betrayed by post-war compromise. Following the death in 1964 of Palmiro Togliatti, Gramsci's successor as leader of the PCI, two factions had emerged, embodied in the uncompromising views of Pietro Ingrao and the more emollient approach of Giorgio Amendola. Togliatti's deputy, Luigi Longo, had been elected leader as a continuity compromise, but Nono remained firmly of Ingrao's part. Ingrao had written to Nono early in 1967, encouraging a sense of historical progress:

> I think that music, as a moment of consciousness and expression, as 'action', has its history, its development [. . .] and therefore to participate in this consciousness, to live it fully and richly and not superficially, it is necessary and important in every way to engage with this history, to possess it as far as possible.[6]

Opportunities for engagement were proliferating. Having completed *Per Bastiana*, Nono was finally able to visit Latin America, where rapid political and cultural evolution seemed to be taking place. Modern concepts of democracy were penetrating with difficulty across the continent, battling vested interests and US-incited fear of communism. Revolutionary groups were active with varying degrees of popular support, of militancy, of Marxist ideology and contact with other movements, but the right was in the ascendancy. In that context, Cuba appeared a beacon of liberation, progress and support. Argentina was in the forefront of military repression, with Juan Carlos Onganìa's 'Revolución Argentina' of June 1966. Jorge Pacheco Areco would become President of Uruguay in December 1967, fighting the Marxist National Liberation Movement. In Chile, the incremental reforms of Eduardo Frei Montalva had polarised opinion between those who would support the election of Salvador Allende in 1970

Manifestos

– the first elected Marxist President in Latin America – and the forces that would replace him with Pinochet in 1973. Repressive elements were also at play in Peru, where the reforming government of Fernando Belaúnde Terry would be deposed by the military in 1968.

Keen to develop musical and political connections, Nono travelled to Latin America with his whole family in July 1967. He gave talks, presented recorded performances of *La fabbrica illuminata*, *Ricorda cosa ti hanno fatto in Auschwitz* and *A floresta*, met students and participated in conferences. He began in Uruguay, proceeded to Buenos Aires at the invitation of Alberto Ginastera to teach at the Instituto Torcuato di Tella, spoke to the Asociación Nacional de Compositores de Chile in Santiago and then continued to Lima in Peru. There he was due to give classes from 28 August to 1 September. On 27 August the National Symphony Orchestra gave a concert dedicated to the Guardia Civil, the government's paramilitary instrument of repression. Nono was reported as saying, 'As the National Symphony Orchestra dedicated their concert to the Guardia Civil, I dedicate my course to the guerillas massacred by the Guardia.'[7] He was arrested at his hotel, detained for 36 hours and put on a plane to Mexico by state security. Nono was unbowed: 'I am a communist and don't regret my words. I have given concerts and expressed my ideology in numerous countries, and this is the first time it has caused a problem.'[8] The event caused a stir in Italy – a committee of artists asked for political intervention – but Nono continued to a more welcoming climate in Havana, where on landing he declared: 'the new culture of Peru is that of the guerillas'.[9] For the next two decades, Nono's reference point in Cuba would be the Casa de las Americas, a literary and artistic institution that acted as a vehicle for Latin-American radical thought and art. It was founded and directed by Haydée Santamaria, a leader of the revolution, who would figure importantly in Nono's next stage work, *Al gran sole carico d'amore*.

He returned to Cuba at the beginning of 1968, for the Cultural Congress held in Havana, 4–11 January. In the meantime, the assassination of Che Guevara had galvanised revolutionary sentiment: 'the supreme example of the contemporary revolutionary intellectual' was Castro's judgement at the Congress.[10] His notes and interviews show that over the next three or four years Nono absorbed Che's writings avidly. A highly publicised event, Castro had used the highly publicised congress to demonstrate Cuba's cultural independence from the Soviet Union and its leading role among non-aligned 'Third World' nations.[11] It is important to recall that to radical thinkers this term had very positive connotations, quite different from the condescending 'underdeveloped' connotation of current usage: it denoted a way forward free from the ossified positions of the Cold War. 'The integral growth of man' was a key theme of the Congress, which included contributions from venerable figures such as Sartre, Russell, Herbert Read and Ernst Fischer. Nono had been instrumental in organising an Italian delegation that was to include Calvino, Pestallozza, Einaudi and Feltrinelli.[12] While there, he befriended Carlos Franqui. From peasant origins, Franqui was poet, journalist, art critic and editor of the clandestine newspaper that was now the party organ, *Revolución*. Franqui had arranged for the Parisian *Salon de Mai* art exhibition to show in Havana a few months earlier – a clear statement against socialist realism. He would remain in exile following events later in 1968, and work with Nono in Italy. This flourishing of Cuban independence would be short-lived – Stalinist factions reasserted control soon after – but it is significant that Nono's warm and enduring relationship with Cuban culture was formed during this window of vision and optimism.[13]

In February 1968 Nono was in West Berlin to take part in the anti-war demonstration organised by the *Sozialistische Deutsche Studentenbund* (SDS) – one of the largest such demonstrations in Europe, coming just two weeks after the Tet offensive punctured any sense of American

Manifestos

invincibility in Vietnam. The streets were a sea of red flags with tens of thousands of demonstrators, while around the hall of the International Vietnam Congress a banner displayed Che's dictum: 'the duty of the revolutionary is to make the revolution'.[14] The student leader Rudi Dutschke made a strong impression on Nono; he cited Duschke's conviction that students and intellectuals should be talking with workers, rather than about them, as a principle of the new culture. This was a time of heroic figures. The embodiment of social and human struggle, physical and intellectual endeavour in a single figure was clearly significant for Nono. He declared his intention to write a work for the recently assassinated Che Guevara:

> not so much to glorify him as to establish Che the theorist, Che the thinker. A music that grows from a new consciousness, so that the world sees itself with new eyes. [...] the avant-garde isn't just a technical apparatus, it's also knowing how to move, how this apparatus should move. The avant-garde – that is art, science and politics, wound together within a social structure, that can work for or against a certain development.[15]

He then crossed to the East, to a conference on Brecht, to see Dessau and in the hope of the Berliner Ensemble organising a tour of *A floresta* in the DDR. Nono would maintain very different relationships with institutions and individuals in the two sides of Berlin – ambivalent in both cases, as if each encapsulated a different paradox of artistic freedom and materialism, social progress and repression. In March, he chaired a conference at the XIII Week of New Music in Prague, in the early days of Dubček's reforms in defiance of the USSR and of new artistic freedom. The 'Prague Spring' would be brutally repressed months later. At the beginning of April, Nono was one of a group of artists who made a new appeal to President Johnson following his announcement on 31 March that he would not seek re-election. On 11 April there was an attempt to assassinate Duschke. The SDS accused the publisher Axel Springer, who had labelled Dutschke 'an enemy of the people', of inciting the neo-Nazi assassin. The next day, Nono and Vedova took part in a protest under the clock in St Mark's Square. Having chased the group through the streets, the police identified the artists as organisers of a breach of public order. Nono saw this as another 'demonstration of the repressive function of the police, a result of the authoritarian and oppressive politics of the centre-left government'.[16] In June, Nono was in Florence for the production of Brecht and Dessau's *Signor Puntila* at the *Maggio Musicale*. A concert of his own music was to take place the following day: *La fabbrica illuminata*, *Ricorda cosa ti hanno fatto in Auschwitz* and *A floresta*. The concert was free, in support of the Florentine industrial workers currently on strike for better conditions, and was followed by a discussion on 'Music, culture and social struggle'. *l'Unità* naturally emphasised the gesture of solidarity; more cynical critics saw an audience of intellectual elite rather than workers.[17]

The Venice Biennale had been brought under fascist control in 1930, since when its constitution had remained unreformed. Progressive artists increasingly saw the Biennale as an instrument of established cultural and political interests, a disquiet that ignited in June 1968 into boycotts and protests. Following the student unrest of previous months, state and police were nervous and prepared. A small demonstration in St Mark's Square encountered police in full riot mode, and the Venetian *Il Gazzettino* unhelpfully published a photograph of Nono 'throwing a chair at the police'.[18] The paper described the event as a battle between 'sinophile' (Maoist) artists and the citizens of Venice; when the march from the student-occupied Accademia succeeded in breaking into St Mark's Square, shopkeepers joined in the fight against them. It noted the particular displeasure with which Venetians identified artists from 'good' Venetian

Manifestos

families, such as Nono and Vedova. Both were identified and charged as ringleaders, but would be acquitted the following February.

Led by artists and intellectuals including Nono, protesters moved on to occupy the Giardini, the site of the exhibition itself. The authorities were determined to open the Biennale at all costs; *L'Avanti* reported over a thousand police and two tanks at the entrance.[19] Following the occupation, the Biennale gardens had to be heavily guarded and identity checks were imposed throughout the exhibition. Many artists threatened to withdraw their work if the police did not leave. An Argentinian artist poured 30 kilos of green dye into the Grand Canal so that it 'ran emerald'; Swedish artists refused to allow their pavilion to open and announced 'The Biennale is dead'.[20] In his design for the Italian pavilion, Nono's friend Carlo Scarpa concealed the fascist columns. The protesters included intellectuals and activists of a new generation; Nono's close collaborators included Massimo Cacciari and Antonio Negri, leaders of a new wave of political–philosophical initiatives. Such events serve to illustrate the disjuncture between the city's cultural status and its small-town conservative ways, the context for Nono's preference for the company of the boat-builders of Giudecca or the industrial workers of Marghera. The following month he sent a telegram to Labroca at the Biennale prohibiting performance of his works because of its 'irresponsible ignoring of new cultural-political requirements';[21] *Per Bastiana* had been scheduled for the autumn festival. In August, Nono led the committee to boycott the Cinema Festival, organising free screenings for workers from Marghera as a counter-initiative.[22] As an indicator of the seriousness of these events, Negri reports that the police planted a bomb at the Lido, the site of the Cinema Festival, in order to declare a militarised zone.[23] Such tactics would soon become more common, with dangerous consequences. Nono's own Venetian federation of the PCI denounced the festival publicly, calling for a full analysis of the role of economic and political power in culture. Mila was sympathetic, but felt it unhelpful to blame the Biennale for the state of contemporary art.[24] These events instigated a period of reflection that would lead to a new constitution for the Biennale in 1973. In a more detailed statement, Nono set out the chain of interest and influence that dominated decision-making in the region, the close ties between cultural, educational and political institutions, and monopoly employers such as Montedison and Confindustria.[25]

Situated action and Venetian counterpoint: 'Contrappunto dialettico alla mente'

In February 1968, Nono was again commissioned to provide a work for the Prix Italia. Once more, the RAI would refuse to include it on barely concealed political grounds. *Contrappunto dialettico alla mente*, a twenty-minute tape composition using texts by Sonia Sanchez and Nanni Balestrini, is one of Nono's most self-contextualising works, a parody of parodies and perhaps a response to *Per Bastiana*. It is more rounded, consciously Venetian both historically and geographically – ironic, even funny, but with the clearest of political messages. Its model is provided by Adriano Banchieri's comic madrigal cycle *Festino nella sera del giovedì grasso avanti cena* (*A little party before dinner on Maundy Thursday*, Venice, 1608). Banchieri was the antithesis of Zarlino – an intensely practical musician with a keen sense of his audience and social context. Nono's title refers to Banchieri's *Contrappunto bestiale alla mente*, a madrigal with at least two levels of comicity. It is *bestiale* both in being sung by drunken revellers imitating animals (cuckoo, owl, cat, dog) improvising counterpoint over a comic cantus firmus, and because it demonstrates the facile nature of counterpoint produced *alla mente*, without reflection or planning. Specifically, this means without the *cartella* or wax tablet on which counterpoint was worked out; in another in-joke – or piece of seventeenth-century publicity – Banchieri's own

Manifestos

treatise on composition was *La Cartella Musicale*.[26] Banchieri was a master of exploiting new technologies – the printing houses of Venice. This cannot have been lost on Nono, whose practice is characterised precisely by a constant, iterative process of inscription and reinscription – whether of text, notes, graphics, symbols or tape – and whose work continually challenges the very limits of the musical ontologies afforded by technology and cultural structures.

Composition through the early summer followed Nono's new practice, bringing together studio recordings – both new and from his existing repertoire – synthetic sounds and location recordings. The recorded and processed sounds of metal tubes and plates remain fundamental to his palette, as well those of the chamber choir and the studio's wave generators. An early plan had been to use tape with a live choir. He recorded in Venice with Zuccheri: sounds across the lagoon, voices in the fish market and the Rialto, and the *Marangona* – the largest bell of St Mark's, that marked the start and end of the working day. In the studio he worked with his established company: Poli, Bove, Vicini, Troni and now Marisa Mazzoni. Many of these recordings are of group performance, such that detail of timing and response remains in the finished work. The texts are an Italian translation of American poet Sonia Sanchez's poem *Malcolm* (a eulogy for Malcolm X), the manifesto of *Black Women Enraged* – a Harlem group opposed to the Vietnam draft – and two passages by the experimental poet Nanni Balestrini. Each of Balestrini's texts consists of twenty-five lines of four interwoven strands: two parallel poems, phrases that start and end in half-words as if extracted from some oblique poetic reference to the main texts, and new Italian-sounding non-words made of phonemes from the current line.[27] Nono may have been reminded of Myakovsky's surreal, resynthesised nonsense texts. Balestrini's words generate a chattering, the unarticulable semantic richness of the crowd. From this material Nono constructs short score-scripts for his actors to perform in the studio: text fragments, canons and orchestrations of vocal sounds made by repeating phonemes, often with careful markings of rhythm, accent and dynamics.

Work at the studio in Milan, from May to July 1968, was therefore concurrent with the protests in Venice. The opening of the Milan Triennale had also been delayed by an artist occupation; Nono addressed the protesters in a public gesture of support. With the perspective of time we can see *Contrappunto dialettico alla mente* as encapsulating Nono's relationship with his own city and people – affection and anger in equal measure. Despite its major political themes and surface resemblances to *A floresta*, this is a much more personal work; conceived radiophonically, it exploits the unmediated communication of that medium. Indeed, Nono may have recalled Scherchen's early advocacy of the culturally democratising potential of radio. The locatedness of the work, its Venetian setting, allows its hybrid sources to be reconciled. Nono wrote to Piccioni, vice-director of radio at the RAI, presumably anticipating disquiet as to his subject matter: 'Banchieri sets texts of his own time relating to his own time.'[28] Avoiding mention of sources other than Balestrini, he diplomatically mentions that he has 'brought everything into relationship with today, to avoid a possible neoclassical game, which I hate'. The anti-racist, anti-war texts not only situate the work in Nono's own time, they situate it in St Mark's square, with the protests of Nono and his comrades.

Banchieri's work is a sharp but affectionate critique of Venetian society. It incorporates cultural affectation, seduction, drinking songs and tongue-twisters, peasant gossip and dialect, passing entertainers and dubious traders. 'Il Moderno Diletto tutti invita a un opera di gusto e favorita' ('Modern Delight invites everyone to a work of taste and enjoyment') stands as an epigram to its introduction. On his copy, Nono writes 'Il diletto delitto modern (Malcom X) ('the delightful modern crime'). 'Like black power' he adds to the end of Banchieri's invitation. Nono lists Banchieri's materials as 'meaningful texts, phonetic texts, marketplace cries, exclamations, madrigal style, various historical forms of counterpoint'.[29] Once taken with the

Manifestos

idea, Nono sees more parallels in Banchieri's use of nonsense words, rhyme and alliteration. He notes the 400th anniversary of his birth. The work is 'Like a homage to Banchieri':

> But in the 'search for a relationship with the kind of musical procedure that Banchieri employed: particular use of the voice, of sonic material of his time, humorous confusion and parody, especially in lyrical and dramatic moments' [. . .] Market cries, onomatopoeic games, phonetic diversions. But in present reality.

Ideology and technique are constantly united: in the various moments of research, of composition, of the determining of responsibility.[30]

Nono articulates Banchieri's lengthy text into three types − phonemes, lyrical and scherzo − and selects five comic vignettes:

- *il diletto moderno per l'introduzione* (modern delight, as an introduction);
- *mascherate di vecchietti* (masques of old folk − a combination of two numbers: a masque of *villanelles*, and a *giustiniana* of elderly Chioggians) − lyrical, phonemes, scherzo;
- *la zia Bernardina racconta una novella* (Aunt Bernardina tells a story) − scherzo;
- *i cervellini cantano un madrigale* (the idiots sing a madrigal) − lyrical;
- *intermedio di venditori di fusi* (intermezzo of the spindle-sellers) − scherzo.

These he adapts into a new dramatic structure, maintaining the articulation into separate numbers of Banchieri's original. As is clear from the sequence and proportions of movement types he describes, Nono's approach to form remains thoroughly rational:

0'00"–0'35"	(introduction) *contrappunto dialettico alla mente*
0'35"–4'59"	*il diletto delitto moderno* (lyrical)
4'59"–9'54"	*mascherata dei vecchietti* (lyrical-scherzo) / *venditori di soffio* (scherzo)
9'54"–14'37"	*i cervellini cantano un madrigal* (lyrical)
14'37"–18'28"	*lo zio Sam racconta una novella* (scherzo)
18'28"–19'50"	(reprise − *il diletto delitto moderno*) (lyrical)

Against a sustained, static resonance a dense canonic counterpoint of actors' voices announces the title of the work. After the introduction, Sanchez's poem begins clearly, but is then pulled in two directions: towards pitchedness, drawn by the slowly evolving clearly pitched background of soprano and metallic resonance, and towards fragmentation into rhythmic complexes of vocal utterances. Behind these successive waves the sustained background functions as a horizon, almost a cantus firmus. They combine through the last minute into a sonic pandemonium in which all the voices of the world seem to participate. The stuttering announcement of 'mascherata dei vecchietti' is a pun; 'venditori di soffio' ('breath-sellers') is a whispered, more sinister sound, into which reconstituted phonemes from 'Johnson', 'casa bianca' and 'pentagono' insinuate themselves. The words and phonemes of Balestrini's texts become verbal virtuosity, counterpointed at different speeds, pitches and distances. They mock themselves, collapsing into streams of stuttering taken up by synthetic sounds. A tense silence introduces a more threatening layering of shouting, whispering, singing, processed and electronic sound. High transposed speech becomes increasingly insistent, until it has transformed into clouds of bird noise, near and distant − the idiots' madrigal − behind which sung and synthetic resonant pitches appear. They draw into focus until voices announce 'I cervellini cantano un madrigale'. This is the only discernible text, returning at a few cue pitches as a marker at regular intervals. The idiots are joined in a play of nonsense phonemes, even studio-produced animal sounds, until low, resonant female voices join at 13'00" heralding a more sustained development. The clear, unison announcement 'Lo zio Sam racconta una novella' directs the attention towards a story to be recounted. A slow, sustained development of solo voices, the bell of St Mark's, water and scraping metal establish the space for its unfolding. In the context of such sophisticated, distanced use of the voice, the directness of the line that eventually comes is a blow, a challenge: 'lo zio Sam vuole te, nigger' ('Uncle Sam wants you, nigger'). Nono attributes the text to Stokely Carmichael;[31] it seems to have emerged in different versions from the Student Nonviolence Coordinating Committee of which he was chairman. It is a warning message to those likely to be recruited for the Vietnam War:

> Uncle Sam wants you, nigger
> Become a member of the world's highest paid black mercenary army!
> Support White Power – travel to Viet Nam, you might get a medal!
> Fight for Freedom (in Viet Nam)
> Receive valuable training in the skills of killing off other oppressed people!
> You cause too much trouble in your ghetto
> Uncle Sam wants you to die in Viet Nam[32]
> The whitey's plan is to do for you in Vietnam
> Stay here and fight for your dignity as men.[33]

Every word is heard in relief against the words, cries and shouts accumulating with the increasingly percussive sonic environment. As they decay, bell resonance remains to introduce the finale, initially a reprise of *il diletto delitto moderno*. It sounds as if this has been a play within a play, but an expanding canon of bell sounds provides a frame within which the entire sonic panoply returns before condensing back into bell resonances, into a single moment in Venice. Aesthetic distance is never allowed to settle into comfort.

This is the most finely heard and constructed of Nono's studio works to this point. Sounds are blended and elided more artfully than before; Nono initially edited and mixed the work for eight channels – two four-track recorders, as in *A floresta* – giving a clarity of perspective. Passages such as the complex of voices after 4'00"–5'00" bespeak a mastery of balancing detail, spectra, dynamics and space such that every element affords attention. Listening is kept in constant movement. Following Nono's own repeated listening in the studio, the listener's attention becomes his primary sonic-sculptural parameter. Sounds other than text-carrying voices are rarely identifiable; 'no naturalismo' is a note that appears across Nono's sketches for recorded material since *Un diario italiano*. The role of text is a key thread through the work. In the first main section the words are clearly audible, but rearranged or overlaid to play either side of the boundary of comprehensibility. In the second, speech itself becomes the subject. Voices are transformed to become something quite other in the third, but in the fourth, Carmichael's shocking central text is clearly declaimed. 'FOR COMPREHENSIBILITY' Nono writes to himself, but the space is richer than a single continuum of voice and word between meaning and abstract sound. This is also a dialectical counterpoint of voices in the mind, a virtual theatre of ideas from the globally momentous to the commonplace, nonsensical or absurd – groups and individuals informing each other, ignoring, conflicting, pulling in different directions. The human voice is the common, unifying element; this is the sound of society.

The soundtrack of struggle

In late September, Nono returned to Latin America, now to Caracas in Venezuela. There he participated in both the first International Music Festival and the Mérida Documentary Film

Manifestos

Festival. The report he published in *Rinascita* in December makes clear that he found the latter more interesting; while the music festival organised sightseeing excursions, that of film 'used the time for screenings, discussions, working meetings on the cultural problems of Latin America.'[34] Highly engaged with the art and politics of that region, he admires the integrity and responsibility, the commitment to the struggle for social justice, of both groups. The filmmakers constituted the more regionally representative body: 'it has been possible to deepen my understanding of the difficult reality and struggle of the Latin-American countries through their new cinema, of worldwide validity and significance in technical, formal, structural and ideological terms'. [35] The role of film in Latin American struggles was something of a cultural model for Nono, and he was keen to support particular artists. According to Calabretto, whose extensive and forensic research is invaluable, the Mexican director Leobardó López Aretche used Nono's music in his 1968 *El jinete del cubo*.[36] Álvarez he seems to have met in Cuba; Nono allowed Álvarez to use extracts from *A floresta* in his 1967 film about the liberation struggle in Laos *La guerra olvidada*.[37] Leo Brouwer, Head of Music for the Cuban Film Institute (ICIAC), advised many of the Cuban directors, and had close contact with Nono. This would continue: Cuban director Humberto Solás used Nono's music in his 1986 *Un hombre de éxito*, particularly *Das atmende Klarsein*.[38]

The unique cultural position of film – its capacity to bring radical or complex ideas and difficult realities to a wide audience – drew Nono to various projects closer to home. In 1964, an unrealised project with Venetian director Tinto Brass, *Ça ira, il fiume della rivolta*, was to encompass twentieth-century revolutionary movements across the world – a perspective with analogies to Nono's works of the early seventies. Nono was unable to reach agreement with Luchino Visconti, who had contacted him in 1966 with a view to collaborating on *Lo straniero*, a version of Camus' novel:[39] 'he shared with me his ideas for the acoustics of the film, from the music to the sounds and speech'.[40] Rossana Rossanda recalled Nono's view on the illustrative use of music in film: 'never use music as a subtitle – Luigi Nono was a wild beast on this [matter]'.[41] In 1972, Nono had engaged positively with Giuseppe Ferrara's *Faccia da spia*, a study of CIA manipulation of financial markets, but this enthusiasm waned at the prospect of scoring to a finished film.[42] In 1973, he reacted with surprise and anger at the news that a director was planning to use his music in a series of television programmes,[43] and he later declined a proposal from Stanley Kubrick to use *A floresta* in *The Shining* (1980).[44] Nono was much more inclined to collaborate on projects that resonated with his own cultural–political view of the role of art, particularly those of the Unitelefilm production company that worked closely with the PCI.[45] He explored his repertory of taped sounds in Vittorio Togliatti's documentary on the Florence flood of 1966, *L'Arno è anche un fiume*.[46] He curated the selection of Vietnamese music for Maria Volonté and Mario Socrate's 1969 *L'offensiva del Tết*, produced with the National Front for the Liberation of South Vietnam.[47] Luigi Pirelli's *Laos escalation* of 1971 would use Nono's *La fabbrica illuminata*, among other extracts, as would his *Un futuro per Genova* of the same year.[48] Parts of *Il canto sospeso* accompany Paolo Gobetti and Giuseppe Risso's 1975 *Lotta partigiana*, a study of European resistance movements in the Second World War.[49]

More intense would be Nono's involvement in *La Fabbrica*, a 1970 film by Alberto Lauriello, Lino De Seriis and Lucio Libertini.[50] Indeed, in a short article for *Cineforum* he describes it as his only experience of working with cinema.[51] Using documentary material edited with great rhetorical and compositional precision, the film reflects the workers' protests of 1969 in Turin, developing the idea of the factory as concentration camp. Protests for lower rent, for housing, against working conditions, the unions, the absolute power of Fiat and its historical relationship

Manifestos

with fascism all figure in this picture of industrial life and struggle. Nono describes three stages of the collaborative process: viewing the documentary material and discussion; proposals, tests and discussion with the directors; editing of the soundtrack to the finished film and further discussion. *La fabbrica illuminata* features prominently, but *Ricorda cosa ti hanno fatto in Auschwitz*, *Como una ola* and *Non consumiamo Marx* are also to be heard, together with popular song, sounds of factory and protest and 'bourgeois' music.

> The collaboration seemed logical to me, as a different way of participating in the cultural–political debate, different to the numerous meeting-debates that to which I have been invited by workers' associations for years. Also because it is quite distant from the concept of self-contained "musical categories", the compartmentalized specialization sought by the bourgeoisie in their division of labour [. . .][52]

'Il Manifesto'

The Soviet repression of the 'Prague Spring', the Russian tanks entering Prague in August 1968, presented a challenge to non-Soviet communist parties. The PCI at first decided to condemn the invasion as a tactical error rather than symptomatic of a deep structural malaise. Enrico Berlinguer, elected as Deputy Secretary at the XII Congress, would distance the Party from the USSR in Moscow later in 1969, the first step towards his 'Eurocommunism', but outright condemnation was not forthcoming. The Soviet action was equally difficult to reconcile on a personal level, as Nono's friend Rossana Rossanda recalls:

> At some point Gigi Nono rang me – he always rang me at night, scaring an aunt who thought that all telephone calls after a certain hour heralded disaster – to complain that we were not attacking Prague strongly enough ('But what's Pietro [Ingrao] doing? What's Pietro waiting for?') – and he was completely dumbfounded when I told him that the invasion was unacceptable. So was 1956 [the Soviet invasion of Hungary]. What did he think socialism was? He was totally confused: But what did I mean, and what about Fidel, and Vietnam?[53]

Nono had developed a warm friendship with Pietro Ingrao, who had been regularly in Venice as the party liaison. Ingrao also noted Nono's difficulty in questioning the Soviet action:

> We discussed the Italian political goings-on together, and especially the revolutions that were breaking out in the third world, towards which Gigi felt particularly drawn. And he, with extraordinary patience and communicative passion, tried to get me to understand his research. [. . .]
> Let's be clear: I always felt the presence of ideology in Gigi, and of a clear sense of social conflict across the world, above all the progress of the revolutions in the third world [. . .] I wasn't always in agreement with Gigi: not just his opinion on the Cuban revolution – too unquestioning for me – but also in his assessment of the USSR, about which my reservations were growing.[54]

Here we must distinguish between the historical materialist and the pragmatist. Nono was not a political pragmatist; his ideology was a vehicle for faith and optimism, an ethical–moral touchstone. The notion of a single organisation to lead the struggle towards a more just world

287

Manifestos

was axiomatic to his communism, and this inevitably led to paradoxes and contradictions in responding to political events.

On 8 February 1969 Nono drove to Bologna with his friend and comrade Cesco Chinello, to attend the XII Congress of the PCI as representatives of the Venetian Federation.[55] At the previous congress in 1966, the Party had elected Longo as Secretary, choosing the path of continuity over the reforms proposed by Ingrao. Since then, major developments had arisen to challenge the party line: the politicised student movement and May 1968, the evolution of workerist and autonomist theory and organisation, and especially the Soviet intervention in Prague. More generally, a flammable mix of industrial and political unrest and uncertainty was brewing in Italy, that would lead to the 'hot autumn' of 1969 and the confusion, fear and despair of the 'anni di piombo', the 'years of lead' of the long Italian 1970s. Among their tasks at the Congress was to present three amendments to the final declaration, one of which had been proposed by Nono: that the cultural policy of the PCI should be to work towards 'a synthesis of class and culture'.[56] They would not be called to speak because, in Chinello's opinion, the leadership preferred not to draw attention to such minor challenges.

The radical rereading of Marx and Gramsci of the early 1960s had roots in post-war Italian thought: that of philosopher Galvana Della Volpe and sociologist Ernesto De Martino, for example. Its immediate political implications had been developed by theorists such as Raniero Panzieri and Mario Tronti in the journal *Quaderni Rossi*. With his concept of the 'social factory', Tronti showed how capitalism had come to dominate not just production but social relations as a whole; the whole of society had become a means of production.[57] The closer cooperation between unions and major industries, as well as between the right-wing Christian Democrats and socialist PSI (not the communist PCI), meant that organised labour had become a facilitator, optimising production for the benefit of capital. Instead, Tronti argued, there must be a necessary antagonism between labour, labour power and capital. The Italian 'economic miracle' had produced a new working class, no longer represented by existing structures. The violent 1962 demonstration of Piazza Statuto in Turin encapsulated the situation. Workers' anger was directed as much at the unions as their employers; like the PCI, the CGIL union was close to their family and social lives, and there was a sense of betrayal.[58]

Discussion in the local federations meant that such ideas were widely diffused, even if they were dismissed by the PCI as a threat to unity. As faith in the ability of party and union structures to address the grievances of workers diminished, especially in the new industries, new forms of worker organisation emerged, with no allegiance to either. The 'mass worker' was identified as a new subject, a new kind of politico–economic actor. As theory and action evolved, strategy diverged. Tronti supported workplace disruption as a means of asserting the central role of the workforce, the 'strategy of refusal';[59] Panzieri saw this as maintaining a state of defeat. Through a new journal, *Classe operaia*, from 1964 Tronti, Negri and others developed ideas as to how the new working class might organise itself organically, spontaneously and locally, to take control and benefit from the contemporary technological state of industry. Two paths presented themselves: 'entryism' – working for change through the PCI – and more direct action. The former proved frustrating, as under the continuity leadership of Longo, Ingrao's more left-leaning proposals were still insufficiently radical.

The tendency known as 'operaismo' ('workerism') found most fertile ground in the newly industrialised north-east of the country, the Venetian hinterland, in the form of 'Potere operaio' ('Workers' power'). It was here that the subsequent and more militant 'autonomist' movement developed, later implicated, however unjustly, in the violent unrest of the 1970s. With the leadership of figures such as Antonio Negri, professor of political philosophy at the University of Padua, the movement gained academic credentials and connected with new student organisations. The Montedison petrochemical works at Porto Marghera, on the mainland of the Venetian lagoon, became a particular flashpoint. Workers' demands bypassed the unions, expressing a solidarity that differential pay agreements had tried to fragment. Disruption through the summer of 1968 brought production to a halt and came to a head with a demonstration of 60,000 people.[60] Nono had taken part with Cacciari and Negri in the actions at Porto Marghera. In the process he had to confront the reality that his participation was welcomed not because of the vital role of culture in the wider struggle, but because his presence as a public figure contributed profile and validity. We must assume that this realisation confirmed his commitment to the PCI and motivated his amendment to Congress in February 1969. More confrontational at the Congress were the ideas for reform put forward by prominent party thinkers such as Rossanna Rossanda and Lucio Magri. Their speeches were scheduled for the opening session, before the meeting had fully got underway; 'the left dies at dawn' was the common conclusion.[61] The lack of support from Ingrao, still seen as the potential leader of internal change, left the reformers isolated and without a voice. At the end of the week, on 15 February, the Congress voted on its final declaration, usually a formality. Instead, there were two votes against and fourteen abstentions, including Nono and Chinello. This must have been a grave personal decision.

The reformers knew their path was blocked within the Party, and decided instead to disseminate their ideas through a new journal, *Il Manifesto*. The first issue appeared on 23 June 1969. Its extraordinary success – 75,000 copies sold immediately – meant that the PCI had to respond. As the first *Manifesto* was published, the magazine *ABC* announced 'the Communist Party splits in two', with a picture of Nono – 'the Chinese', so-called because of his Maoist reputation – protesting at the previous year's Milan Triennale.[62] The final straw came with a *Manifesto* editorial in September, accusing the PCI of having abandoned Prague to the USSR. Nono was publicly implicated in the *Manifesto* project, having supported their aims and contributed to an early issue of the journal. He was named as one of the group accused by the Party of 'factionalism' – attempting to split the PCI – and investigated in early October.[63] At a special meeting of the Central Committee in November 1969, Rossana Rossanda, Lucio Magri, Aldo Natoli and Luigi Pintor were expelled; Ingrao could have argued their case, but chose political survival – a decision he later claimed to regret. Nono also feared expulsion, as he said in a letter to Aharonián in Cuba on the day of the hearing.[64] Again, he chose to stay within the Party. He made the necessary undertakings; the wilier politicians probably saw him as useful rather than dangerous. Nono wrote immediately to Longo and Berlinguer in support of his expelled friends: the Party needs all the intelligence at its disposal to confront the need for change identified by Berlinguer, he wrote.[65] In answer, there came only an invitation to speak with the editor of *l'Unità*.

In the months before the November crisis, Nono had been very active politically, sending reports to the Party from his travels: the communist festival at Châtillon in May; in June to West Berlin to speak with emigrant workers at the Buna chemical plant and then on to a student meeting in Munich; in July to Cuba for the third year in succession. He redoubled his attempts to engage more meaningful meaningfully with culture as a force for historical transformation. In a long letter to Longo and Berlinguer he expressed his dissatisfaction with a meeting of the Cultural Committee, his frustration at the superficiality of the Party's understanding of the potential of culture. They were discussing not the avant-garde, not new forms of creativity but 'provincial programming, mentality, habits and patriotism'.[66]

Berlinguer, elected as Vice-Secretary at the Bologna Congress, would replace Longo in 1972. His 'historic compromise' with the Christian Democrats and his strategy of what became known as 'Eurocommunism' may have set him against more radical reformers, but he would transform the PCI, restore its mass, momentum and sense of relevance; his funeral in 1984 was attended by over a million people. Perhaps Nono had a sense that these more gradual reforms would allow him to continue to work through the Party. The PCI was so deeply embedded in working-class culture that it presented the only viable context for the kind of cultural consciousness-raising he describes in his long letter to the leadership. There was certainly anger in such areas of society, anger that would continue to grow and be exploited through the 1970s, but the new political theory of *autonomia* likely spoke to factory workers no more directly than the music theory of Nono. It was action that appealed, the prospect of taking control, of breaking through the inertia of compromise. The more radical elements of Potere operaio were becoming frustrated with its inefficacy; they now found new momentum and focus with the concepts of autonomism and the leadership of Negri. Activists soon had to choose whether to stay within the Ingroaist left wing of the PCI, or join the more disruptive actions of the nascent autonomist movement. Cacciari would join the PCI in 1969; he describes 'continuous meetings at the home of Luigi Nono with the Ingraoist left'.[67] Negri recalls the high level of discourse of the Venetian PCI, but points to the inherent tensions:

> in a situation like that in the Veneto, however, where there were Luigi Nono, Emilio Vedova, another series of people directly involved, the level of discussion was really high, in terms of quality. [. . .] probably there was on one side a great theoretical intensity, an experience of class struggle that forced us onwards; but on the other, ambiguities remained, because despite everything the Venetian PCI was pretty open, apart from some enormous argument around the great strike of '63, or later around the great regional struggle of '69.[68]

Negri, Cacciari and Alberto Asor Rosa had founded the journal *Contropiano* in 1968, initially intended to further thought on class struggle and its relationship with social structures. With Negri's departure after the first issue, focus turned more explicitly to planning and architecture, giving prominence to ideas evolving at the Istituto Universitario di Architettura di Venezia (IUAV), the group including Cacciari and Manfredo Tafuri. Tafuri's paper *Per una critica della ideologia architettonica* would become particularly influential.[69] Involvement in such lively discussions with a group of young thinkers searching intensely for a clearer theoretical basis for architecture provided Nono with a sounding-board for his own strategies, as well as a challenge to his own coherence of thought. His earlier references to Gramsci, to the organic intellectual, to his actions as a musician being equivalent to those of any other worker, now needed to be elaborated in the context of the intense public political debate of the end of the decade.

In an interview with Rossana Rossanda for *Il Manifesto* in the summer of 1969, Nono presents a clear articulation of possible understandings of the relationship between politics and art. He lists five possible approaches. The first two he discounts easily: that there should be no relationship (Boulez is his example), or that only culture can create revolution (Kagel). The third is that technology might lead revolution; this he also eliminates, citing Stockhausen. Perhaps he does so too lightly, given his own practice; elsewhere he makes frequent references to the need to engage with new technologies, with science and with new industrial means of production. He observes that new audiences – workers, students – find it easier to engage with the sound world of his electronic music than with the earlier serial works. In terms of revolution through listening, through the raising of consciousness, this has proved to be true: Nono's later music with live electronics has found a receptive audience from a much wider cultural constituency than only that of 'classical 'music. Fourthly, he mentions the view that art is so marked as a bourgeois activity that a new culture will only be possible after revolution. Here he is presumably referring to Negri and the more radical workerists, for whom his early enthusiasm seems to have waned as it became clear that their increasingly radical stance set little store by consciousness-raising through culture. Finally, Nono sets out his own position:

> that attempts [to create] culture as a moment of coming into consciousness, of struggle, of provocation, of discussion, of participation. This involves the critical use of language and instruments that are historically received or invented; the denial of any Eurocentric or aristocratic concept of culture and language; [it is] a way of working tested against social forces before, during and after. *Before*, to understand who you are, where you find yourself and why you choose a particular area to work in – that is, how you become a communist (Brecht said that you aren't one, you become one). *During*, to understand how and from what point of view you write and in relation to whom, and why and who for. *After*, to see the result in its various modes of dissemination and reception with different publics, to offer and receive from them provocation, participation.[70]

Elsewhere, Nono acknowledges the paradoxes inherent in his position.[71] We might identify three key issues in an irreducibly complex situation: his role as a bourgeois intellectual, the accessibility of his music to a wider public in terms of both style and cultural infrastructure, and the possibility of integrating popular music from particular cultures.

The notion of the organic intellectual is often cited in relation to Nono, and is clearly fundamental to a Gramscian vision of progress. Through the late 1960s Nono repeatedly makes reference to his desire for provocation and intervention, for discussion with all areas of society. He clearly relishes every opportunity for the exchange of ideas, for sharing his music with non-bourgeois communities. He supports their struggles, but he does not lay claim to being an organic intellectual in respect of Italian factory workers. Indeed, if we are to apply this term to Nono, it should be precisely in relation to the bourgeois audiences for concert music who remained the principle constituency for his work. Being indigenous to the working class is not the only property of the new intellectual described by Gramsci:

> The mode of being of the new intellectual can no longer consist in eloquence, which is an exterior and momentary mover of feelings and passions, but in active participation in practical life, as constructor and organiser, 'permanent persuader' and not just a simple orator [. . .] from technique-as-work one proceeds to technique-as-science and to the humanistic conception of history, without which one remain 'specialised' and does not become 'directive' (specialised and political).[72]

So, while Nono does not claim to be of the working class, we might understand his role as that of organic intellectual in two respects. He is 'native' to the bourgeoisie, the very class whose consciousness is both most in need of being transformed and the most intransigent; and the nature of his work is not intellectual in the traditional sense – it is the technical work of a musician, a composer. Nono's prime mode of thought is musical not theoretical. We should not expect that his various statements on his political engagement as an artist add up to a comprehensive, coherent unified theory. It is more relevant to consider the nature of the intellectual–musical multiverse of which these are contextual snapshots. He contrasts the reception to his work at 'cultural' events – where the issue is whether or not it is music – with that in factories or workers' associations, where discussion focuses on more technical issues of production and dissemination and where he finds more aesthetic openness.

Nono's use of external material – popular or political songs, documentary recordings – is itself a technical compositional matter and highly contextual. Our retrospective view inevitably brings the risk of flattening the range of kinds of work in the late 1960s and their different contexts. In general, there are two reference points: the use of found material in early polyphony and the power of mass political song. Nono was also associated with various aspects of the popular protest song. He befriended and made frequent appearances with exiled Latin-American groups such as Inti-Illimani, collecting many of their recordings. He discounted the direct use of folkloric material in progressive culture, although certain instances challenge this assertion.[73]

The early ethnographic musical projects of Ernesto De Martino and others developed from the same political and methodological roots as the theorists of *Quaderni rossi*, documenting music from the regions, from the resistance, and from aspects of Italian life that were fast disappearing. From such initiatives grew the *Nuovo Canzoniere Italiano* movement that popularised songs such as *Bella ciao* through festivals and recordings. The new generation of Italian *cantautori* – singer song-writers – were able to tap into both of these streams, as well as the commercial success of protest and folk song from America.[74] The LP of Nono's *Non consumiamo Marx* was issued in 1969 by *I Dischi del Sole*, the label of the *Nuovo Canzoniere*. In a further experiment in the medium, Nono collaborated with singer-songwriter Mario Buffa Moncalvo on the LP *San Vittore 1969*. This documents and reflects on the riot at the prison of San Vittore in Milan, in April 1969. 1800 prisoners, many of them political detainees, were held in an ageing facility built for 850, with no access to political news, little access to family and under harsh restrictions including a ban on singing. Over a hundred prisoners were injured as the police and Carabinieri took back control. Moncalvo's songs are interspersed with sounds recalling the environment and protests of the prisoners. Nono's sound design attempts to capture the urgency and energy of the moment: 'Song, voices, texts, sounds in violent continuity signifying continuous invention, shock and alienation, of human passion in revolt tending necessarily to revolutionary consciousness.'[75] Keen to further links with movements in Latin-America, Nono proposed and curated an album of resistance songs and messages of solidarity – *Venezuela in questo momento guerriglia* – that was released in October 1969.[76] These LPs themselves represent Nono's engagement with a new audience through the technical means of the moment, but also his striving to provoke, to engender discussion, to play a part in the moving-on of public consciousness.

Direct action

'*Musica-Manifesto n. 1: Un volto, e del mare – Non consumiamo Marx*'

In May 1969, at the height of these internal Communist Party tensions, Nono presented a new work not at an international music festival but at the *Fête de l'humanité* of Châtillon-sous-Bagneux, a modest communist-run banlieue outside Paris.[77] He was invited as a representative of the PCI to this popular fair similar to the Italian *Feste de l'Unità*. *Musica-Manifesto n. 1: Un volto, e del mare – Non consumiamo Marx* was composed at the Milan studio in March and April. As we have seen, to call a work *Manifesto* had a very specific relevance for Nono at this moment. Its thirty-four minutes are divided into two equal parts; again, Nono confronts his listener with a dialectic, a clear binary balance. *Un volto, e del mare* sets lines from Pavese's *Mattino* for soprano, actress and tape; *Non consumiamo Marx* is for tape alone, using slogans from the Paris demonstrations of May 1968 and recordings of the Biennale protests in Venice. As Stenzl notes, in his extensive interview with Enzo Restagno in 1987 Nono glossed over what might be considered among the most important politically engaged works of the late twentieth century – *La fabbrica illuminata*, *A floresta*, *Contrappunto dialettico alla mente* and *Y entonces comprendio* – but spoke affectionately at length about *Musica-Manifesto n. 1*, which has remained one of his least-performed works from the same period. It is here, says Stenzl, that Nono comes closest to the essence of Pavese.[78]

Manifestos

Nono had already considered setting *Mattino* at least twice: in the project for Dartington, and in *Deola e Masino*.[79] The twenty slogans from walls in Paris are taken from a collection published soon after the riots of May 1968.[80] They had initially been considered for a project in the continuing *Un diario italiano* line: *L'immaginazione prende il potere*.[81] In selecting and organising the Paris slogans Nono finds rich parallels. Indeed, it may have been the first of his selection that initially caught his eye, reminded him of Pavese: reminded him of Pavese: 'The half-open window holds a face' (Pavese), 'Open the windows of your heart' (Paris).

Pavese's poem is an extended Petrarchan sonnet: an octave and two sestets, with the octave divided to give a pattern of 3–6–5–6 lines. Nono selects the same number of slogans and organizes them in a related pattern – 6–6–8 – that will be obscured in the final arrangement of recorded materials. He identifies the themes in Pavese's poem: 'woman, sea, nature, love'.[82] To this we might add 'morning', an image of hope through Pavese's poetry and a clear link with *Per Bastiana*. The Paris slogans are arranged such that they effectively form a new poem with its own sense of direction, in three stanzas of love, life and a call to action. There are connections on every level, including Nono's own pun: Pavese / pavés – poet and paving stones as the twin instruments of expression. 'Sous les pavés la plage!' ('under the cobblestones, the beach!') ran the call to protest. Both parts begin with the opening of a window and end with meditations on the transitory nature of the moment. Pavese concludes with a reflection on the brief opening of the window, the slogans with 'The barricade closes the street but opens the path'. This is Nono's Marxian manifesto; like love, revolution is not a state that can be attained and possessed, but a continuing action. It is an attempt to arrive at the essence of both Marx and Pavese, the truth of the present. The two texts become glosses on each other, two manifestations of the same human–social reality. They are the key to a more complex relationship between sounds, between the voices of individuals and groups. The slogans form an eloquent mediating layer – articulate, poetic peaks in a landscape of mass protest that link the imagery of poetry with the language of the street.

In terms of material, subject, sound and voice the two parts might initially appear to stand in stark opposition, but they constitute a more fundamental whole. Only later in the composing process did Nono decide to separate his materials in this way. He set out with three main groups of recordings. Nono worked extensively with Liliana Poli in the studio, recording new material: vocal sounds from isolated phonemes to whistling and long melismas bordering on bel canto. They experimented with use of the microphone; distance and movement play important roles, as they will in the later vocal works with live electronics. Kadigia Bove read *Mattino* in several versions, with different speeds and intonations, while Poli took isolated vowels and fragments. The Paris slogans were read by actress Edmonda Aldini. Recordings of the Biennale demonstration of June 1968, in which Nono was involved, include sounds at a range of focal distances, from speeches through megaphones and individual shouts to group singing and shouting and the noise of protesters clashing with police. A documentary voice announces the locations other than San Marco: Campo Santa Margherita, Porto, Piazzale Roma. Nono also explored further his existing sonic repertory: the bell of St Mark's, processed recordings of metal tubes and plates with different beaters and microphone placement, the work with Stefania Woytowitcz – made a decade previously – and choral textures. This earlier material constituted a unitary entity from the beginning.

The different materials were edited and mixed on to several preliminary tapes. Their descriptions give clues as to Nono's vision:vision: 'calm/amazement (Liliana – with microphone – for Pavese)' and 'tension – with Biennale'. Square and triangle waves were added to the whistling and vocal sounds; Nono and Zuccheri experimented with the speed and filtering of voices. Nono warns himself: 'Avoid canons in the text! Not canons but superimposition'.[83] As the structure emerges, rough plans and timings are replaced by timed graphical representations of four channels. The essential duality of the work is frequently marked by references to 'Credo' and 'Dies irae'. This seems to refer not to the two sections of the final work, but to the studio-based material using the Paris slogans ('Credo' – statements of belief) and to that based on documentary recordings of the Venice protests ('Dies irae' – here the wrath of the people):

> The slogans of the Paris May revolution of 1968 and the demonstrations against the Biennale in Venice 1968 are phonetic and acoustic elements of a new folklore. The barricade songs of our time, the choral speech and automatization are the marks of my class-war music.[84]

Nono's initial intention had been that the two parts should run simultaneously; before deciding on their sequential presentation, he and Zuccheri experimented with this idea such that the parts bear traces of each other in negative.[85] As indicated by the timings in Nono's sketches, both parts manifest a regrouping of musical forces at the one- and two-thirds points (Figure 9.2). As to their subsequent order, Nono seems to have decided that to end with the Pavese might present a false sense of resolution. The tape of *Un volto, e del mare* begins with whistling – an intimate sound, the opposite of shouting. A soprano vocalise joins the developing counterpoint of whistling, synthetic waves and voices. A slowly shifting harmony emerges from melody as the lines descend in pitch and move closer together, recalling Nono's interval-group construction of the early 1960s and anticipating the spiralling resonances of the late vocal works. Gentilucci describes 'intersecting lines that furrow the space [. . .] the poetic plot seems to traverse the temporal space with sonic signs that emerge from great mother-of-pearl pained backgrounds.'[86] Phonemes begin to appear from 5'30", becoming longer passages of *Mattino* spoken, declaimed or sung: 'another melody, humble and everyday' in Gentilucci's poetic interpretation.[87] Once the most significant words of the poem have become audible, it can begin in full. The interval-

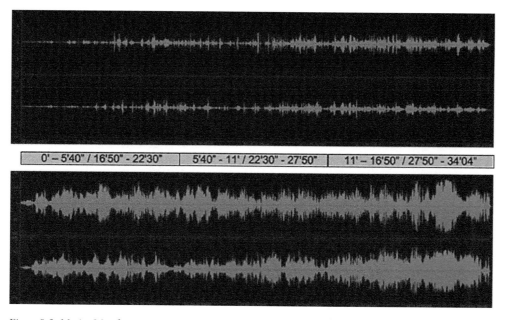

Figure 9.2 Musica-Manifesto n. 1: Sonograms of *Un volto, e del mare* and *Non consumiamo Marx*

based pitch structures of the first part are now replaced by shapes constantly rising like Shepard tones. From 11'00" these are assimilated into a new texture of bell resonances and choral sounds; by 14'00" any residual text has been absorbed into a rich evolving spectrum. This shifts down in register at the opening of *Non consumiamo Marx*, at 16'50": low bell and tube sounds, reverberated and filtered. The first slogan, 'ouvrez les fenêtres de votre coeur', is balanced by the last, 'la barricade ferme la rue mais ouvre la voie'. The slogans appear in relief; however processed, multiplied or otherwise kept in movement, they are always clearly comprehensible at their original speed and pitch. Behind them, shouting, speeches and singing compete for attention; slogans fuse with megaphone voices and we hear the acoustics of Venice. It is important that the slogans are spoken by a woman's voice; for Pavese, salvation and revolution have female form. Pavese's poem refers to 'the tender rhythm of the sea'. Here sound comes in continuous overlapping waves and the waves in three great tides; it reproduces the dynamics of the ocean or a battle. There are moments of near-stasis, of regrouping at 22'30" and 27'50". The mixing is a virtuoso display of orchestration; there is rhythm to the way in which the listener is drawn to the various emerging strands. Against this sea of noise, the return of slogans provides structure and articulation; 'ici, on spontane' returns like the hook in a pop song.

Nono seems to have had three versions of the piece in mind as he worked on it: the four-channel tape with soprano and reciter for live performances, a stereo version for LP and a mono reduction for radio. In one early plan, only the live version was to include *Non consumiamo Marx*, although this was changed. The different media present more than practical questions; they are quite different in terms of the listener's relationship with the work. In particular, the LP was developing its own status and practice as an aesthetic vehicle and object. In performance, Poli and Bove sat among the public for some minutes before responding to the recorded sound with further fragments from *Mattino* as they moved around the hall, returning to their places before the end of *Un volto, e del mare*. 'Arrive at a more lyrical, dramatic form', Bove marked on her copy of *Mattino*. A single recording exists of such a performance, from the Holland Festival in Amsterdam on 30 June 1970. Poli explained her role in detail to Riede in 1986 and to Riegler in 1999,[88] accounts that correspond with notes on the back of a copy of the poem.[89] Following the opening whistles (Nono's term), Bove begins three recitations of the poem – the first fragmented and interrupted, the second less so and the third continuous. Poli joins, singing isolated vowels and words from *Mattino*. The live component is present through the central ten minutes of *Un volto, e del mare*, framed by an introduction and coda of tape alone. Their directed movement around the hall, responding to present acoustic reality, anticipates Nono's final *Post-prae-ludium*. The live performers are absent from the stereo LP version sanctioned by the composer. Clearly, this presents a challenge for further performance; in this respect, the work is less well documented than *A floresta*, for example. Still more interesting is the question of its relevance, its impact. This is not an abstract aesthetic object; even more than Nono's other works it is intended to stimulate discussion and action, to change consciousness. If a fundamental property of the work is its nature as an *intervention*, how do we assess its value as an artwork from without its historical context?

Musica-manifesto n. 1 addresses Nono's own lecture *Historical presence in the music of today* of a decade earlier. There he shows how neither 'autonomous manifestations in which the spirit remains passive in adoration' nor speculative experimentalism 'in which musical experience will have to be satisfied with the future' offer a way forward. He deals with improvisation in similar terms: 'In ancient Chinese music, improvisation was based on written texts in which a parameter was fixed – that of pitch – while the others were left free for improvisation. The performance of such improvisation was always restricted to certain groups, within which those methods were transmitted from generation to generation.'[90] If this describes the role of improvisation in *Un volto, e del mare*, then his broader observation applies to its very nature:

Manifestos

giving life to a work of art is never obedience to a schematic principle (whether scientific or mathematical) but rather the synthesis – the dialectical product – of a principle and its historical realization, that is, the individuation in a historical moment determined absolutely, not before and not after.[91]

Nono would later reflect on the historical models behind the revolutionary structures of *Musica-manifesto n. 1*:

It all resolves into a form–technique–language in which it seems to me there lies the latent form of a Bach cantata. I say this not without a certain irritation, because only years later do I recognise in that way of working a sort of unconscious distortion of the facts of a historical culture that drew me in.[92]

In its use of documentary material and reference to Nono's own political life, *Musica-Manifesto n. 1* can be seen as his most explicit engagement with contemporary events. What is more important in terms of Nono's creative practice, however, is that it constitutes a different kind of aesthetic object, one that seeks to shoulder its social responsibility through new relationships with listening, performing and composing subjects: 'Requiescat in pace musician-aesthetes of restoration: music – non-music', he would say later.[93] The slogans are also imperatives to himself: encouragement and principles for his own practice. Perhaps a distinction can be drawn between *Contrappunto dialettico alla mente* and *Musica-manifesto n. 1*; perhaps they should not be heard the same way. Despite its more personally challenging text, the former retains a greater degree of aesthetic autonomy in its referential form and in its initial conception as a radiophonic work. There the challenge is to the elite who were its initial audience, and the clothing of an artwork was necessary precisely for it to insinuate itself. The audience of *Musica-manifesto n. 1* were the very folk whose voices we hear; the work connects the composer's experience with that of his listeners. Nono would choose to remain within the fold of the PCI, but his own *manifesto* embodies the essence of radical Italian thought. Despite his later finding traces of historical form, his process at the time was that of Tronti's 'organisation without organisation'[94] – the emergent structure of the demonstration and the structural foundation of workerism. There is no resolution, no dialectics; the two parts exist in a necessary antagonism, an inward and outward breath:

I wanted to superimpose and interweave two different kinds of falling in love, that is to say two conceptions, two materials, two techniques, two different uses of the instruments, of the voices, of feelings, so as to provoke a sort of ambiguity between title and text, and sound and song. This conflictual combinatorics of the music is almost like the conflict of feelings that I felt [. . .][95]

Returning from Paris, Nono went straight to the Milan studio to produce the music for a film by Mario Bernardi, *Pace e Guerra*. Bernardi's film explores the bronze 'war and peace' doors made by sculptor Giacomo Manzù for the rebuilt Sint Laurenskerk in Rotterdam. As well as the contrasting images of the doors, we see the city in flames, Manzù's sketches and him working the metal in his studio. Just called *Musiche per Manzù* in his notes, Nono's music is made entirely from his existing palette of materials. There is no text, although his initial sketches mention both *Bella ciao* and *Ave Maria* – perhaps the setting by Verdi that will become so resonant for Nono. Striking sounds from *Ricorda cosa ti hanno fatto in Auschwitz* accompany images of the destruction of Rotterdam; these sounds are gradually replaced by choral voices as peace becomes the subject. Finally, a single voice emerges from the resonance of the bell of St Marks. Through the longest sequence *Manzù lavora* (*Manzù at work*), clear vocal pitches merge with inharmonic resonance in a slow polyphony in constant movement, at the edge of what is consciously graspable – a pre-echo of Nono's later sound-world. Distinctions between event-time and formal time, vertical and horizontal, timbre and pitch are dissolved into a single space of unpredictable dimensions. Its transparency allows the ear to follow the slightest change. Nono's electronic music becomes performative: the sound of human action, of the artist and his materials. He invokes past suffering and faith in the future by embodying that sound in a single individual, the present moment of the sculptor's action.

'Y entonces comprendió'

A major new commission for the RAI was to be part of a retrospective concert of Nono's recent music, to be held in Rome in March 1970. The dedicatee of *Musica-manifesto n. 1* was Carlos Franqui, whom Nono had met at the Havana Congress in 1968. Increasingly visible in the international art world, Franqui was now in Rome. There, Nono discussed plans to use his poetry, based in his experiences of the revolution as a close comrade of Che.

For the new work, Nono planned to 'develop *Musica Manifesto 1 > Musica Manifesto 2*'.[96] 'Just voices', he decides.[97] The resources are listed in detail: tape, Carlos, RAI chorus 'as orchestra', Antonelli's chamber choir, three female singers, and three actresses. Next to a space for three male voices he writes 'NO'. His technical plan includes clarinettist William O. Smith – perhaps in some conducting role – as well as a twenty-four voice choir and two four-track tapes. An associated list, 'micro, modulators, filters, generators', suggests that he was considering live sound processing, now becoming widely used. In the event, the processing would be all on tape, but the sound world Nono creates anticipates that of his live electronic works. Simultaneous use of the tapes of *Un volto, e del mare* and *Non consumiamo Marx* figures in the earliest plans, though later revised. Other tape material was to include a letter from Che read by Fidel, recordings of the singers, actresses and choir, and recordings of 'life of Cuba' 'like Marx'; documentary sound is now an established part of Nono's sonic universe.

This would become *Y entonces comprendió*, written between October 1969 and January 1970. The successor to *Musica-manifesto* but constituted more like *A floresta*, it is the work that most directly reflects Nono's experiences in Latin America, dedicated 'To Ernesto "Che" Guevara and all the comrades of the Sierra Maestras of the world'. Nono's own introduction is clear:

> For:
> a) six female voices live (three sopranos and three actresses), used according to their personal technical and expressive characteristics (a collective choice from experiments in the studio), exchange sounds and words and characterise the five episodes of the composition, in groups or singly,
> b) chorus: episode V
> c) continuous tape: for its composition I used phonetic and semantic material from the six voices; in episode II I also used metallic and electronic material; in episode V there are three quotations from my composition *Non consumiamo Marx*.
> Texts chosen: a) from a cycle of poems by Carlos Franqui, who took part in the Cuban revolution, but to whose openly expressed views against the Cuban government since '71 I am radically opposed.
> b) from the last letter of Ernesto 'Che' Guevara to Fidel (1965)
> c) from the message to the Tricontinental ('67) of the same heroic guerrilla.[98] [. . .]
> The four initial episodes develop themes of: I. mythological joy, 'the horse as magic' (in Cuba the horse is the primary symbol of energy attributable to man); II. revolutionary necessity, 'the wall of the firing squad'; III. collective sadness for the disappearance of the

Manifestos

legendary Camilo Cienfuegos in a plane during a storm, 'Camilo in the air' 'Camilo in the water'; IV. the nocturnal magic of nature, 'sound in the night'; they are resolved in episode V 'the struggle', where we hear the message from Che to the Tricontinental (chorus) simultaneously with phrases from the last letter from Che to Fidel (on tape, various superimpositions of the voice of Fidel himself), together with three quotations from *Non consumiamo Marx* (again on tape: sounds of the street – demonstrations).[99]

The five episodes are titled *Caballo* (divided into four 'legs') (0'–6'35" on the Deutsche Grammophon recording), *Muro* (6'35–12'03"), *Camilo* (12'05"–21'32"), *Noche* (21'32"–26'17v), and *La lucha* (26'17"–32'03").

Franqui supplied about twenty texts, some reflecting on Cuba and its people, others on characters and events from the revolution. Nono recorded him speaking them, experimenting with his voice in the studio. Franqui proposed a structure; the last section is presciently headed 'caminantes' ('traveller') – to become a vital notion in Nono's last years. Nono revised this, adding another layer of documentary material from Che's letters to his children and to Fidel. He assembled a company of an appropriate internationalism and range of voices. Together with Liliana Poli there were Gabriela Ravazzi – a lighter voice – and the American Mary Lindsay. Elena Vicini and Somali Kadigia Bove were now joined by Cuban actress Miriam Accevedo. Having chosen the five episodes that would eventually articulate the work, Nono returned to the studio with his international group of six soloists. For each episode he determined the combination of voices that would work with the texts. Despite his presence in all the plans, William O. Smith is absent from the recordings; this was to be an entirely vocal work. The group improvised following Nono's directions: detailed, emotionally graphical descriptions of the ways he wanted to explore the voice. The sonic and gestural palette has evolved since *A floresta*; 'troppo living', writes Nono of one improvisation.

Nono's descriptions and instructions continue into his analysis of the recordings. They trace his own exploration of the voices he was hearing: 'molten, ecstatic, astonished, joyful, violent, sweet, secure, magic, mysterious' is but one sequence.[100] These recordings are extraordinary documents; some are complete guided improvisations of sensual vocal chamber music. At the same time, Nono's notes make it clear that they are rooted in his personal response to the texts, his vision of Cuba as reflected in them. In this sense these recordings are composed artefacts, however distributed or unfinished. Following the practice of *A floresta*, this process produced two kinds of material: recordings from which to construct the tapes, and experimentally generated sounds and gestures to be incorporated into the live performance.

The tape would provide the stable architecture of the work. Nono worked from nineteen new spools in addition to his existing repertoire. The *Tempophon* was a new addition to the studio's armoury: a device for varying tape speed without changing pitch, affording the composer a degree of independent control of these parameters, albeit at some cost to sonic fidelity.[101] Nono experiments with transforming the female voices into a full range of registral groups. He also works with a sound spatialisation device for the first time.[102] The process of repeated listening, of the critical reassessment and reimagining of recorded sound, is becoming as central to his compositional practice as text analysis or the generation of notation-based material. As with those activities, he accumulates gloss upon gloss of description, analysis and reflection, marking material to be used live. He frequently reconsiders his own technique: 'various sonic planes, with different texts, with different techniques, mobile and not'.[103] The mobility of sound is a constant concern. He works episode by episode, combining four-track submixes into a complex sound theatre. Complexity is itself a constitutive parameter: 'Black is Carlos' preferred colour/not a symbol of mourning/but BLACK against WHITE/FULL against EMPTY'.[104]

Manifestos

After a brief and dramatic introduction, *Caballo* sets out the emotional space of the work. Liliana Poli's voice gradually proliferates to enter into dialogue with itself, Kadigia Bove, and then the others. Simultaneities become polyphonies, then recede to become a single element in the evolving sonic landscape. In the final 'leg', this process slows to a near-homophonic, harmonic texture. *Muro* begins and ends with the sound of metal tubes, a reference sound for Nono from *La fabbrica iluminata* until the works of the early 1970s. Breath-like, it occupies a space between human and artificial, between pitch and noise. Bells and modulated choir bring an almost programmatic, requiem tone to 'muro de piedra' ('wall of stone'), the place of the firing squad. Suddenly the drama has time and place. This is a lyrical, poignant world by comparison with Nono's Auschwitz. Shouted instructions, wordless laments and measured recitation develop over low mechanical noise. *Camilo* is a more processed, rapidly edited sound world; a disorientating mosaic of text fragments. Perspective changes rapidly against a background of processed choir, always distant but moving in and out of focus. *Noche* is its negative, an exercise in close listening and focus. There are references to 'Landino' in Nono's notes for this section, perhaps a response to the early music purity of the monody by Ravazzi on which it is based. *La lucha* explodes with the sound of demonstrations, street noise and protest song. There are three waves of this overwhelming density, through which emerge isolated voices and fragments of Castro reading from Che's letters, terminating in a single clear statement: 'hasta la victoria siempre'. They contrast with the formal blocks and layers of the three *corales*, choral interjections that appear between the first and second waves, together with the third, and then after the tape has subsided, returning attention to the choir and soloists, to the present.

The performance instructions for each soloist are in a set of part-books, each a combination of text and aide-mémoire largely notated by the individual performer. There are sporadic timelines against which the text fragments are written: cues, some melodic shapes, dynamics, use of the microphone, vocal instructions ('whispering, guttural') and accents, but the most common indication is 'take the sound of the tape'. *Noche* is the most sustained example. A solo recording by Gabriela Ravazzi is the basis of the tape, an improvisation of swooping high melismas that return like refrains, balanced by low, warmer melodic phrases closer to the microphone and punctuated by explorations of single consonants – words taken from Franqui's poem *violino notte*. On the finished tape this becomes an expanding, mobile polyphony; in performance Ravazzi then anticipates, echoes and further extends her own voice live before being joined by Mary Lindsey.[105] Lindsey's annotations for this passage, in Italian and English, presumably represent Nono's directions (Figure 9.3).

For the choir there are three passages, *Corale I–III*. In the part books these would appear to be distributed through the work: I after *Caballo*, II during *Muro* and III during *La lucha*. In the performances and recording, however, all three are heard during the final episode, consolidating the difference in kind between that and the first four. The *corales* are constructed quite differently from the rest of the work. Having determined their texts – all passages from Che's *Tricontinental* testament – and overall durations, Nono constructs a different number series for each of the four voices. These are distributed by permutation to individual phonemes such that with rests allocated by a similar process each voice adds up to the same length. The pitch range for each voice covers a major seventh, divided into three bands of a minor third, each of which is further divided into three. The limits of the overall range, given in staff notation, can vary between entries. This allows Nono control over the range and density of the texture. Each sound is then characterised by pitch-band and the distribution of voices across sub-bands, dynamics and arrows representing pitch change. Phonemes may change together, or by individual voice, staggered across the duration. The *corales* are notated on squared paper, like *Per Bastiana*, in

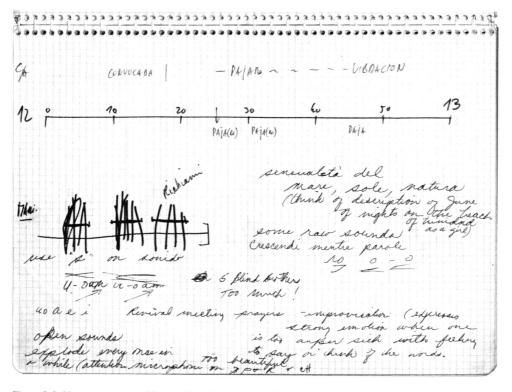

Figure 9.3 Y entonces comprendió: page from *Noche* in part book of Mary Lindsey. (ALN 35.09.02/15. © The heirs of Luigi Nono. Reproduced by kind permission.)

terms of seconds and pitch-band. They have a formal technical quality that establishes a dialectic with the more overtly expressive work of the soloists and tape, an aesthetic distance that creates depth of perceptual field. The sonic image of the *corales* comes from electronic music, but its hidden inner structure derives from Nono's earlier thought and practice, as if to preserve their fundamental otherness to the studio-derived body of the work.

Dramatically, *Y entonces comprendió* is clearer than *A floresta*. There is a locus and subject: Cuba and its people in the present. The five scenes have a natural trajectory, from the culture of Cuba to the struggle for freedom, and there is a central character, Che. The antagonistics of *A floresta* or *Musica-manifesto n. 1* are absent; the faith in the Cuban people and their hero is absolute. This brings about a situation in which expressive, explicit meaning and absolute music are in balance. The model is, once again, Bach.[106] *Y entonces comprendió* is a passion for Che, a work to teach, touch and develop the faith of those who would hear, and to enter under the conscious barriers of those who would not. The emphasis on the human voice – of individuals, groups, the choir of the *corales* and the *turba* of the scenes from *Non consumiamo Marx* – the balance between personal reflective texts and scriptural authority and the formal architecture of the whole all reflect a Bachian model. Nono's highly formalised technical structures for the choruses contrast with the intimacy of the solo vocal material. In an interview shortly after completing this work, he explained his continuing fascination with the voice:

> Of all the instruments we have, for me the voice is the most free, not tied to historically determined scales. If you analyze other cultures, other civilizations and the

different ways of using the voice, not from a Eurocentric standpoint but with a Marxist approach, you realize that the voice has always had the greatest expressive potential, from technical and linguistic points of view. If I often use it processed electronically, especially in recent works, I do so because that is where I find the greatest expressive freedom.[107]

Sonically, *Y entonces comprendió* is a study in the expressive power of the female voice. From the soprano ensemble of *Ha venido*, the experiments of *La fabbrica illuminata*, the five women of *Un diario italiano* and the four who should play Deola to the works of the 1980s, this is as constant a theme in Nono as the beloved–saviour–comrade–muse–lover in Pavese, a figure who merges with nature on one margin (caballo, aria, agua, noche) and with liberty on the other. The two trios have other resonances: the *concerto delle donne* of sixteenth century Ferrara – the performers of Luzzaschi's music – or the three Marys at Christ's tomb. This fascination will be explored further in the late works, where the microphone becomes a microscope and dynamics and register are expanded to their limits. It is also a political concern; voice is the embodiment of identity and consciousness.

With hindsight we can see naivety in Nono's use of Che. But there is also the balance of innocence and complex wisdom that is the persona of Che himself, a persona cultivated by the man before its iconographical commodification, and not coincidentally Christ-like in a catholic-dominated culture. Furthermore, we must recall Nono's constant searching for characters, texts, sound and drama in everything with which he came into contact. His creative world is a musical–dramatic space in which every experience is tested for potential. Che – as filtered through friends in Cuba, the Havana Congress at which Che was culturally beatified and the worldwide debate following his assassination – takes on multiple roles: dramatic subject, rhetorician and theorist, and paradigm of personal struggle. The use of Che's words was of particular importance to Nono – a paradigmatic example of his concern with the relationships of sound, meaning and reference:

> I don't use them as a quotation, it is a simultaneity, a superimposition of eight voices [. . .] you don't listen word by word any more than in a conversation, a meeting, a demonstration, but through contemporary technological means they become pregnant in another way, in another acoustic, where our ear no longer listens only in a naturalistic way.[108]

The institutional performance of protest: 'Voci destroying muros, Ein Gespenst geht um in der Welt'

Cultures of listening, especially in respect of politically engaged art, played an important part in the reception of two major works of 1970–1. *Voci destroying muros* was commissioned for the Holland Festival and performed at the Concertgebouw in Amsterdam on 25 June 1970, the final work in the first of two concerts surveying Nono's work of the previous decade. It requires large forces: two sopranos and two actresses, chorus of sixteen female voices, orchestra of low strings and percussion with quadruple flutes, clarinets, trumpets and horns, and tape. Subsequently withdrawn by Nono, some its material would become part of *Ein Gespenst geht um in der Welt* the following year, which would in turn feed into *Al gran sole carico d'amore* of 1974, the culmination of a long thread of musical–theatrical development.

Manifestos

As its trilingual title suggests, the agenda of *Voci destroying muros* (*Voices destroying walls*) is thoroughly internationalist. A number of possible texts were proposed by Giovanni Pirelli, editor of the letters set in *Il canto sospeso*, who since then had worked to give voice to both Italian workers and post-colonial struggles.[109] Some early Vietnamese selections were then abandoned; perhaps such clear political association would have unbalanced the work. Nono eventually brought together texts from the German communist martyr Rosa Luxemburg, Dutch resistance members Hannie Schaft and Riek Snel, Haydée Santamaria and Celia Sanchez on their experiences at the beginning of the Cuban revolution (the attack on the Moncada barracks, 26 July 1953), and contemporary Italian industrial workers. He had considered the texts from Vietnam for the final section, but preferred to conclude the work in his own here and now. The letter of Riek Snel is particularly poignant: it was provided by the festival's music director, Jo Elsendoorn, her husband. The couple had been interned in a concentration camp; Elsendoorn had escaped but Snel died in Germany.[110] The Italian texts come from a piece of co-research: a selection of statements by women factory workers in Milan in 1965–6 on their dehumanising working conditions and powerlessness as employees.[111]

The architecture of *Voci* is straightforward; the four episodes are arranged chronologically – 1919, 1943, 1953 and 1969, as Nono notes – and are separated by three *ritornelli*. Identifying the everyday struggle of ordinary working people against exploitation with the more dramatic exploits of historic heroes is an important theme. The voices are all those of women. The soloists do not narrate, but speak in the first person. The wall is now explicitly the central trope, whether that of the firing squad, the prison, the barrier to be torn down or perhaps the 'fourth wall' – that between artist and audience. In early plans, Nono imagined the chorus standing behind 'like a wall'.

For musical material, Nono returned to known sources – *L'Internationale, The East is Red, Bandiera rossa* – as well as the Cuban *Marcha del 26 de Julio* (marking the anniversary of the Moncada assault) and the rhythms of protest chants from around the world ('Ho Ho Ho Chi Minh', 'Che Che Guevara'). *L'Internationale* runs as a *fil rouge* through the entire work. Nono divides the melody into eight phrases from which he selects four sequences – phrases 1 and 2, 4 and 6, 7, 8 – of 17, 16, 13 and 14 notes, noting the rhythmic distribution and aggregate pitch set of each.[112] These serve as the main material for the four episodes: one for each. In each episode, new strands are woven from these melodic fragments by processes of permutation and recombination; each of these is then subject to a different degree of augmentation and transposition. Intervals of transposition are derived from the source material. *L'Internationale* becomes a cantus firmus. The resultant monodies are shared between soloists and instruments, with the chorus interjecting fragments of the original – a reminder of the common horizon. The shifts in time, rhythm and pitch of a shared origin create the focus-changing effects of Nono's tape music. Each episode thus has a characteristic melodic, harmonic and rhythmic palette. The articulation of the inner pitch space is in constant movement between chromatic cluster and near-diatonic harmonic field. The choral polyphonies of the *ritornelli* are made of long continuous lines produced the same way but now untransposed. Tightly packed to produce subtle changes of density, they outline a shifting window on a diatonic field.

The choral ritornelli move largely at a uniform rate; the momentum is that of an isorhythmic motet. Within the dramatic episodes there is greater rhythmic differentiation, especially with the figural use of *Ho Chi Minh* in the second, *26 de Julio* in the third and *Bandiera rossa* in the last. The sound of familiar protest rhythms presents the most direct challenge to the listener. Do they represent explicit support for these figures? Or do they embody the spirit of the people who had been chanting their names as the sound of a common defiance, a common desire for change? Balestrini's contemporary fictionalised documentary account of worker unrest in the

Manifestos

Italian 'hot autumn' of 1969 suggests the latter – that few had much idea of the significance of such names.[113] This challenge is not for music analysis to resolve – the question confronts the listener directly: how should they respond to popular frustration, anger, vision, optimism?

There are important technical innovations in Nono's work for *Voci destroying muros*, informed by his extensive work in the studio over recent years. The first four notes of *L'Internationale* are announced by the choral sopranos at the opening, stretched to an impossible slowness and sustained against each other like studio reverberation. A rhythmic looseness is achieved by mixing strict metrical notation with the proportional placing of notes. Nono's manipulation of source material has its roots in earlier procedures, but now he keeps track of the new material thus generated by a system of letters and numbers that allows a more coherent process. Fragments are concatenated, annotated for orchestration and development, on strips cut from manuscript paper, a process recalling the copying and editing of segments of tape. Such a methodical use of fragments will become a vital part of his practice from the end of the new decade. His ideas for the use of the Concertgebouw – the careful disposition of performers and loudspeakers – play a part in his planning of the work at an early stage. The site-specific spatial sketches anticipate those for the late orchestral works.

The concert was to be televised. *Voci destroying muros* concluded the first of two concerts presenting a comprehensive retrospective of Nono's work: *Ha venido*, *Canciones a Guiomar*, *Per Bastiana* and *La terra e la compagna*, performed by the Dutch Radio Philharmonic Orchestra and Choir under Ladislav Kupkovic with a team of six soloists including Poli, Acevedo and Vicini from Nono's regular ensemble. Nono worked on the production with director Krijn ter Braak. The sixteen members of the chorus stood on small stages around the sides of the hall, surrounding the audience; the soloists were on another stage at the centre. As the music on stage ended, the two actresses ran though the hall to fling open the doors – breaking down the wall of the concert hall, as Adlington observes.[114] Their calls to revolution should have been taken up by speech from loudspeakers in the foyers of the Concertgebouw where the composer was handing out pamphlets to the departing audience. They, by all accounts, were somewhat confused. The recording of a speech written by German–Dutch composer and theorist Konrad Boehmer was intended to seed heated discussion; this strategy failed both technologically and aesthetically. The second concert concluded with *Non consumiamo Marx*, now also with a spoken text condemning the US incursion into Cambodia; Nono also felt the need to add an insert to the programme explaining that the performance of *Voci* had not been as intended.[115]

Following *Voci* there was 'some polite brief applause mingled with a few half-hearted boos', reported *The Scotsman*. Adlington provides a comprehensive litany of negative critical response; interestingly, critics seem to assume that Nono was addressing a working class entirely absent from the Concertgebouw.[116] It does not seem to have occurred to them that they, the enlightened bourgeoisie or perhaps even a newly classless society, might benefit from any increased awareness. More likely, the ideological criticisms conceal verdicts of taste; the critics did not find *Voci* exciting. Cadieu's reference to early polyphony echoes an interview with Nono prior to the performance, in which he cited Josquin's *La Déploration de Johannes Ockeghem* as a model, an exquisite lament.[117] Anticipating a political thrill, the audience was faced with stark historical and present reality. The *Internationale* does not figure as a rousing call to arms so much as a Gregorian tenor or Lutheran chorale subject.

The wider problem seems to have been one of expectation, of the context-sensitivity of engaged music. As Adlington points out, the recent story of Dutch communism was very different from that of the PCI.[118] The Dutch Communist Party had become something of a historical curiosity, while the radical and violence-provoking 'Provos' of the 1960s were an unsettling episode from which the Netherlands had barely recovered. The Holland Festival had

Manifestos

a reputation for challenging and courageous new work; the audience were presumably there for the thrill of being shocked and to enjoy their enlightened status, not have it questioned. Only weeks before, the Dutch cultural establishment and the Concertgebouw in particular had been publicly challenged by the new generation of musicians, the *Notenkrakers*.[119] There had been a strong move to have Maderna appointed as Bernard Haitink's assistant with specific responsibility for contemporary music, a proposal met with equal intransigence from the establishment. In November 1969, the group had interrupted a concert by the Concertgebouw Orchestra and in March 1970 Frans Brüggen had publicly denounced their playing of Mozart as 'a lie, from A to Z'. Alternative performance styles, venues and infrastructure were already emerging, with specialist ensembles for new, early and improvised music. Politics was at the heart of the young composers' work. In 1968 they had organised a 'politiek-demonstratief experimenteel concert'. Members of the Notenkrakers had jointly composed an opera *Reconstructie* for the previous Holland Festival, dealing with the death of Che Guevara. Louis Andriessen's *Volkslied*, premiered just months later, would be based on *L'Internationale*. In short, Holland was by no means suffering from the same cultural ossification as Italy, and an Amsterdam new music audience had considerable experience of politically charged work. The Dutch press, divided between those who took against Nono's musical language and those underwhelmed by the less than radically charged event, were united in regarding the premiere as unsuccessful.

The technical problems reported by critics – noisy cameramen and faulty loudspeakers – must have added to a sense of artificiality. The cameras were intended to move around the performance, to create an atmosphere of live political event for both Concertgebouw and TV audiences. Instead, their difficulties and intrusiveness seem to have sapped the moment of all spontaneity. Dutch radio had to broadcast a recording of the general rehearsal rather than the concert. Critic Klaus Wagner's analysis was perceptive: in the attempt to combine 'pure' art and political agitation, both aspects appeared synthetic.[120] Despite the technological interventions of the production, this was Nono's first work for nearly a decade with no electronic component. While this may have been intended to emphasise the immediacy, the humanity of *Voci*, we also perhaps hear the absence of an element of Nono's sonic palette. For Martine Cadieu the music was reminiscent of Nono's intention to write a liturgical drama: 'bare, sober, pure, radiating tenderness'; it indeed recalled Josquin or Ockeghem.[121] William Mann of *The Times* was at both concerts of Nono's music. '*Y entonces comprendió* and *Per Bastiana* contain the most convincing, musicianly electronic music I can remember hearing: intricate, dramatically self-assured, forward-looking, but most importantly packed with real musical ideas that you are interested in hearing about.'[122] Of the new work he said: 'Even in this incomplete first performance the vitality of the music was strong, the invention characteristic but perfectly fresh. A certain shock-effect came across, though much less than the composer intended [. . .]'.

Nono's distributing pamphlets after the concert must likewise have been confusing; this somewhat dour music had not had the spirit of a 'happening'. The event was, after all, a retrospective presentation of his recent work, a way of historicising the present. The weight of this very reputation and record must also have become clear at the Pro Musica Nova festival of politically engaged music in Bremen the same month. *Musica-manifesto n. 1* appeared with works such as Kagel's *Klangwehr* for shouting military band. A production of *Intolleranza* at Nuremberg in May raised a similar paradox. Entitled *Intolleranza 70*, its political references now incorporated Vietnam, but the production related explicitly to German theatre of the 1920s. Praise for the production was universal. The radio reported a perfunctory demonstration, but then the audience enjoyed the opera 'in their dinner jackets and evening dresses [. . .] and went out to eat afterwards as if they'd just seen *Der Vogelhändler* [an operetta]. [. . .] It was artistic and not political reasons that brought Luigi Nono's *Intolleranza 70* to Nuremburg.'[123] From a

Manifestos

southern European perspective, Nono seems to have felt that political consciousness was approaching the crest of a wave, a specific historical moment when explicit communication was appropriate and necessary. Instead, the consciousness of a cultured Dutch audience was in a different phase. We might even see this as a victory for those conservative forces in the West that since the 1950s had sought to use the promotion of avant-garde art as a political tool. Having initially been presented as a mark of individual 'freedom', the political in art was becoming fully aestheticised, distanced, individualised, even commodified – a cultural badge with a frisson of danger, but otherwise made safe. To avoid being historicised, contextualised and disarmed, Nono would have to find another way for his music to do its work.

In the meantime, an opportunity to rethink the *Voci* project came with a new work for West German Radio (WDR) – with the exception of stage music, his first German premiere since the 1950s. This wave of performances in Germany was important to Nono; a recent review of the *La fabbrica illuminata* LP had described him as 'a half-forgotten avant-gardist who should be rediscovered'.[124] Nono returned to the compositional starting point of *Voci destroying muros*, but with a revised brief, a different aesthetic perspective and a more developed compositional approach. *Ein Gespenst geht um in der Welt* is for soprano, choir and orchestra – no actors, slogans, recorded speeches or demonstrations, although the chorus still surrounds the audience. Despite the directness of its message, the new work is a more conventional aesthetic object; it affords a more straightforward relationship with the listener. The title is a universalisation of the opening of Marx and Engel's *Manifesto*. The musical sources are those of the preceding work: *L'Internationale*, *Bandiera rossa*, *Marcha del 26 de Julio* and *The East is Red*. Now, however, they also supply most of the texts; the only piece of narrative remaining is that of Santamaria and Sanchez describing the battle for Moncada. The politics are now implicit in the material; there is no hectoring, no explicit reference to the here and now. The music has to carry more of the consciousness-raising argument.

This commission was itself representative of the new place of political art within institutional culture; whatever its 'content' and despite the frisson of resistance, such work was made safe by its very inclusion. In Germany, as in Italy, frustration at the lack of deep change following the events of 1968 was leading to a more dangerous decade. Otto Tomek, Nono's producer at the WDR since 1954, recalled the mood:

> The first performance took place in the aftermath of the movements of '68. The WDR was then in the politically sensitive situation of being seen in some circles as a left wing, red radio station, and therefore had to behave carefully. And now Nono was saying explicitly that he understood music as a function of historical class war. [. . .] So we had to get special approval from the general director Klaus von Bismarck to print Nono's introduction in the programme booklet.[125]

Even in the new Germany, a reference to class war had to be approved by a descendant of the founding *Reichskanzler*. *Ein Gespenst geht um in der Welt* is in four parts, the second of which is framed by two ritornelli:

A   *Bandiera rossa* (L'Internationale, Bandiera rossa) – soprano, choir, orchestra
A' *Per i compagni morti* (L'Internationale) – choir SAT
B   *26 de Julio* (Marcha del 26 de Julio, L'Internationale) – soprano, choir, orchestra
B' *Per i compagni morti* (L'Internationale) – choir AT, 4 clarinets
C   *L'oriente è rosso* – (The East is Red, L'Internationale) soprano, choir, orchestra
D   *Riflessioni* – choir, orchestra

Manifestos

Source material is given in parentheses. Texts are those of the source songs except for *26 de Julio*, the dramatic core, which uses the words of Sanchez and Santamaria describing the attack on Moncada. *Riflessioni* is a textless development of the preceding material.

Early work focused on *L'Internationale* and *Bandiera rossa*, with a sound world divided between 'spectre' and 'reality'. In one sketch, arrows connect 'reality' to 26 July – events in Cuba. The ritornello structure of *Voci destroying muros* persists, now as choral movements marked in his notes 'come sta' ('as it is'). In fact, these are the least mediated or fragmented passages of polyphony. Their number is reduced to two as the new architecture emerges. The final *Riflessioni* adds an additional frame to the main body of the work, a vital layer of architecture and aesthetic distancing. Whereas *Voci destroying muros* had ended by inviting the listener to join the struggle, here politics emerges from and returns to music. In his role as musician, Nono must have concluded that this was a more effective way of asserting the equivalence of musical and political modes of action.

The technical resources of *Voci destroying muros* are developed more fully and coherently as Nono explores the implications of his studio work for his score-based practice. The starting points are those of the tape works: time, register and sources, and the interplay of 'fixed' and 'mobile' sounds. He returns to manuscript paper to begin deriving the threads for this fabric from the four songs. For the listener, the degree of recognisability of this material is perhaps the most significant parameter – not merely quotation or reference but a continuously variable property in terms of time, pitch, colour and complexity; the emergent product of a range of techniques. Nono takes great care over the apprehensibility of known musical material. As in his use of text, recognisable features become nodes in intersecting networks of image, significance and reference.

Individual phrases of the source songs are atomised in terms of durations, intervals and aggregate pitch-set. Each element generates a unique set: the first line of *L'Internationale* a full major scale, the third and fourth a dominant scale and the fifth adds chromatic elements; *The East is Red* is pentatonic. For each, Nono allocates a unique set of possible transpositions from a super-set of seconds, fourth, sevenths and ninths. In a first stage of generation, a group of new strands is produced by permuting the durations differently in each of several voices, augmenting them by different factors (1–7 – i.e. producing lines of different lengths) and beginning some with a rest to avoid regular alignment. Pitches are permutations of the aggregate pitch-set and selected voices are transposed by the allocated intervals. To navigate and articulate pitch and duration spaces, Nono returns to graphical–spatial models, to symmetrical and cyclic patterns of arrows. Together with the original songs, this provides the main corpus of material with which he constructs layers, blocks, sound complexes or passages of sustained, homogeneous polyphony. The transposed aggregate pitch-sets allow the resultant harmonic field to move between varying degrees of diatonicism and the full chromatic, often articulated by register. At some moments this produces a local bitonality, elsewhere a heterophony of variable density or layers of tight motivic interweaving.

These processes generate long, seamless monodies. Movement within such lines is achieved by fragmentation – cross-cutting between different lines, their transpositions, or the original itself – and by a technique Nono describes as interpolation. The initial process tends to produce a preponderance of long durations, often several bars. To introduce areas of more intense rhythmic activity, he applies a recursive, fractal principle: durations may be subdivided into shorter values by applying the same proportions internally, and additional patterns of semiquavers are added to the shortest values. At these moments, pitches are repeated either singly or in a short sequence from the generating material. The textures thus generated fall into two main types: heterophonic and polyphonic. In the latter, different strands produced from the same raw material are woven together, usually within the same register and pitch-field, to produce a layer that might be presented alone – as in the choral ritornelli – as part of a more complex mosaic, or in a clear relationship with its complement. The central section of *The East is Red* (bars 187–210) is a clear instance of the latter; four flutes and four clarinets play mirror images of each other, at a semitone distance. In heterophonic passages, parts are notated proportionally in all but the central voice, as in *Voci destroying muros*. The line may thus be blurred in pitch by a constant tendency to chromatic accretion or dissolution, forming layers usually bounded by a maximum of a fourth. Steps sometimes come from the prevailing pitch set, in which case the heterophony tends to new figuration. Notes suggest that the stretching and compressing in time may be an idea inspired by the recently acquired Tempophon at the Milan studio.

Figure 9.4 shows an example of this detailed working. The first two solo soprano notes come from the end of the monody derived from a transposition of the fourth phrase of *L'Internationale* – reversed from his initial sketch, presumably to achieve a satisfactory interval contour (Figure 9.4b). Those in bars 213–16 are the opening of the monody from the fifth phrase (Figure 9.4a), expanding about the centre of the aggregate scale in the sequence 3 6 2 7 8 (Figure 9.4c) (Nono's version of *L'Internationale* is in B♭). The fifth note, D, forms a pivot with bars 217–18, a direct quotation of bars 5–8 of *The East is Red*. The most salient notes of bars 217–18 are the central elements of the aggregate scale: G–A. The initial note of each phrase is sustained in the choral sopranos with an expanding and contracting movement through a symmetrical pattern of major and minor second above and below the central pitch. Three phrases are also shadowed a fourth by the altos a fourth below. There is a shift of perspective in bar 217 as the soprano figure now seems to elaborate a central pitch sustained in the chorus.

This technical palette affords Nono a wider range of choice than in the previous work. There are echoes of earlier dramatic works at the opening, with its drums and *col legno* strings, extreme dynamics and the clear choral statement of the text, with no hint of the underlying material. The first full episode follows, in which phrases from *L'Internationale* and *Bandiera rossa* constantly emerge and submerge within a sea of rhythmic development and registrally defined bands of heterophony. The stark, tightly wound polyphony of the first ritornello *Per i compagni morti* (*For the dead comrades*), with only the text of a solo tenor from the chorus rising beyond

a – *L'Internationale*: bars 33–40

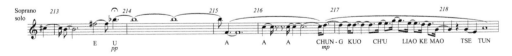

b – *Ein Gespenst geht um in der Welt*: bars 212–218

c – aggregate scale

Figure 9.4 *Ein Gespenst geht um in der Welt*

the *piano* sopranos and altos, seems to exist on another plane. The two ritornelli present the underlying polyphony in its barest form: four-part motets in which the slowest, most regular voice acts as a cantus firmus. Figural rhythm comes only from the choral solo tenor, an everyman singing echoes of *L'Internationale* from the wings. The Moncada episode from *Voci destroying muros* is developed as the dramatic centre; wind and string choirs with *26th of July* material accompany narrative texts set to speech rhythms. The text concludes: 'and in this moment you realize what the fight is', followed by sixteen bars of homogeneous polyphony for the full orchestra *ffff* – an unyielding wall of sound, a mirror built of the *26 de Julio* material, within which two interlocking pentatonic pitch fields exchange colour at the mid-point. From its echo emerges the second ritornello, for tenor with altos doubled by clarinets. Nono's judicious arrangement of fragments is clear: the last high, loud tenor phrase is the opening of both the *Internazionale* refrain and of Verdi's *Va, pensiero*, the anthem of Italian liberation.

The East is Red is primarily vocal – only high woodwind and drums participate in the central polyphony described above. To either side, heterophonic choral lines accumulate to form a different kind of polyphony, that of the multitude. The solo soprano weaves new lines across the texture throughout this movement, an expressive, individual counterpoint to its more organised mass voices. *Riflessioni* functions as a meta-work; it comments on the previous material and events. There is no text and the soloist is silent. Its mosaic of sound complexes is reminiscent of Nono's construction of the early 1960s; heterophonic layers and blocks of polyphony pass rapidly between extreme states. It is richer in detail than the main body of the work and the derivation of material less transparent. The last waves of accelerando and crescendo coalesce into a sustained low chromatic band of F♯–B complemented by a high band of C–F, the final diminuendo of which dissolves into *ppp* drum rolls echoing the opening – not so much a fading as a reminder of their constant presence. In terms of Nono's sonic iconography, perhaps we hear the need for constant vigilance.

In *Ein Gespenst geht um in der Welt* we can see technical innovations fundamental to Nono's late style. In reflecting on *Voci destroying muros* he has fully engaged with and reconceived his earlier compositional universe, rearticulating that space and introducing new models following his work in the studio. Rather than the patchwork of individual panels of a decade earlier, these fragments now derive from a few long passages of music. Their slow, aperiodic temporal patterns incorporate local traces of rhythm and their pitch space is articulated primarily in seconds and fourths, looking forward to Nono's later harmonic universe. While the new work is doubtless more finished, more satisfactory than its predecessor, in some respects it is also less radical. It is dramatically more coherent, musically richer and more detailed, but in the process is more easily assimilated as a conventional concert work, as narrative and document rather than a challenge to consciousness. Perhaps the two should be heard together – regarded as complementary responses to the challenge of engaged art at a crucial moment.

Solidarity in a new culture

Music and reality

An awareness of this new cultural problem, of the changed circumstances within which his music would be understood, emerges from correspondence concerning its performance. Nono continued to resist approaches from Labroca at the Biennale – who, despite its wider restructuring, would remain music director until 1973 – and he reacted angrily to suggestions that his music might be played in junta-ruled Greece. In a letter to Roman Vlad, he explained in detail his refusal to have *Intolleranza* performed at the Maggio Musicale festival of 1972, dedicated to 'the resistance and post-war music'. Such initiatives he dismisses as 'cultural–political opportunism'. Resistance is 'a precise destructive–constructive action against Nazism, against anything-goes, against imperialism, for a socialist future', a struggle informed by Marx and Gramsci; officially sanctioned 'enlightened liberalism', motivated by the cold war, is an insidious enemy.[126] Still, in 1977, Nono and Pestalozza would have nothing to do with an otherwise wide-ranging publication on 'Music and Politics' produced by the Biennale.[127]

At the end of the decade there would be much discussion of Nono's 'abandoning' of the political orientation of his music, especially at the time of the string quartet *Fragmente* in 1980. Nothing could be further from the case. What we see at the beginning of the 1970s is an intense searching for new ways to make music relevant, to contribute to the raising of consciousness which is the only means by which to move towards social change. This is a thoroughly historical materialist approach; as circumstances change, so must one's response. The contextualising and historicising of the political in art is itself a tactic to defuse, to individualise and disarm – a fact increasingly clear to Nono. To be associated with a genre of 'political art' was not the way for his music to do its transformational work. A reformulating of his outward role and his inner relationship with musical material dates from this point, the beginning of a long trajectory that, far from becoming more 'abstract', becomes ever more subversive of social and cultural structures, more directly material in its relationship with sound, and more precisely aimed at individual consciousness. There may be less apparent ideology – indeed, seen in this light the subsequent *Al gran sole carico d'amore* becomes a very different work – but the resistance, the raising of consciousness, happens in ways that themselves resist such cultural distancing effects. The acts of musical production and reception are Nono's new planes of resistance, areas less subject to intervention from the institutions of culture. Far from being in any way abstract or formalist, such an approach relates more directly with the subject. In fact, a Marxist rationalisation would only come later, in the form of more recent theory such as Badiou's *affirmationist art*: a call for resistance to the twin dangers of imitative populism and individualisation or infinite difference.[128]

In letters and interviews of this period, Nono often refers to a 'new culture'; references to Gramsci abound. His frequent use of the expression 'political cultural' reflects this renewed interest. Neither literature nor ideology come about through parthenogenesis, says Gramsci; they require human intervention, the creation of history, 'the revolutionary activity that creates the "new man" – that is, new social relationships'.[129] The meetings and conferences of previous years, largely organised through contacts in the PCI, had accelerated – a series of twenty-five events in Tuscany in 1970, for example.[130] They now developed into a more structured initiative. A new organisation, *Musica/Realtà*, was headed by Nono and his friends Maurizio Pollini, Claudio Abbado, Armando Gentilucci and Luigi Pestalozza, and supported by the left-wing leadership of Reggio Emilia. In collaboration with groups such as public libraries and the 'cultural circles' of factories, they would present live and recorded performances, workshops, discussions, popular music and educational events from 1973 through the decade. Their activities extended through Emilia Romagna, Tuscany and Umbria, as well as at La Scala in Milan, where under Abbado there was a concerted effort to expand the constituency of Italy's most conservative cultural institution.

The nature of Nono's militancy, of his view of his role as a musician, was evolving with its social and political context. He explained his sense of responsibility to fulfil the Gramscian role of 'new intellectual' in a letter of April 1971: 'This practice, and not just a choice or "pure" conscience, has developed increasingly for me over recent years as a result of my participation

Manifestos

in the political–cultural struggle of the working class, with all the contradictions and responsibilities, subjective and objective, of a militant musician.'[131] This had personal implications: 'I have learned from the workers to organise life differently and to find in culture a new creativity, a new conception of life and thought, of discovery and love.'[132] Re-establishing a broad cultural (and hence political) role for music was a vital part of his work and that of the group that would become *Musica/Realtà*, to which end music had to renounce its apparent privilege and reconnect with a new audience. 'When Gramsci talks of the intellectual, I don't understand it as a category apart [. . .] but as object and subject, participant and agent in a historical, geographical social context which must be analysed and for which there are no models.'[133] As Nono re-engages with his musical and political aims, they seem more integrated. He explains in a letter to Abbado, almost conspiratorial in tone:

> With you two [Abbado and Pollini] I have rediscovered the certainty and responsibility of our work. We are creating its function together. [. . .]
> and together we have the capacity, fantasy and will to overturn an old situation and create a new one. [. . .]
> I am convinced that we have in our hands the new musical development for struggle, not only in Italy
> but for the world struggle[134]

Musical understanding and activity are themselves instruments of raising consciousness, of social change, in 'the new musical development for struggle', in the new culture that Nono would describe as a 'culture of transformation'.[135] This is subtly different from the emphasis of recent years. It has important implications for the relationship of music and subject – composing, performing or listening. These would become evident in the works Nono was planning with Abbado: *Como una ola de fuerza e luz* for piano, soprano, tape and orchestra, premiered at La Scala on 28 June 1972, and the azione scenica *Al gran sole carico d'amore*, presented there in April 1975.

The support of Abbado and Pollini for the PCI and its aims was expressed publicly.[136] Like that of Nono, Pollini's art is founded on first principles; like Nono, his family background was one of art and architecture. Pollini made his political stance clear, from concerts for striking workers, demonstrations against fascist terrorism in 1969 and his very public opposition to the war in Vietnam, through to his 2006 concert 'in defence of the constitution' prior to Berlusconi's attempt to divide Italy by referendum. He and Nono had met at the premiere of *A floresta* in 1966. A telegram to Pollini succinctly expresses Nono's view: 'you demonstrate and indicate to everyone how the Gramscian musician constantly intervenes creating new function communication choice quality of music in life'.[137] Abbado and Nono had known each other since the Biennale of 1960; Abbado's appointment as Music Director of La Scala in 1968 and his express intention to encourage new music led to Nono's commissions.

In June 1971, Nono travelled to Chile for three months, at the moment when Salvador Allende's reforms were in full flood. He was invited to participate in *Operación Verdad*, Allende's initiative intended to bypass right-wing and external interference by bringing artists and intellectuals to Chile to experience for themselves the people, their culture and current situation. Among the many artists and activists he met, Nono was particularly struck by Luciano Cruz, a young leader of the *MIR* Revolutionary Left Movement who had been able to come out of hiding during Allende's presidency.

Manifestos

A wave of strength and light

In September, Nono began to work with Pollini on the composition that would become *Como una ola de fuerza y luz*, recording with Zuccheri at the Conservatory in Milan. His material was now Pollini's very musicianship – his sound at the piano, the behaviour of his hands. In his notes, Nono considers the relative weights and repetition rates of fingers, the span of the hand and the possibilities of different combinations of seconds and thirds. He invents the raw material in the studio: single notes in all registers, trills in multiple voices, chords of seconds, fourths, sevenths and ninths (the transposition intervals of *Ein Gespenst*) and chromatic blocks, continuous or separated. During this period, events intervened to change the course of the emerging work; in September, Nono received a letter from Chile informing him of the death of Luciano Cruz. From this point, the new composition becomes a response to the life and death of Cruz; this is to be a much more personal statement than recent political works, and one rooted in Nono's own listening to Pollini's piano timbre.

On returning to the studio, Nono had Pollini work only in the lower and middle registers of the piano. They recorded every pitch of entire octaves in middle and low registers: separate notes with and without pedal, semitone intervals with different dynamic shapes, repeated notes with varying pedalling and dynamics. Notes remind Nono to avoid recorded pedal noise; in fact, such performance artefacts will become an integral part of his next work for Pollini. The most characteristic pitch materials are tritone near-clusters and the open interval of a minor ninth: the hand in its closed and extended positions. They tried different contact microphones, ring modulation and filtering, producing sounds described in Nono's notes as 'marimba' or 'cimbalom'. Nono and Zuccheri continued through the weekend without Pollini. With engineer replacing maestro at the keyboard, they discussed the existential implications for the work should any of Zuccheri's notes make it on to the tape! As he uses these recordings to construct second-stage material – that which will be used to build the performance tape – Nono distinguishes between sounds to be spliced together ('taconamenti' – dialect for a patchwork) and those to be multiply over-recorded ('giosse' – 'drops' in Veneto). The former often combine the attack of one pitch with the resonance of another; the latter use different degrees of microtonal pitch-shifting. Such precise use of individual pitches across the entire range of the piece seems to anticipate digital sampling techniques of the 1980s. Here, however, Nono is not reproducing a virtual piano; rather, he is forensically examining the precise sound that Pollini produces from each key. He added a solo soprano to sing a poem dedicated to Cruz by his friend Julio Huasi, an Argentinian writer whom Nono had also met in Santiago.[138] The work's title – *Like a wave of strength and light* – comes from the poem. Nono reduces its 42 lines to three nearly equal stanzas, and then to its final tripartite form: a repetition of *Luciano!*, the main eight-line body and a parting benediction. The body consists of eight reordered fragments from Huasi's extensive eulogy. All the specific references to Chile, to Cruz's achievements, are omitted. The first and last line of Huasi's poem – 'Alto como la patria y joven como la revolución' – is reduced to its second statement, for example. Nono effectively builds a new, personal text, its references to wind, earth, wave and light echoing Pavesian themes. The final reference to bells – in the middle of Huasi's poem – recalls analogous moments in recent works. The combination of bells and waves takes us directly to Nono's own sound world, his own geographical environment. The Bulgarian soprano Slavka Taskova came into the studio to record guided improvisations: many versions of the name Luciano Cruz with a wide range of expression, both complete and in its separate phonemes, as well as lines from the poem and passages in Bulgarian. Nono wanted to incorporate the person of Taskova into the fabric of the work – her identity as a musician and the inflections of Bulgarian folk music in her voice – as

Manifestos

he had with Pollini. Characters seem to emerge as he listens to her; he categorises passages from the recording as 'niña' or 'mujer' (girl or woman). As with the piano, the recorded vocal material develops in two main ways: edited sequences and polyphonies of note, phrase and gesture, and textures of multiply processed moments – dense layers of piano resonance or choral sound of variable thickness. The mixing and editing work is finer than before. Rhythm and movement in the tape are products of a vast number of actions on the elemental recorded materials. 'The new music is emerging with a violence I have never known', he wrote to Abbado in November.[139]

Form, tape and solo parts developed together from the studio experience, although timings on sketches for the solo parts suggest that they were fully worked out only after the tape had found its final form. Nono's formal conception was fundamentally dramatic: 'music with a programme? and why not? where the title relates directly to the sonic structure', he wrote for a recording.[140] Crucially, in his sketches he puts himself into this drama; the main distinction is between 'them' and 'us/me'. In his first ideas, 'they' are Taskova and Pollini – girl/woman/comrade, boy/man/comrade – while the tape represents 'us/me'. The orchestra is an extension of both; it mediates between the two. There is an initial programme for the tape through the first part of the work: 'news arrives – distraught – sad – violent – struggle – memories human and political'.[141] For 'them', the soloists, Nono implements a kind of *Affektenlehre*. He describes three voices for each:

Slavka:	Mauro:
a) girl	a) man – comrade – us
b) woman	b) dolce espressivo
c) calls – arianna	c) intimate[142]

'Arianna' is a clear reference to Monteverdi's operatic lament, but remains a voice more distant than that of Pollini, which now approaches the subjective. Nono then designs a plan of permutations and combinations of orchestra, tape and soloists. It is impossible to reverse engineer the finished work to see to what extent this plan persisted, but it is clear that such a model informed his thinking in the construction of the tape and solo parts. These appear to have been substantially complete by December 1971, when Nono left to spend a month in Chile, Uruguay and Cuba. The orchestral parts were written back in Venice in early 1972; they develop their own structures from the previously finished materials, between which they constitute a new layer. While the tape is continuous, the solo parts are constructed as individual episodes. The final form maintains its dramatic structure. It divides clearly into two parts; soloists dominate through the first (soprano, piano, then briefly together), the orchestra in the second. The score is notated entirely in seconds (5/4 at $\quarternote$ = 60), facilitating the compositional process of constantly moving between recorded and notated material.

Como una ola de fuerza y luz is unique in Nono's output in being explicitly programmatic, and therefore warrants narrative discussion. The composer supplies epigrammatic descriptions of the four main sections.

1 – 'invocation commentary lament for Luciano'

0' – 2'30" orchestra + tape

As often with Nono's openings, sound seems to create itself; here it appears as unexpectedly as the news of Luciano's death. A full quarter-tone cluster of F♯–C in high wind and strings reduces to a single G♭ across a series of dynamic waves from the base level of *ppp*. Against this, a layer of voices on tape begins from F♯, expands down to C then dissolves in the opposite direction; a principle of complementarity is established at the outset. Internal movement is generated as instruments and voices cycle through the diminishing or expanding pitch space.

2'30"–4'15" I: *interno – dolce*: soprano + tape

Against waves of female chorus, the soprano's three initial cries of 'Luciano!' follow a simple pattern of intervals, their rhythms derived from varying degrees of short-long, the initial iamb of 'Lu*cia*no!' Intentionally or otherwise, Nono's initial pitch sequence consists of a mirror of the opening of Monteverdi's *Lamento d'Arianna*, its central fourth inverted (Figure 9.5). The ascending minor seventh C–B♭ that is the highpoint of Nono's soprano passage likewise mirrors the descent from the melodic peak D of Monteverdi's *Lamento* to the accented low E that starts the next bar. Nono's following bars outline an inverse symmetry, fill in the missing diatonic steps from the model and add a major second, which only appears as the final interval of Monteverdi's line, to the interval set. Depth of field is provided by the tape in three levels of use of Taskova's voice: long lines of close voices outlining the melodic pitch set, a more distant, less focused layer of female chorus, and heavily processed sound that attempts to break through into the foreground.

Figure 9.5a Monteverdi: *Lamento d'Arianna*: opening

Figure 9.5b *Como una ola de fuerza y luz*: soprano, 2'30"–2'55"

4'15"–6'30" II: *duro deciso*: soprano + tape

The non-linearity of the text – reordered fragments from the first few lines of Huasi's poem – is unfolded in interweaving of strands of song and repeated-note speech rhythm. Here we see a new relationship between non-composed recorded material and symbolic musical reasoning. De Assis has demonstrated the origins of this section in Taskova's Bulgarian folk music-informed improvisation.[143] What emerges is a pitch structure based on two inversely near-symmetrical diatonic pitch sets – the principle of complementarity used with the song material of *Ein Gespenst*. On the tape, Taskova's voice establishes chromatic pedals from the central chromatic overlapping area, until it anticipates the high G♯ that begins the second paragraph. This begins immediately with 'como una ola de fuerza y luz'. Entirely on high B/G♯, its minor third stands out in a melos otherwise built solely of fourths, seconds, sevenths and ninths. The sustained cry – 45 seconds in total – is cross-cut with short repeated-note interjections.

Manifestos

2 'presence – absence of Luciano'

6'30"–13'20" piano, orchestra + tape

Here we hear most clearly that the materials for piano and orchestra were produced separately; Nono's new technique incorporates simultaneity and fragmentation on vertical as well as horizontal axes. The alternation of piano and orchestra – Luciano and a world coming to terms with his loss – is paralleled in the different dynamics of their musical development, transcended in the third lament that follows. Piano and orchestra each enter eight times. On the levels of both form and gesture detail, this alternation is governed by a wave motion, a reference to the title but also a new fundamental component of Nono's technical repertoire. The extreme contraction and expansion of the piano sections is counterbalanced by the more architectonic orchestral interventions. The waves lap across each other. The piano sometimes continues under the orchestra, self-absorbed until it reasserts itself, while timpani, bass drum and tam-tam become extensions of the piano's low register. A slower-moving layer of twelve double basses *sul ponte* is introduced with the seventh orchestral passage and remains after the eighth. Their fundamental pitches saturate an entire octave, while their overtones dance with those of the low piano and mix with the higher components of the tape sounds. Unlike the complex dynamic detail of the wind, this layer follows a sequence of diminishing unison crescendos; the waves lose energy incrementally, as if the power of the orchestra were finally fading under the tireless insistence of the piano.

Nono explores the compositional space between recorded sound – the elemental gestures that he had elicited from Pollini – and his techniques of notation-based manipulation. As in the studio, time and register are his initial concerns. The piano is restricted to its lowest two octaves; the orchestra generally occupies the upper of these, sometimes compressed still further to an augmented fourth. Within these ranges, pitch perception is limited; the dense sound complex is articulated in terms of colour, articulation and dynamics. The material is primarily rhythmic, set out clearly by Nono in a series of six rhythms with their retrogrades.[144] These would appear to have some origin in the recorded material; relationships appear constantly between tape and live piano. They are carefully mediated, combining the sequences of accelerating repetition and short-long groups from the studio material with Nono's standard starting-points of expanding or diminishing values and internal symmetries. He uses the same principles in their superimposition and development into folds of kinetic energy. An additional rhythmic feature stands out from this material in its regularity: three equal repetitions that De Assis identifies as a 'Lu-cia-no' motif.[145] Within the pitch regions for each section, Nono uses clusters, shapes of major and minor seconds and single notes to differentiate rhythmic layers with varying degrees of definition. The interlocking internal symmetries of the orchestral sections confirm their essentially static nature against the dynamism of piano development.

13'20"–14'25" – soprano, piano + tape

A new chromatic polyphony emerges from the subsiding piano tremolos, condensing to rhythmic unison below the third soprano lament. It is impossible not to hear the tolling bells described in the text. The soprano's opening symmetrical rising and falling semitones again recall Monteverdi's lament, as does the major/minor second ambiguity of her final phrase of 'juventud'.

Manifestos

3 '"the long march" ascending into the heights'

15'32"–25'17"

Following the central tape episode, the 'long march' – an unapologetic Maoist reference – cuts through the work like a diagonal stripe across a painting by Antoni Tàpies.[146] The tape pursues its own narrative with sounds more highly processed than in the first part. In the orchestra these ten minutes are an inexorable climb from polyphony in the depths of the orchestra to chromatic clusters in rhythmic unison above the range of clear pitch perception, narrowing to a single pitch. Society moves towards a new state. Until the final piccolo clusters dissolve, the rhythmicised blocks of sound move upwards in bands of an augmented fourth. Blocks move between dense chromatic bands and unisons that draw the ear to emergent figuration. Nono's approach is uncompromisingly rational: each step is a ten-second unit with its own colour and internal organisation. Subdivisions of the beat and duration values are derived from permutations of different number series, modulated by his technique of expansion and contraction. As well as a registral escape, this trajectory is also a kind of retrograde, a path back to the clarity of the opening. On the way, it passes through degrees of clarity and unanimity of organisation, rhythmic and dynamic – new socio-musical structures. The orchestration also changes in blocks of instrumental colour. As the orchestra moves into the middle register, for example, the busy, high-energy low brass, bassoons, strings and percussion are suddenly replaced by an evenly paced, focused, *pp* texture of clarinets, violas, timpani and amplified harp in near rhythmic unison (17'10"). Twice the piano marches with the orchestra, a quite different relationship from the previous section, renewing the energy of the march to commence its next sequence of steps with a tutti *fff* (18'45" and 20'27").

4 'collective explosion in the certain presence [of Luciano]'

25'38"–30'04"

The explosion takes two forms: extreme clarity in the orchestra and extreme virtuosity in the piano. It is transparently cathartic. The orchestra sustains the total chromatic, divided into two hexachords and presented in only three forms: separated by minor ninth for the first 40 seconds, contiguous in the middle register for the following 70 and with their initial registers reversed in the final thirty. Balance and complementarity govern the musical space. Within this, crescendos, diminuendos or sustained dynamics at *fff* or *ppp* are drawn by separated blocks of sound in multiples of five seconds. Each follows one of Nono's elemental sound shapes: start together, end together or both. The piano, now amplified, sustains a formidable energy *fffff* through each of its twenty-seven bars – the age of Luciano Cruz. Full of double trills, uneven chordal tremolos, palm-wide clusters, polyrhythms in widely distant registers and dyads the span of Pollini's hand, it finally emerges into the high register. The piano returns to its full low octave, the base sound of the work, for a final, still gesture following which the last block of the orchestra dissolves. The sudden acoustic silence is a shock, leaving the ears raw to discover the tape filling the space with female choirs at every level of aural perspective.

Nono was no pianist; 'I studied Pollini's fantastic technique', he later said.[147] The virtuosity of Liszt is the clearest model. Perhaps Pollini showed him the *Harmonies Poétiques et Religieuses*. *Funérailles*, with its low tolling tremolos, is Liszt's response to the defeat of the Hungarian uprising in 1848. Its successor, *Miserere après Palestrina*, begins with the text printed over the instrumental melodic line and then pursues a long trajectory from the top to the bottom of the keyboard, contrasting chordal blocks with rapid figuration. An earlier work *Lyon*, from *Album d'un voyageur*, was motivated by the aftermath of a workers' uprising in that city in 1834, for which Liszt performed a benefit concert. The song of the uprising emerges through its intensity: *Vivre en travaillant ou mourit en combatant*. Fistfuls of notes in extreme registers sustain a long *ffff*, *rinforzato*, *crescendo* leading to tremolos in the highest octaves and pounding chords in the lowest. There is no further evidence, but these works provide models of both pianism and structure. More broadly, Nono's closeness to Pollini and Abbado seems to have allowed him to reassess his relationship with Romantic music – the stuff of bourgeois culture. He embarked on a study of Liszt's symphonic poems. Schumann and Mahler, Hölderlin and Nietzsche will become increasingly important to Nono, as will Italian opera of the nineteenth century. In seeking to encourage a new musical culture, he found new richness in his own background, the 'historical continuity' that the organic intellectual should embody.[148] In the context of Nono's conscious self-reinvention, this is entirely consistent with Gramsci's view of the close ties between political and cultural action, and the consequent rediscovery by the 'new man' of the past he has overthrown – the 'Gramscian musician' of Nono's telegram to Pollini.[149]

An explicit programme also invites misinterpretation. At the premiere, at La Scala on 28 June 1972, Mila heard not a society coming to terms with loss and struggling for enlightenment, but the rumblings of war – an uncharacteristic mishearing. His experience of Nono's music led him to expect a more directly polarised drama of oppression and transfiguration, and he found resonances of the renaissance *battaglia* genre.[150] In *l'Unità*, by contrast, Tedeschi felt that Nono had found a state of equilibrium, of reconciliation.[151] The performance at La Scala was a success. Despite the inevitable calls of disapproval from some sections of an audience not known for its radicalism, Nono and his friends were rewarded with clamorous applause and positive reviews.[152] The very fact of the performance was noteworthy: 'either Nono has been tamed or a new wind is blowing through La Scala,' observed Mila.[153] Pointedly, he also referred to the impeccable cut of the blue suit Nono wore over his red shirt. In fact, Mila's 'new wind' hypothesis was true, and would bode well for Nono. The day after this premiere, Abbado and Pollini continued their process of cultural transformation at La Scala with a concert 'in defense of liberty' of Beethoven, Prokofiev and Verdi's *Va, pensiero*, to a packed house of people who could otherwise never have attended such an event. A year later, the trio presented *Como una ola de fuerza y luz*, together with Beethoven's *Eroica* in Reggio Emilia, as the culmination of the first season of *Musica/Realtà*.[154]

Notes

1 Interview with Hansjörg Pauli, 1969. LNII, p. 31.
2 Letter to Dallapiccola, 2 February 1967, in Kämper, 2010, p. 51.
3 Warnaby, 2003, p. 23.
4 'Per Bastiana – Tai-Yang Cheng'. LNI, p. 458.
5 'Per Bastiana – Tai-Yang Cheng'. LN1, p. 458.
6 Letter from Ingrao, 15 January 1967, in Trudu, 2008, p. 111.
7 *El Comercio*, Lima, 31 August 1967.
8 *Expreso*, Lima. 2 September 1967.
9 *El Mundo*, Havana, 9 September 1967.
10 Silber, 1970, p. 321.
11 Castro's speech, the reports of the five commissions and most of the papers are contained in Silber, 1970.
12 Letter to Mario Baratto in Trudu, 2008, p. 123.
13 This period of dissent is described in Ripoll, 1984.
14 Brown, 2013, p. 234.

Manifestos

15 *l'Unità*, 16 March 1968.
16 *Il Gazzettino*, 30 April 1968.
17 For example, Pinzauti in *La Nazione*, 17 June 1968.
18 *Il Gazzettino*, 21 June 1968.
19 *L'Avanti*, 19 June 1968, p. 1.
20 Di Stefano, 2010, gives an account of the opening.
21 *La Stampa*, 9 July 1968.
22 *L'Italia*, Milan, 10 August 1968.
23 Negri, 2004, p. 170.
24 *La Stampa*, 7 September 1968.
25 *l'Unità*, 20 August 1968.
26 For a discussion of the *cartella*, see Owens, 1997, Ch. 5.
27 Balestrini, 2007, contains his complete texts for music. Balestrini's more recent *Tristano* (Verso, London, 2014) develops this logic. Each printed copy is a unique reordering of its two hundred constituent texts. His *L'orda d'oro* (Balestrini and Moroni, 2011) is a detailed insider's account of the Italian protest movement 1968–77.
28 Letter to Piccioni, 31 July 1968, in liner notes to *Luigi Nono: Complete works for solo tape*. Ricordi CD STR 57001.
29 'Contrappunto dialettico alla mente'. LNI, p. 462.
30 'Il potere musicale', 1969. LNI, p. 263.
31 Later Kwame Ture. See: www.kwameture.com (accessed 16 May 2017).
32 This is a variant of the most common form, in which the last two lines are replaced with 'Die Nigger Die – you can't die fast enough in the ghettos . . .'.
33 'Dichiarazione di Luigi Nono', 1968. LNI, p. 244.
34 'Il "Che" vivo a Caracas', 1968. LNII, p. 250.
35 'Il "Che" vivo a Caracas', 1968. LNII, p. 250.
36 Calabretto, 2017, p. 146.
37 Calabretto, 2017, p. 283. *La guerra olvidada* can be seen at: www.youtube.com/watch?v=BtbunBQt5Pc (accessed 3 January 2018).
38 Calabretto, 2017, pp. 159–64.
39 Calabretto, 2017, pp. 139–43.
40 Interview with Fiona Diwan, 1985. LNII, p. 371.
41 Rossanda, 2013, p. 236.
42 Calabretto, 2017, p. 134.
43 Calabretto, 2017, p. 6.
44 Calabretto, 2017, p. 70.
45 Much of the Unitelefilm archive is available at: www.aamod.it/ (accessed 3 January 2018).
46 Calabretto, 2017, pp. 323–34. Available at: www.youtube.com/watch?v=SACuWCJSbTY (accessed 3 January 2018).
47 Calabretto, 2017, pp. 292–4.
48 Calabretto, 2017, pp. 292–4. Available at: http://patrimonio.aamod.it/aamod-web/film/detail/IL8300 001319/22/un-futuro-per-genova.html (accessed 3 January 2018).
49 Calabretto, 2017, pp. 262–82.
50 Calabretto, 2017, pp. 216–59. Available at: http://patrimonio.aamod.it/aamod-web/film/detail/ IL8010003526/22/la-fabbrica.html?startPage=0&idFondo= (accessed 3 January 2018).
51 Nono, 1973.
52 Nono, 1973.
53 Rossanda, 2010, p. 312. At this point, Rossanda was Secretary of the Cultural Committee of the PCI.
54 Ingrao, 2006, p. 265–6.
55 Chinello, 2008, p. 267.
56 Chinello, 2008, p. 263.
57 *La fabbrica e la società*. Tronti, 2013, pp. 35–56.
58 Confederazione Generale Italiana del Lavoro, founded in 1944.
59 Tronti, 2013, pp. 236–54.
60 Negri, 1983, p. 120.
61 Chinello, 2008, p. 262.
62 *ABC*, 2 May 1969, pp. 34–5.

Manifestos

63 *Stampa Sera Torino*, 1 October 1969. *Il Giornale di Sicilia*, 1 October 1969. *Gazetta del Popolo*, 2 October 1969.

64 Letter to Aharonián, 25 November 1969, in Trudu, 2008, p. 158.

65 Letter to Longo and Berlinguer, 27 November, 1969, in Trudu, 2008, pp. 158–9.

66 Letter to Longo and Berlinguer, 7 January, 1970, in Trudu, 2008, pp. 161–5.

67 Massimo Cacciari in Trotta and Milana, 2008, p. 830.

68 Antonio Negri, in Trott and Milana, 2008, p. 802.

69 Tafuri, 1969. This becomes the basis of his *Progetto e utopia: architettura e sviluppo capitalistico* (Rome: Laterza, 1973), published in English as *Architecture and Utopia*.

70 'Dopo la contestazione', 1969. LNII p. 44

71 'Colloquio con Luigi Nono su musica e impegno politico'. LNII p. 55.

72 Gramsci, 1971, p. 10.

73 Adlington, 2016, p. 207.

74 Borio, 2013, provides a clear and detailed account of the confluence and political context of rock, folk, folklore, avant-garde and technological music in Italy through the 1960s and 1970s.

75 'San Vittore 1969'. LNI, p. 470.

76 Bermani's highly informative essay on Giovanni Pirelli contradicts itself as to the realization of this project: http://www.iedm.it/istituto/giovanni-pirelli-un-autentico-rivoluzionario/

77 Châtillon had a history of communal activism; it had welcomed miners and their families during the strike of 1963. The 1969 'Fête de l'Huma' is documented on film, available at: www.cinearchives.org/Liste-des-films-669–615–0-0.html (accessed 16 May 2017).

78 Stenzl, 1998, pp. 75–8.

79 In his retyping of *Mattino*, Nono replaces Pavese's 'viso' at the end of the fourth line with the near-synonym 'volto', as in the opening line. It's not clear whether this was intentional, but it persists through Nono's work on the piece.

80 J. Besançon (ed.), 1968. *Les murs ont la parole. Journal mural mai 68*. Paris, Tchou.

81 Breuning, 1998, p. 214.

82 'Musica-Manifesto n. 1: Un volto, e del mare – Non consumiamo Marx'. LNI, p. 468.

83 ALN 33.03.01/4r.

84 Interview with Wolf-Eberhard von Lewinski (1970). LNII, p. 81.

85 Nono confirmed this on more than one occasion: interview with Enzo Restagno, 1986. LNII p. 526; Kropfinger, 1991, p. 118.

86 Gentilucci, 1987, p. 164.

87 Gentilucci, 1987, p. 164.

88 Riede, 1986, p. 84. Riegler, 1999, pp. 109–11.

89 ALN 33.02.01/02r.

90 'Presenza storica nella musica d'oggi', 1959. LNI, p. 51.

91 Seminar on music and political engagement, with Michele Straniero, 1969. LNII, p. 48.

92 Interview with Enzo Restagno, 1986. LNII, p. 526.

93 Interview with Mario Gamba, 1988. LNI, p. 468.

94 Tronti, 2013, p. 264.

95 Interview with Enzo Restagno, 1986. LNII, p. 526.

96 ALN 35.03.01.

97 ALN 35.03.01/03.

98 16 April 67, a supplement to the magazine *Tricontinental*, written while Che was fighting secretly in Bolivia.

99 'Y entonces comprendió'. LNI, p. 472.

100 ALN 35.03.02/1v, 2v.

101 Produced by the Eltro Automation Company in 1967.

102 'San Vittore 1969'. LNI, p. 470.

103 ALN 35.04/02r.

104 ALN 35.04/02v.

105 Some transcriptions are given in Ramazotti, 1995.

106 Ramazotti, 1995, p. 30, finds an explicit reference to Bach in an associated project.

107 Interview with Hartmut Lück, 1970. LNII, p. 78.

108 Interview with Hartmut Lück, 1972. LNII, p. 109.

109 Besides his literary projects, Pirelli was active in financially supporting progressive publications

ventures, including *Quaderni rossi*.

110 Adlington, 2016, p. 182.
111 Iotti, 1966. *Milano: parlono le donne lavoratrici* was published by the Commissione Femminile della Federazione Comunista di Milano, 1968. Nilde Iotti was the first woman deputy in the Italian parliament and the partner of Togliatti.
112 ALN 36.04.01/01.
113 Balestrini, 2013, p. 87.
114 Adlington, 2016, p. 184.
115 Adlington, 2016, p. 185.
116 Adlington, 2016, pp. 185–7.
117 Interview with Martine Cadieu, 1970, in Stenzl, 1975, p. 238.
118 Adlington, 2016, p. 188.
119 Adlington, 2013, pp. 59–96.
120 Frankfurter Allgemeine Zeitung, 14 July 1970.
121 *Le Monde*, 15 July 1970.
122 *The Times*, 6 July 1970.
123 West German Radio report, 12 May 1970, ALN.
124 Frankfurter Rundschau, 5 June 1969.
125 Tomek, 2004.
126 Letter to Roman Vlad, 17 October 1971, in Trudu, 2008, pp. 186–8.
127 Messinis and Scarnecchia, 1977, p. 10.
128 Badiou, 2006, pp. 143–147.
129 Gramsci, 1977, vol. II, p. 733.
130 Interview with Hartmut Lück, 1971. LNII, p. 106.
131 Letter to *Le Monde*, April 1971, in Trudu, 2008, p. 181.
132 Interview with Wolfgang Becker-Carsten, 1972. LNII, p. 98.
133 'La funzione della musica oggi', 1972. LNII, p. 116.
134 Letter to Abbado, 8 November 1971, in Trudu, 2008, pp. 188–90.
135 Seminar at Columbia University, 1979. LNII, p. 230.
136 *l'Unità*, 5 May 1972.
137 Undated telegram to Pollini, ALN.
138 The poem is a condensed version of Huasi's *Luciano*, published with the journal *Punto Final*, Santiago, 31 August 1971. This and reports of Cruz's life and funeral are available at: www.archivochile.com/Homenajes/html/luciano_cruz.html (accessed 31 October 2017). A further article in *Punto Final* explores the relationships between the MIR and Allende, available at: www.puntofinal.cl/665/mir.php (accessed 31 October 2017).
139 Letter to Abbado, 8 November 1971, in Trudu, 2008, pp. 188–90.
140 'Como una ola de fuerza y luz'. LNI, 480.
141 ALN 38.02.02/02.
142 ALN 38.02.02/03.
143 De Assis, 2006, vol. I, pp. 70–1.
144 De Assis, 2006, vol II, p. 33.
145 De Assis, 2006, vol. I, p. 76.
146 Tàpies had visited the Nono home in Venice when he was awarded the UNESCO prize in 1958. Their friendship continued and the Nonos visited his studio in Barcelona in 1983.
147 Interview with Frank Schneider, 1977. LNII, p. 226.
148 'La funzione della musica oggi', 1972. LNII, p. 117.
149 Gramsci, 1977, vol. II, pp. 733–4.
150 Mila, 2010, p. 289.
151 *l'Unità*, 29 June 1972, p. 7.
152 Archive recording, ALN.
153 Mila and Nono, 2010, p. 287.
154 The introduction by Nono, Abbado and Pollini can be seen at: www.youtube.com/watch?v=6p QCTw73PtE (accessed 31 October 2017).

10

AL GRAN SOLE CARICO D'AMORE

A long-awaited sunrise

In the continuous search for dramatic subjects, Nono had been discussing a new work with Abbado and Pollini.[1] A letter to Abbado from November 1971, while they were working on projects for Reggio Emilia and *Como una ola de fuerza e luz*, refers to the possibility of a new opera.[2] 'Finally opera' says Nono in a telegram to Abbado in May 1972, as soon as the score of *Como una ola* was complete.[3] This would become *Al gran sole carico d'amore* (*In the bright sunshine heavy with love*), dedicated to Abbado and Pollini, and premiered at La Scala on 4 April 1975. Nono revised the work in 1977 for a further production at La Scala the following year; we will discuss the score in this final version. The title is taken from a poem by Rimbaud, *Les mains de Jeanne-Marie*, that appears at the centre of the first act. It also recalls a line from *L'Internationale*, one of the work's musical sources; the second verse of Bergeret's 1901 translation begins 'un gran stendardo al sol fiammante' ('a great flag in the blazing sun'). The Red Flag itself is heavy with love. When Paolo Grassi, co-director of the Piccolo Teatro, became superintendent in 1972, the commission was one of his first acts.

The difficulty of the role of collaborator on Nono's theatre projects was well established. One is reminded of Gramsci's own way of developing ideas: 'Ordinarily, I need to set out from a dialogical or dialectical standpoint, otherwise I don't experience any intellectual stimulation. [. . .] I want to feel a concrete interlocutor or adversary.'[4] Here, as before, the dramaturgical essence and text components were primarily Nono's. As the designer of the first production, David Borovsky, observed, Nono was involved in every aspect of the work. At the same time, Stenzl has pointed out that the entirety of the drama is in the score itself.[5] Nono needed to find a director with an understanding of his by now well-developed if informal theory of a new music theatre, of the azione scenica. Wladamiro Dorigo, then director of theatre at the Biennale, had seen the work of Yuri Lyubimov's Taganka Theatre in Moscow, and proposed Lyubimov as a partner. Once he had seen the Taganka for himself, Grassi readily agreed.

Lyubimov had founded the Taganka in 1964, following a production of Brecht's *The Good Woman of Szechwan* that had transformed the Russian theatrical tradition. Instead of producing conventionally dramatic works he had developed a repertoire based on poetry, on adaptations of prose and on devised theatre. Lyubimov was both a skilled survivor and a thorn in the side of the Soviet cultural establishment – the personification of continuous resistance. His productions followed Brecht's principles; according to Russian theorist Smeliansky, Lyubimov's

Al gran sole carico d'amore

actors 'punched an enormous hole in the so-called fourth wall'.[6] They reached beyond the stage, dissolving boundaries with 'real life'. Technology played an important role – Lyubimov had trained as an electrician – as did the simple but dramatically structural stage design of his designer Borovsky. In a renowned production of Pasternak's translation of *Hamlet*, which Nono saw in Moscow, a single curtain provides both scenery and furniture. Like Nono, Lyubimov had a company of artists with whom he had developed a close understanding and who were a vital part of his working process. The popular singer–songwriter Vladimir Vysotsky made a particular impression on Nono. Song was an important part of Lyubimov's productions. His socially critical adaptation of Gorky's novel of the 1905 revolution *The Mother* incorporated the song of oppression and rebellion *Dubinushka (The Cudgel)*, made famous by Shalyapin shortly after the publication of Gorky's book.

Nono wrote to Lyubimov in November 1972, describing the work he had in mind and the nature of the proposed collaboration:

> it won't be an opera, in which first the musician writes it, then the conductor comes to conduct it, then the director who stages it etc. but a collective work from the outset. That is, a work that grows together between us.[7]

He visited Moscow the next month to meet Lyubimov; both Lyubimov and Julia Dobrovolskaja, their translator, recount Nono's emptying his enormous portfolio of sketches onto the floor at the Taganka, to explain his ideas.[8] Their collaboration required official approval, which the Minister of Culture, Yekaterina Furtseva, was reluctant to provide; she had banned Lyubimov's *Alive* in 1968. Both were blacklisted, explains Dobrovolskaja: Nono was a dodecaphonic Maoist, Lyubimov a generally difficult artist with whom the administration had found an accommodation. Lyubimov had particularly come under suspicion for his production based on Mayakovsky, a heroic figure for Nono.[9] Eventually, Nono found a new route via the PCI; he persuaded the recently appointed national secretary Enrico Berlinguer to ask Brezhnev to intervene, and the project received full official backing.[10] Returning to Russia with his family, Nono spent three weeks working with Lyubimov at a rural 'Centre of Creativity' in Ruza, outside Moscow. There they stayed in the dacha of Tikhon Khrennikov, leader of the Union of Soviet Composers, with whom Nono had already established a fractious relationship in 1963. Dobovrolskaja recounts some of the frictions that arose from Nono's clear-speaking on issues such as the ignorance of Denisov's students at the Conservatory, their reverence for the decadent Rachmaninoff and the replacement of the USSR by Latin America as the centre of socialist cultural transformation. Initial discussions with Lyubimov were not straightforward. Nono had a much wider experience of theatrical innovation outside the USSR; indeed, Peter Brook's telephone number appears on early plans for the new work. However, they found a constructive working relationship, maintained through Lyubimov's subsequent visit to Nono in Venice.

Much of the content of *Al gran sole carico d'amore* had been considered by Nono prior to this collaboration; with Lyubimov it would find structure, focus and a unifying dramatic concept. The kernel of the new idea had been the centenary of the Paris Commune of 1871. Nono put Marx's *The Civil War in France* and Brecht's *The Days of the Commune* at the centre of various textual constellations of more recent situations: Rosa Luxemburg, the great strike of 1943, the revolution in Cuba, industrial strife in Turin, the events of 1968 and the continuing war in Vietnam. As he worked with text extracts, forms and proportions, the challenge seems to have been to balance such a clear central subject with a mosaic of historical references. He begins to think of specific voices, members of his expanding informal company. He associates characteristics and emotions with five of the sopranos of recent works 'like a quintet in Verdi'; the multiple everywoman of *Un diario italiano* persists, although they will become four. 'MAKE IT LINE BY LINE – THEN TECHNIQUE', he reminds himself.[11] At this stage, it was already clear that the central figures would all be women. The structural models Nono mentions are interesting, described as 'closed forms': Berg's *Lulu*, Brecht's *Jasager* and *Neinsager*, and Malipiero's *Sette Canzoni*. The last, a Venetian work, is a series of seven self-contained miniature music–dramas that Malipiero said were 'born of the struggle between two sentiments – fascination by the theatre and boredom with [traditional Italian] opera'.[12] '8 tapes – 8 materials – 8 sources' are identified in one highly developed graphical plan: 'Marx, Commune, Brecht, Vietnam, Cuba, Che, 4 sopranos, demonstrations', characterised by different instrumental colours and sound shapes (Plate 1).

Lists of possible texts are assembled for each. Drawings of stage designs for an abandoned three-act version (beginnings in Europe, events in Cuba, present in Europe) recall his early fascination with constructivist and futurist theatre of the 1920s. They suggest planes of action at variable angles – horizontal to vertical – and a performance surrounding the audience. Most tellingly, these shapes recall his designs for form, sound complexes or musical lines. Nono still had Svoboda in mind. His plans for projections anticipate the eventual balance of two acts: 'I: same situation – UNITARY. II: various situations – SIMULTANEITY – MANY-SIDED RELATIONSHIPS.'[13] The substantial forces planned from the outset – large and small choirs *spezzati*, groups of vocal soloists and a full orchestra – would remain. An idea to use an ensemble of amplified instrumental soloists would have to wait for *Prometeo*, and the multiple tapes accompanying different groups would be rationalised to a single four-channel tape.

Operatic architecture

Nono's initial timetable for the year shows how he intended to distribute the writing of three acts through 1973. In the event, the refurbishing of La Scala put back the premiere to the following season, and composition continued into 1974. Grassi, nervous about public reaction in such politically fragile times and initially unconvinced by the title, was keen to see a libretto without delay.[14] Together, Nono and Lyubimov designed a carefully balanced structure of two acts embodying Nono's unitary-simultaneity concept – an orthogonally binary model of the kind that has supported his architectures since *Canti per 13*. They worked on the floor, on multiple sheets of paper taped together, to see form and detail. A premonition of *Prometeo* stands out on one such sheet: '?SOLO ASCOLTO!'.[15] Rimbaud's poem and the self-defence at trial of the communard heroine Louise Michel bring individual voices to the first act, Pavese's Deola and Gorky's Mother to the second.

The first act reflects on the Paris Commune. For all its complexity, it retains a clear architecture both overall and within scenes. The nine scenes fall into three groups of three – the context and facts of the Commune, the experience of the Communards, the aftermath – surrounded by broader reflections on revolution. The texts of Brecht, Marx and Lenin on the Commune dominate the opening scenes. The words of Tania Bunke, killed fighting with Guevara, and Che himself are woven into the first two scenes as a reminder of continuing relevance. Four of the scenes (1, 5, 6 and 9) have a clear ABA structure. Only the third, combining texts from Lenin and Brecht, approaches an operatic narrative drama, building to the central plane of reflection and personal experience. Rimbaud's poem and Louise Michel's memoirs stand at the centre of the act, framing Brecht's *Resolutions* in scene 5. The wall returns as a symbol of oppression in scenes 7 and 8, the massacre of the Communards, where the tape becomes the only source of sound.[16] The act concludes with the firm resolution of Michel and

Al gran sole carico d'amore

The Mother's prediction of continued revolution. Four interspersed orchestral *Riflessioni* provide an additional layer of architecture, a parallel commentary.

The second act takes a different approach. Rather than a single bounded event, the multiple stories told here are of endless resistance rooted in human love. Rather than an extinguishing, it ends with statement of inextinguishable hope. The basic locus of the act is that of Gorky's *Mother* in the failed revolution of 1905. From there it shifts temporarily to the industrial suburbs of Turin in the 1950s – with documentary texts and the voice of Pavese's Deola – to the 1953 battle for Moncada in Cuba and to contemporary camps in Vietnam. This act also has a parallel instrumental structure, the *schieramento della macchina repressiva* ('array of the machinery of repression'), a brief but insistent orchestral signal that appears in almost every scene as a reminder of the constant enemy that unifies these individual dramas.

The dramatic rhythm and fragmentation of narrative strands owes much to Brecht, as Nono acknowledged.[17] Another frequent reference through this period is the *Kino-pravda* ('film-truth') of Dziga Vertov, short documentaries from the early 1920s anticipating his own self-reflective *The Man with a Movie Camera* of 1929: 'From his films I have learned how our sense of time has got faster. We need much less time than before to observe and recognise something; we are able to apprehend simultaneous events and to establish autonomous relationships.'[18]

Nono constructs the score as a sequence of autonomous compositional units – between one and eight for each scene. This is a pragmatic approach to such a large and complicated undertaking, but also ensures that inappropriate musical teleologies, unities or relationships do not disturb the dramatic balance. Each unit has its own internal logic. Timings are noted scrupulously, in numbers of bars or in seconds; the overall form is under constant review and, as with his recent works, there is a four-channel tape to incorporate.

With Nono's emphasis on the role of women, the female voice dominates. Male soloists appear as historical figures or prophetic voices rather than subjects: Thiers, Favre and Bismarck in the scene at Montmartre, Gorky's Pavel or the words from prison of Fidel, Dimitrov and Gramsci towards the end. Of the main female characters, only The Mother is associated exclusively with a single voice, a solo alto; the case of Haydée Santamaria is different, as will become clear. Tania Bunke, Louise Michel and Deola are represented by a group of four sopranos, as are groups of Vietnamese women, comrades and Communards.

> Deola is not just Deola, but a moment in life which expands our understanding of Louise Michel. Louise Michel is not just a heroine but part of a process of transformation; she is also Deola for a transitional moment. [. . .] The Mother is both the mother of 1905 and the mother of the time of Turin.[19]

Other groups of Communards, workers, emigrants and comrades are given voice by combinations of soloists, small choir and the full choir. Apart from the imported material in the Moncada scene, the only role taken entirely by the full choir is that of 'workers today' – an explicit gesture of unity, solidarity and the identification of the composer with the listener. A variable association of identity and numbers of performers with dramatic roles reinforces a Brechtian distancing; it avoids the identification of performer with character. It opens questions of the relationship of individual and group, and of the uniqueness of the individual subject; we may all constitute a single subject (workers today) or a single subject may have multiple identities (the four sopranos). These are not only dramaturgical decisions, however – they have fundamental compositional consequences. There is a continuum of focus, of degree of identity and subjectivity that can be manipulated like those of pitch, space or figure.

Al gran sole carico d'amore

Nono incorporates new resistance songs into his material – *Non siam più la commune di parigi*, *O fucile, vecchio mio compagno* and *Dubinushka* – in addition to his recent repertoire – *L'Internationale* (itself a product of the Commune), *Bandiera Rossa*, *26 de Julio* and *The East is Red*. They afford Nono two important parameters: the degree to which figure is cognisable, and the degree to which it is then heard to be referential. Much of the essential musical fabric is created following the practice established in *Voci destroying muros* and *Ein Gespenst geht um in der Welt*. Phrases of a song are analysed for their interval and rhythm content and aggregate pitch set. New lines are spun from this material on various rhythm bases, using both the original pitch set and a transposed chromatic complement (as far as possible). The transformation of melodic material into compositional pitch-matrix represents a stage between the perpetual inner motion of the all-interval series and the multiple parallel worlds of Nono's later use of the scala enigmatica, notably in *Fragmente-Stille, an Diotima*. The scales thus produced are variable-breadth sources of local melodic charge with which he can generate material that is more or less distinctive or recognisable. Similarly, the rhythms produced from found material may be used formally in constructing complex sound shapes, or figurally to provide forward motion. The iterative self-multiplication of interval patterns anticipates the shifting, constrained harmonic universe of *Prometeo* and beyond.

Textures of one or many voices are woven from such threads which Nono then uses to populate the scenario in question, differentiated by thickness, colour, speed, dynamics and figural focus. To generate more complex, less integrated rhythms, he devises a method of changing rhythm base according to the preceding interval. He maintains sculptural control; such a process may generate one or several layers of polyphony that might reduce or condense to a single voice, or it may produce a single line that can proliferate into a complex polyphonic texture.

In *Ein Gespenst*, Nono described his source materials as 'historical class signals'.[20] Here, they assume dramatic roles, not as leitmotivs (although he does use this term in one sketch) but as agents of class struggle. They embody shared consciousness for the group and symbolise the strength of that commonality for the individual. The opening *Come preludio* presents the elements of the musical argument. A solo soprano traces a line from the polyphony of the large choir, the group of four from the small choir, before their lines separate and develop autonomy. Against this, percussion and *col legno* strings begin to assemble a rhythm that emerges in the second part as *Non siam più la commune di parigi*, now in a prolation canon with permutations of its rhythmic components. The third and fourth beats constitute the kind of sequence of diminishing durations that has been Nono's *ex nihilo* starting point since *Variazioni canoniche*: ♩ ♩ ♩ ♪ ♪. He abstracts them, multiplies by different rhythm bases and builds a permutation square to generate sequences not in the original. This simple example typifies Nono's exploration of his known technical space in *Al gran sole*; he finds new connections rather than new methods. This material alternates with 5/8, quarter-tone-based sound complexes descended directly from those of *Canti di vita e d'amore*, before becoming the more mediated source of the first scene proper.

A similar musical drama is played out more fully in scene 5 of Act I, where the opening of *Canti di vita e d'amore* returns almost entirely to accompany the rising of the Commune. Divided into sections, it alternates with the insistent rhythms and unison choral lines of the *Resolutions of the communards*, derived from *Non siam più*. The sequence of brief texts at the centre of the following scene, the *Episodio di Montmartre*, most approaches narrative dialogue – here between a soldier, an officer and a communard. Nono designs the overlap of dialogue graphically, in shapes like those of his sound complexes, before he maps them out with speech rhythms. Underneath, a sequence of transposed phrases from *O fucile* provides continuity and direction. The same song provides the material for the central setting of *Les mains de Jeanne-Marie* in scene 4, a choral aria. The relationship is made clear at the start of the second verse. While the choir sopranos present the song as a vocalise, the group of four sopranos hocket a new line as a descant, a rearrangement of the elements of the original (Figure 10.1). Its pitch set is shifted a tone higher, the rhythm is based on quintuplets rather than semiquavers, and the dynamic envelope is different, enhancing the perceptual separation between the two layers. Chromatic grace notes avoid unintended tonal implications. In a further layer, flutes, clarinet, amplified harp, bells and marimba add a gloss to the whole with a more fragmented hocket of gestures made from the same material.

Figure 10.1 Al gran sole carico d'amore: Act I, bars 379–81

The texts of Pavese play a crucial role:

> Of course Deola is a prostitute, but not only that. From one situation Pavese develops many others: it is about the relationship with death, with man, with a city, with a historical moment, with love, with beauty. For me, Pavese is a kind of prism that breaks the light into different colours. And when his poems come into contact with other texts they develop a new light to shine on the others.[21]

A similar technique is extended to generate the music of Deola in Act II: the first four scenes incorporate settings of passages from Pavese's *Canzone* (1931), *I mari del Sud* (1930), *Fumatori di carta* (1932) and *In the morning you always come back* (1950). It forms a continuous substrate uniting the revolutionary contexts of Paris, Russia and Turin. A phrase from *Non siam più la commune di Parigi* – of nine elements including the final rest – is used at original pitch, transposed up an augmented fourth and down a perfect fourth (Figure 10.2a). This produces three five-note pitch aggregates; one is exclusive, the other two overlap by three elements (Figure 10.2b). There are four different durations, expanded by Nono on to four time-bases; he will also use a quintuplet base (Figure10.2c). He produces three times three non-repeating cycles of pitch and duration sets, then repeats the process to generate a total of six lines of twenty-seven elements. Their difference in length results from the differing combinations of rhythm base and duration value. Nono then divides the whole result into nineteen individual melodic segments on the basis of shape, gesture and proportion (Figure 10.2d). The only structural traces that remain are the six start points. These he reorders to create a polyphony for four sopranos. Most units are used, some twice, and some are transposed by the intervals of the source material: semitone, tone and fourth (the opening minor sixth is not used). The transformation between this state of material and the final setting of poetry is the space where Nono is most free. None of this is used unchanged. The first passage 'Le nuvole' (scene 1) is entirely for four sopranos. It begins with the model but gradually departs as Nono sees new possibilities: grace notes

Al gran sole carico d'amore

Figure 10.2a From *Non siam più la commune di Parigi*

Figure 10.2b Pitch sets

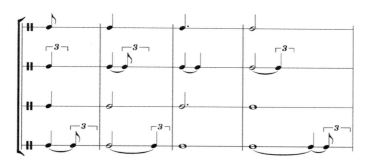

Figure 10.2c Basic durations

Figure 10.2d Segments 7–12

Figure 10.2e From Act II, scene 4
Figure 10.2 Al gran sole carico d'amore: derivation of Deola material, Act II

transform harmonic implications and add new gestural rhymes, pitch coincidences are exploited and rhythms are changed, particularly by extending the ends of phrases. The same material is developed more freely in the following two passages 'E io penso alla forza' (scene 2) and 'Lo spiraglio' (scene 4); both begin as solo lines, expanding into the quartet only at their ends. 'Lo spiraglio' ('the glimmer') is represented by the turning of the three notes of segment 7, repeated at the beginning of each of the first two three-line sections. A bell picks out isolated notes to create a melody on another time-plane, as does a solo alto with the quartet of 'Le nuvole'. Figure 10.2e shows the continuation of 'Lo spiraglio' with material from segments 9, 7 and 12. The setting of text may be a late stage in preparing the score, but Nono's initial analysis of its semantic and sonic properties has informed every musical decision. This newly confident approach to folding, fragmenting and redistributing material will become important in his next stage of development, notably in *Fragmente-Stille, An Diotima*.

The massive, all-encompassing twelve-note *schieramenti della machina repressiva* descend directly from similar moments in *Il canto sospeso*, *Intolleranza* or *Ricorda cosa ti hanno fatto in Auschwitz*. They occupy aural space entirely, eliminating all trace of other musical life, but are empty, lifeless themselves; they afford no development, musical or otherwise, no engagement even in the last prolonged accumulation to the assassination of The Mother. In contrast, the orchestral *Riflessioni* of Act I have clearly articulated forms. They are tightly contrapuntal constructs, balances of mirrors and forward development, exchanges of clearly differentiated colour and pitch-set. Fermata of varying lengths draw attention to their formal nature. These are not transitional or programmatic moments, but invitations to the listener to reflect on events.

In Act II, scene 3, 1950s Turin is represented by the documentary texts from *Un diario italiano*. Here the orchestral *Riflessioni* that ends *Ein Gespenst* is arranged to incorporate choirs and soloists. Some of the voice-leading is changed to create more vocal lines and there are minor changes to orchestration to enhance definition (and perhaps help an opera house choir to find pitches). The clear perspectives of colour of the original allow straightforward substitutions by vocal groups. The solemn four-part motet *Per gli operai morti* which concludes the scene is one of the ritornelli *Per i compagni morti* from *Ein Gespenst*, and will return, transposed, as *Continuità dell Madre* at the end of the work. The three Moncada episodes of Act II, scene 5 are taken directly from the same work, their proportional rhythms now notated precisely. The

Al gran sole carico d'amore

massive sustained *fff* body of orchestral sound that ends the first act is that which concludes the Moncada section of the earlier work. Its unstoppable energy now stands in contradistinction to the brutal but lifeless *schieramenti*. In scene 6, the words of Vietnamese women replace those of *The East is Red*, in the central symmetrical passage from that section of *Ein Gespenst*. Here, the soprano lines are condensed differently from their underlying counterpoint. An ensemble of prisoners – a gesture to Dallapiccola, perhaps, but also to Verdi – presents texts by Gramsci, Dimitrov and Castro: expressions of faith. Gramsci sings Nono's own stark contemporary warning – 'You are driving Italy to ruin. It's up to us communists to save her' – his speech rhythms made clear by timpani and all the upper strings. As Dimitrov and Fidel sing their parting words, the motet-like movement of male chorus doubled by muted trombones settles on a perfect fifth – an archaic sound, thoroughly in the Italian operatic tradition – followed by the tolling of low bells.

The *schieramento* that begins the last scene is not the brief symbolic presence of its immediate predecessors. The body of sound intensifies inexorably over a minute to culminate in the assassination of The Mother, the act that causes the people to rise and revolt against its oppression. Such violence can only be temporary; the voice of The Mother will remain. From the vocal glissandi accompanying her death emerges the harmonic-lyrical clarity of her memory and 'continuity'. A wide-ranging wordless soprano monody, derived like the Deola material above, is answered by The Mother herself. She intones a phrase from *L'Internationale* – 'non più servi ne padroni' ('no more servants nor masters') – the source of the accompanying motet, and then sings it rhythmically, followed by another fragment, 'Su lottiamo' ('Let's get up and fight'). In being isolated, the reference of this rhythmic-melodic shape, the start of the chorus, is unmistakable: Verdi's 'Va, pensiero', the chorus of the Hebrew slaves, the cherished patriotic song of a free and united Italy. There could be no clearer line of communication to Nono's audience at La Scala. He may also have had in mind the performances of *Nabucco* in East Berlin, when the public would applaud Verdi's chorus loudly for their own liberation. Finally, only the female chorus remains. Mirroring the sounds of the male prisoners (Gramsci, Dimitrov, Fidel) at the end of the previous scene, they dissolve to two perfect fifths separated by a semitone, to a single fifth and then a single note. Nono leaves the outline of his future pitch universe hanging in the air.

A national event

At the beginning of 1975, with the score completed and *Al gran sole* entering production, Nono found himself embroiled in a public debate even more heated than he had imagined. The infrastructure of Italian culture was undergoing upheaval. It could clearly not be maintained without major change. At a conference at Turin in January, Grassi proposed a new model by which La Scala would become the hub of a network of regional opera houses. The suggestion met with accusations of cultural colonialism, but the discussions encompass the full range of political issues, of which the opera house stood at the symbolic core: regionalism, funding for culture, the prioritising of high art music over popular culture and the expensive maintaining of a heritage.[22]

Nono's association with La Scala, and with Abbado and Pollini – who could hardly be dismissed as avant-gardists – put him at the centre of Italian cultural life. Their LP recording of *Como una ola* was released in January 1975 to enthusiastic reviews. In early February, Nono made his first visit to Portugal, invited by the newly legalised Portuguese Communist Party following the 'carnation revolution' and the overthrow of dictatorship a year earlier.[23] His message was clear: 'For me, music, as much as a moment of creation, of selecting acoustic

Al gran sole carico d'amore

material, is an act of understanding of our historical situation.'[24] On his return, he participated in a youth festival *Musica per la libertà* at the Palazzo dello Sport stadium in Rome, marking the thirtieth anniversary of liberation and expressing solidarity with contemporary liberation struggles. Artists from folk to free jazz, singer–songwriters to Latin-American 'nueva canción' groups such as *Quilapayun* and *Inti-Illimani*, performed to a crowd of some 15,000.[25] The performance was to include the Italian premiere of Nono's *Per Paul Dessau*, written in December 1974 for the composer's 80th birthday and presented in the DDR. The wrong reel was in his suitcase on his return from Portugal, so he introduced the final part of *Il canto sospeso* instead; it was soon drowned by calls and whistles from an audience used to other forms of music. Nono interrupted the performance and addressed the crowd:

> Comrades – I understand there's a certain difficulty, but we communists must be convinced, aware, that we must use all the means of culture at our disposal. We must use all means, not just the guitar – from the guitar to political song to electronic music to instrumental music – and not abandon ourselves to facile triumphalism or political simplicity. Communist culture is a serious fact, a fact that brings obligations. As Gramsci says, great intelligence can be difficult, but remember that we need all our intelligence, all the means at our disposal, if we are to bring about the cultural hegemony of the working class.[26]

As he spoke, a captivated silence turned to rapturous applause.[27] Through their various encounters at such events, a warm friendship developed between the Nonos and the Chilean musicians of *Quilapayun*. Exiled to France since the Pinochet coup, they often used the texts of Julio Huasi in their popular-political songs. Their ethos is clear in the liner notes to their album *Basta*, recently released in Italy: 'Bourgeois society wants art to be another factor contributing to social alienation; we artists should transform it into a revolutionary weapon, until the contradiction that currently exists between art and society is finally surpassed.'[28] Nono amassed a considerable collection of nueva canción recordings through the early 1970s.

In late February, at a meeting to discuss to subsidy for La Scala, the leader of the Christian Democrat group in Milan – Massimo De Carolis – announced that for Nono's new opera the theatre was to be draped in red flags, that its famous choir was to sing *Bandiera Rossa* and that Lyubimov had been expelled by the USSR for being too left-wing. Grassi refuted these distortions, but the DC sensed that the world of theatre, so central to Italian culture, had been dominated by the left since the war, and planned a counter-attack. Perhaps emboldened by the 'historic compromise' they intended to lay claim to some of this power. In the absence of constructive proposals, a kind of capitalist realism became the threat: to divert performing arts funding into crowd-pleasers and education, and to transform the theatres into multi-purpose venues. Meanwhile, La Scala, with its 750 employees, was facing bankruptcy; the orchestra could only be paid until the end of March.[29] Loans had fallen due, the receivers had been called in and the government subsidy had as yet failed to materialise. The socialist major Aldo Aniasi responded to further threats by making La Scala and the Piccolo Teatro autonomous, with himself as President. He and Grassi responded to an 'invitation' to reconsider their programme by cancelling performances of Verdi and Puccini rather than Nono; Grassi described the reduced budget as a state of 'pre-agony'.[30] They asserted artistic independence, supported by protests by musicians and theatre workers, a petition from artists across the country and outcry from the press. 'Who's afraid of Luigi Nono?' asked the conservative *Corriere della Sera*, pointing out that the whole episode was a mark of the power of Nono's work.[31] In a further attack, the DC suggested that Nono's opera was an act of propaganda ahead of forthcoming elections;

Al gran sole carico d'amore

the PCI were also holding a general rehearsal for their XIV Congress in Milan in March.[32] Grassi answered that Nono's opera, first planned for the previous season, was programmed for entirely artistic reasons, just like the new works commissioned from Béjart, Maderna and Berio. It was the DC who had 'instrumentalised' Nono's opera politically, he observed.[33] Pestalozza noted the difference between the debate over Nono's work and the undisputed, almost simultaneous production of Manzoni's *Per Massimiliano Robespierre* in PCI-run Bologna.[34] For both composers, 'the theatre is a witness of a willingness to confront, of a participation and awareness of the here and now, according to a concept of consciousness and participation which is then realized in music'.[35]

Meanwhile, Nono, Lyubimov and Borovsky were presenting their work at factories, cultural centres and schools around Milan; the *Corriere* nervously noted Lyubimov's red scarf.[36] Another interviewer described his subject: 'Luigi Nono likes to joke, but when he speaks about music he becomes nervous and doesn't control a barely perceptible stammer.' Nono expressed his hope that tickets would be made available to students, workers and unions:

> My works must be performable anywhere: on the street, in the piazza, in a sports hall. [. . .] I am not remotely interested in one-sided polemics of the fascists and the silent majority. It is true that my opera must be also understood politically. This is the source of the ideological battles, which I obviously expected. I do not retreat, but I maintain that my reasons are musical and not oratorical.[37]

The premiere at the newly renovated Teatro Lirico on 4 April was a major public event. Curiosity had spread far beyond the world of opera. Lyubimov's production and Borovsky's sets contributed importantly to its success; in every interview Nono insisted on the collaborative nature of their work. The sets, lighting and movement of people across the stage recalled the geometric, constructivist drawings made during their intense periods of working together. The theatrical visions of Myakovsky are clearly present. The planes of action mirrored Nono's structures. In the more linear first act, the chorus moves almost on the vertical, appearing on suspended, tilting shelves through the height of the stage. They come to life as if from the serried coffins of the infamous images from the Commune. In the second, more fragmented act, movement takes place on the horizontal as groups continuously reconfigure. Twenty minutes of applause followed the performance to a packed audience of eighteen hundred: 'a prolonged party of which the motor was now the applause of the public, its passive subjects the composer, performers and collaborators, or rather co-authors'.[38] 'It would have continued if the safety curtain had not been brought down.'[39] The Italian press was unanimous: it was 'a triumphant premiere – a victory for culture',[40] a work of 'elegy and hope',[41] 'twenty minutes of triumph',[42] 'a colossal lay oratorio'.[43] Despite ungraciously mentioning the cost, the presence of 'intellectuals' and the performers' informal dress, even the *Corriere* had to admit that 'Milan decreed a great success to Luigi Nono. The launch of his new opera finished in glory.'[44]

A Gramscian opera?

Nono had three essays printed in the programme, all from over a decade earlier: *Presenza storica nella musica d'oggi*, *Possibilità e necessità di un nuovo teatro musicale* and *Text – Musik – Gesang*.[45] In terms of the historical roots of his music, his vision of a new theatre and the relationship between music and text, Nono seemed to be presenting his new work as the fruit of a long period of development. 'For a new musical theatre' is the programme's subtitle. *Al gran sole* is not only political in its subject and nature. To write what was to all intents and purposes an opera, especially in this febrile climate, was itself a political act – to do so for the heart of Italian cultural life, La Scala, even more so. Its stories of the persistence of human faith, courage and optimism through tragic setbacks reflect events during the process of composition: the death of Allende and subsequent repression in Chile (from which Nono's friend Huasi narrowly escaped), and the death of Maderna during the writing of his own *Satyricon*. The work had occupied Nono fully; asked about the surrounding scandal, he found it 'irrelevant, risible, absurd and ignorant'.[46] Other political events were more relevant. Confronted with the imperialist resurgence of 1973, manifest most clearly in Chile, stagnation and repression in the USSR and the 'strategy of tension' in Italy – terrorism, industrial strife and five governments in two years – Berlinguer led the PCI to a 'historic compromise'. Beginning with a series of articles in *Rinascita* in the autumn of 1973, he proposed the setting aside of sectarianism so that the PCI and elements of the DC could work together towards stability and progress. Berlinguer was confronting material reality and taking steps to move it in a positive direction. While they might have chosen different steps, this had been substantially the plea of *Il Manifesto*. This was an enormous step in Italian Communist thinking, and one that Nono supported. In 1975, he would be elected to the Central Committee of the PCI. Berlinguer's strategy led to the PCI winning over one third of the national vote in the elections of 1976, unprecedented for a West European communist party. This pragmatism continued in a policy of national solidarity, the PCI only withdrawing support for the Christian Democrat government with the kidnap and murder of Aldo Moro in 1978.

The evolution of the Party must have prompted Nono to reflect on his own continuing process of transformation during the composition of *Al gran sole*: 'In this way my ring modulators will no longer produce incomprehensible 'avantgardism', but music that can speak to the hearts of people today.'[47] This was the aspect observed by Giorgio Napoletano, then cultural secretary of the PCI and latterly President of Italy:

> an opera which is something new in the multiplicity of its contributions and in the maturity of the effort to communicate with the public. [. . .] At the same time, the urge to communicate a high ideal, political and human message [. . .] has been pursued with rigour, without renouncing the fruits of Nono's long and laborious research into the language of music, and without ever falling into declamation or facile political ostentation.[48]

Subsequent commentators have focused on *Al gran sole* as a textual and musical assemblage. References to collage are misleading; Nono took issue with such techniques in several occasions. For the listener, this is no more collage than the *Mass in B Minor*. For Nono, *Al gran sole* is the product of a continuous process. There is certainly no external reference of the kind of Berio's *Sinfonia*. To see the reuse of material as compositionally problematic is to fetishise the organic, integral uniqueness of the work.[49] The 'class sound signals' of revolutionary songs work differently. They constitute a constellation of entry points for the listener. The texts, on the other hand, are quite explicitly assembled. They are all voices that for Nono are heroic, from the anonymous factory worker to Marx and Che. There is no requirement for the listener to place these words further, to relate them externally; any dialogic property is not essential to the work.

Despite its revolutionary impact, important elements *of Al gran sole* link it directly to the tradition of *melodramma*: from the explosive crowd scenes to the solemn wisdom from prison, and above all its essential vocality. Such connections are not ironic or referential. If the work is to be tested in Nono's own terms, then we must consider the extent to which it is

Al gran sole carico d'amore

Gramscian.[50] This twin state – revolutionary internationalist music theatre and Italian melodramma – constitutes a contradiction of the kind Gramsci saw as necessary for the artist; without this, he becomes 'sectarian'. The theatre is itself a model for social collaboration; it becomes a creation that transcends the individual artist. Unlike literature, music and the other arts tend towards a cosmopolitan language for an international elite, says Gramsci. But by working as a collective, it is possible to bring understanding to a wider audience.[51] This is the activity Nono was engaged in, not the politicking. Other clues are in Nono's own markings in Gramsci's writings: 'Art is always related to a specific culture, in struggling to reform which one works to create a new art, to modify the whole man.'[52] The opera house was both a symbol and a model of Italian culture, the current turmoil surrounding such institutions a microcosm of the turmoil outside. Gramsci's circumspect view of the power of *melodramma* was well known; he saw it as the Italian equivalent of the novel. He writes of the Italian tendency to *melodrammatise* events as a constraint on cultural evolution. A new language, he says, should be 'lively and expressive, but at the same time sober and measured'.[53] His view of popular song points precisely to its role in *Al gran sole*: 'What distinguishes the popular song of a nation or a culture is not its artistic origin or historical origins, but its way of conceiving of the world and life, in contrast with official society.'[54]

Gramsci's view of history informs the very structure of *Al gran sole*: history is not deterministic or mechanical.[55] Like Nono, he has faith that transformation is possible, but it requires acts of courage and creativity. Like Nono's temporal structures, these acts are both cyclic and teleological; history is both synchronic and diachronic. The passages of *Continuità* at the end of each part – of the Commune and of The Mother – point to their persistence; they become part of a cumulative force for transformation. This approach to history will itself be transformed with the central role of Benjamin's theory in *Prometeo*. Gramsci's own explanation that transformation is the product of incremental individual actions, not of imposed ideology, presages *Prometeo* itself: 'A collective consciousness, a living organism, only forms through the multiplicity that results from the uniting of singularities: one cannot say that "silence" is not a multiplicity.'[56] His analogy is the orchestra itself. Writers have pointed to *La fabbrica illuminata* as embodying Gramscian principles.[57] With Nono's intensified engagement with Gramsci's writings and the relationship of his new work with what Gramsci identified as the essence of Italian culture, *Al gran sole* is the full embodiment of this influence.

There are more general concerns: Nono's contributing through his work to the development of a new cultural hegemony, and his role and responsibilities as an intellectual engaged in raising consciousness. Making scores stood at the centre of a network of cultural and political activities. From the conferences with Pestalozza through the 1960s, *Musica/Realtà* and the events surrounding *Al gran sole*, to discussions with groups of workers or artists from Latin America to the USSR, such events should not be understood as 'outreach' or 'educational'. They are integral to the work itself. Reports all indicate that Nono listened as much as he talked. His listening provided motivation, material and trajectory for the thought that would produce music. Gramsci's view of culture encompassed not merely works of art but the modes of thought of a people in a historical moment. The contiguity of Nono's music with other aspects of his thought, the analogies between processes and principles, are therefore quite conscious: 'As Gramsci said, participation in reality, the maximum invention in this reality.'[58]

According to Gramsci, 'Creating a new culture does not only mean making "original" discoveries as an individual, it also, especially means the critical deepening of truths already uncovered or "socialized".'[59] The historical roots of Nono's music had been a vital part of his thought from the beginning, but they were perhaps less a part of a mainstream cultural consciousness still grounded in residual Romanticism. In *Como una ola* and *Al gran sole* we see a new confidence to address that consciousness directly. Paradoxically, as the world, the economic–social reality, changed, so would Nono's relationship with Gramsci. While we might still see his later work and self-image as an artist as underpinned by well-established Gramscian principles, references to Gramsci in interviews become sparser and themselves romanticised. In *Al gran sole*, the figure of Gramsci, imprisoned, separated from his loved ones and from the party that is the instrument of his thought, becomes as powerful as the texts themselves. For the later Nono, Gramsci becomes a poet-hero.

Under a common flag: 'Für Paul Dessau'

In 1969, Nono had expressed his intention to write a work for Paul Dessau's seventy-fifth birthday.[60] He had known Dessau since 1952, and their warm friendship had evolved through Nono's regular visits to the DDR since 1958. As a senior and reliable party member, Dessau was permitted to attend events in the West. The two were thus able to exchange ideas and experiences with a considerable degree of understanding and openness. Dessau negotiated an artistic relationship between sincere public communism and a more critical personal understanding of the DDR; it was perhaps his very proactive role in East German cultural life that allowed him to create such a space.[61] Despite his solidarity with musicians in the DDR and their struggle to build a socialist state, Nono had no time for the doctrine of socialist realism or 'bureaucratic' structures – the 'frozen monsters' of his *Guai ai gelidi mostri* a decade later. For his part, Dessau had condemned the temporary banning of Nono's music by the DDR in 1963 as 'a stupid move, staged by some 'Eskimo''. [. . .] We however hear your music with the free, fresh, open, trained, loving ears of communists, who want to help the world change.' [62] He referred to Nono as 'a great person, a real communist, who screams at what is going on and loves tenderly what is dear to him.'[63] Nono describes his friend in a contemporaneous report on music in the DDR:

> Dessau is the foundation of current musical development [in the DDR]. [. . .] In Dessau the vast understanding of current problems is based on that great resourcefulness that derives from his wide musical experience, his struggle as a militant, always full of irrepressible enthusiasm, of real wisdom and constant motivation.[64]

Dessau's eightieth birthday in 1974 presented another opportunity. It was agreed that Nono should write a new work for the official birthday concert. Presented by the Akademie der Künste der DDR, Deutsche Staatsoper Berlin and the Berliner Ensemble, the event was billed as 'Solidarität zum 80. Geburtstag von Paul Dessau, Solidaritätsmatinee'. In an early announcement, Nono's contribution was entitled *Von Lenin bis Allende (Eine Montage)*.[65] Perhaps this had been agreed in the echo of *Como una ola*, before the overthrow of Allende in September 1973; the focus had changed by the work's premiere the following year.

The work performed on 15 December, now called *Für Paul Dessau*, is Nono's last piece for tape alone. Made in Milan during work on *Al gran sole*, its four channels were mixed to stereo for presentation in Berlin. Like the larger work, *Für Paul Dessau* deals with the past and present of the worldwide human struggle towards a socialist future. Its strength lies in its balancing of two planes: extrovertly public and intimately private. This was an official occasion, and the texts are public declarations on global matters by world figures. At the same time, the work is a private conversation between Nono and Dessau; we can see traces of some of its references, but of many others probably not. The two shared the experience of negotiating an honest relationship between these two worlds. The principle voices are those of Lenin, Che, Castro and Lumumba,

Al gran sole carico d'amore

heard in documentary recordings – speeches that together cover the international diffusion of communism and its development though Dessau's lifetime. Lenin – on the Soviet and the Red Army – represents the foundation of the common political context of the two friends. Lumumba's 1961 talk – the last before his assassination – recalls a shared memory: they had listened to Dessau's 1963 *Requiem für Lumumba* together in 1965, when both were in Berlin working on music for different productions of *Die Ermittlung*.[66] Castro's Second Declaration of Havana (1962) brings the defiant optimism of Cuba, and Che's speech in solidarity with the people of South Vietnam is a reminder of continuing struggles; the premiere of *Für Paul Dessau* came only weeks before the US Congress refused President Ford's request for additional funds to support the South Vietnamese government. The Third World – the world beyond Europe, Russia and China – is thus the principle locus of the work, the source of energy of its vision of freedom and justice. The addition of the voice of martyred German communist leader Ernst Thälmann links it to the history of German communism and recalls one of Dessau's best-known songs, *Die Thälmann Kolonne*, recorded in 1937 by Ernst Busch in Barcelona during the Spanish Civil War.

To these documentary recordings, Nono adds material from his own archive at the Studio di Fonologia: *Il canto sospeso*, the protests of 1968 (*Non consumiamo Marx*), and his recent recording sessions with Pollini and Slavka Taskova (*Como una ola*). Dessau had expressed admiration for all three pieces.[67] An initial five-minute graphical plan expands to over seven as he assembles the tape in the studio with Zuccheri.

Nono plots a polyphony of the four main orators in three sections of about two minutes each, framed and separated by brief passages of instrumental and electronic sound. At moments they surround the listener in a unified polyglot gesture, as in the initial addressing of their respective constituencies. Elsewhere, more clearly intelligible statements are given a particular emphasis by their combination or sequence. Hoffmann finds a clear focus to each of the three sections: struggle and a call to action, hope and faith in change, and new consciousness and vision of a socialist future.[68] The short opening and closing passages reinforce this: the work opens with assertive brass and percussion from *Il canto sospeso*, and ends with high soprano voices floating in the clear air. The recording of Thälmann later in the first section, the only text in German, has a different voice; his 'most brotherly and revolutionary greetings to the Congress' seem addressed directly to the Berlin audience, or perhaps to comrades everywhere. It is followed swiftly by Che's 'and the struggle in South Vietnam begins anew', as a reminder of the continuous task.

Nono's handling of the intelligibility of these texts mediates their sheer quantity and immense political weight. Moments of clarity emerge as individual spoken phrases float free from the mass of voices. The different degrees of presence of the materials creates a deep sonic perspective. Pollini's low piano attacks are the closest to the listener; they articulate the more distant layers of orchestral and vocal sounds. Modulation and reverberation are used to create dense sound complexes, but also to elide the different kinds of material. The anonymous voices of the people shape the path of the whole – they are its motivating energy and sonic foundation. Sounds of protest are prominent through the first section, balanced by dense choral textures. High soprano figure begins to emerge in the second section, preparing clear, focused final sounds; the demonstrations are absent in the third as society organises itself. *Für Paul Dessau* is a manifesto of faith in humanity and personal friendship.

Notes

1 Weber, 2009, p. 81.
2 Letter to Abbado, 8 November 1971, in Trudu, 2008, pp. 189–90.

Al gran sole carico d'amore

3 Telegram to Abbado, 21 May 1972, ALN.

4 Letter to Tatiana Schucht, 15 December 1930, in Gramsci, 1977, vol. I, p. 369.

5 Stenzl, 1998, p. 89.

6 Smeliansky, 1999, p. 33.

7 Letter to Lyubimov, November 1972 in Trudu, 2008, p. 195.

8 Dobrovolskaja, 2006, p. 196. Lyubimov, in Degrada 1977, p. 52.

9 Smeliansky, 1999, p. 40.

10 Letters from Berlinguer, 6 March 1973, 1 June 1973, in Trudu, 2008, pp. 200–1.

11 ALN 40.05/04.

12 Waterhouse, 1999, p. 826.

13 ALN 40.06/14dx.

14 Letters from Grassi: 28 January 1974, 21 August 1974, ALN.

15 ALN 40.07/06.

16 Nono surely knew *La Muralla* by Cuban poet Nicolas Guillen. Inverting the wall as symbol of oppression, it becomes an object of hope, built by hands of all colours working together. As a song it was a firm fixture in the politically charged repertoires of Latin-American 'nueva canción' groups, including both *Quilapayun* and *Inti-Illimani*, whose work Nono knew well.

17 'Luigi Nono e Luigi Pestalozza a proposito di *Al gran sole carico d'amore*', 1975. LNII, p. 210.

18 Interview with Sigrid Neef, 1974. LNII, p. 199.

19 Zehelin, Grewe and Nono, 1978.

20 'Ein Gespenst geht um in der Welt'. LNI, p. 476.

21 Nono, in Zehelein, Grewe and Nono, 1978.

22 *Il Popolo Lombardo*, 23 January 1975.

23 A full account of the visit is given in De Assis, 2015.

24 *Diario de Lisboa*, 3 February 1975.

25 *l'Unità*, 19 February 1975. Borio, 2013, p. 31.

26 From the documentary film *Musica per la libertà*, Luigi Perelli, 1975. Available at: http://patrimonio. aamod.it/aamod-web/film/detail/IL8600001518/22/musica-liberta.html?startPage=0&idFondo= (accessed 3 January 2018). The performance of *Inti Illimani* and Nono's intervention were then incorporated in *Per un'Italia diversa*, a film by Antonio Bertini documenting the transformation of the Italian political landscape in 1975, when under Berlinguer's leadership the PCI had taken eleven million votes in the June regional elections.

27 *Il Corriere della Sera*, 20 February 1975.

28 Liner notes to *Basta*, recorded June 1969 in Chile, released in Italy 1974 by *I dischi dello zodiaco*, ALN.

29 *Corriere d'Informazione*, 26 March 1975.

30 *Il Mattino* 27 February 1975.

31 *Corriere della Sera*, 26 February 1975.

32 *Le Ore*, 12 March 1975.

33 *Avanti!* 23 March 1975.

34 Like *Al gran sole*, Manzoni's work is based on an assemblage of historical texts. Pestalozza and Virginio Puecher assisted Manzoni with the texts and dramaturgy.

35 *Rinascita*, 14 March 1975, p. 43.

36 *Corriere della Sera*, 6 March 1975.

37 *Corriere d'Informazione*, 26 February 1975.

38 Massimo Mila in *La Stampa*, 6 April 1975.

39 *Il Corriere della Sera*, 6 April 1975.

40 Rubens Tedeschi in *l'Unità*, 5 May 1975.

41 Mario Messinis in *Il Gazzetino*, 6 April 1975,

42 *Il Giorno*, 5 April 1975.

43 *Il Lavoro*, 6 April 1975.

44 *Il Corriere della Sera*, 6 April 1975.

45 Degrada, 1977, p. 24.

46 *Il Corriere della Sera*, 6 March 1975.

47 *Il Corriere d'Informazione*, 26 February 1975.

48 *l'Unità*, 6 April 1975.

49 For instance, Vogt, 1985, an otherwise perceptive analysis.

Al gran sole carico d'amore

50 For further discussion, see Noller, 1989, and Lüderssen, 2007. For an introduction to Gramsci's cultural theory in English, see Crehan, 2002.
51 Gramsci, 1977, p. 731.
52 Gramsci, 1950, p. 189.
53 Gramsci, 1977, p. 1739.
54 Gramsci, 1950, p. 126.
55 Gramsci, 1977, p. 1770.
56 Gramsci, 1977, p. 1771.
57 Stenzl, 1975, p. 433. Lüderssen, 2007, p. 100.
58 'Musica e Teatro', 1966. LNI, p. 210.
59 Gramsci, 1977, p. 1377.
60 Letter to Dessau, 6 June 1969, in Hoffmann, 2016, p. 201.
61 Tischer, 2009.
62 Dessau, 2000, p. 102.
63 Dessau, 2000, p. 88.
64 'Come si fa musica nella RDT'. LNI, p. 317.
65 Hoffmann, 2016, p. 225.
66 Dessau, 2000, p. 121.
67 Hoffmann, 2016, p. 210.
68 Hoffmann, 2016, p. 212.

11

WAVES

'..... sofferte onde serene ...'

Dealing with the practical and personal dynamics of an opera house had left Nono exhausted but keen to get back to making music in a more creative environment. 'A tidal wave' is how he referred to the enormous, inflexible organism that is an operatic production.[1] He wanted to return to a direct, intimate productive relationship. Nono had already described such a new work to Stenzl before the opening of *Al gran sole*.[2] It was to be called *Notturni-Albe*, for piano and tape. The title is rich in associations: the importance of Chopin in Pollini's musical persona, Pavese's symbolic dawns and the new beginnings of a reinvigorated, post-opera house creativity. There were already hints in *Al gran sole*; Act II is prefaced 'La notte è lunga ma già spunta l'alba' ('The night is long but already dawn is breaking'), and at its centre is Pavese's poem *Lo spiraglio dell'alba*, sung by 'Deola – Alba amore'.

The revolutionary poet Vladimir Mayakovsky and his lover Lilya Brik were the poetic and emotional protagonists in Nono's imagination. There is an ambivalence in Nono's abiding fascination with Mayakovsky and Brik: alongside the intensity of their relationship, of Mayakovsky's Futurist-grounded creativity and of his literary–political organising, there is also the poet's suicidal despair of ever being understood or relevant. The ideas of Mayakovsky, of Lilya and of her husband Osip Brik – the three effectively constituted a family – also have theoretical implications. Brik's *Sound Repetitions* of 1917 presents an understanding of poetry rooted in sound and the physicality of the poet – the 'rhythmic impulse'.[3] Sonic and semantic are inseparable. His analytical approach – modulating rhythmic networks of sound, meter and meaning – is so resonant with Nono's that it is difficult not to posit an influence. Despite his formalist stance and insistence on the vital role of technique, for Brik, 'Art is first and foremost a social phenomenon. Changes in the psychology of the artist and the public, and changes of artistic forms are but a reflection of deeper changes which take place in the social nature of art.'[4]

Exploring piano and pianist

On 3 and 4 September 1975 Nono was back in the Studio di Fonologia with Pollini, preparing the work that would become ..... *sofferte onde serene ...* for piano and tape. They had intended to present the new work in a small town in Lombardy as part of *Musica/Realtà*.[5] This would

Waves

have been not just a political gesture – resistance to the 'hierarchy' and 'exclusiveness' of musical life – but fully in keeping with the intimate nature of the work itself. Pollini had already programmed a performance for Turin in the autumn.[6] Eventually, it was premiered in Milan on 17 April 1977, after the piece had followed a quite different trajectory.

In the studio they seem to have begun with no prepared material. The five reels of tape contain a new exploration of the sounds Pollini draws from the instrument. High, low, single notes, repeated notes, tremolo and chords – they investigate the possibilities as before, but now there are differences in Nono's responses, in what interests him. The interaction in the studio is less formalised, more intimate musically and personally. Nono's requests to Pollini and his three successive layers of analysis of the tapes are now more like his way of relating to singers. He is less interested in the piano as an abstract sound-producing device and more concerned with the particularities of Pollini's playing. Their talk of 'those sounds which are usually lost in the hall' presumably refer to earlier conversations, the experience of *Como una ola*. This is now material that originates entirely in Pollini's possession, as it were: the release of the pedal or the modulation of the decaying vibration of the strings as the dampers return, for example. As well as this attention to sonic and performance detail, Nono is using the kind of language he had used with the non-musicians of the living theatre in *A Floresta*. As Pollini improvises, Nono interrupts him. He observes that Pollini tends always to look for a line, instead of which Nono asks him to think of the notes and groups as isolated events – 'trying not to construct a line'.[7] It is unfortunate that tape was still not to be wasted in the 1970s – much of the conversation is cut. In a montage by Zuccheri we hear Nono asking for sevenths and ninths. The incidental sounds fascinate him, particularly the pedal. He explores this further by repeatedly releasing the pedal with different silently depressed chords, having Zuccheri work with Pollini to dampen the pedal resonance, or to add to the sound with a beater on the wood or strings. Already they describe certain sounds as 'bells'. They experiment with the speed of note-repetition, with the particularities and limits of Pollini's touch and this instrument. Periodic repeated sounds produce changing modulation effects. The body of the piano becomes an acoustic space within which sounds form, move and resonate. The middle register, the zone of clearly perceptible figure, interests Nono less than the extremes, in which they experiment with the colour effects of differently constituted clusters: hard and dry in the high registers, complex and resonant in the low. He has Pollini try combinations wider than an octave. One particular pitch construct draws his attention – D E♭ E, G G♯ A – which he then explores, spread across the entire keyboard in different configurations. Polarisations emerge between dry *fff* attacks and quiet, sustained resonance, between groups and single sounds.

The tape seems to have been constructed, at least provisionally, before Nono began to compose the score in Venice. He categorises and selects from the recordings to plan a simple arch form: outer sections of complex percussive sounds produced by Pollini and Zuccheri together, within those the passages of 'Mauro solo', and at the centre material from the fifth reel, described in his notes as 'isolated groups'. His abbreviation already suggests a formal idea from *Prometeo*: 'IS+LA', 'island'. The passages with both Pollini and Zuccheri making sounds he describes as 'Toni e Bepi' – the hapless pair who are the butt of a hundred jokes in dialect, the Venetian Mutt and Jeff. A comic tape montage by Zuccheri illustrates the creative joy shared in these days.

The final tape, edited by Nono alone, retains this basic structure.[8] The first (0' –2'45") and last (11'49"– 13'40") sections both use the low, widely separated percussive attacks created by Pollini and Zuccheri together.[9] We hear Zuccheri's beater on the wood, Pollini's individual releasing of individual pitches within a complex, and in the final strokes the resonance not of the strings but of the case itself. The opening section becomes a more complex exposition with

Waves

the superimposition of material from the fourth section (9'17"– 11'49"): sparsely repeated notes and clusters in different registers. It establishes both the sonic world and the base pitched resonances of the piece. The pitches of the second section of the tape (2'45"– 4'50") are more varied and widely spaced, often expanding into narrow pitch bands and micro-rhythms. Their 'pure' piano sound draws attention to careful editing of attacks and resonances (as in *Como una ola*), the acoustic modulation of decay and some microtonal pitch-shifting. Beginning in the high register, they follow a continuous downward trajectory until the final low clusters introduce the denser, more dynamic central section (5'00"– 9'17"). Here the thud of a pedal release becomes an almost regular heartbeat. Above it, single low notes and rolling tremolos accumulate to dissolve at 6'25" to leave a space gradually filled by high, repeated rhythmic figuration. From the centre of the work at 6'50" this is underpinned by more slowly repeating bell-like clusters that develop their own logic and resonances until their energy too dissipates unevenly, like the decaying strokes of a peal. The waves of gentle low pulse that return in the final section are no longer disturbed by the initial turbulence, as if the actions of the live pianist have responded to, reordered and absorbed wave patterns to restore equilibrium.

'. . . the infinite smile of the waves'

Between the initial recordings and working on the score, tragedy had struck Maurizio and Marilisa Pollini – the work's dedicatees – and Nono had lost both his parents within three months. The death of Dallapiccola shortly before the premiere of *Al gran sole* must also have been a sad preparation for a year of loss.

> As my friendship with Maurizio Pollini deepened, together with the astonished awareness of his pianism, a harsh wind of death brushed across "the infinite smile of the waves", in both my family and the Pollinis'. This fellowship brought us still closer together in the infinite smile of ..... *sofferte onde serene* ... .[10]

Commentators have often pointed to the shape of the title itself; suffering and serenity are balanced by the waves. Work continued, but now with a deep personal significance. The diaries of Franz Kafka became an important touchstone as Nono sought to confront his own turmoil. An extract from the work's programme note describes the environment of its composition:

> In my home, on Giudecca in Venice, sounds arrive continuously from different bells, with different reverberations, different meanings, day and night, through the fog or the sun.
>
> There are the signals of life on the lagoon, on the sea.
>
> Calls to work, to meditation, warnings.
>
> And life continues in the suffering and serene necessity of 'the equilibrium of the profound interior', as Kafka says.[11]

The piano part is likewise composed in five main sections, falling into three nearly equal parts. In an early sketch headed *Fantasia*, Nono sets out the initial pitch material developed from Pollini's augmented octaves. Isolated high notes and low clusters are articulated into three sequences of elements which are then organised into self-balancing structures (Figure 11.1). This forms the basis of the opening twenty-five bars, a sequence of five five-bar gestures. Figure 11.2 shows the first. The first three and the last gesture have the same basic shape; they work their

Waves

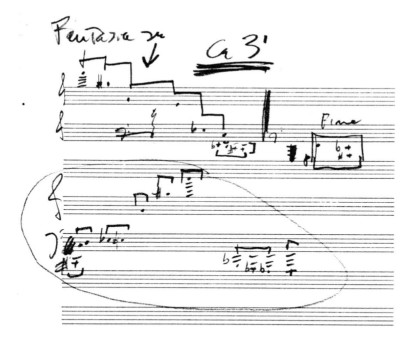

Figure 11.1 ..... *sofferte onde serene* ...: initial pitch material. (ALN 42.04/01rdx (detail). © The heirs of Luigi Nono. Reproduced by kind permission.)

way downwards through the pitch fields. The elements of Nono's pitch field remain in their original registers with the exception of elements 4–5 – C D E♭ E – which move up an octave during the second gesture and another octave in the fifth. Individual layers are sometimes thickened chromatically, which both draws attention to a particular layer and threatens the dissolving of its identity through a process of entropy. The additional B♭ in the right hand seems to serve a balancing function between its G♯ neighbour and the A above. Rhythms are spun from a minimal nine-element set of single and double attacks, displaced through the beat in divisions of 3, 4 or 5. We hear Nono's fascination with the acoustic artefacts of Pollini's fast repetition. In the opening bars these rhythms populate a clear structure of proportional layers in four registers, presumably by Nono's technique of interpolation:[12] 3 beats (A), 6+ beats (G♯), 12 (B–E♭) and 24 (low cluster). Only the fourth gesture (bars 16–20) follows a different pattern, a tight contrapuntal structure that stays within a middle register chromatic cluster F♯–B♭ until its final three chords (*fff ff pp*), which expand by a semitone in each direction. At the beginning of the fifth gesture we hear the clearest contrast between taped sounds of pedal and wood, followed by the live piano alone. Throughout the opening section the listener's attention is constantly drawn to the resonant space marked out by the polyphony of rhythmic streams. There is no figure beyond non-linear repetition. Sudden changes in dynamic produce internal hierarchies and fleeting polyphony between layers; Nono is sharing his own process of listening anew.

The second section is the same length. In contrary motion with the tape, it ascends through the full range of the piano, recalling the 'long march' of *Como una ola*. As it begins, the low acoustic piano brings high pitches on the tape into relief, filtered as if heard underwater. As the roles are reversed, low pedal sounds and notes transposed below the range of the piano draw attention to their higher non-harmonic partials. De Assis' exhaustive account shows how Nono analyses his own material from the opening to identify pitch sets and rhythmic figures that are

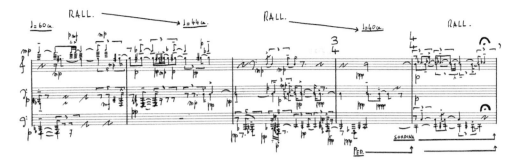

Figure 11.2 ..... *sofferte onde serene* ...: bars 1–5. (Reproduced by kind permission of Casa Ricordi.) For detail see Plate 2.

recombined and superimposed to produce new material.[13] Melodic figure begins to emerge at bars 37–8: like the title, a mirror pattern B♭ B♭ A♭ B A♭ B♭ B♭. Above the deep waves, the surface moves only in narrow intervals.

The central section (bars 50–101) is itself an arch and is effectively a development. A base sonority of fourth or fifth with augmented fourth is announced immediately, the root of a sequence of pitch sets that Nono recombines to generate the entire section. The whole is the product of three polyphonic textures, three interacting wave systems. We now hear not only multiple layers but multiple parallel dramas, brought into focus at moments such as the repeated interventions in bars 62–5 and their consolidating into a single high E at bar 73, static over the slowly repeating chords of the tape. Its compressed, latent energy is released in the twelve bars of energy of the Höhepunkt, a high, percussive canon in three voices, each beginning with a development of the opening rhythm of the piece and outlining a stretto of rising chromatic patterns. It is interrupted by a repeated *ffff* low cluster D–A♭ (bars 86–8), the axis about which the piece turns, in the echo of which the coda of this section returns quietly to the opening material, now distributed stably across registers.

The last two sections constitute a coda and its final echo. Nono extended his first draft of the fourth section by inserting receding waves of repeating notes. Outside these passages, it moves from the minor ninths of the very opening (bar 141) via a registrally distributed cluster F–B to open major ninths F♯ G♯ B♭ (bars 170–4), repeated gently as if to placate the waves below. At bar 138, the tape echoes the piano immediately. In this section the close relationship between Nono's score and Pollini's recordings is clearest. There are delays of the live notes, repeated as if to assert their being the same gesture, but also anticipations – something that will no longer be possible working only with live electronics, a direction of temporal travel that will be lost. Chopped chords, low clusters and pedal noises on the tape all defy the acoustics of the live piano and give perspective to its sustained sounds. As silences open up, the sudden presence or absence of residual resonance on the tape changes the shape of the acoustic space for the live piano and the listener – as if somebody had just walked into the room. Final pedal repetitions on tape mark time as residual movement is reabsorbed into a central A–C♯ cluster.

'. . . a man searching for truth'

That ..... *sofferte onde serene* ... remains one of Nono's most approachable works is partly a function of frame, scale and perspective. Nono and Pollini carry the listener with them without explicitly challenging the conventional listening stance appropriate to Pollini's core repertoire. This allows an intimacy and spontaneity to be shared with the listener unimpeded. Indeed, if the pianism of *sofferte* has a parallel, it might be in the wide-ranging polyrhythmic layers of Cecil Taylor. Not by coincidence were there reports of the tape being heard in performances by the virtuoso improvising group AMM. Other elements of Pollini's current repertoire are also heard. He had recently been performing Liszt's late *Nuages gris, Unstern!, Die Trauergondel* and *Richard Wagner–Venezia* – all included in the Milan recital – and we can assume that Pollini shared his understanding of this music with Nono.[14]

..... *sofferte onde serene* ... was heard twice in the concert: to end the first half and as an encore. As well as the Liszt pieces, Pollini's tour-de-force included Webern's *Variations* and Boulez's *Second Sonata*; Nono could not have been in more intense company. 'A programme of stupendous coherence' reported *l'Unità*, 'the warm reception and clamorous calls for Nono and Pollini were repeated with still more conviction'.[15]

Mila saw the work in the context of Nono's development:

> There was lively anticipation and curiosity; Nono deprived of his two most stable assets, the human voice and political engagement, and furthermore finding himself face to face with an instrument like the piano [. . .]. For Nono, who has many enemies, it was in a way a test: the test of being a 'pure' musician and not a political tribune [. . .]. The test was passed with flying colours. Triumphantly, indeed, according to the audience verdict, given in a hall packed especially by young people [. . .]
>
> For the first time Nono presented himself not as a man certain of the truth but as a man searching for truth, and above all who lives instead of fighting, who allows himself to live, with all that it brings, with plural visions of things and the world, with different perspectives, and thus with inner enriching and maturing.[16]

One might take issue with Mila on certain points – there is no voice as such, but human presence is at its most intimate, and as Nono explicitly equated composition with political action, *sofferte* must be considered a radical act – but his report gives a fair summary of its reception.

To posit a unique moment of return, reflection or reinvention in the composing of *s offerte* would be to ignore their role in Nono's established practice. Clearly, the composition of *Al gran sole* was both a major task and the culmination of a trajectory of more than a decade; in some respects *sofferte* is its complement. In its musical focus and personal significance, and in the freedom of thought these afforded Nono in the composing process, *sofferte* stands between two great spans of creative development. It also gives us a compact picture of his repertory of ways of thinking about composing at that critical moment. ..... *sofferte onde serene* ... is rich with poetic and technical metaphors, all of which and more Nono doubtless had in mind.

More than any other of his works, *sofferte* presents a specific sound image. This is no soft-focus postcard; his own environment provides the context for confronting suffering as much as seeking serenity, especially at the violent centre of the work. The bells and waves are not heard through alleys and *campi*, but across water, at the edge of Giudecca where the bells of four churches modulate each other's echoes across the canal, each with their own pitches, periodicity and schedule. Both on the wide Giudecca canal and beyond Nono's studio, looking away from the city across the lagoon, interference patterns are generated by waves on all levels: the surface disturbance of wind, the deep swell of storm and the wakes of everything from seabirds to cruise ships. Breathing quasi-periodicity and modulating wave patterns are emerging as important in Nono's re-evaluating of his elemental materials and models. Here, the fleeting single-pitch rhythmic figures summon attention like light briefly reflecting from waves at different points in the field of vision, disappearing as soon as they are located. Below, rhythms are the inner, visceral swell of departed vessels – past presences – or distant calls.

This is Nono's first work for a decade not to incorporate some kind of referential material, his first 'abstract' instrumental work since the mid-1950s. The source is his work and friendship with Pollini. Taking pitches and gestures from Pollini's recordings and combining them with his own essentialist approach to the generation of material – displaced or permuted successions of one, two or three attacks on different temporal planes, chromatic expansion, canons and mirrors – he begins a process of proliferation. Material begets material, a process shaped and constrained by designing hierarchical structures in units of bars, beats or seconds with clear formal trajectories. Writers often refer to the role of fragment in Nono's approach from the time of *sofferte* onwards. To describe the small units he manipulates as fragments suggests that they function as pieces of something larger, a presence never heard in its entirety. His process here – as in the Deola passages, as in the later *Risonanze erranti* – might better be understood as one of folding. Material is produced linearly then folded, reconstituted and folded again such that new simultaneities and figures emerge, to themselves become subject to the same process. New relationships and trajectories are formed across time- and pitch-space, a new manifestation of Nono's constant tendency to have time working in all directions, to and fro and simultaneously, within a forward-moving musical architecture – the essence of counterpoint, in fact.

..... *sofferte onde serene* ... represents above all an intensification of Nono's listening to the particularities and movement of sound. Just as the surface texture is generated by the interaction of superimposed waves, he is now interested in the finest details of how resonances modulate each other, in interference. The blending and ambiguity of piano and tape are enhanced by projecting the tape part from a loudspeaker underneath the piano. The studio-manipulated sounds return to resonate through their source; the instrument becomes a resonator, the space within which sounds and actions interact. Clearly heard physicality and sonic materiality are brought into a close, present relationship. Composer and listener alike are increasingly sensitised to presence, to sonic reality and human action. The 'work' as an abstraction has receded from experience.

Nono's initial pitch material reveals another private reference, a response to the loss of his mother. He would be explicit about his use of Verdi's 'scala enigmatica' in the subsequent string quartet *Fragmente-Stille, an Diotima*. The scale is the basis of Verdi's *Ave Maria* of 1889, published as one of the *Quattro Pezzi Sacri* in 1898. Invented by Adolfo Crescentini, it had been presented a year earlier as a compositional challenge in the Milanese *Gazzetta Musicale*. The *Ave Maria* is, significantly for Nono, one of the works with which Verdi returned to composing after a long silence; Nono had transcribed it during Scherchen's course in 1948. It thus had profound significance both personally and in terms of the development of his view of musical space. As articulated by Nono, the scala combines chromatic and whole-tone segments with a major/minor third ambiguity. This is precisely the tripartite interval pattern he had used to construct the series of *Epitaffio n. 2* in 1952. His articulation of the scala becomes the foundation of *Fragmente-Stille, an Diotima* and is key to the pitch universe of *Prometeo*. In a comparison with his initial sketch we can see that in ..... *sofferte onde serene* ... Nono is already exploring its potential (Figure 11.3a–b).

Prometeo emerges as a material project from Nono's conversations with Massimo Cacciari during the difficult period between the first experiments with Pollini and the conception of ..... *sofferte onde serene* ... . The name of *sofferte* will reappear in the final version of Cacciari's texts for *Prometeo*, inserted at a later stage into the adapted words of *Isola 5°*, where the voice of Prometheus himself remains silent. Perhaps this later context – one of a network of countless

Figure 11.3a Fragmente-Stille, an Diotima: Nono's articulation of the 'scala enigmatica'

Figure 11.3b ..... sofferte onde serene ... : rationalisation of Figure 10.1

references through and beyond *Prometeo* – tells us something about the personal significance of ..... *sofferte onde serene ...* :

> that in this storm the gaze
> lingers to arouse that which is broken
> that in it our voices
> are waves, tormented and serene
> this is MIRACLE

Aftershock: 'I Turcs tal Friúl'

In May 1976, while Nono was working on *sofferte*, a major earthquake had struck the Friuli region. It killed nearly a thousand people and was felt in Venice itself. Further tremors continued through September. Pier Paolo Pasolini grew up in the Friuli town of Casarsa, north-east of Venice, to which he returned during the fascist occupation and allied bombing. There he wrote in *Friuliano* dialect, including an allegory of the sparing of Casarsa from Turkish destruction, *I Turcs tal Friúl* of 1944. In a gesture of solidarity, it was decided to present this for the first time in Venice, in a co-production by La Fenice and the Piccolo Teatro of Udine, the regional capital. The play was performed on 16 November in the desanctified church of San Lorenzo – a year after Pasolini's death and in the space where Nono's *Prometeo* would be premiered a few years later. The performance began with projections of images from the earthquake, making clear the parallel between that disaster and the ravaging of the Friuli by the Turkish army in the late fifteenth century. The further analogy with fascism is implicit in Pasolini's text, and in its use of dialect both as a form of resistance and as the embodiment of the soul of a people.[17]

In the spirit of a medieval passion play, the townspeople become a chorus for which Nono contributed two musical interventions performable by actors rather than professional singers. A two-part note-by-note trope on the Kyrie *Cunctipotens genitor*, from the treatise on free organum *Ad organum faciendum* (c. 1100), is set for sopranos and altos. It returns as the people pray for salvation. Against this, Nono writes a *Coro dei Turchi* for male voices and percussion. The intimidating speech rhythms become figure, in the manner of *Fuçik* or *Memento*. The monotone chanting is accompanied by timpani rolls and percussive accents. Traces of Nono's tendency to permutation are heard in the arrangement of subdivisions within the beat of the text, and in the patterns of one to three consecutive accents or rests in the percussion. The text of the Turkish invaders invokes the moon. While the people are saved, a deep human empathy emerges; their enduring tragedy is that they are caught between two kinds of superstition.

Waves

'Con Luigi Dallapiccola'

If any work could be described as pivotal, it must be a new composition that emerged from Nono's relationship with La Scala. He had worked intensively with the percussion group of the orchestra, led by timpanist David Searcy, whose timpani statement of *Non siam più la comune di Parigi* had opened *Al gran sole*. Indeed, a reviewer had noted the timpanist at that premiere: 'dressed like a hippy, with a headband to keep still his flowing blonde mane'.[18] *Con Luigi Dallapiccola*, for six percussionists and live electronics, was finished in the spring of 1979 and premiered at La Scala on 4 November. Dallapiccola had died in February 1975 while Nono was rehearsing at La Scala; Nono had felt a deep kinship with him and his music since his earliest studies. Dallapiccola was originally from Istria, opposite Venice on the Adriatic coast – a place that had passed between the Venetian republic, Austro-Hungary, fascist Italy and Soviet-dominated communism. His music, often dealing with oppression and freedom, had been Nono's first contact with serialism. A dedication appears in Nono's working draft: 'In the continuing presence of a "brother" of pure human, moral and musical rigour, Dallapiccola, a new study of specific language begins and a new beginning for *Prometeo*.'[19]

At the head of the finished score Nono presents the 'fratello' motif from Dallapiccola's opera *Il Prigoniero*, a work begun before the end of the war and given its stage premiere by Scherchen in 1950. This motif – F E C$\sharp$ – is the symbol of hope through the opera, but also an affirmation that hope is realised through brotherhood. Again, Nono is reconnecting with his own past. This had been the fundamental timpani motif in the second of Nono's 1948, *Due liriche greche*: *Ai dioscuri*, a work written fully in the light of Dallapiccola in which the percussion carry much of the musical argument. Nono is clearly remembering the important part played by Dallapiccola in his own development; perhaps the brotherhood is theirs. Resonances with Dallapiccola ring through the new work. In his student analysis of the *Sex Carmina Alcei* Nono noted the last of Dallapiccola's *Canti di Prigionia*: *Congedo di Girolamo Savonarola* for choir and percussion. He observed how the parts diverge from their serial origins – two note-rows and the *Dies Irae* – to construct different kinds of canon. Dallapiccola's later work may also have been in mind: his fascination with the difficulty of expressing a certainty 'after all the question marks',[20] and particularly his last opera *Ulisse*. The latter must have been a reference point for Nono as he began work on *Prometeo*; Dallapiccola's libretto of wandering and questioning is likewise synthesised from several sources, its scenes arranged in a formal architecture, the music shot through with canon and mirror.

Percussion instruments play a crucial role in many of Nono's works since *Polifonica-Monodia-Ritmica*, often as bearers of rhythm, signifiers of power or the *suoni fissi* with which Nono highlights strands of pitch. Now he pays intense attention to the detail of percussive sounds. He listens to Searcy as he listened to Pollini. The kind of physical gesture, the beater and its placing, the attack and decay of sounds are all noted with precision. He notices the acoustic modulation of the great gongs built for *Turandot*. Having considered and rejected the use of ring modulation with live piano, he now returns to the idea. In any case, it is clear that amplification will be necessary to exploit some of the smaller sounds. For the first time since the mid-1960s, there is no mention of tape. Nono seems to be searching for a more present, plastic, responsive situation. He uses four pick-ups on the larger instruments, their signals sent to three ring modulators, each with an associated frequency generator. As well as drawing the listener's ear to the slighter sounds, his use of ring modulation amplifies the differences between strokes; it becomes a sort of hyper-real coloration. Live electronics enter Nono's musical-conceptual discourse, bringing symbolic, performative and studio modes of musical imagining and reasoning into a single unified space.

345

Waves

Nono categorises the instruments demonstrated by Searcy as metal, skin or wood, noting which might carry the 'fratello' motif. The polyphonic potential of two marimbas fascinates him – four players using different kinds of stick – although he warns himself to 'be careful of the Africa effect'.[21] Working on interlocking patterns later in the process he writes 'not Vivaldi!'[22] Ways of striking the large pitched metal plates that will eventually carry the fratello motif also receive much attention. Kirchert describes the use of percussion here as 'demilitarised'.[23] A deleted early draft of bars 61–75 moves towards unison rhythms. Perhaps this was too reminiscent of the role of large percussion groups from *Fučík* to *Al gran sole*.

The pitch material is constructed of the three-notes of the fratello motif with their transposition by an augmented fourth, also used by Dallapiccola in his subsequent *Canti di liberazione*: F E C♯, B B♭ G. One is reminded of Scherchen's few-note composition exercises; there is a path from the three of this piece to two in *A Carlo Scarpa* and a single pitch in the last *Post-prae-ludium*. In his programme note, Nono recalls that Scherchen showed him Dallapiccola's 'extreme, specifically musical intelligence [. . .] of compositional wisdom, of the conflictual contemporality of signs and thoughts' in the *Canti di liberazione*.[24] These structural pitches are distributed in extreme registers such that frequencies produced by acoustic interference and ring modulation are equally present to the ear. Metal plates and timpani, crotales and triangles produce a central aural field of overtones and undertones. Ring modulation generates sidebands around the input frequencies at the distance of the modulating frequency. High-frequency ring modulation creates additional artificial components within this aural field, the manipulation of their volume from the mixing desk modulating the natural decay of the acoustic instruments. Only the passage for two marimbas (bars 37–57) and that with tubular bells towards the end (90–104) bring the pitch argument clearly into the middle register. The rhythm space is organised analogously. Movement takes place in isolated sequences of strokes, in fast subdivisions of the beat or on a slow pattern such that rhythmic figure is generally an emergent property of their interaction. There is a continuum between fast, notated repetitions, the player-driven repetition of rolls, the instrument-driven repetition of the serrated bamboo and the low-frequency ring modulation. The slow acoustic amplitude modulation of the decaying resonances of low instruments adds another layer of wave motion; techniques such as the use of a Chinese cymbal against the plate gong draw attention to these phenomena.

Con Luigi Dallapiccola is constructed in fragments of five or six bars, punctuated by silences, resonances and single-bar gestures. In an attack-based sound world, Nono's earlier concept of 'negative rhythm' is appropriate. His technique both returns to the number squares of early works and provides a model for the more complex aphorisms of the string quartet to follow. Having conceived a basic form and sequence of movement and colour, his construction of the pattern of attacks and durations for each section is largely spatial. A three-dimensional number rectangle contains two sets of permutations of 1–7 for each of six voices – duration values for sounds and silences. Against each, another symbol represents divisions of the beat from 2–8. From this, Nono constructs two six-part rhythmic polyphonies, one beginning with rests – *A veloce* of seven bars – the other commencing together – *B calmo* of eight. Each voice in each such matrix consists of seven 'positive' values, and hence seven rests. These two-dimensional notated rhythmic planes are almost square, therefore, and Nono devises a new, plastic approach to building his forms. Indeed, one can see this sculptural, accumulative treatment of small forms as having dimensionality greater than that of his previous more horizontal polyphonic fabric. Such an understanding is consistent with Nono's emerging view of musical time. In moving around this space, he not only allows himself repetitions, mirrors, diminutions, augmentations and superimpositions, but also to move diagonally through the matrix. Nono will return

Waves

```
    3   5   7   6   1   4   2
  5   4   6   3   7   2   1
    4   1   2   7   5   3   6
  2   4   7   6   5   1   4
    1   6   3   2   4   7   5
  4   1   3   2   6   5   7
    5   7   6   4   3   7   1
  3   6   4   1   2   7   5
    6   3   4   5   2   1   7
  7   5   1   4   3   6   2
    7   2   1   3   6   5   4
  1   3   5   7   4   3   6
```

Figure 11.4a Con Luigi Dallapiccola: three-dimensional number square

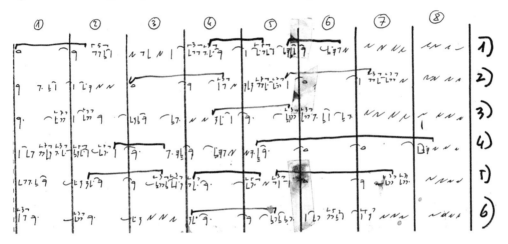

Figure 11.4b Con Luigi Dallapiccola: B *calmo* material, derived from square. (ALN 43.03.02/08. © The heirs of Luigi Nono. Reproduced by kind permission.)

Figure 11.4c Con Luigi Dallapiccola: Crotales 1, bars 29–34

Figure 11.4 Con Luigi Dallapiccola: derivation and use of B *calmo* rhythm matrix

repeatedly to these two passages of material; their richness, balance and fundamental coherence is such that they become part of his repertoire of generative musical behaviours.

Figure 11.4 shows the number square behind the *A* and *B* rhythmic materials, and Nono's use of the *B calmo* material in the 1st crotales line at bars 29–34. The rhythm initially comes from the fifth bar of the *calmo* material: two beats of voice 2, two of voice 6, the bar repeated

Waves

but with different numbers of repetitions. Bars 31–2 follow the same principle, now continuing to voice 3 and 6 of *calmo*. The number of attacks oscillates between one and three. In bar 33, Nono repeats the pattern of the previous two beats, varying attacks to avoid figural imitation, and then mirrors those. The first two beats of bar 34 are both an echo of the previous pattern and the continuation of the *calmo* material, now again from voice 2.

Nono further develops the principle of modulating waves so characteristic of *sofferte*. Varèse's 1931 *Ionisation* is an obvious model for this work; he had first heard it at Darmstadt in 1950 on the occasion of his meeting with Varèse and just after a performance of Schönberg's *A Survivor from Warsaw*, so the memory must have been etched deeply. In the 1979 interview mentioned above, Nono recalls how Varèse had shown him various percussion instruments on his visit to New York in 1965, and that in Cuba, where Varèse had learned much about percussion, Fernando Ortiz had shown him how to listen to their fine differences of sound.[25] In his copy of Varèse's *Écrits*, Nono would later mark the reference to interlocking waves. He described *Con Luigi Dallapiccola* as '. . . a study of the simultaneity of waves, of surfaces in which every now and then there occurs not a counterpoint between lines but emerging relationships between waves which arise and others that disappear.'[26] Acoustically, compositionally and electronically, the musical surface is a product of modulation, of the interference of waves. One such additional layer is generated here by note repetition. Two to four repeated attacks may replace the single event of the base polyphony, beginning from its start or its end; where they are used, these values are cycled or permutated. By the same principle, numbers of grace notes may be added to the beginning or end of values. Individual events are thus themselves fragments, carried along by interfering wave systems. Nono creates the conditions for each section, then navigates his way through according to prevailing formal needs.

The work is effectively in two halves, each consisting of two main sections surrounded by an introduction and coda. In keeping with its origins in the two short six-voice passages (*A veloce* and *B calmo*), it is constructed in five- and six-bar sections, punctuated by short gestures, extended by mirrors, silences and time for resonance to decay; 'remember the relationship between percussion and sound production' he notes to himself. Pauses are more frequent than in *sofferte*. They take on a different, more active quality with the performers free from the time-jacket of a tape. As well as its own colours and gestures, each section uses a distinct balance of rates of time and ranges of duration to create a wide variety of pacing and internal movement. This motion is also cyclic. Following the separate, ritual gestures of the opening, rhythmic momentum builds to a peak as woodblocks mark out the patterns of two marimbas in bars 47–57. Then the fast, detailed movement of crotales either side of the silent central bar 67 is replaced in bars 77–83 by long overlapping durations filled by regular crotale and triangle figuration, which themselves give way to eight bars of continuous ring-modulation of the plate gongs. A new cycle of increasing rhythmic figuration begins until it dissolves back into the bamboo sounds of the opening. Clarity of pitch follows an analogous architecture. All six pitches are most clearly present in the two-marimba passage, which moves from the 'fratello' set to its transposition; in between, attention shifts repeatedly from one to the other via superimpositions, almost like tonic and dominant. Crotales also carry all six pitches. The outer sections of the work are constructed of the 'fratello' triad alone, presented in rhythmic figure by the timpani, with melodic clarity by tubular bells, slowly and modulated by the plate gongs. In a later draft, Nono marks the underlying slow-moving pitch structure of the gongs like an X-ray of the aggregate surface.

The structure of the opening section (bars 1–21) makes the six-bar pattern clear: bars 1–3 (bamboo, sleigh-bells and plates) are echoed by 19–21, bars 4–10 are interrupted by a bar's silence, a pivotal bar of silence is also introduced at bar 11, and bars 12–18 are unbroken. The opening gestures – scraped bamboo, plate gongs, bass drum, sleigh-bells triangles and lion's roar – remain outside the space of percussive figural rhythm. High and low sounds mark the edges of a wide frequency spectrum, coalescing in their aggregate reverberation through the silences that separate the fragmentary statements. Two six-bar passages of more rapid figural development follow (22–7, 29–34), dominated by crotales, triangles and tom-toms. They are separated by a single bar of resonance (28) and end with two more (35–6). The section for two marimbas and woodblocks (37–60) alternates sustained chords with increasing fast repetition. Each passage is introduced and interrupted by drums, bells and triangles. Crotales, plates and bass drum provide a coda to the first half (61–6) before a bar of silence marks the mid-point. Three separate three-part gestures – each of crotales, triangles, timpani – form a new introduction to two sections for crotales and triangles (71–6, 77–83), the second of which becomes even figuration marking out a slow rhythm. This dissolves into the most static, most Varèse-invoking point: four bars, repeated, of sustained plates and lion's roar with phased crescendi of ring modulation, decaying into silence (84–8). A new clarity emerges as rhythm is re-established; tubular bells mark out the 'fratello' motif through the sound of drums and woodblocks, interrupted by triangles (94), three bass drum strikes (97) and bamboo and sleigh bells (103–4). Rhythmic movement is polarised in a coda (105–12) in which crescendos of lion's roar and bamboo weave through a texture of fast repeated figures from tom-toms and timpani. From the echo of their final *ff*, crotales, tubular bells and plates resonate to nothing (113–15).

'Fragmente-Stille, an Diotima'

The process of knowledge

During the 1978 production of *Al gran sole*, dramaturg Klaus Zehelein introduced Nono to the recent Frankfurt edition of the works of the early Romantic German poet and philosopher Friedrich Hölderlin. Hölderlin already figured in Cacciari's exploration of radical Romanticism, *Krisis*, largely through Heidegger's essays of which Nono also had several copies.[27] The new Hölderlin edition – only completed in 2008 – was a milestone in philology. It presents Hölderlin's writing in the context of his working process, with its drafts, parallel alternatives, amendments and corrections. Its spaces of multiple parallel possibilities fascinated Nono.[28]

> In the reproductions of the manuscripts, I saw how Hölderlin thought and composed. How he put different fragments of thought side by side, at the same time. This is fantastic. He writes something first in German, then suddenly here a quite different idea in French, then something else again, as if he really wanted to fix in space the simultaneity of thought we have within us. I think this is a general problem today. When I hear something, I hear something else at the same time, sounds of a different nature which don't belong to the others. It is also the problem of different planes of sound.[29]

This was one model of *process* of which Nono now spoke often. In conversation with Zehelein he already hints at *Prometeo* and his collaboration with Cacciari:

> today I am much more interested in the process of knowledge than in the results of a process. Taking part in a process is more important to me than establishing the consequences. In collaboration with a young Italian philosopher I am trying to develop a processual thought, to grasp the development from Aeschylus to today as a process.

Waves

It's a matter of everyone growing, developing and finding new knowledge, instead of something being shown didactically that simply has to be accepted.[30]

Text and voice, always underlying Nono's thought, had already played a part in his initial thinking about *Con Luigi Dallapiccola*. While experimenting with Searcy, he had considered having the percussionists sing short passages of Hölderlin, and then that they might sing or whistle vowels while consonants were to be supplied by the percussion – a development of his earlier vocal ensemble technique.[31] Clearly, *Prometeo* was already at the front of Nono's mind while working on *Con Luigi Dallapiccola*. 'AS A PROLOGUE/ FRAGMENTS – SILENCES', he noted in those sketches, anticipating his next project, a string quartet.[32]

Fragmente-Stille, an Diotima was Nono's response to a highly significant commission: from the city of Bonn for the 30th Beethoven Festival. It is dedicated 'mit innigster Empfindung' ('with innermost feeling') to the LaSalle Quartet, who gave the premiere in Bad Godesberg on 2 June 1980. Led by violinist Walter Levin, the quartet were renowned for their performances of modern music, from authoritative interpretations of the second Viennese school to new works such as Ligeti's *String Quartet No. 2*. Friends of Nono since the Darmstadt of the 1950s – they had been performing Webern while Nono and Maderna were teaching composition in 1958 – a work for the LaSalle had long been in discussion. The dedication, borrowed from Beethoven, was initially to have been the work's title. Nono later explained its relevance: just as the *Molto Adagio* of Beethoven's Quartet op. 132 is a song of thanks in the Lydian mode, so Nono's quartet is a song of thanks using Verdi's 'scala enigmatica'.[33] The extraordinary multi-section form of that movement must also have been a model. It continued to serve as an important reference for Nono; in addition to his several copies of the score, he bought another in Freiburg in 1983. He may also have recalled Beethoven's previous use of the expression in the final Andante of the Sonata op. 109, where it is preceded by the instruction *Gesangvoll*.

At the family summer home on Sardinia, Nono prepared material for a meeting with the quartet in September 1979. With them he covered much of the ground he had surveyed with Kolisch decades earlier – harmonics, double stops, bow placement and pressure – but less stable sounds were also of interest now. An early decision not to use microphones is significant, as *Fragmente* becomes a study in presence and listening. In his notes he explores in detail the possible combinations of open strings across the quartet. This pattern of open fifths will provide a grid of harmonic reference and resonance. The work's sequence of composition is reflected in its fundamental bipartite architecture; in December, Nono was able to send the quartet the first half of *Fragmente* and in January 1980 it was finished.

The *Fragmente* and *Stille* of the title are clear in the work's formal pattern. Fragments – from a single chord or gesture to a handful of bars or a brief passage notated without metre – are frequently punctuated and usually separated by silent or sustained fermata of varying lengths, on a 12-element scale from a brief comma to 'endlos'. At its premiere, *Fragmente* was a work of some 30 minutes; by the time of a Deutsche Grammophon recording a few years later, after more experimentation with the length of pauses, it lasted 38 minutes. 'an Diotima' refers to the extracts from Hölderlin printed in the score, which are:

never to be spoken aloud during performance
under no circumstances to be taken as programmatic performance indications
but many other moments, thoughts, silences 'songs'
of other spaces, other skies
to otherwise rediscover the possible, do not 'say farewell to hope'
The players should 'sing' them inwardly, in their autonomy
In the autonomy of sounds striving for a 'delicate harmony of the inner life'[34]

Waves

Reading is a form of active listening — remember St Augustine's astonishment at the silent reading of St Ambrose. These silent fermata are listening gestures. Nono's decision to have the texts printed in the programme at the premiere was very significant in terms of his understanding of the nature of the work; voice is present, however silently. *Fragmente* carries forward Nono's concern with voice and text; it also points back to the vital moment of the soprano entry in Schönberg's Second Quartet, a crucial moment in music history and in Nono's personal narrative.

While Hölderlin is the only author whose words appear in the score, the quartet is suspended in a rich network of poetic and historical references. As we have seen, Nono was already considering the idea of incorporating fragments of Hölderlin in an instrumental context before starting work on the quartet. However, detailed notes also suggest very specific links between the early stages of the new work and fragments from the diaries of Kafka. The many annotations in his copy reveal the intensity of the resonance Nono found in Kafka's descriptions of the ways in which a continuing, often vertiginous state of existential disorientation also reveals new imaginative spaces. Dreams play an important role in Kafka's reflections: 'only dreams, no rest', he comments. Nono copies this into the earliest sketches for his new quartet, while associating other references with specific structural elements.[35] The suicide of Lilya Brik in August 1978 brought Nono back to the potential subject of her relationship with Mayakovsky, and before beginning work he informed his friend Julia Dobrovolskaja in Moscow that he would dedicate the quartet to their memory.[36] This intention was superseded, but references remain in sketches that anticipate Nono's final violin works:

> love – sweet – passionate – violent
> anger (present impossibility > Mayakovsky /continuity > Lili/isolated/together)
> exasperation
> utopia > serene > nostalgia/of present anger/future in the present[37]

The choice of Hölderlin seems to have been a later decision, taken once work on the score was substantially underway. This decision is clearly significant in terms of Nono's understanding of his own work. He saw in Hölderlin's work a model of process, of the non-finite nature of expression. A faith in love, in humanity, is its guiding spirit, a sentiment embodied in Nono's instruction above. Perhaps more importantly there is a sense of transformation through tragedy in Hölderlin that the more existential Kafka does not offer. Diotima is also a central character in Robert Musil's *The Man without Qualities*, which had only been published in full in 1978, half a century after its long gestation. In Nono's opinion '*The Man without Qualities* is a great manual of composition, for composers.'[38] He often referred to the title of a chapter in Musil's novel: 'If there is a sense of reality, there must also be a sense of possibility.'[39] Musil describes the infinite worlds that populate the perception of his protagonist, Ulrich: 'Nothing is, to him, what it is; everything is subject to change, in flux, a part of a whole, of an infinite number of wholes presumably adding up to a super-whole that, however, he knows nothing about.'[40]

Regardless of specific texts for the new work, Nono seems to have identified key common features of their process. Nietzsche and Wittgenstein are the twin poles of Cacciari's recent study of negative thought, *Krisis* (1976).[41] His book develops ideas set out in his earlier *Pensiero negativo* (1973), of which Cacciari had already given his friend a typescript in 1972, dedicated to Luigi Nono 'Meister in der Mahlerkunst'.[42] Fin-de-siècle Vienna is seen as a moment of crisis generating radical new ideas from which important lessons can be learned for our time. Mahler is an important reference in the nexus of figures Cacciari and Nono were now discussing – the complement of Schönberg, perhaps. Nono and Cacciari would frequently refer to Wittgenstein's work on the limits of language, but his questioning of logic itself is still more important to the evolving thought of both of them. In particular, the incapacity of dialectics to reframe questions or remodel spaces of thought, experience or potential becomes a major challenge. An early explanation by Cacciari is uncharacteristically succinct:

> The form of the dialectic is the form of the negative that is affirmed positively – the recoverable contradiction. The whole system posits itself and maintains itself in terms [nel segno] of negativity: a movement of universal alienation is the true-real [vera-reale] totality.[43]

Dialectics are dismissed as a system for maintaining the status quo. The implications are as concretely political as they are logical or aesthetic. Indeed, Cacciari's *pensiero negativo* will be crucial in the development of Vattimo's more post-modern *pensiero debole* and Negri's radically political *autonomia*.

In a discussion at Columbia University, New York, during the composition of *Fragmente*, Nono explained: 'This is why I refer to Wittgenstein. My work implies an attempt to understand and develop a new kind of logic, even if it might seem that we are in a phase of irrationality because we cannot yet understand its underlying principles.'[44] In working on *Prometeo*, Nietzsche's figure of the Wanderer will become an important reference for Nono, but his extensive study of Nietzsche through this period, part of his ongoing conversation with Cacciari, suggests another link. Nono's copy of the letters includes Nietzsche's *Letter to my friend, in which I recommend that he read my favourite poet* of 1861:

> Also you do not know [Hölderlin's] *Hyperion*, in which the harmonious movement of his prose, the sublimity and beauty of the characters, made upon me an impression like that of the wave beat of a troubled sea. Indeed, this prose is music: soft melting sounds interrupted by painful dissonances, finally expiring in dark mysterious funeral songs.[45]

Waves of memory

Wave and interruption are the musical essence of *Fragmente*. It brings together the structural modulation of *Con Luigi Dallapiccola*, the sonic and metaphorical waves of *sofferte*, and the physical movement of the string players. In early notes he writes:

[Continue the . . . waves . . .]
But for strings – percussion

        – sustained sounds
        – microstructures > fragments motifs – <u>interrupted</u>
ALWAYS   – fields   harmonic
INTERRUPTED!   timbral
                               dynamic
                               attacks and ends of sound (ARCO!!!)
                               of fragments[46]

Nono was immediately clear as to his sources. For primary pitch material he returns to the 'scala enigmatica' of Verdi's *Ave Maria*. As Nono noted in his analysis of all its transpositions, the aggregate nine-note scale presents three chromatically adjacent augmented fourths. He commented on Verdi's advanced age; life's rhythm occupied him, and perhaps relationships with his late parents and friends constitute the 'geheimere Welt' ('secret world') of the first text fragment. *Malor me bat* from Petrucci's 1501 edition, attributed to Ockeghem, is another source and another private reference to his earliest development; Maderna had orchestrated it as part of the *Odhecaton* project with Nono and the other students over thirty years earlier, and the score in Nono's hand was subsequently published by Scherchen (Figure 11.5). A page of transpositions of the scala enigmatica, apparently from the composing of *Fragmente*, appears in Nono's sketches for *Prometeo*. On another page, next to a series of transpositions of the scala enigmatica to the open strings of the quartet, Nono notes 'with tritones!!! or open strings', generating intervals additional to the seconds, sevenths and ninths that dominate the scala.[47] These options persist through the work; the harmonic world is an interference pattern between a compositional–theoretical construct and the physical, acoustical properties of its realisation on the four string instruments. It is the product of the modulation of the scala enigmatica in a pattern of transpositions, additional augmented fourths, the open strings of the quartet and, at a certain point, *Malor me bat*. Only the F and B of *Malor me bat* are not present as open strings. Its Phrygian mode exploits the tension between perfect fifth and augmented fourth, the principal elements of Nono's harmonic language here.

Figure 11.5 Ockeghem: *Malor me bat* from Petrucci *Odhecaton*, 1501

He maps out the network of personal significance, of his own loss:

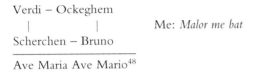

We might see this first rectangular arrangement of references as a two-part formal plan; *Malor me bat* appears in the second part of *Fragmente* and – as Carola Nielinger-Vakil has pointed out – the non-linearity of that part contrasts with the more orderly organisation of the first.[49] The fundamental material is more contiguous with *Con Luigi Dallapiccola* than their surfaces might suggest. Nono divides the scala enigmatica into three groups with distinctive interval content. The first group A is an inversion of the 'fratello' motif (Figure 11.6).

Figure 11.6 Fragmente-Stille, an Diotima: scala enigmatica

In early experiments with generating material, Nono refers to a sequence of three dreams in Kafka's diaries – 'I dreamed today [...] Besides this, I dreamed [...] Then I dreamed' – [50] designated, like the scala, as *A*, *B*, *C*.[51] This recalls his description of *Al gran sole* as 'yesterday, today and tomorrow, superimposed, anticipated and fragmented.'[52] 'Kafka – harmonics. Ockeghem – flautato sounds', he writes below; elsewhere, 'today I dreamed' appears twice next to high, sustained notes.[53] These two elements also appear together on other pages, suggesting perhaps that *Malor* might materialise from such a dream moment, just as Kafka's dream descriptions develop very specific images. In fact, *Malor* will appear in a different voice, equally unworldly: low viola, *dolcissimo*, *sottovoce*, *al tasto*. High, sustained flautato and harmonics figure as a strand through the work, however, such that Kafka's dreams remain a constant presence.

'Fragments – not aphoristic!!!', he warns himself.[54] The fragments are to be passing glimpses of possible worlds, not self-contained concise definitions. An early drawing suggests two approaches to fragment construction – a characteristic binary form-scheme of two orthogonally related views in sequence. In the first, five elements are cut in sequence at different angles 'like the attack of tape sound'; in the second, continuous waves intertwine through five further sections (Figure 11.7). These will characterise the two parts of *Fragmente*.

As this early plan evolves, fragments are cut together, alternated and reversed. The pattern of pauses does not always correspond to fragment boundaries. Numbers in the published score

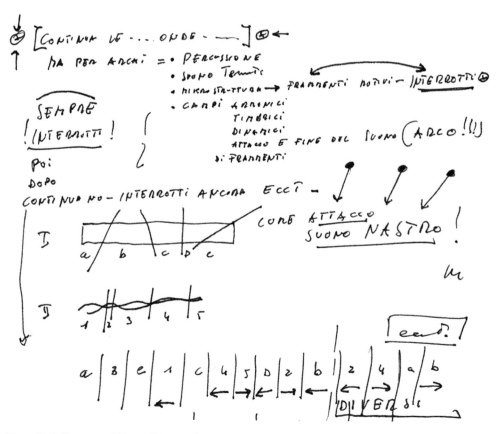

Figure 11.7 Fragmente-Stille, an Diotima: fragment patterns. (ALN 44.04.03/13 (detail). © The heirs of Luigi Nono. Reproduced by kind permission.)

are rehearsal numbers, not identifiers of fragments; they derive from page numbers of an earlier draft. Given Nono's working method there is therefore a relationship, but one obscured by subsequent compositional decisions. They divide almost symmetrically, however: numbers 1–25 lead to the central hiatus, followed by fragments 26–52. Nono's initial architecture remains visible: in Part I, materials alternate, overlap or elide; in Part II they are continuously interwoven. Cross-cut, sequential relationships are followed by continuous parallel development: the binary horizontal–vertical balance we have seen frequently. Initially, each fragment is characterised by its transposition of a set from the scala, a set of rhythmic subdivisions, playing techniques and articulations. Rhythm derives from the *A veloce* and *B calmo* rhythmic planes of *Con Luigi Dallapiccola*.[55] From the underlying rhythmic polyphony, Nono might select different lengths or depths of block, focus on a single line, or compress multiple lines into one. The rhythm bases – divisions of the beat – may diverge or be unanimous. At the highest structural level, the work is the product of the modulation of three waves: the performed score, silences and the read texts. Spree maps the work in terms of its 13 tempi of ♩ = 30 to 240. He sees a clear formal balance in the arrangement of fragments: 7–11–7–1, 7–11–7–2.[56]

The wide differences between lengths of silence create uncertainty and anticipation; for Elzenheimer they constitute a 'dramaturgy of silence'.[57] Because of the quietness of the music, the small detail of its actions, attention is drawn to the slightest sound or movement and to the resonances in the room itself. The sounds are often at the limit of audibility, some of the pauses very short, so the boundary between sound and silence is often unclear and escapes reflection. The music itself denies reduction or compression; there are few cues or markers by which memory can be searched. Constant timbral instability and ambiguity means that figure is induced, implied, distantly remembered, rather than consciously perceived or recognised. New relationships thus arise in the process of listening. The musical surface is supported by networks of mirror and imitation, but the additional modes of interference often make these inaccessible to the conscious ear. Reflection is drawn back to the sonic experience itself. This is inherent in the nature of the music. Listening is constantly drawn to the physicality of performance – to extremes of register, dynamic or the rate of change of playing technique, but especially to the long sustaining of quiet sounds with their internal rhythms of players' breathing or changes in arm tension. Nono's notes to the players acknowledge this: 'naturally the sound quality changes, but so beautifully as a love has seldom appeared – Hölderlin – Diotima.'[58] During the moments of sustained stasis, player and listener are reminded of the unavoidable inner mobility of performed sound, even when attempting to deny time. During the silent fermata, the ear is drawn to rehearse, to reconstruct what has just been heard, but a tension is created between this process and that of expectation. Reflection, anticipation and interpretation modulate the music in the process of listening

The background rhythmic fabric is also woven as for the previous work: polyphonic matrices generated by permutations of 1–7 'positive' values and the same number of rests, through which Nono can trace multiple paths as he did earlier through number squares. The structural equivalence of sound and silence is thus built into the rawest material. This pattern is obscured as he takes sequences from different starting points and across lines. Figure 11.8a shows such a structure using quavers; other versions are built with beat divisions of 4, 5, 6 and 8. Each of the six voices consists of six patterns of crotchets and quavers separated by rests. This becomes the basis of the opening fragment. Using rhythm sequences from here, a four-voice passage is constructed using pitches permuted from the central *B* whole-tone set of the scala enigmatica transposed to B – <E♭ F G A> – followed by a transposition <E F♯ G♯> to complete a chromatic augmented fourth band; Figure 11.8b gives the top line. Figure 11.8c shows a later stage, a draft of the first violin part of the opening begun within a four-part elaboration of the same rhythmic and pitch material, but then developed as a solo line. In addition to added tritones and open strings, further pitches and rhythms (on the lower line) are adapted by imitation and from the other parts. The final first violin part (notated on three staves, the practice throughout this score) is shown in Figure 11.8d. This is the product of several waves of process: addition and substitution by tritone, fluctuation of rhythm base – for instance, the opening quintuplets – patterns of fermata, registral displacement, tempo variation and the compression of several strands of polyphony into a single line. As in his earliest works, Nono weaves a single line through a polyphonic process, but now the degree of polyphony itself becomes more plastic. Dynamics and articulation, playing techniques and the pattern of fermata add further modes of interference.

The first seven fragments are effectively a violin monody, selectively filtered and reverberated by the other three instruments. In the fifth, a rapid tremolo figure is introduced that becomes

Figure 11.8a Six-part rhythm matrix[59]

Figure 11.8b From lines 2–3 of Figure 11.8a[60]

Figure 11.8c Intermediate stage[61]

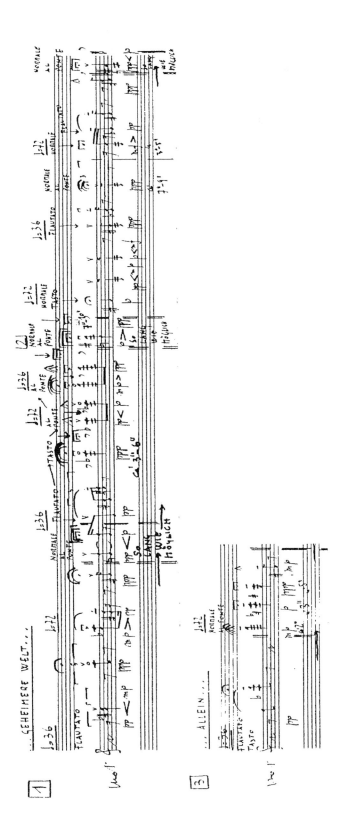

Figure 11.8d Final score. (Reproduced by kind permission of Casa Ricordi.)
Figure 11.8 *Fragmente-Stille, an Diotima*: derivation of violin I, opening

Waves

characteristic of this middle-register material derived from segment B of the scala: *alla punta, aperiodico, al ponte*. Real polyphony arrives in the eighth fragment – '. . . wenn aus der Tiefe . . .' – as cello and viola introduce wide, leaping gestures of major sevenths and minor ninths developing the chromatic segment C. In his sketches, Nono maps their distribution across the full range of the quartet graphically, with permutations of arrows in different directions. Against this, moments of high sustained harmonics and *flautato* use the pitch-shape of segment A. Quarter-tone shading adds to the sense of these sounds being at the limit of pitch discrimination. Through close analysis of pitch materials and their associated text fragments, Carola Nielinger-Vakil identifies the central set B from the scala enigmatica as 'Diotima' material. The first set A (<F♯ D B♭> from a scala on F♯) she associates with the idea of 'Stille', its high, sustained shimmering with dream references in Kafka and with sounds described by Nono as 'mirages'. The last set C (<C♯ D E♭> from a scala on E♭), leaping up from the low register, she identifies with 'Tiefe'.[62]

These three strands are cross-cut at different speeds and angles through the first twenty-five fragments, pursuing the suggestion of Nono's early drawing. As the central tremolo layer works its way to dissolution, the musical argument condenses into an alternation between fragments of high stillness – the sound kept constantly mobile through slight modulation of timbre, rhythm or pitch – and highly articulated, interrupted rhythmic movement across the whole range of the quartet. In fragment 25, an echoed unison rhythm (from line 5, bar 2 of Figure 11.8a) almost becomes a refrain before with an 'endlos' sustained triad (18–21 seconds) we arrive at the farthest point of Nono's orbit: near-stasis.

The central hiatus is interrupted by the same tutti rhythmic gesture as began the final fragment of the first part: a brief return of the tremolo *alla punta, aperiodico, al ponte*, now slower and with a crescendo. It is a re-emergence from the shadow that introduces a recommencement from the same place as the beginning: '. . . heraus in Luft und Licht . . .' ('outwards into air and light'), with the instruction 'mit innigster Empfindung' (no. 26). In a more sustained structural echo, it continues by outlining in clear crotchets and quavers the rhythm of the opening fragment of the work; it is a moment of new inner discovery, of new departure. The four instruments take their unison rhythm from line 2 of Figure 11.8a; they all contribute equally to the sonic aggregate based on segment B of the scala, all playing *arco normale* for the first time, largely in double-stops. The fragment is a self-contained structure of mirrors disguised by octave displacement. In each part the dyads of the central bars are reflected about the last beat of the third bar; passages to either side of this are exchanged (vln I/cello, vln II/viola), and the instruments all end the fifth bar with their own dyad from the first. This coming-into-the-light is a moment of such fragility that the most 'normal' quartet sonority thus far strikes the listener as the most extraordinary. From here, the three pitch segments are now all developed from the scala on C. All strands of material now shift by quarter-tones as well as semitones, as their exploration intensifies. As indicated in Nono's early diagram (Figure 11.7), the second part develops a more involved, intermodulating relationship between elements, as if through a process of exchange rather than alternation the quartet body is able to glimpse more distant worlds, new possibilities. As he sketches the sequence of fragments, the labels 'A', 'B' and 'C' give way to 'Luft' and 'Laut'.

Unstable sounds are an important feature throughout: constellations of *gettato* attacks, or the uncertain speaking of *legno + poco crine* (with the wood of the bow and little hair). Like the touch of Pollini in *sofferte* or the breath of Roberto Fabbriciani in subsequent works, Nono thinks of the bow as the point of contact between idea and material sound; the instrument is a resonator. Apart from a single brief pizzicato passage, the entire work is articulated by the

Waves

speed, placing and pressure of the bow: *legno, crine, battuto, flautato, saltato, balzato, gettato*, moving between bridge and fingerboard, *sf* or *sotto voce*.

Certain fragments achieve a dynamic stability between layers of different sounds. At no. 47, for example, all four voices alternate *balzato* double stops with *normale* harmonics in out-of-phase cycles of rhythm bases 3, 4 and 5. This returns as no. 49, extended and with rapid crescendos beyond their original *piano* limit to *ff*. Recognisability has an important function here. These two passages are separated by the fragment of *Malor me bat*, distinguished by its rhythmic unison. The viola haltingly presents a version of the opening of the melody, *sul tasto*, never more than three notes without a pause. The cello sustains *flautato* as a shadow with constantly changing harmonies while the violins add percussive sounds or noise from the bridge or wood. *Malor me bat* thus appears in an extraordinary light, through a window in the central narrative, a wormhole through memory and time.

A single line of silent text returns as a refrain through the second part. '. . . das weisst aber du nicht . . .' ('but you do not know') occurs five times, each a brief two- or three-bar fragment in rhythmic unison, based on the central whole-tone pitch set with semi- and quarter-tone transpositions. Each is marked *arco normale, mit innigster Empfindung, sotto voce*. These clearest references to Beethoven develop a rhythm of moments of inner emotional intensity (nos. 34, 36, 38, 43, 45). This obsessive return is like Nono's reminder to himself of his new space, very different from that of the first part. It is a motto of his evolving ethos, the 'goalless searching' described by Lachenmann, that characterises Nono's late music.[63] The last occurence is followed by '. . . wenn in die Ferne . . .' ('if into the distance', no. 46), a knot tied in Nono's semantic network; 'das weisst aber du nicht' is the last line of the poem that begins 'Wenn aus der Ferne . . .', the text of no. 16. This resonance frames the body of *Fragmente*; it is followed by the tripartite unit of *Malor me bat* with its symmetrical surrounding fragments (nos. 47–9). Nono builds a further frame: the second text of no. 16, '. . . aus dem Aether . . .', is answered at no. 50, after the *Malor* sequence, by '. . . zum Aether hinauf . . .', as if to confirm that this is a new journey. The second part is framed symmetrically: the *rallentando* 5/4 bar from the end of no. 26 returns *accelerando* at no. 50, as if to announce a coda. The final sound of the work consists of slowly decaying high harmonics – D, G, A: pitches of the three common open strings of the quartet – as if the sounding body of the quartet as a single instrument remains reverberating while *Fragmente* continues its path, disappearing from our view.

The texts accompanying these final fragments return to the serenity of sea and river ('. . . in Grunde des Meer . . .', '. . . an Neckars friedlichschönen Ufern . . . eine stille Freude mir . . . wieder'). Despite the composer's injunction, performers and listeners cannot avoid the connection. There are several such moments: at nos. 19–20, unison strokes with a crescendo to *ff* at 'wenn in einem Blick . . . und laut. . .' are followed by sudden *ppp* in the highest registers of all instruments at '. . . wenn in reicher Stille. . .'. Most moments are less onomatopoeic; the situation approaches the madrigalian relationships of Nono's vocal works, where common nodes emerge between evolving musical and textual structures. Here he has constructed a network of textual fragments from single words to phrases, a web of meaning-potential made up of the resonant peaks of intense reading rather than a hiding a secret narrative. A musical 'translation' was of no interest to him.[64] Nono searches for connections within his textual network as he does in his musical material; 'Wenn aus der Ferne', for instance, comes from two different poems. He takes forty-nine fragments from fifteen poems.[65] The greatest number – also fifteen, probably not by coincidence – come from the longest of Hölderlin's *Diotima* poems, *Leuchtest du wie vormals nieder*. A single word, 'allein', is taken from *An Diotima*. Their sequence presents traces of structure. The three fragments from *Götter wandelten einst* begin and end the first part (nos. 2 and 25) and end the second (no. 50), suggesting that the last

Waves

two fragments (51–2) should indeed be regarded as a coda. An alternating sequence of fragments from *die Eichbäume* and *Wenn aus der Ferne* (before no. 34 to after no. 39) constitutes a consolidated group.

Two years later, Nono described the process of composition to Wolfgang Rihm:

> he spoke long and expressively about the completely free process of development, the improvisation of discovery, memory (especially his beloved teachers Maderna and Scherchen) and his particular state of agitation during the work (he was shattered, turned inside out, perhaps with the vocabulary of Nietzsche: harried, blown around by the wind). During the work he never knew in one moment what the next would bring. The great constellational idea, that derives from the visual appearance of the Frankfurter Ausgabe and is represented ideally with its printing technique, together with intensive reading of Wittgenstein, gave him the courage to develop this fragment-form. Signs, figures, strewn across the surfaces[66]

Diotima, the poetic figure inspired by Hölderlin's impossible love for Suzette Gontard, is also the absent voice whose understanding of Eros is recounted by Socrates in Plato's *Symposium*. Hölderlin's fullest literary development of his love is in the briefroman *Hyperion* (1797–9), of which Nono kept himself supplied with copies. Allwardt's beautiful essay draws parallels between *Hyperion* and *Fragmente*; she shows how Hölderlin's imagery turns to song and sound as he approaches the limits of speech.[67] References to being silent abound – an act, not a withdrawal. Nono's *champ d'action* is the area just beyond speech. Maderna's *Hyperion*, which he probably heard at its premiere at La Fenice in 1964, must also have been in Nono's mind. Flautist Severino Gazzelloni, the protagonist in Nono's own *Y su sangre*, played the wordless role of the poet; perhaps this informed Nono's thought as he began to work with Roberto Fabbriciani later in 1980.

Hölderlin's use of classical models, his involvement with Greek liberation, his enthusiasm for the early stages of the French Revolution and his disappointment at its betrayal must all have recommended him to Nono. His reading of Heidegger's work on Hölderlin was also clearly influential. At the moment when the very possibility of poetry was most urgently being questioned, Heidegger saw Hölderlin as the voice that could 'speak the words that bring a new world into being', in Coetzee's paraphrase.[68] For Heidegger, Hölderlin's response to the passing of the Gods – the very subject of Nono's *Prometeo* – was to reconfigure poetic and human time.[69] Writing of his own composition of *Hyperion*, Hölderlin spoke of an 'eccentric orbit', a moving forwards and backwards within time's arrow, that recalls Nono's approach to time and the direction and teleology of inner structures.[70] *Fragmente* is an exercise in making linear a multiplicity of potential times;[71] it anticipates the island-form of *Prometeo*. Introducing the work in Bonn, Nono described:

> fragments that don't conclude and that don't reveal themselves in some later moment of synthesis, but that rather show particular moments of potential, of life, and which develop further, also conflictually, where no dialectical movement is possible, just an emerging of various different possibilities, potentials, forces or such moments [. . .] which together offer a great multiplicity of thought, of life, of existence. Rather than when through a dialectical moment there comes a synthesis, a goal, a revealing – it is more important for me to develop these contradictions, dissents, conflicts further. There is this need of the Wanderer – Benjamin, Nietzsche – for whom there is no fixed moment but just a constant searching.[72]

Both technical obsession and political dogma he described as 'bureaucratic thought'; 'Schönberg taught us to think, not to compose', he continued. Above all, *Fragmente* is Nono's response to the notion of the unsayable; Wittgenstein, Nietzsche and Cacciari are as present as Hölderlin. *Fragmente* embodies the mystical, in Cacciari's sense, but this is not the magical. Developing his exploration of Wittgenstein, Cacciari relates this distinction to Schönberg:

> 'Profundity' and 'mysticism' would be opposite concepts in this respect, also in Schönberg. The 'profound' is the incomprehensible and unsayable that one attempts to say [. . .] The 'mystical', however, is the clarity with which one warns of the non-sayable that embraces language. [. . .] The 'mystical' is not spoken. The mystical is thus 'disenchanted'. And precisely from that disenchantment is born the act of faith: it is revealed in full comprehensibility, to the degree that this is possible only by recognising the non-sayable [73]

Like all Nono's work, *Fragmente* is transformational, not utopian. It requires the participation, the active listening of performers and listener alike; it draws them in to become fellow Wanderers, constructors of meaning. Lachenmann, with whom Nono would shortly end a protracted estrangement, articulates this quality:

> it is not just the composed score of the *Diotima* quartet which puts across this music's message: it is the perception of its reflection in our inner selves, across the space of silence and also remembrance, reflection, self-discovery as opened up by the fermata which he piles up in constantly changing, almost artless configurations.[74]

Far from any metaphysical 'turn', the achievement of *Fragmente* lies precisely in the materiality of its experience. 'I have in no way changed; the soft, the private also have their collective, political side. Thus, my string quartet is not the expression of some new retrospective line, but my current experimental condition: I want to say the largest, most agitating things with the smallest means.'[75] *Fragmente* makes material the limits of the sayable; this is what makes it a key work in Nono's *oeuvre*. It is irreducible, it denies the compression of musical experience and challenges cognitive representation. It is a song suspended in webs of presence and absence, listening, making sound and making meaning.

'Fragmente' and criticism

Critics were unprepared for *Fragmente*. Max Nyffeler's introduction to the first broadcast summarised many of their questions:

> It is not just a question of Luigi Nono's transformation into his opposite [. . .] How is it that Luigi Nono, member of the political commission of the central committee of the PCI, can in his composing be led by ideas that have nothing to do with the image of the politically-engaged composer we have developed of him over the last two decades? [. . .] Has the composer turned away from revolution and social development in his string quartet? Is this a case of resigned fleeing from the world, as we have seen spreading among composers recently? Or a symptom of the ideological softening of the Italian left in the grip of Wojtyła and the Socialist international, whereby an ideological retreat is accompanied by an aesthetic regression?[76]

Waves

With a little reflection, a more nuanced response emerged. In particular, a 1981 edition of *Musik-Konzepte*, motivated by renewed interest in Nono in the German-speaking world, contained essays by Pestalozza and Metzger addressing such questions directly. 'Turning-point Quartet?' asked Metzger's title. The notion of interiority in listening, proposed by Barthes in 1976, had assumed greater currency with the advent of the Sony Walkman in 1979.[77] Metzger, Pestalozza and, shortly after, Doris Döpke found clear arguments to refute the idea of an inward 'turn' that persisted as a response to Nono's quartet; they each identified time as key to its understanding. Pestalozza saw a risk in Nono's 'annihilation of time [. . .] not in the sense of an antihistorical metaphor, but really into nothingness as a negation of everything beyond experience.'[78] 'All too seductively, the quartet points the way to integration' he says, 'But it still resists it.' Metzger's more technical treatment focuses on the anti-dialectical nature of *Fragmente*; for him, the silences recall Adorno's notion of listening acts, they are 'the opposite of demagogy'.[79] Döpke, writing shortly after the premiere of *Prometeo*, disagrees with Pestalozza. She finds an echo of Benjamin's *Theses of History*:

> [*Fragmente*] seeks to decipher in the past the potential that indicates the future, to reunite the debris of that which has been destroyed in a new constellation in order to launch a pre-naissance of liberty and happiness.
>
> Here is precisely the aim of Nono's string quartet; its temporal structure is designed for this purpose: it is not 'the annihilation of time' but on the contrary an attempt to arrest it.[80]

'Fragmente', Hölderlin and the caesura

Quietness does not reflect quietude; fragmentation is not the product of resignation. Nono's insistence on the continuing political essence of his music must be taken seriously. Döpke is quite correct to see a role for Benjamin here, but he is part of a wider nexus in Nono's thought-world that has very specific implications for *Fragmente*. In his *Remarks on Oedipus* – notes on his own translation – Hölderlin identifies the caesura as a key component of tragic poetry:

> In the rhythmic sequence of representations, in which the tragic transport exhibits itself, that which one calls the *caesura* in poetic metre, the pure word, the counter-rhythmic interruption, is necessary; precisely in order to counter the raging change of representations at its summit so that it is no longer the change of representations but the representation itself which appears.[81]

He describes this on both metrical and formal levels; for him, the interventions of Teiresias constitute the crucial structural caesura in both *Oedipus* and *Antigone*. A century later, Benjamin would identify an analogous moment in Goethe's *Elective Affinities*: 'That sentence, which to speak with Hölderlin contains the caesura of the work and in which, while the embracing lovers seal their fate, everything pauses, reads: "Hope shot across the sky above their heads like a falling star".'[82] For Benjamin, the caesura is fundamental to Hölderlin's theory of art. Indeed, Hölderlin's formulation of the relationship between philosophy and poetry is a pre-echo of Nono's non-distinction between his compositional and political thought, and of *Prometeo* itself:

> Thus those who are enlightened and those who are not must finally make common cause, mythology must become philosophical, to make the people rational, and philosophy must become mythological, to make philosophy sensuous. [. . .] Only then will equal development for all of our powers await us, for the particular person as well

Waves

as for all individuals. No power will again be supressed, then general freedom and equality will reign among spirits![83]

In particular, Benjamin emphasises the power of the *expressionless* – an anticipation of Lachenmann's description of Nono's fermata as 'artless' – and its fragmenting nature:

> The expressionless is the critical violence which, while unable to separate semblance from essence in art, prevents them from mingling. It possesses this violence as a moral dictum. In the expressionless, the sublime violence of the true appears as that which determines the language of the real world according to the laws of the moral world. For it shatters whatever still survives as the legacy of chaos in all beautiful semblance: the false, errant totality – the absolute totality. Only the expressionless completes the work, by shattering it into a thing of shards, into a fragment of the true world, into the torso of a symbol.[84]

He equates the expressionless to:

> that caesura, in which, along with harmony, every expression simultaneously comes to a standstill, in order to give free reign to an expressionless power inside all artistic media. Such power has rarely become clearer than in Greek tragedy, on the one hand, and in Hölderlin's hymnic poetry, on the other. Perceptible in tragedy as the falling silent of the hero, and in the rhythm of the hymn as objection. Indeed, one could not characterise this rhythm any more aptly than by asserting that something beyond the poet interrupts the language of the poetry.[85]

Adorno takes this up in his meditations on Beethoven's late style, a direct resonance with *Fragmente*:

> Then comes the equivalent of Hölderlin's concept of the caesura. This is the moment when subjectivity intervenes in the formal structure. Stated in terms of expressive structures, it is the moment of decision. [. . .] [the caesura] has a technical pre-history running through Beethoven's entire *oeuvre*.[86]

In developing Benjamin and Adorno not just to understand Beethoven but to develop a whole theory of classical style, Spitzer reminds us that the caesura 'is an expressly *rhythmic* device (Hölderlin's "counter-rhythmic rupture"), albeit at several orders of abstraction; thinking of drama as a kind of "rhythm," and of the interruption of a rhythmic sequence (the "onrushing change of representations") as itself "rhythmic."'[87] The caesura unites the metrical, the temporal and the dramatic-structural planes.

The silences, then, are not mere frames for the 'content' of *Fragmente*, not just room for reflection or echoic memory; this music is neither 'quiet' nor apolitical. They are caesurae – acts that embody a power, a violence beyond expression, the intervention of the subject and the moment of decision.

'Fragmente', Hölderlin and Marx

While the recent Frankfurter Ausgabe, drawing attention to process and parallel possibilities, was clearly a catalyst for Nono, his relationship with Hölderlin had deeper roots. Hölderlin's reputation as a radical thinker had been developing for some time on the German left, and particularly in the DDR. Through the nineteenth century, Hölderlin had been seen as eccentric to the German literary canon – perhaps in deference to Schiller and Goethe's dismissal of him as 'dangerous' and 'gloomy and sickly' respectively.[88] After the defeat of the First World War, he was adopted as an icon of heroic, patriotic idealism, a line developed under national socialism. An alternative view was proposed by Thomas Mann in 1923, who suggested that the German spirit would be complete if Marx had read Hölderlin.[89] Georg Lukács' essay *Hölderlin's Hyperion* of 1935 was a turning point in the left's understanding. He presents the poet as a radical thinker: 'Jacobin principles constitute the whole atmosphere of his poems. Only he whose perspective is dulled or blinded by class conformity will not perceive this all-determining atmosphere.'[90] For Lukács, Hölderlin's tragedy had been that Germany was not yet mature enough for a bourgeois revolution; unlike Hegel and Goethe, he was unwilling subsequently to compromise the principles of the French revolution to negotiate with an emerging bourgeois structure. Hölderlin's work is thus revolutionary and tragic in equal measure. Lukács shows how Hölderlin's thought remains emphatically pre-dialectic in this respect – an important property in the light of the non-dialectic turn that was emerging in the documented thought of Nono and Cacciari.

Brecht had adapted Hölderlin's *Antigone* in 1947, his attention having recently been brought to the poet by Hanns Eisler while both were working in California[91] – Eisler set fragments from Hölderlin in his *Hollywood Songbook*. Closer to Nono was the 1969 adaptation of Hölderlin's other Sophocles translation, *Oedipus Tyrann*, by Heiner Müller – widely regarded as Brecht's natural successor in the DDR. Müller had collaborated closely with Nono's recently deceased friend Paul Dessau. 'What counts is the example – death means nothing', he wrote on Dessau's death.[92] Müller was known to Nono through organisations such as the Akademie der Künste der DDR and would soon work with him: as a reciter in *Prometeo*, and then in developing other potential projects. Mayakovsky was also an important reference for Müller; to complete the loop, his poem *Majakovski* incorporates the end of Hölderlin's *Die Hälfte des Lebens*. Müller's *Germania Tod in Berlin* – written in 1971 but not produced until 1978 – combines scenes from German history with others from German mythology in a non-chronological sequence. His theatre pieces make frequent use of non-linear fragmentary episodes, encouraging those witnessing the performance to take different perspectives, to become a democratic audience. The influence of his dramatic strategies on *Al gran sole* was already clear; in a telegram of early 1974, Müller had warmly recalled their conversations.[93] Now his fragment technique was more developed, and presumably the subject of discussions with Nono in Berlin. Nono must have been aware of Müller's notion of the 'synthetic fragment', itself evolved from Brecht's epic storytelling. Brecht quoted Döblin: 'Unlike the dramatic, you can cut the narrative into so many separate pieces as though with scissors.'[94] Jameson describes Brecht's approach to fragmentation and resequencing as 'autonomisation'. His summary of its functioning in modernist literature applies equally to *Fragmente* and Nono's late fragmentation technique:

> Modernist autonomisation includes within itself the twin contradictory (yet dialectically identical) tendencies of the work towards minimalism on the one hand, and the mega-structure on the other. For if the logic of the work's production lies in analysis – in the literal sense of the Greek term *ana-luein*, to break up – it is all one whether the ultimate ideal consists in that least common denominator of a kind of silence that stands in a Beckett play for aesthetic purity, or on the other an addictive and well-nigh infinite expansion of the work which, as in Musil, needs no particular closure, even though 'incomplete' may not be the word for it.[95]

Waves

Nono had a copy of the 1971 biographical play *Hölderlin* by Peter Weiss, with whom he had worked on *Die Ermittlung*. Weiss' play builds on Pierre Bertaux's 1969 book, *Hölderlin und die Französische Revolution*, relating Hölderlin's work directly to that revolutionary impulse. Weiss explores Hölderlin's unwillingness to compromise enlightenment ideals by negotiating with bourgeois or military responses, or to dissolve the fundamental interconnectedness of his emotional, creative, philosophical and political life:

> I wanted to describe something of the conflict that arises in a person who suffers to the point of madness from the injustices, the humiliations in his society, who completely supports the revolutionary upheavals, and yet does not find the praxis with which the misery can be remedied.[96]

Herein lie the strength and tragedy of Hölderlin, illustrated by Weiss in a series of imagined versions of real encounters. Only the final scene is fictional, even if historically feasible: into the tower-room of the elderly, isolated Hölderlin comes Karl Marx. Perhaps in his words we find something of the political essence of *Fragmente*:

> Marx:
> It was my encounter
> with your works
> and especially Hyperion
> that with one blow
> shattered all my attempts[97]
> Two paths can be taken
> to prepare the way
> for fundamental change
> One is
> the analysis of the concrete
> historical situation
> The other
> the visionary formulation
> of deepest personal experience
> . . .
> I submit to you
> that both paths are
> equally valid[98]

Notes

1 Interview with Enzo Restagno, 1986. LNII, p. 478.
2 Stenzl, 1998, p. 92.
3 Ensenzberger, 1974, p. 39. Steiner, 1986, pp. 128–51.
4 Ensenzberger, 1974, p. 50.
5 Interview with Gerhard Müller, 1977. LNII, p. 222.
6 Mila and Nono, 2010, p. 303.
7 ALN tape 67.
8 De Assis, 2006, vol. I, pp. 190–207, documents the editing sequence.
9 Times refer to the CD of the performance tape published with the 1992 edition, Ricordi 132564.
10 '..... *sofferte onde serene ...*'. LNI, 482.

Waves

11 '..... *sofferte onde serene* ...'. LNI, 482.
12 See discussion of *Ein Gespenst geht um in der Welt*, above.
13 De Assis, 2006, vol. I, pp. 222–223.
14 *La Stampa*, 16–5–75.
15 Rubens Tedeschi in *l'Unità*, 19 April 1977.
16 Mila, 2010, p. 303.
17 Calabretto, 2001, explores the textual context in detail.
18 *Corriere della Sera*, 5 April 1975.
19 ALN 43.07.01/01.
20 Luigi Dallapiccola, quoted in Fearn, 2003, p. 127.
21 ALN 43.01/04r.
22 ALN 43.03/13rx.
23 Kirchert, 2006, p. 157.
24 'Con Luigi Dallapiccola'. LNI, p. 485.
25 Interview with Renato Garavaglia, 1979–80. LNII, p. 240.
26 Interview with Renato Garavaglia, 1979–80. LNII, p. 241.
27 Cacciari, 1976.
28 'Comporre oggi'. Interview with Wilfried Gruhn, 1984. LNII, p. 323.
29 'Comporre oggi'. Interview with Wilfried Gruhn, 1984. LNII, p. 323.
30 Zehelein, Grewe and Nono, 1978.
31 ALN 43.01/01.
32 ALN 43.01/13.
33 Klaus Kropfinger, 'nessun inizio – nessun fine [. . .] Estratti da colloqui con Luigi Nono', 1987. LNII, p. 455.
34 Performance instructions to *Fragmente-Stille, an Diotima*. The quotes are from Hölderlin's letters to Suzette Gontard.
35 ALN 44.04.01/02vsx.
36 *l'Unità*, 10–8–78.
37 ALN 44.04.03/12.
38 'Comporre oggi'. Interview with Wilfried Gruhn, 1984. LNII, p. 323.
39 Musil, 1995, p. 10.
40 Musil, 1995. p. 64.
41 Cacciari, 1976.
42 Cacciari, 1973.
43 Cacciari, 'Sulla genesi del pensiero negativo' 1969, in Mandarini, 2009, p. 58.
44 Discussion at Columbia University, November 1979. LNII, p. 233.
45 Nietzsche, 1996, p. 5.
46 ALN 44.04.01/13
47 ALN 44.06.01/1sx.
48 ALN 44.04.01/01vdx. The final 'o' of 'Mario' is ambiguous in Nono's handwriting. His intention is made clear in a nearby comment: 'Maria madre – Mario padre.'
49 Nielinger-Vakil, 2010, p. 132.
50 Kafka, 1948, pp. 119–20.
51 ALN 44.04.01/02vsx.
52 Interview with Enzo Restagno, 1978. LNII, p. 541.
53 ALN 44.04.04/01dx, 03vdx.
54 ALN 44.04.03/12.
55 Confirmed in Nono, 1980.
56 Spree, 1992, p. 139.
57 Elzenheimer, 2008, pp. 140–9.
58 Cited in Allwardt, 2004, p. 75.
59 ALN 44.05/06sx-dx.
60 ALN 44.06.01/02.
61 ALN 44.06.03/01r.
62 Nielinger-Vakil, 2010. Hers is the closest and most detailed analysis of *Fragmente*. It must be read bearing in mind that Nono's decision to use specific texts from Hölderlin was taken *after* composition was well underway.

Waves

63 Lachenmann, 1999, p. 27.
64 Nono, 1980.
65 Linden, 1989, pp. 92–143, provides a full concordance with the original contexts. Nono takes texts not from the Frankfurter Ausgabe but a bilingual edition (Hölderlin, 1979). Michael Hamburger's collection (Hölderlin, 2004) is the most complete collection of translations, although for 'Leuchtest du wie vormals nieder . . .', see Appelbaum, 1995, p. 46.
66 Rihm, 1990, p. 3.
67 Allwardt, 2004. Benjamin's recent translation of *Hyperion* is excellent (Hölderlin, 2008).
68 Coetzee, 2006.
69 Heidegger, 2000, p. 64.
70 Beiser, 2008, p. 405.
71 'Infinito, inquieto, incompiuto'. Interview with Lothar Knessl, 1988. LNII, pp. 471–6.
72 Nono, 1980.
73 Cacciari, 1976, p. 112.
74 Lachenmann, 1999, p. 24.
75 Cited in Metzger, 1981, 112.
76 Quoted in: Metzger, 1981, p. 93.
77 Barthes, 1985, p. 250.
78 Pestalozza, 1981, p. 9.
79 Metzger, 1981, p. 93.
80 Döpke, 1987, p.111.
81 Hölderlin, *Remarks on Oedipus* (1803), in Bernstein, 2003, p. 195.
82 Benjamin, 1996, pp. 354–5.
83 Hölderlin, *Oldest Programme for a System of German Idealism* (1796), in Bernstein, 2003, p. 187.
84 Benjamin, 1996, p. 340.
85 Benjamin, 1996, p. 341.
86 Adorno, 1998, p. 64. Here the 'decision' refers to 'The Difficult Decision' that is the title of the last movement of the Quartet op. 135.
87 Spitzer, 2006, p. 227.
88 Fehervary, 1977, p. 15.
89 Fehervary, 1977, pp. 51–2.
90 Lukács, 1968, p. 145.
91 Calico, 2008, p. 97.
92 *Neues Deutschland*, 2 January 1996.
93 Telegram from Heiner Müller, 29 January 1974. ALN.
94 Jameson, 1998, p. 55.
95 Jameson, 1998, p. 58.
96 Peter Weiss, quoted by Robert Cohen in 'Introduction' to Weiss, 2010, p. 10.
97 Weiss, 2072, p. 198.
98 Weiss, 2072, pp. 200–1.

12

VERSO *PROMETEO*

'Das atmende Klarsein'

Breathing anew

During his visits to Milan through 1978, Nono had begun to discuss musical ideas with the flautist Roberto Fabbriciani, then playing at La Scala. They had met after a performance of Camillo Togni's *Blaubart*, in which the solo flute has a dramatic role on stage – an anticipation of their subsequent collaboration.[1] Fabbriciani was a student of Gazelloni and rapidly becoming one of the most original and creative of new music virtuosi. He travelled to Venice to work with Nono, and together they not only experimented with sonorities, techniques and gestures, but established the basis for a new kind of relationship between composer and performer, one that in their case would last a decade.

Friends and colleagues tell of Nono's difficulties through this period. The issue was not how to turn away from fundamental principles, but rather how they were to be sustained, evolved and realised in a changed political, cultural and personal world. In conversations with people such as Cacciari he was developing new theoretical understandings, and his increasing dissatisfaction with the empty, conventionalised 'artistic' behaviour of institutions and musicians alike is well documented. There seems to have been frustration at not yet having identified the conceptual models with which he could respond musically to these new challenges. Through the period of intense collaboration with Fabbriciani and others, of the development of *Prometeo* and beyond, the renouncing of 'resolution' would become axiomatic. The ineffability of compositional concept and musical experience would evolve into a principle of mobility – 'goalless searching' as a permanent state. He would address the paradoxical situation of fixing details in tape and score so fine that they risk becoming arbitrary, through new relationships with performers and the performance situation, and with live electronics.

In the Studio di Fonologia, Nono and Fabbriciani recorded the improvisation that would become the basis of the next work – *Das atmende Klarsein* for bass flute, choir and live electronics – which would eventually be premiered on Florence on 30 May 1981. Despite the good offices of the universally admired Zuccheri, the Milan studio was in decline. There had been no director since 1973, and even then the RAI had been reluctant to invest in new technology; it would close with Zuccheri's retirement in 1983.[2] Nono was aware of recent advances elsewhere; he had met John Chowning and seen recent work with artificial intelligence at

Verso Prometeo

Stanford.[3] He had been invited to work at the Experimental Studio of the SWF at Freiburg, founded a decade earlier by its director, Hans-Peter Haller. Nono and Fabricciani worked in Milan on 1 and 2 December 1980. In these recordings the instrument becomes a filter for breath, singing and whistling; sounds are bent, opened or closed until they dissolve. Fabbriciani's improvisation explores his vast range of extended techniques and virtuoso gestures. Sensing that they had reached the limits of what was possible there, they decided to drive straight to the Black Forest. Fabbriciani recounts how Nono was too excited to enter the new studio directly. Instead, they walked in the forest for a day and found the hotel that would effectively become Nono's second home for some years: the Hotel Halde, high on the Schauinsland mountain. Fabbriciani remembers the moment clearly: as they entered the studio 'Nono trembled with emotion and excitement, but also nervousness as to this next phase.' Haller demonstrated and explained the equipment. 'Nono was astonished, he marvelled. With great humility, timidly, slowly he began to work with these machines, to reimagine sound and embark upon a path that was completely new.'[4] Haller also describes the occasion in detail:

> After about two and a half hours Nono wandered pensively, silently around the studio and sat on the piano stool with his head in his hands, concentrating. After a little while he suddenly stood up, continued his walking around, came up to me timidly and said "my friends call me GIGI!" – the studio visit was over. Before he left, he said he would like to come back, and asked whether we might have time for him over the next few weeks.[5]

This relationship would continue through the decade, to Nono's last works. Haller describes it as a situation of continuous and mutual learning and research.

Nono's sense of wonder is revealed in meticulous notes from his introductory sessions with Haller. Most importantly, the potential of this technology was contiguous with the fundamental operations in which his own musical thought was grounded. It afforded mobility of sound on the very axes of manipulation of musical ideas that supported his compositional practice, but on the finest of levels, with control, responsiveness and – above all – in real time, in performance. Pitch could be transformed by a harmoniser, rhythm and time by delays, timbre with filters, spatial position by the Halaphon (invented by Haller and Peter Lawo) and acoustic space by reverberation. Logical relationships between different sound sources could be established using a gate. The levels of compositional intervention and the nature of the sonic material may be quite different, but the dimensionality of this musical thought-space still has much in common with Nono's established practices – indeed, with his historical models.

In January, Nono and Fabbriciani began work in the Freiburg studio with an arrangement of three microphones to capture key-clicks, breath sounds and the full complex spectra of multiphonics – the intimate physicality of performance. The performance is inherently spatial; the distribution of different sounds through the body of the instrument becomes clear in these recordings, as does the inner polyphony of various layers of activity – breath, fingers and resonance. They started with ring modulation, as in *Con Luigi Dallapiccola*, but soon abandoned its persistent artificiality for the more natural products of transposition, delay and spatialisation. Fabbriciani introduced other musicians to their research; improvising trombonist Giancarlo Schiaffini was the first to join them. The collaborative process is described by Fabbriciani: a continuous conversation, the embracing of error and the rejection of the banal.[6]

Prometeo – its shape, its means and its very nature – was the motivating idea behind all Nono's activity through this period: arguably since the completion of *Al gran sole* and explicitly since *Con Luigi Dallapiccola*. Nono's arrival in Freiburg marked the beginning of an intensification

Verso Prometeo

of focus and clarity. In August 1980 Cacciari had written with new suggestions for *Prometeo*: extracts from the second, fifth and seventh of Rilke's *Duino Elegies* (1922), poems he had returned to having written about Rilke in *Krisis* (1976). He initially proposed that these fragments might be used to link the elements of *Prometeo*, 'rather like the lines from Hölderlin in your quartet.'[7] When Nono undertook to present a new work at the Florentine *Maggio Musicale* festival of the following spring, Cacciari proposed an autonomous textual structure in Greek, Italian and German, combining the Rilke fragments with ancient Orphic poems to accompany the dead – texts first conceived for the *Prologo* of *Prometeo*. Memory is key: beyond the dwelling of Hades, we will find the fountain of Mnemosyne where the waters flow clear, the Orphic fragments tell us. Cacciari's texts were reduced and reassembled by Nono into a network of fragments, articulated by nodes of semantic, phonetic or referential resonance.[8] Parts of what became *Das atmende Klarsein* – the title is taken from Rilke's seventh *Elegy* – would in any case be incorporated into *Prometeo*. For bass flute, chamber choir and live electronics, it was intended to be included in the initial 1984 version in its entirety. Early plans related to a version of the *Prologo*: for flute, trombone, percussion and choir, with recordings of the bells at Freiburg. The prospect of an autonomous composition for Florence suggested a more focused project.

The title *Das atmende Klarsein* (*breathing clear-being*) reflects Nono's own sense of being able to breathe once more. In his work on architecture, Cacciari would relate these lines of Rilke to the space left by the destruction of place or dwelling: clarity rather than consolation.[9] Here, breath is the origin of sound. After the short choral introduction, distinct words are heard rarely; phonemes are superimposed or widely separated in time in a vocal texture of extreme transparency. A few phrases recur as beacons: 'ins Freie' ('into the open') and 'ein reines Fruchtlands' ('a pure land of fruit') reinforce the sense of landscape, of a new environment in which life is more possible. There is a natural continuity with the 'heraus in Luft und Licht' of *Fragmente*. The studio, Rilke, Fabbriciani and his new physical environment all seem to have allowed Nono to renew his own sense of active listening – an experience to which he refers repeatedly in interviews. This fundamental reacquainting with the physicality of composition responded to the challenges that had arisen, without being in any way a 'solution' (such an idea would be anathema), and opened a vast new area of musical imagining. The landscape of the imagination becomes contiguous with that of the environment. Nono's room at the Hotel Halde looked down through the valley, across forests bent by the wind. Fabbriciani describes his fascination with this landscape: high, remote, silent but for the wind:[10]

> Emission is breath, *anemos*, source of life and it is the generating force of *Das atmende Klarsein*. The vitality of this piece is set in the freedom of an intoxicating breath. I remember the walks with Gigi along the paths of the Black Forest near Freiburg: he breathed deeply inviting me to do the same, as if taking on a new life.[11]

The contrast with Giudecca is clear, but Venice is not replaced; the two environments constitute an important, musically material creative dialectic.

Nono's new compositional world required new models for its navigation. Following subsequent thought in philosophy and science, we might describe it as a space of potential, rather than one of forms and materials.[12] Giordano Bruno's notion of an infinite universe would become central to the wide-ranging reconstitution of Nono's conceptual repertoire. Alexander Gosztonyi's recent book on the concept of space was an important source of ideas.[13] Gosztonyi examines the relationship of space and time through the history of thought, and the co-evolution of conceptual models with developments in philosophy and science. His detailed

Verso Prometeo

studies of non-Euclidean models and the implications of recent philosophy are directly relevant. Haller, with whom Nono discussed Gosztonyi's book, rationalises its significance for Nono's work in terms of geometrical space, sound space and time space.[14]

'. . . a sense of the possible'

Nono's compositional practice now embodies his theoretical vision: multiple paths through a vast imaginative space that together allow the listener to perceive aspects of its many dimensions. 'It is not the contents of the texts that are reproduced musically but paths,' he says of *Das atmende Klarsein*. 'The work does not give form to images or words but to the way in which they are combined, to what they suggest, and to what disturbs them.'[15] He works separately on instrumental material for Fabbriciani and on the choral text settings. *Das atmende Klarsein* consists of eight continuous sections through which chamber choir and bass flute alternate; they overlap only in the decaying resonance of each section. Fabbriciani reports Nono's rationale: 'the choir and the flute never encounter each other because one is nostalgia for the past and the other nostalgia for the future'.[16] This points to a fundamental property of Nono's late music: as focus on the present moment intensifies, so does awareness that in both aesthetic and material, compositional terms this moment is a product of acts of memory and imagination. These possible worlds of present and future have to be navigated in parallel for the present to have any sense; there is no single 'true' version of either, and neither can be known in their entirety. The present is suspended between these imaginative projections; at the end of the decade, *La lontananza nostalgica utopica futura* will be Nono's most explicit exploration of this state. 'But how to burst in to the non-temporality of life?' asks Cacciari:

> How can life remove itself from the merely negative, from the nihilism of duration, where the past does *not* exist, the future does *not* exist, and the present is past as soon as it is thought? [. . .] The very experience of the far-stretching desert of time can make us all tend to listen to a non-temporal dimension of time. There is a *Nunc* of the creature which is mysteriously close to that of the divine image; a *moment* of the creature, elusive, a *sudden meanwhile* (zwischen zwei Weilen), which no-more and not-yet fail to capture, which shatters duration, which is the exception to its rules. This Nunc opens out ins Freie; through its narrow door, almost invisible, elusive, we open out ins Freie.[17]

Nono asks for 'fragility' in the voices, but also impeccable intonation with no beating between unisons.[18] The 'non-temporality' of these transparent vocal textures is also in their impossible sustaining through slow tempi and the long fermata; for Nono they represent 'an ideal of classical antiquity'. Fabricciani's flute is in constant vibration, however slight or extreme – in a continual now.

The two types of material – for chorus and flute – develop in separate, complementary ways, but they have common origins. As in the preceding works, two short passages of rhythmic polyphony provide the temporal frameworks, compressed or stretched as necessary. He selects these from a series of seven-voice rhythmic fabrics constructed of permutations of seven duration values (3–9), each at one of seven subdivisions of the beat (1–7) with each value followed by the same duration as a rest.[19] Again, annotations indicate that Nono conceives of these passages as a contrasting pair, whatever their eventual use. The marking of one as 'buio' (darkness) suggests that the other denotes clarity in some way. The derivation of pitch material is new. Fabbriciani gave Nono tables of possible and workable multiphonics. Nono uses those

Verso Prometeo

by Pierre-Yves Artaud and Thomas Howell to number sequences of multiphonics for piccolo and bass flute, carefully notated with their pitch inflections.[20] These serve as pitch material for choral and instrumental areas of the work respectively. Nono organises candidate sonorities from piccolo and bass flute according to their interval content: for each he groups those rich in tritones, seconds, sevenths and ninths, and those based on fourths and fifths.[21] In selecting the piccolo sonorities for the chorus, Nono avoids those with octaves and rationalises microtonal inflections.[22] These are combined with the minimal intervallic language distilled through the process of *Fragmente*: perfect fifths, augmented fourths and minor seconds, which are also prevalent in his choice of multiphonic material. As far back as *Variazioni canoniche*, these can be seen as Nono's primary grids for traversing pitch space. Thirds have become exceptional events in his harmonic-melodic matrix of this period. Choir and flute are different projections not entirely of the same pitch complexes – piccolo- and bass flute-derived sequences naturally diverge – but of material generated by the same physical–acoustic activity. From these materials he abstracts sequences of dyads to produce a background layer that is not strictly polyphonic as before, but an evolving sequence of sonorities of one to four voices, expanding and contracting, mostly entering or moving one voice at a time in seconds or fifths. Its characteristic motion is directional but not teleological, an organic behaviour that moves forwards one step at a time. No one point of rest is prioritised over any other.

Choral and flute sections each move forwards in their own rhythm – two perspectives that on the surface make no attempt at synthesis. Only the continuities of pitch between the first and second, third and fourth sections hint at underlying common foundations. Sound is generally continuous. Metrical and temporal rhythm become a single parameter; in both flute and choral material the common measure is breath. The flute passages are naturally articulated this way; changes of pace or insistent evenness, rapid exhalation or near-impossible sustain become the principle rhetorical factors. The choral sections are striated with one, two or three fermata in almost every bar – a positive image of the grid of silences in *Fragmente*. Over sustained sounds rather than silences, these range in duration from 2 to 17 seconds – an enormous challenge for the singers, whose constantly changing dynamics generally remain within the range *pppppp* – *p*.

The first two sections mark out the terms and positions of the discourse. The opening chorus presents the background material most clearly. Like the beginning of *Fragmente*, this is essentially a refracted monody. It is difficult not to read its text – 'nach spätem Gewitter das atmende Klarsein' ('after a late storm, the deep-breathing freshness')[23] – as autobiographical. A dynamic range of *ppp* – *pp*, open intervals, clear text setting and long sustained pauses, often on a single note, allow the ear to open itself to full attentiveness. The sound is constantly in motion, both internally and between pitches, which move slowly and by step, sliding sideways between fifths and fourths. The initial F♯–C♯ returns inverted in the middle of the first section to follow a path that hints at the descending complement of the opening, foreshadowing the expansion of the second flute section (Figure 12.1). This interval pattern – two-fifths or fourths separated by a semitone – will assume significance in subsequent works as the portal to Nono's harmonic thought-space.

The transition between the first two sections shows their contrast in texture but also their common origins. At the opening of the second section, the solo bass flute elaborates a mirror of the first chorus, exact to begin with. Short, sharply characterised gestures proliferate around this structure, recalling the initial recordings in Milan: extremes of dynamic of speed, articulation and timbre, using lip, tongue and throat modulation. As these gestures pursue their own development, a new bifurcation emerges; their urgent forward motion is regularly interrupted by *lentissimo pppp* phrases of harmonics overblown from a single sustained low pitch, as if to

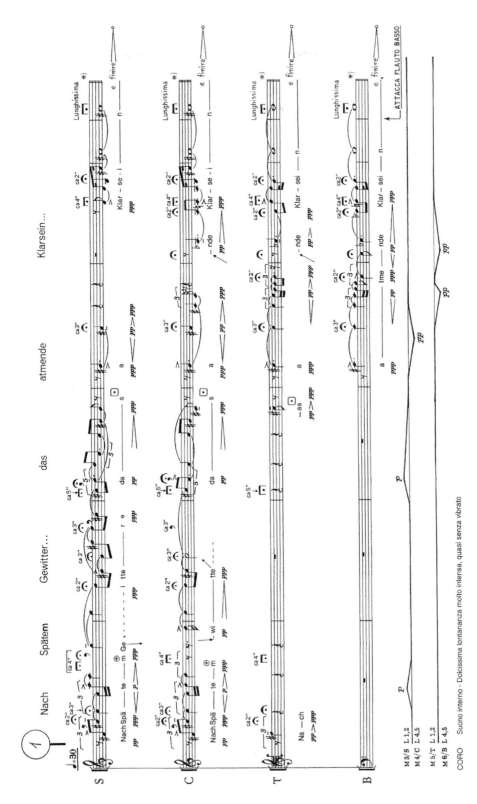

Figure 12.1 *Das atmende Klarsein*: bars 1–7. (Reproduced by kind permission of Casa Ricordi.)

Verso Prometeo

restore the primacy of the open intervals. In going beyond the initial mirror and evolving into a line of continuous multiphonics, the flute seems to explore a space prior to the work itself.

Their relationship having been established at the first transition, chorus and flute pursue different trajectories. In the second choral entry, the Greek texts are interspersed with Rilke. Phonemes are still heard sequentially, but here words are more divided among voices, using the technique introduced in the first chorus: individual voices are frozen on a pitch and vowel, as if the music occupies a space of multiple rates of time. The Greek texts are almost derhythmicised by long durations and the pattern of fermata. These windows in the forward flow of time are analogous to the phrases of harmonics in the first flute section. The third and fourth choral sections are derived using the process seen in the Deola material of *Al gran sole*. The opening choral and flute sections become raw material, divided into numbered events from which Nono creates new sequences, adjusting voicing and rhythms. The process is more akin to folding than fragmentation. It brings elements of the background world into new relationships; memory is reconfigured. It encourages us to hear the 'original' as one temporal path through the totality of possibilities. Although organised differently, the use of text confirms this. While the voices maintain a single aggregate rhythmic unison, the texts now overlap such there may be up to four simultaneous phonemes – an additive synthesis that seems to expand the human capacity for language.

The second flute section establishes a clear pattern of movement in three-bar units of a single note, separated by commas. The derivation from Nono's earlier all-interval series is heard clearly at the opening. He builds a wedge-shaped sequence of dyads contracting from octave C–C to unison F♯–G♭, but in quarter-tones, in thirteen steps. Through this he makes twelve three-dyad passes, each a semitone step (i.e. taking every second dyad, a 'salto a 2'), alternating higher and lower pitches. Thus, the first half of the movement, marked A in the score, moves by semitones from a minor 7th B–C♯ to A–E♭, then backwards, expanding again on the other quarter-tone grid. Dynamics and the amount of breath noise are in constant motion. Part B moves forwards twice through the second half of the sequence, but now *sempre p*. Melodic and timbral instability increase as the pattern is pulled inwards to its fixed point attractor; pitches are drawn back temporarily to their previous state, and, once stable, they resist clear definition by the addition of whistling or ambiguity as to their octave. Delays enhance the sense of a narrowing spiral, as do the quarter-tone shifts of the flute's pitch-grid. The flute's final F elides with the opening C–F fourth of the third choral section, the first statement of a word that will return again and again: 'ascolta' ('listen'). Likewise, articulated as units of a single breath, the third flute section is the negative of its predecessor. Sustained, barely inflected pitches are replaced by a nervous murmuration of breath sounds, rapid key movement and what Nono and Fabbriciani call 'aeolian' sounds – unstable whistle sounds, resonances that barely speak. The player's breath is now subject to constantly changing acoustic modulation. Microtonal harmonisers render pitch contours still more ungraspable. As Evans points out, such multiple sounds never speak simultaneously; they have their own inner temporal displacement, a fragility that connects the listener to the process of sound-production.[24] There is an inherent uncertainty to such modes of production. The continuous resistance to representation, reduction or commodification is now at the level of the sound itself. Finally, the flautist improvises over the tape produced by Nono and Fabricciani in Milan, using material from that recording – a last fold in time, to a state before the work emerged as an entity or even a possibility.

The close sonic focus of the second and third flute sections reflects Nono's collaborative research with Fabbriciani at Freiburg and their investigation of the possibilities of live electronics. Sound processing is used subtly, without drawing attention to itself. Nono explained the object in this first use of live electronics as:

Verso Prometeo

not only the processed sound as a unitary perceptual phenomenon, or the sound treated and fixed on tape, but the 'live-natural' sound of the choir and the bass flute and, *in the same instant* and not in temporal or visual succession, its becoming other, its germinating both as a compositional spectrum and as a spatial dynamic.

fantastic diversity and multiplicity of sound *in the same instant*, possible, in other words, like that of thought, of feelings, of creativity.

we should listen to Musil 'if there is a sense of the real, [. . .] then there must also be something which we will call a sense of the possible'.[25]

We hear Nono's voice in this text. In his speech and writing, his natural syntactic tendencies now approach those of his music ever more closely. Fabbriciani describes his voice at the time: 'Sometimes he spoke so quietly you could hardly hear him. Gigi would say "look, now there's snow on the mountains everything changes, even the acoustic." And then he would speak even more quietly.'[26]

Sound is distributed through six channels, surrounding the listener. The disposition of processing changes section by section; during each one only the levels of processed and unprocessed sound are controlled live. There is no obvious sense of sound being added, except perhaps with the canon created by delays in the second flute section. Here, slow pitch change in combination with the constant internal movement of sound creates a phasing, a searching for a new relationship, between the flute and its own echo. In the first and final sections for flute, the sound moves circularly around the room in opposite directions and at different and changing speeds, as if it has no single point of origin. The choir is only amplified during its third entry, when, as in the third flute section, sound is transposed by roughly a quarter tone in both directions. The resultant beating and phasing keep the sound in constant motion, a development of the concept of mobility Nono had realised in previous scores by the dynamic microtonal thickening of lines.

As Haller points out, these treatments expand the perceptual space inhabited by the music. He describes the phenomenon as 'the modulation of acoustic space'.[27] Like other aspects of the composition, the physical sound space becomes a many dimensioned space of potential in which time and physical position are as mobile as every other dimension. Nono's frequent reference to Musil is indicative of his reconceiving of his own creative space. The twin dangers of the arbitrary and the 'bureaucratic' recede as he reconfigures his map of the possible. The actions of performers in non-notated contexts will be the product of long discussion and preparation, mutual understanding and trust. There will be no 'indeterminism'; these actions will be as determined as any score, but more closely so in respect of the circumstances, the individuals and the moment of their determining.

In its dual, parallel paths, *Das atmende Klarsein* embodies Nono's conscious rejection of synthesis, of resolution, and provides a clue as to the continuing political consciousness of his music. Rather than a 'turn' in Nono's work, the changes in his working environment and practice facilitate a renewal of his radical stance. To see this as a response to the immediate political situation – the collapse of the historic compromise between the DC and the PCI at the end of 1980 – would be to over-simplify, to banalise Nono's thought. We have already considered the critique of dialectics embodied in Cacciari's concept of *pensiero negativo*. Such a stance also has roots in the radical re-reading of Marx led by Mario Tronti, whose 1966 *Operai e capitale* laid the theoretical foundations for Italian workerism and for the progressive tendencies within the PCI. There, Tronti asserts that the search for a dissolution of the boundaries between workers and capital is misguided, that such a goal is actually an instrument of capitalism itself. Instead, it is their antagonism that is the potentially productive force, that must be

Verso Prometeo

maintained.[28] Nono addressed the non-dialectial nature of *Das atmende Klarsein* in a conversation with Philippe Albèra:

> I find the term 'dialectical' obsolete nowadays; the idea that things lose their specificity to approach a common result has been superseded. I think there are different situations, different characteristic tendencies, different functions and potentialities, and that this diversity is a powerful force for invention, transformation, the emergence of new sensibilities. It is not unanimity. At the moment there is a harmful tendency not to argue, not to debate, to reduce everything. [. . .] [Instead] it is the continuous confrontation, continuous exchange, the transformations, the polycentrism, the rejoicing in properties [that are] against amorphousness. It is necessary to change certain categories of thought: what is the working class? Is the terminology still valid? What is a class? Political action, union action, change with the realities imposed by the times.[29]

For Cacciari,

> *Das atmende Klarsein* can only be understood thus: the production of a sound without knowing, presenting a challenge as to why the next sound instead of nothing [. . .] No scheme, no dialectic, no series relates one sound to another, if not their pure participation in the world of silence.[30]

It is the complement of *Fragmente* and the essence of *Prometeo*. *Das atmende Klarsein* will stand as the likely *Esodo* of *Prometeo* through much of its composition – the final emergence of the eternal Wanderer into clarity. As always, Nono's imperative is to bring philosophical and compositional issues together, such that their implications and affordances become a single field of action. Nono and Cacciari have not yet identified the vital role of Benjamin's *Theses of History*, but the dynamic nature of time and the importance of memory have become central to opening the vast multiple spaces of the now. In addressing this in compositional terms, Nono is also confronting the memory of his own musical thought, his own behaviours, including the internal inconsistencies and paradoxes they inevitably produce.

'Io, frammento dal Prometeo'

Nono's intense engagement with new theory, models and techniques reconfigures the space of his own thought, adds to the repertoire of mechanisms for its navigation and permits the emergence of new musical concepts. He was clearly acutely conscious of this process. Immediately on completing *Das atmende Klarsein*, Nono announced to Fabbriciani that he now knew how to approach *Prometeo*, and shortly thereafter he agreed with Haller to continue work in the Freiburg studio on the next project: *Io, frammento dal Prometeo*, a commission for the Venice Biennale in the autumn of 1981.[31] Clarinetist Ciro Scarponi had joined Nono's research at Freiburg, as had a succession of vocalists. At Fabbriciani's suggestion, Scarponi had been invited to Giudecca to play for Nono: 'The first thing Nono said to me was "Look at this score on your own for twenty minutes then I'll come back and see what you can do." [. . .] Probably they were sketches for *Prometeo*.' Nono was very enthusiastic: 'It's not possible! Nobody could do these things for me before! [. . .] These pianissimi on the contrabass[. . .]! I'll expect you at Freiburg in three days!'[32]

Verso Prometeo

That this more complicated work was ready for its premiere in Venice the same September is an indication of the advanced state of Nono's preparation for *Prometeo*. For three solo sopranos, 12-voice choir, bass flute, contrabass clarinet and live electronics, it develops a passage from Cacciari's evolving text – Prometheus' encounter with Io – and will form the basis of section a) of *Isola 2°*. The text derives from Aeschylus' episode in which Io, fleeing the wrath of Hera the wife of Zeus, recounts her sufferings to the bound Prometheus and asks him to predict her fate. His eventual prophesy that it will be the son of Io and Zeus to overthrow Zeus and release Prometheus is not yet heard. A form-sketch for *Prometeo* from 1981 shows the important role of the Io episode. Between the opening *A* 'Prologo' and the final *A* 'Eko – Fine Utopia – Wanderer' come episodes for Prometeo (marked 'Utopia') and Io ('violenza – eros – ASCOLTA').[33] Despite the significant changes the text will undergo, this episode is already seen as pivotal, as the moment of epiphany; it is the moment when Prometheus chooses to prophesy rather than rebel. This is the *drân* referred to by Cacciari, the seed of 'drama', the decision on which everything turns.[34] In an interview, Nono explained how he understood these characters:

> the idea emerged to focus everything on the figure of Prometeo. But just as a model, a figure emblematic of wandering, of seeking. That's why alongside the fragments of Aeschylus there are others from Euripides, Virgil, Hölderlin, Nietzsche, Benjamin. *Prometeo* is just an island in an immense archipelago of wanderers, of travellers in consciousness. [. . .] Each wanderer is at the same time the mirror of the other, each one a fragment of the perennial wandering of us all.
>
> [. . .] [Io] is also a creature obliged to be a wanderer, following her exile. She also fights with the divinity, and in a way seeks struggle, persecution. But above all she is a restless mirror of the eros of Prometeo, which she makes him acknowledge. The restlessness of Io reveals itself as that of Prometeo. And, if you like, the restlessness of sweetness, of tenderness.[35]

Cacciari sets out the words of Prometeo and Io in parallel, together with those of a third figure, Mitologia. For this abstract third figure, Cacciari brings together the third stanza of Hölderlin's *Schicksalslied* (Hyperion's *Song of Fate*), the sixth of Pindar's *Nemea* odes and lines from Euripides' *Alcestis*. In an early form-plan, Muthos (to become Mitologia) was to surround the entire drama with words of Hölderlin.[36] Mitologia is 'the logos that wants to penetrate the mythos, which tries and tries again to understand, in its own text, the dialogue between Prometeo and Io, the originary affinity that he has revealed.'[37] Mitologia meditates on the common ancestry and irremediable division of gods and men. By this device Cacciari creates a space of ideas, emotions and relationships analogous to Nono's sonic space; Mitologia is a reflective surface. Nono's introduction sets out the origins of the work in notions of space: 'A moment of restless research in spatiality, in conflict between various probabilities of technology, of thoughts, of feelings. For me, *Prometeo* is "fragmenting" in space, not visual, but all to be listened to.'[38]

Like *Das atmende Klarsein* in its initial form, *Io, frammento dal Prometeo* has nine sections. This pattern emerges early in the process, and sections are characterised spatially from the outset. The premiere was not to be in a concert hall but in a large sports venue, for which Nono conceived an arrangement of nested sonic spaces. The performers are in the centre, arranged asymmetrically about the conductor, ringed by an inner set of loudspeakers, the audience and then another circle of loudspeakers. The near circle used Nono's preferred technique of projecting the loudspeakers upwards, to create an indirect sound. An additional more distant

Verso Prometeo

pair of loudspeakers creates a front-back axis across these two circles. Each listener thus has a different aural perspective on the work. An unrealised plan was to have a further circle of trombones, perhaps a memory of Gabrieli at San Marco or the passage to Hades of Monteverdi's *Orfeo*. The work is marked 'a più cori' ('for several choirs') as if to emphasise its Venetian provenance. To the delays, harmoniser and Halaphon, Nono now adds reverberation, filters and a vocoder. The vocoder's spectrum-shifting allows useful transposition by intervals beyond the microtonal chorusing of the harmoniser: up to three semitones in each direction. 'Think!' he notes, 'audio-computer.'[39] These are not effects; the Freiburg equipment allows Nono to perform compositional operations in real-time. Pauses in almost every bar of the choral sections enhance awareness of the speed of change, of the physical–virtual acoustic and of the trajectories of physical sound and musical idea.

Pitch material is again built from perfect fifths separated by a semitone, the building blocks of Western music. Inverting or changing the order of fifths allows other intervals to enter the discourse: fourths, augmented fourths, major thirds. Many structures of both pitch and rhythm derive from the same sources as the first two choruses of *Das atmende Klarsein*.[40] Fragments are inverted and reversed, selected and folded into new sequences to shape the form that Nono has determined, then folded more tightly along new lines for further use. At each stage the fabric thus produced is rearticulated, develops new internal structure. Elsewhere, such constructs become the basis for new patterns. Figure 12.2 shows examples of the use of the opening intervals of *Das atmende Klarsein* in *Io, frammento dal Prometeo*. In a first rendering, the original is compressed then projected through a kaleidoscope of mirrors (Figure 12.2a). The second part of this is divided to set text fragments 20 and 21 in the next stage (Figure 12.2b); the placing of text subsequently changes. These are separated in the subsequent folding to the final score; note the fifth-semitone pitch relationship with the preceding bass flute insert early in section I (Figure 12.2c). In section VI, the independent materials of woodwind and sopranos begin from the same starting point, then separately pursue ever-expanding cycles of fifth-semitone chains in sequences of changing transpositions (Figures 12.2d–e).

The nine sections are characterised by the dynamics of their musical spaces. Movement in physical space by means of sound diffusion and the Halaphon is important, but inseparable from other aspects of musical behaviour. Nono's conceptions of the movement of sound through physical space, of musical argument through local and formal time, and of structure through its various dimensions are all developed spatially. An initial series of nine distinct sound designs – patterns of movement in which sound distribution directly reflects compositional architecture – was refined in favour of more subtle use of spatialisation. Experimentation may have shown that the perception of sound space has a complex relationship with the materials; movement is not figural except when it approaches the kind of banal effect that Nono was anxious to avoid. More interestingly, Nono seems to have assimilated these models into the compositional fabric of each section. The fundamental pattern was retained in the configuration of musicians and loudspeakers described above.

The formal pattern is again fundamentally one of alternating chorus and instruments, but this is overlaid with a constant blurring of the distinctions between voice and instrument, text and non-text. Voice and language remain central concerns. In the first section, Io and Prometeo are heard in succession and in clear dramatic juxtaposition. The initial words of Io are sung by female voices with interruptions from bass flute, followed by those of Prometeo by male voices with contrabass clarinet. The solo instruments are clearly identified with the two characters. Io is diffused in the inner circle of loudspeakers; Prometeo contains her from the outer. The use of six voices for each establishes their mythical, multiply present status. The division can be dissolved at madrigalian moments such as the addition of women's voices on Prometeo's

Verso Prometeo

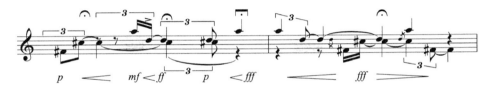

Figure 12.2a Early sketch[41]

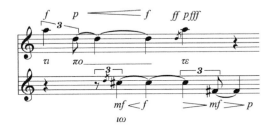

Figure 12.2b Text fragments 20 and 21[42]

Figure 12.2c Section 1, bars 10–11

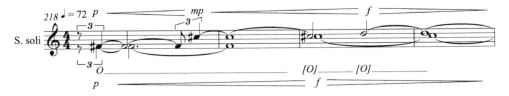

Figure 12.2d Section VI, opening – sopranos

Figure 12.2e Section VI, opening – bass flute
Figure 12.2 *Io, frammento dal Prometeo*: development from *Das atmende Klarsein*

Verso Prometeo

'aurora'. At this early point in the work, the stark contrast between vocal and instrumental colours obscures their origins in common material. This will reveal itself as the listener is taken along a path of focused listening, a process that begins with the brief instrumental second section. There is no sound processing here other than spatialisation. The instruments are diffused to opposite corners of the room to retain their autonomous characters, but the sonic animation arises from their extreme dynamics and multiphonics at the edge of resonance – the inherent rhythm of the very act of making sound. We begin to hear inner voices, even the shapes of words, within the complex envelopes of woodwind notes.

The third section brings a corresponding transformation. The female choral voices sing the cry of Io – 'BURN ME in fire, BURY ME in earth, FEED ME to the monsters of the sea'; 'ARDIMI, SPROFONDAMI, DAMMI' – the rhyming key words return like an incantation. Their phrases are descanted, continued and interrupted by a high solo soprano vocalise rising to G above top C. Once again, Nono's writing for soprano recalls Mina; just weeks after this premiere, Pestalozza compared Mina to Maria Callas and Cathy Berberian, and mentioned that Nono had wanted to write for her.[43] A few years later, while reaffirming his lack of interest in commercial popular music, Nono admitted that: 'Perhaps Mina is an exception. With her voice she was able to produce very interesting very high sounds.'[44] Here, the highest soprano notes are often marked 'flute'; the line is quiet but constantly in movement. Io becomes an individual, intimate character of multiple manifestations, whereas Prometeo remains rooted in his mythical, choral status. While the choral voices now begin to be transposed through the inner circle and slightly delayed through the outer, as if to slow the speed of sound across space, the soloist is projected directly front and back. The unity of voice and instrument is confirmed in the fourth section for solo soprano and bass flute, the wordless soprano now entering the flute's register to cover a range of over three octaves. The two sounds fuse in a monody, its intervals led either melodically or by multiphonics.

Clear text setting returns in the central fifth section. Here and in the seventh, Io and Prometeo are heard together as quasi-independent groups of male and female voices with no instrumental elaboration. Their material develops independently as they present parallel texts. They proceed largely through a process of alternation, almost suggesting a dialogue. There are other hints of their arising from the same essence: their opening phrases are almost mirrors, and sometimes the apparently autonomous melodic-harmonic succession of one will complete the intervallic logic of the other. Individual words emerge, but their continuity is subsumed within a broader progress, as in Nono's renaissance models. A long wave motion is again present in the words of Io with the recurrences of 'PLACA' ('appease'). The positions of the opening chorus are reversed: while Prometeo's voice is static in the centre, thickened by the harmoniser, that of Io dances around the outer circle. Mitologia's meditation on their situation arrives in the sixth section with the last stanza of Hölderlin's *Schicksalslied*: 'But we are fated to find no foothold, no rest'. The music develops on two simultaneous but independent planes: two solo sopranos and the woodwind have independent scores and separate sound worlds. The sopranos set out a clear monody-biphony. In continuous tempo and without pauses or registral extremes, its irregular polyphony is compounded by a long delay. In contrast, the woodwind's progress is halting, the noise components of their multiphonics emphasised by vocoder transposition. The vocoder resynthesises by filtering one sound – here pink noise, adding to the inherent noise of instruments at the edge of resonance – with a spectrum derived from another but which can be shifted in pitch. The spectrum here is that of the contrabass clarinet. Its pitch shift is the inverse of the pitch direction of the bass flute; as the flute plays lower, the transposition moves higher. However discrete its sonic impact in this case, such inner, real-time interactivity is a major innovation in terms of the relationship between composition and performance.

Verso Prometeo

The apparent difference of sound world masks the origins of vocal and instrumental layers in the same material – a clear analogy with Io and Prometeo, men and gods. The dichotomy of the choral fifth section resumes in the seventh. Now melodic and rhythmic figure emerge from the underlying interval pattern with increasing shape and urgency, overlapping more closely. Rhythms coincide with increasing frequency producing dense composite textures that approach homophony. This greater simultaneity persists as the waves subside, leaving only the cries of Io.

The following section for woodwind alone is marked 'sospeso' in Nono's notes; they also refer to its 'chorality'. The instruments take on the simplicity of the sopranos at their previous interjection in section six, following lines of open intervals and semitones – often overblown fourths and sevenths or underblown lower twelfths, but with slighter, slower movement of the sound than before. It is diffused through two interlocking halves of the room, the sound set in slow motion by the phasing and detuning of the harmoniser. The sonic essence of the whole work is presented here as a slow-turning mobile, a suspended song.

The final section adopts a new tone in setting words from Euripides: his chorus on the power of fate, following the burial of Alcestis. Nono divides the text into four passages separated by sequences of pauses. These are then subdivided such that each harmonic unit is presented as a static object. Seven such objects consist of pairs of fifths in semitone relations; the other four, two augmented fourths a semitone apart, act as formal markers ending the first two passages, starting the third and at the centre of the last. This is a clear outline of the harmonic/melodic landscape of *Prometeo*: two-fifths separated by a rising semitone, as at the start of *Das atmende Klarsein*, or by a falling semitone to produce two tritones, the shape *T* that Nono adds to the scala enigmatica as he sets out his materials for *Prometeo*. In the scala enigmatica on C, the first three elements of both are present as <E B C>, <E A♯ B>.[45] The choir is now a single polyphonic entity of up to twelve parts. Its articulation of slow-moving harmonic fields recalls both the inner life of the woodwind multiphonics and Venetian choral falsobordone – the opening of Monteverdi's *Vespers*, perhaps, as if to indicate the origins of the entire spatially oriented alternating of vocal and instrumental, intimate and epic.

Performing the new work in a sports arena was significant for Nono. 'Towards the new use of space' was his immediate answer when asked about the direction of his work: 'The choice of the Palasport is no coincidence. [. . .] It is the space itself that becomes a musical instrument. Spatial components become musical components.'[46] His description of multiple routes through space and time reflects his engagement with ideas such as those of Gosztonyi, but the specific location was also important to Nono – a venue, as he points out, that would normally accommodate pop stars and, more crucially, their non-Biennale audiences.

'Quando stanno morendo: Diario polacco n. 2'

Music of continuous resistance

Far from consciousness-raising, ideology, liberation or resistance, the last stages of the cold war in its various proxies had become a raw struggle for power. The Soviet occupation of Afghanistan was now an offensive war; Reagan had authorised covert US military activity in El Salvador and the funding of the contras in Nicaragua. In Eastern Europe there were some signs of change. The leaders of Charter 77 in Czechoslovakia were in prison, but in Poland the Solidarność union, formed in 1980, seemed to be leading resistance. Karol Wojtyła had been elected Pope in 1978 and a confidant Polish national consciousness was rapidly emerging. A month after the premiere of *Io, frammento dal Prometeo*, Nono was in Hungary, where the

Verso Prometeo

government of János Kádár had been in place since the uprising of 1956. Jürg Stenzl heard his contribution to the UNESCO-sponsored International Musicological Congress in Budapest at the beginning of October 1981. He describes Nono's talking of:

'the search to find something, but not certainty [. . .] to break open mental and cultural cramps (Wittgenstein) with a conscious search for new solutions.' He didn't just put forward a new 'culture of listening', but cited El Salvador, Afghanistan and especially Poland as examples of attempts 'to resolve conflict using the examples of old dogma and mental cramp'.[47]

As Stenzl observes, the official report has a different emphasis:

He stressed the significance of artistic freedom, the autonomous nature of music, and the importance of social commitment, the role of experiment with a sense of responsibility to society. He spoke of new music and its new kinds of links with the public, and of the neglect of such matters by his country's musical institutions[48]

Nono's introduction to *Quando stanno morendo: Diario polacco n. 2*, premiered in Venice a year later, sets out its origins in this particular historical moment:

In October 1981 the directors of the Warsaw Music Festival invited me to compose a *Diario polacco 2* for the festival that should have taken place this year. Then came December 13. I have heard nothing more of the friends who invited me. The committee has been dissolved, the festival has not taken place. I wanted to write this Diario even more. I dedicated it to my Polish friends and comrades who in exile, in secret, in prison, in their work, resist – hope even if desperate, believe even if incredulous.[49]

On 13 December the government of General Jaruzelski had declared a state of emergency, having declared martial law and placed the leaders of the Solidarity movement under arrest. *Quando stanno morendo: Diario polacco n. 2* was instead premiered at the Venice Biennale on 3 October 1982, conducted by Roberto Cecconi. It was not the expression of a new dawn that Nono might have first anticipated, but a much darker comment on repression and an assertion of resistance.

Quando stanno morendo is written for four female voices (two sopranos, mezzo soprano, alto), bass flute, cello and live electronics. It is in three parts (I–III), each divided by Nono into three sections (a–c) – nine in all, like the previous two works. The first and third parts each present three poems in succession and are primarily vocal. Part II presents a single poem and is dominated by instrumental sound. Cacciari prepared the texts: Italian translations of poems from Eastern Europe and Russia by Czesław Miłosz, Endre Ady and Aleksandr Blok in the first part, Boris Pasternak, Miłosz and Velemir Khlebnikov in the third and another by Khlebnikov as the centrepiece. Of these poets, only Miłosz was contemporary – a Pole working in the USA whose work was little known in his own country until he was awarded the Nobel Prize for Literature in 1980. His poem that opens this work, 'My faithful language', is a meditation on homeland and memory. The sorrowful words of Ady and Blok come from the beginning of the century when both saw a desperate need for political change in their countries, Hungary and Russia. Pasternak's 'But, after a while, we will come into the light' is a powerful affirmation of faith in the face of despair. The two poems of the early Futurist Khlebnikov (1885–1922)

Verso Prometeo

combine these sentiments in the most explicit, graphical expressions of resistance. His poems mark the pain of the beginning of the Soviet Union just as the current repression in Poland was symptomatic of its end. 'The poets that we quote live in apocalyptic anguish', say Nono and Cacciari in their note; in terms of Cacciari's intellectual project the poems are products of crisis.[50] The overall dramatic sequence might appear to present a dialectical emotional trajectory in its purest form: suffering, reaction, hope.

Nono's approach to building the work is architectonic, rational. Having established a sense of form and poetic shape, his continuing research in Freiburg is now focused on identifying appropriate sound materials: vocal and instrumental gestures, modes of performance and sound processing. As the sound world of each section becomes clearer, so do its requirements in terms of material. Certain decisions are in place early in the process: the monody of Part I and the choral finale. Nono seems to work against a background matrix of potential score-based material from which he is confident of sculpting specific structures. His various shorthand headings give indications as to how he conceived of the different sections. The three sections of Part I are together invariably marked 'Monodia'. Part II is called 'Invettiva' (Invective) at one stage, IIIa and IIIb become 'high' and 'low' and IIIc 'Finale'. Informal indications for three sections – 'mikro, makro, armonia' – recall his earlier *Polifonica – Monodia – Ritmica*, the sequential presentation of different perspectives of a compositional essence.[51] Nono plays with the ambiguity of 'mikro': he plans shapes for small-scale movement of performers relative to the microphone in the same way as he constructs designs for spatialisation. Plans – soon dissolved – for equal numbers of fragments, spatial designs and movement are perhaps less a remnant of serial thought than an attempt to build a three-dimensional matrix within which he can move freely.

In the same sketches he sets out the basic components of Part I: fragments, fixed spaces and movement.[52] Each section is a single presentation of the same monody. The original form is heard in Ic; it is divided into 18 fragments and reordered, with changes of register and some amendments, to produce the first two sections. In a characteristic balance of progressive and recursive time, Nono constructs them as if they were parallel potential paths through a single polyphony. He seems to have abandoned an initial strict permutation to build two distinct lines related by structural rhymes, as if to draw analogies between the poems of Miłosz and Ady: laments for two different East European countries in two centuries. Thus, in both Ia and Ib fragment 18 (the final E–B of Ic, bars 78–81) appears at analogous points (bars 5–6, 38–9); the clearly figural semiquaver G–A♭ (fragment 6, bar 63 in Ic) occurs near the end of both Ia and Ib (bars 28, 52). Against this, there is continuous sonic development through Part I. The fragments of Ic are separated by rests of up to five semiquavers, sometimes stretched, compressed or overlaid in Ia and Ib. Over this is laid an expanding and contracting pattern of fermata: up to five counts of the slow ♩ = 40–46 tempo, that may occur on sounds or rests and articulate each section differently. Occasionally the monody broadens; Nono retards and anticipates notes and durations to create brief coincidences that blur the flow of time. In Ia, salient words are emphasised with such madrigalisms: two notes on 'notte' (bars 5–6), three on 'avessi' (14, significant as a conditional – the tense of potential) and 'nella memoria' (16–18), and four on 'patria' (22–3).

The inner life of the monody develops progressively through the three sections. Its base dynamic level is *pppppp*, with constant slight variation; the amplification should not obscure the acoustic sound. The varied internal rhythms of superposition, overlapping and exchanging of voices, movement relative to the microphone, opening and closing of vowels, microtonal inflections and the paths and speed of the Halaphon keep the line in continuous movement. Soprano 1 remains in the central axis while the others move between different orbits, sometimes

Verso Prometeo

joining her as the distant fixed point. One by one voices begin to be filtered. The use of gates allows Nono to construct logical relationships between performance parameters. The levels of soprano 2 and alto are controlled by that of the mezzo soprano – her volume and position relative to the microphone. A more conscious mode of interactivity emerges in Ib, where the two instrumentalists begin to breath into their microphones, their level and rhythm notated in the score. The breath of the flautist controls the speed of movement of the Halaphon, the cellist's the level of signal now to be delayed. The inputs to these processes, the voices to be treated, are determined by programme changes numbered in the score. As the sound picture becomes richer, reverberation is added to widen the sonic canvas. The highest voice remains stationary, while the others now move through the outer circle. A wider spectrum of vocal sounds also emerges, from the near-sine wave of whistling to the noise of breath-inflected production or the distortion of raucous, grating singing. Only soprano 1 remains immobile and unprocessed as the interaction and changes of processing accelerate through Ic, the monody itself: Blok's 'once more once more the snow'. One by one the three lower voices are coloured. Together their degree of delay and speed through the exploding and imploding orbits of the Halaphon are manipulated by the instrumentalists' breath, reaching a climax on the F♯–C♯ of 'stelle' ('once more it is mirrored by the stars', bar 75) before what is effectively a coda as 'senza tramonto' ('without sunset') comes to rest on a unison high B.

Roles are reversed in Part II – the negative of the outer sections. Soprano 1, perhaps the voice of the subject, the protagonist of Part I, is silent here. It consists of three parallel layers, each occupying their own registral, timbral and gestural space, each with its own sound processing. Cello and bass flute are suddenly a constant presence. The cellist needs four instruments for the work, three of them in Part II. For each section the strings are tuned in quarter tones about a central pitch: F, F♯ and C respectively. Using a technique developed by Frances-Marie Uitti, Nono's collaborator at Freiburg, the player uses two bows simultaneously, such that inner and outer pairs of strings are notated with different rhythms. Both cello and bass flute are transposed down an octave and heavily amplified, the opposite pole to the high, light vocality of Part I. In addition, the bass flute is delayed by 2", the cello by 5". Their sound is oppressive, static, diffused around the entire eight-channel circle. Initial swells build to *fff*, covering every other sound in IIa, followed by a crescendo from *p* to *sfffff* through IIb and maintained at that room-vibrating level to the end of IIIc. Their rhythms develop in waves of intense activity, apparently derived from the *A veloce* material of *Con Luigi Dallapiccola*. Despite such rhythmic unpredictability, the delays create another level of mechanical inevitability. High above this, soprano 2 quietly traces a long vocalise in three stanzas. Sometimes doubled by mezzo soprano, the line often rises to high E, sustained *pp*. In outline similar to the previous monody, this is more evenly spaced, using integer values of 5–8 beats. Durations and distances are such that the ear registers interval and pitch rather than figure. In each stanza, a high B♭ functions as a trigger for a recitation of Khlebnikov's 'Mosca, chi sei?' ('Moscow, who are you?') – an impassioned denunciation of a previous inhumane Russian bureaucracy as 'orthodox wolves'. The first two hearings are fragmentary, the third complete but drowned by the downward spirals. Only the second promises to be audible, at which point the fragmenting, disorientating effect of the sample reverser becomes clear, as if language contradicts itself. Soon even this is swamped by the wall of instrumental sound.

The high voices are likewise consumed by the sound, but they occupy a different space from the poem. Nono instructed that they 'should sound real but distant [. . .] the song anticipates that of IIIa) b) c).'[53] Not only memory is at work in Nono's management of time; the potential for the future exists in the present. The first two sections of Part III are autonomous concertante movements. Soprano 1 returns in the central axis, anticipating the second line of Pasternak's

Verso Prometeo

poem – 'we will come into the light'. This is the inverse of the question of Part II, 'Moscow, who are you?' – here she is the oppressed, or perhaps all of us. The poem is artfully truncated to become a more abstract vision of hope, emphasising imagery that could be from Pavese: 'the sun of dusk/will call us to the window'. Descanted by the first soprano's opening melodic arch, soprano 2 and mezzo soprano sustain a long near-unison line that, like Nono's earlier layers of pitch, wants to divide, to expand to fill pitch space. At moments it sounds as if the bandwidth of a filter is opening, at others like the moment of speciation from heterophony into polyphony. The simultaneity is more historical: 'Machaut', notes Nono in the score. An extraordinary new sound emerges from the final flute harmonics of IIIa: the cello, now tuned normally, is sounded just with the release of finger pressure from the string. Heavily amplified and reverberated, this is transposed down by an octave and by an inharmonic resonance of something less than a major thirteenth. Described in the sketches as 'bells', this sound fills the room, the bass flute contributing to its spectrum. It becomes the beginning of the alto's solo rendition of Miłosz's poem 'Send your second soul beyond the mountains', as well as its acoustic context. Accompanied only by sustained pitches from the instruments *pppp* – providing both bass and springboard for the melody – the intimacy of the poem is balanced by its formal, clear setting. In even crotchets, the alto *pppp* develops a symmetrical series of permutations of the background melodic material. Phrases expand from four notes to twelve and back, the last two phrases mirroring the opening.

Only in IIIc, the final section, is there harmonic or choral writing. The four unaccompanied voices move together, first outlining three parts and then four for the final word 'sing'. They now move together spatially, circling from the corners in both directions; there is no need here of the central axis, the distant imagination. As Stenzl points out, such endings are a trope in Nono's work: *Canciones a Guiomar*, *La fabbrica illuminata* and *Al gran sole*, for example. [54] Khlebnikov's poem connects directly to the foundations of Nono's art, to *Il canto sospeso*, to *Fučík* and to Schönberg's *A Survivor from Warsaw*:

> When horses die, they breathe
> When grasses die, they wither,
> When suns die, they go out,
> When men are dying, they sing songs.

Song, the embodiment of faith, is suspended to be taken up by others, by us.

Far from the polyphonic proliferation of his text-setting elsewhere, in Part I and in the Finale Nono transcends declamation through a state of hyper-clarity. The temporal separation of phonemes is such that their perceptual assimilation into words and phrases is difficult. In these passages each sound becomes an object of contemplation; the listener creates and explores the potential musical figure or textual narrative in their own perception. Nono's own historical time can be traversed in multiple directions. Above all, it seems to be a gesture of faith, of the coming together of human spirit, the raising of consciousness and the emergence of new vision. Trichords, dyads and unisons are stated in clear four-beat units, shifted by semiquavers like the high voices in IIIa. Only at 'sing' (bar 85) do four-part, two-beat chords appear, a brief *mf* echoing back to the *pppp* base level. Nono's sketches suggest that this section is a coda, added to the main harmonic body. Sallis shows how up to this point Part III can be rationalised in terms of the scala enigmatica on B♭, F and E♭, and how Nono had first intended to set the entire poem with a sequence twice as long.[55] These final chords fall outside that explanation, reducing to the sound of breath and a final dyad C–D. There is no single goal, no unique horizon.

Verso Prometeo

Part III also represents a compressed image of the whole: high, low, harmony. The balanced form of *Quando stanno morendo* – a bridge, its keystone marked by the sample-reversal of 'Mosca, chi sei?'– echoes Nono's current interest in the music of Bartok. In Budapest and Venice he gave talks to mark Bartok's centenary. Such a view is supported by his emphasis on Bartok's use of microtones, microrhythms and proportion.[56] Nono identifies his notion of tempo parlando, of the natural flow of time of the voice, the relationship between microintervals and 'microtimes', including examples of amplitude modulation, and Bartok's use of slow tempi to define open musical spaces.[57]

It is debatable to what extent to which the generative matrix that produces Nono's melodic constructs – fifths/fourth, augmented fourth, tone and semitone – is formal. It is certainly not mechanical; in this piece above all, any formulaic process he perceives emerging is anathema, an example of 'bureaucratic thought' – a term weighted with significance in Italian Marxist critique, but especially in this historical context. There is craft, technique, but its interruptions, nonlinearities and adaptability are crucial. 'Break everything' appears frequently in his workings. 'Not mechanical' he regularly writes across pages of process and material through this last decade. Here, Beyst sees a combinatorial map; Sallis suggests the scala enigmatica as the root source.[58] The scala certainly provides the source material; 'BASE: T', Nono writes, referring to the pattern of two tritones separated by a semitone (Figure 12.3). Augmented fourth and fifth, their semitone difference and the ninth produced by two-fifths suffice to define an entire harmonic/melodic world. In this space, augmented fourths represent a kind of oscillating stability, never still but leading only to each other. The fifth is more grounded, but its inherent root-fifth inequality and capacity to populate the entire chromatic space through self-replication give it a different energy and mobility. To this is added Nono's tendency to expand a single pitch-point outwards into microtonal and chromatic space. These few behaviours together produce the complex dynamics of Nono's late harmonic multiverse.

Nono planned the sound projection specifically for the Scuola Grande di San Rocco, a rectangular space covered with the works of Tintoretto. Collegiate rather than sacred, this had been an important venue for public performance in sixteenth- and seventeenth-century Venice. Ten loudspeakers are arranged as inner and outer four-channel circles, with an axis of the remaining two channels passing centrally through the space. This latter is used, with appropriate processing, for the most distant sounds. At least four levels of diffusion are thus available, from the acoustic sound of the performers to processed sound creating new imaginary spaces as it appears to come from beyond the confines of the room. As Beyst has observed, the percept is the modulated product of acoustic, electronically sculpted and imaginary spaces.[59]

San Rocco may have been a favourite freelance venue for Giovanni Gabrieli, but here the reference is earlier: 'con dadi (Josquin!!!)' ('with dice') Nono writes across the opening of his monody (Plate 3). These framing sections of *Quando stanno morendo* are a motet. Their monody is a tenor; polyphony is to be found in the continuous variation of space, colour and internal rhythm that inhabits it. The reference to Josquin also has a practical component; randomisation is here an act of resistance.

The final section of *Quando stanno morendo* had a further echo. Directly after its completion, in September 1982, Nono prepared a version for the four singers alone for a performance at a November concert in Cologne organised by the Association internationale de défense des artistes: 'Contemporary composers write for disappeared Argentinian artists'. He replaced the text with the words '¿Donde estás hermano? ('where are you, brother?'). The tempo is reduced still further to $\downarrow$ = 30–34, the dynamic to an almost constant *ppppp*, punctuated only by two monolithic chordal cries. These 36 bars thus last some eight minutes – a sustained meditation on the immanence of loss.

Verso Prometeo

Subversive humanism

Mila wrote that in *Quando stanno morendo* 'the liturgical intonation of the voices, treated with live electronics, and the mystical obscurity of the performances become a kind of ritual'.[60] It is perhaps an inner *Canticum Sacrum*; indeed, a 1992 Biennale performance took place in San Marco, where Nono had heard the premiere of Stravinsky's work. The broader sequence may recall Monteverdi, but the sonic gesture of the final two sections is closer to Bach's *Agnus Dei* and *Donna Nobis Pacem* – the end of the Mass in B Minor in miniature. In terms of Nono's materialism, 'et homo factus est' is perhaps the underlying credo.

This work poses fascinating questions in terms of Nono's evolving relationships with politics, dialectics and secularism. *Quando stanno morendo* and its successor of the following year, *Guai ai gelidi mostri*, are powerful statements against repression; they are both explicitly political in this sense. Only in *Quando stanno morendo* is the object of Nono's anger – Moscow – made specific, although it would not be unreasonable to see the very Venetian nature of the subsequent work as implicating Italy and his own immediate milieu. Following the premiere of *Quando stanno morendo*, a debate in the communist press revealed a range of interpretations. In his review, Pestalozza praised the music but appeared to take issue with Nono's explicit condemnation of Moscow.[61] He took exception to Nono's personal identification with the texts, which he saw as quasi-religious and yet integral to the mystical quality of the work as a whole; Nono and Cacciari's 'apocalyptic anguish' remains problematic for him. In rebuffing a dismissive reply by Rubens Tedeschi in *l'Unità*, Pestalozza points to his own earlier writing on Bach's Passions, in which we hear 'a Bach not religious but profane, who with his music speaks of real men, of their suffering which is human not divine'.[62] In this observation we find a straightforward key to the political-mystical nature of Nono's work.

How are we to understand the tripartite form of *Quando stanno morendo* after Nono's repeated assertions of the irrelevance of dialectics? Perhaps Pestalozza, after earlier years of deep discussion with Nono, was fundamentally correct. The work's final section – beginning with Pasternak's 'But, after a while, we will come into the light' – is not a resolution, a synthesis, but rather an assertion of faith in humanity that pre-exists, survives and subverts particular suffering. This may also be Pestalozza's deeper sense: that there is less emphasis on material progress here, that this faith approaches the metaphysical.

Such a view is not without foundation. The expressive microtonal and timbral inflection of Jewish, Islamic and Andalusian singing is an important influence on Nono's vocal writing, as he often acknowledges in interviews through this period. It is increasingly grounded in philosophical reflection, as he and Cacciari pursue a more rigorous engagement with Jewish and Middle-Eastern thought. The vocal expression of other cultures fascinated him, and the sonoscope at the Freiburg studio, a device for producing a continuous sonogram in real time, offered a way of studying the evolving pitch content of a sound in analytical detail. Nono studied Jewish song in particular; he had all ten volumes of Idelsohn's *Thesaurus of Hebrew Oriental Melodies*. For Nono, Jewish music is rich in connections: with Schönberg, with Poland, with resistance to oppression, with pre-Christian history. Not by coincidence, as he works towards *Prometeo*, he studies musical cultures with strong connections to deep historical roots. The intense sense of history and moment embodied in the texts of *Quando stanno morendo* will be further interrogated and refined as Nono and Cacciari work on *Prometeo*. In their introduction to the Venice performance, Nono and Cacciari argue that the poetic act subverts death itself. There is ambiguity in their description of the locus of this poetry: the Eastern Europe of political turmoil, the poets' Russia, the barren mountain-top of Aeschylus' tragedy, or Venice itself? Poland, like Venice, stands at the border between two cultures and two histories:

Verso Prometeo

It is time to free this poetry from the passive, hypocritical stereotype of collapse, of disillusion, of anguish following the shipwreck of 'revolutionary hope'. [. . .] Just to despair is intellectual pessimism – just to believe is bureaucratic trumpeting.

This poetry has its place: where Europe is both border and bridge to Asia; where it constantly resists in itself, in its own, in its ethos, and constantly discusses and questions itself.[63]

'. . . peace is doubtful disquiet'

Reconciliation

There had been little contact with Helmut Lachenmann since 1964. He had invited Nono to contribute to the new *Zeitschrift für Musiktheorie*, to no avail. Their paths had crossed at some events – notably a frosty encounter after a shared concert in München in 1971 – and ten years later Lachenmann wrote to thank Nono for Fragmente: 'You and I know that I have everything to thank you for.'[64] At the beginning of 1983, a new channel of communication opened through Freiburg composer Cornelius Schwer, who had attended Nono's seminars at the Hochschule in 1980–1, went to study with Lachenmann in Stuttgart and was working at the SWF studio in Freiburg. Schwer mediated a reconciliation, communicating the two composers' willingness to see each other. On 12 February 1983, Nono telephoned Lachenmann to say that he would be at his house in Leonberg in an hour. He stayed for four days, visiting the sites of Hölderlin in the area, and so rekindled what became one of the closest and most constant friendships of his otherwise difficult last years.

In the same month, Nono felt it necessary to write a circular letter to several friends and colleagues in Germany and Italy – from Heiner Müller to Berlinguer – refuting a rumour that he had demanded a fee to attend a concert in East Berlin in December 1982.[65] The actual reason was the quality of the sound equipment available. This episode is interesting not because of the detail or the unlikely accusation, given Nono's record of unstinting support for colleagues in the East and comprehension of their precarious situation. What is fascinating is a glimpse of the fragility of status and the brittleness of trust within that world, and the lengths to which individuals in the DDR would go to protect or advance their reputation.

'*Omaggio a György Kurtág*'

Through the spring of 1983 Nono was working at Freiburg towards the following year's premiere of *Prometeo*. A commission for Cologne in October also had to be fulfilled. An extraordinary ensemble was emerging from such intensive research with a group of dedicated performers. A new relationship of composer with musicians was part of Nono's developing view of musical thought, set out in a talk entitled 'L'errore come necessità' ('Error as necessity'):

Diversity of musical thought.

Not musical formulas, rules or games.

A musical thought that *transforms* the thought of the musicians, rather than offering them a new profession of making so-called contemporary music [. . .] the work of research is infinite, in fact. Finality, realization, is another mentality. [. . .] Often conflicts break out during the research process or rehearsals. But these are very emotional moments. Then there is the ritual of the concert.

Verso Prometeo

Perhaps it is possible to change this ritual. Perhaps it is possible to reawaken the ear.

To reawaken the ear, the eyes, human intelligence, the maximum of externalised interiority.

That is what is needed today.[66]

In the same talk of that spring, Nono puts forward three vital ideas: the difficulty of listening to silence – to others – rather than projecting one's own ideas, the importance and particularity of space, and the role of error – an idea derived from Wittgenstein and reinforced by his experience of experimentation in the studio. A concert in Florence in June presented an opportunity to bring his research to the public. The framework was titled *Omaggio a György Kurtág*, but the music was a guided improvisation of the kind the ensemble had been developing in the studio. Nono had recently met Kurtág in Budapest, and in 1979 Kurtág had composed a choral *Omaggio a Luigi Nono*. Only three years later would Nono create a more defined version, the basis of the subsequent published edition. His key collaborators were involved: alto Susanne Otto, flautist Fabbriciani, clarinettist Scarponi and tubist Schiaffini.

The Florence performance seems to have been an attempt to bring to the concert platform the intensity of listening and extremes of control of the group's research in the studio – 'static virtuosity' is Borio's expression.[67] The isolated phonemes of Kurtág's name provide phonetic material for the alto, but voice and instruments – four different ways of producing sound with air – often become indistinguishable as they move imperceptibly from still, pure sounds through the noise of breath to silence. The music is given life by the slightest modulation of pitch or dynamic. The performers explore the full range of techniques and live electronics with which they had been experimenting in the studio: 'shadow' sounds, 'aeolian' (whistle-tones), 'Tibet' (filtering by changing mouth-shape), whistling, pitched breath.

For the Florence performance on 10 June 1983, musicians may have used material from Nono's recent *Quando stanno morendo*. As Nono finally constructed a score for *Omaggio a György Kurtág* in 1986 – post-*Prometeo* and now in Berlin – his notes suggest he returned to the monody of Part I of *Quando stanno morendo* as a source. Plate 3 illustrates the layers of remediation. Durations relate to the *B Calmo* matrix, subject to further fragmentation and interpolation. Notions of 'reuse' are inapplicable here. This ensemble of soloists and the rhythmic material relate directly to *Interludio 1°* from *Prometeo*, and Nono's experiments in the studio through these months – particularly his examination of timbre with the sonoscope.[68] *Prometeo* must be understood not as an autonomous compositional project but as Nono's own journey. From at least 1979, he is mapping an evolving personal musical–technical universe, however flexible or informal, within which he can explore ideas and instantiate performances.

In its final version, *Omaggio a György Kurtág* consists of fourteen sections lasting some 18 minutes. One third of its 149 bars are silent. The tempo moves between 30 and 60, even during the long silences, two of which should last for more than a minute. The first of these follows the longest passage of sustained sound – nine bars – through the end of which the alto outlines a fifth G♯–C♯–G♯ as if to emphasise the sonic palindrome of the text: Gy-ö-rgy The phrase ends 'as if interrupted, suspended' – the most elemental of songs, suspended through the long reverberation that follows. The notated pitch range is kept tightly in the low middle register, the range of the alto; only the tuba sometimes descends below. These are the registers Nono had identified in working on *Interludio 1°*. Early sketches use three voices, suggesting that the tuba does indeed sometimes become the third. Only the fricatives and plosives of Kurtág's name emerge from the compressed dynamic range: *pppppp* – *mp*. Vowels are assimilated into the ensemble wind palette. These constraints allow the ear to focus on variation and movement of

Verso Prometeo

pitch and timbre, to detect slight changes of spectral content. Sounds move independently, rarely joining in homophony but accumulating dyads and triads some of which are captured in a long reverb (50") such that we hear their decay to nothing; in a live performance we attend to the very edges of the physical acoustic space. There are rhythmicised repetitions and changes of intonation but only very rarely does melodic figure emerge, and then usually of only two notes.

However sparse on the page, this piece makes intense and sustained demands on the performers, both in terms of individual control and as an exercise in ensemble. This is perhaps the respect in which it pays homage to Kurtág, whose music is likewise grounded in the creative role of the performers and their interaction, in a deep awareness of the action of music-making. Describing the parallels for the major celebration of Nono's work at the Biennale in 1992–3, Philippe Alberà wrote:

> For Kurtág and Nono, the work is above all *mediation*. It inscribes itself in history and in the present, which it articulates critically. It does not deny its contradictions, rather it is from these that it derives its strength. [. . .] The music exceeds the notation, because the work does not 'reduce' to the notes of the score. It is embodied in the gesture of the musician who reinvents the music in the moment.'[69]

Of the published scores, *Omaggio a György Kurtág* is perhaps that which most closely embodies the sense of collective work that subtends Nono's research of this period. In this synthetic approach to timbre and language we hear the fruits of Nono's experimentation in the studio. With the sonoscope he could identify the 'pure', sine wave-like components of vocal or instrumental sound, the role of noise in timbre and articulation, the overtone content that would encourage or inhibit the blending of timbres and the fine modulation of intonation that is fundamental to the musical languages in which he was now interested.[70] Nono now frequently refers to 'suono mobile' ('mobile sound') in his notes, interviews and instructions to performers. Here, in addition to performance instructions such as unstable modes of production and the use of breath noise, there are frequent indications of 'microintervalli' or 'aperiodico'. More even than before, sound is never a 'note' in his late music; the inner lives of sounds become compositional material, but they constantly resist control or representation.

'Guai ai gelidi mostri'

The seed for the new Cologne work came with a series of paintings by Emilio Vedova: . . . *Cosidetti Carnevali* . . . (. . . *So-called Carnivals* . . .), an *opera aperta* begun in 1977 but not yet made public. By the end of 1983 they numbered some 64, but by 1991 there were ten more. According to Fabrizio Gazzarri:

> When his friends Luigi Nono and Massimo Cacciari went to visit him in his studio, as they often did then, they expressed their enthusiasm at the sight of these works which were so Vedova-like and yet strikingly different and unexpected. Nono, impressed by these works which addressed issues parallel and related to his own research at that time, asked Vedova if he could publish some in the programme of his concert that was to take place in Cologne a few months later: 'For Emilio this was finally the moment to liberate the [. . .] *Cosidetti Carnevali* [. . .] and allow the outside world to know them.'[71]

Verso Prometeo

Vedova explained the title: 'Carnival interests me in its gestural, the fantastic, the "uncomposed", the dynamic, the irrational, in its being emotive, organic, frenetic, dramatic, in its ambiguity, its "liberatingness", the "anything is possible" for a few hours.'[72] In 1960 the spontaneity and plasticity of Vedova's practice had been a model for Nono's new adventure in the electronic studio. Following decades of shared development, Nono now found a new resonance in his friend's work, as well as a direct, intuitive empathy – a counterbalance to the theoretical–literary conversations with Cacciari. The *Carnevali* are discrete paintings – not process, sculpture or mobile – and yet they challenge both their dimensionality and their unique identity. Vedova's recent *plurimi binari* were arranged at angles to each other in large groups. The *Carnevali* escape their dimensionality by extending into other planes – locally, in assemblages of other objects, and structurally by spreading into additional surfaces or into the supporting structure itself. Other materials emerge from the painted steel or canvas plane: wood, paper, plastic and rope found in the alleys and canals but especially carnival masks – flattened, torn, threatening, questioning. They were collected for him by Vedova's students at the Accademia, where in 1982 he held a happening-ritual to celebrate the death of carnival, necessary for the germination of new life. These are works of expressive, visceral gesturality, but there are hints of formal structure in the traces of shape and the masks challenge the viewer to metaphysical or semantic interpretation. Suggestions of Venice penetrate their abstraction: architectural features (Vedova's first subjects, some fifty years earlier) and water. Form and spontaneity are in a dynamic dance, they and the viewer in a constantly mobile relationship. Nono wrote to his friend 'they provoke me to feel other vibrations which I can't yet reach – but I know that they're there: unanticipated and unpredictable – but they're there and one waits – I felt and <u>feel</u> I <u>must</u> (not may) discover "unanticipated and unpredictable music" for the *Carnevali*'[73]

The composition of this unanticipated music is woven through work on *Prometeo*. As Nono works with wind and vocal soloists in Freiburg through March and April 1983, he marks certain sounds and ideas 'für Köln'. He interrupted his research in April and May to give courses in Barcelona, at the Miró Foundation, and in Lisbon. His sound examples for these talks included *Songs of the Humpback Whale*. At once abstract and expressive, these sounds transmitted through an alien medium are surely to be heard in Nono's wind writing for the three wind soloists. Back in Freiburg in May he worked with string players, especially double bassist Stefano Scodanibbio and cellist Frances-Marie Uitti. Cacciari's Vedova-inspired texts arrived in June, with Nono back in Freiburg after the Florence performance of *Omaggio a György Kurtág*. In *Guai ai gelidi mostri* we see Nono's collaborative practice in microcosm. In August he was in Venice listening repeatedly to the Freiburg tapes; 'study better, do better', he writes to himself.[74] He annotates his notes from the spring on the recordings of instrumental and vocal sounds and electronic transformation, commenting on materials for *Prometeo* and 'Köln' – the new work has as yet neither title nor 'notes'. From these, he assembles an A2 sheet for each element – singers, wind and strings – which he takes back to Freiburg at the end of August to work again with the musicians. Through September he experiments further with these elements until he can write 'fissato' ('fixed') on certain materials. After half a year's planning and listening, only later in September – a month before the performance – does Nono begin to work with music notation, at the same time as beginning rehearsals. At the heart of his process is the recursive reintensification of listening; listening and imagining are inseparable actions.

Guai ai gelidi mostri (*Woe betide the cold monsters*) was premiered in Cologne on 23 October 1983. Cacciari's texts consist of four assemblages of fragments from Gottfried Benn, Lucretius, Carlo Michelstaedter, Nietzsche, Ovid, Pound, Rilke, Benjamin and Franz Rosenzweig. Despite their complexity of source and language – Italian, German, Latin and English – these

Verso Prometeo

texts achieve a new unity as many-dimensioned poems. Zarathustra is heard at the opening – 'The state is called the coldest of all cold monsters' – and Cacciari's new assemblages of text trace paths beyond the state to 'where man is not superfluous', ending with echoes of 'Pone Metum' – 'cast away fear'. The resistance of *Quando stanno morendo* here becomes more allegorical. Carnival exists in a double bind; its irrationality serves to show the arbitrariness of order, the absurd banality of the quotidian. In being less politically specific, the darkness of *Guai ai gelidi mostri* invokes the resistance of everyman. Since *Il canto sospeso*, the degree of political specificity of each work is carefully calibrated in terms of both aesthetic goals and current circumstances.

Entitled *In Tyrannos!*, *Lemuria*, *Das grosse Nichts der Tiere* and *Entwicklungsfremdheit*, the new texts correspond to the four parts of the sonically continuous work. For Cacciari, these:

> are the four dimensions which every moment of [Vedova's] cycle embodies, interrogates and transforms in its own way.

> *In Tyrannos*: the cry that wants to liberate itself from the idol of the 'what-was', from the gaze turned to the *paupertas horrida* of the 'power' of the what-was, which corrupts everything, which predicts death, which eliminates every light. The what-was inters the destiny of man. [. . .]

> *Lemuria*: from this night there emerge figures, unwelcome guests and spirits. When it can no longer be dark, the Lemuri threaten from the forest of shadows. They are the guardians of the what-was [. . .] The cry *in tyrannos* still resounds, but its echo seems to disperse, its hope to become more desperate. [. . .]

> *Das grosse Nichts der Tiere*: perhaps the animals know or anticipate it. Perhaps in the eye of the animal is preserved the open,[75] which the 'interred' word is unable to express. [. . .] Only from this *epoché* of the discourse can new word germinate.

> *Entwicklungsfremdheit*: is this the new word? That everything that exists is not born to die? that everything which tends to form is not superfluous vanity? that a song that is really 'convinced', measured, shaped, beaten fibre by fibre on the anvil, is not merely prey to Chronos? [76]

Once again, it is song that survives darkness and time.

Few of their words appear in the fragmentary contralto entries – generally, no more than two at a time. Long durations and slow tempo mean that even here the phonemes are widely separated. Text is presented at the pace of the tenor of a liturgical motet, its components too separated to cohere into a semantic percept; it becomes a symbolic object of contemplation through sound. Nono's notes refer to the singing of a cantor in a synagogue. In contrast with *Quando stanno morendo*, instrumental sound now dominates. *Guai ai gelidi mostri* is a harmonic–spectral work, a study for *Prometeo* that constantly reflects the act of listening back to the subject. There is little for the conscious ear to reduce to figure, little in the mid-range of pitch or rhythm. It is built of three layers: three winds (flute/piccolo/bass flute, clarinet/contrabass clarinet/E♭ clarinet, tuba/piccolo trumpet), three low strings (viola, cello and double bass) and two low altos (descending an octave below middle C). The instrumental groups will become the soloists in *Prometeo*. Live electronics expand this chamber music intimacy into new layers of physical and aural space. This is a polychoral conception, but in Nono's notes it is the string group that is referred to as 'coro'. The layers function as unitary sonic entities. Polyphony emerges from their slow-moving relationship and in the micro-detail of their inner spectral

Verso Prometeo

development, both acoustic and processed. 'Not silences but depths – amplified space,' he notes. 'Break programmes break fragments break continuity.'[77]

The string sound is the most continuous. Indeed, it functions as a continuo group, its aggregate sound and energy kept in constant movement by the rotation of the bow (*arco mobile*), movement between bridge and fingerboard, changing resonance and spectrum, and microtonal variation. Often in rhythmic unison, the integration of the string timbres is such that even when in higher registers there is a sense of a low common fundamental. Bass flute and contrabass clarinet are used in their lowest registers, punctuated by rhythmic overblowing that emphasises high, inharmonic partials. The tuba provides the most direct link with vocal sound, and is often pitched high in the alto register, above the woodwind. Piccolo and E♭ clarinet operate at the other extreme, frequently with multiphonics and joined by the tuba player on piccolo trumpet – actually a rare piccolo flügelhorn from Schiaffini's collection. The two androgynous voices emerge together from this instrumental texture, defining clearly characterised fields of no more than five pitches, word by word.

The fundamental material for the strings and low wind remains that of the monody of *Quando stanno morendo*, divided into 32 fragments (the number varies slightly according to need and context) and disposed vertically and horizontally. Fifths, tritones and semitones characterise all harmonic movement, but the traces of sequence remain, folded and refolded, such that the harmonic successions within each layer develop their own logic. While common patterns emerge, each layer pursues its own inexorable harmonic orbit, creating resonances, echoes, attractors and coincidences. Given the preponderance of fifths, this generates moments of near-tonality. The formal balance of the previous work is also reversed. Here, the weight (173 of 272 bars) is in Part I. A single string chord repeated across five bars, followed by a bar of silence, constitutes Part III. In Part IV, the woodwind become still more the extension of the voices, but also begin to alternate with the strings, sharing the sustaining of continuous sound.

The base level is *ppppp*, from which there is continuous slight movement. The other extreme appears in the dramatic gesture that closes both Parts I (five statements) and II (three), with brief pre-echoes in Part I. At these moments, the lowest open strings *fffff* alternate with the highest *ppppp*, accompanied by high woodwind multiphonics (piccolo and E♭ clarinet) and piccolo trumpet. At these points the winds threaten to feed back, to take over the acoustic space entirely. The ear instinctively protects itself. These are undisguised moments of violence – disturbing fractures in the prevailing sonic environment like Vedova's masks breaking through the canvas.[78]

Cacciari's essays of this time presumably hold traces of his conversations with Nono. His reflections on the role of Carnival are rooted in a multi-layered conception of time: 'Time no longer appears as a transition from Nyn to Nyn, from moment to moment, but as a complex of clips [. . .] of irreducible singularities.' There is no one past or one future: 'In their complex [. . .] past, present and future are simultaneously and continuously in play.'[79] As in the case of Cacciari's texts for *Guai ai gelidi mostri*, or the identity of many of Nono's later works, there is no 'whole' to be grasped fully or uniquely. Carnival is a moment that 'renews, recreates', in which 'all energy must be brought to expression, to assure the continuation of life.' The interruption of Carnival 'liberates us from old unambiguities'.[80] Such moments are outside 'normal' time – *kairos* rather than *chronos*. Cacciari describes them as 'ectopic' to measured time. Of all the inversions of Carnival, the mask is the most enigmatic, both terrifying and liberating, that 'points to new possible forms'.[81] If carnival is an interruptive moment of death and rebirth, for Nono listening holds the potential for a continuous such act. Cacciari's thought never reduces to a system, but here we see three faces of time, the co-existence of which is vital to Nono's later work. Chronological, moment-to-moment time is punctuated by 'ectopic' events

Verso Prometeo

that need have no implications for chronos or for each other; the listener, however, is drawn to build relationships. But these two categories describe kinds of connection within a third, multi-layered, fully networked temporal space in which no particular direction is privileged. The explosions of sound are moments of mask, of kairos, ectopic but vital to the other layers which themselves present new trajectories through a space that exists outside this particular work.

More generally, form is articulated harmonically. At the opening, while the strings set out the principal intervals <E B♭ B> across their full range (the incipient interval set T as present in the scala enigmatica), the piccolo adds two-fifths to the upper note, as if to present another simultaneous possible path. Part I falls into three sections, the first two of 65 bars each, both ending with a silent bar, the third of 42. In the strings, the fifth E–B is clearly established as an important attractor at the opening (bars 1–9) of the first section and ending (126–8) of the second, as well as effectively being a goal of Part IV (258–63); its appearance in the second section of Part I demonstrates Nono's formal use of harmonic recognisability. As well as the fifth E–B, the scala enigmatica on C contains the key to both of Nono's superimposed fifth patterns: B♭ (> F) and C (> G). Open fifths emerge regularly from the harmonic progression. Successions by fifth stand out as perfect cadences (A–E in bars 133–5 to D–A in 136–9). Elsewhere, low fifths underlie a slowly shifting melody-generated spectrum (bars 182–92) reminiscent of the contemporary work of Grisey. The kernel of *Das atmende Klarsein* reasserts itself at the very end; the last vocal entry F♯–C♯ (bars 266–8) is echoed in piccolo multiphonics, followed by its resolution in the final high D–A.

Vocal material is derived from that of *Io, frammento dal Prometeo*. Voices and woodwind are more rhythmically articulated than the strings but move at the same harmonic pace, slowly enough to become a formal harmonic rhythm. Some pitch areas are sustained for over a minute. Wertenson shows how Nono uses dice to generate random multipliers of his basic durations and shorter additional values to avoid an unvarying time-grid.[82] The durations are generally in multiples of 1–5 of 1–6 beats (at ♩ = 30–34). Values may be negative (replaced by rests) or articulated internally by Nono's technique of 'interpolation' – fitting other rhythmic material within a given duration. In addition, shorter value rests (♩ or less) are taken from the original rhythms of the monody in which the start of individual fragments is variably offset, thus displacing the onset of some pitch groups.

Physical, virtual and historical spaces

In Nono's late work we find two methods for producing random sequences, and both are present in *Guai ai gelidi mostri*. The first is known in probability theory as an 'urn' model. Having articulated a body of material and numbered its elements, Nono would tear up the list of numbers, throw them down and pick them up randomly – each item can only be selected once, so the sequence generated will have the same length as the original. In this we might see traces of serial thought. The second is the use of dice to generate a potentially infinite sequence of numbers (1–6 or 1–12); a pair of dice was a regular part of Nono's composing environment. These techniques are used for two purposes: to reorder a body of material – to articulate its monadic nature – or to introduce variation into patterns of values. Here we see both cases. More than two decades previously Nono had railed against what he saw as the abdication of composerly responsibility in the use of aleatoric techniques, so how can these practices now be reconciled with his ethos? In fact, the arbitrary plays no part in the use of these techniques. They may provide a way of navigating Nono's temporal multiverse, a space in which multiply-networked objects exist simultaneously – as with the sequence of monody-derived pitch sets

Verso Prometeo

here – or be used to break 'bureaucratic' structures, to prevent things lining up or balancing too evenly. In the extension of durations in *Guai ai gelidi mostri*, this is a way of achieving artisanal handmade-ness while avoiding the banality of taste – like the edges of Vedova's brushstrokes.

References to 'Josquin' and 'dadi' abound in the Nono's sketches of this period. In Petrucci's 1514 print of Josquin's *Missa Di dadi*, probably an early work, pairs of dice (2:1, 4:1, 6:1, 5:1) represent the augmentations of the tenor (Morton's chanson *N'aray je jamais mieulx que j'ay*) in movements up to the *Sanctus*.[83] It seems unlikely that Nono's interest would only extend to a device for generating augmentation values, particularly during work on *Prometeo*, when his critical relationship with history was at its most intense. Osthoff's pioneering work on the construction of textures in Josquin had figured in Nono's earliest research.[84] His engagement with this repertoire was such that it is impossible to gauge the extent to which influences are conscious, but certain resonances with the *Missa Di dadi* stand out: Josquin's obsessive returning to the perfect fourth D–G; the focus on low countertenor/contralto voices; the augmentation of longer values while retaining the original and recognisable shorter values of melodic figure (as in Josquins' *Sanctus*); the interplay between the clear use of head-motifs, canon and longer term structural devices. Nono's reuse of his own polyphonic material also has a precedent in Josquin: textures from the *Missa Di dadi* reappear in the later *Missa Pange lingua*. Likewise, his fragmentation of a source monody: in the *Missa Malheur me bat*, Josquin explores segments of the source one by one, repeating them in different mensurations. Maderna emphasised the importance of text in Josquin.[85] Presumably, this was a view that he and Nono discussed in their early research; it is consonant with Nono's Schönberg-derived understanding of the music–text relationship as transcending conscious audibility. Here, as in the earlier music, the relationship moves along a continuum between abstraction and listener-ascribed depiction. The key words of the first section of *Guai ai gelidi mostri* are examples of the latter: 'tiranos', 'stato', 'gelidi mostri of death', all to fifths or fourths. Its opening words 'in tiranos' return in retrograde to end Part I. Josquin uses his entire chanson only at the *Osanna*, the elevation of the Host, after which it is no longer needed. In *Guai ai gelidi mostri*, hope comes in Part IV as the three sonic strata come into a new balanced and integrated relationship.

The live electronics here use the same palette as in *Quando stanno morendo*, but more subtly. As Nono's research for *Prometeo* developed, transpositions and filter frequencies are manipulated in greater detail; he defines 48 different filter frequencies, always avoiding tempered semitones but often outlining an augmented fourth. The voices are subject to no processing beyond reverberation, and are diffused through a pair of loudspeakers in the centre of the room, either mounted very high or facing upwards such that the sound should seem to come from the heavens. The eight remaining channels are again arranged as inner and outer groups. Unlike many of his contemporaries, Nono imagines the diffusion of sound through three dimensions. He preferred asymmetrical loudspeaker placement and would vary the relative height and location of performers and loudspeakers between performances to explore the full acoustic potential of the room.[86] Movement between near and far spaces, often distinguished by the presence of processing, provides an additional layer of formal architecture. By Part IV, all instrumental sound comes from the farthest corners.

Among the sketches is another clue to Nono's spatial conception of the work: a postcard reproduction of Giovanni Bellini's late *Sacra Conversazione* altarpiece of 1505, from San Zaccaria in Venice (Plate 4). Around the central figures of Mary and Christ are four saints – two female and two male, arranged symmetrically. Below them a girl plays the viola da braccio, an individual, intimate personification of the angelic choirs of earlier altarpieces. Nono separates out the male saints with black lines; they are not part of his mise-en-scène. Four elements

Verso Prometeo

remain – parallels, perhaps, with those of *Guai ai gelidi mostri*: the choir (in the person of the viola player), two female saints mediating between humanity and deity, and the centre of creation in its most compassionate human form. The fourth area marked by Nono is the cupola above the central figures. Bellini's use of space and architecture, the play of inside and outside, are remarkable. The cupola is itself a virtual inner space, symbolic of infinity. Columns suggest a common, unifying inner space, while to both sides and behind there are glimpses of an outside world beyond. There is no simplistic mapping, but the topology of Bellini's conceptual architecture is that of *Guai ai gelidi mostri*.

As he prepares for *Prometeo* Nono moves between physical, musical–technical and conceptual spaces, clarifying and refining its motivations; his note for the premiere of *Guai ai gelidi mostri* reveals some of this reflection:

> being infinitely disposed to the surprising, the unusual, to the opening up to discussion even with the maximum of uncertainty (certainty in uncertainty) with the maximum of doubtful disquiet (peace in doubtful disquiet) – infinite searching is more important than finding
>
> listen!
>
> how to *listen* to the red and white stones of Venice as the sun rises – how to *listen* to the infinite arch of colours on the Venetian lagoon at sunset – how the *listen* to the magical undulations of the Black Forest: colours silences, the natural *live* [electronics] of the seventh heaven.[87]

Notes

1 Fabbricciani, 2008.
2 Scaldaferri, 1997, p. 87.
3 Interview with Renato Garavaglia, 1979–80. LNII, p. 246.
4 Interview with Roberto Fabbriciani, 24 April 2007.
5 Haller, 1995, p. 116.
6 Fabbriciani, 1999, p. 9.
7 Letter from Cacciari, 19 August 1980. ALN.
8 Nono's manuscript arrangement of texts is reproduced in Auner and Shreffler, 2016, p. 44.
9 Cacciari, 1993, p. 174.
10 Interview with Roberto Fabbriciani, 24 April 2007.
11 Fabbriciani, 1999, p. 11.
12 Agamben, 1999, pp. 177–242, explores potentiality as a property of art and the artist. The concept of space of potential is developed in Delanda, 2011.
13 Haller, 1991, p. 36; Gosztonyi, 1976.
14 Haller, 1995, p. 149.
15 Nono, cited by Stenzl, 2003.
16 Cescon, 2002, p. 100.
17 Cacciari, 1990.
18 Richard and Mazzolini, 2005, vii.
19 ALN 45.08.02/06–07.
20 Artaud, 1980; Howell, 1974.
21 ALN 45.08.01/04–05 (bass flute), 08–09 (piccolo).
22 The tables of piccolo sonorities are reproduced in Durazzi, 2005, pp. 207–8.
23 From Stephen Mitchell's translation of the *Elegies* in Rilke, 1982.
24 Edwards, 2008, p. 235.
25 'Das atmende Klarsein'. LNI, p. 487.
26 Cescon, 2002, p. 110.

Verso Prometeo

27 Haller, 1995, p. 124.
28 Tronti, 2013. Toscano, 2009, explores the wider implications of what he describes as Tronti's 'Copernican revolution' in Marxist thought.
29 Interview with Philippe Albèra, 1987. LNII, p. 427.
30 Cacciari, in *Verso Prometeo*, LNII, pp. 354–355.
31 Cescon, 2002, p. 100.
32 Ciro Scarponi in Cescon, 2002, pp. 117–18.
33 ALN 45.04/02r.
34 Cacciari, 1984a, p. 20.
35 Interview with Dino Villatico, 1981. LNII, p. 261.
36 Reproduced in Jeschke, 1997, p. 224.
37 Cacciari, 1981, p. 22.
38 'Io, frammento dal Prometeo'. LNI, p. 488.
39 ALN 46.02/10.
40 A full account of correspondences in the first movement of *Io, frammento* is given in Melkert, 2001, pp. 92–3.
41 ALN 46.08.01/01.
42 ALN 46.09.01/03sx.
43 *l'Unità*, 8 November 1981.
44 Interview with Fiona Diwan, 1985. LNII p. 370.
45 ALN 51.21.02/04.
46 Interview with Renato Garavaglia. *l'Unità*, 24 September 1981.
47 Stenzl, 1998, pp. 102–3.
48 Breuer, 1982, p. 6.
49 'Quando stanno morendo. Diario polacco n. 2'. LNI, p. 490.
50 Doati, 1993, p. 8.
51 ALN 47.05.01/01.
52 ALN 47.05.01/08.
53 Richard and Mazzolini, 1999, p. x.
54 Stenzl in Doati, 1993, p. 11.
55 Sallis, 2006.
56 Breuer, 1982, pp. 5–6.
57 LNII, pp. 515–21.
58 Beyst, 2004; accessed 3 January 2018. Sallis, 2006.
59 Beyst, 2004.
60 Mila, 2010, p. 316.
61 *Rinascita*, 8 October 1982.
62 *l'Unità*, 15 and 16 October, 1982.
63 'Quando stanno morendo. Diario polacco n. 2'. LNI, p. 490.
64 Postcard from Lachenmann, 28 September 1981, in De Benedictis and Morsch 2012, p. 137.
65 Letter to various recipients, including Heiner Müller and Berlinguer, 23 February 1983, ALN.
66 'L'errore come necessità', 1983. LNI, p. 523.
67 Borio in Doati, 1993, p. 67.
68 'Verso Prometeo'. LNI, pp. 393–4.
69 Doati, 1993, pp. 74–6.
70 'Verso Prometeo. Frammenti di diari'. LN I, pp. 385–6.
71 Gazzari '. . . Cosidetti Carnevali . . .' in Celant and Gazzarri, 2013, p. 29.
72 Vedova, quoted in Barbuto and Rorro, 2007, p. 148.
73 Letter to Vedova, 20 March 1983, reproduced in Gabetti, 1990, pp. 16–19.
74 ALN 50.04.02/11.
75 'L'aperto' – Hölderlin's 'Freie'.
76 Cacciari in Celant and Gazzari, 2013, pp. 47–50.
77 ALN 50.03.02/10.
78 Wertenson (2011) adopts the notion of 'acoustic masks' from Canetti. This may depart somewhat from Canetti's own concept, but introduces a very suggestive image.
79 Cacciari, 1986, p. 9.
80 Cacciari, 1986, p. 43.

Verso Prometeo

81 Cacciari, 1986, p. 47.
82 Wertenson, 2011, p. 62.
83 Long, 1989, presents a detailed study of structure and symbolism in the *Missa Di dadi*.
84 Osthoff, 1952.
85 Fearn, 1990, p. 314.
86 Haller, 1995, p. 152.
87 *Guai ai gelidi mostri*. LNI, p. 491. 'massimo di incertezza' etc. are clearly puns on his collaborator's name.

13

A TRAGEDY OF LISTENING

Inception

Prometeo was intended to be a third azione scenica. It would evolve into an entirely new kind of musical entity, no less dramatic but vaster, more intimate and more pluridimensional. Like *Al gran sole*, *Prometeo* emerges directly from the echo of its predecessor. It would be premiered in Venice on 29 September 1984 and substantially revised for a production at La Scala the following year, both conducted by Claudio Abbado. Below we will discuss the score of the revised, 1985 version. Nono's thinking about *Prometeo* is the context for his work for a decade before, and its implications inform his work thereafter. Over three decades later, it has become one of the most performed major works of the late twentieth century, despite the extraordinary demands it makes of performers and listeners alike.

Cacciari places the start of their project in the summer of 1975, in the months immediately following the premiere of *Al gran sole carico d'amore*.[1] Together, Nono and Cacciari re-read Aeschylus' *Prometheus Desmotes* (*Prometheus Bound*). The first and only remaining tragedy of Aeschylus' trilogy, *Prometheus Bound* tells the story of the Titan's punishment for challenging the tyranny of Zeus, by being chained and tortured on a far mountaintop for eternity. We learn that Prometheus had not only saved humanity by stealing fire from the gods, but had given to man the tools of reason and reflection, and therewith technology, science, art and philosophy. He further angers Zeus by revealing that he knows the secret of the god's own downfall. These details emerge through a series of encounters with Hephaestus (his reluctant imprisoner), Oceanus (who implores him to recant), Io (likewise a victim of Zeus) and Hermes (who, when he fails to extract Prometheus' secret, announces destruction). According to Cacciari:

> however innumerable the 'epiphanies' of this myth are in our civilisation, none 'communicated' that which Nono wanted to express in that moment of his life and of his work. It was a moment of disappointment that did not want to be transformed into disillusion; of disenchantment, that did not want to give in to resignation.[2]

An understanding and manifestation of the myth – the materials, form, means and nature of the work – would evolve with Nono's reflection on the nature of his own activity. Significant is an article by Pavese he must surely have known, written shortly before the poet's suicide in 1950 and the source of much debate in the left-wing literary world.[3] It might appear superficially

A tragedy of listening

that nothing could be farther from the specificity of the epic, socially engaged works of Nono's initial trajectory than the timelessness of Greek myth. However, Pavese seeks to rehabilitate myth at the centre of art, and suggests that the redefinition of myth is the foundation for each new epoch of artistic practice, the seed of every poem. The creation of a new work is potentially the construction of both a new aesthetic and a new ethos; in their absence, the work is simply a re-expression of something we already know and will lead *away* from the questioning that is the responsibility of the artist. The reinterpretation of myth and the process of continuous questioning frame Nono's late work.

The path from *Prometheus Bound* to the full text, concept and structure of *Prometeo* was long and complicated.[4] A definitive version of Cacciari's text would arrive at the end of 1982. To describe it as a libretto is misleading; it is at once the formal architecture, conceptual framework and semantic surface of the work, thoroughly assimilated into the process of composition. Through the series of countless exchanges, analyses and iterations an evolution can be traced in three main stages: Nono's reading and analysis of *Prometheus Bound* together with Cacciari's *Polemics* (1977), a full compound but linear text (1978) and the final version (1982).[5]

Nono's own Italian edition of *Prometheus Bound* is covered in notes. He seems initially to have planned to ignore the choruses. The second episode was the focus of Nono's attention: Prometheus' account of the tools of thought, culture, science and technology he has brought to man, and his intimations of a secret that will destroy Zeus. There are indications of soloists, of a children's choir, and of a political interpretation with Prometheus as liberator. Goethe's depiction of Prometheus' heroic resistance to the gods is a clear model at this stage. Marx's amplification of Goethe's understanding would have been particularly resonant for Nono: 'Prometheus is the most eminent saint and martyr in the philosophical calendar.'[6] Cacciari's view was somewhat at odds. In early 1977 he provided Nono with a pair of texts – interpretations, assemblages of references, position statements – just marked *Polemica A* and *B*, which presumably encapsulate their discussions: meditations and explorations of Aeschylus' character, his actions and situation and their implications.

For Cacciari, the separation of men and gods is the crisis in which the myth originates. Prometheus and Zeus have a common origin in Gaia, mother earth herself, who Cacciari suggests is represented by Aeschylus' chorus. That man should have the all-illuminating fire goes against the natural law that governs both men and gods. The central feature of this story is not Prometheus' rebellion – an inevitability, in Cacciari's view – but the reconciliation of man and Zeus to come in the third part of Aeschylus' work, *Prometheus Pyrphóros*. Prometheus will reveal his secret to Zeus, who thereby avoids death. Their reconciliation, celebrated as the origin of human art, thought and technê, marks the acknowledgement by both that they are subject to Nomos (law) and Dike (justice) – cosmological, not divine. Zeus has escaped death, but his youthful freedom to arbitrary action is now constrained; man can no longer be deprived of fire, but this light condemns him eternally to the very cycle of *works and days* (Hesiod's title) that it makes possible. He no longer has secrets from god. There is no hope of a redeemer or messiah, no further Achilles (the son of Io and Peleus), who has been condemned to mortality by this pact. The wider, natural law – the foundation of the life of man – is not Kantian, based in morality, but it is necessarily political. It condemns man to his eternal wandering. Prometheus is equated to Ulysses in this respect, a crucial association for the eventual structure of the work. Moses also becomes an important figure, and Schönberg's unfinished opera a continuous reference. Both Cacciari and Nono were increasingly engaged with Jewish thought; while the world of *Prometeo* is ruled by *Ananke* – natural law or destiny – the future pact between Prometheus and Zeus is perhaps analogous to the covenant between God and man. Interpretations by Hesiod, Pindar, Hölderlin, Goethe and Schönberg are adduced

A tragedy of listening

in Cacciari's text. *Polemica A* ends with a reference to Mahler's *Das Lied von der Erde*, *Polemica B* with questions:

> But does all this not mean: transitoriness, indeterminacy, the impossibility of theorising this 'dwelling' and its relationships with Zeus and Dike as 'well-founded' – ? is this relationship not a 'collection of fractures? And is it not <u>a priori</u> possible that all this should be a 'trick' – that the 'feast' of reconciliation itself is a trick? Technê, work etc., where are they 'well-founded'?[7]

Conversations with Cacciari and Franceso Dal Co continued until ideas became more concrete in the spring of 1977. The texts were the basis of a month-long experimental project in Prato with the *Laboratorio di Progettazione Teatrale* recently founded by Luca Ronconi, then head of theatre at the Biennale. Nono saw this moment as the real beginning of *Prometeo*.[8] 'Discover relationships', Nono writes on one copy of Cacciari's document. He articulates the texts in four columns: Aeschylus, Greek sources, German sources, and the words of Cacciari.[9] In November, Nono arranged these texts compositionally, ordering them spatially, often in parallel, and looking for relationships, resonances and structure – a 'disposizione grafica tentativo' ('draft graphical arrangement').[10]

Following further discussion, a new text arrived from Cacciari early in 1978, subjected immediately to the same treatment.[11] The drama now assumes its initial shape: *Prologo, Episodio I–VI, Esodo*. As Nono and Cacciari exchange annotations, the composer seems to answer his friend's concerns: 'not disenchanted, but listening to new possibilities'.[12] Hesiod's *Theogony* – an earlier version of the myth – sets out the pre-human chaos and origins of the gods, and establishes Gaia/earth as the universal mother. Fragments from his *Works and Days* describe the eternal toil of man and the inevitable cyclic rhythm of his life and world. The new figure of Mitologia provides reflection within the drama, as discussed in the context of *Io, frammento*. Muthos, the basis of Mitologia, represents story – narrative and causality – and Nomos the naming and order of things. Nono continued to work graphically – retyping, cutting and rearranging, and developing ideas with Cacciari. Figure 13.1 reproduces an early plan for the first part: the episodes of Prometeo, Efesto, Io, Mitologia (never a single voice) and i nomi (the names) followed by a concluding chorus. 'Everything in the air, high, suspended', he writes of the opening.

A revised version, incorporating Nono's suggestions, arrived in July 1978 – to the family summer home in Sardinia, where Nono worked on it through July and August.[13] The incorporation of Greek script adds an additional layer of structure and perspective. While not yet named as such, Cacciari's map of the paths and relationships between the episodes anticipates their later concept of 'islands' (Figure 13.2). It introduces a crucial spatial property to the emerging *Prometeo*. Nono will return to this drawing as he imagines the disposition of music in space – perhaps reflecting on the fact that it was drawn on notepaper from the Chamber of Deputies, the lower house of the Italian parliament, to which Cacciari had been elected in 1976.[14]

In a new 'disposizione grafica', sheets of text are cut and pasted so that Nono can see the shape, complexity and proportions of the drama.[15] In a note he quotes Cacciari's rispost to Wittgenstein: 'of that which you cannot express, you must not remain silent'.[16] A symmetrical six-episode form was evolving, with the parallel figures of Prometheus, Achilles and Ulysses in the central episodes. Around these, the chaotic cosmos of the *Prologo* would be mirrored by the new space of the *Esodo*, the terrain of Prometheus the Wanderer. Against this contraction and expansion, the narrative density developed symmetrically about the mid-point. A central

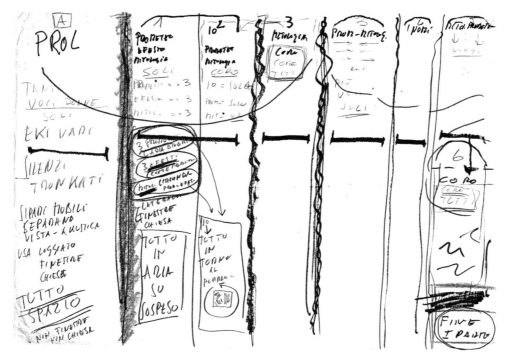

Figure 13.1 Prometeo: early plan of first part. (ALN 51.18.02/0001. © The heirs of Luigi Nono. Reproduced by kind permission.)

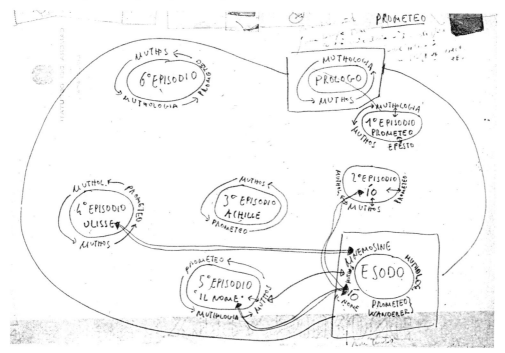

Figure 13.2 Prometeo: drawing by Cacciari, 1978. (ALN 51.04.01/20. © The heirs of Luigi Nono. Reproduced by kind permission.)

A tragedy of listening

interludio formed the keystone. This classically balanced whole was to be interrupted by development on another dimension.[17] At a certain point, he deletes 'episode' and substitutes 'fragment', in a matrix with form on one axis (prologo, I–III, interludio, IV–VI, esodio) and forces on the other ('fragments inserted', 'canzone', space, voices, instruments).[18] The canzone will become the Benjamin-derived texts of a new figure: Maestro del Gioco.

Second and third arrangements of the texts follow, in which Nono's increasing fascination with fragmentation is evident.[19] The passages from Aeschylus are still intact and central, but around them the other texts are fragmented in a simultaneous, discontinuous choreography of ideas. References to other musical sources, Nono's personal music–historical framework, now appear more frequently. Mahler is a frequent reference, an important figure in Cacciari's writing at the time and presumably in their conversations. In *Krisis*, he describes Mahler as 'the real contemporary of Wittgenstein'.[20] '!think of Mahler today!', Nono tells himself.[21] He begins to see the emotional drama in terms of colours – perhaps the product of his own graphical practice, but a property to become part of the theatrical vision. Structural ideas were thus already advanced while Nono was still working on *Con Luigi Dallapiccola* at the Milan studio, before the revelations of Freiburg and the new language of *Das atmende Klarsein*.[22] He discussed theatrical possibilities with various directors including Ronconi, Tadeusz Kantor and Peter Brook, but the idea of any narrative staging seems to have dissolved as he considered possible theatrical scenarios, a process described by Cacciari as 'emptying' that would continue through early productions of *Prometeo*.[23]

An unpublished interview given while he was still working on *Fragmente* gives a snapshot of Nono's evolving thought:

> I have been thinking about Aeschylus for quite some time. My perspective on the figure of Prometheus has broadened through the conversations with Massimo and with Francesco dal Co: how the myth of Prometheus has been understood in various times, especially in terms of the relationship between laws and their transgression for a new formulation. Prometheus is not seen as the rebel, the liberator as in Schelling or Schiller. I am interested in the struggle between the foundation of the principles of life and the continuous dynamic that leads to their overcoming in a relationship of continuous conflict.
>
> Whereas in *Gran sole* there was an intersection of various moments, of texts etc., here there are sort of 'islands' in continuous transformation; there are continuous journeys between these 'islands' that introduce new perspectives, new cognitive angles. There will not be a succession, a traditional development of scenes but a complex superposition, with returns, utopian perspectives that recall each other continuously.[24]

This text still presented two major issues in terms of Nono and Cacciari's conception of the work. First, it still presented the myth as a linear narrative, when simultaneity had, according to Cacciari, become Nono's obsession. He seems to have been searching for a kind of monad:

> a research aimed at eliminating any narrative structure; he had a sense of being able to condense – into a single point, hence the notion of 'instant'– all possible developments without unfolding them, without developing them such that they would inevitably become chronological-narrative.[25]

This is Nono's Musil-derived idea of the 'sense of the possible'. At the same time, the double bind of Hesiod's *Works and Days* condemns man to the unending cyclical nature of chronological time. Second, the assemblage of sources still lacked an additional stratum of critical understanding

A tragedy of listening

– one closer, perhaps, to their own ideas, and one that would allow a broader space for reflection and tension.

Nono and Cacciari had been contemplating solutions for some time. References to Benjamin and the 'Maestro' appear in early sketches, and Nono was already thinking in terms of 'islands' in 1979–80. *Fragmente* opened new paths of thought, and *Das atmende Klarsein* a revitalised practice; work on *Prometeo* thus took on a new energy and urgency through 1981. Cacciari revised and amended the texts until on Christmas Day 1982 he presented Nono with a definitive version. The episodes were replaced by five *Isole* (islands) interspersed with two *Stasima* – choral commentaries. In addition, Cacciari had introduced a set of twelve poems for the figure of Maestro del Gioco (Master of the Game), paraphrases of aspects of Benjamin's 1940 *Theses on the Philosophy of History*.[26] These afford a means of articulating, interrupting or interconnecting the views of time inherent in the other texts: cyclic, chronological, 'ectopic' or eternal. Benjamin suggests a model orthogonal to the continuous, teleological narrative of Enlightenment history, one based on discontinuity and interruption. He introduces the concept of 'weak Messianic power'. Grounded in a materialist view of history in which any concept of 'absolute' redemption plays no part, Benjamin's weak Messianic power is the historically formed potential of every moment for 'fulfilment and redemption': 'The past carries with it a temporal index by which it is referred to redemption. [. . .] Like every generation that preceded us, we are endowed with a *weak* Messianic power, a power to which the past has a claim'.[27] It is weak because in every moment it may remain unrealised or fail.[28] It is a constellation of instants of potential: '[The historian] establishes a conception of the present as the "time of the now", which is shot through with chips of Messianic time.'[29] This is one of the most crucial intellectual challenges of Nono's later work: how to reconcile concepts of temporal simultaneity and infinity with a teleological understanding of time necessary for any concept of political or personal progress? How to then realise this in the sequential time of music? His exploration of these questions is informed by his reading of Bruno and Gosztonyi, for example, but also increasingly of theologian/philosophers such as Martin Buber and Franz Rosenzweig. Rosenzweig's *The Star of Redemption*, with its emphasis on revelation and redemption in the here and now, was now an important reference for both Nono and Cacciari.[30] Responding to this challenge is fundamental to Nono's thought on *Prometeo* – the strongest indication that his Gramscian foundations have evolved, not been abandoned. That Nono identifies with the Wanderer seems clear – the wandering, as we shall see, is goal-less but not undirected.

The paths through a map of this new musical–architectural space – perhaps an explanation for Abbado – gives a sense of its multi-dimensionality (Figure 13.3). Five islands (each in a different colour), three interruptions (orange) and two stasima (choruses, in blue) are framed by a *Prologo* and *Das atmende Klarsein*. The Maestro del Gioco is a continuous presence, as are air, breath and wind. Josquin and Gabrieli are underlined prominently.

Prometeo is mentioned in the letter in which Cacciari proposes the extracts from Rilke and Orphic hymns for *Das atmende Klarsein*, and in which he summarises his view of Nono's relationship with text and thought:

> What they [certain musicologists] understand is the dissolution (really: dis-solve – and, therefore, critical – no sudden illumination) of the relationship of the metaphysical with the signified – what they will never understand (as good 'avant garde' [. . .]) is how everything is still given in the 'sign' [. . .] and thus certainly also <u>Fabbrica</u>, also <u>Floresta</u>. The 'revolutionary' side of what you're doing today seems to me to be precisely in the non-resolving (still peacefully and [. . .]) of the metaphysics of the signified in her 'sister', the sign [. . .] That it should be difficult, and painful, I can understand [. . .][31]

A tragedy of listening

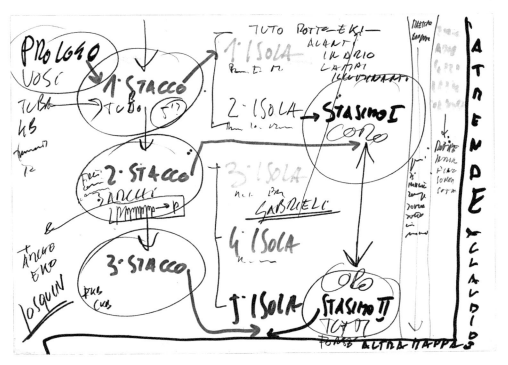

Figure 13.3 Prometeo: map of final structure. (ALN 51.18.03/001. © The heirs of Luigi Nono. Reproduced by kind permission.)

Nono was thus presented with a very specific compositional challenge: how to bring the performer and listener to engage with the musical/poetical reality of the immanent present within the sequential context of musical times, structures and actions. The simultaneous doing and comprehending of a musical act in a multiple present in which none of its possibilities are denied becomes the central concern of *Prometeo*. For Cacciari, this concern with the moment of revelation is precisely what makes it a *tragedy*. The present moment becomes a node in structural and historical networks:

> At the opposite of a sole *movimentum*, common to all, an arhythmic succession of points, arbitrary, naked of their own sounds, is that of *Prometeo* which flattens paths, creates vast 'free' equal spaces, destroys presuppositions. In its laws, the past is simply has-been [. . .] and the present is a plane from which we stretch 'everything together' out into the future [. . .]. Instead, the time [of *Prometeo*] [. . .] is polyphonic: its dimensions are presented simultaneously; the past of this line, of this idea, of this thought, of this single word can be the future of another. The present is not a plane common to all, but the unrepeatable instant, clear and alive, of this singularity. Like the Angelus Novus [Benjamin's image from Klee], it sings a moment, but this moment is unique and unrepeatable, and for this uniqueness and unrepeatability it is necessary.[32]

The very possibility of action in the present is opened to Nono's exploration by the new theoretical and technological tools at his disposal. This is the search for the Rilkean *Augenblick*, the word that may not be anticipated or recalled.

A tragedy of listening

The space of *Prometeo* occupies Nono from the start. How to combine the massiveness and openness of the mythical landscape? What are the sonic properties of the Olympian mountains, of Ulysses' boundless sea? He collects images of temples: Greek temples from Athens, Olympia, Corinth, Paestum, but also others from Knossos, Ur, Persepolis, Abu Simbel. He is particularly fascinated with those in south-west Sicily, at Selinunte and Agrigento. On the images he plays with lines, structures, forces and balances, particularly the careful construction of asymmetry. Broken or missing pieces draw his attention as points of gravity with multiple possible lines of attraction, with spaces of potential. He marks points of gods emerging from stone. These are titanic objects, massive sounding volumes, touched by those who felt in touch with their gods. His lines, vectors of movement and energy, recall those of Klee's *Pedagogical Sketchbook*, which he was reading closely at the time.[33] As he draws and redraws the form of *Prometeo*, Nono balances the asymmetries of forces in different ways reminiscent of his annotations of Greek friezes. The theories of colour of Goethe, Runge, Kandinsky and Itten also begin to figure in Nono's working, as he searches for ways to articulate its many dimensions.[34]

'Fragments wandering in space' is how Nono describes an early plan.[35] He builds from elements rather than materials; they are indeed monadic. His fundamental resources are consistent with the vision of the earliest works. In this respect *Prometeo* signals an entirely different path to the figure-based contemporary operas of Stockhausen. Lengths of rhythmic fabric are woven from permutations of repeated note-values and rests, different lines shifted through metrical space relative to each other. These are used as whole beats and in divisions up to septuplets. The earliest of these passages seem to date from the same time as the *A Veloce* and *B Calmo* sources of *Con Luigi Dallapiccola*. Nono follows his established practice, building polyphonic matrices from the base materials through which he traces paths to produce folded, variegated rhythmic sequences. These repetition-based patterns will reappear as premonitions of references to Schumann's *Manfred*, and in the slow, ritual repetition of the group of solo strings. They also shape the echoes of vocal passages, articulations and interruptions staggered between the four orchestral groups. A page of transpositions of the scala enigmatica is marked 'PROMETEO'. Possible voicings of overlapping subsets follow, against one of which he writes 'Gustav'.[36] The harmonic/melodic universe of *Prometeo* is again articulated by seconds, fourths and fifths. The scala enigmatica and *Das atmende Klarsein* serve as maps and materials. This is now Nono's meta-stable space: infinite, and yet with only certain paths available from each point, as in a tonal system. In some respects it fulfils a function analogous to that of his earlier all-interval series.

As in other works, the composition of each component of *Prometeo* is rooted in the meticulous gathering and indexing of materials, however heterogeneous they may be. Naturally, there are common features, but a vital component of this process is its very singularity, its unique relationship with the particular context and materials in question. Nono's iterative, graphical cycle of development and filtering of ideas, materials and models is fully in evidence. With *Prometeo*, however, there is an additional reflexive layer; Nono documents its composition in an extensive series of photographs. These reveal much about the importance of his working environment in Venice and at the Hotel Halde near Freiburg. An image of some of the many materials with which he surrounded himself in his Giudecca studio shows photographs of the stones of Venice – patterns of marble that are at once organic and full of exquisite symmetries – alongside classical images, family photographs and sketches for the architecture of *Prometeo* (Plate 5). In another picture his desk looks more like that of a designer or architect as he works on plans for the lighting of the islands in San Lorenzo (Plate 6). He took countless pictures of the changing landscape of the Black Forest, of the mountains in different weather conditions,

A tragedy of listening

through his window at Hotel Halde. His room there was likewise hung with plans and drawings (Plate 7). Such images had become portals to new areas of Nono's imagination:

> Listen to the stones, the red bricks. Listen to the dark, listen to the way the sky is a creature of the stones, of the bricks, the water. To know how to see and hear the invisible, the inaudible. To arrive at the minimum level of audibility, of visibility.[37]

Production

A contract was signed in September 1983. *Prometeo* was to be a co-production; premiered at the Venice Biennale in September 1984, it would be presented at La Scala the following season. Claudio Abbado would conduct and Renzo Piano – architect of the Centre Pompidou and IRCAM – was engaged to design the performance space. In their first telephone conversation, Nono asked Piano not for stage design but for a 'musical space'.[38] By December 1983, Nono's vision of *Prometeo* had assumed material, physical shape. The Biennale proposed the desanctified church of San Lorenzo as a venue that could be adapted for such an ambitious project; the stones of Venice became his instrument:

> Venice is a complex system that affords precisely that pluridimensional listening [. . .] the sounds of the bells are diffused in various directions: some combine, are conveyed by the water, transmitted along the canals [. . .] others vanish almost completely, others connect to other signals from the lagoon and the city itself. Venice is an acoustic multiverse, the opposite of that hegemonic system of transmitting and listening to sound that we have been used to for centuries.
>
> [. . .] the reawakening of the faculty of listening to silence does not arise only from solitude of nature, from being solitary, but rather and often from within the crowd, the loudest sonorities [. . .] so no Manichean opposition of word–silence, word–sound, sound–silence [. . .]
>
> Now I feel as if my head *were* San Lorenzo [. . .] I feel that I occupy it and try to be fully occupied by the space [. . .]
>
> The fact is that my head no longer belongs to me at the moment, it lives in this problem. And the work – which is not there yet, of which the means of composition and the sounds are missing – already lives, *it is already a work of listening!*[39]

Nono outlined his plans to Abbado and Piano in detail, in a letter that gives a sense of the breadth, coherence, intensity and urgency of Nono's vision. He envisages a raised floor above loudspeakers projecting upwards, walkways around the space at three heights along which vocal and instrumental soloists could move, six platforms at different heights for the islands and four further asymmetrical positions for the orchestral groups:

> sounds read the space/creating new spatial dramaturgy/from minimal spatial variation/to the whole space completely full of original sounds and processed with live electronics [. . .] Not opera/no director/no scenographer/no traditional personages/but dramaturgy-tragedy with mobile sounds that read discover empty fill the space [. . .]
>
> Venetian school/A. G. Gabrieli/Church of San Marco/cori spezzati/compositions for up to 18 choruses dislocated at various heights – positions/up to 40 separate

407

A tragedy of listening

voices/Striggio – Tallis (English)/Ockeghem (Flemish)/ + live electronics and computer today/entirely your invention/between acoustics/various spaces/various movements/various islands/maps routes navigation by surprise/means material colours YOURS/then we look at the possibility of using 8 Siemens projectors out of focus/little focus/projection of colours chosen by us and Vedova/new technique for glass not slides/not fixed/not static/never frontal/but anamorphic – Colours: I amuse myself studying Goethe/Runge/Itten/Kandinsky

[. . .] a continuously mobile space/times: not the unique – unitary of tradition but different, conflictual times

[. . .] not solutions but many possibilities like many navigational paths to find with the stars and with the deep sea – Movement almost like the foam of a hurricane – cyclone – sailing before the wind[40]

For Piano, one challenge was to 'avoid the risk that the architecture should become a "protagonist" to the detriment of the music, which is the fundamental perceptual experience for the audience'.[41] Nono's metaphors were well aimed. Piano, a keen sailor, developed a structure like the upturned hull of a boat – a second nave, standing within that of San Lorenzo, that became known as the 'arca'. Curved panels of wood laminate contained the performers and audience on four sides, mounted in a steel structure above a floor raised by three metres 'like a keel'.[42] Galleries at heights of 2.4, 4.8 and 7.2 metres were connected by stairways. A raised platform high between the central pillars accommodated sound equipment, with Nono, Haller, Alvise Vidolin and their assistants (Plate 8). The bi-vaulted ceiling with a central screen dividing the church presented a challenge, but this became integral to the nature of *Prometeo*: there should be no 'complete' view or 'ideal' position from which to listen. This was to be 'an archipelago at the centre of which is the public', but, as Piano observed, the whole system cannot be seen from any one point in an archipelago.[43] Instead, the effects of the whole are experienced through changing partial views, through the actions of wind and waves; this was to be the role of Nono's music in the space. The non-continuous panels contributed to this sense of fragmentation; they also gave another acoustic dimension – the surrounding stone space of the church itself. Piano likened his structure to:

> a violin, or better, a lute or a mandolin: a musical instrument on such a large scale (8 or 9 thousand cubic metres) that it can contain the entire performance, including the public. The music that it holds naturally sets into vibration this enormous sound box, and with it the performers and the audience, literally integrated into the sounding body.[44]

The tension identified immediately by Piano would emerge in other quarters. Nono had been discussing *Prometeo* with theatre director Jürgen Flimm, who had directed *Al gran sole* in Frankfurt, but soon realised that any directorial stamp would compromise the notion of a tragedy of *listening*.[45] Vedova had been involved in discussions from early stages, and, as we have seen, colour was now an integral part of Nono's imagining. They worked together on the idea of projecting light through specially made coloured glass – a thoroughly Venetian plan. Ideas naturally proliferated in Vedova's imagination. He produced a series of sketches of light in movement in which signs and symbols begin to play a role; Cacciari described this development with enthusiasm.[46] However, the active role of lighting in the initial production was diminished, and – with the exception of certain aberrations not sanctioned by Nono – subsequent instantiations of *Prometeo* would dispense with extra-sonic components altogether.

A tragedy of listening

A sketch of the arrangement of the islands episodes in the asymmetrically divided space of San Lorenzo shows how Nono had imagined them to be lit in different colours (Plate 9). Vedova's projections would evoke the stained glass of earlier mystical spaces, of the history of San Lorenzo itself.

Nono and Haller's accumulated experience was now such that the composer could work largely away from the studio; his visits were less frequent during the final stages of composition. He was, however, now also working at the Centro di Sonologia Computazionale of the University of Padova, with the 4i machine of Giuseppe Di Giugno. A development of the 4x that Di Giugno had built for IRCAM – in particular, for Boulez's *Répons* – the 4i allowed real-time control of complex digital sound processing. Nono worked with Alvise Vidolin to design wind sounds that could be synthesised, filtered, reverberated and spatialised in real time. While abandoned after the initial production of *Prometeo* – there was insufficient space for the underfloor loudspeakers in Milan – this element is fundamental to Nono's conception of the work: the wind through the Black Forest, across the Adriatic, or as the force that steers a course across a mythical Aegean irrespective of the will of man. References to wind abound through the notes and sketches, and the 4i has its own line through Nono's working score.

Construction of Piano's 'ark' began in late August 1984. Haller and the studio equipment arrived at the end of the month, but only in the second week of September could they begin installing the twenty-four loudspeakers. Two weeks remained for rehearsal. Haller's journal documents the process in some detail, including an unfruitful boat trip to Murano to source Venetian glass for the electronically processed bell sounds, with Nono at the rudder. In the event, cheese domes from Freiburg performed rather better.[47] While acknowledging their impeccable performance, Haller also comments on the behaviour of the orchestra – The Chamber Orchestra of Europe – at rehearsals. This is of more than anecdotal interest; it raises interesting questions about Nono's use of the orchestra, especially in the late works. The very effective orchestral writing in *Prometeo* demands the highest level of concentration and technical control from performers. In contrast with the permeable boundary between solo vocal and choral writing, however, there is no overlap with the highly personal and engaging parts for the instrumental soloists. His concentration on particular instrumental detail is such that the fluidity between individual and group so important in other aspects of Nono's music is less in evidence when dealing with the orchestra. The movement of performers was incrementally reduced through rehearsals and subsequent productions, initially due to the additional noise created but subsequently as part of the focusing on sound and refining of the electronics.

Nono invited his friend Heiner Müller as the male reciter for the Venice and Milan performances. Müller's idea of the 'synthetic fragment' had been important in the development of Nono's *Fragmente*, he had produced his own translation of Aeschylus' *Prometheus* in 1969, and Nono had attended the first West German production of his recent *Verkommenes Ufer Medeamaterial Landschaft mit Argonauten* in 1983. Müller's ideas on theatre continued to inform Nono's thinking through work on *Prometeo*. He noted several passages on the importance of history in Müller's work in a recent interview: 'the impact of ideas, and of the idea of history, on human bodies. This is indeed my theoretical point: the thrusting on stage of bodies and their conflict with ideas.'[48] 'I don't think a play can be good unless you burn your ideas in the writing process,' is also underlined. In a letter from Venice during the first production of *Prometeo*, Müller described it as 'an attempt to compose light'.[49]

Prometeo. Tragedia dell'ascolto was premiered in Venice on 25 September and repeated over the following three days. Just a month later, Nono was back in Freiburg refining the electronics and making substantial revisions to the score, work that would continue in parallel with several other projects through the early months of 1985. In Milan, Piano's structure was reassembled

A tragedy of listening

at the Ansaldo, the large ex-industrial space used as the workshop for La Scala, for six performances of the revised score that began on 25 September, a year after the premiere.

Nono would participate in further performances of *Prometeo*: in Frankfurt in August 1987, at the Paris Festival d'Automne the following October, and in the Kammermusiksaal of the Philharmonie in Berlin at the end of August 1988. Since then, it has become one of the most performed major works of the late twentieth century. It stands at once in the tradition of Western art music, poses a direct challenge to that tradition and indicates possible ways forward – not just for the art form of music as currently constituted but ways of listening, of understanding, of being in the world. The technical and technological questions of how to combine situatedness and personal experience, the *hic et nunc*, with the 'work' as a meta-stable entity have exercised composers and theorists increasingly over subsequent decades.

That these and subsequent productions (apart from an aberrant instance in Brussels) have been primarily listening experiences – unstaged apart from the disposition of performers and loudspeakers, free of theatrical interpretation or distraction – seems entirely in keeping with Nono's wishes. It is a shame that Piano's ark – the acoustic performing–resonating–listening space for which *Prometeo* was conceived – still languishes in a Milan warehouse. It is to be celebrated, however, that an authoritative performing score of *Prometeo* has finally been produced, due largely to the tireless advocacy of its editor, André Richard. He has been able to distil the essential additional information needed to complete the 1985 score as a performing edition – through his initial work with Nono as choral director in 1981, later direction of the live electronics in his role as Director of the Experimental Studio of the SWF, in gathering the accumulated wisdom of Nono's collaborators, and as artistic coordinator on most, if not all, subsequent productions. The necessary breadth of that experience is itself an indication of the range of issues involved.

Major aspects still resist notation, however. Pauline Driesen considers a view of *Prometeo* as an 'opera aperta' in two respects: in Nono's own reworking of the score, its fixed points determined by circumstance as much as any sense of 'termination', and in the light of the fact that even then it has to be reimagined and sonically reconfigured in each new environment.[50] This is an interesting limit-case to consider as a thought experiment. Prometeo is certainly part of a continuous development in Nono's thought; there is indeed an archipelago of music and ideas through which he plots a particular course, one of which the listener builds a partial and moving image from their own perspective. As we will see, however, the composer's formal decisions as he moves through the *Isole* are highly rational, and can be seen as developments of his long established practice. Richard points to the challenge of specifying the live electronics for his edition.[51] This brings into focus the ways in which *Prometeo* resists being fixed, resists reduction or commodification. This resistance is more than a requirement to adapt. The fundamental integration of live electronics and performance space with compositional strategies demands a profound engagement with the performance practices and ethos of the work. Every performance is a rehearing for performers and audience alike, a common personal and social act of listening and seeking to understand. The recent words of Nuria Schoenberg-Nono offer the most concise summary: '*Prometeo* is the key work of his life [. . .] his aesthetic and ethical manifesto.'[52]

The full forces required by the 1985 version are: 2 soprano, 2 alto and tenor soloists, male and female speakers, chamber choir, two trios of instrumental soloists (viola, cello, double bass; flutes, clarinets, alto trombone/euphonium/tuba), percussion ('glasses'), orchestra divided into four identical groups, and electronics. Two conductors are required. The distribution of texts and performers through the movements is summarised in Figure 13.4.

A tragedy of listening

Prometeo, Tragedia dell'ascolto (1985 version)

Prologo
Tutti
Speakers: Hesiod *Theogony*
(with fragments from Aeschylus *Prometheus Bound*, Sophocles *Trachiniae*, Hesychius *Lexicon*) [These sources are developed from Cacciari's 1978 text]
Soloists and chorus: Cacciari *Maestro del gioco I & II* (based on Benjamin's *Theses on the Philosophy of History*)

Isola 1°
Chorus, string trio, orchestras
Chorus: 'Mitologia' (Cacciari)
[Aeschylus *Prometheus Bound* ('Prometeo' and 'Efisto') printed in the score through the orchestral passages]

Isola 2°
  a) *Io – Prometeo*
      SSAAT soloists, chorus, b flt, cb clt, string trio, orchestras
      Aeschylus *Prometheus Bound* ('Prometeo' and 'Io')
  b) *Hölderlin*
      SS soloists, speakers, b flt, cb clt
      Hölderlin *Hyperions Schiksaalslied*, Pindar *Nemea Ode VI*
  c) *Stasimo 1°*
      SSAAT soloists, chorus, orchestras
      Euripides *Alcestis*

Interludio 1°
Alto, flute, clarinet, tuba
Cacciari *Maestro del gioco IV & V* (based on Benjamin's *Theses on the Philosophy of History*, Euripides *Alcestis*)

Tre voci a
SAT soloists, b flt cb clt euphonium, glasses, 4 violins from each orchestra
Cacciari *Maestro del gioco VII, VIII & IX* (based on Benjamin's *Theses on the Philosophy of History*)

Isola 3°- 4°- 5°
Isola 3° SSAA, wind trio, string trio, orchestras
Sophocles *Oedipus at Colonus*
Isola 4° SSAAT soloists, wind trio (b flt, clt, alto tbn), string trio
Sophocles *Oedipus at Colonus*, Hölderlin *Kolomb, Achill*, Hesiod *Work and Days*, Schönberg *Moses und Aron*
Isola 5° wind trio (piccolo, Eb clt, tuba)
texts printed in the score, from Aeschylus *Prometheus Bound*, Nietzsche *Menschliches, Allzumenschliches*, Hölderlin *In lieblicher Bläue*, Schönberg *Sechs Stücke für Männerchor*
Eco lontano chorus, orchestras

Tre voci b
chorus
Cacciari *Maestro del gioco X, XI & XII* (based on Benjamin's *Theses on the Philosophy of History*)

Interludio 2°
orchestras (low instruments), glasses

Stasimo 2°
SSAAT soloists, wind trio, string trio
Aeschylus *Prometheus Bound*, Cacciari *Maestro del gioco*, Schönberg *Moses und Aron*

Figure 13.4 Prometeo: form

A tragedy of listening

'Prometeo. Tragedia dell'ascolto'[53]

'Prologo'

Prologo maps out the multidimensional space of sound, ideas and references navigated through the rest of the work. It establishes the discourse of *Prometeo*, and thus warrants consideration in detail. Through some 20 minutes it presents both the materials from which the rest will emerge and the full range of vocal and instrumental forces. It establishes the environment for *Prometeo* in many respects, including Nono's own working practice. Work on *Prologo* continued from his first responses to Cacciari's proposals to the revisions of 1985. If the concept of *Prometeo* begins in 1978, the practice that produces it starts with Nono's arrival in Freiburg at the end of 1980. The iterative, daily process of repeated listening to experiments and materials with his collaborators in the studio – live or in the countless recordings – becomes one with his listening to the new sonic environment of the Black Forest, and that in turn leads to a reintensified awareness of the 'acoustic multiverse' that is the Venetian soundscape. While an acute aural imagination is manifest throughout Nono's work, the transformation of consciousness through listening now becomes the foundation of his practice – a present, active reality. This is the ground for other more theoretical explorations; it is what he shares through *Prometeo*, its anticipations and echoes, and is at the political, humanitarian core of the music of his last decade.

Nono already started developing *Prologo* from Cacciari's 1978 text. 'su tutto: UNRUHE' ('disquiet everywhere') says a note on the opening, establishing the base state of the work.[54] Next to it, a drawing of form shows four parallel layers of structure, across all of which runs the continuum 'Prometeo – Wanderer'. A series of interruptions are marked as 'high wedges'; they will become the brief pre-echoing references to Schumann's *Manfred*. Nono articulates his forces as choruses, instruments and, for the first time, computer. References to percussion, pick-ups and ring modulation place these sketches in 1979, during the composition of *Con Luigi Dallapiccola*. Cacciari's additional texts – to become those of Maestro del Gioco – are referred to as 'canzone', analysed and re-ordered as an additional dimension (Figure 13.5).

He worked on the final score of *Prologo* from early in the final phase of composition – that is, from the time of *Das atmende Klarsein* in 1981 – and revisions continued until the Milan production of 1985. Drafts, experiments and preparatory works reach different stages of completion. An early choral setting of the *Prologo* text is developed from reordered fragments of *Das atmende Klarsein* – elaborations of the original material in which the texture expands and contracts with the intensity of the words, sequences of movement and density rhyming like lines of poetry.[55] *Io, frammento dal Prometeo* develops a passage from an earlier version of Cacciari's text, with its role for Mitologia, and sections of that work were subject to a similar process of fragmentation. In another undeveloped draft, a tenor monody sets the first of Cacciari's poems, tracing a line through the opening of *Das atmende Klarsein*.[56] None of these initial ideas enter the final score in their entirety, but traces remain – perhaps memories of his first thoughts as he begins again. In the abandoned tenor monody, for instance, he adds a quintuplet rhythm to the sustained note on the word 'aria'; flutes add that figure to the sustained chorus 'aria' in the final score of *Prologo* (bar 58).

As often, Nono sets out his fundamental materials on a single sheet – a map of the space *Prologo* and much of *Prometeo* will explore. To the articulation of the scala enigmatica familiar from *Fragmente* he adds a pattern of two fifths separated by a semitone, producing two tritones (T) (Figure 13.6). Each unit is associated with an element of the drama: T 'Gea' (Gaia), B 'Dei' (gods), C 'uomin.' (men), B+C 'una' ('one' – the origin in Cacciari's first texts) and A

A tragedy of listening

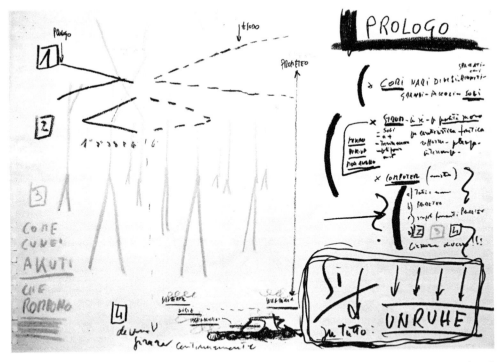

Figure 13.5 Prometeo: *Prologo*, early sketch. (ALN 51.14.04/01. © The heirs of Luigi Nono. Reproduced by kind permission.)

Figure 13.6 Prometeo: interval material for *Prologo*[57]

'Mitologia'. Together with the musical–semantic network of *Das atmende Klarsein*, these constitute a prime source, a point of origin.

The first sixteen bars were added as an introduction to the final score of *Prologo*. Sopranos and altos of the *coro lontanissimo* begin with the name of mother earth – 'Gaia' – across two-fifths separated by a tone: F–C, D–A (a set present in the scala enigmatica on C♯). The processed 'coro lontanissimo', transposed down an augmented fourth and with a long reverb, is diffused through distant loudspeakers, their sound reflected from walls or ceiling. Gaia represents a world beyond gods and man. The musical fragment was chosen early in the process: 'Fruchtlands' and 'di cielo (stellato)' – earth and heaven – from *Das atmende Klarsein*, 'aurora' from *Io, frammento dal Prometeo*. Female voices are then replaced by the violins of all four surrounding orchestras, who expand the sustained D–A microtonally and registrally. Architectural and pitch space are established immediately, together with a force of diffusion, of

A tragedy of listening

entropy; such dissolution of clear intervals into natural sound is characteristic of *Prologo*. The shaded, dissolving fifth alternates with two interjections by the combined orchestral groups at the other extreme of complexity. In these, hollowed-out repeated rhythms are delayed differently from the four directions as a chromatic whole is built, missing only F–C in bars 8–9 – the negative of the opening – and then just F. The second choral entry maps out C♯–F♯, C–G, now expanded by wind as well as strings, diffusing the pattern through a wider timbre space. 'egeinato' ('bore') is thus set to the interval pattern 'T' of Gaia, appropriate as the account of the earth's progeny begins. The four orchestras as a body are the only element in *Prometeo* to be heard with no electronic processing (although they are the source of the four amplified solo instruments in *Isola 1°*). If their natural sound, encircling the performance space, can be seen to represent Gaia, then the expansion of voices into instruments, the absorption and dissolution of their clear musical figures, seems to reflect a relationship between man and nature.

As well as the spaces of pitch and architecture, these first few bars establish the polarised modes of time between which the musical–conceptual events of *Prometeo* are suspended. A photograph of a temple frieze from Corfu has fish-like humans emerging from the water on one side, over which Nono has written 'waves, voices'. On the other side stands a group of superhuman figures. Both look to the centre, which is missing. There Nono writes 'Prologo' (Figure 13.8a).[58] As Nono pointed out, this is the moment described by Hölderlin in which 'the gods are dead and the new gods are not yet born'.[59] Two musical references occupied Nono in particular: Mahler's *Symphony No. 1* – not by coincidence *'The Titan'* – and the overture to Schumann's 'dramatic poem with music' *Manfred*. They seem to represent respectively the unarticulated, unending time of Gaia – ur-time before Cronus – and the ungraspable fleeting moment that can be reflected only in memory. These are the 'empty' or 'homogeneous' time and 'now-time' of Benjamin's *Theses on History*. Neither can be possessed or measured. Annotations in his copy of Mahler indicate features of specific relevance: the out-of-time opening bars, free of figure and harmony; the pedal A sustained for 56 slow bars; the descending fourth motif (mirrored in Nono's ascending fifth) and the minor second thus formed against the sustained pedal; the fact that these bars themselves constitute a clear historical reference to Beethoven's Ninth Symphony; the suggestion of parallel tempi in the clarinet cuckoo call (another Beethoven reference); and the changing spatial distance of the trumpet calls. *Das Lied von der Erde* and *Das Klagende Lied* are also mentioned through Nono's sketches. He refers to the opening of Mahler's First Symphony in an interview with Cacciari, as well as Mahler's concept of 'Naturlaut' ('sound of nature'), which Nono describes discovering in the Black Forest: 'music of nature, based on resonant silences of inaudibility'.[60] The close connection between experience, culture and memory is a central concern here, and the world of Mahler and Musil reflects obsessively on that inescapable space.

Manfred, the protagonist of Byron's 'metaphysical drama', is also a Promethean character. Schumann's overture begins with a single bar of three rapid syncopations from the full orchestra. *Rasch, crescendo*, harmonically ambiguous, they have passed before the ear can process them. Only in the silent fermata that follows can they be rehearsed in memory. If the opening of *Prologo* recalls Mahler directly, the three slow syncopations that emerge from the near complete chromatic of bars 8–11 are a premonition of a memory of Schumann to come. There are further pre-echoes: at bars 40–1, 64–6, 96, 183–7 and 196–7. Some are slow such as to become almost static, in others the urgency of syncopation begins to emerge. Only in the final orchestral intervention (bar 202) will the reference become explicit, at Schumann's tempo of $\bullet = 152$, a moment of anamnesis.

These modes of time mark out the space of the body of *Prologo*, which is produced by the overlapping waves of five elements: the full orchestral *Manfred* events, chorus and vocal soloists

A tragedy of listening

echoed by instrumental groups from all four orchestras, the two reciters, the wind soloists (with the struck, electronically processed glass bowls) and the trio of solo strings. The fluctuating tempi of the actions of gods and men (singers and orchestral groups) and the now-time of *Manfred* move across the mythical time of the speaking voices and the groups of string and wind soloists, all proceeding at the sub-rhythmic rate of ♩ = 30. This temporal architecture can be understood in terms of Nono's earlier sketches: parallel layers of 'fragments wandering in space' interrupted by the proto-*Manfred* interventions from all four orchestral groups.[61] Under the reverberation of the introduction, the reciters begin to read Hesiod's genealogy: from Gaia and Uranos, through Cronus and the first generation of Titans to Prometheus and the second. Divided into thirteen fragments, the text is an incantation, both a memory and an invocation of the gods – an old testament against which comes Cacciari's Benjaminian new testament. The male and female voices speak in a constantly phase-shifting heterophony: Nono's 'waves of voices'. Detuning, filtering and projection through the highest loudspeaker add to the alienation of an archaic language. We hear the ancient sound of a people telling their story to themselves as much as to their listeners.

The coro lontanissimo illuminates names from this spoken litany. These were largely added in the 1985 revision, using moments from *Das atmende Klarsein* as Melkert has shown.[62] These and lines of the first two Maestro del Gioco texts are taken up by groups from the orchestras – always with the same instrumentation from all four directions – reflecting, echoing, reverberating or rhythmicising to keep the names in constant motion. At 'non resiste nell'eco della voce' ('does the voice not endure in its echo'), for instance, the final *mp* choral fifth D–A is echoed across a wide range as C♯–G♯, *ppppp* – a Doppler-shifted echo. Elsewhere, all four orchestral groups offer external elaboration of the vocal material: articulating starts and ends, delaying and diffusing in pitch and space, adding timbral complexity (muted brass, strings *crini e legno sul ponte*) or reducing to the near-sines of flutes. Perhaps these moments constitute the response of Gaia to the hubris of gods and men. Such instrumental expansions of voices contrast clearly with the full orchestral interventions. High voices echo the name Uranos, *pppp*, using the G♯–F♯–C♯ of 'Gewitter' ('storm') from *Das atmende Klarsein*; it emerges from speech as the filter settings changes to reveal higher components. They repeat the reference, framed by the first calls of 'Ascolta', the beginning of *Maestro del Gioco 1*. Its opening augmented fourth is the interval of Unruhe, of disquiet. Oceanus – the great river encircling the world – is absent from the reciter's litany, but presented by the chorus as a perfect fifth B–F♯, to become an important point of reference throughout *Prometeo*, the horizon relative to which pitch- and interval-space are navigated. A sketch shows the layers of this musical-mythological world (Figure 13.7).

References to 'echo' or 'echo rhythms' abound in Nono's sketches. In *Prologo*, Nono's echo technique is clearly in evidence in the relationship between voices and orchestras. The simple principle of echo unites space and time, moment and memory; it is key to the sound world of *Prometeo*. This is a development of his early rhythmic techniques, a rationalisation that affords Nono a continuous plane between unison periodicity and polyphonic rhythmic complexity, and a way of unifying long-term, almost formal durations with local rhythmic figure. The primary sustained material moves between choir and vocal soloists – a movement between far and near, group and individual. The four surrounding orchestral groups articulate and punctuate with homogenous timbres – strings, woodwind, brass – together, or staggered such that the sound moves around the hall. In these interventions we hear a synthesis of Nono's earlier sound-complex shapes and tight polyphonic construction. Each is unique; echoes of the beginnings and ends of notes develop their own rate of delay, sometimes using different divisions of the beat or adding internal repetitions. We see another influence of the studio on

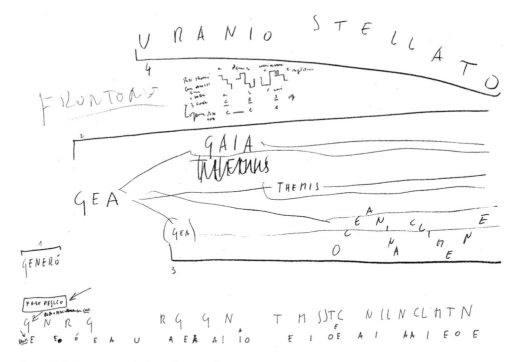

Figure 13.7 Prometeo: mythological strata of *Prologo*. (ALN 51.15.01/05. © The heirs of Luigi Nono. Reproduced by kind permission.)

his thought: here, 'echo' can be understood as the component of early reflection in reverberation. The relative direction, intensity, initial delay, repeat and decay rates of such reflections characterise a space to the ear; the intuitive acoustics of listening construct an image of physical space. By manipulating these in his score, Nono creates a sense of constantly shifting space – sometimes incrementally, sometimes suddenly, cinematographically. In this way he also creates continuity with the electronic transformations and movement.

At the mid-point of *Prologo*, the names that represent a turning-point in the history are entrusted to the chorus, they become song: Cronus (son of Gaia and Uranos, castrator of his father) and Rhea (parents of Zeus), then Japetos (their son, Titan of mortality) and Clymene, the parents of Prometheus. Otherwise the old text – Hesiod – does its work through being spoken; the new – Benjamin/Cacciari – requires listening, demands attention in its song. Chorus and solo voices present the first two Maestro del Gioco texts. Four times they repeat their adjuration 'Ascolta' ('listen'). This echo of the opening exhortation of the Rule of St Benedict would not have been lost on Nono: 'Obsculta, o fili, præcepta magistri, et inclina aurem cordis tui' ('Listen, my son, to your master's precepts, and incline the ear of your heart'). It unites the act of listening and acceptance of the law, two key concepts of *Prometeo*. 'Obsculta!' Is the watchword of the Benedictine order, for which the great monastery of San Giorgio was built on the island adjacent to Giudecca. It was for its refectory that Veronese's *The Wedding Feast at Cana* was painted, depicting the painter's fellow artists as musicians, listening attentively to each other.

Two of Nono's annotated images relate to these poems (Figures 13.8b–c). The picture from Selinunte marked 'Ascolta' hung on Nono's studio wall as he worked on *Prometeo* – a reminder, an instruction to himself.

Figure 13.8a Frieze from Corfu[63]

Figure 13.8b Temple at Selinunte[64]

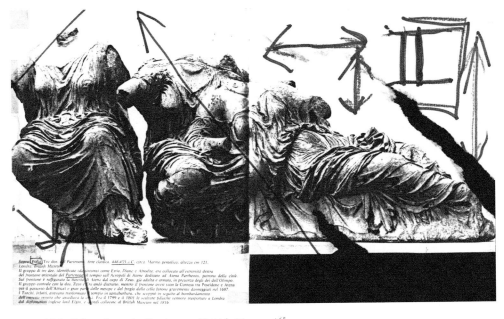

Figure 13.8c Frieze from the Parthenon (British Museum)[65]

Figure 13.8 Prometeo: annotated photographs from Nono's sketches

A tragedy of listening

The text passes between soloists and chorus; the differences are of perspective, proximity and the subtle differences within groups of voices. Each passage has its own path through the pitch space, but there is evidence of a larger architecture, of layers of networks across the smaller units. The B–F♯ of Oceanus returns on 'echo', 'silenced' and 'secrets', for example. Passages of text are built from sequences of discreet vocal or instrumental units. Within these, symmetries and balances are evident on all levels. As in earlier vocal works, even where the complexes of pitch and rhythm are constructed prior to text setting, there are clear signs of sculpting the raw material to poetic ends. On 'volto', for instance ('the face of the beloved'), Nono builds a structure of interwoven symmetries (Figure 13.9). Such moments interrupt the near-becalming of time, otherwise resisted only by the physicality of singing.

Figure 13.9 Prometeo: Prologo, bars 129–31, solo SAT

The naming of Prometeo heralds the last line of the first Maestro del Gioco text and the centre of *Prologo*. The chorus emerges from the most abstract sounds of the solo winds; 'suoni eolien acutissimi, mobile micro, con suono ombra' ('highest possible aeolian sounds, moving relative to the microphone, with a shadow sound') he directs the bass flute, as if Prometeo arrives with the wind itself. The continuation of this reference establishes a link between the two levels of text: the wind soloists echo 'nell'ali [. . .] dell'angelo' ('in the wings [. . .] of the angel', bars 165, 175), with the glasses rung evenly like a Sanctus bell. Prometeo 'gives hope to man, is an angel' states Cacciari's *Polemica A*. He is the Klee-inspired angel of history of Benjamin's theses, the Angelus Novus which had been symbolic for Cacciari since his earliest writings; already in 1964 Cacciari and Cesare de Michelis had founded a journal of critical theory, *Angelus Novus*. The sound world of the second Maestro del Gioco text is then transformed – more vocally continuous, more human. Two sopranos replace the soprano, alto and tenor soloists of the first; the chorus sing close to the microphone, sometimes covering their mouths with their hands, their voices no longer transposed or moving in space.

The two groups of instrumental soloists mediate, comment, but remain with the speakers in the tempo of mythical time. The solo wind trio and glasses enter at 'Urano' (bar 24) – the sky. Their sounds are the most unworldly, moving along a continuum between the filtered white noise imagined for the real-time electronic sound of the 4i machine and barely focused, unstable pitched sound dissolving into its higher harmonics. Variation of articulation, dynamic, movement and modes of flutter-tongue introduce destabilising artefacts. Quarter-tone detuning introduces further inner mobility to the processed sound, while the glass bowls are transposed down two octaves with long reverberation to become other-worldly bells. The low string trio enters at 'Oceanus' (bar 41). As in *Guai ai gelidi mostri*, they constitute a single body, always in

A tragedy of listening

rhythmic unison. The extraordinarily long durations of their sounds – beyond that of echoic memory – are kept in constant motion with change of technique, timbre and intonation. Each of their nine entries has its own slow rhythmic figure – repeated with slight variations of dynamic and articulation – and its own colour. Together they sound like a sixteenth-century lyrone, its harmonics and sympathetic strings drawing attention through the glistening of higher partials rather than notated pitches. This is enhanced by filtering by whole tone steps (section B of the scala enigmatica, Nono's reference to the gods) in high and low registers, moving in opposite directions around the space. Early in his sketches, Nono considered 'v[io]la da gamba with Benjamin/like evangelist in Matthew – John/a la John Dowland'.[66]

'Everything in waves', say early notes.[67] The waves of different layers – speakers, singers, string and wind soloists – aggregate into the formal dynamics of *Prologo*. At the climax of the movement, 'questa debole forza' ('this weak power'), they align. This prepares the two clearest orchestral *Manfred* interjections at the end of the movement: a double pre-echo (bars 196–7), its four rhythmic components becoming three with the dynamic sequences *fff p sff sff*, and the dense, microtonal, clear statement at bar 202. Between them, the vocal 'weak power is given to us' stands quietly alone, its phonetic components compressed. Tuba and bass flute emerge from the reverberation of the final *Manfred* interjection; 'do not lose it' is the final choral warning, as the string trio continue their ceaseless turning on a time scale beyond everyday human experience.

'Isola 1°'

The solo strings continue their independent journey of slowness in constant timbral movement through *Isola 1°*: 'vary acoustic spectra by register, by field, by interval and micro-interval – Mobile – varying intensity', they are instructed. They now pass through two channels of delay with feedback to form a denser encircling mass, moving in opposite directions around the space at different speeds. Above them, a polyphony of form plays out a silent dialogue as the drama commences. The length of this movement – equal to that of *Prologo* – reflects the vastness of the barren mountain landscape in which it takes place. The surrounding orchestras build harsh, monumental blocks, violent eruptions and expanses of near-nothingness. Only later in the movement will continuous instrumental sound be interrupted by voices: the coro lontanissimo giving voice to the reflections of Mitologia.

Threads through this virtual drama are connected by tempo, which changes frequently, often bar by bar. Orchestral interventions ($\bullet$ = 30, 44, 56, 60, 72 or 88) are separated by static fifths of the *Prometeo* horizon B–F♯ at $\bullet$ = 30, sustained by a single amplified instrument from each orchestra: trumpet, horn and two violins. These moments become windows on what Christine Mast calls the 'mythical time' of the slower tempo, a tempo below human rhythm.[68] This fifth is shifted or blurred by quarter tones to a semitone lower, as if to draw attention to its slow movement around the space and gradual expansion across a wide range. Nielinger-Vakil see this constant pull towards B♭–F as techne, Prometeo's contribution to humanity and man's move away from the natural origins of Gaia.[69] The dynamics of these sustained moments are changed only from the mixing desk; they have an unworldly life. In these bars we sense the force of Prometheus in his silence. Above them, his exchange with his torturer Hephaestus, from Aeschylus, is printed in the score: 'The given texts are never to be read! But listen to them (and make them "felt") in the 4 orchestral groups, in the 3 solo strings'. Against Hephaestus' detailing of his punishment, Prometheus asserts his achievement, his empowering and liberating of man. His own first words point to his own silencing, however: 'Know: although seeing they did not see, although hearing they did not hear.'

A tragedy of listening

The orchestral fragments are organised in a modular bar structure based on (1 3 5 7 10 12 14 24), using the same values to subdivide longer passages by tempo. Lengths change in the final score as Nono reconciles the layers and material. The rhythmic and pitch resources are developed from those in *Prologo*. Now the patterns of repeated divisions of the beat – whether sounds or rests – are polarised with long, sustained values using the same moduli of numbers of beats as the bar structures. Dynamics and articulation are also more extreme – *ppppp* to *fffff* – their patterns distributed differently according to the same moduli. The orchestral passages thus open up the space between the times established in *Prologo*. The texture is in constant movement within and between the groups; harmonies are often shifted between orchestras with microtonal shading, exaggerating the sense of movement. The composer shows his hand in adapting the structures to produce spatial effects. In bars 59–62, for example, he inserts a retrograde pattern so that a pitch complex passes down through one group then back up through another.

As in any substantial, complex architecture – a large fugue or motet, perhaps – there is a constant play between inexorable and intervention. Large architectonic gesture is balanced by tight microstructure. The division of material between groups is in constant play; they become one, two or four orchestras, sharing, reflecting, turning or opposing. Tempo changes produce variations of energy in the performance regardless of the chronometric length of sounds. The most minimal movement of the slowest sustained sounds is enough to alert the ear to the forward motion of time; the unpredictable onset and dynamics of repeated notes tenses the ear against further events, new information, and yet such sounds remain ungraspable, available to consciousness only in memory. This is a pattern not of contrast but of unpredictable transformation of sonic landscape – of its time, energy, scale and movement – that presents a constant challenge to the ear, to attention and to the sense-making activity of musical listening. In *Prometeo* above all, Nono's art does its transformational work physiologically.

The insistent, repeated rhythms of the shorter passages at ♩ = 88 derive from the *Manfred* material. Despite their loudness, only at bars 21, 53 and 258–62 does the reference make itself explicit. Through these final bars of *Isola 1°*, an accelerando and crescendo from *fff* to *sfffff* accompanies the coming into rhythmic alignment of the full orchestral forces, like a hyper-real magnification of the accumulating energy of Schumann's opening bars. The threefold repetition in Schumann recalls that of the shadow of Manfred's beloved in Byron's 'metaphysical drama' – her echo, perhaps – calling his name as she disappears. 'I live but in the sound' is Manfred's reply.

The only voice we hear is that of Mitologia, questioning the power of Prometheus. In these words from Cacciari's original text we find another instance of his post-dialectical thought: if in challenging the gods Prometeo were to present himself as their equal, nothing would fundamentally change. With the figure of Mitologia and the ideas from Benjamin, Nono and Cacciari are challenging Goethe's representation of heroic resistance. Heavily reverberated, the quiet, still clarity of timbre and figure of the coro lontanissimo stand in marked contrast to the turmoil from which it emerges. The orchestras establish the context for Mitologia. F then B♭, *pp*, *fff*, separated by silence, are stated as clear pitch centres in bars 99–101. Stretched by eighth tones to a semitone in each direction, they confirm a shift of the discourse away from Gaia towards Prometeo. Monumental seven-bar walls of orchestral sound, *ffff*, the harmony shifting with a new attack on each beat, surround the listener before and after the first vocal entry. Their initial announcement of the name Prometeo moves from the F–C that was the opening of *Prologo*, its origin, to the B–F♯ that is the current horizon. Together they form the tritone interval pattern T that Nono had early associated with Gaia. These two bars and their final reprise (bars 111–12, 254–5) thus map out the essential space of the work (Figure 13.10). They

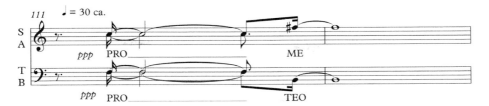

Figure 13.10 Prometeo: Isola 1°, bars 111–12, coro lontanissimo

are echoed rhythmically by muted brass with woodwind and strings. The four central interventions are unaccompanied and adopt material from *Das atmende Klarsein;* 'ascolta, ascolta' appears as in the previous work.[70] Using a different bar pattern (2 2 4 6 6 4) the first four of the six Mitologia interruptions are announced by relatively extended, consistent orchestral passages (of 7, 7, 1+6, 7 bars), the last two by passages moving up and down the tempo scale. With longer musical units a clearer architecture seems to consolidate, as Mitologia asserts the inevitability of a higher law to which both gods and men are subject. Only Mitologia bears witness to Prometeo's silent chaining, challenging his arrogance and naiveté just as Goethe's Prometheus scorned the gods: 'Listen – do you think your fire is omnipotent?'.

'Isola 2° (Io-Prometeo, Hölderlin, Stasimo 1°)'

The three successive sections of the third part – *Isola 2°* – balance the three cross-cut elements of the sixth – *Isola 3° – 4° – 5°* – and the three interwoven voices of the fifth and seventh – *Tre voci (a)* and *(b)*. Nono traverses his ocean as a 3×3 formal multiverse reminiscent of the bipartite strategy of *Fragmente* or the orthogonally related formal components of works in the 1950s. *Io-Prometeo*, the first section, is the crucial exchange that was the basis of *Io, frammento dal Prometeo*: the moment when Prometeo decides to prophesy rather than rebel, when in effect his humanity is asserted. The second section *Hölderlin* presents texts from the poet's *Hyperion's Schicksalslied* together with extracts from Pindar, a meditation on this new state. With words adapted from Euripedes' *Alcestis*, *Stasimo 1°* comments on the turning point of the drama and is the third section of *Isola 2°*.

In *Io-Prometeo* the identification of contrabass clarinet with Prometeo and bass flute with Io remains from the earlier work. From the beginning, their complex but distinct sonic variation, beginning and ending their first phrase together, suggests a more intimate dialogue than the slow-moving amplified fifths that previously stood for that between Prometeo and Hephaestus. These sounds are the product of movement of mouth and breath; they stand between speech and the unsayable. The instrumental language is that of their parts in the earlier work – quiet, unstable breath, overblown or modulated sounds alternating with clear multiphonic intervals – but now recomposed. Long delays on the woodwind soloists play with memory, but their sound is otherwise unprocessed; they are the most present characters in this respect. Both the woodwind soloists and string trio tend to the 'mythical time' of ♩ = 30, but now instead of proceeding independently at their own pace they move with the tempo waves of singers and orchestras.

Io, frammento dal Prometeo was conceived before the incorporation of Benjamin's *Theses* created an additional frame and dimension for *Prometeo*. This episode is, of course, crucial, and its larger context makes different demands. Here, Nono completely reworks the setting and distribution of the dialogue between Prometeo and Io, adapting twenty-seven short fragments

A tragedy of listening

from parts 1, 3, 5 and 7 of the previous work.[71] Prometeo's words are now sung by solo tenor. His voice is filtered to create a sense of otherness; his line emerges from or expands into the chorus. The distinction between one and many is fluid. At moments, the chorus cover their mouths with their hands and pitch is notated graphically; we seem to hear distant masses. The virtuoso and emotional soprano extravagances of the earlier work are replaced by a more distanced perspective, a more fluid boundary between male and female voices. Pairs of soprano and alto soloists carry the words of Io. Behind them, female voices of the chorus burst into whoops and cries, their hands now used as moving megaphones. As the whole chorus joins the solo tenor, the roles seem to fuse. Since his first encounters with the poetry of Pavese, for Nono the encounter of man and woman has been a turning point in consciousness, whether personal or political. Constantly changing electronic transposition of the vocal ensembles enhances the sense that the individual personages are embodied in the many, that identity is a dynamic property not limited to a single being – a long-standing trope in Nono's music.[72] Rapid spatialisation creates uncertainty as to their very locus. The distribution of phonemes between voices, reaching back still further into Nono's past, increases the impression of mobile distributedness.

The sonic perspective is transformed. In general, the interventions from subgroups of all four orchestras begin and end together, and consist of only two internal rhythmic voices. This produces polyphony rather than movement, very different from the complex delays and multiple rhythmic subdivisions of the previous movements. Each intervention has its own colour: choirs of muted brass, muted trombones with cellos sul tasto, violas and bassoons, flutes and violins. These properties give unity and autonomy to the interventions. Electronic movement of the soloists remains, but the larger surrounding body – the orchestral groups – seems to stand still, to listen as one, to focus attention on the protagonists. The number of such interventions was reduced in the 1985 version, enhancing this concentration. Five massive, single *Manfred* orchestral attacks are spaced almost equally across the movement as three markers, like a tempo, a passage of time, beyond human perception. The first two remind us of an additional presence whose identity becomes clear in the last triple intervention as Io sings of 'Cronus, the jealous God'. At the *Manfred* tempo of 152, the three syncopations of that urgent moment are each magnified differently: the first rapidly echoed between two pairs of orchestras, the second in rhythmic unison from only half the groups (4 and 2), the last a double attack in which two groups (4 and 3) are then joined by the others, crescendo to *sffff*. Cronus is a living, moving presence.

The string trio again generates a unified sound, but now discontinuous and high – the negative of its previous role. Their sustained high harmonics with additional inharmonic content (*sul tasto*, *al ponte* or *crini & legno*) create a harmonic penumbra. Electronic detuning and the alternation of reverberated and non-reverberated sound create a constant ambiguity: a continuous sonic presence at the edge of conscious perception. At several points the solo string trio contributes to the incipient pitch content of the woodwind soloists – at the edges of hearing in terms of frequency and volume, blurred by long delays and resonated by filtering. After Io's final words, their sound comes into focus on a high B against the bass flute F♯ – the horizon of *Prometeo*, but now inverted.

Hölderlin sets the text of section VI of *Io, frammento*: Cacciari's adaptation of the last stanza of the poet's *Hyperions Schicksalslied*, his lament for humanity's separation from the gods, together with words from Pindar's *Nemean Odes* describing the fate of the 'fratelli infelici'. This is the moment of Achilles from Nono's early plans, the end of utopia; it is Achilles who should fulfil Prometheus' prophecy. Cacciari's initial explanation is helpful in understanding this crucial dramatic nexus and the relevance of Hölderlin:

A tragedy of listening

He [Achilles] – as only Hölderlin understood – uniquely among the Homeric heroes – not 'fraudulent' like Ulysses, like Prometheus, not violent like Menoetius, like Ajax, not greedy like Agamemnon – is the impossible utopia of the most originary and 'hidden' mythical-tragic Greek thought.

Thus, Prometheus does NOT 'rebel'.

He prophesises. Utopia is reduced, hidden, postponed. Zeus governs – no longer unformed – no longer a 'young' power – but 'well-founded'. But this is realised only in the <u>reconciliation</u> with Prometheus-Ulysses. [. . .] Ulysses is 'home'. But 'home' is reached only because he has revealed to Zeus the secret of Gaia–Themis. The world of thought originates in this death of the utopian myth, preserved as mere memory in the figure of Achilles.

Thus begins the work and days of mortals.[73]

Hölderlin is a sustained four-part invention for two solo sopranos, the two woodwind soloists and the two speakers – the most continuous passage to this point in *Prometeo*. The woodwind now play clear pitches despite changes of timbre, multiphonics and breath noise. Within the continuous sound, dynamics are in constant motion and articulation is exaggerated by proximity to the microphone. With long delays, the voices circle the space in opposite directions at different speeds; there is movement, but no escape. Bass flute and contrabass clarinet modulate each other's sounds by means of a vocoder, resynthesising them according to the other's timbral characteristics. The total sound cannot be disaggregated, but its continuous evolution has the inevitability of unending directionality: 'the suffering fall blindly like water from cliff to cliff', in Hölderlin's poem.

The two sopranos recall *Io, frammento*. There is ambiguity as to their separate identities; their relationship moves between near-canon, heterophony and a single line diverging through parallel possible paths. The opening section outlines precisely the initial pitch space of *Das atmende Klarsein*; the first 72 bars of the soprano duet are adapted directly from *Io, frammento*. It continues with a long descent, the aggregate soprano line taking over a minute to pass through two octaves. Perhaps this is a reference to Brahms' setting of the same text, as Lydia Jeschke has suggested; Cacciari mentions the work in an essay from this time.[74] The various versions of Brahms' long descending phrase 'ins Ungewissene hinab' ('down into the unknown') hint at the scala enigmatica. As the voices turn around 'Blindlings wie Wasser von Klippe zu Klippe' at full volume, the woodwind produce an expanding and contracting pattern of synchronised or alternating crescendos and decrescendos, an inexhaustible breathing.

The second part of *Hölderin* marks a moment of bifurcation. The sopranos commence a new, micro-tonally inflected line with a text from Pindar's *Nemean Odes*: 'one of man, one of god, race of god, unhappy brothers'. Bass flute and contrabass clarinet (its mouthpiece removed) return to the mouth sounds of *Io*: breath, throat and tongue. They trace a harsh, forceful polyphony of faster rising and falling patterns in which pitch is barely perceptible. Meanwhile, the speakers reprise Hölderin's text – the female voice reorders the words like a variable delay, a shifting canon – as if to make sure that its terrible words remain in consciousness. 'Fratelli infelici' ('unhappy brothers'), the sopranos' final words, come to rest on a tritone F–B – still in constant microtonal movement, but a point of arrival, while the woodwind complete their passage from clarity to decaying noise.

Dramatically and musically, *Prometeo* thus approaches a point of near stasis. For the first time, all spatial movement stops. *Stasimo 1°* was incorporated into *Isola 2°* in the 1985 version, perhaps to emphasise the structural role of the *Interludio* that follows and ensure the balance of the whole. It is the first choral commentary; in Greek drama the stasimon is a dramatically static

A tragedy of listening

chorus, performed from the orchestra. The chorus carries lines from Euripides' *Alcestis* – the last section of *Io, frammento* – on the inevitable, implacable rule of Ananke, the law above gods and men, equal to Gaia. This fragmented temporal mosaic stands in absolute contrast with the continuity of *Hölderin* and of the following *Interludio*. It is woven from three strands, cross-cut to produce a spezzato form characteristic of multi-choral Venetian music: text-carrying passages for singers and orchestras, quiet sustained orchestral moments marked 'ricordo lontanissimo' ('distant memory'), and loud *Manfred* interjections. Interspersed are four silent bars of increasing length (1", 3", 4", 7"), affording reflection.

There is no utopian dream; gods and men are subject to the same law. Cacciari described this pivotal acknowledgement in his initial text:

> Zeus knows, acknowledges the 'originary' law of Ananke – that which Gaia had revealed to Prometeo – and recognises <u>himself</u> within the limits imposed by that law. Man is also included – and he does <u>not</u> rebel. In Aeschylus, Prometheus stands in an indissoluble relationship with that originary law, much more powerful than Zeus.
>
> Man has fire. And with fire he can realise the works and the days. [. . .] These works and these days are <u>tragic</u> – because they have no 'hope': in Ananke they are inexorably in conflict. But the existence of Zeus is also <u>tragic</u>. He survived, tearing his secret from Prometheus – but at the cost that he too should acknowledge his conflict in Ananke.[75]

Textual architecture is clear and follows the tripartite structure of the ode. The three lines each of strophe and antistrophe are sung simultaneously, apart from their final rhymes 'la piega' and 'la placa'. The five words of the concluding epode are set separately, spaced evenly through the second half of the movement; the first three are preceded by *Manfred* interjections, the fourth and fifth by moments of 'ricordo lontanissimo'. The passages of text are marked 'sonar e cantar' –'play and sing' in Venetian. A reference to Gabrieli in the sketches makes the association clear.[76] All four orchestras play together; as they play, the instrumentalists sing the material for their group, quietly, distantly, perhaps into their instrument, at octave transpositions where necessary. This creates a vocal haze around the whole, further enhanced by slight electronic transposition; the stasimon emerges from the orchestra, as in Greek tradition. Each of these nine passages has a unique instrumental colour, with slight variations of orchestration between the orchestras to reinforce their spatial separation. The musical material is reordered from the entirely vocal final section of *Io, frammento*. The eight vocal parts of that movement are redistributed among voices and instruments. No more than four are sung at any given moment, producing a tighter, more clearly polyphonic vocal texture, with the other parts distributed among the particular instrumental combination. Soprano and alto soloists expand the number of voices, doubling lines or adding a retrograde. Inner echoes and mirrors add greater density, but nonetheless rhythmic clarity and slow tempo allow both polyphony and the aggregate text to be heard.[77] This movement has been the subject of intense analytical attention. That it is rooted in Nono's harmonic universe of fifths, semitones and microtonal expansion is clear. Melkert maps the derivation of passages from *Io, frammento*.[78] Jeschke shows the inner workings in detail and identifies its origins in the Gaia element of Nono's material.[79] Nielinger-Vakil goes further to trace the origins of all three strands of *Stasimo 1°* in sequences of fifths moving by tone and semitone, on the basis of the harmonic architecture of the previous work.[80]

The four instrumental 'ricordi lontanissimi' are sustained *ppppp* at registral extremes with microtonal inflection. The first is echoed after a reprise of the final words of the first three lines, most prominent of which is 'Orfeo' – man's strength and weakness is his inability not to look

A tragedy of listening

back. Memory is playing an increasingly active role, while the final *Manfred* interjections of *Prometeo* now begin to suggest a transformation of their force. These appear as two groups of three, mostly at the *Manfred* tempo of ♩ = 152. In the first, an assertive statement from orchestras 3 and 4 is preceded by a pre-echo from orchestra 1 and followed by a weaker, slower echo from orchestra 2, the three separated by choral passages. Such moments will be replaced by echoes and memories ('ricordi lontanissimi') for the remainder of *Prometeo*. Following a further 'cantar e sonar', two *sfff crescendo* statements – their fast syncopation shared differently between the orchestras to generate movement – are separated by the same chord, *piano*, at slower tempo.

Stasimo 1° marks the end of the ungraspable instant and the onset of the replacement of the present by memory; these are the arrows directed across the centre from either side in Nono's frieze (Figure 13.8a). Time moves forwards and backwards from the now of the text: 'Neither the voice of Orpheus, nor Thracian enchantment calms her, neither altar nor statue nor blood sacrifice bends her. She knows no shame; inaccessible, she holds the summit.'

'Interludio 1°'

This summit, the still now, is marked by *Interludio 1°*. The renouncing of utopia is balanced by the 'weak messianic power' of every instant. *Interludio 1°* maintains its position from Nono's early formal plans, and as befits the absent centre of the Corfu frieze, it is the quietest music in *Prometeo*: *pppppp*, 'at the limit of audibility'. According to Stenzl, he described it as the 'axis of the work, as the eye of a needle towards a "new Prometeo"'.[81] A motet for alto, flute, clarinet and tuba, it sets brief phrases from Cacciari's *Maestro del Gioco* IV and V, together with words from Euripedes' *Alcestis*: 'nothing [stronger] than Ananke I found'. As the keystone, these are now words of permanence – the strength and inevitability of Ananke. Cacciari's opening enjoinment – 'Do not lose it [. . .] this weak Messianic power' – is heard with studied, measured clarity. This is the only mention of the key concept from Benjamin's *Theses* – a direct obligation on the listener. Benjamin's idea is captured in the sonic metaphor from Cacciari's fourth poem: 'endures the echo [of] past silences'.

Flute and clarinet are instructed to play 'without overtones'. These are the pure sounds that Nono studied with the sonoscope at Freiburg, in the registers he noted.[82] The ensemble is that of *Omaggio a György Kurtág* and the *Machaut–Ockeghem–Josquin* precursor of *Risonanze erranti* – Nono's most intimate musical circle. In an article for the premiere, Nono describes how such performance requires extraordinary awareness of the instrument. In these registers – the lowest ranges of flute and B♭ clarinet, highest of the tuba – the three instruments together produce 'a spatial listening without a beginning and without a directional source.' The sense of a single resonant object is enhanced by the tight register within which the parts move: tuba and alto share almost the same space (7th F♯–F, 6th G–E), of which clarinet and flute slightly extend the limits, but both constrained to a fourth (E♭–A♭, C–F). In addition to its timbral purity, the music denies temporal gravity; it is a still central point. This contrasts with the noisiness of *Hölderlin* or the formal complexity of *Stasimo 1°*; it is the opposite pole to the 'maximum disquiet/maximum dynamicity' of *Prologo*.[83]

'Machaut – monovalori' appears on an early plan.[84] The carefully constrained strictness of early motets is in mind, as befits the rule of fate and necessity. The instrumental parts are constructed of separated, measured notes. Their lengths and those of the intervening rests are derived from the earlier *A veloce/B calmo* material by eliminating shorter values and redistributing the remainder between voices, a process randomised using Nono's torn paper technique – echoes of the past. *Interludio 1* is ludic in that the composer's actions follow rules, but also in that the context itself disallows any wider teleology. The 1985 version compressed Nono's initial tapestry slightly, to strengthen this crucial moment. While harmonically the four parts trace a path through the established pitch universe, the disconnectedness of their events focuses listening on each new move. For the soloists, the production of each note is physically critical, on the edge of non-production; listening becomes an empathetic action. The instrumental sounds move slowly around the space at different rates, their sounds echoed distantly, while each note of the alto is heard from a different loudspeaker, with some phasing and transposition. These words have no origin; they are timeless and universal.

'3 voci (a)'

3 voci (a) presents lines from VII, VIII, IX of Cacciari's *Maestro del Gioco*, set for soprano, alto and tenor soloists, the solo euphonium (with woodwind and glass interventions) and the four violins from each of the four orchestral groups, each violin with a separate part. In the score Nono is explicit: '3 different acoustic planes – not to be united'. Text fragments are arranged in a double permutation (IX VIII VII VIII IX VII) with a final repeat of the opening 'Ascolta' from IX.

The fragments of Maestro del Gioco, and hence of Benjamin's *Theses on history*, are a response to the situation reached in *Isola 2°*, the end of utopia; they are a development of the call to 'weak messianic power' of *Interludio 1°*. These words selected from Cacciari's texts are images of hope, but also of action: 'Listen. Seize this moment.' The singers move only by fourth or fifth, augmented fourth or semitone, except when joining another voice. Their clear intervals and carefully separated phonemes recall early polyphony. Even where distributed among the voices, the words are clear; their separation across time allows the images evoked to find form in the listener's mind. Certain entries are marked by the glasses, heavily amplified and transposed down, delayed and reverberated to ring through the movement.

Until the final 'Ascolta', the violins provide a continuous sonic halo, its density, shape and position slowly morphing but in high intervals at the edge of hearing; we sense a changing of acoustic, of atmospheric pressure, rather than harmony. A change of bow position from *tasto* to *ponte* marks the halfway point and subtly moves the listener into a new acoustic space. It is also a characteristic Nono formal device: continuity set against binary symmetry. Following the opening soprano invocation, all three layers begin together from the same fifth E♭–B♭. The absolute unity, the law of Ananke, of *Interludio 1°* now proliferates into the parallel orbits of a multiverse, each with its own rhythm, its own trajectory through pitch space. The violins pursue a course of high fourths with additional harmonics adding tension and ambiguity. The descending sequence (on B♭, A, G♯, F) is reordered in the second half (A, G♯, F, B♭) to arrive where it began. New layers are added or subtracted in steps, some sounds sustained for nearly a minute.

The euphonium player constantly sings a fifth above the note played; the delayed sound is transposed down a fifth and fed back to produce a further transposition. Two voices of delay move around the space in opposite directions. Thus, an enormous, all-encompassing universe of fifths accumulates incrementally as the euphonium pursues its inexorable journey. Its rise and receding about the central point provide the clearest architecture of *3 voci (a)*. The impenetrable wall of sound, of noise, that develops represents a Höhepunkt of *Prometeo* in terms of sustained volume and saturation; in rehearsals, Haller heard a Dies Irae.[85] Benjamin's words are not to be ignored. The notated euphonium part also moves through patterns of accumulated fifths, shifting chromatically to cover the entire space. Their root moves by step down to B♭ at the centre of the movement – the B♭–F that has been pulling against a B–F♯ axis from the beginning – to return almost symmetrically. The euphonium follows a slow, regular breathing

A tragedy of listening

rhythm. The proportions of exhale (note) and inhale (rest) change gradually with the dramatic architecture of the movement: from 5:4 slow minims at the start, to 2:1 at the ·climactic moment and 1:3 at the end. It arrives finally at the B–F♯ horizon of *Prometeo*, echoing ever more distantly after the other actors have run their course – perhaps a ship continuing its journey across this ocean.

Moments of 'eco ricordo lontano' continue the pattern begun in *Stasimo 1°*. Bass flute and contrabass clarinet – breath, harmonics, unstable 'transition' sounds, fluttering – interrupt the progression of both singers and euphonium, but not the violins. The first separates 'a blink of an eye [. . .] an instant'. Such moments are pre-echoes of the more complex, sustained sounds that herald words from *Maestro del Gioco IX* as euphonium and violins begin their return journey: 'angels break in – sometimes – angels – crystal – of morning – purple wings beat'. They repeat their fluttering under the second 'angeli'. This is clearly Benjamin's *angelus novus*, the angel looking back at history but drawn towards the future, the angel that according to Cacciari's early texts is Prometeo. Hope is in every moment, every individual, but this requires constant awareness, constant action, constant listening.

'Isola 3° – 4° – 5°'

These three of Cacciari's islands are woven together to make a fabric very different from that of *Stasimo 1°*. Rather than the monumental, confining complexity of that movement, here we journey between the islands, recalling the map of Nono's early plan. Prometheus is unbound, has become the Wanderer. The *Isole* fall upon each other with wave-like regularity. Eight instances of *Isola 4°*, nine of *Isola 5°*, and ten of *Isola 3°* are further interspersed with seven passages of 'eco lontano' from *Prologo*. Nono selects from an enormous body of text, so let us hazard a gross reduction. In *Isola 3°*, Prometeo echoes the words of Mitologia: that he should return to Athens with his fire, to make 'festival and tragedy' with Zeus. 'i nomi' ('the names') give Prometeo advice for his journey home across the sea in *Isola 4°*. In *Isola 5°*, Mitologia and Prometeo consider the miracle that is the law above justice and injustice. Scored for vocal soloists, the wind and string trios and orchestras, the three islands are clearly distinguished, but there is a degree of sonic commonality not present in *Stasimo 1°*. In particular, the three wind soloists participate in all three, albeit in very different ways.

The most continuous vocal thread selects from the three parallel texts of 'the names' in *Isola 4°*: words from Sophocles, Hölderlin, Schönberg and Hesiod set for all four female vocal soloists and tenor. The eight passages are built from sixteen fragments. Each is an example of Nono's technique of folding and filtering materials to produce a polyphony of variable density, a single sound object with an envelope that might grow from one to many real internal voices. Two further layers add to the sense of multiplicity. Solo instruments, particularly the wind, echo the voices in irregular, halting quasi-canon or mirror, each note crescendo or diminuendo such that its origin or direction is ambiguous. Other instrumental soloists follow graphical directions to breathe into microphones. By means of electronic gates, their sound is used to control the spatialisation of the singers, whose voices are thus in constant movement; the words are swept along by breath. The whole sets out from a call to Prometeo – 'at the end is your journey' – which marks out an inversion of Nono's interval shape 'T' (G D C♯ G♯, descending) with both canon and mirror. Musical and textual networks sometimes come into alignment at salient moments. 'The voice of god calls you/where the blue sky opens' (bars 55–7) develops through a crescendo to an F♯ major triad, resolving to a bare fifth A–E. With reference to the 'bora' – the terrible wind of the Adriatic – bass flute and alto trombone have their longest notes with continuous extreme changes of dynamic (bars 76–86). Uniquely, at 'your words/in its silence' (bars 119–21), there is no accompanying breath, no movement. In the simplest fragment – 'tell the angel of the accumulation of memories' (bars 204–12) – the second solo soprano adds a high, rising major sixth on 'il cumulo' to what is otherwise a soprano monody. The only break in the otherwise seamless vocal texture comes at 'wait' (bars 235–47).

In the first version, words from *Isola 5°* were set to a polyphony of pitched speech from the chorus. This was removed in 1985 to leave just the layer of piccolo, high E♭ clarinet and tuba or alto trombone. Sparse, high, unpredictable woodwind multiphonics, close to the microphone, are heard above tuba multiphonics produced with the voice – not the steady fifths of *3 voci (a)* but a moving line producing constant changes of overtone. These are the slightest of sounds, but produced with great effort, their emergence marking the silence that surrounds them. *Isola 5°* punctuates the other two islands with voids, spaces for the unsayable to sound: 'the truth of the blue silence'. 'Miracolo' – the regular refrain of the absent text – is Nono's initial description.[86]

The silence and emptiness of *Isola 5°* stand in absolute contrast to the continuous, all-enveloping sound and developing fullness of *Isola 3°* – two images of the same truth. 'CENTRALE – TUTTO CAMBIA' ('central – everything changes') writes Nono as he begins work.[87] *Isola 3°* announces itself with a sudden change in acoustic environment: a homophonic vocal entry, the four voices echoed by wind and viola, framed by sustained Cs, *pppp*, moving slowly between the violins and trombones of the four orchestras. At the top and bottom of clear pitch discernment, they constitute a bounding sonic presence. Through this first entry, 'Prometeo' is set to a mirror, like a cantus firmus from which the other voices expand with his words and with those of Mitologia: 'now return/at the end is my journey' (Figure 13.11). *Isola 3°* returns in a regular pattern like a series of pillars. Each time, an additional pitch is added to the orchestral backdrop such that it begins to compete with the voices and soloists for the foreground. Pitch space is filled incrementally, in symmetrical steps; the distant initial Cs expand registrally and chromatically. Once added, voicing and orchestration remain unchanged such that a dense wall of sound accumulates over the ten instances. In contrast to the other islands, this is a clear direction; Prometeo's resolve consolidates to become absolute. Against this evolving plane, textures of voices and echoing instruments are based around simple materials – generally, no more than one or two real parts. The surrounding trombone bass recalls Gabrieli, but Nono was also studying the giant motets of Striggio and Tallis. The text is the most linear, taken from a single source: Sophocles' *Oedipus at Colonus*. As it unfolds, we hear the abstract, non-figured orchestral presence as the gradual consolidation of Prometeo's vision of his future: 'on the sea my rudder will be a thousand blue sails/here you will say from an altar with Zeus/festival and tragedy/and no god will be able to take this fire from me'. The movement ends with the quiet, slowly turning saturation of chromatic space.

The accumulation of the past – the view of Benjamin's Angelus Novus – is present as moments of 'eco lontano' ('distant echo'): fragments from the *Prologo*, their edges torn or

Figure 13.11 Isola 3° – 4° – 5°: alto soloists, bars 36–41

A tragedy of listening

blurred by the orchestras, are remembered wordlessly by the coro lontanissimo. The first, third and last recall *pppppp* the absent words 'non vibra qui ancora un soffio dell'aria che respirava il passato' ('does a breath of air that breathed the past not still resonate here'). In between, the others rise in agitation to the *sfff* 'quasi grido' (almost screaming') of the fifth – a reminder of the constant presence of the terrible power of the past.

In their constant return, the three islands mark the infinity of the sea across which Prometeo must journey, the uncharted wasteland in which there is only Ananke – the law – and in which we are forever drawn into the future, while having agency only in the moment and seeing the accumulation of the past. The various textual sources find common resonance in images of sea, blue sky, wasteland. Nielinger-Vakil's essay finds their poetic–philosophical roots in Hölderlin via Heidegger and Cacciari.[88] As Nono pointed out, performers and listeners are united in Piano's arc, a 'ship of fools', wandering the ocean – not gods, but without fear and free to think.[89] 'The world of thought has its origins in the death of the utopian myth', states Cacciari's initial *Polemica*.[90] 'You are invincible in the wasteland of the sea', *Isola 4°* concludes.

'3 voci (b)'

Nono worked on the (a) and (b) parts of *3 voci* together. As so often with Nono's binary constructions, they share certain planes and co-exist orthogonally on others. Following the journey of *Isola 3° – 4° – 5°*, the three last movements together constitute the 'esode', the exodus of Nono's early plan, although this architectural clarity only emerges with the 1985 version. Chorus, orchestra and soloists make their statements in turn, a compound picture of the transformative power of the weak messianic force in every moment, of the emergence of clarity from nothingness.

3 voci (b), for chorus alone, presents X, XI, and XII of Cacciari's *Maestro del Gioco* texts. It cycles up and down between them, framed by 'Ascolta' at the beginning and 'Ascoltali' ('listen to them') thrice at the end – the ritual form established in *3 voci (a)*. Shorter and simpler than its predecessor, the twenty-four one- to six-bar fragments of *3 voci (b)* step through a tempo range of 30, 60 and 120. Dynamics are likewise discontinuous and change with tempo: *ppp*, *p* and *fff* respectively. The short fragments all consist of rhythmic figures from a similar range of values, producing an effect of shifting through rates of time and distance enhanced by the different spatialisation of the three strands: still but distant, slowly moving, and randomly crisscrossing at speed. This is a sequence of moments, of instants, of events, of 'secret breaths', as the texts describe. Some are almost brutal in their intensity, others of absolute stillness. The three poems speak with the same voice: an instruction to listen, a celebration of the weak power given to us, of the moment, of the silence. They are united in their chorality, their humanity – 'puro – Josquin', Nono remarks – but also structurally, their origin as a single continuous monody.[91] This idea is clear in an early sketch headed 'Motetto a1: 3 testi / 3 spazi'.[92] Each fragment has its own global shape and inner architecture; 'attento – eki', Nono notes. Among the echoes, palindromes, canons and mirrors, moments of homophony stand out: 'Ascolta quest'attimo' ('listen to this moment'), *fff*, followed by 'una debole forza' ('a weak force'), *ppp*, in which the voices expand from each other one by one. Likewise, a bare sustained octave, *ppp*, framed by silence – the only unit with no text – follows the polyphonic 'un'opera dal movimento delle opere' ('a work out of the movement of works).' *Prometeo* refers to itself.

Individual fragments remain within a pitch set of fifths with adjacent semitones generating further fifths. In preparation for *Interludio 2°*, harmonic and melodic tensions are brought together; there is ambiguity between the additional semitone as a 'structural' interval and the tendency of the core intervallic unit here – the fifth – to wander chromatically or to dissolve

A tragedy of listening

microtonally, as it will do in the following movement. Nono constructs a sequence of patterns of 3 to 5 notes using tritone T, fourth/fifth, tone and semitone.[93] This is both what Nielinger-Vakil describes as the harmonic 'monad' of *Prometeo* and the key to navigating an entire pitch universe. Each pattern is matched with a retrograde.[94] He reorders these pitch sets and from them constructs a line marked 'monodia'.[95] The four voices proliferate from this monody, sustaining or repeating pitches such that each fragment outlines a single set. The original relationships remain clear: the opening set C♯ G♯ F♯ C (bars 1–4) is mirrored as G D C F♯ (bars 10–14). Nono then recomposes the whole, adjusting text and texture and adapting its inner workings to the work's broader architecture. This is clear in the last three fragments – one of each strand. At 'questa debole forza' (bars 76–81), the pitch set changes at the last word to the Promethean shape of two-fifths a semitone apart – C♯ D G♯ A – maintained through the following 'ascoltali'. This is echoed a tone lower in the final fragment, establishing the *Prometeo* B–F♯ horizon and preparing its C–G complement for the start of the following *Interludio 2°*.

'Interludio 2°'

Interludio 2°, added for the 1985 production, builds an environment for the following *Stasimo 2°* in its new role as the last movement. Sonically, spatially, musically and metaphorically it prepares the ground. Indeed, it is the most programmatic moment of *Prometeo*; it is difficult to describe this movement except in terms of the infinite, sparse desert/ocean/mountain range that is the work's landscape. This is the space in which the soloists will find strength for their wandering in the final *Stasimo*. It is marked out by only the low instruments from all four orchestral groups (cello, double bass, bassoon, horn, trombone), punctuated by tolling from the solo glasses transposed electronically. In the five minutes of *Interludio 2°* Nono uses only a low fourth G–C, the twenty available voices smearing the two notes microtonally by up to a tone in either direction. In the rocking of their blurred edges, these eighteen possible pitches afford the brief, emergent occurring of the other fundamental intervals of *Prometeo*: semitone, tone, augmented fourth, fifth.

Waves of energy shift this minimal sound in pitch, time, dynamics, articulation or space. Its detailed inner canons and mirrors produce ripples of movement and interference patterns, just as the effects of wind across water or sand are modulated by invisible forms below. These waves move through a scale of eight tempi, from ♩ = 30 to 72. The deep fundamental pitches are such that the ear registers changes in modulation, beating or spectrum rather than notes. There is no figure, no 'word' textually or musically. Perhaps this is an echo of Moses' final lines in the completed part of Schönberg's opera: 'Unrepresentable God! Inexpressible, many-sided thought! [. . .] Oh word, thou word, that I lack!' The 51 bars of the movement are made up of two equal parts. In each, a more complex pattern of breaking waves is followed by two that successively lose mass and energy to find calm, these larger waves separated by silences. The central moment is thus marked by the densest, strongest and most unified wave, followed by its diminishing after-echoes. The phasing of attacks of the three glasses – transposed down and heavily reverberated – likewise comes into alignment as equilibrium is found, and finally they strike twice together. There is no mistaking the reference here: this is a Venetian sound of bells heard across a wide canal, reflecting from distant buildings, only the lowest frequencies penetrating the fog such that it becomes impossible to place their source.

Sonically, *Interludio 2°* is perhaps the most quietly radical moment of *Prometeo*. Technically, it is unexceptional in the context of Nono's practice, and yet there are resonances of the listening experiments of Pauline Oliveros, Maryanne Amacher or even La Monte Young, of the mobile sounds imagined by Vicentino in the sixteenth century and of recent generative art.

A tragedy of listening

'Stasimo 2°'

It had long been Nono's intention that *Prometeo* should end with a version of *Das atmende Klarsein*, in many ways the musical seed of the entire project. This idea was abandoned during rehearsals in Venice. As if the new form had finally detached itself from its origins, Nono decided that *Stasimo 2°* was its natural ending. However integral to the conception of *Prometeo*, to continue with the earlier work would have been both to suggest an inappropriate resolution and to open new questions. *Stasimo 2°* remained in its initial version from 1984. Written just for the ensembles of soloists – five singers, three wind and three strings – the second stasimon is, like the first, marked 'a sonar e a cantar'. On this occasion, these words read more as a description than an instruction. Instruments and voices move through the same pitch space with the same slow rhythmic motion; the wider compass of the instruments and brief moments of string articulation form a timbral halo around the text-carrying voices. The processed sound of long reverberation is static, heard from the highest and farthest loudspeakers. Of all the elements of Cacciari's text, Nono gives *Stasimo 2°* the most complete and continuous setting. There is no overlapping or compression of words, as if these must be understood with absolute clarity: the many names of the law have but one form.

A sequence of nineteen pitch sets of between two and five elements follows the harmonic orbit of *Das atmende Klarsein*.[96] The very stability of this sequence allows us to see a simple logic at its core: fifths are balanced either side of a central augmented fourth (F–B, plus B♭, F♯). Within the inner symbolism of *Prometeo*, the superimposition of the two-fifths might be seen as the co-existence of Gaia and the techne of man. Elements of this sequence are replaced or added by the two forces inherent in this structure, fifths and semitones. Internal voice-leading arises from subsets of these pitch groups, which Nono reorders to create clearly distinguished shapes – a combination of his polyphonic weaving and folding, and the sound shapes of his early choral works. There is generally some continuity between successive pitch sets, which he disrupts by changing the sequence. At 'divisio' ('division, bar 13), for example, he jumps from the second to the last set, to work his way back from this disjuncture. Only the tenth (twelfth of his original order) contains no fifth, used at 'apre molteplici vie' ('opens multiple paths'); its two augmented fourths (D–G♯, B♭–E) could go in many directions. Delays add to the polyphony from this point, but also bring memory into the argument. For each pitch set he plans a series of between three and nine different voicings, distributed among the three core ensembles, always *pppppp*. Some are homogeneous and tightly compressed in pitch, others use timbral difference to mark wide distances across five octaves from the depths of the bass tuba to a soprano high F. Several of the pitch sets are diatonic; he carefully avoids voice-leading that might imply tonal sixth or seventh chords. Each sound lasts from one to seven whole beats at a tempo fluctuating around ♩ = 46, their starts offset by 0–3 semiquavers. These sounds – one for each phoneme of the text – are generally either separated by rests or move between ensembles, such that the occasional moments of melodic continuity emerge with considerable expressive power: 'è il trasgredire il rifondare è l'abbattere' ('it is the transgressing, the refounding, the tearing down', bars 33–44) reminds us powerfully of the political implications of *Prometeo*.

Once a strong architecture and the parameters of the musical language are decided, Nono becomes a madrigalist when working on vocal detail. Vocal phonemes are often coloured instrumentally. 'ri-cor-da' at bars 88–9 becomes a mirror, a memory, in miniature. Its opening 'r' is accompanied by strings *sul ponte*, the long vowel by the wind and the final plosive by strings *battuto legno-crini*. 'Silenzi', the only moment for voices alone, is carried by a three repetitions of a single chord, the last *quasi bocca chiusa*, and each followed by an incrementally lengthening silence. From 'apre molteplici vie' to the end, at least two of the four-note root

A tragedy of listening

set are present, and often more. The balance rotates between three stable axes: B♭–F, F–B or B–F♯. The final reference to Ananke, the law – the uncomposed last words of Schönberg's *Moses und Aron*: 'è nel deserto invincibile' ('it is invincible in the wasteland') – echoes to the remaining fifth B–F♯, the horizon of *Prometeo*. The preceding lines could refer to *Prometeo* itself: 'it opens multiple paths/it urges us to reawaken that which is broken/to renew silences/it transforms and recalls/it flashes'.

In Cacciari's 1985 *Icone della Legge*, contemporary with the revisions of *Prometeo*, *La Bocca di Mose (The Mouth of Moses)* is a meditation on the Moses of Freud and of Schönberg; Cacciari thanks Nono for his hand 'in this chapter, the book and all the rest.' The silence he describes in his conclusion is that of Nono (quite different from that of Cage, as Nono had observed):

> The word which is missing is the name, that sound – missing is the word capable of expressing the silence without betraying it, to express the silence as silence, to hear the inaudible, to hear it truly in as much as it is truly inaudible.[97]

Notes

1 Cacciari, 2002, pp. 24–5.
2 Cacciari, 2002, p. 24.
3 'Del mito, del simbolo e d'altro'. Pavese, 1990, pp. 315–22.
4 Jeschke, 1997, pp. 52–60, surveys the textual sources, reprinting *Polemica B* at pp. 278–86. Comisso, 2008, sets out the sequence of their development, from the sketches. Cacciari, 1984a, is his contemporary statement on *Prometeo*. Such ideas are explored further in Cacciari, 2001 (first published in 1990), which develops his concept of 'negative thought' through various aspects of Greek tragedy. A meditation on Aeschylus' Prometheus in dialogue form (pp. 359–80) may echo some of his conversation with Nono, to whom Cacciari dedicates a note in his second edition. Cacciari's more recent views are found in Cisternino, 2002, an interview from 1992, and Cacciari, 2002.
5 This differs from Comisso's (2008) articulation of the evolution of the text of *Prometeo*.
6 Marx, 2008, p. 15 (1841).
7 Jeschke, 1997, p. 286.
8 Interview with Renato Garavaglia, 1979–80. LNII, p. 245.
9 ALN 51.02.04.
10 ALN 51.02.05.
11 ALN 51.03.03.
12 ALN 51.03.07/03.
13 ALN 51.04.01.
14 ALN 51.38.02/14v.
15 ALN 51.04.02.
16 ALN ALN 51.04.05/01.
17 ALN 51.14.04/01.
18 ALN 51.17.01/10.
19 ALN 51.05.01–04, 51.06.01–04.
20 Cacciari, 1976, p. 113.
21 ALN 51.16.02/23.
22 The extensive formal plans in (ALN 51.14.03) contain references to Zuccheri, the percussionists of La Scala and the technology of *Con Luigi Dallapiccola*.
23 Cacciari in Cisternino, 2002, p. 26.
24 Interview with Renato Garavaglia, 1979–80. LNII, p. 245.
25 Cacciari in Cisternino, 2002, p. 24.
26 Benjamin, 1973.
27 Benjamin, 1973, p. 246.
28 For a full and clear discussion, see Benjamin, 2005, pp. 40–5.
29 Benjamin, 1973, p. 255.

A tragedy of listening

30 See, for example, the very opening of the book Cacciari was working on during the last stage of preparation of *Prometeo: Icone della Legge* (Cacciari, 1985, p. 13).

31 Letter from Cacciari to Nono, 19 August 1980, in Impett, 2004, p. 32.

32 Cacciari, 1984a, p. 20.

33 Klee, 1968.

34 Johann Wolfgang von Goethe, *Zur Farbenlehre*, 1810. Philipp Otto Runge, *Farben-Kugel*, 1810. Wassily Kandinsky, *Über das Geistige in der Kunst*, 1911. Johannes Itten, *Kunst der Farbe*, 1961.

35 ALN 51.17.01/01v.

36 ALN 51.21.02/04.

37 'Ascoltare le pietre bianche'. I suoni della politica e degli oggetti muti. Interview with Franco Miracco, 1983. LNII, p. 295.

38 Piano, 1984, p. 55.

39 'Verso *Prometeo*', 1984. LNII, pp. 349–51.

40 Letter to Abbado and Piano, 6 December 1983, ALN. The later part, quoted here, is reproduced in Cecchetto and Mastinu, 2005, pp. 102–3.

41 Piano, 1984, p. 55.

42 Piano, 1984, p. 60.

43 Piano 1984, p. 58.

44 Piano, 1984, p. 59.

45 Haller, 1995, p. 162.

46 Cacciari, letter to Nono, 4 July 1984, reproduced in Cecchetto and Mastinu, 2005, pp. 104–5. Some Vedova sketches are reproduced in Vedova, 2005.

47 Haller, 1995, p. 164.

48 Müller, 1982, p. 39.

49 Heiner Müller, letter to Erich Wonder, 1985, in Müller, 1990, p. 225. During preparations for a production of *Prometeo* in Frankfurt in August 1987, Nono would hear Müller's own *Die Befreiung des Prometheus*, with music by Beethoven and Rihm.

50 Driesen, 2011.

51 Available at: www.ricordi.com/en-US/News/2017/05/Prometeo-Richard-new-edition.aspx (accessed 1 October 2017).

52 Nuria Schoenberg-Nono interviewed in *Corriere della Sera*, 26 May 2017.

53 The 'listening score' accompanying the col legno CD release of *Prometeo* is invaluable in grasping its form and texts.

54 ALN 51.14.04/01.

55 ALN 51.17.05, 51.17.06, 51.17.07.

56 ALN 51.17.08.

57 From a sketch reproduced as the inside back cover of Cacciari, 1984.

58 ALN 51.09.02/18.

59 Interview with Renato Garavaglia, 1980. LNII, p. 245.

60 'Verso *Prometeo*', 1984. LNII, p. 349.

61 ALN 51.17.01/01v.

62 Melkert, 2001, pp. 122–5.

63 ALN 51.09.02/001.

64 ALN 51.09.04/007.

65 ALN 51.09.03/002 (detail).

66 ALN 51.17.01/06.

67 ALN 51.14.04/8–9.

68 Mast, 2008, p. 755.

69 Nielinger-Vakil, 2015, pp. 252–3.

70 Melkert, 2001, pp. 154–7.

71 A full concordance of the reuse of material is given in Melkert, 2001, pp. 160–78.

72 Alvise Vidolin describes the technique in Doati, 1993, p. 45.

73 Cacciari, *Polemica A*. ALN 51.02.02/03–04.

74 Jeschke, 1997, 218.

75 Cacciari, *Polemica A*. ALN 51.02.02/04–05.

76 'Stasimo I alla Gabrieli a cantar e sonar'. ALN 51.33/01.

77 Jeschke, 1997, 119–123.

A tragedy of listening

78 Melkert, 2001, pp. 173–182.
79 Jeschke, 1997, 107–116.
80 Nielinger-Vakil, 2015, pp. 274–277.
81 Stenzl, 1998, p. 111.
82 'Verso *Prometeo*'. LNI, pp. 393–394.
83 ALN 51.18.01/04.
84 Reproduced in Jeschke, 1997, p. 63.
85 Haller, 1995, p. 177.
86 ALN 51.28.01/03.
87 ALN 51.28.01/01.
88 Nielinger-Vakil, 2015, pp. 295–307.
89 Interview with Enzo Restagno, LNII, p. 525.
90 ALN 51.02.02/04.
91 ALN 51.56/05sx.
92 ALN 51.29/01.
93 ALN 51.56/01.
94 Nielinger-Vakil, 2015, p. 310.
95 ALN 51.56/03.
96 ALN 15.59/03rsx.
97 Cacciari, 1985, pp. 176–7.

14

RESONANCES

Echoes

The architecture of silence: 'A Carlo Scarpa, architetto, ai suoi infiniti possibili'

Two major architecture-mediated encounters inform Nono's development. If the second was the cultural–political debate centred on the Istituto Universitario di Architettura di Venezia through the 1970s, the first was his early friendship with Carlo Scarpa (1906–78), also a professor at the IUAV. Their relationship dated back to Nono's youth, when he would exchange the more formal atmosphere of his home for long evenings of lively discussion with artists and architects at Scarpa's apartment – effectively his second home at one stage.[1] As the young couple moved to Giudecca the friends saw less of each other, and once Scarpa had transferred to Asolo in 1962 they would not meet again. It was, however, through Scarpa that Nono encountered some key figures and ideas. Scarpa introduced him to Japanese art and architecture, to the balance of nature and modernism in the work of Frank Lloyd Wright, and to the Viennese modernism of Wagner, Hoffmann and Loos – central to the thought of Cacciari. Aspects of Scarpa's ethos would become fundamental to Nono's practice: the relationship with and intervention in history, and with that of Venice in particular; the crucial role of artisan skills in shaping materials, and the importance of recognising and respecting the nature of those materials. Especially characteristic of Scarpa's work is that the design of every detail is treated not only with the same attention, but with the same approaches as the architecture of form; both are developed through tireless iterations of sketches. Like Palladio before him, Scarpa was known for his care for materials and for his close working relationship with the craftsmen who formed them. Scarpa's early experience was designing for the Venini glass company; the diffusion of light and colour remained important to his work. Nono may have had this in mind when imagining the coloured light-diffusing glass for *Prometeo*. Like Nono, Scarpa was quintessentially Venetian and yet retained an outsider's radical stance with respect to his profession. Scarpa shared his multi-sensory enthusiasm for the spaces of his city. Their mutual interest is confirmed by a postcard of an auditorium he sent Nono from Japan in 1956, prophetic in terms of Nono's polychoral orchestral piece premiered in Tokyo thirty years later.[2]

Resonances

During the final months of preparation for the première of *Prometeo*, the Accademia in Venice presented a major exhibition of Scarpa's work. Prior to its opening in June 1984, Nono would doubtless have been party to discussions and to the renewed consensus as to Scarpa's importance; its curator, architectural historian Francesco Dal Co, was part of Nono and Cacciari's intellectual circle, and likewise from a well-established Venetian family. Nono must have recalled his early conversations with Scarpa as he took stock of the full range of his friend's work at the exhibition.

One of Hans Zender's first acts as the newly appointed Music Director at the Hamburg Opera was to commission an orchestral piece from Nono. Nono's response, *A Carlo Scarpa, architetto, ai suoi infiniti possibili*, was premiered by Zender with the Hamburg Philharmonisches Staatsorchester on 10 May 1985. It seems to have emerged remarkably complete and fully fledged in the context of his working practice through this period; indeed, it points directly towards his final orchestral work, written for Tokyo: *Non hay caminos, hay che caminar . . . Andrej Tarkovskij*. As with Scarpa's own designs, the surface simplicity of *A Carlo Scarpa* leads the subject to spaces of infinite detail and dimensionality – the infinite possibilities or possible infinities of Nono's title. Even the appellation *architetto* is rich in significance. Like Nono, Scarpa had little time for 'professional' qualifications; he did not hold the title 'Architetto' – he was usually addressed as 'Professore' – and this did, in fact, impact on the kind of commission Scarpa would receive.[3] *Architect* is thus a highly significant, respectful form of address.

After the complex responsibilities of the performances of *Prometeo* in late September 1984 and Nono's immediate return to the studio for revisions, the clarity of focus on *A Carlo Scarpa* must have been reinvigorating. He worked with some speed. The full outline of rhythmic material is dated November 21; by 13 December a fair draft was complete. A week later, Nono wrote to Zender that he was driving the score to Ricordi in Milan and outlined his subject:

> Carlo Scarpa is a Venetian architect genius [. . .] – a fascinating man – a great friend, especially when I was 18–25 – so often in his house where Signora Nini made me so welcome [. . .] some months ago there was a major exhibition at the Accademia – his drawings – plans – projects – built and not. simply a surprising discovery for everyone – and he just lived here (often without money) [. . .][4]

In the ten minutes of this work 'for microtonal orchestra', Nono uses only the two notes of Scarpa's initials: C and E♭ ('Es' in German: S). However, each of these may be varied by up to six-sixteenths of a tone upwards or seven down (C is lowered by up to ten), spanning nearly a tone in total. This conception of variable-breadth pitch is now finer-grained than the more static clusters of *Prometeo* – in the string interruptions to *Stasimo I*, for example, where quarter-tone differences enhance the impression of spatial distance. It recalls the frequency bands Nono imagined for his earliest experiments with technology in *Omaggio a Emilio Vedova*. Huber mentions Nono showing him a passage from Fritz Winckel's work on psychoacoustics – a book contemporaneous with *Omaggio* – that 'helped him in overcoming the problem of "unity"'.[5] This was shortly after Nono's earlier work with instrumental frequency bands in *Per Bastiana*. Winckel discusses the degrees to which microvariation of frequency contributes to the perception of unity of pitch across octaves, and how sounds mask or synthesise with each other. Nono's approach in *A Carlo Scarpa* now also reflects his recent experiences with live electronics, with the variable bandwidth, resonance and unpredictability of filters.

Appropriately, Nono begins with an entirely architectonic structure. He plans a rational pattern of sections – CCSS mirrored, CCS mirrored – cross-cut with two instances of CS to generate further internal mirrors (Figuren14.1a).[6] Their durations are to be 2, 3 or 4 times a

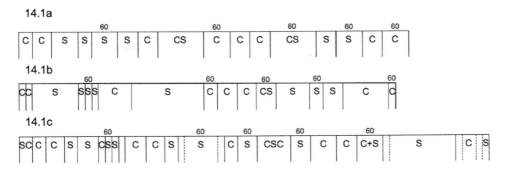

Figure 14.1 A Carlo Scarpa, architetto, ai suoi infiniti possibili: evolution of form (tempo ♩ = 30 except where noted)

basic modulus – a 3/4 bar in the first instance – with a multiplier of 7 for the CS sections. For each section he plots a different arrangement of registers, bar by bar, the octaves numbered 1–7; the two CS sections use the full spectrum. This gives him a clear picture of the frequency bands; often one group is stable in the centre while the other moves around it or veers to one or both extremes. He marks spectral rhymes between sections. Across the basic tempo of ♩ = 30, he lays an accelerating pattern of sections at ♩ = 60, occurring after 4, 3, 2, 1 and 1 passages at the slower tempo, and a further grid of measured pauses. He designs three possible rhythmic voices for each register, taken directly from the *B calmo* material used since *Con Luigi Dallapiccola*. On two pages of sketches, therefore, he determines the essential shape of *A Carlo Scarpa, architetto* – form and material are one.[7]

The artisan approach to shaping materials so important to Scarpa can be traced through the evolving morphology of Nono's score. A second plan amplifies the contrast between long and short sections and enhances a sense of formal development (Figure 14.1b).[8] The placement of double-tempo sections makes correspondences with the initial plan clear, and shows how in the final score (Figuren 14.1c), the last two of twenty-two sections become a coda. The opening and closing sections now constitute a symmetrical frame. The basic modulus becomes 4/4 and the multiplier of 7 is replaced by 5 (bars 26–30 and 37–41), avoiding excessive formal disjunction and making the coda more extraordinary. Bars 26–30 are framed by two empty bars, part of an additional grid of silences that also separate the pitches of the coda. Binary balance and symmetry abound. The second bar is rhythmically a near echo of the first. The two most percussive, rhythmically figural C sections at bars 17 and 20 are followed by the fully sustained S passages at 23 and 25. The central CSC section is framed symmetrically in terms of pitch and tempo, but the proportions of the surrounding C sections are different, modulated by other structural dynamics. The piece now comprises 71 bars. The final long pause – 'as if to continue to listen to presences, memories, colours, breaths' – constitutes a 72nd unit, an active, immanent event with no clear endpoint that reminds the listener of their participation in the remembering of Scarpa. He was 72 years of age when he died. Even this numerology is a tribute; Scarpa often based designs around the number of letters in his own name.

For each voice in each section, Nono constructs a unique rhythm from his remediated material. Taking the single bar as a unit, each rhythm is constructed of one-bar cells of one to four elements, in triplet, semiquaver or quintuplet subdivisions. These are arranged in different kinds of symmetry: mirrored, in augmentation or diminution, using altered subdivisions or by inverting positive and negative (note and rest). In the first full draft he reconsiders the uniform density: 'not always *a 3* – varied to the end'.[9] Even where not immediately perceptible, the

Resonances

internal symmetries reinforce the sense of autonomy of individual sections. In expanding his raw rhythmic material to the final form, Nono cuts, stretches and adds new mirrors as the timbral and emotional shape emerges. As in Scarpa's work, these signatures appear on every level. The distinction between detail and form is just one of perspective; there is no intermediate level.

The two notes are articulated in two ways: sustained (arco strings, flutes, clarinets and brass, timpani roll) and percussive (pizzicato and col legno battuto strings, staccato winds, tuned percussion and triangles). Just as the pitch focus of the two notes is dissolved to varying degrees, so the pitch clarity and noise content of the timbres of the two kinds of sound are constantly varied. Nono uses the sustained instruments in two ways: as 'fixed' and 'mobile' sounds. Fixed sounds are homogeneous groups of four instruments. To generate the constantly varying mobile sounds, he distributes the sustaining instruments through a 4×12 matrix, read in four directions. Harp, celesta, bells, triangles and timpani constitute a separate group from the first sketches. That the number twelve should still have a structuring role is indicative of how it had become an integral dimension of his thought at an early stage. Huber sees Fibonacci sequences in the overall architecture, the orchestration, the presence of triangles and *battuti* in different sections, and in the range of dynamics (8 values of *p* or less, 5 *mp* or greater, 13 in total).[10] Rather than a coherent formal system, these traces should perhaps also be seen as evidence of a mode of proportional thought developed through previously conscious processes. As with Nono's use of rhythmic proportions, such relationships are used to generate organic expansion and contraction without the arithmetic modularity of multiplication and division. The distribution of events between sustained and percussive sounds produces multiple layers of timbre from which rhythmic voices briefly emerge as they dynamically coalesce into coherent sequences: 'Remember Stasimo II – change timbre!!! quality, technique, dynamics'.[11] 'No percussion' at certain points suggests that their presence or otherwise has formal significance. Some sections emerge or retreat slowly to silence, the start or end of others is marked by unison percussive strikes. The lower, noisy, resonant percussive sounds recall the sound world that emerged with ..... *sofferte onde serene* ..., but now the association is different: 'The bells of Halde in the forest – low sounds'.[12]

Each section has its own pattern of microtonal expansion, often creating symmetries across the form as a whole. In bars 37–41, downward expansion descends beyond the semitone, as if to balance the upward interval of CSC. In two sections the *suoni fissi* state the central pitches with no such shading: 52–5 (C) and 56–66 (S), which surround the sole section in which the pitches appear simultaneously. In the final section, 67–71, the central pitches are entirely absent, while in each ensemble entry the sixteenth-tone shifts are symmetrically above and below. Elsewhere, microtonal deviation is balanced differently across octaves giving variable degrees of tension to the registral shape that emerges. Bars 17–19 and 20–2, for example, use the four lower octaves. In bar 23–4 only the lowest of these remains, to which the very highest is added, outlining the full range. Framed by the two bars of silence, bars 26–30 rise by step through all seven octaves, followed by a harsh restatement of the limits of pitch by piccolos and trombones in 32–22. A near symmetry is created as bars 34–6 move down through the registers *pppp*, to be arrested by *ff battuti* strings from the echo of which emerges the central CSC section (37–41), '*p possibile*, at the limit of audibility'.

The eleven bars that precede the final reverence appear not to derive from Nono's initial material. Instead, the hitherto repressed, disconnected rhythmic implications are allowed to develop their own logic. Played by the percussion alone above a sustained timpani E♭, this is the moment of clearest reference to the memorial role of the work, not unrelated to the fragmenting funeral march of the *Eroica*. It also has echoes of the music of Japan, perhaps a further personal resonance. Scarpa became increasingly fascinated with Japanese culture, and it was there that he died in an accident in 1978, so the reference may be quite explicit. The ritualistic sequences of pitch and percussion recall the slowly evolving music of Noh, with its formal counts of beats and silences, or perhaps, as Huber has suggested, the courtly music of Korea.[13]

The interference patterns of sections, silences, fermata, pitch change and percussive rhythm imply multiple flows of time: some static, some proceeding at different rates or in different directions. The listener is taken through a landscape of almost monumental blocks constructed of the juxtaposition of shards of different materials – 'nuclei', Huber calls them. Scarpa's designs are fragmented; the subject's attention is kept in continuous movement. Nono may have had in mind Scarpa's last and most personal project, the *Tomba Brion* (1969) in the Veneto plain. Likewise a monument, it is also a form of separate shapes and spaces. It takes inspiration from the temple complexes of Kyoto in its apparent lack of a centralised plan, its close relationship between built and natural. There is no single perspective; it is rather to be inhabited as the subject walks through its discontinuities of space and form. Space and time are articulated with absolute clarity, yet there is no reducible modularity, no hierarchy of large and smaller elements. Attention shifts continuously between fine detail and the architectonic – finding form in the former, detail in the latter. Flowing water is a further reminder that the experience of architecture is also dynamic, temporal. Like the forest recalled by Nono, the monument is surrounded by the sounds of nature in their richness and unpredictability; like the evolving patterns in wood, stone or metal beloved of Scarpa, those of Nono's 'nuclei' resist all formalising.[14]

Stefan Drees understands *A Carlo Scarpa* in terms of time frames beyond the scope of the work itself: biographical, composed (objective), performed (subjective) and the times of memory.[15] He reads a specific biographical narrative into the work's form.[16] A more general analogy is supported by Dal Co's observation that Scarpa's life was punctuated by silences 'which seem like acts of objection to the current banality of architectural "discourse"'.[17] Federico Goffi-Hamilton makes a related observation about the fragmentation, speed and direction of time in the works of both artists.[18] Nono would likely have been conscious of these parallels. Like Nono, Scarpa had a keen awareness of history; many of his projects were interventions in historical buildings or for museums. The role of memory is not a modernist construct; it is unavoidable as the subject negotiates a relationship with a work. This notion is explicitly fundamental to *Prometeo*, but underlies all Nono's later work. Histories are a continuous presence; the specious present is merely the centre of a broader perspective, like the central pitches of *A Carlo Scarpa*.[19] Writing about Scarpa for the 1984 exhibition, Dal Co gives a suggestion not only of the architect's work, but of conversations in which Nono must have participated, of their discourse, which touch directly upon important aspects of Nono's work at the time. Questions of history, memory, time, form and process are inextricably interwoven:

> For the most part the projects of Scarpa present themselves as precarious systems. Involuntary recall, which breaks in from memory and upsets the plan [. . .] points to evidence of a privileged relationship with experience, with the 'past'. [. . .]
>
> Scarpa's fragmentation is the conclusive expression of his dissatisfaction with habit. Habit becomes the sediment of the linear experience of time in practice, where the fragment is in dialogue with the moment and is the instantaneous extension of memory.[20]

'A Pierre: Dell'azzurro silenzio, inquietum'

Early in 1985 Nono was back in Freiburg reflecting on *Prometeo*, preparing a new version for the La Scala performances scheduled for September. The 60th birthday of Pierre Boulez was on 25 March, to be marked by a concert in nearby Baden Baden – home of both Boulez and the SWF – on 31 March. Perhaps Nono saw the invitation to contribute a piece as an opportunity to cement a friendship that, during the three decades since the dedication of *Canti per 13*, had been far from untroubled. His friends Fabbriciani and Scarponi were working with him in Freiburg, and he had a vast store of notated and recorded material that he had developed with them. *A Pierre: Dell'azzurro silenzio, inquietum* is therefore for contrabass flute, contrabass clarinet and Haller's live electronics. The two soloists reprise their duet roles from *Io-Prometeo*, although with the lower flute the two spectra are more fused and, counter-intuitively, more of its high partials come within the audible range of electronic processing.

As with *A Carlo Scarpa*, Nono worked quickly. His sketches first mention the piece in Freiburg on 15 January, while together with revisions to *Prometeo* he was developing ideas for a new work with Cacciari; *A Pierre* was finished in Venice on 20 February. There is again a close proximity between form and detail, although here the relationship is more occluded by the extended woodwind techniques and live electronics. The score is marked 'a più cori', and in his initial plans Nono added an amended version of his Gabrieli motto: 'cantar e sonanze – assonanze'.[21] Is he looking for assonances between his music and that of Boulez, or is this an idea for an internal structural principle? That Nono should announce the polychoral nature of one of his most intimate works is intriguing, however.

On the surface, the sound world of *A Pierre* could hardly be more different from that of Boulez; it seems to resist figure entirely. However, the constrained, intimate context draws the listener to attend to the inner complexities of the sounds. On the contrabass instruments, the constant, unstable, high-register mobility of pitch, timbre and rhythm produced by the extended techniques comes down into the frequency range of conscious listening. This generates movement that weaves itself into a choral texture to be delayed, transposed and spatialised by the electronics. Infinite levels of activity lie beyond the apparent stillness and slowness ($\quarternote$ = 30) – the 'infinite breaths–feelings–thoughts–tragedies' Nono ascribed to Boulez in talking of this piece.[22] A clue to his compositional approach is in another note: 'Several choirs in continual transformation by vocal formants – timbres – indeterminate spaces and some possibilities of transformation by live electronics.'[23]

Formants – the characteristic spectral peaks of a voice – were an important topic of research at IRCAM. Nono had been there with its director Boulez the previous November, in preparation for performances of *..... sofferte onde serene ...* and *Guai ai gelidi mostri* in March 1985. The term also has significance in Boulez's earlier compositional theory, as he explored paths beyond serialism.[24] Here it seems to point to the relationship between the extended techniques of the surface – harmonics, multiphonics, whistling 'aeolian' sounds, unstable over- and under-blown timbres that approach noise or silence – and a deeper structural skeleton. There is now a continuum between compositional technique and electroacoustic transformation. The flute and clarinet become real-time, acoustic filters, working through the harmonic potential of an underlying series of low fundamentals. Apart from a single *forte* moment of high whistling and overblown clusters, the entire work moves between *p* and *pppp*, focusing the attention of both performers and listeners on the slightest of physical actions. The framework is essentially a piece of two-part counterpoint. The upper part (contrabass flute) is largely in a spectrally harmonic relation to the lower (contrabass clarinet), such that their changing timbres fuse. This is especially evident where they are in a twelfth relation, the strongest partial of the clarinet, as in the very first and last dyads. Fifths and ninths dominate, with wide octave displacements. Sometimes the harmonic role of the contrabass clarinet is clear – for example, as it moves from C in bar 31 (anticipated by its twelfth in 30) through A♭, F#♯, F to its lowest B♭ in bars 49–51. At other moments it is aurally implicit – in bars 24–5 a low B♭ is suggested by high harmonics on the B♭ sounding length. Elsewhere it recedes further: instead of a sustained E♭

through the last four bars, the clarinet moves down through higher components of an E♭ harmonic series to rest on B♭, the twelfth. The live electronics generate downward transpositions of a tritone and minor seventh, producing a degree of harmonic separation; three bandpass filters act as additional formants on the delayed signals.

The upper rhythm is a permuted rhythmic diminution of the lower. Nono's sketches refer once again to Josquin's *Missa Di dadi*. In Josquin's Mass, the proportions represented by the dice printed by Petrucci above each section may be understood singly or doubly, and the number six has particular significance as the end of the game – the Sanctus, in that case. Here, Nono follows an analogous principle, perhaps as a pun on Boulez's earlier dodecacentricity. Values of one to thirteen beats are spread across the 60 bars which, as in the previous work, represent Boulez's age. Durations of 1, 2 and (mostly) 3 beats become rests. Those of 4, 5, 6 and 8 are given to the flute, those of 7 to both instruments, and – as befits a slower structural bass – the clarinet takes 10 and 13. The additional sounds of the various playing techniques are rhythmicised to generate subdivisions and additional voices, usually by contiguous values (e.g. 3, 4, 5). The 13-beat phrases of the clarinet always consist of 7+5 or 5+7, separated by a beat rest. The terminating number 12 is scrupulously avoided, but the whole texture is divided by pauses into twelve sections. The pauses follow a similar logic; with the final pause, the twelve of the manuscript score are made up of 3' of 2", 3' of 4"and 5' of 6".

In *A Pierre*, the live electronics and the physical instruments – long perforated tubes, far removed from 'normal' acoustic optimisation – are both ways of processing the breath of the performers. It could be heard as a vocal piece, but unvoiced, with no need of text. It is, above all, human; inner actions become surface. In his note on *A Pierre*, Nono refers to 'another "memoria" of visionary luminosity [. . .] of images from Elem Klimov's film *Farewell to Matyora* [. . .]'.[25] He had known Klimov, secretary of the Union of Soviet Filmmakers, since 1966. The imagery of Klimov's 1981 story of an island community threatened by a new hydroelectric project has much in common with that of Tarkovsky's later films: a tree, the surface of water, a burning house. In other respects, *A Pierre* is the complement of *A Carlo Scarpa*. Its intimacy balances the monumental nature of the previous work, and they are almost of the same length. As the twin pitches of *A Carlo Scarpa* tend constantly towards evaporation, so the underlying structure of *A Pierre* promises to condense into focus from each breath; both works maintain a dynamical, critical, unstable balance. The paradox of producing a highly prescriptive score for performers with whom he had such a close relationship must also have struck Nono. He takes a quite different approach in the series of solo *Post-prae-ludia* he would soon commence, and the detailed scores of the final violin works serve as material for the performer to render a more open architecture.

In a talk from the same months, Nono was explicit about the relationship of thought and music in his work: 'Music is not just composition. It's not artisan work, not a profession. Music is thought.'[26] Cacciari would later concur, from his own perspective: 'Music and philosophy follow the same principle of working, that of construction and deconstruction. They are both systems for arriving at a poetical structure.'[27]

'Risonanze erranti. Liederzyklus a Massimo Cacciari'

Musical precursors

The third work to emerge from the echo of *Prometeo* is perhaps its truest complement. *Risonanze erranti. Liederzyklus a Massimo Cacciari* found its final form two years later, in the performances of its third instantiation in Berlin and at the Paris *Festival d'Automne* dedicated to Nono in

Resonances

October 1987. Written for his closest associates – mezzo soprano (Susanne Otto), bass flute and piccolo (Fabbriciani), tuba (Schiaffini), five or six percussionists and the live electronics of Haller's Freiburg studio – the concepts embodied in *Risonanze erranti* were germinating during the final stages of work on *Prometeo*. Important components date from mid-January 1985, while he was in Freiburg working on revisions for the Milan production. These were busy weeks: as well as *Prometeo*, there were the performances in Paris and premieres of *A Carlo Scarpa* and *A Pierre* to rehearse. A new production of *Intolleranza 1960* – its fifth instantiation, and the third in German – was to be presented in Hamburg in February and March. Meanwhile, the live electronics and a score for *Omaggio a György Kurtág* also had to be prepared. *Risonanze erranti* would emerge from two projects that develop side by side through the early months of that year: an as yet textless piece for a Duisburg concert in May 1985 for mezzo soprano, flute/piccolo/contrabass flute, clarinet in C/contrabass clarinet and tuba/euphonium, and a song cycle dedicated to Cacciari for the same forces with the addition of double bass, intended for a commission for Cologne in December. In a sketch during the composition of *A Pierre* in January, he lists them separately as *Machaut–Ockeghem–Josquin* and *Liederzyklus*.[28] As they develop, each project informs the other until they become fused, a process catalysed by the poetry of Melville and Bachmann used in the final work. [29]

In both projects Nono returns to his founding musical experiences to explore his most recent thinking. Schubert and Schumann had figured importantly in his early work with Maderna,[30] and at least since the initial fragmentation of text in *Il canto sospeso* he had been guided by Schönberg's early views on the relationship between music and text.[31] A song cycle was a natural response to the networks of texts and ideas he had developed with Cacciari. Three cycles of four songs each were envisaged, woven into a single web ('broken between each other').[32] At its most Mahlerian point, the vision included alto and bass soloists, the obligato flute and tuba, and additional strings and wind. Only the first cycle evolved to have musical form. It was to use two texts from *Das atmende Klarsein* (*Atmendes* and *Dasein*) and two from *Prometeo* (*L'infranto* and *Inquietum*); Nono was also intending to revisit the poetry of Pavese and Quasimodo. The musical skeleton is worked out in full, a characteristic balance of mirror and increasing complexity.[33] The proper material of each song lasts 23 bars; in addition, five bars of the fourth are cut into the first, five each of the third and fourth into the second, ten each of the first two into the third and ten of the first three into the final song. These interruptions are to be 'broken further [. . .] many pauses [. . .] not whole.' Polyphony increases with structural complexity. *Atmendes – tuba & Susanna –* is an almost continuous monody with some marking of parallel transpositions. The central line of *Dasein – Susanna, tuba & flauto –* is more interrupted, and is accompanied by a more fragmented rhythmic counterpoint. The melos of both is built of augmented fourths and perfect fifths – the space of *Das atmende Klarsein* and *Prometeo*. The lines are constructed of overlapping internal mirrors and echoes, rhythmic and intervallic. The voices of the last two songs – in three and four parts respectively – are more equal and notated rhythmically. For *Inquietum*, he plans to use four crotales, to become a vital part of the sound world of *Risonanze erranti*. Only *Atmendes* is realised in full; the mezzo-soprano monody, with detailed notes as to the use of the microphone and sound processing, is heard within a soundscape of breaths, harmonics and ghostly echoes from all three wind instruments.

A draft of the *Machaut–Ockeghem–Josquin* piece was finished in Venice in May 1985 – material for the Duisberg performance that month, for alto, contrabass flute, contrabass clarinet and trombone.[34] On a title page, presumably added later, he names it *Risonanze erranti (vaganti)* – resonances not only wandering but also drifting. The three chansons of source material are rich with association for Nono, all dealing with loss and grief. He knew them from his earliest studies: Machaut's *Lay de plour*, Josquin's *Adieu mes amours* and again Ockeghem's *Malor me bat*

Resonances

– the last two both from Petrucci's *Odhecaton* that Nono and Maderna had worked on with Scherchen. He separates the melody from each into 23 fragments, the same number as the bar-length of each of the four songs of his incipient cycle.[35] Using the monody construction from *Guai ai gelidi mostri* he rearranges these – apparently by his casting-to-the-wind technique – into a single line, adding rests and fermata.[36] From this he builds a new four-voice motet, its 121 bars divided into 44 short sections. The texture is sparse, an exercise in minimal counterpoint recalling the fabric of its historical models. The sequence of fragments is compressed from the monody, but all are subject to a process of erasure, hocket and displacement. Notes are often replaced by rests – their negative – to reduce figure to its minimal recognisable form; distances are augmented. Rarely do more than two voices coincide, and any simultaneity is the product of echo, doubling or transposition. Vestigial imitation becomes transforming resonance. The fragments are disposed across alto, tenor and bass registers; transpositions are largely by fourth in the flute, major ninth in the clarinet. This rarely generates pitches beyond the diatonic scope of the original material. The rhythms are those of the originals, their constituent parts separated, redistributed or augmented, but not made more complex.

At the beginning of the year, Haller had introduced Nono to the newest addition to the Freiburg studio's armoury: the Publison *Infernal Machine*, now able to handle the crucial reverberation processes for the revised *Prometeo*. 'Music computer' Nono writes in his notes, 'SAMPLING'.[37] As well as being able to perform the processes with which he was acquainted – reverberation, transposition, delay – with greater precision and flexibility, the new Publison could record and process substantial samples in real time, a step change in live digital sound processing. The final work does not use this technique in its bald form, but the idea of sampling clearly informs Nono's thought as he constructs his score-based material. The *Machaut–Ockeghem–Josquin* score is not a first draft of *Risonanze erranti*, but a coherent resource of 44 sound samples to be mined and processed in the new work. Compositional process and digital sound processing are contiguous; Nono's thought can flow freely between them. Acoustic space and the spaces of time and memory are the structures through which the materials of *Risonanze erranti* flow, are transformed and experienced.

Poetic catalysis

In February 1985, back in Venice, Nono had begun to work through Herman Melville's 1866 collection *Battle Pieces and Aspects of the War* – reflections on the terrible cost of the American Civil War. Melville's formative influence on Pavese constitutes a further resonance.[38] Rhythm, word and phoneme count and internal resonances of sound and meaning inform Nono's reduction of the poems to a skeletal trace, but the words he selects echo the imagery of Pavese. He also returned to the poetry of Ingeborg Bachmann, whom he had known since 1953. Bachmann had visited the Nonos in their new home in 1956, and in 1958 she had asked Nono's advice on her essay *Musik und Gedichte*.[39] There she proposes a new relationship between music and poetry; as in her other criticism, Bachmann insists that in reinventing their language, artists must confront the moral and spiritual challenges of their time. Perhaps Nono had this essay in mind when selecting her last published poem, *Keine Delikatessen* from 1963, a questioning, doubting meditation on identity and the creative process. From the two literary sources he condenses fragments – rarely more than two contiguous words – that together constitute new semantic–phonetic networks, new textual entities that have resonance both in their original contexts and for Nono personally. In their abstraction from original reference, isolated word sequences become powerfully political in their new, intensely personal context – 'my country's ills', 'Pain [. . .] slave [. . .] pain [. . .] crime'.

Resonances

In his plan for the Cologne performance, initially scheduled for December 1985 but postponed to March 1986, Nono lists the elements of both projects under the new heading *Risonanze erranti*.[40] The new work is the product of the encounter between the two incomplete projects, fuelled by their latent musical energy. To find its shape, he sets out the new texts vertically, in parallel, separated by *Machaut–Ockeghem–Josquin*. Three of Melville's poems are represented in the final version: *Misgivings*, *The Conflict of Convictions* and *Apathy and Enthusiasm*. A single additional enjoinment from Melville's posthumous *Pontoosuce* – 'but look [. . .] hark' – recalls the 'Ascolta!' of *Prometeo*. Each of these three poem-traces is followed by a fragment of Bachmann's text, marked *Bachmann 1, 3* and *4* in the score. *Bachmann 2* is inserted into the second Melville poem, wordlessly so as not to interrupt; the voice is replaced by piccolo as if in embodiment of Bachmann's question: 'Soll ich [. . .] Metapher [. . .] mit einer?'. A fifth Bachmann section follows the fourth as an epilogue. Into this mosaic are cut twelve short fragments adapted from the *Machaut–Ockeghem–Josquin* material, only one of which is more than five bars long. Some of the dislocated words from these chansons are now sung: individual words – 'ahimé', 'adieu' – or fragments – (mal)'heur' – become sighs as much as echoes of text.

The fabric is constructed using Nono's fragment technique, woven together in the kind of acoustic-referential network of resonances and memories hinted at in his first sketches. The *Machaut–Ockeghem–Josquin* passages are sampled, abstracted and condensed from the Venice material, a fourth stage of remove from the source editions. While the tempo elsewhere fluctuates constantly, these sections are at a regular ♩ = 30. In Figure 14.2 we see how the first such section of *Risonanze erranti – Ockeghem 1°* – is sampled from the four-voice material, and that in turn from the source. Figure 14.2a shows three bars from Ockeghem's chanson, the fragments numbered by Nono, with the filtered version from his re-sampled monody below. This appears as fragment 10 of the four-part *Machaut–Ockeghem–Josquin* score, the Venice version prepared for Duisberg in May 1985 (Figure 14.2b), and then in bars 38–9 of the final score of *Risonanze erranti* (Figure 14.2c). Played softly by crotales, it emerges as a memory from their sequences of dyads and triads in the surrounding sections; Nono adds the text to encourage vocal phrasing. The quotation is harmonised using the same fundamental intervals of *Risonanze erranti*: fifth, augmented fourth, minor second. Each sound is delayed slightly further; the last is a secondary resonance of the preceding harmonising D, to which are added the characteristic intervals.

Subsequent sections focus on one, two or three intervals, the melos reaching its fullest extent at the central 'Ahimè' in bar 214. Voice and fragments of text emerge from the sparse instrumental counterpoint. The highly concentrated expression is itself at the centre of a network of reference: 'doloroso wie "remember me"', 'con pianto interno (Gesualdo)' appear as performance instructions. As well as Purcell and Gesualdo, in rehearsals Nono encouraged echoes of Verdi and Wagner.[41]

The Melville fragments derive more freely from the same musical material. Textually and sonically, they have the widest expressive range; these are the passages that afford the most emotional engagement with the listening subject. Their dramatic trajectory is balanced about an extended fulcrum on the repeated words 'Past [. . .] slave [. . .] pain [. . .] crime'. The uniform eight-bar structures of the initial version are amended slightly in the final score for sonic and dramatic reasons. Largely diatonic lines are at the centre of evolving folds of the fundamental intervals, their inversions and transpositions, as well as chromatic expansion of the frequency band, enhanced by microtonal electronic transposition. Thus, in the opening section the vocal line is generated from the first two samples of the *Machaut–Ockeghem–Josquin* monody (Figures 14.3a–b). The start of sample 2 is followed by sample 1 in retrograde, then sample 2 continues likewise reversed, with the final B echoed. We see the detailed directions of Nono's

Figure 14.2a Risonanze erranti: Ockeghem *Malheur me bat*, fragmented and filtered

Figure 14.2b Risonanze erranti: bars 21–2 of *Machaut-Ockeghem-Josquin*

Figure 14.2c Risonanze erranti: crotales, bars 38–9
Figure 14.2 Risonanze erranti: use of *Machaut-Ockeghem-Josquin* material

Figure 14.3a Risonanze erranti: samples 1–2 of *Machaut–Ockeghem–Josquin*

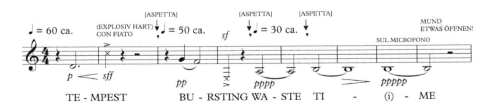

Figure 14.3b Risonanze erranti: alto, bars 1–8
Figure 14.3 Risonanze erranti: opening – derivation from *Machaut–Ockeghem–Josquin* samples

Resonances

vocal writing, which is supported by chromatic expansion and movement between breath and pitch in bass flute and bass clarinet.

Layers of grief and loss mirror the constantly changing sonic spaces; each provides perspective on the others. In avoiding complete immersion in any one of them, the whole resists despair. This is where the strength of *Risonanze erranti* lies, and what makes it more than the sum of a set of settings. The role of the early polyphonists here seems to be to transcend grief. The words of Melville express a common anguish, a latent resistance. The tragedy of Bachmann's words is in their isolation. These passages are more inward – expressively and structurally still more self-contained. Here Nono seems to develop the *Liederzyklus* material – the three notes of *Bachmann 1* are the opening of *Atmendes*: A G♯ D. There they begin an extended melodic mirror; here, with separations and echoes, they suffice alone to carry 'Nicht(s) mehr [. . .] mir' ('nothing more [pleases] me'). The subsequent Bachmann passages are equally focused. In the second, the piccolo replaces a mute voice, traversing the same pitch set twice. The third, the darkest, uses only an octave C. The alto follows the syllabic rhythm of the five words 'Einsehn gelernt [. . .] Hunger – Tränen – Finsternis' ('[I have] learned an understanding – [with the words that are there for the lowest classes] – hunger – shame – darkness'). The wind anticipate each word with a single note. The fourth builds a mirror on an inversion of the three notes of the opening. The last is interrupted twice – by Machaut's 'pleu[re]' and Ockeghem's 'Malheur'. Traces of twelve-tone thought remain behind the focus on intervals. While Nono eventually changed the last note, Bachmann's final words were to be set to a hexachord that is both its own complement in inversion and contains the twin essences of pitch behaviour; the fifth/minor second pattern is continued by both another fifth and a chromatic expansion around D/C♯.

Each fragment inhabits its own acoustic space, a function of orchestration, texture and electronic processing; the latter changes with almost every fragment. The spatialisation and movement of sound are more architectural than in *Omaggio a György Kurtág*. Each of the brief *Machaut–Ockeghem–Josquin* passages has its own pattern of spatialisation; Nono refers to the multiple spaces within which these memories are hidden.[42] He draws them for Haller, for the June 1986 performance in Turin, but was dissatisfied. 'In Turin it was static', he notes, and proceeds to re-examine every parameter possible for real-time sound processing.[43] One might even posit some influence from Boulez's recent *Répons*, following Nono's visit to Paris in early 1985.[44] Here there is an analogous circular triple layering of space and material.[45] The alto is heard from the stage but also from two loudspeakers at the centre of the room. Distance and position relative to the microphone are carefully determined, modulated by actions of hand or tongue. The vocal writing sometimes recalls that of much earlier works – *Canciones a Guiomar*, for example, likewise with its constellation of *suoni fissi* – but its detail now magnified under the sonoscope. The alto's material is echoed, anticipated, commented, extended or replaced by the two wind instruments, their relationship to the vocal material further shifted in pitch, time and space by the electronics. Harmonics, 'aeolian' and breath sounds, notes at the limits of register, of dynamics or of speaking, produce a timbral continuum between instruments and voice. Their spectral overlap, observed by Nono with the sonoscope in the preparations for *Prometeo*, here becomes a harmonic/timbral foundation.[46] The percussion – Sardinian shepherd bells, bongos and crotales – provide a more distant resonance, often at the limit of pitchedness or rhythmic definition, but never pure noise, echoing, counterpointing or providing a sea of sound from which figure emerges. Nono's contiguous treatment of notated material and live sound processing is clearest in the percussion. In the fourth section (bars 27–35), for example, a single bongo impulse is delayed incrementally in triplets then semiquavers, each instance echoed in another part at a delay of one and two beats. The whole is then subject to eight electronic delays of 5–9", transposed by minor sevenths and major ninths. Together with the

Resonances

4" alto reverberation, these fill the space to the beginning of the next section. The spatial processing of the percussion is Nono's most active use of the Halaphon, circling or zig-zagging across the space.

In many respects, *Risonanze erranti* is the most successful work of the post-*Prometeo* moment. 'Less of a departure', suggested Spangemacher after the premiere, 'than a work at the border'.[47] It finds a balance between expressive freedom and compositional coherence, between being embodied in the actions of particular performers and its abstract status as a work. It possesses a significant feature of Western art music: multiple possible paths of long-term structure are combined with comprehensible local figure. The Cologne version was repeated in Turin in June 1986, together with the revised version of *Omaggio a György Kurtág*. Nono ended his programme note: 'Schubert's WINTERREISE, p – fff –ppp –f – ffffff – ffff in my heart.'[48] Among other resonant spaces are the pastoral sounds of Mahler – again mentioned in Nono's notes – and the expressiveness of later Verdi and early Schönberg. As Spangemacher observes, text is much clearer than in *Prometeo*. In Nono's last text-based works, he achieves a new transparency.

The changes that Nono made between his first complete version for Cologne and that heard in Berlin and Paris in the autumn of 1987 recall the dramatic cut made by Scherchen to *Polifonica–Monodia–Ritmica* decades earlier. Two major sections of Melville ('Lonesome [. . .] loneliest dead' from *To the Master of the Meteor* and 'implacable sea' from *Pebbles*) are removed from before the fifth and final Bachmann passage, along with three fragments of *Machaut–Ockeghem–Josquin*. This must be a judgement based on the dramatic sequence, not the length of the work as a whole; the final version has exactly the same number of bars as the first. There are some new echoes, but the difference is mostly made up of additional time for the twin layers of resonance: percussion and live electronics. These changes provide important indications as to how *Risonanze erranti* works in practice. The fragments contain sufficient trace of figure – melodic, rhythmic or semantic – that the listener is drawn to find pattern, to make sense. The absence of repetition or even continuation leaves the ear engaged, but with only echoic memory to reflect upon. The long silences, fermata, barely figural percussion passages and non-figural electronic resonances stretch beyond the limits of echoic memory and conscious reflection. The ear rehearses and redraws the listener's memory such that its patterns begin to weave with the much longer term traces of individual experience and understanding. This is no poetic conceit or metaphor; it is a cognitive, phenomenological approach to composition. Nono shapes time and acoustic experience such that individual and shared perceptions interact. In this respect, subject and society remain a driving dialectic. Long silences in the concert hall are as culturally challenging as political rhetoric. They draw attention to the shared present and to the transformative power of shared reflection. Active listening is not an optional desideratum – it is now a structural, structuring component of Nono's language.

Spangemacher suggests that Bachmann's meditation on the loss of poetry itself reflects Nono's own state at this time. Any doubt is not only that of uncertainty, however; it is also the awareness of multiplicity, of parallel identities and times. Nono's response to this is not, like Bachmann, to renounce the struggle. Instead, his work constantly restates commitment to particular moments and situations. The dedication to Cacciari is more than titular. As Nono began work in 1985, continuing discussions with his friend must have encompassed Cacciari's forthcoming book, *Icone della Legge*.[49] At the outset, Cacciari observes how philosophy ignores its own motivating impulse: human fear of death. The loss of oneself – death – can only be known vicariously, through the subjective loss of others. This is what unites the themes of loss and identity in *Risonanze erranti*. Imagination and memory are fundamentally the same activity – in composing, as in listening. Cacciari's epigram is a quote from Schönberg:

Resonances

And instead imagine:
that there is a law:
such that you should have to hail such a miracle!
And that there should be those who rebel,
is nothing but trite banality.[50]

'Der Wanderer'

At the end of his fair copy of *Risonanze erranti*, Nono writes: '1985 Venezia Freiburg Köln Milano Berlin 1987' – a fair summary of his path through this period. This itinerant life and the practice of developing works through the process of concert giving set the pattern for his final years. He was combining the life of a touring musician with an intense schedule of new compositions. Being part of a touring ensemble brought its own tensions: between the creative, experimental imperative of composer and the pragmatic, rehearsed requirements of high-level performance. A performance of *Guia ai Gelidi Mostri* in Perugia in October 1985 was abruptly terminated when Nono discovered that the Freiburg engineers had put limiters on the mixing desk between rehearsal and concert. The dynamics and economics of new music were changing rapidly through the 1980s. Nono had an increasing role as a senior figure in international cultural life – both as a representative of a now historicised post-war modernism and as a visionary mapping the potential of a new cultural–technological world. Performances, commissions and public appearances were now more closely connected. His copious notes show that Nono was constantly planning and replanning projects into the future. There is little difference in kind between his plans for new works and notes on specific compositional ideas; more than ever, this is now a continuous, evolving creative pursuit, of which individual 'works' are situated realisations. Highly productive as this period certainly was, the irregularity of such a rhythm of existence and prolonged periods away from the care available in Venice were beginning to impact on his health. Specifically, the liver illness that had troubled him since the hepatitis of his youth was now recurring with increasing frequency and severity. This provoked moments of irascibility, understandable to those close to him, but sometimes disconcerting to others.

Since 1984, Nono had been discussing the possibility of a residency in Berlin with the Deutscher Akademischer Austauschdienst (DAAD). His visits were already frequent, his connections with German cultural life close; in November 1985, he had been in the DDR for events marking the European Year of Music and the International Year of Youth. The plan came to fruition in January 1986, when he joined the DAAD Berliner Künstlerprogramm. His stay would be extended through the following year, and then into 1989 through his election to the Wissenschaftskolleg, the prestigious Institute for Advanced Study in Berlin.

Residence in Berlin brought little stability. In January 1986, he was in Buenos Aires; in October he would return to Havana. In May, he informed the DAAD that he would be travelling for some weeks, for projects in Munich, Venice, Turin, Milan and Freiburg – he had finished the first version of *Risonanze erranti*, was revising the score of *Omaggio a György Kurtág* and planning a work based on the poetry of Edmond Jabès.[51] Respite from such a schedule did not mean staying still. In August, he took a boat trip to the north of Greenland, enthusiastically describing new colours, new sounds and new sensations in postcards to his friends:

alone in front of the sea, its colours and the pole star. That special sea was neither frozen nor dark, but a continuous transformation between indescribable colours filtered between the clouds, between the icebergs. The spectacle was nothing like

Resonances

what you read in books: white, dark, grey or dark blue ghosts moved around, slowly becoming bright with emerald green or a topaz never seen before. Other unforgettable things: the sounds, the violent explosions you heard when the icebergs detached from the glaciers, snapping. It's just coincidence, but I had taken the score of Varèse's *Arcana* to study again, and I found myself hearing it amidst the violence of nature.[52]

He may have embraced constant inner disquiet as a productive force, but that clearly made it no less costly, reinforced as it was by constant geographical mobility and fuelled by illness and professional demands. A nourishing environment for dialogue was crucial to him. Returned from Greenland, he wrote to Abbado:

often I am tempted, especially in continuous periods of deep depression, to throw away everything – nearly everything – or really everything – not because I can't see what I have attempted or 'achieved', but I increasingly feel the lack of physical – vital – moral – intellectual air to breath (this is also why I tried to look for them among the icebergs in Greenland) [. . .]
Freiburg, the studio, the Black Forest keep me going –
Berlin, the 'superorganised' standardisation of musical life (including practical aspects [of life]: a real infernal game!) is heavy – but here my study [. . .] also continues to let me feel other AIR other SPACES other POSSIBLE LIVES[53]

Berlin afforded a rich intellectual context with which Nono was already well acquainted; now he could participate more fully. Political debate in Germany had also found a new intensity – very different from the torpor into which that in Italy was receding – and Berlin was its natural epicentre. In February 1987, Nono accepted an invitation to participate in the Moscow International Forum for a Nuclear Weapon-Free World, an extraordinary meeting of intellectuals, artist and scientists. Guests ranged from Normal Mailer and Yoko Ono, to representatives of New German Cinema such as Kluge, Herzog and Fassbinder, recently freed dissident Andrei Sakharov and nuclear experts such as Frank von Hippel. Surreal as the gathering may have been, Mikhail Gorbachev addressed the forum and acknowledged its role in shaping events.[54] In the midst of his development of the ideas of perestroika and of nuclear disarmament negotiations with the US, this must have seemed a moment of optimism. For Nono, it may have restored faith in the capacity of communism to reinvent itself and its goals, and to adapt to historical circumstances. On 8 March he was in Berlin to take part in a panel discussion on *Film, Literature, Music* at the Berlin International Film Festival and to present Klimov's *Farewell to Matyora*. Such activities seem to have lifted his spirits; he reported them to his friend Giacomo Da Re in Stuttgart:

I've been in Moscow for the international forum, then here a week with Klimov – NEW Soviet film-literature/music. I'm working on various projects, also in the DDR – and here morale and work good! With new ideas and new times. I've been in Rome, Milan, Zurich, Freiburg – WORK – WORK – WORK.[55]

On his trip to Spain in October 1985, Nono had been in Toledo, where he had seen written on a monastery wall: 'Caminantes no hay caminos hay que caminar' ('Traveller there is no path there is only travelling'). As has often been noted, this is a paraphrase of a poem by Machado that Nono himself had considered setting some years previously, but abstracted from that context the phrase struck Nono with its personal resonance[56]. As a formulation of a present

Resonances

truth it opened up a future space of potential. It is, he told Restagno in March 1987, 'the *Wanderer* of Nietzsche, of continuous searching, of Cacciari's *Prometeo*'.[57] It would provide the thread through his next phase of work.

Notes

1 Interview with Philippe Albèra, 1987. LNII, p. 422. Drees, 1999, pp. 25–6. Interview with Nuria Schoenberg-Nono, 20 September 2013.
2 The postcard is reproduced in Goffi-Hamilton, 2006, p. 292.
3 When Frank Lloyd Wright landed at Venice airport in 1952, he was greeted by a delegation from the IUAV. 'Which one of you is Scarpa?' he asked. None was; not officially being an architect, Scarpa had not been invited.
4 Letter to Zender, 13 December 1984, quoted in Drees, 1997, p. 25.
5 Winckel, 1958; Huber, 1999, pp. 25–6.
6 ALN 52.01/04.
7 ALN 52.01/05sx-dx.
8 ALN 52.01/08.
9 ALN 52.03/01v.
10 Huber, 1999, pp. 2–22.
11 ALN 52.03/02vr.
12 ALN 52.02/01.
13 Huber, 1999, p. 29.
14 Murray Grigor's documentary film *The Architecture of Carlo Scarpa* (1996) includes footage of the Brion cemetery.
15 Drees, 1998, p. 87.
16 Drees, 1998, p. 84.
17 Dal Co and Mazzariol, 1984, p. 24.
18 Goffi-Hamilton, 2006, p. 192.
19 James, 1890, p. 609.
20 Dal Co and Mazzariol, 1984, p. 27.
21 ALN 53.01/06.
22 'A Pierre: Dell'azzurro silenzio, inquietum'. LNI, p. 496.
23 'A Pierre: Dell'azzurro silenzio, inquietum'. LNI, p. 494.
24 For example, 'Form' in Boulez, 1991, pp. 90–6.
25 'A Pierre: Dell'azzurro silenzio, inquietum'. LNI, p. 495.
26 'Altre possibilità di ascolto', 1985. LNI, p. 531.
27 Cacciari in Röller, 1995, p. 13.
28 ALN 53.01/01–02, 54.04/11.
29 The sequence of work is described in Ramazotti, 1997.
30 Interview with Enzo Restagno, 1987. LNII pp. 489–91.
31 Schönberg, 1974 (written in 1912).
32 ALN 54.04.01/10.
33 ALN 54.09.02.
34 ALN 54.11.01.
35 54.07/01–03.
36 ALN 54.09.01.
37 ALN 54.05.02/25v.
38 Pavese translated *Moby Dick*, and discusses Melville's work in his essays on American literature.
39 Since 1953, Bachmann had lived in Rome. The circumstances surrounding her early death there in 1973 had been the subject of wide public interest in Italy. She and Nono had been introduced by Henze, with whom Bachmann collaborated on *Der Junge Lord*. Their relationship is recounted in Larcati, 2002.
40 ALN 54.02/01.
41 Stenzl '*Risonanze erranti*' in Albèra, 1987, p. 200.
42 ALN 54.16.02/05r. Haller, 1995, p. 185.
43 ALN 54.19.01/03r.

Resonances

44 Nono refers to Boulez's research in a later programme note to *A Pierre*: 'silent technological labyrinths to climb to the spacious light' (*'A Pierre: Dell'azzurro silenzio, inquietum'*. LNI, p. 495).

45 In *Répons* (1981–4), a central group of soloists is surrounded by the orchestra. The live electronic processing is projected through loudspeakers that encircle players and audience.

46 Interview with Wilfried Gruhn, 1984. LNII, 321. Cacciari, 1984, p. 7.

47 Spangemacher, 1986, p. 44.

48 'Risonanze erranti. Liederzyklus a Massimo Cacciari'. LNI, p. 498.

49 Cacciari, 1985.

50 Cacciari, 1985, p. 11.

51 Letter to DAAD, 22 May, 1986.

52 Interview with Enzo Restagno, 1987. LNII, p. 521.

53 Letter to Abbado, 7 September 1986, ALN.

54 Wittner, 2003, p. 397. Gorbachev's speech to the forum was circulated to the UN. Available at: http://repository.un.org/bitstream/handle/11176/60420/A_42_132%3BS_18701-EN.pdf?sequence=21&isAllowed=y (accessed 15 November 2017).

55 Letter to Giacomo Da Re, 15 March 1987, in Trudu, 2008, p. 271.

56 *Proverbios y Cantares* XXIX.

57 Interview with Enzo Restagno, 1987. LNII, pp. 561–2.

15

POSSIBLE WORLDS

'1° Caminantes . . . Ayacucho'

'. . . in an infinite space and with innumerable voices'

In early 1982 Nono had been invited by the director of the Münich Philharmonic, Hubertus Frantzen, to write an orchestral work for the opening of the new Gasteig concert hall, planned for 1985. The orchestra, led through the 1980s by Sergiu Celibidache, was not known for its enlightened radicalism. Organist, writer, dramaturg and cultural animateur Frantzen was at the height of his intense work to build new audiences and to extend the reach of culture; a commission from Nono must have promised the perfect balance of radical cultural intervention and masterwork. Abbado was to conduct and Frantzen planned a week of events around the premiere to mark the composer's sixtieth birthday. Pollini was to be invited; the new work was to be for piano, orchestra, electronics and perhaps choir. Fully occupied with *Prometeo*, Nono saw no reason to supply Abbado with the requested 'concept' until the present project was finished; eventually, the date of the premiere slipped and Abbado was unavailable. An additional project enters Nono's plans at this point: an unrealised work with Abbado and Pollini for Berlin, where Abbado was to become chief conductor of the Philharmonic in 1989. On the same page, Nono lists the three works that would make up the *Caminantes* sequence: 'Caminantes [. . .] Munich/no hay caminos [. . .] Tokyo/Hay que caminar Berlin 1988'.[1] He describes the sequence: 'continuous, continuous, fragmented'.[2] The Munich work was finally presented on 25 April 1987 under Djansung Kachidse. *1° Caminantes . . . Ayacucho* for mezzo soprano, bass flute, small and large choirs, organ, three orchestral groups and live electronics is a setting of *Ai principi dell'universo*, a poem from Giordano Bruno's cosmological tract *De la causa, principio et uno* (*On cause, principle and unity*) of 1584.

Nono appears to have given the distant project scant attention in 1982, but the few early notes do suggest a clarity of sound concept and realisation that characterise the work he returned to four years later. He envisaged a work for:

> 10 groups [. . .] solos or groups [. . .] voices and instruments distributed in the space or on the podium | perhaps: all the strings nomadic | others in groups 5 4 | voices in groups 5 6 | think about programmes organised on the computer | perhaps: *pppppp-ppppp-pppp-ppp-pp-p* and <u>silences</u> [. . .] all circles | in groups: tbn hn cl fl [3]

452

Possible worlds

'TRADITION IS DARMSTADT' states an enigmatic note to himself, as if recalibrating his own perspective before commencing work – 'echoes and others – mutations!'[4]

There is no indication that Nono gave the project further consideration until 1985, when he contemplates writing for Susanne Otto and the Freiburg chamber choir and first mentions the possibility of a text from Bruno. His copy of *De la causa, principio e uno* is also dated July 1985. In its biographical introduction, Nono underlines each place, every movement on Bruno's journey. To a degree their itineraries are parallel – Bruno moved continuously, from Italy to France, England, Germany and back to Venice – but more fundamental is the sense of the Wanderer, of the constant search for dialogue and understanding. In his reading of philosophy, Nono searches for vision, for new conceptual models. His is not a formal, reductionist response. There is no point in looking for a world-view that is somehow mapped into musical form, a point he made in a talk while working on *Caminantes*:

> I always enter the Freiburg studio with 'no idea'. No programme. This is fundamental because it means the complete abandoning of logocentrism, giving up the notion that there must be an idea that precedes the music, the idea as that which must be realised or expressed in the music or the story that must be told 'in music'.[5]

Nevertheless, there are aspects of Bruno's work that seem to have resonated very specifically with Nono's concerns at this time. Bruno is fundamentally a materialist; he cannot ignore the radical implications of what is known in his own time. Briefly put, if the earth is not at the centre of the universe, then there may be many such worlds and there is no reason to posit a boundary: '[innumerable worlds] manifest and proclaim in an infinite space and with innumerable voices the excellence and majesty of their first cause and first principle'.[6] If there are infinite material worlds, there is no place for hypothetical other worlds; thus, if a motivating spirit exists, it must be found in everything as a universal soul. Divine and earthly, creator and created are inseparable; there is no need for a mediating figure or institution, no need to fear the imaginary. The rational soul stands at the centre of a universal intelligence. Bruno argued unsuccessfully that his work concerned natural philosophy, not theology. The inquisition's disagreement was an equally material political response: he was burned at the stake in 1600. In the context of Nono's intellectual cosmology, Bruno might be considered the complement of Gramsci; his search for enlightenment is individual rather than political and organisational.

Bruno's radical Copernican cosmology is fundamentally spatial; for Bruno, the hermetic metaphor of rising through concentric spheres had been broken open. The possibility of being exists everywhere, realised dynamically in created forms in a process of continuous transformation. There are no hierarchies, no separate ideal forms or ideas independent of their material manifestation. This is especially relevant to Nono's relationship with his own working process at this stage, and to the relationships between different elements that evolve within a work. In Bruno's terms, 'act' and 'potency' coincide. Constant movement and continuous evolution explore and give form to the potential of the infinite space: 'the void does not exist in the sense of a space with no matter in it, but rather a void is a space in which different bodies move and succeed each other'.[7]

'Ars combinatoria'

Caminantes is above all a spatial work, in which sound is continuously present and in constant movement. Its form derives from the intersection of three quasi-autonomous layers: the orchestral groups and choirs, organ, and soloists. It is the emergent product of simultaneous worlds, of wave systems moving across each other. Formally and semantically, the choirs mediate between instruments and soloists; the organ assumes a more independent role. An early sketch describes soloists and organ as 'autonomous'.[8] While the main work of composition took place between November 1986 and the beginning of 1987, some crucial decisions were taken while Nono was working in Freiburg in the early summer of 1986. He must have been aware that his various impending journeys would leave little time for such a major project. The conceptual foundations were laid not in score or text, therefore, but while Nono was experimenting with soloists in the studio. To produce the detailed structure, minimal materials are developed using concepts evolved through this studio practice: reverberation and diffusion, spatialisation, echo and delay, multiple pitch-shifting and sampling – the reuse and reordering of materials. The thought processes of technology are now fully absorbed into Nono's notation-based practice; they bring a new robustness to the process. Nono had been sent pictures of the Munich Philharmonic rehearsing in their new hall, on which he sketched the constitution and layout of three groups of voices and instruments ('cantar – sonar'). With these came details of the new four-manual organ. He took notes on the organs in the Munster at Freiburg: four instruments in different locations, all playable from a central console. The dedication *Ayacucho* also appears at this time. In June 1986, there were massacres at three prisons in Peru as the new president, Alan García, imposed his rule by repressing revolts by supposed members of the Maoist *Shining Path* guerilla group. Nono had visited the Ayacucho region in 1967; one of the poorest rural regions of the country, Shining Path had begun their action there in 1980.

As he began work in earnest, Nono once again planned a nine-part architecture, each section characterised in detail in terms of pitch, register, orchestration and overall dynamic shape. Plans show tempo sequence and timings adding up to the 35 minutes of the final work. Both choirs are present, but there is as yet no mention of soloists or text. The journey, in a space of a few weeks, from these single-page maps to a full detailed score represents a significant technical challenge. Bruno's anti-dogmatism seems to guide Nono as he explores his relationship with his own fully assimilated technical repertoire; 'eliminate mechanical process!!! follow your nose!!!' he writes in dialect ('vai a usma!!!').[9] *1° Caminantes . . . Ayacucho* and its orchestral pair, *2° Non hay caminos, hay que caminar [. . .] Andrej Tarkovskij*, were to be the last works in which Nono's long-established, post-serial polyphonic techniques play a part. The act of composition remains one of resistance, but now of resistance to his own habits of thought. While many techniques relate to those of the studio, other cognitive and graphical models still reflect aspects of his early mature works. In this very relationship we see a distance travelled. They are no longer fundamental to the work's poetic DNA; they don't embody any kind of essence. Compositional processes have been refined, abstracted and distanced to become, like the machines in the studio, a set of ways of dealing with the basic properties and transformations of sound. An individual output has no particular authority or weight; Nono is free to experiment, guess, edit, discover or discard. This is the maturation of a long process rooted in his discussions with Cacciari on the limits and necessity of language games and formal systems.

The distribution of forces in the final score (Figure15.1) largely follows the pattern of Nono's initial sketch. Groups A and C, in the galleries to left and right, are nearly symmetrcially constituted of brass quartet, percussion (bass drum, bongos and crotales) and chamber choir (low voices to the left, high to the right). The central group B is itself distributed symmetrically: two groups of brass and woodwind quartets (there are no double reeds) surround the string section; behind them two groups of *suoni fissi* (harp, bells and bongos) flank the timpani. The large choir is behind the stage, in front of the organ. Live electronics distribute the sounds of the two soloists around the hall. An early idea was that Fabricciani should walk around the hall with a radio microphone – the seed of Nono's later *Découvir la subversion* and *BAAB–ARR*. To

Possible worlds

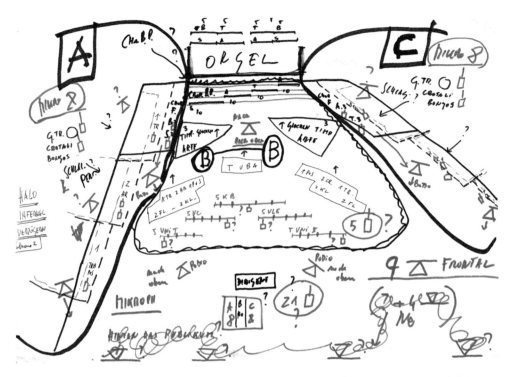

Figure 15.1 1° Caminantes . . . Ayacucho – spatial distribution (from draft score) (ALN 55.03.02/06. © The heirs of Luigi Nono. Reproduced by kind permission)

his established armoury of processes, Nono adds an innovation from his research with Schiaffini: sound is gathered through a microphone placed inside an otherwise silent tuba, such that, like that of the singers, wind and organ that carry most of the musical argument, the sound of the room itself is coloured by a physical resonant body. He stipulates minutes of inactivity on stage before the first sound is made, time for the room itself to develop character in the ear of the listener.

Figure 15.2 1° Caminantes . . . Ayacucho – basic pitch material

For the main body of performers, Nono uses only five pitches (Figure 15.2). He marks the letters A, C and H (the note B in German notation) in AyACuCHo, leaving G [iordano] B[runo].[10] This would be insufficient to explain their derivation. Melkert suggests possible origins in the *scala enigmatica* or Nono's own all-interval series. To this, Döllinger adds the significance of the number 5 in various aspects of *Caminates*; there are five tempi, five subdivisions of the beat, and Nono begins with building blocks of five bars. We might also note that these are harmonics 12–15 of the fundamental C. To seek clear confirmation of such intriguing ideas is to fall into the formalist trap that Nono so consciously avoided. They are part of a poetic process of allusion and resonance, neither arbitrary nor formal, closer to what

Possible worlds

Bruno describes as magic – processes for passing between different spheres – than referent or formula. The pitch set has well-defined intervallic properties: the tight knot of smaller intervals is bounded by a single fifth (never inverted) and a single major third. There is no augmented fourth. This provides a clear stable horizon relative to Nono's current ever-orbiting, side-slipping pitch language of semitones, fourths and fifths. In general, the open fifth and the chromatic cluster are used as two distinct elements; the set is rarely heard as a single entity. In selecting and voicing pitches, Nono takes his cue from the registral ambiguity of organ mixtures. By expanding semitones to sevenths and ninths, and varying the spectral content of playing techniques (sul ponte or tasto, for example) he moves sound masses freely in register and colour.

Sound is kept in continuous movement spatially, but also by detailed modulation of pitch, colour and timing – lessons learned from technology. The listener's awareness of the performance space being brought into vibration is enhanced by the slow basic tempo of ♩ = 30, regularly interrupted and arrested by near-silence. Nono had used microtones since *Canti di vita e d'amore*, notably in *Per Bastiana* (1967). Here he develops the retuning technique of *Quando stanno morendo*. Five players are required for each of the five string sections, one for each of the five source pitches. Each player uses four strings tuned to eighth-tone variants of their particular note. Microtonal clusters around each pitch are thus available in each group of strings. Nono invents a notation to indicate which string or pair of strings to play. In addition, the entire string group is sometimes shifted by all players stopping all four strings at the same position. This produces transpositions in semitone variants of unison, fifth and octave (min. 2, +4, 5, +5, maj. 7). Only the augmented fourth transposition has no pitches in common with the original set. The fine control of microtonal focus reflects not only Nono's work with technology, but also his recent fascination with the expressive intonation of Jewish and Arab singing. His ingenious technical solution seems to have engendered some resistance from the orchestra, protective of their instruments.[11] Wind and brass vary the pitch by quarter tones, such that the definition of the initial pitch set can be dissolved to cover almost the whole space apart from the range D–E. The semitone transpositions of *suoni fissi* (harps, bells, crotales, timpani) mark clearer shifts of horizon, most prominently with their repeated unison C♯ at the opening of the central section at the choir's 'procedere'.

Suoni fissi, together with bongos and bass drums, generate passing points and clouds of rhythm that emerge from or tend towards periodicity before dissolving. The acoustic phasing of their resonance, especially through near-silences, is contiguous with the acoustic microtonal modulation of instruments and live electronic processing of choir and soloists. Staccato interventions from strings and wind mark intervals and hiatuses of time across slowly changing sustained layers, repeated string arpeggios skating across their surface.

The tripartite spatial structure informs Nono's thinking about material. Internally, forces are divided into choir, orchestra and percussion. Time is marked out in terms of three tempi – ♩ = 30, 60 and 120 – to which 44 and 88 are later added as intermediate stages (♩ = 45 and 90 are not standard metronome marks). Some of the operations by which Nono derives his material appear graphically related to those of thirty years earlier: matrices, permutations, rotations and reorderings. However, this is now a process of triangulation rather than production, of sculpture or architecture rather than conventional composition. He works inwards from various faces of the poetic idea, inventing, solving, reconciling, and framing appropriate decisions to be taken.

Rhythmic detail is again derived from the *A veloce* and *B calmo* material of *Con Luigi Dallapiccola*; Nono identifies three types of figure within each. Figure 15.3, from section 2, shows how Nono uses material from *B calmo* (see Figure 11.4b) to generate pitch, dynamic, rhythmic and spatial mobility while sustaining a single G in the four trumpets ranged across the

Possible worlds

Figure 15.3 1° *Caminantes . . . Ayacucho* – trumpets, bars 36–40

space. Ten fragments from the source are used in their original sequence, marked in Figure 15.3 with Nono's notation. Some have additional rhythmic articulation; the first and last units of I4 are untied, while the beginning and end of III2 are broken into semiquaver triplets. II4 is hollowed out to leave only its start and end points. Starts and ends are often marked in other voices, creating opportunities for rhythmic figuration and spatialising. These microstructures are arranged about the centre of the passage, the only silence at the end of bar 38, such that they create both symmetry and forward motion. II3 is mirrored; its start is rearticulated to left and right in both semiquavers and triplets. The triplets are echoed at the end of the mirror and again with the elaborated end of II2. The three semiquavers that begin I4 together shift the sound from left to right. At the end of the fragment and again at the end of the passage, eliding IV4 to IV3, they are offset by a semiquaver as if to mark the movement of sound through space. Incremental delays or similar rhythms with different beat divisions are frequently used to trace the movement of events through space. Moments of near-regularity draw the ear to follow their direction, as at the very opening. With a slight further increase of the temporal distance, single events proliferate into polyphony.

From early sketches, the organ is referred to as *continuo*. It maintains precisely this role, sustaining one, two or three notes for periods ranging from five to thirteen bars. Pitches come from either the fifth C–G or the chromatic A–B♭–B. They range across the instrument's entire compass, although they begin at the lowest possible C and end on the highest B. Nono selected his twenty-eight combinations and their registration from a systematic analysis of the available intervals – a sort of long-range additive synthesis. The planning of time, of bar numbers, tempi and durations, also seems to have begun when considering the organ part, such that it has a fundamental continuo role within the compositional process. As with other aspects of *Caminantes*, the clear formal structure is increasingly modulated as composition progresses. Through much of the work, a ten-bar modulus is clearly in evidence; elsewhere, it is interrupted, prolonged or accelerated. The rate of change doubles to every five bars – Nono's initial plan – through the final two sections, exploring permutations within the high octave chromatic cluster. In general, the organ pursues its own course, but macrostructural fermata or interventions generate points of coincidence. Registration changes with every pitch change except through the final sections, where the *höheflöte* blends with acoustic woodwind.

Possible worlds

There are few indications of text or soloists until Nono begins to draft the whole in detail. Form, text-setting and the soloists' role evolve together in the course of the process. Mezzo soprano and bass flute are two faces of a single entity; their sounds and identities are fused. The vocalist sings, 'Always directly into the microphone. Always *ppppp* = almost as if *mormorando*, whispering into it.' The bass flute should follow the singer 'like a foggy spectrum, which sounds a) differentiated b) confused'. At moments, the voice develops a rich noise spectrum, the flute sound morphs into a syllable, or the two together generate additional artefacts through slight shifts in pitch or time. Both inhabit a liminal space between sounding and not-sounding. As with much of Nono's music since *Fragmente*, notions of interiority are misleading. This sound world illuminates the act of speaking, of exteriorising, as much as withdrawal. While they share Bruno's poem with the choirs, the soloists' musical path is entirely independent. As if to reconnect with the moment of the work's conception in 1982, Nono returns to the long monody that forms the first part of *Quando stanno morendo* (Plate 3). The aggregate line of alto and flute parts is taken from a draft skeleton of that movement: three sequences of its eighteen fragments almost in their entirety.[12] Some note sequences thus return two or three times; Nono mediates this carefully. The soloists' first three-note fragment ('Errante stellae', F♯–F–B, bars 76–81) should occur again at 'm' (bar 176); only the last note is used, to avoid a clear melodic rhyme. It returns in full across 'Olimpe, Iovem', almost at the end (bars 291–4). Octaves are sometimes altered to reshape the melodic contour; the original rhythms are adapted where appropriate, but their more figurative properties are largely retained. Reflections, repetitions,

Figure 15.4a 1° *Caminantes . . . Ayacucho* – monody from sketches for *Quando stanno morendo*

Figure 15.4b 1° *Caminantes . . . Ayacucho* – alto solo, bars 78–115

omissions and prolongations reinforce the sampling paradigm. Figure 15.4 shows how the initial phrases of the soloists derive from the monody. The repetition of the instruction 'spectate' ('behold') is underscored by a fold in the line, which circles once more on 'orbem' ('world'). Brief semitone shifts (the flute B♭ in bars 119–23) reflect the shifting gravitational pull of the main body. The long, almost cadential E–B pattern that is prominent in the earlier work (it ends the third section) receives particular attention. It would appear twice: E is omitted on the first occasion, the B extended to three times its length on 'somni' ('sleep', bars 153–9); it should then provide the soloists' last two notes, but they are both lowered by a semitone (bars 295–8). The soloists' material is distinguished not only by its melodic properties – chains of seconds, fourths and fifths, and a figurative rhythmic middle ground that stands out from the sustained layers and rhythmic punctuation of the main body – but also by its long-term coherence. This infinitely forward-moving dynamic contrasts with the formal blocks of the three orchestral groups; each provides a point about which the other can rotate.

Caminantes follows a formal journey, not a plan. The relationships of forces, text and form emerge as Nono assembles the whole. Nono had paid careful attention to the transitions or gaps between the nine sections in his sketches; now these become fissures through which transforming forces emerge. Figure 15.5 shows how Bruno's poem is distributed through the work. The opening expands from a single note, an organ low C, and a single bass drum pulse. Percussion mark out space and time and the strings pitch, constructing the matrix within which the choir to left and right can present their text, syllable by syllable, in a monody the intervallic edges of which are blurred and overlapped to dissolve into polyphonic patterns. A brief tutti

---

GIORDANO NOLANO
AI PRINCIPI DE L'UNIVERSO

I (1) Lethaeo undantem retinens ab origine {5 – organ} **II** (36) campum
Emigret o Titan, et petat astra precor. {1 – organ}
III (71) **Errantes stellae, spectate *2 procedere in orbem**
Me {5 – soloists} **IV** (111) **geminum, si vos hoc reserastis iter**. {4 – soloists}
V (141) [procedere in orbem
Me geminum, si vos hoc reserastis]
Dent geminas **somni portas** *laxarier usque,*
Vestrae **per vacuum me** {silent fermata} **VI** (180) **properante vices:**
Obductum tenuitque diu quod tempus avarum,
Mi liceat densis promere de tenebris.
{10 – soloists} **Ad partum properare tuum, mens aegra, VII** (221) *quid obstat,*
Seclo haec indigno sint **tribuenda** *licet?* {3 – soloists}
VIII (268) *Umbrarum* **fluctu terras** *mergente*, cacumen
[promere de tenebris.
Ad partum properare tuum, mens aegra,]
Adtolle in clarum, noster Olimpe, Iovem.
[quid obstat,
Seclo *haec* indigno] **IX** (307-24) [Adtolle in clarum]

Key: Main sections in Roman numerals (bar numbers in parentheses)
       Choral text in plain, [repeated text in square brackets]
       Alto text in bold
       Omitted text in italics
       Interludes in curly brackets {length – instrumentation}

Figure 15.5   1° Caminantes . . . Ayacucho: distribution of Bruno's text

Possible worlds

hiatus and crescendo, separated by fermata and repeated, introduces forty seconds of static, high organ bare fifth, almost inaudible at first under the resonance of the preceding sound. These *ppppp* interjections could be seen to stand for silence. There is no nothingness; there are always layers beneath. They are sonic panels – seemingly static, but creating spectral colour and time to pay attention to fine artefacts of tuning, phasing or acoustic.

In contrast with the left–right interplay of the first section, the second immediately inhabits the entire space. Intense instrumental rhythmic and dynamic activity surrounds the central choral address to the sun – quiet, sustained, as dramatic as the parting of storm clouds to reveal a heavenly sun in a Tintoretto. Just a single bar of the organ fifth – eight seconds, now slightly shifted in colour – occupies the stillness that introduces the third section. The symmetrical *suoni fissi* set out an introductory rhythmic unison, not spatially staggered now but setting a unanimous stage for the entry of the soloists. Their material begins to be woven into the form. On the first 'spectate' ('behold', bars 86–90), the alto, accompanied by flute breath and whistling sounds and against a static organ cluster, moves by fifths down to a low D. This pre-echoes the gap before section four (bars 106–10) where the soloists now continue over the following organ panel 'procedere in orbem' ('proceed towards the heaven'). The dramatic tutti crescendo of bar 136 is by now established as signifying the end of a section. This time, however, the soloists continue through the intervening space alone, the listener's ear straining to hear the absent organ. 'reserastis iter' ('opened the path') is their text as they float through one of the work's first silences.

The twelve lines of Bruno's poem fall into five units: six couplets, of which the third and fourth run together. Nono's initial analysis shows that he saw this as the central weight of the text; the balance seems to have shifted slightly in the course of composition. While the soloists continue with the fifth and sixth lines of the poem, the other voices repeat the previous lines, 'procedere', the sound moving inwards from chamber choirs to the central group and back out. This forms a clear central pillar to the work, with unequivocal middle C♯s at regular eight-second intervals, supported by harps and bells. It marks the point both of greatest unanimity and of farthest departure from the main pitch material, the apoapsis of the work. These bars are echoed at the next transition (bars 175–9), now on B♭ and repeating the text of the previous transition, 'reserastis'. There are 140 bars to either side of this section, which marks its own centre with an implied transition at bars 163–4, a dramatic choir and percussion crescendo (B♭ B C♯), followed by a sudden fermata and *pppp* strings. The central pillar is thus solidly framed, binding together its opposing architectonic and forward-driving forces. We also find ourselves at an extraordinary node in Nono's rich network of references: while stylistically there are echoes of Stravinsky's Venetian serial works or even the *Symphony of Psalms*, the formal gesture recalls the *Adagio non troppo ma divoto* of the last movement of the *Choral Symphony* – its still, slowly turning fulcrum at 'über Sternen muss er wohnen' ('Surely he lives above the stars').

Text and instrumental music take increasingly divergent trajectories, and the poem itself begins to be hollowed out, reduced to its most resonant phrases. The soloists' first line of section six dissolves, overtaken by a repeated brass and drum ritornello. Low brass then carry the semantic weight of 'de tenebris' as clearly as for Monteverdi's Caronte. The following transition is expanded to ten bars by the soloists as they create additional space for their own journey, half over a very low organ fifth, half over the highest possible B, the positive and negative of a *ppppp* chiaroscuro. The orchestra responds with a purely instrumental seventh section. Clearly defined blocks of colour, density and activity lead to a second Höhepunkt: brass and woodwind state long, quarter-tone inflected Gs *ffff* followed by a silence, sustained G–C clusters and a flurry of rhythmic activity, the whole repeated four times faster, *ppppp*. The brief final transition (bars 265–7) consists of just one word from the soloists – 'tribuenda' –

Possible worlds

against the high B that will be the organ's ultimate goal. As the soloists continue, the choirs echo their words from the sixth section. These would seem to be two autonomous layers, but Nono finds textual–musical nodes and resonances as madrigalian as those of his vocal works of the late 1950s. The 'te' of 'tenebris' ('darkness') and 'terras' ('earth') coincide as both lines make their point by descending chromatically from the same B. The choral echo of 'adtolle in clarum' ('rise into the light') that constitutes the final section escapes the darkness of 'tenebris'. The last word of the penultimate line, 'indigno' ('unworthy'), is set to an insistent middle C, which opens to a chromatically extended fifth on 'adtolle'. The last 'clarum' is built from quarter-tone bands around the B♭ below middle C, B and A in successive higher octaves. Finally, while the organ sustains its highest B, flutes and sopranos fade their high A.

To regard Nono's late musical language as non-teleological, not goal-directed, might almost appear to be a truism.[13] While the motto 'non hay caminos' seems to point at precisely this state, *Caminantes* suggests a richer situation. In some respects it presents a paradigmatic example of the play of forces that subtends much of Nono's work: against a rotating background layer, one structure displays classical symmetry within clearly constrained orbits of pitch and rhythm, while another moves constantly forwards through its entire space. The underlying pitch trajectory, from the gravitational centre of the lowest C and its fifth to the highest chromatic band, also implies significant movement – structural/grammatical or semantic/illustrative or both. Bruno's multiverse has no single horizon, reference or end-state. Their absence does not imply lack of impulse or direction, however; every step is a directed searching through a space of infinite dimensions, a searching of which the work is a compound trace. One could see *Caminantes* as a journey as dramatic as that of *Prometeo* or the emigrant of *Intolleranza*. Continuous resistance is no longer a property with which the composer hopes to imbue the work; it is embodied in the sequence of acts of composition. Gerhard Koch's review of the premiere captures some of the work's richness:

> Nono has once again succeeded with a great work in which worlds of ideas and sonic spaces permeate each other so fascinatingly that one might imagine the Gasteig Philharmonic contained both San Marco and the sounds of Bruno's cosmos. [. . .] especially in the range of dynamic and timbral possibilities, expanded more widely than for a long time, and the hovering 'tutto lontanissimo' matched by hard percussive signals that remind one of Japanese Gagaku music, but also of Boulez's *Rituel*.[14]

Nono's programme note is a map of the thought-world from which *Caminantes* emerges. He lists its landmarks: Vicentino, Brouwer and Varèse; the Toledo inscription; the encounter between Jewish and Islamic cultures in Andalucia; radical creative thought in Berlin and Russia in the 1920s; repression and massacre in Ayacucho; Giordano Bruno; the Venetian school and polychoralism of the sixteenth century; the cosmology-inflected acoustics and combinatorial musical processes of Athanasius Kircher and the new hall in Munich, enriched with live electronics.[15] But if ideas are not reflected in reduced formal schemes – mapped to music – or as philosophical principles of composition, how might we understand Nono's musical navigation of an increasingly complex intellectual cosmos? Space and movement in the kaleidoscope of metaphors and images offered by Gosztonyi's book seem to offer a key. The hermetic magic inherited and embraced by Bruno involves a network of talismanic references that connect and give access to different forms of knowledge – wormholes in the space–time–wisdom continuum. References are related to each other by what Frazer would call 'sympathetic magic'.[16] This is redolent of compositionally conventional practices of imbuing a musical text with personal meaningfulness; Bach's numerology and the use of BACH by other composers constitute one

Possible worlds

such strand. In the same period, Nono was interested in the work of thirteenth-century Catalan philosopher Ramon Llull, which suggests a more formal model for the architecture of his intellectual space. He had accumulated much of Frances Yates' work, which sets Llull and Bruno firmly in the hermetic tradition, but which also explores their work as systems for mapping and exploring knowledge in the search for new truths – for *remembering, reflecting and reasoning*, to use Bruno's expression.[17] In his *Ars Magna*, Llull evolved a system of reasoning based on combining and synthesising ideas, a notion taken up by Bruno, adopted by another of Nono's references, Athanasius Kircher, and developed by Leibniz into his *ars combinatoria*. Nono's copy of Leibniz's early writings may also be relevant to *Caminantes*; there, Leibniz uses organ registration as a model for the ars combinatoria. Llull's vision has been seen as a precursor of modern computer programming, and Nono's own ars combinatoria is a contemporary, dynamical networked construct.

The word and its absence

'Découvrir la subversion. Hommage à Edmond Jabès'

During his visit to Paris in February 1985, Nono had immersed himself in a recent publication by Jewish French–Egyptian poet, Edmond Jabès, *Dans la Double Dépendence du Dit*.[18] This would bear fruit over two years later in a new work – *Découvrir la subversion. Hommage à Edmond Jabès* – presented on 5 October 1987 at the Paris Festival d'Automne dedicated to Nono's music. Performed the day before the final version of *Risonanze erranti*, the new work is closely related to its predecessor in sound and constitution: alto, tuba (Otto and Schiaffini) and live electronics remain, now joined by bass, horn and reciter. The nature of *Découvrir la subversion* as a musical construct is radically different, however. In contrast to the increasingly precise score of the earlier work, this performance was effectively an improvisation guided by a graphical score and Nono's direction; it was nevertheless the fruit of a compositional process equally as intense and extensive.

Jabès' short, dry questioning style offers no answers and affords no reduction; as poetic form, it is descended directly from radical philosophy. To transcend or escape self and yet be able to act is at the ethical heart of aesthetic behaviour, and Nono's abiding concern. For Cacciari, Jabès suggests a model; in his *Dans la Double Dépendence du Dit*, for example, 'Jabès breaks the 'pact' of Lévinas between the other and the face. The absolute other is also that which is other to every face.'[19]

Jabès' philosophical poetry takes up themes explored in the virtuoso performance hermeneutics of thinkers such as Derrida or Cacciari, but in a direct poetic voice. The recurrent imagery from nature – deserts, snow – recalls Pavese. Like Bachmann's *Keine Delikatessen*, like Cacciari's recent writing, it addresses (to hazard an absurd reduction) the very possibility of the book or the subject, the double bind of the word and silence, of the necessity and impossibility of writing. The meaning, the power of the word lies in its gaps, its margins. Jabès' gentle, incisive erudition combines the biblical and the modernist. In early 1986, back in Paris, Nono had moved on to his earlier *Le livre des questions*, now reading and annotating with a view to using texts in a new work.[20] He met Jabès on the same visit, and Jabès gave him a copy of *Le Parcours*. Both books became candidates for a new work, both presented structural problems: 'Difficult: concluded phrases!!! How to fragment them???'.[21] Having considered using both Arabic and Hebrew texts in their original, he eventually alighted on Jabès' 1982 *Le Petit Livre de la subversion hors de soupçon*.[22] This appealed to Nono on every level: the epigrammatic lyricism of the poetry, development of his investigation of Jewish thought from Schönberg

Possible worlds

onwards, of continual questioning, and above all the notion that the very act of challenging the impossibility of writing is both a subversive act of resistance and a moral obligation. In a sense, Jabès' explicit confronting of the obligation to write post-Holocaust poetry connects to Nono's earliest work.

In Jabès' *Le Petit Livre de la subversion hors de soupçon* Nono found that he 'theorises continuous interrogation, continuous questions, continuous doubts, continuous research [. . .] ancient memory, discoveries of ancient memory [. . .] the technology of today allows us to rediscover our past in a new way, to study it'.[23] Jabès' book extends the biblical interdiction of representation to writing in general; Nono's musical response was immediate.[24] *Découvrir la subversion*, the resultant work, persists only in its sketches and the fact of its performance. Perhaps we should likewise see Nono's use of material generated in the course of the research process in interaction with certain musicians as a process of structural self-effacement. The book, the text, as Jabès points out, is always too late:

> To go into the silence is to measure oneself against the unknown, the unknowable.
> In no way to learn what one doesn't know, but on the contrary to unlearn, to be
> ultimately nothing but an antenna for the infinity into which we sink. [25]

The shape of the new work began to emerge through 1986, gaining momentum during long visits to the studio in Freiburg. In the course of determining the musical constitution of *Jabès*, material had been proliferating. In Berlin in April 1986, a month after the Cologne *Risonanze erranti*, Nono constructed another monody of fifty-one 1–3 note segments using principally the material from *Dasein*, resampled and reconstructed, and reanalysed in colours according to their interval content.[26] This was intended for Susanne Otto, or perhaps two altos, perhaps with trombone; there now seems to be a central thread of production almost independent of particular works. From this material Nono constructs a new self-contained passage for low voice and horn, with tam-tam and bass drum; this again is 'to be fragmented – don't forget'.[27] He plans five segments of material, arranged in seven sections, intended for five texts from Jabès as yet to be determined.[28] This he contemplates resonating across two registers: alto and horn, bass and tuba. This core orchestration is repeated in another list of plans. To map the sequences of polyphonic density he returns to the number squares of his earliest works: permutations of 1–4, read in different directions.[29] In the same month, Nono considers a passage of piccolo material 'for Jabès', using the same interval palette but now in continuous multiphonics.[30] This is covered in layers of reflection and analysis and marked 'III' – perhaps a reference to the piccolo instance of the *Pre-Postlude* project already being planned, and thus a link between *Das atmende Klarsein* and the very last works. The essence of *Découvrir la subversion* was already established eighteen months before its performance, therefore.

While planning the works to come, Nono appears to set out a lexicon of gestures deriving directly from his humanist vision:

break *sff*	open <	fling wide *fffff ppppp* <	close	into itself
violento −	*dolcissimo*			
today	utopia			
utopia	today [31]			

In early summer and again in December, back in Freiburg, Nono worked in detail on the sound material, now experimenting with the overlap between horn (Martin Walz) and tuba, and exploring still further the range of vocal sounds with Susanne Otto and the team of engineers. A polyphonic weave of four soloists and four asymmetrically positioned loudspeakers is the basis. Transpositions, modes of spatial movement for groups of soloists, delay and reverberation times are all considered in detail. Instrumental and vocal material is all sketched in terms of a perfect fifth F–C. Nono is becoming expert at achieving a seamless relationship between live and processed sound, and at using the electronics to fragment material and space still further; there are no static 'effects'. Two particular ideas emerge from this research that are significant for the final shape of the work. As voices of processing accumulate, Nono pays careful attention to the point of crossover between an elaborated solo line and the emergence of a unitary choral texture, a perceptual transition. As with the final version of *Omaggio a György Kurtág*, space is now structurally related to performers and material. The sound of each soloist has its own inner spatial extension, but these are articulated as two pairs:

Su[sanne]:	———	near space less wide
c[o]r[no]:	———	
Basso:	———	near space more wide
G[ian]C[arlo]:	———	

Fabricciani does not feature in the list of performers sent by Nono in the spring of 1987 – the four soloists and a reciter – but in the draft scores and the performance itself he moves across the stage in the course of the piece, changing from piccolo to bass flute. For *Découvrir la subversion* Nono selected nine short passages from *Le Petit Livre* to be read in the original French (he had also considered Arabic and Hebrew), and nine to be sung in German.[32] In the 16 minutes of the Paris performance of 5 October 1987, recorded for radio, these are distributed across seven scenes of sound processing. It begins with half-sounded notes at registral extremes; isolated traces of figure surround the whispers of the reciter. A harmonic palette emerges as notes coincide, close enough in register to be assimilated as intervals. This process and the electronic transposition create a language of fifths and semitones, inflected by microtonal variations. The transition from solo to chorus is clear in the fourth section, where sounds and phonemes proliferate and coalesce into a polychoral polyphony. Sibilants are echoed, moved through the space to merge with breath sound from the wind, while the reciter intones at a low pitch, bringing speech and instrumental sound closer. The minimal notated pitch material outlines a clear structure, a trajectory describing both the fifth, the work's fundamental interval, and the semitone that separates the components spatially (Figure 15.6).

Figure 15.6 *Découvrir la subversion* – outline pitch structure

Possible worlds

The blank page

Haller sees the performed state of *Découvrir la subversion* as an initial sketch using a set of building blocks still to be refined into a score.[33] However, given Nono's direction of travel and Jabès' poetry, there is no reason to see this performance as an experiment on the way to a never-to-be-completed score. Many of the elements planned in detail through the previous eighteen months emerge clearly in performance. As we have seen, certain elements were as developed, the fruit of as much research, as those of *Risonanze erranti*, but other aspects were embodied in the shared knowledge of composer and performers, and become determined through rehearsal and performance. It is not the degree of composition that is different, but the distribution of that composition through time, individuals, technology and inscription. If *Risonanze erranti* stood at the border, *Découvrir la subversion* may have been a step into a new territory. That Nono was confronting a new state of the work-text while composing *Dècouvrir le subversion* is suggested in some words he underlined in his first encounter with Jabès:

> This absence of place, as it were, I claim as my own. It confirms that the book is not my only place, at once the first and the last. Place of a <u>non-place</u>, more vast, that I inhabit.
>
> [. . .]
>
> To hear a word is to hear it above all in its echoes, in its infinite prolongations. The book is built on this hearing.[34]

'Le blanc . . . la subversion' repeatedly emerges through the opening section of the Paris performance. The blank page is the subversion, the act of compositional resistance. What is absent is not the work – it exists, in its performance and in the recording that Radio France should release – but the commodity. The work's ontological status and its publishability – its status as definable, traceable intellectual property – are two separate questions. *Découvrir la subversion* was not an experiment, but one of an infinite set of possibilities characterised by their presence, their immanence to a given place and moment, rather than abstraction. It is – to paraphrase Jabès – conceived as a network of questions, not a construct of answers. Nono suggested such a view in an interview with Philippe Albèra during the Festival d'Automne:

> *For you, doing, living, communicating the experience is more important than arriving at a fixed form . . .*
>
> Absolutely! The great love, physical and intellectual, is in the moment of work, of study, in the errors that you make and from which you discover fantastic things. Afterwards, the interest is related to the possibility of still being able to change things. And then you have to abandon the whole thing, perhaps in a slightly brutal way, to follow other beginnings.
>
> *There's a link between this fundamental attitude and the fragmentary writing of your works, the obsession with the fragment: the refusal to organize a discourse, a logical discourse . . .*
>
> The logic of discourse is something terrifying for me. The taste for formulation, the formula, provokes an almost physical reaction in me. Hence my current interest in Edmond Jabès: his words always have multiple meanings, they are never unequivocal, meaning isn't fixed once and for all. Musil also talks about this: often one chooses a solution, a path, from the range of possibilities but in an instant one abandons other, perhaps more fertile possibilities.

Possible worlds

> *So it's these choices that determine an identity . . .*
>
> Perhaps . . . People talk a lot about identity . . . but whose? Of what? Personally I have many doubts in this respect. I have discussed this at length with Jabès . . . [35]

At root, the work of both Jabès and Nono is the lyrical expression of the relationship between continuous doubting and fundamental faith, mediated by warm humanism. In the work of both, the non-identity of the spoken and written word becomes increasingly important. Their meetings were warm; 'It was as if the writing, understood all at once, melted into the music', said Jabès.[36] Together, they discussed the ways in which the human voice can convey parallel states: the complex emotional truths embodied in the microtonal inflections of the Cantor in the synagogue, for example. The subtle vocal expression of Bellini – likewise, in Nono's view, a composer on the fringes of Western culture – was also of great interest at this moment. Nono's intimacy with the voice was a central thread of his work since the earliest settings of Quasimodo. Through *Risonanze erranti* and especially *Découvrir la subversion*, his last vocal work, he renewed this attachment; we can only wonder where these new fascinations would have led.

The Committee assembled after Nono's death to oversee editions of his music decided that *Découvrir la subversion* existed only as a preliminary exercise, as a 'compositional idea not yet defined in a score'.[37] They passed a similar verdict on Nono's last *Post-prae-ludium n. 3 'BAAB–ARR'*. While one can understand how the various concerns, viewpoints and interests of the committee might lead to this conclusion – as well as the challenges involved in producing a performing edition – several factors suggest that this is a view that fails to keep pace with Nono's own development. First, there are the material circumstances: the profile of the occasion, the years of thought and preparation, and above all the personal responsibility of Nono's relationship with Jabès. Then we must look at Nono's subsequent path: the solo works soon to follow, each open in different ways. Most importantly, we should listen to Nono's own words at this time. As we have already seen, that composing should be the defining of an idea in music runs absolutely counter to his ethos. Multiple paths and parallel possibilities are axiomatic. He adopts a thoroughly phenomenological approach to musical experience: when you hear music, he asks his listeners, are you listening to the sound of the performance, or to some putative score?[38]

The notion of fixing music independently of its lived experience is becoming antithetical to Nono's evolving ethos. As with the perceived 'turn' of *Fragmente*, this is doubtless a further stage in Nono's personal, philosophical development, but it is far from abstract metaphysics. He is confronting the practical impossibility of fully determining the music he is now imagining and experiencing, outside of the moment and context of performance. This is neither chance nor improvisation: events *are* fully determined in the moment of their instantiation through Nono's direction, materials and preparation relating to the specific work, and the intense experimentation with his close collaborators. He is also searching for a way of dealing with a thoroughly musicianly perception: that the transformational power of music lies not in notes on a page but in the pre-conscious link between sound and mind.

The writings of orientalist and philosopher Henry Corbin figured importantly in Cacciari's *L'Angelo Necessario* of 1986. In the same year, Corbin's 1960 study of Zorastrianism, Sufism and Persian mysticism, *Corpo spirituale e Terra celesta*, was published in Italian.[39] It deals with the *mundus imaginalis*, the domain proper to the artist. Nono quotes from his heavily annotated copy in his 'autobiographical interview' with Enzo Restagno in 1987: 'We have to admit that there are sounds perfectly perceptible to the imagination which are not transmitted by the vibration of air; they constitute the imaginary part of sound, sound as it exists in its pure state

Possible worlds

in the *mundus imaginalis*.'[40] Sound is the bridge between the physical and the beyond-physical. 'Mila is right when he says of me that the battle goes on,' said Nono in an interview during the Festival d'Automne, 'I hope for continuous transformation.'[41]

'Post-prae-ludium n. 1 "per Donau"'

A new work had been scheduled for the Donaueschingen Festival in October 1987 – an annual event with a central role in the history of post-war new music. Performed by Giancarlo Schiaffini with Haller and the Freiburg studio at Donaueschingen on 17 October, the score of *Post-prae-ludium n. 1* for solo tuba and live electronics was written quickly but its gestation was much longer. The idea of a sequence of solo pieces is first mentioned in a sketch that appears to be from 1982. The 'post-' and 'pre-' elements are sometimes listed for different instruments, as if they might surround something else. Low brass often play an important role in Nono's music, a direct connection with his Venetian forbears. In *Prometeo*, trombones ground and colour the timbre of the four orchestral groups, and Schiaffini's role is central. *Interludio 1°* was initially to be for tuba solo, and the most intense sonic kernel of *Prometeo*, *3 voci (a)*, is made of multiple transpositions and folds of the euphonium, building from Schiaffini's near-sine wave to complete sonic saturation. Besides Schiaffini's regular participation in Nono's chamber ensemble, other possible compositions had been discussed: a quartet for the October 1986 trombone festival organised by Free Music Production in Berlin, and a piece for trombones and voices for the opening of the Berlin Kammermusiksaal a year later. Well acquainted with the free music community, especially in Berlin, Schiaffini introduced Nono to an ethos of music-making quite different to that of other new music virtuosi.[42]

He had been in Paris with Nono for the Festival d'Automne in early October. There were performances almost daily: six performances of *Prometeo*, a concert with *Il canto sospeso* and two programmes of recent chamber works with live electronics. Over the previous few weeks, Nono and his closest collaborators had been involved in two performances of *Prometeo* in Frankfurt and several concerts dedicated to his music at the Settembre Musicale festival in Turin. Meanwhile, Nono was finishing a major orchestral score for Tokyo the following month. As the Donaueschingen premiere approached and Nono decided not to attend the festival, some kind of score was urgently needed. Before Schiaffini left for the Black Forest, Nono gave him the three pages that constitute the work's text.[43] 'Rudi (Rudolf Strauss, engineer at Freiburg), has the programmes that we worked with on Wednesday morning', he writes.

Experimentation in the studio had continued since *Prometeo*. With Schiaffini, Nono explored simultaneous falsetto singing and playing, extreme registers and dynamics, half-valve techniques – destabilising the acoustics of the instrument to allow glissandi and tremolo – jazz-influenced vibrato that evolves over the course of a note, and the sounds of whales.[44] All of these play a part in *Post-prae-ludium n. 1*. The score consists of a matrix of trajectories through various sound spaces, times, materials and gestures, situated within a broad formal architecture of electronic transformation. The 14-minute work is in two clear halves. In the first, seven possible colour-coded paths are provided, criss-crossing through four staves of different kinds of material: half-valve, sung falsetto, vibrato, and playing and singing together, all in the high register of the instrument.[45] At tempi of ♩ = 30 or 60, each might take roughly a minute or thirty seconds. It is indicative of Nono's conception of his material, of its possible worlds, that some notated elements are not reached by any of the given paths; they remain latent potential. Four sections follow, each elaborating a single pitch with microintervals and half-valve modulation, moving between impossibly long sustain and rapid, nervous interruption. In each, Nono's notated

Possible worlds

suggestions and textual description give only indications as to how the performer might respond to the evolving sonic environment. Their clear pitch centres (F5, C1, F4, D–A4) cover a four-and-a-half octave range. The selection of these pitches was quite pragmatic: Nono asked Schiaffini which were the highest, lowest and loudest notes on his 6-valve F tuba. The uneven waves of swirling, canonical delays of the first part are now replaced by long reverberation of phased and low-pass filtered sound. Despite the title's reference to the Danube, what we hear is the Venetian lagoon in fog, the spatial ambiguity of sound and slow waves moving out towards the Adriatic to the edge of European culture, the view from Nono's study on Giudecca: 'sospeso sempre più . . . allontanado sempre più'.

At Donaueschingen, *Post-prae-ludium n.* 1 was premiered in a programme with Boulez's . . . *Explosante-Fixe* . . . and Stockhausen's *Solo*. The festival seems to have been hoping for a historic reunion. Instead, Nono took the trans-Siberian train to Japan, clearly exhausted. 'Danke grazie an EUCH ADIEU L.N.', he ends the score. 'Do what you will with it', were his parting words to Schiaffini.[46]

During the festival in Turin, Nono gave a uniquely retrospective and remarkably full account of his work in an 'autobiographical interview' with Enzo Restagno.[47] In an interview for the Festival d'automne he presents a very concise picture of his trajectory to this moment, of his political engagement and his view of the current state of communism:

> Sartre spoke of 'engagement'. Canetti of 'civic responsibility' . . . in every period we have a different relationship with history, with the political context. My 'engagement' arises from the war, from the time in which Mussolini was in power. The avant-garde came from Russia, with poets such as Velimir Khlebnikov and Mayakovsky and painters such as Tatlin and Malevich. Through the great cultural adventure of the Weimar Republic and that in France, from Monet to Duchamp, from Rimbaud to Apollinaire up to Edmond Jabès today, I have always tried to find a balance – even if sometimes it's gone a step too far – between innovation in ideas and language. An interventionist approach, and engagement which has not prevented my opposing that enormous catastrophe which the communist regime has been, which has disappeared and killed generations. I have tried to opt for doubt, for incessant questioning in the face of creative ideas, of innovation, of contemporary thought.[48]

'2° No hay caminos, hay que caminar . . . Andrej Tarkovskij'

Distillation

Nono had long been an admirer of the films of Russian director Andrei Tarkovsky. *Solaris* (1971) and *Stalker* (1979) were already cult films when Tarkovsky came to Italy to make *Nostalgia* in 1983, before producing his last film *The Sacrifice* in Sweden in 1986. Most resonant for Nono had been the non-linear autobiography of *The Mirror* (1975) and especially the early *Andrei Rublev* (1965, but repressed in the USSR until 1971). Against the long backdrop of Russian history, in *Andrei Rublev* Tarkovsky composes a sequence of non-narrative events between which resonances and polyphonies emerge. As personal and historical narratives run concurrently, apparently arbitrary, enigmatic events assume symbolic significance. Rublev himself rediscovers the spiritual power of icons against a backdrop of violent upheaval. As in all Tarkovsky's films, the subject perspective is often unclear – this effectively forms part of Rublev's own continuous searching – and long durations, many with no apparent forward motion, afford the viewer reflection on their own role. Tarkovsky's famously long shots are

Possible worlds

often accompanied by music – not background music, but as object of contemplation – and Bach provides his constant reference. A particular recommendation came from Abbado, with whom Tarkovsky had directed *Boris Godunov* at Covent Garden in 1983; from then on, *Boris* would become a crucial operatic reference for Nono. In January 1987, a month after Tarkovsky's death, Nono wrote to Dobrovolskaja, presumably after seeing his just-released *The Sacrifice*:

but now ANDREI TARKOVSKI

Yesterday, here in Zürich, I was moved by his great poem – tragedy – tragic – it is our time, our here and now, our WHERE? FROM WHERE? TO WHERE? For a long time I haven't been so OVERWHELMED AND AMAZED FEELINGS – SYMBOLS – REAL – UNREAL – VISIONS – FAME – FOLLY – PROBLEMS TEARS INTERNAL – EXTERNAL – SPACES MADDENING MAD and US?[49]

A similar commission to that of *Caminantes* had arrived from Tokyo in March 1985, while Nono was in Freiburg revising *Prometeo* and preparing *A Pierre*. The new Suntory Hall was to open in October 1986, and a prestigious programme of new works was planned. Berio, Cage, Lutosławski, Messiaen and Xenakis were also invited, as well as Toru Takemitsu, the artistic advisor, who wrote to Nono urging him to accept.[50] The contracted premiere for the opening month was never a realistic prospect, and agreement was finally reached for the following season. On 28 November 1987, Ken Takaseki and the Tokyo Metropolitan Symphony Orchestra presented the second work in Nono's *Caminantes* sequence: *2° No hay caminos, hay que caminar . . . Andrej Tarkovskij*, a 25-minute work for seven 'choirs' – orchestral groups.

Yasui Architects' Suntory Hall develops the 'vineyard' arrangement pioneered by Scharoun's Philharmonie in Berlin.[51] Multiple overlapping terraces allow a large audience to surround and feel close to the performers while retaining the privileged aspect of the podium. The Tokyo hall offered more possibilities than that in Munich. Space is central to Nono's initial notes; his immediate ideas concern the distribution of forces and the movement of sound. Materials will be reduced to a minimum to realise this dynamic, sculptural conception. The main compositional work seems to have begun during July 1987, before Nono travelled to Frankfurt for the performances of *Prometeo*. In Giudecca he reminded himself 'remember – sounds – clouds – isolated and in continuous waves'. Returned from Frankfurt, he wrote to Lachenmann that he had reached an impasse:

again I'm in crisis: what is Frank.[furt] and Prom. [eteo]???/again new conflicting thoughts/again I can't 'fix' a single note (and I must for Tokyo)/again in a STORM at SEA_ /again Manfred_ Schlegel [*Lucinde*] can tell me something/again this maddening waiting.[52]

Work continued while he was in Turin in September for the Settembre Musicale, the first of the two major festivals dedicated to his music. He travelled directly to the second, the Paris Festival d'Automne, an intensely busy fortnight, where he finally began to draft an orchestral score.

Some abandoned ideas tell us much about Nono's conception of the work. For much of its development, Roberto Fabricciani was to move about the hall along set paths, his sound diffused electronically: 'Roberto vagabondo'. After Nono's prolonged and intimate collaboration with Freiburg, planning such an arrangement at a distance and with little rehearsal must have seemed impractical. This image is the seed of the solo piccolo piece of the following year,

Possible worlds

however. As well as the ever-present Halaphon, there are intriguing references to sampling.[53] Elsewhere, Nono considers using a tape he refers to as 'Müller'. This likely refers to the tape described by Alexander Kluge, a project by Nono and Heiner Müller for a tableau before Act V of *King Lear: Zwischenmusik für Grosse Gesangsmaschinen.*[54] In the Freiburg studio, Nono had assembled a tape of non-singing sounds – the unconscious sounds of breathing, preparation and effort – from recordings of singers in performance.[55] He planned to work further with Müller in the studio. In addition to a large library of his work, Nono had recently been much impressed by Müller's 1977 *Die Hamletmaschine* – a landmark work of theatrical self-deconstruction then set as music theatre by Wolfgang Rihm in 1987.[56] The influence of Kluge himself is also evident in this new approach to hearing opera.

Plans for electronics were soon abandoned, but this makes little difference to Nono's emerging idea. He continues to plan the architecture of the piece graphically, in terms of movement in space; as he begins to work with material, Nono seems to discover that the patterns of movement he has imagined can be realised acoustically.[57] The sound world revealed to him by working with the Freiburg studio has now become part of his compositional thinking independent of new technologies; this is a major part of his poetic re-empowering following the epic of *Prometeo*. Nono's sketches for *No hay caminos* demonstrate a continuous reassessment of his own practice. As he finds himself pursuing well-trodden technical paths he looks for fissures in his own habits of thought. Private compositional processes have become material, have acquired their own plasticity. The continuous writing out of tables, listing of possible combinations – most of which will be redundant – seems to be an exercise in concentration or meditation, a path to engaging with the work, for finding its essence and his own focus as much as a technical means for deriving its detail. In the context of Tarkovsky, we might see these as symbolic objects, as signs or traces of forces at play which may not reveal themselves on the surface. In these workings we see the ars combinatoria to which Nono referred, an example of the 'divided representation' identified by Vesely in the practices of contemporary architecture.[58] The musical object is no longer developed and projected by means of its 'image', but as the product of the interaction of a heterogeneous range of more algorithmic processes that are manipulated as the concept evolves and the work emerges. Inscription as a score happens at a late stage, but that process remains a vital moment of mediation for Nono and of state-change for the work.

'Continuo' occurs frequently through the sketches, although early plans involving the Suntory Hall organ were abandoned. The continuity of sound is emphasised by the grid of interruption – moments of absolute statis. There is no equivalent to the organ layer of *Caminantes*, but in some respects the formal timbral mosaic of that element provides the clearest model for *No hay caminos*. Its sixteenth-century influences are clear; not only Gabrieli and Josquin, but particularly three of Nono's companions on his trip to Greenland: his early notes refer frequently to Tallis, Striggio and Victoria. The 40-part polychoral motets of Tallis and Striggio provide models of the way minimal harmonic change draws attention to inner movement, and of the inherently spatial nature of polyphonic complexity. In Tallis' *Spem in alium*, Nono calculates proportions of bars and beats and marks the one moment of rhythmic unison.

The seven choirs of *No hay caminos* are constituted thus: 1 (behind the podium): 3 trombones, timpani, bass drum; 2 (podium): 5-part strings; 3–6 (two to each side): solo violin, flute; (3 and 5) or clarinet (4 and 6): trumpet, bongos; 7 (to the rear of the hall): solo viola/cello/double bass, trombone, timpani, bass drum. The main body of strings is in the centre, supported by a choir of brass and percussion. Four high choirs mark the sides and the rear choir is a reduced echo or mirror of the front two. 'a cantar e sonar' he writes, like the stamp of a Venetian

Possible worlds

polychoralist. It also reminds us that pitch and rhythm remain his starting points, brought to life by the continuous movement of timbre, and that the voice is Nono's fundamental model of sound production.

Open fifths are his elemental initial material: 'AnDrEj tArkovski', which with G become the open strings of the violin. This is reduced to G and D – initially assigned to the two elements A and B described below – and then to G alone. A variable pitch focus quantised in quarter tones is planned from the start; three quarter tones to either side provide a possible bandwidth – perhaps the resonance or Q of a filter – of a minor third. The single note retains its identity under constant changes of focus, perspective and speed of sound. Perhaps this is an example of what sixteenth-century composer and theorist Nicola Vicentino describes as a special category of sounds – those that are at once stationary and mobile.[59] Nono made frequent reference to Vicentino, who re-examined Greek music theory to propose a 31–note division of the octave. Nono's continued references to the opening of Mahler's *First Symphony* also find their fullest expression here: temporary aggregates of pitch and rhythm drift across a single pitch at varying speeds, each remaining a suggestion, a space of potential. The note G assumes a symbolic role. It stands for 'Gigi', of course, as it had as far back as the *Due espressioni* of 1953. As he briefly considers possible texts, 'about me' is one candidate.[60] But G is also *sol*, sun: 'sol sole saul sale de la terra' ('salt of the earth'), he writes at the top of his working draft.[61] 'Sounds transform feelings, feelings transform sounds', he says in a programme note.[62] There seems to have been some kind of transformation since the 'senza sole' he noted for the projected *Liederzyklus* in the darkest moments of 1985.[63] Now, a red circle at the centre of an early page of notes is marked 'sun – turning continuously'.[64]

Nono's red sun is also an acknowledgement of Japan, of the different cultural context for his new work and of the influence of Scarpa. The clarity of focus on detail, minimal materials and sharp juxtaposition of very slow and very rapid events all seem to address his Japanese audience directly, and constitute a further clear homage to his architect mentor. The form of *No hay caminos* is equally Venetian; the twenty-one marked sections outline a polyphonic architecture constructed like layers of different columns in a Palladian façade, their spaces revealing a further formal intertwining.

Expansion

The twenty minutes or so of *No hay caminos* fall into five main parts. As in recent orchestral works, the base tempo is ♩ = 30, deviations from which are its multiples 60 and 120. Each of the first four parts concludes with a section using the faster tempi. The fifth part concludes with a compound ritornello that almost precisely reprises the others in the sequence 2 3 1 4 – a characteristic Nono expanding series – apart from some changes in spatial distribution. As often with Nono, multiple waves of structure modulate each other. The form can also be seen as a bipartite structure with a coda. Bar 120 is the first moment at which G is heard completely without microtonal variants – a moment of stability or arrival. Bars 121–64 present a compressed version of the same trajectory, followed by two chords presenting the full microtonal set across the entire orchestral range (Figure 15.7).

Formal durations and rhythmic detail again both derive from the *A Veloce/B Calmo* material from *Con Luigi Dallapiccola*. The original six-part textures are five and eight bars long respectively. At Nono's default tempo these represent durations of 40"and 1'04". In an additional version of A, the parts are staggered by one bar, extending its duration to 1'20"; B is amended by adding A and B – 1'44"–which is then treated as two 52" subsections. These become the formal building blocks for *No hay caminos*; Figure 15.7 shows how the twenty-one marked sections of the work relate to this substructure. Within the non-ritornello sections there are few deviations: a bar is lost from 19–30, balanced by an additional bar of silence in the corresponding section of the next main part, at bar 67. The 1'36" structure of 19–30 is echoed at 144–55. In the long central section, bars 88–93 consist of 40" passages for percussion and strings, staggered by one bar. For each of the four durations he designs a distinctive pattern of sub-units to be fleshed out with material taken directly from A and B.

Figure 15.7 2° *No hay caminos, hay que caminar . . . Andrej Tarkovskij*: structure

Possible worlds

Rhythmic detail also comes from A or B accordingly, produced by a two-stage hand-crafted process. Nono's spatial permutations have become material; he makes multiple photocopies of A and B, cuts them horizontally into voices or vertically by bar and reassembles the pieces with tape to produce new textures. Through these he traces paths – single voices or complex textures – to sculpt the texture and movement he wants, using echoes, symmetries and reflections build coherent local structures. A single duration or rhythmic figure might provide a rhythmic unison for many voices, perhaps staggered in time as it moves across space, or mapped on to different subdivisions of the beat so that each choir has a clearly differentiated behaviour. Elsewhere, these values become a hollowed-out skeletal structure about which expanding and contracting waves of fast-repeating notes mark their beginnings and ends. These nervous, fleeting, mobile patterns are difficult to capture in consciousness; they leave their trace without affording rehearsal by the listener. The isolated accented pulses that often end a section both mark the formal division with absolute finitude and leave an acoustic after-image through the silent fermata that follows, obliging the listener to hear a relationship across the divide.

As well as two modes of duration/rhythm, there are two of pitch development: the main line of continuous expansion and contraction around the central G, and the separate, contrasting timbres of the four ritornelli. 'Rompi' – 'break' – is how he marks the ritornelli in his notes. Each section is characterised by the ways in which Nono explores his tightly constrained pitch material: as a rich timbre across several octaves, as a single frequency band of variable width or as a micro-scale. He begins by considering arrangements of the seven pitches across seven octaves – three to either side of a middle G – as well as asymmetrical 1- 2- 3- and 4-note subgroups across octaves or within a single register. The appearance of each pitch is balanced by its registral complement, mirrored about the central G4. He makes a selection from these subgroups, organised into a 7×4 grid. Through this, he traces a path to produce a sequence that will be the pitch structure of the non-ritornello sections.

The initial G in the central position is rendered mobile by its surrounding quarter-tones, proposed hesitantly by the lateral choirs in succession. The different subdivisions and offsets of groups of bongo attacks seems to announce that time can move at different speeds in different places. At bar 6, G–G♯ is spread vertically across three octaves, almost static for the first 52"subsection as it emerges from a *sul ponte* pre-echo from the rear strings, taken up by the main body and then the trombones to the front. As the side choirs elaborate, this is balanced during the rhythmically active second subsection by horizontal G–G♭ at bar 14. *Arco battuto* on open strings establishes a continuum between strings and percussion. The full low cluster of the passage at bar 19 – two octaves below the centre, in static, separated unison statements from the front choirs – is mirrored four octaves higher in that at bar 33, again in the main strings. They are separated by a single *fff* statement in bar 32, pre-echoed by the high lateral voices. The reflection at bar 33 approaches the other end of the spectrum: the pitched strings – a combination of *tasto* and *ponte*, both *arco lentissimo* and *ppppp* – are accompanied by the pure tones of *flautato* and the near-noise of *dietro il ponte*. Bars 41–53 develop bars 6–18, the initial G♯ an octave higher, spreading at the 52" point to add a stretched octave below, and adding a horizontal elaboration of the G♯ at bar 51. Strings front and rear initially accompany the lateral bongos with rich noise played behind the bridge; the layer of pitched sound dissolves as rhythm evolves. Percussion rhythmic unison interruptions around the entire space, *fff*, remind the listener that moving worlds can come into alignment to powerful effect. The four-octave spectrum is shifted down to its lowest point at bar 54, beginning with a stark low unison from all the trombones, and is balanced by the high G♭ (shaded only at its beginning by a quarter tone) of bar 68–75, the only single-pitch section of the work. Even within a single location and pitch there is constant movement, the oscillating spectral shading of *ponte* and *tasto ppppp* punctuated by *sff pizzicato*; 64 seconds of sustain draw the ear to fine detail. The long passage bars 80–109 actually consists of four of Nono's structural building blocks. A high, wide frontal string dyad expands into noise *dietro il ponte* to the sides, separated by intense lateral percussion activity from three low quarter-tones that develop to a quiet, intense string rhythmic unison. High, shifting dyads circle to the sides, building to a cluster again separated by percussion – now sparse – from the second low cluster, this time *sffff*. The high, three quarter-tone shape is echoed to either side, *ppppp*, at 110, before returning in the main strings at 121, effectively a reprise of the opening, then expanded to semitones in a further echo at 129, the harmonics of half the low strings articulated by the others 'behind the bridge, fast up-bow, like trembling human voices'. Bars 139–43 are entirely rhythmic until the last beat when loud low G♯s from front and rear cross with high Gs from either side. A kind of resolution is established as the trumpet Gs, now *ppppp*, are assimilated into the medial string resonance of the last such section.

The outer ritornelli (I and IV in Figure 14.10) are the only two instances of Nono's full seven-octave distributions. The first expands symmetrically as it rises above the lowest G. It passes quietly and rapidly from the rear, along the sides to a loud unanimous statement by the full forces, with only the lowest G left to dissolve. IV is an extended complement; almost the retrograde of I, it mirrors itself for the highest possible G to dissolve. III is itself almost a palindrome, *sffff* rhythms framing moving, sustained *ppp* chords, all from the high lateral choirs. In contrast, IV – the spectral inverse of I – is low, frontal and directional: five increasingly loud notes separated by fermata, in which a five-note cluster reduces to three and then to the only insistent lone G of the work, its abrupt end followed by seven seconds of silence.

Each section creates movement within its own clearly differentiated space of pitch, register, texture, density and spatial behaviour. Each is an autonomous, coherent sound-event with its own inner life. The sequence affords a balance of contemplation and drama that addresses its Japanese audience. Such a conception is clearly informed by the studio, but also by a sonic–analytical approach to acoustic music. In a interview in March 1987, Nono effectively denied the influence of the 'spectralists' – Grisey and Dufourt, for example – referring instead to early discussions at Darmstadt, but he listed the scores of Lachenmann and Kurtág among his travelling companions.[65] The relationship between these formal elements also recalls that between lines of texts or points of imitation in late sixteenth century polyphony – particularly in Victoria, another of Nono's companions in these months, and specifically the highly formalised *Tenebrae responsories*. Only two sections – the opening and bars 121–8 – exhibit melodic polyphony with imitation and continuity of line. The minimal oscillation moves slowly and regularly between lateral choirs, delayed and inverted. It recalls the Ambrosian response for Good Friday used by Victoria and noted by Nono in his initial sketches – *Tenebrae factae sunt* (*Darkness fell*) – the opening of which turns about G. Still more precisely, it traces the precise outline of *Veni creator spiritus*, the chant analysed by Scherchen at the beginning of his course in 1948 (Figure 15.8). Nono was clearly aware of such allusions: 'Mai Gregoriano!' he notes on his working draft.[66]

Figure 15.8 2° *No hay caminos, hay que caminar* . . . Andrej Tarkovskij: bars 2–3

Possible worlds

Sun, sacrifice and angels

The long train journey across Siberia must have reminded Nono of Tarkovsky's landscapes, as well as representing a physical break from the Western cultural milieu in which he had recently been intensely and exhaustingly immersed. Nono appears to have read the script of Tarkovsky's *Sacrifice* in May 1987, while contemplating the new work in Berlin, and likely had a video copy. Sound and music are central to Tarkovsky's conception of film. Through *Sacrifice*, there are constant sonic indications of events or dramatic dynamics beyond the image – a cognitive polyphony – as well as a clear musical architecture: the sound of the shakuhachi framed by *Erbarme dich* from the *St Matthew Passion*. Calabretto describes the use of sound and music in *Sacrifice* as 'never an amplification of the image, but rather forming a score that interacts with the story on film.'[67] Sound creates spaces of narrative and perspective: distant sounds of an impending air attack, local sounds such as the ticking of a clock, the modulation of these perspectives in the vibrating of glasses on the table. The singing of Swedish shepherds forms an other-worldly bridge between such environmental sounds and music. Tarkovsky's views on sound and music in film afford material resonances with Nono's work. The architecture of *No hay caminos* is essentially one of refrain. For Tarkovsky, 'the refrain brings us back to our first experience of entering that poetic world, making it immediate and at the same time renewing it. We return, as it were, to its sources.'[68] Fundamental to his highly composed use of sound is the elimination of everyday or environmental noise: 'as soon as the sounds of the visible world, reflected by the screen, are removed from it [. . .] then the film acquires a resonance.'[69] Here, Nono creates focus on movement, on timbre and the inner life of sounds by excluding all but a single note. The ways in which he draws attention to the constant shifts of intonation, spectral content and register of a single note in *No hay caminos* refer also to the shakuhachi; they relate this major orchestral score directly to the quasi-ephemeral solo piccolo piece developed over the following year. He seems to be responding to Tarkovsky's sense of the possible:

> I have a feeling that there must be other ways of working with sound, ways which would allow one to be more accurate, more true to the inner world which we try to reproduce on screen; not just the author's inner world, but what lies within the world itself, what is essential to it and does not depend on us.[70]

Such parallels are interesting but naturally incomplete. Nono gives us no clue as to where his path diverges from that of Tarkovsky. What is equally instructive about Nono's thought, however, is the enthusiasm with which, having identified such an empathy, he would search for creative resonances.

Long shots of slow movement, periods of near-eventlessness, abrupt changes and violent interventions, focus on apparent abstraction that proves to be part of material reality – Tarkovsky's tropes all serve to engage the viewer as reflective subject. 'The allotted function of art', he wrote, 'is not to put across ideas. [. . .] The aim of art is to prepare a person for death, to plough and harrow his soul, rendering it capable of turning to good.'[71] Dialectical engines – individual/group dynamics, personal/historical trajectories, architecture/poetry – generate the energy with which Tarkovsky sculpts time. Time is the medium on which cinema is impressed, and yet, following Eisenstein, poetry is its essence. Social, material consciousness and spirituality are inseparable. Likewise, the political and the artistic: a work that expresses only political truth becomes one-dimensional. We hear Nono echoed in Tarkovsky's words: 'The artistic image cannot be one-sided; in order to justly be called truthful, it has to unite within itself dialectically contradictory phenomena.'[72] If the Church represented malign

Possible worlds

conservatism in Italy, it had connotations of individual freedom in the USSR. The nature of Tarkovsky's work may allow more sight of its religious underpinning, but surely a similar conflictual relationship subtends Nono's thought. 'The meaning of religious truth is hope,' wrote Tarkovsky.[73] As often in his films, symbols provide portals between parallel worlds in a Bruno-like multiverse. The irreducibility of such elements is a vital property in works that would both explore and subvert their own logic.

Only after the first performance of *No hay caminos* did Nono come across Tarkovsky's essays, collected as *Sculpting in Time*. One essay in particular, *Art – a yearning for the ideal*, is heavily annotated: 'Art does not think logically, or formulate a logic of behavior. [. . .] It very often happens that a great work is born of the artist's efforts to overcome his weak points; not that these are eliminated, but the work comes into existence despite them.'[74] 'No schemes but invent, dream' writes Nono in his notes for Tokyo. Both film and music are supremely technical time-based forms; these are the reflections of mature artists confronting the ways in which they have assimilated their own techniques and practices.

The sculpting of time is effectively the sculpting of memory: 'Time and memory merge into each other, they are like the two sides of a medal.'[75] We might crudely identify three levels on which memory works though Nono's music. It acts structurally, within the work, in its manipulation of aurality, in echoes, mirrors and architecture. Each thought is also situated in its own network of cultural–historical memory, of music, poetry, thought and events. All these are audible to those who would hear. Of a third, middle level of personal memory we have only clues, yet it is perhaps from here that the music draws much of its strength. In Lachenmann's words: 'Hopefully you don't just listen, but you open your inner self to *No hay caminos* . . . or *Guai ai gelidi mostri*. You have to discover and unfold qualities of understanding with which you will live thereafter. It tears you open, and you are changed for the rest of your days.'[76]

Nono's programme note draws together all these modes of memory in its catalogue of associations: technical, historical, cultural and personal. He selected Maderna's orchestration of *Odhecaton* to begin the Tokyo concert. Its score, from over three decades earlier, is in Nono's own hand. *No hay caminos* was followed by Sciarrino's *Allegoria della note* and Webern's *Six Pieces for Orchestra* op. 6; it stood as the highly compressed, constantly turning centre of an image of Nono's own historical context.

Nono would stay in Japan for some days, discussing ideas with young composers at Tokyo University. As it did for Scarpa, this experience marks a major expansion of his aesthetic consciousness. In a public discussion with Takemitsu, Nono made clear the importance of his journey across Siberia (accompanied by Dostoyevsky):

> After a very particular year of work, I needed to cross unknown country. [. . .] For me this journey has also been a ceremony in the ancient sense, between the desire for something new and sacrifice, to make, to develop this desire to find other things. Solitude in the sense of sacrifice, to be 'far from', to then be able to find new encounters in Tokyo.[77]

He clarified his view of Tarkovsky's last film, and notes what seems to be a resonance with *Prometeo*:

> *Sacrifice* is a thought with different times of different ceremonies: visual, acoustic, photographic, dramatic [. . .] and disquiet when everything is subject to discussion [. . .] it is a great openness of Tarkovsky in the very moment when he was most ill: openness to nature, to human thought, towards a new world order. This dramatic

Possible worlds

quality, the son Petr who finally speaks and says: 'Daddy, why was there the word in the beginning?'[78]

Nono's productivity through this period, his commitment to making music and sharing ideas, bespeak an intense faith in art and humanity, and yet perhaps Tarkovsky's description of the main character of *Sacrifice* has resonances with Nono's more difficult moments:

> Alexander, an actor who has given up the stage, is perpetually crushed by depression. Everything fills him with weariness: the pressures of change, the discord in his family, and his instinctive sense of the threat posed by the relentless march of technology. He has grown to hate the emptiness of human speech, from which he flees into a silence where he hopes to find peace.[79]

As nuclear destruction threatens, Alexander offers to God – in whom he has declared not to believe – to sacrifice everything he loves, including his son (mute almost throughout), if it might be averted. Giovanni Morelli's perceptive and poetic essay finds more precise parallels between the narrative, symbolism and dimensionality of *No hay caminos* and those of *Sacrifice*. He draws an analogy between Alexander as an avatar for Tarkovsky and Nono's own creative condition:

> like no other musician of today, Nono discovered, or rather set out to discover, more in the doing than in the telling, that which a fuller formulation might term 'the pathos of still making music', surviving the terminal illness of the evolution of musical language: the progressive extinction of the possibility of aligning *idea* (gesture, thought, affect etc.) and *form*.[80]

Furthermore, Morelli sees the spatiality of Nono's composition as reflecting the modes of movement of Tarkovsky's film: its horizontal and vertical axes, its cruciform and circular potential, and the threads of its sonic polyphony. Calabretto understands the movement of *Non hay caminos* rather as that of the movie camera as the artist explores his subject.[81] While *Non hay caminos* is certainly not a musical version of *Sacrifice*, we might identify further resonant detail in the references to Japan (the 'Japanese tree', the ideogram it resembles, Alexander's kimono, the idea of nuclear explosion and the sound of the shakuhachi)[82] and the conflictual but inescapable relationship with Christianity (Leonardo's *Adoration of the Magi* and Bach's *Erbarme dich*).

In the earliest study of this work, Leblanc notes the resemblance between the distribution of choirs and patterns of movement forms drawn by Nono and the 'Tree of Life' of the *Sefer Yetzirah*, the earliest text of Kabbalah.[83] He sees a further echo of the barren tree that has a central symbolic role in Tarkovsy's *Sacrifice*. The *Sefer Yetzirah* had fascinated Nono since he discovered it in Granada in 1985; he had discussed questions of the Kabbalah with Jabès, and in an interview while working on *No hay caminos* he describes how his interest in Jewish thought had deepened his understanding of Schönberg.[84] The cosmological tree was also adapted by Athanasius Kircher, another of Nono's references at this time. The analogy is corroborated by Cacciari's contemporaneous use of the same image of Talmudic angelology to understand Klee's *Angelus Novus*. Only Michael and Gabriel are fixed points, 'all the other Angels sing their hymn and then disappear, to return where they were created, in the river of fire (Daniel 7:10)'.[85] Cacciari anticipates Nono's programme note reference to transformation: 'The music of the angels accomplishes, therefore, the miracle of this spiritual transformation of

Possible worlds

the numerus sonorous of the spheres, of the astral necessity, "de li etterni giri" ("of the eternal turning" – Dante, *Purgatorio*).'[86]

Berlin

Nono's election to the Berlin Wissenschaftskolleg for the academic year 1988–9 permitted him to sustain the tri-polar existence of the previous two years, moving between Berlin, Freiburg and Venice. The research project he proposed reflects his ongoing fascination with the voice and its use in different cultural contexts, in different spaces and particularly in the operas of Bellini.[87] Nono had been fascinated with Bellini since his studies with Maderna, but now he saw the Sicilian composer as representing a radical alternative to northern rationalism in his use of the voice and extra-European cultural influences.

The effort required by his own intensive research was significantly increased by increasing bouts of illness, leaving him with little patience for those less engaged. In March 1988 it was announced that Nono was to act as Guest Professor of composition at the Hochschule der Künste.[88] Three months later he resigned, citing the 'fossilisation' of the institution and its incapacity to prepare students appropriately. His specific requirements are interesting: 'For my teaching it is essential that there is at least a constructive openness, as well as some awareness of the significance of space in composition, of electronics and computer science.'[89] In May, he had attended the Leningrad performance of *No hay caminos* and spoken with students from the conservatoire. In July, he was in Granada for the Curso Manuel de Falla – not a course as such, he insisted, because composition cannot be taught. He expressed his long-standing interest in the use of the voice in flamenco, but despair at the conservatism of Spanish culture.[90]

If the institutions of music tried his patience, Nono's circle of German filmmakers and dramatists afforded dialogue and stimulus. Gorbachev's new policies had freed Eastern European states to plot their own course; Berlin was at the centre of the rapid developments that ensued. As an artist working on both sides of the wall, Heiner Müller's work – dealing critically with recent German history and with the attempt to build a socialist state – was now of wide public interest. Nono collaborated in producing the music for Müller's *Der Lohndrücker* at the Deutsches Theater, which ran for 72 performances from January 1988 to September 1991, through the collapse of the Berlin wall in November 1989.[91]

In 1987, in a letter to Lachenmann, Nono had mused about the possibility of making a version of Schlegel's *Lucinde*.[92] Schlegel's unfinished utopian work begins 'by destroying at the very outset all of that part we call "order", so as to remove it, and explicitly claim and actually affirm the right to a charming confusion.'[93] In some respects, this experimental novel, with its 'confused sheets' and abrupt shifts of mode and voice, is the source of the fragmentary, multi-perspectival approach to theatre, literature and film of Heiner Müller and Alexander Kluge.

Nono first mentions filmmaker, author, theorist and cultural commentator Alexander Kluge in 1985, in relation to Kluge's experimental cinema workshop in Munich. Together they planned a multidisciplinary seminar to be held in Baden-Baden.[94] Kluge, having studied music and law, had worked with Adorno's Institute for Social Research; it was Adorno who directed him to film, and Kluge became one of the leading lights of New German Cinema, alongside Herzog, Wenders and Fassbinder. Nono was first impressed by Kluge's writing. His books bring Müller's kaleidoscopic, democratising approach to a personal level, through transmedial sequences of texts, images and documents that 'encourage readers to become active "co-producers" in the meaning-making process.'[95] The same spirit characterises Kluge's films: 'The film takes on its existence in the spectator's head.'[96] 'Cinema has a temporal structure like that of music', Kluge had noted in 1976.[97] In a 1986 Berlin speech that Nono may well have heard,

Possible worlds

Kluge outlined an ethos that he would certainly have sympathised with: 'writers do not become political by sticking to a particular political praxis but by helping to recuperate (in the form of stories [Geschichten]) what is considered unpolitical as a political matter.'[98] Particularly significant for Nono was Kluge's 1964 novel *Schlachtbeschreibung* – a mosaic of different perspectives on the battle of Stalingrad. Nono's view is inevitably *Prometeo*-inflected:

> don't give definitions, don't give solutions, don't demonstrate an agenda, but give the maximum possible information, such that everyone can relate or connect, like supplying many means and then seeking to help arrive at the islands [. . .] to circulate, to move, to transport, to transform.[99]

In 1983, Kluge's film *Die Macht der Gefühle* (*The Power of Emotions*) had won the FIPRECSI critics' prize at the Venice Film Festival. In a characteristic assemblage of documentary, historical and fictional material, Kluge questions the institutionalised association of music with emotions. Verdi and Wagner are particularly prominent as he searches for alternatives to the inevitability of tragedy that social and economic forces conspire to reinforce; opera begins in hope and ends in despair. He deconstructs plots and finds unconventional perspectives. The physicality of singing fascinates him, as does that of the opera house: an institution related to those of technology and the military. He describes opera as 'the power-plant of emotions', a theme he returns to in later films: 'For years I have been working through literary and filmic means to change opera stories: to disarm the fifth act. [. . .] We must work to develop an *imaginary opera*, to bring forward an alternative opera world.'[100] Nono knew this work while he was working on *Prometeo*, therefore.

By the late 1980s, Kluge was interested in television, as a format and as a mode of communication. His many-voiced, fragmented approach persists in his TV productions. In late 1988, Miriam Hansen reported on Kluge's current projects, including the culture show *10 vor 11* – half-hour programmes juxtaposing short fragments, in the spirit of his historical documentaries:

> composer Luigi Nono has supplied the series with forty two-minute operas for adaptation. These miniatures will alternate with presentations of writers [. . .], conversations with the editor [. . .], portraits of actors [. . .], or just a series of outtakes [. . .]. *10 vor 11* is coupled with a programme of news analysis produced by the magazine *Der Spiegel*.[101]

In fact, Nono's involvement was not quite so direct: 'In Munich, Nono brought me a cassette of some experimental recordings made during the rehearsals for some of his concerts. I had asked him for short fragments of music for my cultural programmes. Over time, I created about forty two-minute soundtracks which proved very valuable for my television broadcasts.'[102] Their exchanges were clearly significant for both Nono and Kluge, however. Just as fragmentation, multiple networks of reference and constant shifting of perspective play important roles in Nono's late works, Kluge's subsequent broadcasts and films develop ideas from their discussions. Calabretto lists twenty-four programmes by Kluge that explicitly include music by Nono: some incidental, others featuring specific works such as *La Fabbrica Illuminata* and *Al gran sole*.[103] Kluge's *Achtung, Orchesterperspektiven!* of 1990 includes excerpts from *Siegfried* recorded as Nono had described to Restagno in 1987, using different sonic perspectives from stage, hall and orchestra pit. Several further films would emerge from Kulge's ongoing project of opera as *The Power-Plant of Emotion*, exploring plot, institution and the physicality and emotions of

Possible worlds

the performers themselves.[104] This incorporated *Der imaginäre Opernführer* (*The Imaginary Opera Guide*), written under the name of Xaver Holtzmann – a Calvino-like structural conceit that purports to survey 80,000 operas as a single score. Kluge's televised conversations with Heiner Müller frequently deal with opera.[105]

Nono's close connection with life in Venice remained important, however. At the end of 1988 he wrote to Girolamo Federici, secretary of the local PCI federation, that he would be back in the new year to renew his membership for 1989: 'Here: hard study – snow – beautiful encounters'.[106]

'La lontananza nostalgica futura'

A short history: Berlin

In the autumn of 1988, the Berliner Festwochen honoured their temporary resident with a 'Composer Portrait' series. As well as two performances of *Prometeo* on 30 and 31 August, two days of concerts on 3 and 4 September presented a broad range of recent and earlier music, together with two newly commissioned works for soloists: *La lontananza nostalgica futura – madrigale per più 'caminantes' con Gidon Kremer*, for violin with an eight-track tape, and *Post-prae-ludium 'BAAB–ARR'* for the solo piccolo of Fabricciani, scheduled to incorporate live electronics.

Kremer describes the hours before the premiere in minute detail; tension and trust emerge from his account with excruciating clarity. He arrived at Nono's Berlin apartment on 31 November, two days before the performance, without having seen a note. Nono, excited and enthusiastic, played him the tape:

> With his unique sonic imagination, Nono heard me in the most unexpected way, yet nonetheless I recognized my impulse. I was enthusiastic and asked him for the promised solo part. In response he showed me, nervously, apologetically, some bits of manuscript paper: here a line, there four bars, there three lines, and said with almost fatherly calm: 'No problem, no worry, I've got it all. Tonight I'll write it.' There were still 36 hours to the premiere.[107]

The next day they worked together, Nono writing in one room, Kremer practising in another. He had to decipher the extreme range and dynamics, the timings of multiple lengths of fermata and the very specific performance instructions with which the score is replete: 'con crini, senza vibrato, suoni mobile' is Kremer's example. New sections became illegible as Nono's ink ran out and he resorted to ball-point – a trivial event, but one that draws attention to the situated nature of composition, the role of context and sequence in the production of a work. Kremer gave up; Nono promised the remainder by that evening when they would reconvene in the Kammermusiksaal of the Philharmonie for a full technical rehearsal. A new practical challenge presented itself: the score now consisted of several large double sheets. How was Kremer, still reading new material, to negotiate this in performance? Kremer saw Nono's distributing of the work between music stands around the hall as a pragmatic avoidance of the performance being articulated by page turns. He was to move between these positions just as Nono mixed and spatialized the tape through loudspeakers throughout the space. 'To wander – is the goal' is how he understood the new piece.[108] It is not clear to what extent this mobility was part of Nono's initial conception, but it now became fundamental to the formal and performative nature of the work. Nono's enthusiasm increased as they realised the spatial and

Possible worlds

theatrical nature of the work – a feedback resonance that repeats itself through accounts of his collaborative working process.

He then suggested that Kremer perform the work without tape. This marks an important new stage in the performativity of Nono's practice, in his listening and in his close collaboration with performer and acoustic. His new piece for Fabricciani would realise this new vision. Following the general rehearsal, it was decided to retain the tape. Kremer's account also points to the intensity of personal relationships, particularly the attentiveness with which the Freiburg team would respond to Nono's ideas and requests. Kremer did perform *La Lontananza* solo later the same weekend, following Nono's disagreement with another scheduled performer. Both performer and composer were pleased with this slightly shortened version, but Nono subsequently decided that *La Lontananza* should only be performed with the tape. In January 1989 Nono revised his score for Ricordi from the manuscripts used by Kremer for the initial performances – snapshots of an evolving idea, perhaps, rather than stages towards a definitive text.

The work was performed as a duo between Kremer and Nono. One observation is particularly telling: 'The premiere succeeded. Nono had created a music never imagined, never heard before, avoiding every vulgar or familiar sound.'[109] Nono had remediated Kremer's own past – and, by virtue of Kremer's commanding position as a virtuoso, the past of the violin itself. Nono was less pleased with the performance – he felt that it had been too much a matter of accompanying Kremer with the tape, and insisted that in future performances the two elements should work as equal partners.[110]

Kremer's account is rooted in a conservative view of the relationship between composer, text and performer. The many stages of Nono's sketches present a very different narrative. It was not without time pressures, as lists of days remaining before Kremer's arrival attest; there was *Prometeo* to rehearse, as well as other works with live electronics. But this was a densely reasoned process, the fruit of months of contemplation. The direct and explicit relationship with his earlier work allows a clear comparison of practice. Many of the considerations and conceptual models of the early works can still be traced here, but their distribution through the compositional process and through the nature of the work itself is quite different. The performative nature of composition has now been fully assimilated to the extent that it becomes contiguous with performance. Fragmentation, movement and the role of the space itself were integral to the work's conception from the outset; the production of a score is one situated moment in its evolution.

A long history: Freiburg

We might consider the emergence of the work in five discrete stages, each informed by its own circumstances and motivation: initial recording with Kremer, constructing the tapes, the cyclical process of producing the violin part, directing the assembling of the whole in performance, and subsequent revisions to the score.

The two had been introduced in 1987 by a mutual friend, violist Charlotte Geselbracht, who had participated in *Prometeo* with the Chamber Orchestra of Europe. Before working with Kremer in the studio, Nono had then begun to plan a work for solo violin accompanied by groups of four violas, four cellos and four double basses. Using a modulus of 56", he plotted an architecture of time and density. Pitch material was to expand the open strings of viola and cello – C, G, D, A – with tritones and microtonal variation. He returned to his notes for *Varianti*. For Kremer's solo part, Nono's ideas are articulated spatially and in terms of movement, as five areas of bowing on the string. 'a sonar e a cantar' he repeats to himself.[111] This embryonic

Possible worlds

project perhaps reflects Kremer's initial suggestion that Nono should write a contemporary Venetian companion to Vivaldi's *Four Seasons*. A list of four *post-prae-ludia* planned for 1988 suggest that the larger project was soon dropped: Kremer, 2 percussion, voices, Roberto.[112] While effectively abandoned as the new work took shape, aspects of these initial plans inform its development. Kremer recalls their initial meeting, in Freiburg in the spring of 1987:

> Conversation soon [. . .] took a quite aleatoric path. Names such as Tintoretto, Schnittke and Webern, Florensky, Tarkovsky and Gorbachov surfaced, changing around. It was about politics, love, religion, philosophy, and everything seemed to flow together into one theme: the spiritual responsibility of the artist in the world. You never knew in what direction the next turn in the dialogue would lead. The only clear thing was the movement of searching. [. . .]
>
> To formulate [a concept of Nono] I would have to talk of vibrations, associations, perspectives and intensities. Without wishing to mystify Nono, the metaphor that occurs to me is that of the magnetic field, with its attracting and repelling energies. [. . .] Everyone who came into contact with him felt it. He himself would be moved by it, responding spontaneously to a situation or an idea.[113]

Having agreed on a project, they were unable to find time to work together until the following year. On 15 February 1988, they began five days of work in the Freiburg studio, recording continuously for hours every morning. As Kremer began to play, to warm up in the studio, he probably assumed that none of his initial gestures would be of interest. For Nono, the sound of a great violinist daily renegotiating a relationship with instrument, body and acoustic must have been fascinating. The tapes document the whole process. With quiet concentration, he asks Kremer to play high and as quietly as possible. These high sounds, sustained to focus on their inner life, are followed by the fifths and microtonal variations of Nono's initial plan. Kremer continues with high phrases – mostly extracted from the core solo repertoire, but recorded closely to reveal subtones, additional partials, bow noise and instability – and the percussion of attack. He explores every technique, mode of playing and attack imaginable. While phrases from Beethoven, Bach and Bartok begin to emerge, the obsessive repetition of practising draws attention away from figure or reference to the particular sonic qualities of each sound, to the nature of individual connections. Kremer digs deeper into his repertoire: virtuosic displays such as Heinrich Wilhelm Ernst's *Étude* on *The Last Rose of Summer* and more personal works such as the *Partita* of Vytautas Barkauskas. As the artists relax into their project, Kremer plays longer passages – entire movements of Bach, of Schumann – stopping to focus on sounds that fascinate or trouble him. This auto-archeological process seems to have been as interesting to Nono as the material itself. As Kremer searches for sounds and gestures, and then rehearses his own actions, these tapes explore an entire strand of Western music as embodied in one musician.

The day before, in preparation for the recordings, Nono planned the types of sound he hoped to elicit from Kremer. He lists six groups of material – perhaps not coincidentally the same number as individual *leggii* or sections of the final work. The first already has an internal drama anticipating the finished piece: 'furioso, sognando, dubbio/abbandono'.[114] Nono's notes and their recorded fragments of conversation show how they discussed gesture and rhetoric rather than notes or composers. He immediately begins to plot parallel narratives of live and recorded sound: above, he writes 'DRAMMA'. 'Choice: how?', he asks himself.[115] The presence of Kremer is vital. Their work in the studio is not an abstract pre-compositional generating of material, but an act present in the music. The physicality of the studio itself is to

Possible worlds

be represented, he notes: incidental sounds of windows, doors, chairs and microphone stands, some of which find their way into the final tape. The exploration is essentially of Kremer's own musicianship; only later does Nono begin to intervene, to ask for specific sounds from beyond the conventional palette: wood, noise, distortion.

Nono edited the tapes in late June 1988, with Haller's assistance. New schemes of categorisation evolve as he rehears the recordings. His process is graphical as usual: timed descriptions of the tapes are covered with layers of comments and connections, further analysed in colours such that structure and pattern begin to become clear. Sounds are characterised by origin (voice, Gidon, noise), composer (Bach, Vivaldi, Schumann), playing technique (balzato, armonici) or description (motivi), until clear groupings emerge. 'Motivi' – 'figure' – plays an important role in this process of organisation; the management of recognisable shape becomes a powerful compositional parameter.

Nine new tapes were assembled from these threads. Nono's notes refer to them as *Grundband* (foundation tape), *Krak* (sounds of the studio: door, glass partition, table, breathing), *Schumann* (including extracts from the violin version of the Cello Concerto – part of Kremer's own searching for new expression), *Wort* (including dialogue between Kremer and Nono), two called *1000 Kremers* and three further mixes (*Mix 4–6*). The occasionally distinguishable dialogue of *Wort* brings the searching of the studio into the moment of performance; only isolated words emerge clearly, but the intonation of questioning pervades. In *Krak* we hear the physical, incidental activity but also another acoustic. Nono's suggestion in the score that the tape was produced 'without any manipulation of the live recording' is not strictly true. These tracks were sculpted with the full Freiburg armoury of transposition, reverberation, filters, delays, spatialisation and layering. *1000 Kremers*, for example, is created using multiple delays with microtonal transposition. Only the *Grundband* remained unmodified: 18 minutes of Kremer's direct sound. Other tapes were as short as 1'20". In assembling a single eight-track tape, Nono had to reconcile this variation in duration. With *Varianti* already in mind, he considered using the sound-complex archetypes developed thirty years earlier – a symmetrical architecture, for example, with the shortest *Mix* at its centre. Such a solution would have inhibited the flexibility of performance he sought, however. Instead, material was repeated to extend all eight tracks to the full 61 minutes. André Richard – Haller's successor as director, who assisted at the premiere – describes them as four pairs:

Tracks 1 and 2: very dense, multiply overlayed harmonic material.
Tracks 3 and 4: original sounds of various techniques, single notes and fifths.
Tracks 5 and 6: voices, words, sounds of doors, chairs etc., also violin sounds.
Tracks 7 and 8: high sounding melodic material. Melodies in harmonics, fast tremolo, bouncing and thrown bow – spiccato, gettato.[116]

All these threads are thus continuously available in performance. 'These eight paths are entirely autonomous, I composed them so as to allow the perception of different times and qualities, aiming not for a unitary result but for a multipolarity of elements.'[117] They should not be heard all together, but rather form a rich resource from which the co-performer builds new polyphonies of variable density – not unlike the dense polyphonic fabrics from which Nono would weave new strands and textures in earlier works. Distributed through eight loudspeakers around the hall and mixed live, this allows the co-performer – initially Nono – to explore Kremer's sound world together with the violin soloist. With Kremer's movement, their exploration is also a spatial navigation of a jointly created space of potential; a new sonic–spatial–dramatic–referential polyphony is created in the act of performance. The multiple

Possible worlds

space-times of the work extend simultaneously through the tracks of the tape, sequentially through the violin part but then reordered by the soloist. Early plans for live electronics were reduced to a single intervention: the sustaining of the last note – a high G – of the sixth and last part while the soloist leaves the stage.

The six separate sheets or 'leggii' ('music stands') of the violin part are, like the tape, the product of a process of folding – a complex laminal structure, the final stage of which is determined by the violinist's movement between music stands during the performance. The sheets of the score are distributed by the performer among six music stands arranged around the hall. Additional stands are placed to enhance the sense of multiple possible sources. The only constraint is that the last sheet, *leggio VI*, must be next to a microphone and that the performer must be able to make their exit from this position. Freedom in taking time for movement and great flexibility of tempo mean that the internal timings of performances will vary widely, and coordination with any sound projection plan can only be approximate. Nono's tempo indications are sometimes in precise steps, elsewhere indicative, or in the case of the final leggio 'tempo 30 > 140'.

The six leggii derive from several heterogeneous layers of thought. The idea of working in fragments is present from the earliest sketches, as is a sequence of registers moving from low to high and ending with the entire range. These Nono associates variously with different techniques and colours: arpeggios, sustain, harmonics. A scheme of 'autocitazione' ('self-quotations') from *Varianti* also forms part of this conception. Fragments from the solo part of *Varianti* provide material – transformed and elaborated, but still recognisable at various moments. Two pitch structures modulate these sources. A chromatic scale covering four and a half octaves of violin range is numbered in permutations of 1–12. He also writes out all transpositions of the *scala enigmatica* in ascending and descending forms, grouped in tritone-related pairs. He plans a trajectory to explore their combination and selectively adds open strings to produce the interval language characteristic of *La lontananza*: seconds and ninths, fifths and tritones. The *scala enigmatica* provides a background source, transpositions and permutations forming a polyphonic web of possible paths within a meta-harmonic/melodic universe. Its role is now akin to that of the all-interval-series in the late 1950s. Kremer's account of Nono's excitement about the tape rings true; through the editing process and subsequent listening, he abstracted gestures and figuration from their referential context, modulating them with structures on other parameters. The presence in the score of material from the studio recordings gives the line a more physical, violinistic character than that of *Varianti*. It is densely woven with elements of Kremer's virtuosity: harmonics, characteristic dotted rhythms, *accelerando* and *precipitando* figuration, polyphonic sustained double stops, percussive *sffff* double stops. The bow is in constant movement of position – between bridge and fingerboard – and pressure: *flautato, tallone, crini + legno*.

Physicality is also central to Nono's engagement with his own text – an iterative cycle of listening, planning, writing, numbering, cutting and taping. Extended passages of material and shorter fragments emerge from his initial ideas, to be immediately divided and rearranged. A first continuous draft of some 157 bars, forensically reconstructed by Stefan Drees, presents a sequence of three kinds of material in almost equal proportions: fast-changing violinistic figuration with frequent harmonics, sustained double-stops with one open string and very long, high sounds.[118] This Nono cuts into thirteen fragments, to be rearranged into seven longer sections. Rewriting, recutting and reassembling using additional fragments and adaptations from *Varianti* produces the six sheets of the score used by Kremer in Berlin: *leggio I–VI*. Notated notionally in 4/4, this now extends to 333 bars.

For a performance at La Scala a month later, Nono rebalanced the six sections with some rearrangements of material. He revised and clarified some of the notation – also an irresistible opportunity to add further development. In moving from the initial performing scores to a version for publication, finished in January of the next year, Nono concentrates on the autonomy and coherence of the individual *leggii*. As a madrigal, perhaps, each part should present a satisfactory whole. The work now receives its full title: *La lontananza nostalgica utopica futura – madrigale per più 'caminantes' con Gidon Kremer*. The addition of 'utopica' qualifies the abstract 'futura' to balance the richer 'nostalgica'. It avoids the risk of appearing to be a nostalgia for past visions, a very material issue in the Berlin of 1989. It is a clear statement of faith: a concrete utopian future must be based in understanding of the past and the material reality of the present – the very stuff of this work.

Revisions were substantial. Each *leggio* of the final version is more focused, better characterised and structurally more self-sufficient than in the Berlin and Milan scores. Nono rebalances material between leggii. He elaborates and adds detail, often using his favourite devices of mirror and echo. Rhythmic detail is added to create new inner rhymes, straightforward repetition is eliminated and the whole is paced with a pattern of fermata of different lengths. The tape remains as before, but Nono retracted his suggestion that the violin part might be performed alone.

The folds of memory

The opening gesture of the Berlin, Milan and final versions is unchanged from the first continuous draft. This is the gesture with which the soloist begins part B of *Varianti*, and ends that work with its mirror (bars 83–4, 305–6) (Figures 15.9 and 15.10). The first versions of *La lontananza* open as if a new variant were just beginning; the mirror images spin from past to future. These notes connect *La lontananza* to the past just as the quasi-infinite sustain of the final high G leads to the future. The work itself is in continuous transformation – it will be

Figure 15.9 *Varianti*: solo violin, bars 83–4 (reproduced by kind permission of Schott Music)

Figure 15.10 *La lontananza nostalgica utopica futura*: leggio I, bar 1 (reproduced by kind permission of Casa Ricordi)

different at the next hearing – and the transformative power of music continues after the particular listening experience.

Leggio I then presents the sound world of *La lontananza* in outline: high harmonics, seconds and a dotted rhythm that becomes prevalent in this final version. Long sustains at a base *ppppp* are interrupted by percussive attacks *sffff* and cross-string sweeps. It shows signs of its revised order. In bar 24 (of 29 notated bars), the initial F is elaborated with a dotted rhythm which, in conjunction with the opening gesture, recalls Kremer's use of the second subject of Brahms' *Violin Concerto*. It is then extended by another phrase taken from *Varianti* (F–E–F♯ bars 118 – 121, mirrored at 269–70). This is framed in bar 25 by a new mirror of the preceding phrase which now reveals itself as a further shape from *Varianti* (bars 92–4), elaborated chromatically and with a trace of Kremer's open-string harmonics (Figure 15.11).

Figure 15.11 La lontananza nostalgica utopica futura: leggio I, bars 23–5. (Reproduced by kind permission of Casa Ricordi.)

The length of melodic shapes is extended in *leggio II*, interrupted by fast repetition of double and triple stops. As the architecture of the work evolves, new structural patterns emerge as important. Two gestures receive particular attention, referred to in his notes as 'intonatio' and 'rompi'. 'intonatio' figures importantly in plans for the tape. In the studio, Nono asked Kremer to play open strings – the sound of tuning, of initial contact between musician and instrument – to which he then adds microintervals, seconds and tritones, building the characteristic interval space of *La lontananza*. A sequence of such gestures provides the formal articulation of the final version of *leggio II* – echoes of Kremer's preluding in the studio (Figure 15.12).

The changes from the Milan version reflect Nono's careful restructuring. There, the first gesture of *leggio II* came after another opening phrase, and in reverse: D–D/G. The new version opens with the ur-gesture of the violin. Distributed through *leggio II*, the cycle moves up through the strings before beginning again. A new final gesture covers this entire compass from

Figure 15.12 La lontananza nostalgica utopica futura: leggio II, 'intonatio' figures

the open G and unites this with another important thread of *leggio II*, repeated sevenths or ninths. The sequence as a whole thus corresponds to Nono's original register-plan. His term 'intonatio' is itself rich in association: tuning, certainly, but also the statement of a cantus firmus before a motet, for example. 'rompi' appears to refer to the pattern of *sfff* attacks – often seconds or ninths, usually *sul ponte* – that punctuates all but the third leggio. Their distribution develops with the shape of the six sections, to form an additional grid of cohesion.

The scala enigmatica rises to the surface in *leggio III*. Combinations of transpositions together with open strings are allowed to develop uninterrupted in sequences of 2- and 3-part polyphony. The rhythmic simplicity of these slowly moving voices is in marked contrast with the outer leggii. This is part of what was initially the fourth leggio, now given clearer focus. It is framed by its last third being a fragmented, reordered reprise. The final low open strings are new in the revised score, and mirror the opening of *leggio II*. This still centre of *La lontananza* is *tutto ppppppppp, quasi inaudibile, flautato crini leggerissimo*. *Cantando* is a frequent direction throughout *La lontananza*, but *leggio III* is a moment of 'sonar e cantar'. The violinist is asked to 'sing dolcissimo where possible: unison, 8ve 5th with visionary serenity "la lontananza utopica" almost: looking for the sound'. This utopic moment is neither nostalgic nor future; it is one of presence, but presence is itself a state of searching.

In contrast, *leggio IV* is the most virtuosic episode, bringing together material from the original third and fifth sections. Its arresting opening arpeggiati are the loudest sounds of

Possible worlds

the entire work, their syncopated repetition an echo of the *Manfred* moments in *Prometeo*. Largely in harmonics, the whole is marked *alla punto velocissimo arpeggiato*, its rapid alternation between *tasto* and *ponte* punctuated by occasional hints of figure. These moments find their realisation in *leggio V, con suono molto pregno di canto*. The gestural balance is reversed now: fast ascending and descending arpeggios decorate a long line in constant microtonal movement, until they coalesce into an independent strand of development. The alternation of gesture and sustain continues into *leggio VI*, they approach each other, becoming a series of increasingly elemental figures of reducing complexity. Into this process, Nono inserts a final burst of velocissimo energy – itself a mirror – and an additional pattern of bars' rest. This sound world seems to absorb the occasional hints of melodic figure or violinistic figuration. It explores itself, searching for a new future, entering more deeply into individual sounds as it recedes from audibility. The final leggio comes increasingly to rest on high sustained *flautato*, moving between *tasto* and *ponte*, until the performer slowly leaves the stage under the electronically sustained final note.

Throughout the work, the soloist is instructed to play with a sound 'variable by intervals of less than 1/16 (of a tone), searching for itself, or searching for the sound, varying it every time'. As Sciarrino observes, the direction at the end of each sheet is equally vital to the spirit of the piece: 'walks slowly, halting sporadically, as if searching for rather than going directly to [the next] stand'.[119]

The rich web of musical and personal relationships is as much Nono's as Kremer's. He is physically present in the work; his voice is often heard on the tape, gentle and resonant. Nono's musical relationship with Kremer is very different from that with Fabricciani or Schiaffini. In Nono's work with his long-standing colleagues, composer and performer find a more unified voice, such is the depth of their mutual experience. With Kremer, he has to consciously construct a dialogue. Further performances must inevitably be shaped by the relationship of individual interpreters to this material. Their own experience is drawn in to the work's present; they cannot remain 'objective'. The mobility afforded by this space is made clear in a comparison of Kremer's 1990 recording, with the tape mixed by Sofia Gubaidulina, and that made a decade later in which the work's dedicatee, Salvatore Sciarrino, projects the sound with violinist Melise Mellinger. The former is dense and emphasises violin sounds, as if the performers are anxious not to lose any of Nono's material – quite understandable, so soon after the composer's death. Sciarrino's reading is more spacious and spatial, more selective. It focuses on individual sounds and gives greater prominence to percussive, abstract sounds and dialogue. We hear polyphony rather than density.[120]

As Sallis has pointed out, the mechanisms of *La lontananza* – sampling, reuse, duplication, collage, reference – might suggest understanding the work in terms of 1980s postmodernism. However, this is in no way an 'end of history' work. It is intimately concerned with personal and common musical histories and their potential for pointing to possible futures. The 'specious' present is an ungraspable, unrepeatable moment in which past and future might join to catalyse a transformation in the subject.[121] Nono points to this in his title: the madrigal is an intimate work, a rich polyphony of intra- and extra-musical references. Sciarrino, to whom the work is dedicated as an 'exemplary traveller', suggests its title be understood thus: 'the past reflected in the present (nostalgica) brings about a creative utopia (utopica), the desire for what is known becomes a vehicle for what will be possible (futura) through the medium of distance'.[122]

The notion of *lontananza* arrives via Sciarrino's own 1977 work *All'aure in una lontananza*. Sciarrino traces its origins to baroque poetry, and the common starting point for Nono and Kremer was Vivaldi. The constant references to breaking and fragments in Nono's sketches are in some ways misleading. This is not a destructive process but rather one, of folding, distributing,

Possible worlds

layering and annealing, of bringing together a wide network of elements into a single *hunc et nunc*. A more appropriate model might be Deleuze's conception of Baroque thought as an infinite folding, presented in *Le pli* (*The fold*) of the same year with suitably musical images:

> the Baroque represents the ultimate attempt to reconstitute a classical reason by dividing divergences into as many worlds as possible, and by making from incompossibilities as many possible borders between worlds. [. . .] In short, the Baroque universe witnesses the blurring of its melodic lines, but what it appears to lose it also regains in and through harmony. Confronted by the power of dissonance, it discovers a florescence of extraordinary accords, at a distance, that are resolved in a chosen world, even at the cost of damnation.[123]

Mila was moved by the Milan performance. Gone, he said, were the static, massive aspects of *Prometeo*:

> Sound, with its mysteries, its inner life, is the terrain and field of Nono's music since *Prometeo*. [. . .]
>
> It is a familiar, sincere Nono who speaks about this piece, for once safe from grand political, social or philosophical ideals. But not without ideals. They are more simple ideals, more human, more on the level of we who don't have wings to fly through the storms of great heights and stay with our feet planted on this dear good earth, like the 'travellers' to whom he entrusts this madrigal.
>
> 'La lontananza nostalgica-utopica/is my friend and makes me despair/in constant disquiet' [from Nono's programme note][124] Who ever expected to hear such a disarmed confession from Nono, so simple, so sincere? The 'content' of the work is here.[125]

Perhaps Mila had forgotten a letter from Nono some years earlier, writing about *Fragmente* while he began work on *Das atmende Klarsein*:

> I want to write to you about the quartet [. . .]
> there are many secret reasons
> among them some remain secret, and I have written to you about this_
> others_
> Hölderlin = past − present − future −
> Gods − magic − utopia or nostalgia[126]

The score of *La lontananza* may have been written at speed, but its germination had taken nearly a decade.

'Post-prae-ludium n. 3 "BAAB–ARR"'

The morning after the premiere of *La lontananza*, on 4 September 1988, Nono returned to the Kammermusiksaal to present another new work: another Post-prae-ludium, now for solo piccolo and titled '*BAAB–ARR*'. *La lontananza* and *Post-prae-ludium n. 3* '*BAAB-ARR*' form a pair. *La lontananza* is one of Nono's most densely constructed scores. It achieves its freedom in the present by allowing the performers to draw on a richly networked space of 'potentiality', to use Agamben's term. In '*BAAB–ARR*' that space is constituted very differently. This work highlights the superficiality of conventional shorthand distinctions between improvisation and composition. This is not to suggest that they are identical, but rather that in his practice, Nono had come to acknowledge the complex paths by which a work becomes inscribed in culture, text or technology, and in specific individual experience. If the role of the performative has long been central in Nono's practice, we now see an emerging acknowledgement that composition is itself a performative act.

Completing two new works, rehearsing and participating in several performances and being expected to maintain a public presence must have constituted a stressful period – a situation exacerbated by bouts of illness and disagreements over the complex production and performance details of *Prometeo*. In late July, Nono had worked with Haller in Freiburg on the technical plan: 'Nono's basic idea was for the flautist to walk around the concert hall, pausing by 4 microphones (between loudspeakers 1–4).'[127] Each microphone would be associated with a particular sound process: modulation, delay, amplification and spatialisation. The image of the flautist moving as he performs, filling a space with music, was with Nono since seeing Gazelloni in Maderna's *Hyperion*. It must have been reinforced in his first encounter with Fabricciani, watching Togni's *Blaubart*. The itinerant flautist is a mythical figure in many cultures. As space becomes Nono's main conceptual framework, he explores this idea in several projects: *Découvrir la subversion* and the sketches for *Caminantes* and *No hay caminos*. Initial plans for *Prometeo* had involved the movement of musicians, but with *'BAAB–ARR'*, *La lontananza* and its successor *"Hay que caminar"*, this becomes an integral part of Nono's thought. In his own notes, Nono initially considers sets of three pitches, but a repertory of seven modes of sound production: 'pure' stable sound, flutter tongue and tremolo with pitched breath, movement relative to the microphone, sound ↔ whistling, sound mixed with air, very high 'aeolian' sounds, low pitched breath with or without flute.[128]

In the event, he took a radical decision and reduced the outward complexity of the new piece to a minimum, eliminating the live electronics. For fifteen minutes, Fabricciani played a single note – B♭ – exploring every modulation, articulation and colour at his disposal, with Nono directing his performance and his movement around the hall. Fabricciani recalls the concert:

> The extraordinary thing is that in this piece there is no technology, despite the fact that we worked for days in Freiburg on technological experiments for this piece. Then once we were in Berlin we didn't use the technology, we played it with just live flute. [. . .]
>
> Nono was not very well [. . .] [and there were] technical problems. But all the same the piece was performed trying to convey the musical thought as far as possible. The beautiful thing is that the main aim was to project the sound in space [. . .] to direct the sound in the environment according to how we wanted it to move. We had always done this with electronic means, but for the first time we did it without and the result was exceptional.
>
> I moved around throughout the piece, but independently of my movement the sound itself moved, pulled; I projected the sound in various directions in the hall. Not only was I not static, but the sound didn't come only from where I was – you could hear it much more from down there, now here, another sound from elsewhere. This way of directing the sound spatially was possible because of the study made in the Freiburg years: that is, to conceive of spatialisation by means of different kinds of sound production.[129]

Possible worlds

The decision not to use electronics may have been circumstantial and unanticipated, but it seems to have been the catalyst for a major shift in Nono's understanding of the evolving state of his practice and imagination. A critic's ear-witness account gives a sense of the occasion:

Nono allows the space to participate. Flautist Roberto Fabricciani [. . .] wandered through the space while he was playing, crossing the gangways between the audience sections, turned in circles, leaned up or down – all of this following a plan fixed by Nono – and returned to the stage. The most amazing thing about this highly original piece is that it consists of a single note, a Bb. A note which, however, is subject to modulation on an incredible multiplicity of levels. It is a play with this single note, from a barely audible pianissimo to a brilliant fortissimo. It is an exploration of all the interpretative possibilities of the piccolo. Changing production techniques, vibrato, harmonics, blowing over the embouchure hole – all of this supported by the constantly changing acoustic of the room as the performer moves around – give the composition an enormous range of colour that allows one to forget that it is actually all the same note. Richness of sound replaces melody here.[130]

Wolfgang Schreiber confirmed the positive experience: 'Here again, by means of slowness and extreme differentiation the thought and music of Nono produce a result of absolute strength.'[131] Perhaps there is a clue to the sound world Nono imagined in a talk he gave a few months later, when he was the featured composer at the Avignon Festival:

if you take a sound, Bb. Today, with technology, with live electronics, it is possible to use a part of the sound, a part of the air, or, suddenly, the whole sound, with a particular direction or intensity, until it ends with just a breath. Now it is no longer just a Bb, but the flautist is using his breath nearest to a Bb and the live electronics allow us to bring it into movement. Today, with technology, we can achieve all this from a single note, which we used to consider very precise, uniform, unitary. Think of the historical techniques of Japanese woodwind and Korean flutes, with which they could obtain similar results. Take Tarkovsky's film *Sacrifice*, for which Takemitsu wrote the flute part using an Indian flute, without technology, using just the potential of breath, of the mouth, and not only the whole embouchure.[132]

Nono conflates two notions here: Takemitsu wrote a piece with alto flute called *Sacrifice* in 1962, but Tarkovsky's film uses shakuhachi recordings by Watazumido-Shuso.[133] Nevertheless, these are important reference points as he explores the acoustic potential of a world expanded in the studio. *Post-prae-ludium n. 3 'BAAB–ARR'* may indeed be unperformable without Nono's direction, and there is insufficient basis for a published score, but the recording referred to by the editorial committee that made such a decision is a document of exceptional significance. It marks a crucial moment in Nono's development, but also in the evolution of the very ontology of the Western 'work', of the relationship between imagination, text, action, situation and experience, and should be made publicly available.

'"Hay que caminar" Soñando'

Having completed the revision of *La lontananza* in January 1989, Nono turned his attention to a new project he had discussed with Kremer: a work for him and his violin duo partner Tatiana Grindenko. *"Hay que caminar" Soñando* was finished at the beginning of March 1989. In three

Possible worlds

sections, it reprises the multiple music stands and itinerant performance of the solo violin work – 'Moving at the end of each part, searching them out, as if looking for a path'.[134] Nono also returns to the score of that work, adding to its dimensionality, as Jeschke suggests, but creating something entirely new in the process.[135] The piece is entirely acoustic, but in its extremes of speed, dynamic, register and timbre the experience of the studio is assimilated and transcended; with such performers, Nono can hope for a fineness and sensitivity of control beyond the scope of live electronics.

All of the material in *"Hay que caminar"* derives directly from *La lontananza*, apart from a series of inserts marked in the score with square brackets: sustained diads outlining the scala enigmatica. Each violin part of each the three sections of *"Hay que caminar"* is constructed primarily of fragments from one of the six sheets of *La lontananza*. Nono segments each of the sheets of solo violin writing, as he has done with previous monodies. He begins by identifying twelve segments in each – perhaps an unconscious modulus – such that the two parts might stay in phase. However, the uneven length of natural units means that some require more, up to 21. These he reorders and adapts to produce the three separate sections (leggii) of the duo.

The printed edition is misleading, if not simply wrong, in its numbering. There, the three sections (leggii) are marked:

1: 1 (1st vln), 4 (2nd vln)
2: 2 (1st vln), 5 (2nd vln)
3: 3 (1st vln), 6 (2nd vln)

The actual numbering should be:

1: 1 (1st vln), 6 (2nd vln)
2: 2 (1st vln), 5 (2nd vln)
3: 3 (1st vln), 4 (2nd vln)

These numbers are the sheets of *La lontananza* from which the material is derived. This sequence also constitutes a characteristic Nono pattern, moving symmetrically inwards from the outside to converge on the centre. Nono is very aware of the musical and personal context of this new work. He omits the first page of leggio I and most of the last of leggio VI from his source materials. Thus, the outer moments of *La lontananza* are not present, as if to confirm that *"Hay que caminar"* has separated itself, has evolved its own autonomy and inner life.

Haas finds a possible anachronism in the fixing of scores for Nono's late works.[136] We might see a bifurcation in his practice: if '*BAAB–ARR*' represents one pole, then *"Hay que caminar"* is its complement. This is Nono's most score-based compositional process for years, in that there is no immediate experimentation with the performer, no work in the studio, no protracted graphical or symbolic process. This is far from 'paper' composition, however. If anything, the process of *"Hay que caminar"* most closely resembles a much earlier image of the composer: material and structure both fully internalised, an acute aural imagination, pen and manuscript paper. The reasons are several: Kremer's schedule and Nono's intensifying bouts of illness, certainly, but also perhaps a sense of liberation, of having emerged from periods when the sheer weight and intensity of musical and extra-musical thought, process and reference sometimes made action excruciatingly difficult. He has now arrived at a very direct relationship with sound, whether in the concert hall or on paper. We hear this in his choice, aligning and modifying of materials. His sources now consist only of the trace of *La lontananza* and the scala. As the duo partners each plot new trajectories through their individual spaces, they find new resonances, echoes and interactions, until at the end of each of the three sections they unite, finding focus in the same material.

Possible worlds

Each section has its own internal structure, its own behavioural dynamics as the two violins search for new sounds within their particular worlds and for new relationships with each other. In the first, the upper line is derived entirely from leggio I, the lower from leggio VI; they find agreement in the final G♯–C♯ that are a direct import from neither. In the second, the parts enter a common trajectory. For most of this section (bars 1–46), the upper part comes from leggio II, the lower from V; for bars 47–65, the upper part joins the lower in using material from V. This closer orbiting is maintained through the third section. Through bars 1–19 they both use fragments from leggio IV, through 20–48 from leggio III.

Nono's strategy for selecting fragments also varies between sections. Fragments are used only once, except where they are shared: the unison ends of sections one and two, and at the moments of closest integration in the opening bars of the third. In the first section he limits himself still further, only using fragments 3–11 of the two source sheets (leggii I and VI). In the second, all the material appears: 20 and 21 fragments respectively from leggii II and V. The two violins find their closest involvement in the third section, and this is where we most clearly see Nono's compositional craft at work. He begins by juxtaposing two fragments that begin with a rhythmic unison. Their following gestures are fused by superimposing a common grid of long fermata, beat by beat. In bar 6 he introduces a mirror to give form to the consolidation of two fragments between the two voices. Through the following three bars a high D is almost continuously present, again by means of the phased sharing of two fragments, as if a local attractor were emerging. Such stability can only be temporary: the D is repeated and echoed about two fragments that share an open A (bars 10–11) as this intense activity rapidly disperses to create the space through which the scala enigmatica will move.

There is a clear architecture to the use of the scala enigmatica across the three sections, however then reassembled in performance: it ascends in the first, descends in the last. In the first, the pattern of inserts outlines the scala on C in its ascending form twice with consecutive but non-overlapping diads. The second section has no explicit reference, but in the third it is the first violin alone that traces the descending scala in a series of separated, overlapping diads. Each is marked *ponte* or *tasto, crini e legno, ppppp*. They share these instructions with many other sounds, but the sustained intervals become an audible thread for the listener. Nono considered this as he began work: 'where possible AM [Ave Maria] a due corde'.[137] 'Emphasize them!', instructs Nono's preface, in an apparent contradiction to the performance indications that creates an interesting challenge for the performer. His notation of the scala elements – in square brackets – suggests that this thread should inhabit another dimension, perhaps of colour and intention rather than volume.

There is a further fold implicit in Nono's instructions: the sequence of combinations given in the score is only a suggestion, so the two violinists might each choose to play their three sections in a different order. The folding of the past into the present makes possible the search for the future. We hear traces of Scherchen, *Varianti, Fragmente*, work in the Freiburg studio, all finding new associations, opening new possible paths as they reassemble through their different orbits. *Soñando* – dreaming – is a state outside any causal sequence of past and future, a state in which paths to utopia might be imagined. A different account of time is needed to approach this work. Lisa Baraitser explores a taxonomy of modes of suspended time, a common feature of human temporal experience: staying, maintaining, repeating, delaying, enduring, recalling, remaining, ending.[138] She identifies these in practices of care that take time. The notion of caring is at the heart of Nono's ethos; embodied in and afforded by the work, caring is required of all involved for it to realise its transformational potential. If the argument is powerful in Baraitser's case studies of visual art, how much more applicable would it be to music, and particularly to this music built of the very suspension of time? Stenzl finds a more concrete dramaturgy; he sees the performers' walking as a connection with reality, against which *soñando* represents the maintaining of utopia in a time in which the great ideologies have been taken apart.[139] Nono is writing in Berlin just as the political and popular pressures mount that would lead to the fall of the Berlin wall in November 1989.

New models now present themselves in Nono's constantly evolving, enriching and complexifying sense of musical space and time. The stretching and folding of a chaotic attractor was one of the central images of the new chaos theory, widely disseminated and discussed through 1986–7.[140] Nono's membership of the Wissenschaftskolleg in Berlin would doubtless have exposed him to such ideas. More personally, Nono had been introduced to the work of visual artist Anselm Kiefer, whose works often develop over time subsequent to their leaving the artist's studio. Incorporating found materials and references to recent history, Kiefer's surfaces might transform rapidly, through burning, or over a long period with the oxidisation of lead ('the only material heavy enough to carry the weight of human history'). Nono had visited Kiefer at his studio in Buchen early in 1988. He brought back a copy of the catalogue recent exhibition of Kiefer's work in Amsterdam, focused on 'the recuperation of history'.

Kremer had hoped to give the premiere at his summer festival in Lockenhaus. This was postponed due to Nono's continuing illness; 'only the doctors knew how ill he was', wrote Kremer.[141] *Fragmente* was now in the repertoire of the Arditti Quartet, who played it in Berlin while Nono was working on *"Hay que caminar"*. Violinists Irvine Arditti and David Alberman gave the first performance of *"Hay que caminar"* at the conservatory in Milan on 14 October 1989 – *soñando*, to develop Stenzl's suggestion, during the very last, potentially explosive weeks of East German communism.

Unexplored worlds

Despite increasingly debilitating illness, the intensity of Nono's compositional activity was undiminished through the early part of 1989. Two projects in particular had been gestating in his imagination and were beginning to become material. In their different ways, both related to Helmut Lachenmann, with whom Nono now had regular and warm contact. They exchanged ideas and books. In March 1987, Lachenmann had sent Nono a copy of *Stammheim*, a recent book on the imprisonment and trials of the militant group Red Army Faction, whose initial leaders – Andreas Baader, Gudrun Ensslin, Horst Mahler and Ulrike Meinhof – were active between 1970 and 1972. The book's author, Pieter H. Bakker Schut, was their defense lawyer. Members of the group were tried for murder and for forming a terrorist organisation in a long process at the Stammheim prison from 1975 to 1977. By the time of their trial, itself of doubtful impartiality, some of them had been held in solitary confinement from three years. Lachenmann had known Ensslin as a child, and her letters would appear in his *Das Mädchen mit den Schwefelhölzern*. Meinhof was a very eloquent communist journalist, drawn to this circle with the attempted assassination of Rudi Dutschke in 1968. Her apparent suicide in 1976 was much disputed.

This may have been the work Nono had in mind when in a list of projected post-prae-ludia, probably in September 1988, he mentions one for voices featuring actress Hanna Schygulla, with whom he planned to work in the Freiburg studio.[142] More concretely, it is implied shortly afterwards in a proposed programme for a future concert in Cologne: the various solo and duo pieces would be performed (those for tuba and piccolo, with new pieces for percussion duo, voice and double bass), followed by the premiere of a major new work for the various instrumentalists with André Richard's Solistenchor Freiburg. Sketches for *Post-prae-ludium Stammheim* now begin to appear, and in January 1989 Haller sent Nono a full technical

Possible worlds

outline. In April, Nono informed Wolfgang Becker at the WDR that he was working on *Leopardi*.

As often, two texts triangulate the essence of the work. From *Stammheim* Nono selects no explicitly political statements or events but rather the reflections of Ulrike Meinhof on her solitary confinement: the disorientation, pain, loss of sense of self, loss of voice and language.[143] The human, the imperative to defend the human, is always Nono's subject; the political is an inevitable, contextual consequence. Meinhof's words are counterposed with a well-known canto by Leopardi: *L'infinito* (1819), a meditation on solitude. In its imagery of trees, hills, the sea and a distant beloved, Leopardi's poem seems to pre-echo Pavese. Nono did not reach the stage of drafting a score, but the materials he leaves suggest that in the very difficulty of composing he refined the process to what had effectively always been its core elements. From his analysis of the natural rhythms and voices of Leopardi's canto he distils a set of number patterns and a single dotted crotchet impulse, incrementally shifted by increasing rests. The scala enigmatica generates the pitch universe, but now it seems to be approached melodically, as a scale rather than as a matrix. For *Leopardi*, Nono plans a cycle of intervals from the scala – four steps upwards and four down, either alternating against a fixed upper or lower pedal or in contrary motion – on C, F♯ and G. If the rhythmic atomism recalls that of *Ritmica*, this pitch world has echoes of Nono's Eimert-influenced use of the all-interval series: a continuously self-regenerating dynamic.

The broader concept of *Stammheim* develops recent work and has some intriguing new threads. The spatial arrangement and movement are mapped like those for *Découvrir la subversion*. The six members of the chamber choir (SSAABB) are distributed around the performing space, at the rear of which are the two percussionists. Solo alto, flute and trombone weave different paths through this space. 'Orfeo' is written across one sketch. On another: 'hearing yourself /hearing space/headphones|Aristoxenes'. 'A la Mondrian' he writes on the page of basic pitch material. Mondrian had fascinated Nono since the Biennale exhibition of 1956, as he wrote to Steinecke at the time. Now he found in Mondrian a new model for the pluridimensionality of form, as he intended to explore in a parallel project.

From early in 1988, 'Arditti' begins to appear in Nono's plans of work. 'Quartett-Arditti' and then 'Quartetto (Arditti) + voce (Susanne) Testo?' are listed in plans dated 15 January. 'ARDITTI Quartetto con 4 voci canti <u>1789</u>' says another. These refer to a new commission from the Festival d'Automne to mark the 200th anniversary of the French Revolution in 1989. The commission for Nono was confirmed in July 1988: a new string quartet with alto soloist. To trace a line from the revolution of 1789 through Schönberg's own Second Quartet – its soprano soloist announcing 'the air of other planets' at the very moment of the dissolution of tonality – must have been an exciting prospect. Both Nono and Lachenmann were to be part of a *Cycle de Créations* planned by the festival. Their works were to be presented in the same concert; for both composers this would be a second string quartet. There are the beginnings of work on pitch material, a suggestion of multiple tempi and naturally indications of a spatial concept.

Nono's rediscovery of Mondrian seems to have been a turning point; he bought Jaffé's study of the artist in March 1989. Two works fascinate him: *Composition, 1916* and *Composition in line* (1917). In both, the mark is limited to many short vertical and horizontal black lines, their intersection and superposition. In the earlier work the lines vary in thickness, and behind them another pattern of areas of three colours plays with our perception; the 1917 painting is more uniform and only in black and white. In both cases the whole seems to have form, yet its edges are not clear. There is no centre; hidden dynamics seem to modulate direction and perspective. The eye is not permitted to stay still, but no direction of travel is privileged above another in terms of figure, texture or rhythm. Around both images Nono draws a bounding line – oval

Possible worlds

and rectangle respectively —connecting the numbers 1–4, presumably the members of the quartet (Figure 15.13). It appears that the players would mark the edges of this rich, decentred and decentering dynamic fabric.

Already in *Krisis* Cacciari had identified Dutch mathematician L.E.J. Brouwer as an important contributor to Wittgenstein's thought on the limits of formal systems. In his study of challenges to understanding of the nature of law, *Icone della Legge* (1985), Cacciari explores Brouwer's 'intuitionism' in more detail, and Nono begins to make reference to Brouwer from that point. For Brouwer – whose first published work was on art – 'there are no non-experienced truths'.[144] Mathematics is a mental construct, he says, and he distinguishes his intuitionism from classical mathematics, which, he says, believes in unknown truths.

With Nono's renewed interest in Mondrian, a powerful new resonance emerges. Mondrian was acquainted with Brouwer's thought through their common friend, mathematician and

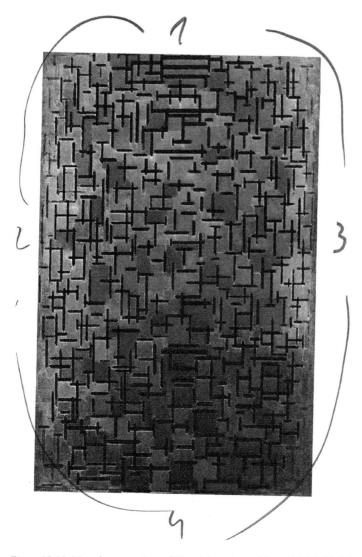

Figure 15.13 Nono's annotation of Mondrian *Composition, 1916* (Jaffé, 1971, p. 93)

Possible worlds

theosophist M.H.J. Schoenmaekers. Schoenmaekers viewed nature as a balance of opposing forces. His reduction of these forces to vertical and horizontal lines begins to enter Mondrian's work while he was writing *Neoplasticism in Painting* and producing paintings such as the two selected by Nono. For Mondrian, intuition offers a view of 'that incomprehensible force which is universally active and that we therefore call "the universal"'. The work of art is thus 'the subjectivisation of the universal'.[145] Time and space develop crucial roles in the process of its realisation:

> Composition leaves the artist the greatest possible freedom to be subjective – as long and insofar as this is necessary. The rhythm of relationship of color and dimension (in determinate proportion and equilibrium) permits the absolute to appear within the relativity of time and space.[146]
>
> [. . .] in life — time always upsets complete equilibrium; and — in art — rhythm relativises the pure expression of relationship.[147]

Nono had been thinking about this in late 1987, when in Paris he observed that 'Brouwer [. . .] overturned the conception of mathematics as based on unity, introducing the notion of contemporaneity'.[148] In Tokyo, he told Takemitsu about 'Brouwer, the great friend of Mondrian. One of the things they said was that it is not true that between two points the most direct connection is a straight line.'[149] As he began work on a second string quartet a year later, Nono seems to have been contemplating an important step in the evolution of his musical thought, a view that would address the central compositional issue of the relationship between theory, technique and intuition – between formal process and poetic insight. It would do so in a way that appealed to both his own tendency to the essentialising of material, and to his need for multiple times and spaces, multiple simultaneous possibilities: a new mode of polyphonic conception, at once a reconnection with his earliest instincts and a move into a new way of imagining music.

In June 1989, the new quartet was announced in the *avant-programme* of the Festival d'Automne, to be played by the Arditti Quartet. Nono referred to his spatial–polyphonic idea in a talk given at Avignon, where he was the featured guest at the Centre Acanthes of the Avignon Festival in late July:

> At this point we have to begin to talk about space, because in all the things I have talked about this is the important element that motivates continuous or discontinuous transformation [of sound]. Take a painting by Mondrian: where is the centre, the end, the limits, the beginning?[150]

His presence at Avignon was greeted with great fanfare in the French press; Nono's international reputation was at its height. He had insisted on going against medical advice, however. He was hospitalised in Paris, from where in September he wrote to Mimma Guastoni of Ricordi that despite some improvement his illness was serious – 'not simple hepatatis' – and long-term, but that nevertheless he was reading and working on the second quartet.[151] Sadly, instead of that work, at the Paris concert of 20 October Lachenmann's new *Reigen seliger Geister* was accompanied by a performance of *"Hay que caminar"*, a week after its premiere in Milan.

Nono was transferred back to Venice, where, despite more sustained medical attention and periods in hospital, his health continued to deteriorate. Warm messages of encouragement and support arrived from around the world. In December he received the news that he was to be awarded the prestigious *Grosse Kunstpreis Berlin* by the Akademie der Künste. He was too ill to

Possible worlds

travel to the presentation in March, or to the weekend of his recent music organised by the WDR in Cologne in April. Nono died on 8 May 1990, surrounded by his family, in the house of his birth. Stenzl reports that a few days before his death, Nono had asked to hear Bach's *Komm, süsser Tod.*[152]

Reports estimate a thousand people at the short memorial held at the church of Santo Stefano on 11 May. Fabricciani, Scarponi, Schiaffini, Susanne Otto and André Richard with members of the Solistenchor Freiburg performed choruses from *Das atmende Klarsein, Interludio 1°* and *Tre voci b* from *Prometeo* and Verdi's *Ave Maria*, before a small flotilla accompanied Nono from Zattere to the cemetery island of San Michele. 'He was buried on the island of San Michele, under the cypresses, not far from Igor Stravinsky, on a clear day "di gran sole"', recounted *La Repubblica*.

The national and international press reported this extraordinarily moving event widely, inevitably paying attention to the large presence of well-known musicians, politicians, artists and public figures. They then faced the impossible challenge of distilling Nono's contribution in words: 'The sound of humanity' (*Il Gazzetino*), 'The poet of sound' (*La Repubblica*), 'The poet of materialism in music (*La Stampa*), 'Explorer of sound' (*Corriere della sera*). Fellow musicians, musicologists and critics were keen to share memories and pay tribute, such that within weeks the press attention to Nono would itself be sufficient material for a book.

There are, of course, no last words; interest in Nono and his work, awareness of his relevance and resonance of his music have grown exponentially since that moment. Among the mourners on 11 May were Nono's comrades from the PCI, from his own Sezione Che Guevara on Giudecca, where he had been a member since 1952. It seems appropriate to hear the spontaneous reactions of his friends and comrades from the party. Just weeks before Nono's death, secretary Achille Ochetto had proposed changing the name; the PCI would be dissolved in February 1991. One of those who voted against was Pietro Ingrao. The day after Nono's death, Ingrao wrote this about his friend:

> his bold innovation cannot be separated from cultural and political history, marked by a sharp critical tension towards the forces that dominate in our time. And this goes beyond the purely political, which made Gigi Nono our dearest comrade. Nono confronted the great currents of thought and action that marked the second half of the twentieth century. We are talking about a great European intellectual; about someone who, more than any of us, understood the global dimension which is the context for so many of our problems and conflicts [. . .] Looking at Nono, at his music, at his powers of invention, at the heights of his cultural research, I find strength and hope.[153]

And Rossana Rossanda, the same day:

> I cannot imagine that Gigi Nono is no more, that he doesn't look at us with those wide eyes of a child and doesn't urge us on to do and to talk – music, politics, discovery.
>
> [. . .] Rarely have I known an artist – although the father of Nuria, Arnold Schoenberg must have been like this – for whom the world and humanity and events and ideas were as important as his own creation, or in fact the same thing. [. . .] Gigi Nono belonged to that moment in which notes or words were a way of understanding and fighting for a society in which a human being could be a human being.[154]

Possible worlds

Notes

1 ALN 56.05/14
2 ALN 56.15/12.
3 ALN 55.02/01.
4 ALN 55.02/03.
5 'Altre possibilità di ascolta', 1986. LNI 526.
6 Bruno, 1998, p. 36.
7 Bruno, 1998, p. 116.
8 ALN 55.03.01/17.
9 ALN 55.08.03/3.
10 ALN 55.03.01/05r.
11 Döllinger, 2012, p. 128.
12 ALN 47.07.01.
13 von Massow, 1999; Kisters, 2009.
14 Gerhard Koch, *Frankurter Allgemeine Zeitung*, 30 April 1987.
15 '*1° Caminantes . . . Ayacucho*'. LNI, pp. 499–501.
16 Frazer, 1996, p. 12.
17 Yates, 2002 (1964), 2014 (1966).
18 Jabès, 1984. Published in English in *The Book of Margins* (Jabés, 1993).
19 Cacciari in Röller, 1995, p. 69.
20 Jabès, 1988 (written 1963–5). Published in English as *The Book of Questions* (Jabès, 1991).
21 ALN 56.02/01.
22 Jabès, 1982. Published in English as *The Little Book of Unsuspected* Subversion (Jabès, 1996).
23 'Ideas and acoustics', interview with Agnes Hetényi, 1986. LN II, p. 390.
24 Röller, 1995, pp. 38–44.
25 Jabès in Röller, 1995, p. 21.
26 ALN 56.07.01.
27 ALN 56.08.01, 56.08.02.
28 ALN 56.08.02/03dx.
29 ALN 56.06/03.
30 ALN 56.07.02.
31 ALN 56.05/12.
32 ALN 56.04.02, 56.04.04.
33 Haller *et al.*, 1993, p. 8.
34 Jabès, 1984, pp. 80–81.
35 Interview with Philippe Albèra, 1987. LNII 424.
36 Jabés 1987, p. 12.
37 Haller *et al.*, 1993, p. 11.
38 'Altre possibilità di ascolta', 1986. LNI 528.
39 Corbin, 1986. Published in English as *Spiritual Body and Celestial Earth* (Corbin, 1989).
40 Corbin, 1986, pp. 105–6.
41 Interview with Michelangelo Zurletti, 1987. LNII, p. 449.
42 Schiaffini, 2011, pp. 98–100.
43 Reproduced in the performing edition prepared by Schiaffini: Ricordi 134668.
44 Interview with Giancarlo Schiaffini, June 2013.
45 The diatonic appearance of Nono's indicative pitch-shapes is a misleading artefact of notation; they should on no account be interpreted thus, which with the electronics would produce a diatonic haze.
46 Interview with Schiaffini, June 2013.
47 'Un'autobiografia dell'autore raccontata da Enzo Restagno'. LNII, pp. 477–568.
48 'I future felici'. Interview with Franck Mallet, 1987. LNII, p. 411.
49 Letter to Dobrowolskaja, 31 January 1987. In Esterbauer, 2011, p. 139.
50 Takemitsu was also an admirer of the filmmaker. His own *Nostalghia: In Memory of Andrei Tarkowskij* for solo violin and string orchestra would be presented in Edinburgh just weeks before Nono's new work in Tokyo.
51 Available at: www.nagata.co.jp/sakuhin/factsheets/suntory.pdf (accessed 13 September 2017).
52 Letter to Lachenmann, 24 August 1987, in Nonnenmann, 2013, p. 399.

Possible worlds

53 ALN 58.01/01, 58.02.01/07. Esterbauer, 2011, pp. 55–66, reproduces Nono's sketches of movement and his 'Tavola base' of basic compositional material.
54 Calabretto, 2017, pp. 194–5.
55 Kluge, 1999, 65–6.
56 Letter to Abbado, 27 November 1986, ALN.
57 ALN 58.02.02/01–04.
58 Vesely, 2006.
59 Vicentino, 1996 [1555], pp. 16–17, 225–28.
60 ALN 58.01/11.
61 ALN 58.06/01v.
62 *No hay caminos*. LNI, p. 507.
63 ALN 54.04.01/02.
64 ALN 58.01/11.
65 Interview with Enzo Restagno, 1987. LNII, pp. 531, 535.
66 ALN 58.06/02.
67 Calabretto, 2017, p. 87.
68 Tarkovsky, 1987, p. 158.
69 Tarkovsky, 1987, p. 162.
70 Tarkovsky, 1987, p. 159.
71 Tarkovsky, 1987, p. 43.
72 Tarkovsky, 1987, p. 54.
73 Tarkovsky, 1987, p. 43.
74 Tarkovsky, 1987, p. 41.
75 Tarkovsky 1987, p. 57.
76 Lachenmann, 2004, p. 226.
77 Seminar with Toru Takemitsu, 1987. LNII, pp. 435–6.
78 Seminar with Toru Takemitsu, 1987. LNII, pp. 442.
79 Tarkovsky, 1987, p. 222.
80 Morelli, 1991, p. 136.
81 Calabretto, 2017, p. 96.
82 Lawton, 1992, p. 131.
83 Leblanc, 1987, pp. 202–3.
84 Interview with Enzo Restagno, 1987. LNII, p. 500.
85 Cacciari, 1986, p. 54.
86 Cacciari, 1986, p. 23.
87 Monigatti, 1990, p. 80.
88 *Der Tagesspiegel*, 1 March 1988.
89 *Der Tagesspiegel*, 14 June 1988.
90 Interview in *El Semanero*, Granada, 1–6 July 1988.
91 Wood, 2017, p. 115.
92 Letter to Lachenmann, 24 August 1987, in Nonnenmann, 2013, p. 399.
93 Schlegel, 1971, p. 45.
94 Calabretto, 2017, p. 167.
95 Forrest, 2012, p. 17.
96 Kluge, quoted in Forrest, 2012, p. 14.
97 Calabretto, 2017, p. 167.
98 Kluge and Bowie, 1986, p. 126.
99 *Idee e acustica*. Interview with Ágnes Heyényi, 1986. LNII, 388.
100 Kluge, quoted in Flynn, 2004, p. 138.
101 Hansen, 2012, pp. 389–90.
102 Kluge, 2014, quoted in Calabretto, 2017, p. 181.
103 Calabretto, 2017, pp. 469–475.
104 Kluge, 2008.
105 In one such interview, after Nono's death, Müller describes an opera planned with Boulez. Available at: https://kluge.library.cornell.edu/de/conversations/mueller/film/1934/segment/2050 (accessed 8 November 2017).
106 Letter to Girolamo Federici, 4 December 1988, ALN.

Possible worlds

107 Kremer, 1999, pp. 208–9.
108 Kremer, 1999, p. 212.
109 Kremer, 1999, p. 213.
110 Interview with Paolo Petazzi, 1988. LNII, 466.
111 ALN 59.02/01–04.
112 ALN 59.03.01/01.
113 Kremer, 1999, pp. 203–4.
114 ALN 59.03.01/02.
115 ALN 59.03.01/04.
116 Richard in Haller, 1995, p. 190.
117 Interview with Paolo Petazzi, 1988. LNII, 465.
118 Drees, 1998, pp. 322–67.
119 Sciarrino, 2001.
120 For a more statistical comparison between three recordings, see Bassetto, 2007.
121 The notion of the specious present was introduced by William James in his _Principles of Psychology_, 1890.
122 Sciarrino, 2001.
123 Deleuze, 1992, pp. 81–2.
124 La lontananza nostalgica utopica future. LNI, p. 510.
125 'Nel cuore di Nono, fra I suoni' (_La Stampa_, 4 October 1988), in Mila and Nono, 2010, pp. 321–23.
126 Letter to Mila, 22 June 1981, in Mila and Nono, 2010, p. 192.
127 Haller _et al._, 1993, p. 20.
128 ALN 60.02/01.
129 Cescon, 2002, p. 97.
130 José Agueras in _Die Wahrheit_, 7 September 1988.
131 _Süddeutsche Zeitung_, 7 September 1988.
132 Conferenza all Chartreuse di Villeneuve-lez-Avignon, 1988. LNI, pp. 541–2.
133 Watazumido-Shuso, _The Mysterious Sounds of the Japanese Bamboo Flute_. Everest Records 3289, 1982.
134 Preface to Ricordi edition 134953.
135 Jeschke, 1997, p. 46.
136 Haas, 1991, p. 334.
137 ALN 61.04/01rdx.
138 Baraitser, 2017.
139 Stenzl, 1998, p. 126.
140 For example, Gleick, 1987.
141 Kremer, 1999, p. 215.
142 Interview with Paolo Petazzi, 1988. LNII, 466.
143 Bakker Schut, 1986, pp. 85–6.
144 Brouwer, 1984, p. 90.
145 Jaffé. 1971, p. 62.
146 Jaffé, 1971, p. 39.
147 Jaffé, 1971, p. 91.
148 'Bellini: un siciliano al crocevia delle culture mediterranee', 1987. LNII, p. 432.
149 Seminar with Toru Takemitsu, 1987. LNII, p. 437.
150 Talk at Chartreuse di Villeneuve-lès-Avigignon, 1989. LNI, p. 542.
151 Stenzl, 1998, p. 127.
152 Stenzl, 1998, p. 127.
153 _l'Unità_, 10 May 1990.
154 _il manifesto_, 10 May 1990, ALN.

REFERENCES

Adlington, Robert. 2013. *Composing Dissent: Avant-garde Music in 1960s Amsterdam*. New York: Oxford University Press.

Adlington, Robert. 2016. Whose voices? The fate of Luigi Nono's Voci destroying muros. *Journal of the American Musicological Society*, 69 (1): 179–236.

Adorno, Theodor W. 1980. Commitment. In *Aesthetics and Politics*, 177–95. London: Verso.

Adorno, Theodor W. 1981. *Prisms*. Cambridge MA: MIT Press.

Adorno, Theodor W. 1984. Neue Musik Heute. In *Gesammelte Schriften*, 124–33. Frankfurt: Suhrkamp. Original edition, 1955.

Adorno, Theodor W. 1998. *Beethoven: The Philosophy of Music*. Translated by Edmund Jephcott. Stanford, CA: Stanford University Press.

Adorno, Theodor W. 2002. The Aging of the New Music (1955). In *Essays on Music*, edited by Richard Leppert and Susan H. Gillespie, 182–202. Berkeley, CA: University of California Press.

Agamben, Giorgio. 1999. *Potentialities*. Translated by Daniel Heller-Roazen. Stanford, CA: Stanford University Press.

Albèra, Philippe, ed. 1987. *Luigi Nono, Festival d'Automne, Paris*. Lausanne: Contrechamps.

Allwardt, Ingrid. 2004. *Die Stimme der Diotima: Friedrich Hölderlin und Luigi Nono*. Berlin: Kulturverlag Kadmos.

Anders, Gunter. 1961. *Die Antiquiertheit des Menschen: Über die Seele im Zeitalter der zweiten industriellen Revolution*. Munich: C.H. Beck.

Antonioni, Michelangelo. 1998. *Unfinished Business: Screenplays, Scenarios, Ideas*. New York: Marsillo Publishers.

Appelbaum, Stanley. 1995. *Great German Poems of the Romantic Era*. New York: Dover.

Argan, Giulio Carlo. 1951. *Walter Gropius e la Bauhaus*. Turin: Einaudi.

Artaud, Pierre-Yves. 1980. *Flutes Au Present – Traite Des Techniques Contemporaines*. Paris: Editions Musicales Transatlantiques.

Auner, Joseph and Anne Shreffler. 2016. *Utopian Listening: The Late Electroacoustic Music of Luigi Nono. Technologies, Aesthetics, Histories, Futures International Conference/Workshop/Concerts, 23–6 March 2016*. Edited by Tufts University, Harvard University. Medford, MA: Tufts University.

Baars, Bernard J. 1997. In the theatre of consciousness: Global workspace theory, a rigorous scientific theory of consciousness. *Journal of Consciousness Studies*, 4 (4): 292–309.

Badiou, Alain. 2006. *Polemics*. Translated by Steve Corcoran. London: Verso.

Bailey, Kathryn. 1992. 'Work in progress': Analysing Nono's Il canto sospeso. *Music Analysis*, 11 (2–3): 279–334.

Bakker Schut, Pieter H. 1986. *Stammheim: Der Prozess gegen die Rote Annee Fraktion*. Kiel: Malik Verlag.

Balestrini, Nanni. 2007. *Milleuna: Parole per musica*. Rome: DeriveApprodi.

Balestrini, Nanni. 2013. *Vogliamo tutto*. Milan: Mondadori.

References

Balestrini, Nanni and Primo Moroni. 2011. *L'ordo d'oro 1968–77: La grande ondata rivoluzionaria e creativa, politica ed esistenziale*. 6th edn. Milan: Feltrinelli.

Banchieri, Adriano. 1601. *La cartella musicale*. Venice: Vincenti (facs. Forni, Bologna, 1968).

Baraitser, Lisa. 2017. *Enduring Time*. London: Bloomsbury.

Barbuto, Alessandra and Angelandreina Rorro. 2007. *Emilio Vedova 1919–2006*. Catalogo della mostra (Galleria nazionale d'arte moderna e contemporanea). Milan: Electa.

Baroni, Mario and Rossana Dalmonte, eds. 1985. *Bruno Maderna: documenti*. Milan: Suvini Zerboni.

Baroni, Mario and Rosanna Dalmonte. 1989. *Studi su Bruno Maderna*. Milan: Suivini Zerboni.

Barthes, Roland. 1985. Listening. In *The Responsibility of Forms: Critical Essays on Music, Art and Representation*. Berkeley, CA: University of California Press.

Bassanese, Stefano. 1999. La versione 1965 del diario polacco '58. In *La Nuova Ricerca sull'opera di Luigi Nono*, edited by Gianmario Borio, Giovanni Morelli and Veniero Rizzardi, 95–103. Florence: Leo S. Olschki.

Bassetto, Luisa. 2007. Tra guida e nastro: dialogo tra violinista e elettronica nella Lontananza di Nono. *AAA · TAC: ACOUSTICAL ARTS AND ARTIFACTS: Technology, Aesthetics, Communication*, 4: 105–16.

Beck, Julian. 1965. A letter from the Living Theatre. *The Tulane Drama Review*, 10 (1), Autumn: 214.

Beiser, Frederick C. 2008. *German Idealism: The Struggle Against Subjectivism, 1781–1801*. Cambridge, MA: Harvard University Press.

Benjamin, Andrew. 2005. *Walter Benjamin and History*. New York: Continuum.

Benjamin, Roger W. and John H. Kautsky. 1968. Communism and economic development. *The American Political Science Review*, 62 (1), March: 110–23.

Benjamin, Walter. 1973. Theses on the Philosophy of History. In *Illuminations*, edited by Hannah Arendt, 245–55. London: Fontana.

Benjamin, Walter. 1996. Goethe's Elective Affinities. In *Selected Writings: 1913–1926*, edited by Howard Eiland and Gary Smith, 297–360. Cambridge, MA: Harvard University Press.

Berdiaev, Nicolai. 1955. *The Meaning of the Creative Act*. Translated by D. Lowrie. New York: Harper.

Bernstein, J.M. 2003. *Classic and Romantic German Aesthetics*. Cambridge, UK: Cambridge University Press.

Berry, Mark. 2008. Arnold Schoenberg's 'biblical way': From 'Die Jakobsleiter' to 'Moses und Aron'. *Music and Letters*, 89 (1): 84–108.

Besseler, Heinrich. 1955. Bach als Wegbereiter. *Archiv für Musikwissenschaft*, 12 (1): 1–39.

Beyst, Stefan. 2004. Luigi Nono's 'Quando stanno morendo. Diario Polacco n. 2'. Available at: http://d-sites.net/english/nonopolacco.html (accessed 5 November 2012).

Bianco, Dante Livio. 1973. *Guerra Partigiana*. Torino: Einaudi.

Bobbio, Norberto. 1948. *The Philosophy of Decadentism: A Study in Existentialism*. Translated by D. Moore. Oxford: Basil Blackwell.

Bobbio, Norberto. 1955. *Politica e cultura*. Torino: Einaudi.

Bobbio, Norberto. 1975. *La teoria delle forme di governo nella storia del pensiero politico*. Torino: Giappichelli.

Bobbio, Norberto. 1976. *Quale socialismo?* Torino: Einaudi (trans. A. Cameron, 1998. *Which Socialism?* Cambridge, UK: Polity).

Bobbio, Norberto. 1995. *Destra e sinistra*. Rome: Donzelli.

Bobbio, Norberto. 1997. *Autobiografia*. Rome: Laterza.

Bobbio, Norberto. 2002. *A Political Life*. Translated by A. Cameron. Cambridge, UK: Polity.

Böhmer, Konrad. 1968. Booklet accompanying LP Wergo 60038. CD reissue 1992, WER 6038–2.

Bonuzzi, Luciano. 2003. *Egidio Meneghetti e la cultura medica del suo tempo*. Verona: Cierre / Istituto Veronese per la Storia della Resistenza.

Bontempelli, Massimo. 1942. *G. F. Malipiero*. Milano: Bompiani.

Borio, Gianmario. 2002. 'Liebeslied' di Luigi Nono: microcosmo di futuri sviluppi. In *Schoenberg & Nono: A Birthday Offering to Nuria on May 7, 2002*, edited by Anna Maria Morazzoni, 251–58. Florence: Leo S. Olschki.

Borio, Gianmario. 2004. Tempo e Ritmo nelle Composizioni Seriali 1952–1956. In *Le musiche degli anni cinquanta*, edited by Gianmario Borio, Giovanni Morelli and Veniero Rizzardi, 61–116. Florence: Leo Olschki.

Borio, Gianmario. 2013. Music as Plea for Political Action: The Presence of Musicians in Italian Protest Movements around 1968. In *Music and Protest in 1968*, edited by Beate Kutschke and Barley Norton, 29–45. Cambridge, UK: Cambridge University Press.

References

Borio, Gianmario and Hermann Danuser. 1997. *Im Zenit der Moderne. 4 vols.* Freiburg im Breisgau: Rombach Verlag.

Boschini, Marco. 1660. *La carta del navigar pitoresco*. Venezia.

Boulez, Pierre. 1963. Sonate, Que me veux-tu? *Perspectives of New Music*, 1 (2) Spring: 32–44.

Boulez, Pierre. 1975. *Conversations with Celestin Deliège*. London: Eulenberg.

Boulez, Pierre. 1986. *Orientations*. Translated by M. Cooper. London: Faber.

Boulez, Pierre. 1991. Stocktakings From an Apprenticeship. Oxford: Clarendon Press.

Boulez, Pierre. 1991a. Possibly . . . In *Stocktakings from an Apprenticeship*, 111–40. Oxford: Clarendon Press. Original edition, *Éventuellement . . . La Revue musicale*, 212 (May 1952), 117–48.

Breuer, János, 1982. Musicological Congress of the International Music Council, Budapest 2–5 October 1981. *Studia Musicologica Academiae Scientiarum Hungaricae T.* 24, Supplementum: 507.

Breuning, Franziska. 1998. Luigi Nono's Entwurfe für Musiktheater – von Intolleranza 1960 zu Al gran sole carico d'amore. In programme booklet *Al gran sole carico d'amore*, Stuttgart Opera. Stuttgart: Oper Stuttgart.

Breuning, Franziska. 1999. *Luigi Nonos Vertonungen von Texten Cesare Paveses: Zur Umsetzung von Literatur und Sprache in der politisch intendierten Komposition.* Munich: LIT Verlag.

Brouwer, L.E.J. 1984. Consciousness, Philosophy, and Mathematics. In *Philosophy of Mathematics: Selected Readings.* 2nd edn. Edited by Paul Benacerraf and Hilary Putnam, 90–6. Cambridge, UK: Cambridge University Press.

Brown, Timothy Scott. 2013. *West Germany and the Global Sixties: The Anti-Authoritarian Revolt, 1962–1978.* Cambridge, UK: Cambridge University Press.

Bruno, Giordano. 1998. *Cause, Principle and Unity: And Essays on Magic.* Translated by Richard J. Blackwell and Robert de Lucca. Cambridge Texts in the History of Philosophy. Cambridge, UK: Cambridge University Press.

Buey, Francisco Fernández. 2015. Love and Revolution. In *Reading Gramsci*, 1–59. Leiden: Brill. Original edition, *Leyendo a Gramsci*, Barcelona: El Viejo Topo, 2001.

Busch, Max W. 2005. *Tatjana Gsovsky Choreographin und Tanzpädagogin.* Berlin: Alexander Verlag Berlin, Akademie der Künste.

Cacciari, Massimo. 1973. *Pensiero negativo e razionalizzazione. Problemi e funzione della critica del sistema dialettico.* Padua: Marsilio.

Cacciari, Massimo 1976. *Krisis.* Milan: Feltrinelli.

Cacciari, Massimo. 1981. Io, frammento da Prometeo. In *Dopo l'avanguardia: Festival internazionale di musica contemporanea*, 21–2. Venice: La Biennale di Venezia.

Cacciari, Massimo, ed. 1984. *Verso Prometeo.* Milan: Ricordi.

Cacciari, Massimo. 1984. Verso Prometeo, tragedia del'ascolto'. In *Verso Prometeo*, edited by Massimo Cacciari, 17–22. Milan: Ricordi.

Cacciari, Massimo. 1985. *L'icone della Legge.* Milan: Adelphi.

Cacciari, Massimo. 1986. *L'Angelo Necessario.* Milan: Adelphi.

Cacciari, Massimo. 1990. Das atmende Klarsein. In *Voci enigmatiche* (concert series programme). Turin: De Sono. Associazione per la Musica.

Cacciari, Massimo. 1993. *Architecture and Nihilism: On the Philosophy of Modern Architecture.* New Haven, CT: Yale University Press.

Cacciari, Massimo. 2001. *Dell'Inizio.* Milan: Adelphi.

Cacciari, Massimo. 2002. Per il Prometeo. In *Happy Birthday to Nuria Schoenberg Nono*, edited by Anna Maria Morazzoni. Venice: Private publication.

Cage, John. 1961. *Silence.* Hanover, NH: Wesleyan University Press.

Calabretto, Roberto. 2001. Le musiche di scena di Luigi Nono per I Turcs tal Friúl di Pier Paolo Pasolini. *Ce fastu? Rivista della Società Friulana 'Graziadio I. Ascoli'*, LXXVII (2): 273–86.

Calabretto, Roberto. 2017. *Luigi Nono e il Cinema.* Lucca: LIM Editrice.

Calico, Joy H. 2008. *Brecht at the Opera.* Berkeley, CA: University of California Press.

Calvino, Italo. 2009. Preface to *The Path to the Spiders' Nests* (1964). Translated by Archibald Calquhoun and Rev. Martin McLaughlin. London: Penguin.

Campus, Leonardo. 2014. Italian Political Reactions to the Cuban Missile Crisis. In *An International History of the Cuban Missile Crisis*, edited by David Gioe, Len Scott and Christopher Andrew, 236–57. Oxford: Routledge.

Caprioli, Giovanni. 2007. Indagine filologica e analisi di 'Omaggio a Emilio Vedova' (1960) per nastro magnetioco solo di Luigi Nono. Facoltà di Musicologia, Università degli studi di Pavia.

References

Carocci, Giovanni. 1960. *Inchiesta alla FIAT: indagine su taluni aspetti della lotta di classe nel complesso FIAT.* Florence: Parenti.

Casadei, Delia. 2014. Orality, invisibility, and laughter: Traces of Milan in Bruno Maderna and Virginio Puecher's Hyperion (1964). *Opera Quarterly,* 30 (1): 105–34.

Cecchetto, Stefano and Giorgio Mastinu, eds. 2005. *Nono Vedova. Diario di bordo: da 'Intolleranza' 60 a 'Prometeo'.* Turin: Allemandi.

Celant, Germano and Fabrizio Gazzarri, eds. 2013. *Emilio Vedova: . . . Cosidetti Carnevali . . .* Milan: Skira – Fondazione Emilio e Annabianca Vedova.

Cescon, Francesca. 2002. Das atmende Klarsein di Luigi Nono. Indagine analtica e filologica sulla prima esperienza di Luigi Nono con il live electronics. Università Cà Foscari di Venezia.

Chinello, Cesco. 1996. *Sindacato, Pci, movimenti negli anni Sessanta. Porto Marghera – Venezia, 1955–70.* Milan: Franco Angeli.

Chinello, Cesco. 2008. *Un barbaro veneziano: Mezzo secolo da comunista.* Padua: Il Poligrafo.

Cisternino, Nicola. 2002. Con Luigi Nono . . . per rivedere le stelle. Conversazione con Massimo Cacciari. In *L'ascolto del pensiero: Scritti su Luigi Nono,* edited by Gianvincenzo Cresta, 23–37. Milan: Ruggimenti.

Coetzee, J.M. 2006. *The Poet in the Tower.* 19 October 2006 pp. 69–76. New York Review of Books.

Comisso, Irene. 2008. Luigi Nonos Prometeo, Tragedia del'ascolto. Rekonstruktion der Verarbeitung des Mythos anhand der Textentwürfe zum Libretto der Hörtragödie. In *Musiktheater der Gegenwart. Text und Komposition, Rezeption und Kanonbildung,* edited by Jürgen Kühnel, Ulrich Müller and Oswald Panagl. Salzburg.

Corbin, Henry. 1986. *Corpo spiritual e Terra celesta.* Translated by Gabriella Bemporad. Milan: Adelphi Edizioni.

Corbin, Henry. 1989. *Spiritual Body and Celestial Earth: From Mazdean Iran to Shi'ite Iran.* Translated by Nancy Pearson. Princeton, NJ: Princeton University Press.

Cossettini, Luca. 2009. Le registrazioni audio dell'Archivio Luigi Nono di Venezia: Linee per la conservazione e la critica dei documenti sonori. *Musica/Tecnologia,* 3: 99–112.

Cossettini, Luca. 2010. Introduzione. In *Luigi Nono, La fabbrica illuminata,* edizione critica. Milan: Ricordi.

Crehan, Kate. 2002. *Gramsci, Culture and Anthropology.* London: Pluto Press.

Custodis, Michael. 2004. *Die soziale Isolation der neuen Musik: Zum Kölner Musikleben nach 1945.* Stuttgart: Steiner.

Dal Co, Francesco and Giuseppe Mazzariol. 1984. *Carlo Scarpa 1906/1978.* Milan: Electa.

Dallapiccola, Luigi. 1970. *Appunti, incontri, meditatzioni.* Milan: Zerboni.

Dalmonte, Rosanna, ed. 2001. *Bruno Maderna/Wolfgang Steinecke, Carteggio/Briefwechsel.* Lucca: LIM.

Danks, David. 2014. *Unifying the Mind: Cognitive Representations as Graphical Models.* Cambridge, MA: MIT Press.

De Assis, Paulo. 2006. *Luigi Nono's Wende: Zwischen Como una ola de fuerza y luz und ..... sofferte onde serene ...,* 2 vols. Hofheim: Wolke Verlag.

De Assis, Paulo. 2009. Compositional techniques as a primary generator of dramaturgy. The dramaturgy of sound in the music of Luigi Nono, Venice. Unpublished paper presented at conference 'The dramaturgy of sound in the music of Luigi Nono', Venice, 13–15 June, 2009.

De Assis, Paolo. 2015. Venetian Postcard. In *Estas Sona, esta Linguagem: Essays on Music, Meaning and Society in Honour of Mário Vieira de Carvalho,* edited by Gilbert Stöck, Paulo Ferreira de Castro and Katrin Stöck, 171–82. Leipzig: CESEM – Gudrun Schröder Verlag.

De Benedictis, Angela Ida. 1998. Gli equivoci del sembiante: Intolleranza 1960 e le fasi di un'opera viva. *Musica/Realtá* (55), March: 153–217.

De Benedictis, Angela Ida. 2000. Incontro con Marino Zuccheri. In *Nuova musica alla radio: Esperienze allo Studio di fonologia della RAI di Milano, 1954–59,* edited by Angela Ida De Benedictis and Veniero Rizzardi, 177–213. Rome: CidIm-RAI.

De Benedictis, Angela Ida. 2006. Can text itself become music?: Music–text relationships in Luigi Nono's compositions of the early 1960s. *Ex Tempore: A Journal of Compositional and Theoretical Research in Music* (California State University), 13 (1): 24–48.

De Benedictis, Angela Ida. 2013. The dramaturgical and compositional genesis of Luigi Nono's Intolleranza 1960. *Twentieth Century Music,* 9 (1–2): 101–41.

De Benedictis, Angela Ida. 2013a. 'Intolleranza 1960' di Luigi Nono: Le metamorfosi di un libretto. In *La filologia musicale. Istituzioni, storia, strumenti critici. Vol. 3: Antologia di contributi filologici,* ed. Maria Caraci Vela, pp. 633–56. Lucca, LIM.

References

De Benedictis, Angela Ida and Ulrich Mosch, eds. 2012. *Alla Ricerca di Luce e Chiarezza: L'epistolario Helmut Lachenmann – Luigi Nono (1957–1990).* Florence: Leo S. Olschki.

De Benedictis, Angela Ida and Veniero Rizzardi, eds. (2000). *New Music on the Radio, 1954–1959.* Rome: Rai-Rai-Eri.

De Benedictis, Angela Ida and Veniero Rizzardi, eds. 2010. *Massimo Mila e Luigi Nono: Nulla di oscuro tra noi.* Milan: Il Saggiatore.

De Benedictis, Angela Ida and Veniero Rizzardi, eds. 2018. *Nostalgia for the Future: Luigi Nono's Selected Writings and Interviews.* California Studies in 20th-Century Music. Berkeley, CA: University of California Press.

De Benedictis, Angela Ida and Ute Schomerus. 1999/2000. La lotta con le armi dell'arte: Erwin Piscator e Luigi Nono. *Musica/Realtà*, 60/61: 190–205/152–84.

De Luna, Giovanni. 1982. *Storia del Partito d'Azione.* Milan: Feltrinelli.

Degrada, Francesco, ed. 1977. *Al gran sole carico d'amore.* Milan: Ricordi.

DeLanda, Manuel. 2011. *Philosophy and Simulation: The Emergence of Synthetic Reason.* London: Continuum.

Del Bo, Dino. 1944. *Persona e società nella filosofia di N. Berdiaeff.* Padua: CEDAM.

Deleuze, Gilles. 1992. *The Fold: Leibniz and the Baroque.* Translated by Tom Conley. Minneapolis, MN: University of Minnesota Press.

Deliège, Célestin. 2003. *Cinquante ans de modernité musicale: De Darmstadt à l'Ircam. Contribution historiographique à une musicologie critique.* Brussels: Éditions Mardaga.

Dessau, Paul. 2000. *Let's Hope for the Best.* Hofheim: Stiftung Archiv der Akademie der Künste – Wolke Verlag.

Di Stefano, Chiara. 2010. The 1968 Biennale. Boycotting the Exhibition: An Account of Three Extraordinary Days. In *Starting from Venice: Studies on the Biennale*, edited by Clarissa Ricci, 130–33. Milan: Et al. Edizioni.

Doati, Roberto. 1993. *Con Luigi Nono – Festival Internazionale di Musica Contemporanea 15–16 September 1992, 11–20 June 1993.* Milan: Ricordi – Biennale di Venezia.

Dobrovolskaja, Julia. 2006. *Post Scriptum. Memorie. O quasi.* Venice: Libreria Editrice Cafoscarina.

Döllinger, Christina. 2012. *Unendlicher Raum – zeitloser Augenblick.* Saarbrücken: Pfau Verlag.

Donati, Paolo and Ettore Pacetti, eds. 2002. *C'erano una volta nove oscillatori: Lo studio di Fonologia della Rai di Milano nello sviluppo della Nuova Musica in Italia.* Rome: Rai Radiotelevisione Italiana.

Döpke, Doris. 1987. Fragmente-Stille, an Diotima: Réflexions fragmentaires sur la poétique musicale du quatuor à cordes de Luigi Nono. In *Luigi Nono, Festival d'Automne, Paris*, edited by Philippe Albèra, 98–113. Lausanne: Contrechamps.

Drees, Stefan. 1998. *Architektur und Fragment: Studien zu späten Kompositionen Luigi Nonos.* Saarbrücken: Pfau.

Driesen, Pauline. 2011. Destare l'infranto, rinnovare silenzi. Open form in Luigi Nono's *Prometeo* (1984–85). *Revue belge de Musicologie/Belgisch Tijdschrift voor Muziekwetenschap*, 66: 203–22.

Driesen, Pauline. 2016. Marching with the Times: The Different Revolutions of Mayakovsky and Nono. In *Luigi Nono und der Osten*, edited by Birgit Johanna Wertenson and Christian Storch, 65–96. Mainz: Are Musik Verlag.

Durazzi, Bruce. 2005. Musical Poetics and Plotical Ideology. Ph.D., Yale University.

Durazzi, Bruce. 2009. Luigi Nono's Canti di vita e d'amore: Musical dialectics and the ppposition of present and future. *The Journal of Musicology*, 26 (4): 451–80.

Edwards, Peter Ivan. 2008. Object, space and fragility in Luigi Nono's Das atmende Klarsein. *Perspectives of New Music, 46* (1): 225–43.

Ehrhardt, Bettina. 2001. *A Trail on the Water.* bce film: Munich.

Eimert, Herbert. 1950. *Lehrbuch der Zwofltontechnik.* Wiesbaden: Breitkopf & Hartel.

Eimert, Herbert. 1956. Uraufführung von Nonos 'Canto sospeso' in Köln. *Melos* (December): 354.

Elzenheimer, Regine. 2008. *Pause. Schweigen. Stille: Dramaturgen ger Abwesenheit im postdramatischen Musik-Theater.* Würzburg: Königshausen & Neumann.

Ensenzberger, Maria. 1974. Osip Brik: Selected writings. *Screen*, 15 (3): 35–54.

Esterbauer, Erik. 2011. *Eine Zone des Klangs und der Stille.* Würzburg: Königshausen & Neumann.

Fabbriciani, Roberto. 1999. Walking with Gigi. *Contemporary Music Review*, 18 (1): 7–15.

Fabbriciani, Roberto. 2008. *Flauto in scena.* Monfalcone: Teatro Communale di Monfalcone.

Favretto, Ilaria. 2002. The Italian left in search of ideas: The rediscovery of the political ideas of the Action Party. *Journal of Modern Italian Studies*, 7 (3): 392–415.

Fearn, Raymond. 1990. *Bruno Maderna.* London: Harwood.

References

Fearn, Raymond. 2003. *The Music of Luigi Dallapiccola*. Rochester, NY: University of Rochester Press.

Fehervary, Helen. 1977. *Hölderlin and the Left: The Search for a Dialectic of Art and Life*. Heidelberg: Carl Winter.

Feinstein, Adam. 2004. *Pablo Neruda: A Passion for Life*. London: Bloomsbury.

Feneyrou, Laurent. 2002. *Il Canto sospeso de Luigi Nono: musique et analyse*. Paris: Michel de Maule.

Flamm, Christoph. 1995. Preface: Il canto sospeso. In *Il canto sospeso*. London: Eulenburg.

Flynn, Caryl. 2004. *The New German Cinema: Music, History, and the Matter of Style*. Berkeley, CA: University of California Press.

Forrest, Tara, ed. 2012. *Alexander Kluge: Raw Materials for the Imagination*. Amsterdam: University of Amsterdam Press.

Frazer, James George. 1996 (1889). *The Golden Bough*. New York: Touchstone.

Fuçik, Julius. 1948. *Notes from the Gallows*. New York: New Century Publishers.

Gabetti, Lorenzo. 1990. *A Luigi Nono*. Vienna: Istituto Italiano di Cultura.

Gallehr, Theo. 1966. *. . . denn der Wald ist jung und voller Leben*. Cologne: WDR.

Gärdenfors, Peter. 2004. *Conceptual Spaces: The Geometry of Thought*. Cambridge, MA: MIT Press.

Gazzelloni, Severino and Emilia Granzotto. 1984. *Il flauto d'oro*. Turin: Edizioni RAI.

Geiger, Friedrich and Andreas Janke. 2015. ZUHÖREN = MEER – FISCH – WOLKEN – TIEFES MEER! Zur Rolle Venedigs für Luigi Nonos Musik. In *Venedig: Luigi Nono und die komponierte Stadt*, edited by Friedrich Geiger and Andreas Janke, 9–34. Munich: Waxmann.

Gennaro, Sara. 2004. Interview with Ennio Gallo (video at ALN).

Gentilucci, Armando. 1987 (1972). Musica-Manifesto n. 1: Un volto, e del mare – Non consumiamo Marx. In *Luigi Nono, Festival d'Automne, Paris*, edited by Philippe Albèra, 164. Lausanne: Contrechamps.

Gibson, Ian. 1989. *Federico García Lorca: A Life*. London: Faber.

Gleick, James. 1987. *Chaos: The Making of a New Science by James Gleick*. New York: Viking.

Goeyvaerts, Karel. 2010. *Selbstlose Musik: Texte, Briefe, Gespräche*. Cologne: MusikTexte.

Goffi-Hamilton, Federica. 2006. Carlo Scarpa and the eternal canvas of silence. *Architectural Research Quarterly*, 10 (3–4): 291–300.

Goléa, Antoine. 1960. Review of 'Il canto sospeso', Venice, 17 September. *Témoinage Chrétien*, 30 September 1960.

Goléa, Antoine. 1962. *20 ans de musique contemporaine*. 2 vols. Paris: Editions Seghers.

Gosztonyi, Alexander. 1976. *Der Raum: Geschichte seiner Probleme in Philosophie und Wissenschafte*. Freiburg (i.Br.): Karl Alber.

Gottlieb, Saul. 1966. The Living Theatre in exile: 'Mysteries, Frankenstein'. *The Tulane Drama Review*, 10 (4), Summer: 137–52.

Gramsci, Antonio. 1947. *Lettere dal carcere*. Turin: Einaudi.

Gramsci, Antonio. 1950. *Letteratura e vita nazionale*. Turin: Einaudi.

Gramsci, Antonio. 1971. *Selections from the Prison Notebooks*. Translated by Quintin Hoare and Geoffrey Nowell Smith. New York: International Publishers.

Gramsci, Antonio. 1977. *Quaderni del Carcere: Edizione critica dell'Istituto Gramsci*. 4 vols. Turin: Einaudi.

Grant, M.J. 2001. *Serial Music, Serial Aesthetics: Compositional Theory in Post-War Europe*. Cambridge: Cambridge University Press.

Guerrero, Jeannie Ma. 2006. Serial intervention in Nono's Il canto sospeso. *Music Theory Online*, 12 (1).

Guerrero, Jeannie Ma. 2009. The presence of Hindemith in Nono's sketches: A new context for Nono's music. *The Journal of Musicology*, 26 (4): 481–511.

Haas, Georg Friedrich. 1991. Über "Hay que caminar" soñando. In *Die Musik Luigi Nonos*, edited by Otto Kolleritsch, 325–37. Vienna: Universal Edition.

Haller, Hans Peter. 1991. Klang- und Zeitraum in der Musik Nonos. In *Die Musik Luigi Nonos*, edited by Otto Kolleritsch, 35–49. Vienna: Universal Edition.

Haller, Hans Peter. 1995. *Das Experimentalstudio der Heinrich-Strobel-Stiftung des Südwestfunks Freiburg 1971–1989. Vol. 2*. Baden-Baden: Nomos.

Haller, Hans Peter, André Richard, Jürg Stenzl, Alvise Vidolin, Mimma Guastoni and Luciana Pestalozza. 1993. *A proposito di Decouvrir la subversion. Hommage à Edmond Jabès e Post-Prae-Ludium n. 3. 'Baab-arr' di Luigi Nono*. Milan: Ricordi.

Hansen, Miriam. 2012. Reinventing the Nickelodeon: Notes on Kluge and Early Cinema. In *Alexander Kluge: Raw Materals for the Imagination*, edited by Tara Forrest. University of Amsterdam Press.

Heidegger, Martin. 2000. *Elucidations of Hölderlin's Poetry*. Translated by Keith Hoeller. Amherst, MA: Prometheus Books.

References

Helm, Everett. 1955. Darmstadt, Baden-Baden, and Twelve-Tone Music Everett Helm. *The Saturday Review,* July 30, 1955, pp. 33–35.

Henius, Carla. 1991. Arbeitserfahrungen mit Luigi Nono als Interpret und Veranstalter. In *Die Musik Luigi Nonos,* edited by Otto Kolleritsch, 75–90. Vienna: Universal Edition.

Henius, Carla. 1995. *Carla Carissima: Carla Henius und Luigi Nono; Briefe, Tagebücher, Notien.* Hamburg: Europäische Verlagsanstalt.

Hindemith, Paul. 1942. *The Craft of Music Composition.* Translated by A. Mendel. London: Schott.

Hoffmann, Ingrid. 2016. Für Paul Dessau. In *Luigi Nono und der Osten,* edited by Birgit Johanna Wertenson and Christian Storch, 201–28. Mainz: Are Musik Verlag.

Hölderlin, Friedrich. 1979. *Diotima e Hölderlin: Lettere e poesie.* Translated by Enzo Mandruzzato. Milan: Adelphi.

Hölderlin, Friedrich. 2004. *Poems and Fragments.* Translated by Michael Hamburger. London: Anvil Press.

Hölderlin, Friedrich. 2008. *Hyperion.* Translated by Ross Benjamin. Brooklyn, NY: Archipelago Books.

Howell, Thomas. 1974. *The Avant-Garde Flute: A Handbook for Composers and Flutists.* Berkeley, CA: University of California Press.

Huber, Nicolaus A. 1981. Luigi Nono: Il canto sospeso VIa, b. *Musik-Konzepte* (20): 58–79.

Huber, Nicolaus A. 1999. A Carlo Scarpa. *Contemporary Music Review,* 18 (2): 19–36.

Iddon, Martin. 2007. Gained in translation: Words about Cage in late 1950s Germany. *Contemporary Music Review,* 26 (1): 89–104.

Iddon, Martin. 2013. *New Music at Darmstadt: Nono, Stockhausen, Cage, and Boulez.* Cambridge, UK: Cambridge University Press.

Impett, Jonathan. 2004. The tragedy of listening: Nono, Cacciari, critical thought and compositinal practice. *Radical Philosophy,* 125: 29–36.

Ingold, Tim. 2007. *Lines: A Brief History.* London, Routledge.

Ingrao, Pietro. 2006. *Voleva la Luna.* Turin: Einaudi.

Iotti, Nilde. 1966. Milano: parlano le donne lavoratrici: libro bianco sulla condizione femminile nelle fabbriche. La Commissione Femminile della Federazione Communista di Milano.

Jabès, Edmond. 1982. *Le Petit livre de la subversion hors de soupçon.* Paris: Gallimard.

Jabès, Edmond. 1984. *Dans la Double Dépendence du Dit.* Montpellier: Fata Morgana.

Jabès, Edmond. 1987. Luigi Nono. In *Luigi Nono, Festival d'Automne, Paris,* edited by Philippe Albèra, 11–12. Lausanne: Contrechamps.

Jabès, Edmond. 1988. *Le livre des questions, I: Le Livre des Questions – Le Livre de Yukel – Le Retour au Livre.* Paris: Gallimard.

Jabès, Edmond. 1991. *The Book of Questions: Yukel, Return to the Book. Vol. 1.* Translated by Rosmarie Waldorp. Middletown, CT: Wesleyan University Press.

Jabès, Edmond. 1993. *The Book of Margins.* Translated by Rosmarie Waldorp. Chicago, IL: University of Chicago Press.

Jabès, Edmond. 1996. *The Little Book of Unsuspected Subversion.* Translated by Rosmarie Waldorp. Stanford, CT: Stanford University Press.

Jaffé, Hans L.C. 1971. *De Stijl.* New York: H.N. Abrams.

James, William. 1890. *The Principles of Psychology.* New York: Henry.

Jameson, Fredric. 1998. *Brecht and Method.* London: Verso.

Jeschke, Lydia. 1997. *Prometeo Geschichtskonzeption in Luigi Nonos Hörtragödie.* Stuttgart: Franz Steiner.

Joachim, Heinz. 1957. Luigi Nono: Il canto sospeso. *Neue Zeitschrift für Musik* (February): 103.

Jona, Emilio. 1993. Luigi Nono 'tecnically sweet' – Cronistoria di un'opera mancata. *Musica/Realtá* (40): 129–54.

Josefowicz, Nina. 2012. *Das alltägliche Drama.* Hofheim: Wolke Verlag.

Kafka, Franz. 1948. *The Diaries of Franz Kafka, 1910–1913.* Translated by Joseph Kresh. New York: Schocken Books.

Kahn, Arthur. 1965. *On Escalation: Metaphors and Scenarios.* London: Penguin.

Kämper, Dietrich. 2010. 'Spazio immenso e infiniti mondi' – Zur Frage der Beziehung zwischen Nono und Dallapiccola. *MusikTexte,* 124: 45–56.

Kater, Carlos. 2001. *Eunice Katunda: Musicista brasileira.* São Paulo: Annablume.

Kirchert, Kay-Uwe. 2006. *Wahrnehmung und FMragmentierung: Luigi Nonos Kompositionen zwischen 'Al gran sole carico d'amore' und 'Prometeo'.* Saarbrücken: Pfau Verlag.

Kisters, Ludger. 2009. *Raum und Klang im Spätwerk Luigi Nonos.* Saarbrücken: VDM.

Klee, Paul. 1968. *Pedagogical Sketchbooks.* Translated by Sibyl Moholy-Nagy. London: Faber & Faber.

References

Kluge, Alexander. 1999. Zwischenmusik für grosse Gesangsmaschinen. In *Drucksache N.F.1, 64–66.* Düsseldorf: Internationale Heiner Müller Gesellschaft / Richter Verlag.

Kluge, Alexander. 2008. *Das Kraftwerk der Gefühle & Finsterlinge singen Baß.*

Kluge, Alexander and Andrew Bowie. 1986. The political as intensity of everyday feelings. *Cultural Critique,* 4, Autumn: 119–28.

Kolisch, Rudolf. 1957. Nonos Varianti. *Melos, Zeitschrift für neue Musik,* 24: 292–96.

Kontarsky, Matthias. 2001. *Trauma Auschwitz: zu Verarbeitungen des Nichtverarbeitbaren bei Peter Weiss, Luigi Nono und Paul Dessau.* Saarbrücken: Pfau Verlag.

Kremer, Gidon. 1999. *Obertöne.* Munich: Ullstein.

Krones, Hartmut, ed. 2001. *Stimme und Wort in der Musik des 20. Jahrhunderts.* Vienna: Böhlau Verlag.

Kropfinger, Klaus. 1991. Kontrast und Klang zu Raum. In *Die Musik Luigi Nonos,* edited by Otto Kolleritsch, 115–44. Vienna: Universal Edition.

Kurtz, Michael. 1988. *Stockhausen: Eine Biographie.* Kassel: Bärenreiter.

Lachenmann, Helmut. 1999. Touched by Nono. *Contemporary Music Review,* 18 (1): 17–30.

Lachenmann, Helmut. 2004. *Musik als existentielle Erfahrung.* 2nd edn. Wiesbaden: Breitkopf & Härtel.

Lanzardo, Dario. 1979. *La rivolta di piazza Statuto: Turin, July 1962.* Milan: Feltrinelli economica.

Larcati, Arturo. 2002. Momentaufnahmen eines verschöllenen Gesprächs: Ingeborg Bachmann und Luigi Nono. *Neue Rundschau,* 113 (2): 139–51.

Lawton, Anna. 1992. *Kinoglasnost: Soviet Cinema in Our Time.* Cambridge, UK: Cambridge University Press.

Leblanc, Jimmie. 1987. *Luigi Nono et les chemins de l'écoute: Entre espace qui sonne et espace de son.* Paris: L'Harmattan.

Leibowitz, Rene. 1949. *Schoenberg and his School.* Translated by Dika Newlin. New York: Philosophical Library.

Ligeti, György. 1965. Metamorphoses of musical form. *Die Reihe,* 7: 5–19.

Linden, Werner. 1989. *Luigi Nonos Weg zum Streichquartett.* Kassel: Bärenreiter.

Long, Michael. 1989. Symbol and ritual in Josquin's Missa Di Dadi. *Journal of the American Musicological Society,* 42 (1), Spring: 1–22.

Lowrie, Donald. 1965. *Christian Existentialism: A Berdyaev Anthology.* London: George Allen & Unwin.

Lüderssen, Caroline. 2007. Luigi Nono und Giacomo Manzonis Musiktheater: Politisches Engagement im Zeichen Gramscis. In *Rebellische Musik: Gesellschaftlicher Protest und kultureller Wandel um 1968,* edited by Arnold Jacobshagen and Markus Leniger, 93–107. Cologne: Verlag Dohr.

Lukács, György. 1968. *Goethe and His Age.* Translated by Robert Anchor. London: Merlin Press. Original edition, 1947.

Lukács, György. 1970. Narrate or Describe. In *Writer and Critic and Other Essays,* edited by Arthur Kahn, 110–48. London: Merlin Press.

Machado, Antonio. 1982. *Selected Poems.* Translated by Alan S. Trueblood. Cambridge, MA: Harvard University Press.

Machado, Antonio. 2001. *Poesías Completas.* 2nd edn. Madrid: Collección Austral.

Malina, Judith. 1984. *The Diaries of Judith Malina 1947–1957.* New York: Grove Press.

Malina, Judith. 2012. *The Piscator Notebook.* Oxford: Routledge.

Malipiero, Gian Franceso. 1946. L'armonioso labirinto (da Zarlno a Padre Martini, 1558–1774). Milan: Rosa e Ballo.

Malipiero, Gian Franceso. 1966. Il Filo d'Arianna. Torino: Einaudi.

Malvezzi, Piero and Giovanni Pirelli. 1954. *Lettere di condannati a morte della Resistenza europea.* Torino: EInaudi.

Mandarini, Matteo. 2009. Beyond Nihilism: Notes Towards a Critique of Left-Heideggerianism in Italian Philosophy of the 1970s. In *The Italian Difference,* edited by Chiesa. Lorenzo and Alberto Toscano, 55–80. Melbourne: re.press.

Marchesi, Concetto. 2003. *Appelli di libertà: La modernità del pensiero di un intellettuale della resistenza.* Padua: Centro Studi Ettore Luccini.

Marx, Karl. 2008. Draft of a New Preface to The Difference Between the Natural Philosophy of Democritus and Natural Philosophy of Epicurus (1841). In *On Religion.* New York: Dover Publications.

Mast, Christine. 2008. Luigi Nono 'Io, Prometeo' Zum Entwurf konkreter Subjektivität. In *Luigi Nono's 'Tragedia dell'ascolto' Promoteo, musikalische konzepte.* Frankfurt: Stroemfeld.

Melkert, Hella. 2001. *Far del silenzio cristallo Luigi Nono. Chorkompositionen aus 'Prometeo'.* Saarbrücken: Pfau Verlag.

References

Messiaen, Olivier. 1944. *Technique de mon langage musicale*. Paris: Alphonse Leduc.

Messinis, Mario and Paolo Scarnecchia. 1977. *Musica e Politica: Teoria e critica della contestualità sociale della musica, voci sull'est, testemonianze e letture di contemporanei*. Venice: Marsilio Editori.

Metzger, Heinz-Klaus. 1980a. Das Altern der Philosophie der Neuen Musik (1957). In *Musik wozu: Literatur zu Noten*, edited by Rainer Riehn, 61–89. Frankfurt: Suhrkamp.

Metzger, Heinz-Klaus. 1980b. Zur Verdeutlichung einer Polemik und ihres Gegenstandes (1958). In *Musik wozu: Literatur zu Noten*, edited by Rainer Riehn, 105–12. Frankfurt: Suhrkamp.

Metzger, Heinz-Klaus. 1980c. Das Altern der jüngsten Musik (1962). In *Musik wozu: Literatur zu Noten*, edited by Rainer Riehn, 113–28. Frankfurt: Suhrkamp.

Metzger, Heinz-Klaus. 1981. Wendepunkt Quartett? *Musik-Konzepte*, 20: 93–112.

Meyer-Eppler, Werner. 1949. *Elektronische Klangerzeugung: Elektronische Musik und synthetische Sprache*. Bonn: Ferdinand Dümmlers.

Mila, Massimo. 1945. "Bilancio della guerra partigiana in Piemonte." Risorgimento. *Rivista mensile 1* (5): 412–19.

Mila, Massimo. 1966. Se Saint Just suonasse il clarinetto. *L'Espresso*, 40. Reprinted in Mila and Nono 2010, pp. 279–82.

Mila, Massimo. 1999. *Maderna musicista europeo* (nuova edizione). Turin: Einaudi.

Mila, Massimo and Luigi Nono. 2010. *Nulla di oscuro tra noi: Lettere 1952–1988*. Milan: il Saggiatore.

Monigatti, Ulla, ed. 1990. Wissenschaftskolleg zu Berlin: Jahrbuch 1988/89: Nicolaische Verlagsbuchhandlung/ Wissenschaftskolleg zu Berlin.

Morelli, Giovanni. 1991. Dedicato a una dedica. In *Con Luigi Nono*, edited by Roberto Doati, 131–41. Milan: Ricordi/Biennale di Venezia.

Motz, Wolfgang. 1996. *Konstruktion und Ausdruck: analytische Betrachtungen zu 'Il Canto sospeso' (1955/6) von Luigi Nono*. Saarbrücken: Pfau.

Müller, Heiner. 1982. *Rotwelsch*. Berlin: Merve.

Müller, Heiner. 1990. *Germania*. Translated by Bernard and Caroline Schütze. Edited by Sylvère Lotringer. New York: Semiotext(e).

Müller-Dohm, Stefan. 2005. *Adorno: A Biography*. Cambridge, UK: Polity.

Musil, Robert. 1995. *The Man without Qualities*. Translated by Sophie Wilkins. London: Picador.

Nanni, Matteo. 2004. *Auschwitz – Adorno und Nono. Philosophische und musikanalytische Untersuchungen*. Freiburg im Breisgau: Rombach Verlag.

Nattiez, Jean-Jacques. 1993. *The Boulez-Cage Correspondence*. Translated by Robert Samuels. Cambridge, UK: Cambridge University Press.

Negri, Antonio. 1983. *Pipe-line. Lettere da Rebibbia*. Turin: Einaudi.

Negri, Antonio. 2004. *Negri on Negri: In Conversation with Anne Dufourmentelle*. London: Routledge.

Neidhöfer, Christoph. 2009. 'Inno d'amore'. Serial dramaturgy in Luigi Nono's Der rote Mantel. *The Dramaturgy of Sound in the Music of Luigi Nono*, Venice, 13–15 June.

Nielinger, Carola. 2006. 'The song unsung': Luigi Nono's Il canto sospeso. *Journal of the Royal Musical Association*, 131 (1): 83–150.

Nielinger-Vakil, Carola. 2010. Fragmente-Stille, an Diotima: World of greater compositional secrets. *Acta Musicologica*, 82 (1): 105–47.

Nielinger-Vakil, Carola. 2015. *Luigi Nono: A Composer in Context*. Cambridge, UK: Cambridge University Press.

Nietzsche, Friedrich. 1996. *Selected Letters of Friedrich Nietzsche*. Translated by Christopher Middleton. Indianapolis, IN: Hackett.

Noller, Joachim. 1989. Gramsci e la musica. *Musica/Realtá*, X (30), December: 35–48.

Noller, Joachim. 1993. Diario italiano und La fabbrica illuminata. Über die Zusammenarbeit von Luigi Nono und Giuliano Scabia nebst einigen Anmerkungen. In *Zwischen Aufklärung & Kulturindustrie: Festschrift für Georg Knepler*, edited by Hanns-Werner Heister, Karin Heister-Grech and Gerhard Scheit, 155–70. Hamburg: von Bockel Verlag.

Nonnenmann, Rainer. 2013. *Der Gang durch die Klippen: Helmut Lachenmanns Begegnungen mit Luigi Nono anhand ihres Briefwechsels und anderer Quellen, 1957–90*. Wiesbaden: Breitkopf und Härtel Verlag.

Nono, Luigi 1947. *Concetto e natura giuridica dell'exceptio veritatis*. Facoltà di Giurisprudenza, Università di Padova.

Nono, Luigi. 1973. Note di lavorazione: La musica. *Cineforu*, 13 (119), January: 18.

Nono, Luigi. 1980. *Wie Hölderlin komponierte* (interview with Walter Levin). Cologne: WDR.

Nono, Luigi. 1998. *A floresta è jovem e cheja de vida*. Milan: Ricordi.

References

Nono, Luigi and Giuseppe Ungaretti. 2016. *Per un sospeso fuoco: Lettere 1950–1969*. Milan: Il Saggiatore.

Nono, Mario. 1990. *Luigi Nono nell'Arte e nella vita 1850–1918*. Florence: Morgana.

Osthoff, Helmuth. 1952. Besetzung und Klangstruktur in den Werken von Josquin des Prez. *Archiv für Musikwissenschaft*, 9 (3/4): 177–94.

Owens, Jessie Ann. 1997. *Composers at Work: The Craft of Musical Composition*. Oxford: Oxford University Press.

Palandri, Cecilia, ed. 1997. Il carteggio con Guido M. Gatti 1914–1972. *Studi di musica veneta*, 24. Florence: Leo S. Olschki.

Pauli, Hansjörg and Dagmar Wünsche, eds. 1986. *Hermann Scherchen 1891–1966: Ein Lesebuch*. Berlin: Akademie der Künste.

Pavanello, Giuseppe and Nico Stringa. 2004. *Ottocento veneto: Il trionfo del colore*. Treviso: Canova.

Pavese, Cesare. 1990. *La letteratura americana e altri saggi*. Turin: Einaudi.

Pavese, Cesare. 2000. *Il mestiere di vivere. Diario (1935–1950)*. Torino: Einaudi.

Pavone, Claudio. 2013. *A Civil War: A History of the Italian Resistance*. Translated by Peter Levy. London: Verso. Original edition, *Guerra Civile*. Torino: Bollati Boringhieri, 1991.

Pendas, Devin O. 2010. *The Frankfurt Auschwitz Trial, 1963–1965: Genocide, History, and the Limits of the Law*. Cambridge, UK: Cambridge University Press.

Pestalozza, Luigi. 1981. Ausgangspunkt Nono (nach dem Quartett). *Musik-Konzepte*, 20: 3–10.

Pestalozza, Luigi. 1989. La guerra civile spagnola e i musicisti italiani del dopoguerra. *Quaderni di Musica/Realtà*, 24: 12–23.

Peyser, Joan. 1976. *Boulez*. New York: Schirmer Books.

Peyser, Joan. 1995. *The Music of My Time*. New York: Pro/Am Music Resources.

Peyser, Joan. 2008. *To Boulez and Beyond*, revised edn. Lanham, MD: Scarecrow Press.

Piano, Renzo. 1984. PROMETEO: uno spazio per la musica. In *Verso Prometeo*, edited by Massimo Cacciari, 55–62. Milan: Ricordi.

Piccardi, Carlo. 1977. Luigi Nono. Realta' di un compositore. Film for *Radiotelevisione Svizzera Italiana*.

Piccioni, Leone. 2011. Le Origini della 'Terra Promesssa'. In *Vita d'un uomo*, edited by Giuseppe Ungaretti. Milan: Mondadori.

Pinzauti, Leonardo. 1970. A colloquio con Luigi Nono. *Nuova Rivista Musicale Italiana*, IV (1): 69–81.

Piscator, Erwin. 1966. Nach-Ermittlung. *Kürbiskern* (2): 100–2.

Poli, Liliana. 2016. *Vita meravigliosa. Autobiografia*. Florence: Nardini.

Ramazotti, Marinella. 1995. La questione filologica in Luigi Nono. Studio sulle opere degli anni sessanta e ottanta con particolare riferimento a y entonces comprendiò e Risonanze erranti. Laurea in Musicologia, Università di Pavia.

Ramazotti, Marinella. 1997. La questione filologica in Luigi Nono. studio su Y entonces comprendió (1969–70) e Risonanze erranti (1985–7). *Musica/Realtá* (52): 82–95.

Reader, Roberta. 2016. Luigi Nono and the Porous Iron Curtain. In *Luigi Nono und der Osten*, edited by Birgit Johanna Wertenson and Christian Storch, 97–116. Mainz: Are Musik Verlag.

Restagno, Enzo, ed. 1995. *Berio*. Turin: Edizioni di Torino.

Richard, André and Giuseppe Mazzariol. 2005. Preface. In *Das atmende Klarsein*, edited by Luigi Nono, i–xii.

Richard, André and Marco Mazzolini. 1999. Introduction. In *Quando stanno morendo*, edited by Luigi Nono, i–liii. Milan: Ricordi.

Riede, Bernd. 1986. *Luigi Nonos Kompositionen mit Tonband. Ästhetik des musikalischen Materials – Werkanalysen – Werkverzeichnis*. Munich/Salzburg: Berliner musikwissenschaftliche Arbeiten.

Riegler, Martin. 1999. Utopie und Realität: Luigi Nono's Music-Manifesto N. 1, zu Werkenstehung, Quellenanlage und Liveaufführung. Masters thesis, Geisteswissenschaft, Salzburg.

Rihm, Wolfang. 1990. Fragmente – Stille, An Gigi. In *Archivio Luigi Nono*. Unpublished manuscript in Archivio Luigi Nono, Venice.

Rilke, Rainer Maria. 1982. *The Selected Poetry of Rainer Maria Rilke*. Translated by Stephen Mitchell. New York: Vintage International.

Ripellino, Angelo Maria. 1959. *Majakovskij e il teatro russo d'avanguardia*. Turin: Einaudi.

Ripoll, Carlos. 1984. Writers and Artists in Today's Cuba. In *Cuban Communism*, edited by Irving Louis Horowitz, 456–70. New Brunswick, NJ: Transaction.

Rizzardi, Veniero. 1998. Luigi Nono: A floresta é jovem e cheja de vita. In *Festival György Kurtág*, 34–7. Milan: Milano Musica.

References

Rizzardi, Veniero. 1999. Verso un nuovo stile rappresentativo. Il teatro mancato e la drammaturgia implicita. In *La Nuova Ricerca sull'opera di Luigi Nono*, edited by Gianmario Borio, Giovanni Morelli and Veniero Rizzardi, 35–52. Florence: Leo S. Olschki.

Rizzardi, Veniero. 2002. Una lettera di Luigi Nono su 'Incontri'. In *Schoenberg & Nono: A Birthday Offering to Nuria on May 7, 2002*, edited by Anna Maria Morazzoni, 259–66. Florence: Leo S. Olschki.

Rizzardi, Veniero. 2004. La 'Nuova Scuola Veneziana', 1948–1951. In *Le musiche degli anni cinquanta*, edited by Gianmario Borio, Giovanni Morelli and Veniero Rizzardi, 1–61. Florence: Leo S. Olschki.

Roccia, Rosanna and Giorgio Vaccarino, eds. 1995. *Torino in guerra fra cronaca e memoria*. Turin: Archivio storico della Città di Torino.

Röller, Nils, ed. 1995. *Migranten: Edmond Jabès, Luigi Nono, Massimo Cacciari*. Berlin: Merve.

Rosenberg, Julius and Ethel Rosenberg. 1994. *The Rosenberg Letters: A Complete Edition of the Prison Correspondence of Julius and Ethel Rosenberg*. New York: Routledge.

Rossanda, Rossana. 2010. *The Comrade from Milan*. Translated by Romy Clark Giuliani. London: Verso. Original edition, 2005.

Rossanda, Rossana. 2013. *Il film del secolo*. Milan: Bompiani.

Rothe, Alexander. 2007. Rethinking postwar history: Munich's Musica Viva during the Karl Amadeus Hartmann years (1945–1963). *The Musical Quarterly*, 90 (2): 230–74.

Sabbé, Herman. 1981. Die Einheit der Stockhausen Zeit . . . *Musik-Konzepte*, 19: 6–96.

Sallis, Friedemann. 2006. Segmenting the labyrinth: Sketch studies and the Scala Enigmatica in the finale of Luigi Nono's Quando Stanno Morendo Diario Polacco N. 2. *Ex tempore*, XIII (1), Spring/Summer. Accessed 5 November 2012.

Sanguinetti, Giorgio. 2003. La formazione dei musicisti italiani (1900–1950). In *La cultura dei musicisti italiani nel '900*, 15–54. Rome: Società Italiana di Musicologia.

Sani, Nicola. 1992. Intolleranza 1960, Luigi Nono – Angela Maria Ripellino: Il carteggio. *Musica/Realtà*, XIII (39): 115–29.

Sartre, Jean-Paul. 1949. *What is Literature?* Translated by Bernard Frechtman. New York: Philosophical Library.

Sartre, Jean-Paul. 1976. For a Theater of Situations [1947]. In *Sartre on Theater*, 3–5. New York: Pantheon Books.

Scabia, Giuiano. 1990. Composizione de La fabbrica illuminata di Luigi Nono e lettere del 1964. *Musica/Realtá* (33): 43–68.

Scaldaferri, Nicola. 1997. *Musica nel Laboratorio Elettroacustico*, edited by Quaderni di M/R. Lucca: Libreria Musicale Italiana.

Scarabello, Giovanni. 2008. Gianni Milner e l'impresa del Circolo del Cinema Pasinetti. In *Per Gianni Milner (1926–2005): Volume pubblicato in occasione del terzo anniversario della morte*, edited by Fondazione Ugo e Olga Levi onlus per gli studi musicali, 48–53. Venice: Edizioni Fondazione Levi.

Scarpa, Gino, ed. 1952. *L'opera di Gian Francesco Malipiero, saggi di scrittori italiani e stranieri, con una introduzione di Guido M. Gatti, seguiti dal catalogo delle opere con annotazioni dell'autore e da ricordi e pensieri dello stesso*. Treviso: Canova.

Schaller, Erika. 1997. *Klang und Zahl. Luigi Nono: Serielles Komponieren zwischen 1955 und 1959*. Saarbrücken: Pfau.

Schatz, Hilmar. 1957. Theoretiker des Zufalls: Junge Komponisten dozieren bei den Darmstädter Ferienkursen. Melos. Zeitschrift für zeitgenössische. *Musik* (4): 298–300.

Scherchen, Hermann. 1929. *Lehrbuch des Dirigierens*. Leipzig: Weber.

Scherchen, Hermann. 1946. *Das moderne Musikempfinden, i: Vom Wesen der Musik*. Zurich: Mondial Verlag.

Scherchen, Hermann. 1991. *Werke und Briefe. Band I Schriften I*, edited by Joachim Lucchesi. Berlin: Peter Lang.

Schiaffini, Giancarlo. 2011. *E non chiamatelo jazz*. Milan: Auditorium.

Schlegel, Friedrich von. 1971. *Lucinde and the Fragments*. Translated by Peter Firchow. Minneapolis, MN: University of Minnesota Press.

Schmitz, Arnold. 1950. *Die Bildlichkeit der Wortgebundenen Musik Johann Sebastian Bach*. Mainz: Schott.

Schoenberg, Arnold. 1964. *Letters*. Translated by Eithne Wilkins and Ernst Kaiser. London: Faber & Faber.

Schönberg, Arnold. 1974. The Relationship to the Text. In *The Blaue Reiter Almanac*, edited by Wassily Kandinsky and Franz Marc, 90–102. London: Thames & Hudson.

Schönberg, Arnold. 1975. *Style and Idea*. London: Faber.

References

Schönberg, Arnold. 1995. *The Musical Idea and the Logic, Technique and Art of its Presentation*. New York: Columbia University Press.

Schönberg-Nono, Nuria and Friedrich Spangemacher. 1995. Enthusiasmus, Ernst und Humor. Nuria Schönberg-Nono über das Verhältnis von Luigi Nono und Arnold Schönberg. Ein Gespräch mit Friedrich Spangemacher. In *Stil oder Gedanke? Zur Schönberg-Rezeption in Amerika und Europa*, edited by Stefan Litwin and Klaus Velten, 266–79. Saarbrücken: Pfau.

Sciarrino, Salvatore. 2001. Booklet accompanying Kairos CD 0012102KAI. LUIGI NONO: La lontananza nostalgica utopica futura.

Silber, Irwin. 1970. *Voices of National Liberation: The Revolutionary Ideology of the 'Third World' as Expressed by Intellectuals and Artists at the Cultural Congress of Havana, January 1968*. New York: Central Book Company.

Smeliansky, Anatoly. 1999. *The Russian Theatre After Stalin*. Translated by Patrick Miles. Cambridge, UK: Cambridge University Press.

Smirnov, Andrey. 2013. *Sound in Z*. London: Koenig Books.

Smith, William O. 1994. Interview at Archivio Luigi Nono: Archivio Luigi Nono.

Smith-Brindle, Reginald. 1956. The origins of Italian dodecaphony. *The Musical Times*, 97 (1353): 76–7.

Smith-Brindle, Reginald. 1961. Current chronicle: Italy. *The Musical Quarterly*, 47 (2): 247–55.

Smith-Brindle, Reginald. 1966. *Serial Composition*. London: Oxford University Press.

Smith-Brindle, Reginald. 1967. Current chronicle: Italy. *The Musical Quarterly*, 53 (January): 95–100.

Smith-Brindle, Reginald. 1975. *The New Music*. London: Oxford University Press.

Sohm, Philip. 1991. *Pittoresco: Marco Boschini, His Critics, and Their Critiques of Painterly Brushwork in Seventeenth- and Eighteenth-century Italy*. Cambridge, UK: Cambridge University Press.

Spangemacher, Friedrich. 1983. *Luigi Nono: Die elektronische Musik*. Regensburg: Bosse.

Spangemacher, Friedrich. 1986. Resonanzen des Fragens und Suchens: Ein neues Werk von Luigi Nono. *Neue Zeitschrift für Musik* (5): 43–4.

Spangemacher, Friedrich. 1999. Schoenberg as role model. *Contemporary Music Review*, 18 (1): 31–46.

Spies, Marcus. 1984. Luigi Nono: La terra e la compagna. *Melos*, 46 (3): 19–43.

Spitzer, Michael. 2006. *Music as Philosophy: Adorno and Beethoven's Late Style*. Bloomington, IN: Indiana University Press.

Spree, Hermann. 1992. *Fragmente – Stille: An Diotima. Ein analytischer Versuch zu Luigi Nonos Streichquartett*. Saarbrücken: Pfau Verlag.

Steinecke, Wolfgang. 1961. Kranichstein – Geschichte, Idee, Ergebnisse. *Darmstädter Beiträge zur neuen Musik*, 4: 9–24.

Steiner, Peter. 1986. *Russian Formalism: A Metapoetics*. Ithaca NY: Cornell University Press.

Stenzl, Jürg, ed. 1975. *Luigi Nono: Texte, Studien zu seiner Musik*. Zurich: Atlantis.

Stenzl, Jürg. 1975a. Luigi Nono und Cesare Pavese. In *Luigi Nono: Texte, Studien zu seiner Musik*, edited by Jürg Stenzl, 409–33. Zurich: Atlantis.

Stenzl, Jürg. 1991a. Traum und Musik. *Musik Konzepte: Sonderband 'Musik und Traum'*, 74: 8–102.

Stenzl, Jürg. 1991b. Luigi Nono – nach dem 8. Mai 1990. In *Die Musik Luigi Nonos*, edited by Otto Kolleritsch, 11–34. Vienna: Universal Edition.

Stenzl, Jürg. 1998. *Luigi Nono*. Reinbek: Rowohlt.

Stenzl, Jürg. 2003. 'From the lyric to the dramatic'. Liner notes to Col Legno WWE 2SACD 20600.

Stockhausen, Karlheinz. 1953. Weberns Konzert für 9 Instrumente op. 24: Analyse des ersten Satzes. *Melos*, 20 (12): 343–8.

Stockhausen, Karlheinz. 1963. . . . wie die Zeit vergeht . . . In *Texte zur elektronischen und instrumentalen Musik, Band I*, 99–139. Cologne: Verlag M. DuMont.

Stockhausen, Karlheinz. 1964. Sprache und Musik II. In *Texte: Band 2*, edited by Dieter Schnebel, 157–66. Cologne: Dumont.

Stockhausen, Karlheinz. 1989. *Stockhausen on Music: Lectures and Interviews*. London: Marion Boyars.

Stockhausen, Karlheinz. 2001. *Karlheinz Stockhausen bei den Internationalen Ferienkursen für Neue Musik in Darmstadt 1951–1996: Dokumente und Briefe*. Kürten: Stockhausen-Stiftung für Musik.

Svoboda, Josef. 2006. 'Intolleranza 1960' a Boston. In *SvobodaMagika*, edited by Massimo Puliani and Alessandro Forlani, 145–50. Matelica: Halley Editrice.

Tafuri, Manfredo. 1969. Per una critica della ideologia architettonica. *Contropiano*, 1: 31–79.

Taibon, Mateo. 1993. *Luigi Nono und sein Musiktheater*. Köln: Böhlau.

Tarkovsky, Andrey. 1987. *Sculpting in Time: Reflections on the Cinema*. Translated by Kitty Hunter-Blair. Austin, TX: University of Texas Press.

References

Tartini, Giuseppe. 1767. De' principi dell'armonia musicale contenuta nel diatonico genere. Padua: Stamperia del seminario (facs. Olms, Hildesheim, 1970).

Tischer, Matthias. 2009. *Komponieren für und wider den Staat. Paul Dessau in der DDR*. Cologne: Böhlau Verlag.

Tomek, Otto. 2004. *Luigi Nono in Köln* (exhibition catalogue).

Toscano, Alberto. 2009. Chronicles of insurrection: Tronti, Negri and the subject of antagonism. *Cosmos and History: The Journal of Natural and Social Philosophy*, 5 (1): 76–91.

Tronti, Mario. 2013. *Operai e capital*. 4th edn. Rome: DeriveApprodi.

Trotta, Giuseppe and Fabio Milana, eds. 2008. *L'operaismo degli anni Sessanta: Da 'Quaderni rossi' a 'classe operaia'*. Rome: Derive Approdi.

Trudu, Antonio, ed. 2008. *Luigi Nono: Carteggi concernanti politica, cultura e partito comunista italiano. Vol. III, Archivio Luigi Nono*. Florence: Leo S. Olschki.

Ungaretti, Giuseppe. 2011. *Vita d'un uomo*. Milan: Mondadori.

Ungeheuer, Elena. 1992. *Wie die Elektronische Musik 'erfunden' wurde . . .: Quellenstudie zu Werner Meyer-Epplers musikalischem Entwurf zwischen 1949 und 1953*. Mainz: Schott.

Vedova, Emilio. 2005. Segni–immagini in movimento per Prometeo. In *Nono Vedova: Diario di bordo*, edited by Stefano Cecchetto and Giorgio Mastinu, 93–101. Turin: Umberto Allemandi.

Vesely, Dalibor. 2006. *Architecture in the Age of Divided Representation: The Question of Creativity in the Shadow of Production*. Cambridge, MA: MIT Press.

Vicentino, Nicola. 1996 (1555). *Ancient Music Adapted to Modern Practice*. Translated by Maria Rika Maniates. New Haven, CT: Yale University Press.

Vlad, Roman. 1957. Riflessi della dodecafonia in Casella, Malipiero e Ghedini. *La Rassegna Musicale*, XXVII: 44–53.

Vogt, Harry. 1984–5. 'Al gran sole' carico d'autocitazione – oder: Zwischen Patchwork und Pasticcio; Zur dramaturgisch-musikalischen Gestaltung der 2. szenischen Aktion 'Al gran sole carico d'amore' von Luigi Nono. In *Neuland – Ansätze zur Musik der Gegenwart 5*, edited by Herbert Henck. Bergisch Gladbach: Neuland Musikverlag.

von Massow, Albrecht. 1999. Phänomenologie oder Gehalt? Deutungsprobleme in frühen und späten Werken Luigi Nonos. In *Luigi Nono: Aufbruch in Grenzbereich*, edited by Thomas Schäfer, 96–105. Saarbrücken: Pfau Verlag.

Wagner, Andreas. 1980. *Karl Amadeus Hartmann und die Musica Viva. Essays. Bisher unveröffentlichte Briefe an Hartmann*, edited by Bayerische Staatsbibliothek. Munich: Piper Verlag.

Walsdorf, Hanna. 2003. *Das Ballett 'Der rote Mantel' von Tatjana Gsovsky: Lyrisch-groteskes Spiel zwischen Beifall und Protest*. Munich: GRIN Verlag.

Warnaby, John. 2003. The music of Nicolaus A. Huber. *Tempo*, 57 (224), April: 22–37.

Waterhouse, John C.G. 1999. *Gian Francesco Malipiero (1882–1973): The Life, Times and Music of a Wayward Genius*. Amsterdam: Harwood.

Weber, Derek. 2009. My friend Gigi: Why Maurizio Pollini returns to Luigi Nono's music time and again. *Salon: Magazin zu den Salzburger Festspielen*: 80–1.

Webern, Anton. 1963. *The Path to the New Music*. Translated by L. Black. Bryn Mawr: Theodor Presser.

Weill-Ménard, Diane. 1994. *Vita e tempi di Giovanni Pirelli*. Milan: Linea d'Ombra.

Weiss, Peter. 1966. *The Investigation: Oratorio in 11 Cantos*. Translated by Alexander Gross. London: Marion Boyars.

Weiss, Peter. 1972. *Hölderlin: Stück in zwei Akten*. Frankfurt: Suhrkamp.

Weiss, Peter. 2010. *Hölderlin*. Translated by Jon Swan. Calcutta: Seagull Books.

Wertenson, Birgit Johanna. 2011. Karneval als Interregnum: Zeit- und Formkonzeptionen in Luigi Nonos Guai ai gelidi mostri. *Musik und Ästhetik* (2): 50–67.

Winckel, Fritz. 1957. "Das Ohr als Zeitmesserorgan." *Gravesaner Blätter* 9: 83–98.

Winckel, Fritz. 1958. Die Grenzen der musikalischen Perzeption unter besonderer Berücksichtigung der elektronischen Musik. *Archiv für Musikwissenschaft*, XV (4): 307–24.

Wittner, Laurence S. 2003. *Toward Nuclear Abolition: A History of the World Nuclear Disarmament Movement, 1971–Present*. Stanford Nuclear Age Series. Stanford, CA: Stanford University Press.

Wood, Michael. 2017. *Heiner Müller's Democratic Theater: The Politics of Making the Audience Work*. Woodbridge, UK: Boydell & Brewer.

Xenakis, Iannis. 1956. Wahrscheinlichkeitstheorie und Musik. *Gravesaner Blätter*, 6: 28–34.

Yates, Frances. 2002 (1964). *Giordano Bruno and the Hermetic Tradition*. London: Routledge.

References

Yates, Frances. 2014 (1966). *The Art of Memory*. London: The Bodley Head.

Zacconi, Lodovico. 1596/1622. *Prattica di Musica*. 2 vols. Venice: Carampello. Reprinted 1983. Bologna: Arnaldo Forni.

Zehelein, Klaus, Dietolf Grewe and Luigi Nono. 1978. 'Prozesse – nicht Modelle!' Gespräch mit Luigi Nono. Musiktheater Hinweise. Informationen der Frankfurter Oper (June/July).

INDEX

Note: *italic* page references indicate figures; 'n' indicates chapter notes.

4i machine 409, 418

Abbado, Claudio 123, 309, 310, 312, 316, 320, 328, 399, 404, 407, 449, 452
abstraction 20, 58, 92, 97, 124, 162, 188, 198, 215, 237, 242, 244, 363, 391, 395, 443, 465, 475
Accevedo, Miriam 298, 303
Adlington, Robert 303
Adorno, Theodor W. 84–5, 141–5, 146n60, 219, 249, 254, 273n107, 363, 367n86, 478; *The Aging of the New Music* 141; *Commitment* 219; *Philosophy of Modern Music* 84
Ady, Endre 382–3
Aeschylus, *Prometheus Bound* 399, 403, 409, 432n4
Africa 261
Aix-en-Provence, France 105, 112, 118
Akademie der Kunste der DDR 276, 333, 364
Albèra, Philippe 376, 390, 465
Alberman, David 494
Aldini, Edmonda 293
Alfa Romeo factory 246
Algeria 204, 231
Alleg, Henri 260
Allende, Savador 310, 331, 333
Alquati, Romano 237
Amendola, Giorgio 279
AMM (improvisation group) 342
Andalusian singing 387
Anders, Günther 221, 224–6, 230

Andersch, Alfred 168, 200nn52–3, 205, 206, 209, 218
Ansaldo, Milan 409–10
ANS photoelectronic synthesiser 246
Antonioni, Michelangelo 205, 209, 239; *Le amiche* 205, 209; *Il grido* 205
Arditti, Irvine 494
Aretche, Leobardó López, *El jinete del cubo* 286
Argentina 279
Ars Viva Verlag (publisher) 59, 64, 72, 105, 106, 122, 271
Artaud, Antonin 185–6
Artaud, Pierre-Yves 372
Auschwitz concentration camp 176, 183, 254, 259, 273n107, 274n117
Austria 2, 5, 8n5
L'Avanti (communist journal) 217, 282
azione scenica (staged action) 7, 66, 79, 168, 206, 216, 238, 252, 260, 310, 320, 399

Baars, Bernard 7
Bach, Johann Sebastian 15, 25, 27, 29, 89, 131, 132, 140, 143–5, 181, 206, 225, 243, 300, 387, 498; *The Art of Fugue* 22, 25, 26; *Komm, süsser Tod* 498; *Mass in B Minor* 144; *The Musical Offering* 29, 143; *St Matthew Passion* 143–4, 475
Bachmann, Ingeborg 200n52, 442–7, 450n39
Baden Baden, Germany 72–3, 84, 105, 118, 158, 439–40, 478
Bailey, Kathryn 123, 136
Baille dance 78, *79*

Index

Bakker Schut, Pieter H., *Stammheim* 494–5
Balestrini, Nanni 238, 282, 283, 317n27
Banchieri, Adriano 5, 7, 282–3; *La Cartella Musicale* 5, 283
Bandiera rossa (anthem) 69, *69*, 70, 302, 305, 329
Baraitser, Lisa 493
Bartók, Béla 386
Bassanese, Stefano 259
battaglia genre 316
Beck, Julian 262
Becker, Wolfgang 495
Bedford, David 187
Beethoven, Ludwig van 10, 13, 25, 70, 140, 359, 363, 414; *Concerto for Violin, Cello and Piano* op. 56 13; *Quartet* op. 132 350; *Symphony no. 3 'Eroica'* op. 55 316; *Symphony no. 7* op. 92 70
Beethoven Festival, Bonn 350, 360
Belgium 209
Bellini, Giovanni 395, 478
Benjamin, Walter 332, 362–3, 376, 403–5, 414, 418, 420, 421, 425–8
Berberian, Cathy 249
Berdiaev, Nicolai 14, 19
Berg, Alban 117, 147, 206, 322; *Kammerkonzert* 117; *Lulu* 206
Berghinz, Carlo 11, 12, 13
Berio, Luciano 30, 67, 193, 196, 207, 249; *Circles* 233; *Momenti* 197; *Thema* 198
Berlin, Germany 22, 24, 49, 101–2, 105, 123, 158, 190, 253, 254, 262, 281, 333, 441, 448, 449, 463, 475, 478–81, 485; *see also* East Berlin; West Berlin
Berliner Akademie der Künste, West Berlin 276, 497–8
Berliner Ensemble 66, 281, 333
Berliner Festwochen 101, 480
Berlin International Film Festival 449
Berlin Philharmonie 80, 158, 410, 467, 480, 489
Berlin Wall 218, 231, 478, 494
Bertini, Antonio 335n26
Besseler, Heinrich 144
Beyer, Robert 46, 85, 86
Beyst, Stefan 386
Black Forest, Germany 112, 369, 370, 406, 409, 412, 414
Black Women Enraged (group) 283
Der Blaue Reiter (magazine) 141, 219
Blok, Aleksandr 382, 384
Blüthner Orchestra, Berlin 22
Bobbio, Norberto 12–4, 33n24, 33n26, 33n40, 33nn21–2
Böhmer, Konrad 258, 303
Boito, Arrigo 2
Boito, Camillo 2, 4–5

Bologna, Italy 3, 288, 330
Bontempelli, Massimo 11, 16, 32n10
Borio, Gianmario 90, 98
Borovsky, David 320
Boschini, Marco 5
Boston, USA 270–1
The Boston Globe (newspaper) 253
Boulez, Pierre 70–1, 72, 84, 87, 92, 93, 105, 106, 107, 108, 112, 119n38, 144, 175, 176, 290, 439–41, 446, 451n44; *Aléa* 157, 176; *Improvisations sur Mallarmé* 168; *Le Marteau sans maître* 87, 142, 157; *Polyphonie X* 92; *Sonata* 157; *Structures* 72, 83
Bove, Kadigia 264–5, 274n156, 283, 293, 295, 298, 299
Braak, Krijn ter 303
Brahms, Johannes 21, 423, 486
Brass, Tinto 286
Brazil 25–7, 169
Bream, Julian 232
Brecht, Bertolt 62, 66, 105, 206, 210, 219, 221, 281, 322, 323, 364; *The Days of the Commune* 321; *The Good Woman of Szechwan* 320; *Die Verhör des Lukullus* (with Dessau) 62
Brik, Lilya 337, 351
Brik, Osip 337
British Broadcasting Corporation (BBC) 195, 216, 217, 232
Brook, Peter 245, 254, 321, 403
Brouwer, Leo 286, 496–7
Brüggen, Frans 304
Bruno, Giordano 139, 370, 452–3; *De la causa, principio et uno* 452–3, 456, 458–62, *459*
Buber, Martin 404
Budapest, Hungary 386, 389
Buenos Aires, Argentina 448
Bulgarian folk music 311–3
Bunke, Tania 322
Busch, Ernst 95

Cacciari, Massimo 5, 7, 20, 33n26, 205, 237, 282, 289, 290, 343, 349, 351–2, 361, 368, 370–1, 376, 377, 383, 387, 391–3, 399–405, 412, 414, 418, 420, 422–5, 431–2, 432n4, 441, 447, 462; *Icone della Legge* 432, 447; *Krisis* 351, 370, 403, 496; *L'angelo necessario* 466; *Pensiero negativo* 351
Cadieu, Martine 304
Cage, John 119n38, 157, 175–6, 186, 196, 432
Calabretto, Roberto 286, 475, 477, 479
Caldwell, Sarah 253
Calvino, Italo 99, 145, 176, 177, 206, 207, 252
Campo Sant'Angelo group 237–8
capitalism 211, 217, 245, 246, 288, 329, 375

Index

Cardew, Cornelius 195
Carmichael, Stokely 285
Carocci, Giovanni, *Inchiesta alla FIAT* 239
Castro, Fidel 239, 334
Cecconi, Roberto 382
Cerone, Pietro, *El melopeo y maestro* 81n25
Chamber Orchestra of Europe 409, 481
chance techniques 143, 157, 175, 180, 186, 466
Chile 70, 279, 310, 311, 312, 331
China 277, 279
Chinello, Cesco 288, 289
Chopin, Frédéric 337
Chowning, John 368–9
Christian Democrats, Italy 329, 331
Christianity 10, 14, 477–8
Church of San Lorenzo, Venice 407–9
Ciardi, Guglielmo 1–2
Cingoli, Giulio 242
Classe operaia (communist publication) 237, 288
Cold War 94, 124, 231, 280, 381
collage 186, 243, 245, 262, 331, 488
Cologne 83, 93, 122–3, 175, 178, 197, 218, 252, 386, 388, 390, 494, 498
colonialism 186, 211, 222, 261, 262, 328
colour 6, 38, 40, 43, 46, 63, 68, 74, 90, 108, 111, 132, 149, 184, 197, 228–9, 278, 322, 403, 463, 483–4, 495
communism *see* Italian Communist Party
Corbin, Henry 466
Cornigliano steelworks 245, 246–7, 252, 259
Corriere della Sera (newspaper) 217, 269, 329, 330, 498
Cossettini, Luca 248
Cruz, Luciano 310, 311, 312, 315, 319n136
Cumar, Raffaele 17

Dal Co, Francesco 401, 439
Dalí, Salvador 120n82
Dallapiccola, Luigi 5, 9, 22, 23, 28–9, 30, 32, 35n126, 36, 38, 276, 339, 345–6; *Canti di liberazione* 143, 346; *Canti di Prigionia* 38, 143, 345; *Due liriche greche* 29; *Due Pezzi* 29; *Il Prigioniero* 29, 32, 143, 223, 345; *Ulisse* 345
Dall'Oglio, Renzo 21
Da Re, Giacomo 449
Darmstädter Beiträge (journal) 176, 186
Darmstädter Echo (newspaper) 45
Darmstädter Tageblatt (newspaper) 123
Darmstadt Summer School (*Ferienkürse für neue Musik*) 9, 19, 22–3, 32, 36, 45–7, 52, 58, 59, 71–2, 80n2, 84, 91, 94, 105, 106, 107, 112, 117, 122, 139, 142, 157, 168, 171, 175–6, 177, 185, 189, 191, 195–6, 204, 207
Dartington International Summer School 189, 232, 293

Davy, Gloria 170
De Assis, Paulo 89, 313, 340–1
De Benedictis, Angela Ida 209, 225, 228
De Bosio, Gianfranco 33n31
De Carolis, Massimo 329
Deleuze, Gilles 489
De Seriis, Lino 286–7
Dessau, Paul 62–3, 105, 254, 281, 333–4, 364; *The Thälmann Kolonne* 334; *Die Verhöhr des Lukullus* (with Brecht) 62
Deutsche Akademie der Künste, East Berlin 276, 333, 364
Deutsche Staatsoper Berlin 333
Deutsche Oper 101
Deutscher Akademischer Austauschdienst (DAAD) 448
Diacono, Mario 169
dice 180, 386, 394–5, 441
Di Giugno, Giuseppe 409
displacement matrices 61–2, 68, 74, 78, 88–9, 96, 99, 102, 108, 115, 127, 131, 162, 164
dodecaphony (twelve-tone system) 17, 20, 23, 24, 27, 29, 34n55, 35n110, 37, 47, 58, 62, 67, 73, 75, 84, 86–7, 113, 167, 245, 321, 327, 441, 446
Donaueschingen Festival, Germany 88, 94, 148, 156, 158, 159, 170, 467, 468
Döpke, Doris 362
Dorigo, Wladamiro 320
Drees, Stefan 439, 484
Driesen, Pauline 410
Durazzi, Bruce 117, 231
Duse, Ugo 217
Dutch Communist Party 303–4
Dutch Radio Philharmonic Orchestra and Choir 303
Dutschke, Rudi 281, 494

East Berlin 95, 105, 254, 259, 276, 281, 328, 388
East Germany *see* German Democratic Republic (DDR)
The East is Red (anthem) 277, 302, 305
Edinburgh Festival, Scotland 221–2, 231
Eimert, Herbert 84, 86, 91–2, 107, 118n27, 123, 124, 151; *Lehrbuch der Zwölftontechnik* 86, 151
Einaudi, Giulio 10, 99, 124
Eisenstein, Sergei 179, 181, 205, 206, 208, 238, 475; *Strike* 205; *The Battleship Potemkin* 205; *October* 208
Eisler, Hanns 364
electronic music 46, 92, 150, 152, 157, 169, 183, 197, 246, 290, 300, 304; *see also* live electronics
Elsendoorn, Jo 302

518

Index

Éluard, Paul 94–5, 97, 210, 241
Elzenheimer, Regine 355
England 188, 189
Ensslin, Gudrun 494
Ernst, Heinrich Wilhelm 482
Esenin, Sergei 10
L'Espresso (newspaper) 217–8
essentialism 30, 37–8, 58, 108, 113, 170, 343, 497
ethical principles 13, 32n3, 37, 48, 84, 101, 139, 177, 259, 287, 410, 462
Euripides 377, 381, 424
Experimentalstudio des SWR, Freiburg 368–9, 374, 376, 378, 384, 387–8, 391, 410, 425, 442, 443, 463, 470, 482, 494

Fabbriciani, Roberto 360, 368–71, 374–6, 389, 440, 442, 464, 469, 480, 490–1, 498
Fabris, Gastone 21, 34n79
Fanon, Frantz 261
fascism 7, 10–3, 33n40, 66–7, 231, 254, 287, 344, 345
Favretti, Giacomo 1
Fedeltà d'Italia (newspaper) 12
Fellini, Federico, *8 1/2* 239
La Fenice, Venice (opera house) 10, 14, 18, 26, 74, 237, 344
Ferrara, Giuseppe 286
Ferrari, Ermanino Wolf 3
Festival d'Automne, Paris 410, 441, 462, 465, 467, 469, 495, 497
Fiat industrial action 239–40, 243, 246, 286–7
First International Congress of Dodecaphonic Music 24, 27, 86
First World War 3, 12
Flacius, Matthias 144
Fleischer, Herbert 58
Flimm, Jürgen 408
Florence, Italy 4, 281, 286, 389
Ford Foundation 253
formalism 5, 19, 64, 85, 87, 90, 94, 97–8, 134, 141, 145, 151, 157, 164, 171, 175, 177, 188, 192, 214, 221–2, 279, 300, 309, 337–8, 439, 455, 474
Frank, Anne, *The Diary of Anne Frank* 169, 175, 260
Frankfurt, Germany 63, 122
Franqui, Carlos 280, 297, 299
Frantzen, Hubertus 452
'*fratello*' motif 32, 35n133, 223, 345–6, 348, 353, *353*
Freiburg, Germany 368–70, 374, 388, 409, 412, 439–40, 448, 453, 454, 478, 481–5, 490; *see also* Experimental Studio, Freiburg
Freie Volksbühne, Berlin 254, 273n106
French Revolution 360, 495

Friuli region earthquake 344
Fu ik, Julius, *Notes from the Gallows* 47–8
futurism 7, 69, 206, 250, 322, 337, 382–3
Fux, Johann 20, 28

Gabrieli, Giovanni 6–7, 107, 108, 129, 139–40, 386, 424
Gallo, Ennio 12, 32n3
García, Alan 454
Garufi, Bianca 159
Gatti, Guido M. 16, 33n47, 35n120
Gayer, Catherine 216
Gazzarri, Fabrizio 390–1
Gazzelloni, Severino 72, 186
Gazzetta Musicale (newspaper) 343
Il Gazzettino (newspaper) 217, 281
Genoa, Italy 245, 252, 264
George, Stefan 141
German culture 5, 93, 168, 206, 207, 252, 364
German Democratic Republic (DDR; East Germany) 62–3, 246, 254, 276, 281, 329, 333, 364, 388, 448
Germany 63–4, 66, 75, 83–4, 87, 106, 118n7, 168, 185, 188, 196, 209, 218, 388; *see also* German Democratic Republic; West Germany; *specific places in*
Gertler, André 147
Geselbracht, Charlotte 481
Gesualdo, Carlo 134, 135, 139–40, 444
Ghiringhelli, Antonio 260
Gielen, Michael 46
Giudecca, Venice 158, 176, 188, 198, 239, 282, 339, 342, 370, 376, 406, 416, 468, 469, 498
Glock, William 189, 232
Gobetti, Carla and Paolo 240
Goehr, Alexander 181
Goethe, Johann Wolfgang von 57, 93, 362, 364, 400, 406, 408, 420–1
Goeyvaerts, Karel 84–5; *Sonata for Two Pianos* 85
Gogol, Nikolai, *Dead Souls* 10
Goléa, Antoine 36, 39, 45, 72, 94, 117
Gontard, Suzette 360
Gorky, Maxim 321–3
Gosztonyi, Alexander 370–1, 381
Göttinger Tageblatt (newspaper) 45–6
Gracchi brothers 101
Gramsci, Antonio 19, 65, 97, 99, 143, 242, 246, 264, 288, 290, 291, 309–10, 316, 330–3
Grano, Romolo 21
graph/squared paper 162, 224, 270, 277, 299
Grassi, Paolo 320, 322, 328, 329–30
Greek, ancient, texts/sources 11, 30, 131, 374, 377, 400–1, 406, 423–4
Greenland 448–9, 470

Index

Gregorian chant 23, 38, 79, 344
Grindenko, Tatiana 491–2
groups technique 86–7, 108, 149–50, 160, 178, 294–5, 483
Gsovsky, Tatjana 101–2
Guastoni, Mimma 497
Guerrero, Jeannie Ma 38, 60
Guevara, Che 280, 281, 297, 299, 300–1, 334
Guttoso, Renato 252

Haba, Alois 20, 22
Haitink, Bernard 304
Haller, Hans-Peter 369, 371, 375, 376, 408–9, 426, 440, 442, 443, 446, 465, 467, 483, 490, 494–5
Hamburg, Germany 62–3, 66, 75, 84, 87, 98, 101, 167, 178, 436
Hannover, Germany 63, 101
harmonic wheel 55–6, 57
Hartmann, Karl Amadeus 63, 87, 105–6, 176, 186, 221, 238
Haüsler, Josef 168
Havana, Cuba 239, 241, 280, 297, 301, 334, 448
Heidegger, Martin 360, 429
Heinichen, Johann David 144
Helm, Everett 117
Henius, Carla 216, 245, 248–52
Henze, Hans-Werner 46, 63, 84, 106, 122, 158, 159; *Nachtstücke und Arien* 159
Hertzka, Emil 219
Hessische Rundfunk, Germany 178, 195
Hindemith, Paul 15, 18, 22, 24, 34n88, 38, 57, 60, 72, 212
Höhepunkt (high point of musical tension) 23, 31, 67, 77, 90, 208, 211, 278, 341, 426, 460
Hölderlin, Friedrich 316, 349, 350–1, 359–65, 377, 380, 388, 421–3, 429
Holland Festival 301–4
Hollweg, Ilse 170
Hotel Halde, Freiburg 369, 370, 406–7
Howell, Thomas 372
Huasi, Julio 311, 313
Huber, Nicolaus A. 123, 136, 137, 187, 277, 438, 439
Hübner, Herbert 59, 63, 74, 84, 98, 159, 167, 180
humanism 6, 14, 19, 64–5, 145, 225, 387, 463, 466
Hungary 381–2

Iddon, Martin 72, 175
Ingold, Tim 139, 140
Ingrao, Pietro 279, 287, 289, 498
L'Internationale (anthem) 95, 96, 97, 302–3, 305, 320, 328

internationalism 13, 64, 83, 87, 101, 138, 260–4, 276, 298, 302, 332
International Music Festival, Venezuela 285–6
International Music Festival, Venice 22–3
International Society for Contemporary Music (ISCM) 22, 28, 35n120, 105
Inti-Illimani (group) 292, 329, 335n26
Iotti, Nilde 319n109
Islamic singing 387
Italian Communist Party (*Partito Communista Italiano*; PCI) 64–5, 209, 216, 231, 237, 240, 245, 252, 259–60, 263, 270, 276, 279, 282, 286–90, 292, 296, 309, 310, 321, 330, 331, 335n26, 375, 480, 498
Italian culture 10, 67, 84, 328–30
Italian post-war economy 94, 106, 124, 239, 240, 245, 288
Italy *see specific places in*
Italsider steelworks 245, 252
Itten, Johannes 57, 406, 408
Ivens, Joris 208–9

Jabès, Edmond 13, 448, 462, 465, 466; *Dans la Double Dépendence du Dit* 462; *Le Petit Livre de la subversion hors de soupçon* 462–4
Jacobs, Paul 157
Japan 435, 438–9, 471, 474, 476, 477
Jeschke, Lydia 423, 424, 492
Jewish music 387, 392
Jewish thought 400, 462–3, 466, 477
Joachim, Heinz 123, 134, 135, 143, 168
Jokisch, Walter 101
Jona, Emilio 239, 245
Josquin des Prez 20, 34n77, 95, 125, 135, 180, 277, 303–4, 386, 395, 404, 441; *Adieu mes amours* 442–3
Joyce, James 260

Kafka, Franz 47, 143, 339, 351, 354
Kagel, Mauricio 142, 175, 290, 304
Kahn, Herman 262–3, 267
Kandinsky, Wassily 219
Kantor, Tadeusz 403
Kašlík, Václav 216
Katunda, Eunice 25–7, 29–30, 35n100, 35n110, 35n128, 49, 52, 58, 65, 66, 67, 143; *Negrinho do Pastoreio* 26; *Quartro Cantos à Morte* 26
Khlebnikov, Velemir 382–3, 385
Kiefer, Anselm 494
Kircher, Athanasius 462, 477
Kirchert, Kay-Uwe 346
Klee, Paul 405–6, 418, 477
Klimov, Elem 441, 449
Kluge, Alexander 470, 478–80
Koch, Gerhard 461
Koellreutter, Joachim 25–6, 27

Index

Kolisch, Rudolf 147, 150, 152–3, 155, 158–9
Korean music 439
Krakow, Poland 176
Kremer, Gidon 480–8, 491–2, 494
Kruttke, Eigel 122
Kubrick, Stanley 286
Kupkovic, Ladislav 303
Kurtág, György 389

Labroca, Mario 82n51, 177–8, 208, 210, 215, 265, 308–9
Lachenmann, Helmut 187–9, 211, 218, 252–3, 277, 359, 363, 388, 476, 478, 494, 495, 497
Landini, Francesco 21
Lascelles, George 222
Latin America 25, 279–80, 286–7, 292; *see also specific places in*
Latin squares/'magic square' technique 23, 61, 68, 70, 78, 81n36, 103, 108, 111, 113–4, 137, 151, *151*
Lauriello, Alberto 286
Lawo, Peter 369
Leblanc, Jimmie 477
Leibowitz, René 9, 27–8, 35n112, 45, 84, 86; *Schoenberg and his School* 9, 27–8, 35n112
Lenin, Vladimir 322, 333–4
Leopardi, Giacomo 495
Levin, Walter 350
Libertini, Lucio 286–7
Liceo Marco Polo, Venice (school) 10–2
Ligeti, György 171–7, 236, 244, 350
Liguria, Italy 36, 75
Lindsay, Mary 298, 299, *300*
Liszt, Franz 315–6, 342
The Living Theatre 262–4, 267
Llull, Ramon 462
Lombardy, Italy 337–8
London, UK 195, 217, 231
Longo, Luigi 240, 279, 288–90
Lorca, Federico Garcia 26, 29, 35n128, 66, 70, 100, 105, 106, 120n82, 140; *Casida de la rosa* 67, 73; *Llanto por Ignacio Sanchez Mejias* 73; *The Love of Don Perlimplin and Belisa in His Garden* 101–4; *Memento* 73, 244; *Romance de le Guardia Civil Española* 75; *Tarde* 67, 69, 73
Lorenzi-Fabris, Ausonio De 3, 8n12
Los Angeles, USA 253
Ludwig, Christa 75, 87–8, 120n88
Lukács, György 145, 147n73; *Hölderlin's Hyperion* 364
Lumumba, Patrice 261, 334
Lunc, Lev 10
Lutoslawski, Witold 174, 176
Luxemburg, Rosa 302, 321
Lyubimov, Yuri 320–2, 329, 330

Machado, Antonio 191, 232, 236, 271n17, 449; *Otras canciones a Guiomar* 232–3, 236
Machaut, Guillaume de, *Lay de plour* 442–3
Maderna, Bruno 5, 9, 13, 16, 17–22, 23, 27, 29, 30, 34n61, 35n107, 36–7, 47, 49, 59, 61, 63, 64, 66, 67, 72, 75, 84, 86, 94, 97, 105, 107, 112, 120n100, 175, 191, 195, 196–7, 212, 216, 221, 242, 252, 304, 331, 442; *Hyperion* 242; *Musica su due dimensioni* 71–2; *Notturno* 197; *Quartetto per archi in due tempi* 60, 112, 155; *Satyricon* 331
Magri, Lucio 289
Mahler, Gustav 10, 104, 316, 351, 401, 403, 414, 471
Malina, Judith 262–3
Malipiero, Gian Francesco 3, 9, 11, 15–7, 22, 28, 33n47, 33nn40–1, 34n53, 34n55; *Sette Canzoni* 322
Malvezzi, Piero 124, 143
Manetti family 4, 10
Mann, Thomas 32n6
Mann, William 304
Manzoni, Giacomo 217, 330, 335n34
Marangoni, Luigi 11
Marchesi, Concetto 12
Martini, Arturo 11, 16, 20, 32n9
Masson, André 118
mathematics 10, 16, 93, 142, 186, 296, 496, 497
Matzerath, Otto 122
Mayakovsky, Vladimir 10, 69, 82n70, 177, 206, 210, 238, 337, 351; *Lenin* 66, 67, 69, 70; *La nostra Marcia* 214
Mazzoni, Marisa 283
Meinhof, Ulrike 494–5
Melkert, Hella 415, 424, 455
Mellinger, Melise 488
melodrama 49, 65, 331–2
Melville, Herman 442–7, 450n38; *Battle Pieces and Aspects of the War* 442, 443
Meneghetti, Egidio 12
Messiaen, Olivier 72, 77, 79, 82n77
Messinis, Mario 19
Metzger, Heinz-Klaus 141–2, 146n60, 195, 362
Meyer-Eppler, Werner 85, 86, 92, 163
Meyerhold, Vsevolod 69, 179, 205, 206, 237, 271
micropolyphony 226, 236
microtones 34n51, 386, 456
Mila, Massimo 33n21, 64, 99, 126, 128, 131, 132, 136, 143, 158, 177, 190, 197, 207, 217, 268, 270, 282, 316, 387, 489
Miłosz, Czesław 382, 383, 385
Mina (singer) 248, 273n78, 380
Missa Di dadi (Josquin) 21, 180, 395, 441
Molmenti, Pompeo 3
Moncalvo, Mario Buffa 292

Index

Mondrian, Piet 495–7; *Composition, 1916* 495–6, *496*; *Composition in line* 495–6
Monicelli, Mario, *I compagni* 240
Monteverdi, Claudio 11, 15, 28, 129, 135, 140, 163, 166, 222, 381, 460; *Lamento d'Arianna* 312–3, *313*, 314; *L'Orfeo* 11, 137, 378, 424, 495
Morelli, Giovanni 477
Morricone, Ennio 273n78
Moscow, Russia 259, 321, 387, 449
Motz, Wolfgang 123, 124, 129, 131
Mozart, Wolfgang Amadeus 131, 140
Müller, Heiner 364, 388, 409, 433n49, 470, 478, 480
Müller, Ursula 95
Münich, Germany 63, 87, 101, 105, 289, 448
Münich Philharmonie 452, 454
Munteanu, Petre 216
Murzin, Evgeny 246
musical thought 1, 5, 7, 9, 15–7, 19, 21, 24, 32, 39, 86, 92, 99, 105, 107, 205, 210, 222, 228, 252, 369, 372, 376, 388, 490, 492, 497
Musica per la libertà festival, Rome 329
Musica/Realtà (organisation) 309–10, 316, 332, 337–8
Música Viva (organisation) 26, 63
Musica Viva series, Münich 87, 105
music theatre 7, 66, 79, 99, 101, 106, 144, 168, 170, 175, 177, 183, 204–8, 218–9, 231, 238–9, 244–5, 261, 320, 332, 470
Musil, Robert 351
Mussolini, Benito 33n40
Mussorgsky, Modest 10; *Boris Godunov* 10, 469

Nanni, Matteo 238, 259
Napoletano, Giorgio 240, 246, 331
National Symphony Orchestra, Peru 280
Natoli, Aldo 289
'negative rhythm' concept 90, 346
'negative thought' concept 351, 432
Negri, Antonio 5, 237, 288–9, 290, 291
neoclassicism 2, 28, 186
Neruda, Pablo, *La Guerra* 69–70, 82n71
Netherlands 303–5
Neue Zeitschrift für Musik (journal) 123
Nielinger-Vakil, Carola 124, 353, 358, 366n62, 419, 424, 429
Nietzsche, Friedrich 316, 352, 450
Nirenstein, Alberto 258
Noller, Joachim 244
Nono, Francesco (great-grandfather) 1
Nono, Igenio (great-uncle) 2
Nono, Luigi *184, 241, Plate 7*; childhood 10–11; death 498; illness 448–9, 490, 494, 497–8; law degree 9, 12–5, 16, 21, 32n12, 33n14, 409; marriage 17, 117; at the Venice Conservatory 15–8, 33n40, 33n43; works: *1°*

Caminantes… Ayacucho (1987) 452–62, *455, 457, 458, 459*; *2° No hay caminos, hay que caminar…Andrej Tarkovskij* (1987) 468–78, *472, 474*; *A Carlo Scarpa, architetto, ai suoi infiniti possibili* (1984) 435–9, *437*, 441; *A floresta é jovem e cheja de vida* (1966) 20, 206, 261–71, *269*, 277, 280, 281, 286, 297, 298, 310, 338; *A Pierre: Dell'azzurro silenzio, inquietum* (1985) 439–41; *Al gran sole carico d'amore* (1978) 244, 261, 262, 280, 301, 309, 310, 320–33, *325, 326, 327*, 337, 339, 342, 345, 349, 374, 385, 399, 408; *Canciones a Guiomar* (1963) 231–7, *234, 235*, 303, 385, 446; *Canti di vita e d'amore: Sul ponte di Hiroshima* (1962) 86, 177, 221–31, *223, 229*, 232, 233, 244, 246, 276, 278; *Canti per 13* (1955) 105–11, *109, 110*, 210; *Como una ola de fuerza e luz* (1972) 287, 310, 311–6, *313*, 332; *Composizione per orchestra [n.1]* (1951) 59–63, *60, 61, 62*, 73, 97; *Composizione per orchestra n. 2: Diario polacco '58* (1959) 178–85, *179, 182*, 189, 190, 192, 196, 218, 255, 258; *Con Luigi Dallapiccola* (1979) 30, 32, 345–9, *347*, 350, 353, 384, 403, 412, 456, 471; *Contrappunto dialettico alla mente* (1968) 282–5, 296; *Cori di Didone* (1958) 158, 168–75, *172, 173*, 255; *Da un diario italiano* (1964) 243–4; *Das atmende Klarsein* (1981) 368–76, *373*, 378, 394, 404, 412, 413, 415, 421, 431, 442, 498; *Découvrir la subversion. Hommage à Edmond Jabès* (1987) 462–7, *464*; *Deola e Masino* (1964–5) 281, 293; *Der Rote Mantel* (1954) 100–5, *103*; *Die Ermittlung* (1965) 254–60, *256, 257, 258*; *¿Donde estás hermano?* (1982) 386; *Due espressioni* (1953) 86, 87–93, *89, 91, 92, 93*, 94; *Due liriche greche* (1948) 29–32, *31*, 38, 345; *Ein Gespenst geht um in der Welt* (1971) 244, 301–8, *307*, 313, 324, 327; *Epitaffio n. 1–3 per Federico García Lorca* (1951–3): *Epitaffio n. 1: España en el corazón* (1951) 66–72, *68, 69, 71*, 83, 92; *Epitaffio n. 2: Y su sangre ya viene cantando* (1952) 72–4, *73, 74*, 86, 92, 104, 343; *Epitaffio n. 3: Memento* (1953) 74–80, *76, 77–8, 79*, 86, 87; *Fragmente-Stille, an Diotima* (1980) 20, 21, 23, 152, 180, 185, 309, 324, 327, 343, *344*, 349–65, *353, 354, 356, 357*, 372, 403, 404, 489, 494; *Fu ik* (1951) 47–9, *48*, 59, 60, 66, 194, 244, 385; *Für Paul Dessau* (1974) 329, 333–4; *Guai ai gelidi mostri* (1983) 391–6, 440, 443, 448; *"Ha venido". Canciones para Silvia* (1960) 191, 192, 194–6, *195*, 208, 211, 255, 271, 303; *"Hay que caminar" Soñando* (1989) 491–4, 497; *Il canto sospeso* (1956) 80, 86, 107, 112, 122–45, *125, 126, 128, 129, 130, 133, 134, 137, 138, 139*,

522

Index

142, 152, 158, 160, 167, 168, 183, 187, 195, 215, 255, 327, 329, 385, 442; *Incontri* (1955) 86, 107, 112–8, *113, 114, 116*, 125, 127, 128, 151, 210, 214, 226; *Intolleranza 1960* (1961) 49, 70, 101, 117, 123, 168, 183, 192, 194, 198, 199, 204–19, *208, 210, 212, 213*, 221, 222, 230, 231, 239, 242, 244, 253, 271, 304, 309, 327, 442; *Io, frammento dal Prometeo* (1981) 376–81, *379*, 394, 401, 412, 413, 421, 423, 424; *La discesa di Cristo agli inferni* (lost work) 28; *La fabbrica illuminata* (1964) 206, 236, 244, 245–53, *247, 250, 251*, 259–60, 271, 280, 287, 299, 305, 385; *La lontananza nostalgica utopica futura* (1988) 7, 371, 480–9, *485, 486, 487*, 492; *La terra e la compagna* (1958) 158, 159–68, *160, 161, 164, 165*, 171, 180, 190, 191, 195, 303; *La Victoire de Guernica* (1954) 93–8, *96, 97*, 119n61, 140, 190; *Liebeslied* (1954) 98–100, *99, 100*; *Liriche d'Ungaretti* (partly lost) 21, *22*; *Machaut–Ockeghem–Josquin* 425, 442–7, *445*; *Ma prima che i boschi si dissechino (But before the woods wither*; coll. Pirelli) 262; *Musica-Manifesto n.1: Un volto, e del mare – Non consumiamo Marx* (1969) 287, 292–6, *294*, 300, 303, 304; *Musiche per Manzù* 296; *Notturni-Albe* 337; *Omaggio a Emilio Vedova* (1960) 196–9, 436; *Omaggio a György Kurtág* (1983) 388–90, 425, 442, 446, 448, 464; *Per Bastiana – Tai-Yang Cheng* (1967) 276–9, *278*, 282, 293, 303, 304; *Piccola gala notturna veneziana in onore dei 60 anni di Heinrich Strobel* (1958) 168; *Polifonica – Monodia – Ritmica* (1951) 27, 47, 48, 49–59, *50, 51, 52, 53, 54, 55, 56, 57, 58*, 74, 84–5, 383, 447; *Post-prae-ludium n. 1 'per Donau'* (1987) 467–8; *Post-prae-ludium n. 3 'BAAB–ARR'* (1988) 480, 489–91; *Prometeo. Tragedia dell'ascolto* (1984) 11, 14, 16, 23, 104, 140, 219, 221, 242, 322, 324, 332, 338, 343, 344, 345, 349–50, 352, 353, 360, 362, 364, 368, 369–70, 376–7, 389, 391, 392, 395, 399–432, 435–6, 442, 467, 480; (*3 voci (a)* 426–7, 428, 429, 467; *3 voci (b)* 429–30; inception 399–407, *402, 405*; *Interludio 1°* 389, 425–6, 467, 498; *Interludio 2°* 429, 430; *Isola 1°* 414, 419–21, *421*; *Isola 2°* 377, 421–5, 426; *Isola 3° – 4° – 5°* 427–9, *428*; production 407–11, *411*; *Prologo* 412–9, *413, 416, 417, 418*; *Stasimo 2°* 431–2); *Quando stanno morendo: Diario polacco n. 2* (1982) 381–8, 392; *Ricorda cosa ti hanno fatto in Auschwitz* (1966) *258*, 258–60, 271, 280, 287, 327; *Risonanze erranti. Liederzyklus a Massimo Cacciari* (1986) 441–50, *445*, 462; *San Vittore 1969* (1969) 292; *Sarà dolce tacere*

(1960) 190–4, *193*, 208; ..... *sofferte onde serene ...* (1976) 152, 337–44, *340, 341, 344*, 352, 440; *Technically Sweet* (1963) 239; *Un diario italiano* (1964) 239–44, *241*, 247, 260–1, 285, 293, 327; *Varianti* (1957) 147–59, *148, 151, 152, 153, 154, 156*, 160, 166, 187, 192, 223; *Variazioni canoniche sulla serie dell'op. 41 di Arnold Schönberg* (1950) 9, 11, 21, 30, 36–46, *37, 38, 39, 40, 41, 42, 43, 44, 45*, 48, 59, 86, 180, 271, 372; *Voci destroying muros* (1970) 244, 301–8; *Was ihr wollt* (1954) 105; *Y entonces comprendió* (1970) 297–301, *300*, 304; writings: *Concetto e natura giuridia dell'exceptio veritatis* 14–5; *Die Entwicklung der Reihentechnik (The development of serial technique)* 148–9; *Geschichte und Gegenwart in der Musik von Heute (History and presence in the music of today)* 176, 185–7, 189, 201n74, 295–6; *L'errore come necessità (Error as necessity)* 388–9; *Possibilità e necessità di un nuovo teatro musicale (Possibility and necessity of a new music theatre)* 206, 231, 237–8, 330; *Text – Musik – Gesang (Text – Music – Song)* 131, 135, 139, 143, 163, 171, 185, 189, 195–6, 204, 244, 330

Nono, Luigi (grandfather) 1–4, 6, 7, 8, 12
Nono, Maria (mother; *née* Manetti) 4, 10, 12, 17, 75, 104–5, 339, 343
Nono, Mario (father) 4, 6, 7, 8n12, 8n16, 10, 12, 17, 104–5, 339
Nono, Mario (uncle) 3
Nono, Nuria (wife; Schönberg-Nono) 17, 98, 106, 117–8, 122, 144, 158, 211, 410
Nono, Rina (grandmother; *née* Pruili Bon; *later* Marangoni) 3, 4, 8n9, 11
Nono, Rina (sister) 4, 10, 65
Nono, Serena Bastiana (daughter) 277
Nono, Silvia (daughter) 189, 191
Nono, Urbano (uncle) 1, 8n1, 11
North-West German Radio (NWDR) 63, 83–4, 86, 101, 107, 118n27, 167
'nueva canción' groups 329, 335
Nyffeler, Max 361

Ochetto, Achille 498
Ockeghem, Johannes 20, 21, 125, 304, 353–4, 444, 446; *Malor me bat* 21, 442–3, 444, *445*
opera 98, 107, 122, 159, 168–9, 206
The Opera Company of Boston, USA 253
Ortiz, Fernando 348
Osthoff, Helmuth 395
Otto, Susanne 389, 442, 453, 462, 463, 498
Ozawa, Seiji 277

Pacheco, Jesús López 221, 222, 225
Padua (*Padova*), Italy 10, 12, 32n8

Index

Paik, Nam June 175
Palazzo del Capitano 9
Palermo, Sicily 239, 243
Panzieri, Raniero 237, 288
Paris, France 85–7, 105, 111, 292, 446
Partito d'Azione (action party) 13, 15, 33n24, 33n31
Pasolini, Pier Paolo 240, 344; *Nuove questioni linguistiche* 240; *I Turcs tal Friúl* 240, 344
Pasternak, Boris 10, 382, 384–5, 387
Pavese, Cesare 54, 99, 106, 117, 119n72, 122, 124, 158, 162–3, 168, 190, 194, 200n33, 205, 221, 228–30, 232, 239, 241, 242, 261, 293, 325, 337, 400, 442, 443; *Al gran sole* 190; *Anche tu sei collina* 162–3, 167, 190; *Canzone* 325; *Fumatori di carta* 325; *I mari del Sud* 325; *Mattino* 292–4, 318n78; *Le piante del lago* 247; *Lo spiraglio dell'alba* 337; *La terra e la morte* 159; *Verrà la morte e avrà i tuoi occhi* 159, 190, 222
Peragallo, Mario 82n51
Peru 280
Perugia, Italy 448
Pestalozza, Luigi 126, 186, 246, 252, 258–60, 270, 309, 330, 332, 362, 380, 387
Petrobelli, Pierluigi 10
Pianciola, Cesare 239
pianism 316, 339, 342
Piano, Renzo 407–10, 429
Piccolo Teatre, Udine 344
Piccolo Teatro, Milan 255, 264, 265, 320, 329
Pindar 377, 421–3
Pintor, Luigi 289
Pinzauti, Leonardo 28
Pirelli, Giovanni 124, 143, 255, 261–3, 302, 318n107
Piscator, Erwin 63, 66, 82nn62–3, 206, 208, 216, 254, 258, 262, 273n106
Pivato, Albano (brother-in-law) 12, 13, 33n14
Poland 176, 179, 183, 185, 189–90, 258, 381–3, 387
Poli, Liliana 252, 255, 264, 266, 283, 293, 295, 298, 299, 303
Pollini, Marilisa 339
Pollini, Maurizio 310, 311–2, 314, 315–6, 320, 328, 337–43
polyphonic density 90, 108–9, 111, 114, 127, 129, 136, 151–2, 164, 463
polyphonic integration 61, 90, 92, 105, 212
polyphony of polyphonies 70–1, 119n55
Po river flooding 101, 205, 209
Porto Marghera, Venice, industrial action 7, 245, 289
Portugal 328

Potere operaio (Workers' power movement) 237, 290
Prague, Czech Republic 142, 146n64, 190, 216, 259, 276, 281, 287–9
Prato, Franco 21
Pritchard, John 231
Prix Italia (competition) 245, 252, 282
Proms, London 231
Pro Musica Nova festival, Bremen 304
Publison *Infernal Machine* (studio device) 443
Puecher, Virginio 242, 265–6
punktuelle Musik (music of points) 72, 86

Quaderni rossi (communist publication) 237, 239, 318n107
Quasimodo, Salvatore 29–30, 35n131, 442; *Tre liriche greche* 30, 35n131
questioning 9, 19, 147, 168, 189, 222, 246, 400, 463, 468
Quilapayun (Chilean group) 329

radio 83–4
Radok, Alfréd 190, 207, 216–7; *Lanterna Magika* (with Svoboda) 190, 196, 206, 207
Ravazzi, Gabriela 298, 299
Ravel, Maurice, *Bolero* 102, 103
Reader, Roberta 246
Red Army Faction 494
Reggio Emilia, Italy 260, 263, 309, 316
Rehfuss, Heinz 216
remapping 38–9, *39*, 59, 155, 171, 174, 180, 192
resistance 12–4, 33n47, 64, 95, 97, 99, 124, 132, 135, 143, 169, 177, 198
Restagno, Enzo 292, 468
Richard, André 410, 483, 494, 498
Ricordi (publisher) 270–1
Rihm, Wolfgang 360, 470
Rilke, Rainer Maria 370, 374; *Duino Elegies* 370, 374; *Elegy*, no.7 370, 374
Rimbaud, Arthur 320, 322
Rimsky-Korsakov, Nikolai 9, 15
Ripellino, Angelo Maria 206–7; *Vivere è stare svegli* 207, 209–10, 214, 220n25
Rizzardi, Veniero 24, 61, 81n39, 268, 270
Rognoni, Luigi 113, 117
Romanticism 316, 332–3, 349
Rome, Italy 21, 65, 176, 207, 252, 259, 264, 297, 329
Ronconi, Luca 401, 403
Rosa, Luigi 3
Rosbaud, Hans 98, 106, 112, 117, 158, 167
Rosenberg, Ethel 131
Rosenzweig, Franz 404
Rossanda, Rossana 240, 286, 287, 289, 290, 498
Rossi, Francesco 11

Index

Royal Shakespeare Company 254
Russian culture 3, 4, 10, 14, 69, 196, 206, 207, 320–1
Russia *see* Union of Soviet Socialist Republics (USSR)

Sallis, Friedemann 385, 386, 488
Sanchez, Sonia 282–3, 302; *Malcolm* 283–5
San Marco, Venice 4, 8n15, 11, 13, 15, 387
Santamaria, Haydée 280, 302
Santi, Piero 217
San Vittore prison, Milan 292
Sardinia 350, 401
Sartre, Jean-Paul 204–5, 219, 242, 252
Scabia, Giuliano 237, 239, 240–2, 244, 245, 246, 251
'scala enigmatica' 23, 73, 324, 343, *344*, 350, 352–3, *353*, 355, 358, 381, 385–6, 394, 406, 412–3, 419, 423, 455, 484, 487, 492–3, 495
Scarabello, Giovanni 205
Scarpa, Carlo 6, 8n28, 11, 435–9, 450n3, 471; *Tomba Brion* 439
Scarponi, Ciro 376, 389, 440, 498
Schaeffer, Pierre 85, 87
Schaft, Hannie 302
Schaller, Erika 151, 155, 162, 180–1
Scherchen, Hermann 17, 22–5, 26, 27, 29, 31, 34n88, 36, 45–6, 48, 52, 57, 59, 64, 66, 74, 75, 79, 85, 87, 94, 95, 101, 105, 106, 111, 120n100, 122, 123, 152, 158, 180, 196, 271
Schiaffini, Giancarlo 369, 389, 393, 442, 462, 467, 498
Schillinger, Joseph 186
Schlegel, Friedrich von 478
Schlemmer, Oskar 206
Schmitz, Arnold 143, 144, 145
Schoenmaekers, M.H.J. 497
Schönberg, Arnold 5, 11, 17, 20–1, 22, 23, 25, 32n6, 84, 140, 141, 143, 147, 194, 224, 253, 361, 387, 447–8, 477, 495; *Die Glückliche Hand* 219; *Die Jakobsleiter* 168, 178–9; *Kammersymphonie* 22; *Moses und Aron* 98, 101, 143, 178, 209, 238, 254, 432; *Ode to Napoleon Buonaparte* op. 41 37, *37*, 44–5; *Piano Concerto* op. 42 37; *Piano Piece* op. 33a 37; *Pierrot Lunaire* 22; *Quartet* op. 30 37; 'The relationship to the text' (essay) 141; *Suite* op. 25 23; *Suite* op. 29 37; *A Survivor from Warsaw* 11, 48, 143, 195, 219, 237–8, 348, 385; *Variationen für Orchester* op. 31 117, 148–9
Schönberg, Gertrude 98
Schönberg-Nono, Nuria (wife) 17, 98, 106, 117–8, 122, 144, 158, 211, 410
Schott (publisher) 59, 106, 120n99, 122, 188, 208, 271

Schreiber, Wolfgang 491
Schubert, Franz 21, 141, 195, 442, 447
Schumann, Robert 21, 316, 406, 412, 414, 442, 483
Schwer, Cornelius 388
Schygulla, Hanna 494
Sciarrino, Salvatore 488
Scodanibbio, Stefano 391
Scuola Grande di San Rocco, Venice 386
Searcy, David 345, 350
Second International Twelve-Tone Congress, Darmstadt 84–5
Second World War 11–4, 16, 22
Seghers, Anna 238
Seneca 12
serialism 23, 26, 32, 35n110, 37, 48, 51, 72, 87, 98, 111, 135, 142, 171, 176, 217, 261, 345, 440
Settembre Musicale, Turin 469
Shakespeare, William 105
Shining Path (guerilla group) 454
Siberia 468, 475, 476
Sicilian songs 67
sine waves 172, 196, 197, 247, 255, 390, 467
singer-songwriters (*cantautori*) 292, 321
situations ('theatre of situations') 204–5, 206, 209, 214, 238, 242
Smith, William O. 255, 265, 268, 297, 298
Smith-Brindle, Reginald 123–4, 134, 269
Snel, Riek 302
Social Democrat Party (SPD), Germany 185
socialist realism 142, 198, 206, 333
sound 5–7, 43, 46, 58, 69, 75, 90–1, 96, 127, 167, 233, 249
South-West German Radio (SWF) 72, 83, 107, 117, 158, 168, 440. *see also* Experimental Studio, Freiburg
Soviet Union *see* Union of Soviet Socialist Republics
Sozialistische Deutsche Studentenbund (West Berlin) 280–1
Sozialistische Einheitspartei Deutschlands (German Socialist Unity Party) 62
Spain 66–7, 69–70, 74, 80, 82n71, 231, 449
Spangemacher, Friedrich 27, 258, 447
Spanish Civil War 94, 95, 237–8
Spanish dances 103
Spitzer, Michael 363
Steinecke, Hella 174
Steinecke, Wolfgang 36, 59, 72, 83, 87, 92, 93–4, 95, 97, 98, 106, 107, 112, 117, 122, 124, 148–9, 158, 168, 174, 176, 178, 179, 186, 191, 195–6, 216, 218
Stenzl, Jürg 7, 49, 117, 167, 183, 200nn45–6, 292, 320, 337, 382, 385, 425, 493–4, 498
St Mark's Square, Venice 4, 9, 281–2, 283, 285, 293

525

Index

Stockhausen, Karlheinz 64, 67, 71–2, 83, 84–6, 92, 100, 104, 107, 119n34, 134, 139, 140–1, 157, 158, 175, 186, 188, 195, 252, 265, 290; *Gesang der Jünglinge* 142; *Klavierstück XI* 157, 176; *Kontra-Punkte* 92; *Kreuzspiel* 71–2, 83, 85, 86; *Studie I* 150, 157; *Studie II* 152, 157
Storck, Henri 208–9
Stravinsky, Igor 387, 460
Strehler, Giorgio 264
Strobel, Heinrich 72, 84, 88, 105, 107, 112, 118, 147, 148, 158, 168, 177
Stuckenschmidt, Hans Heinz 45, 117
Studio di Fonologia, RAI, Milan 196–9, 203n152, 208, 242, 245, 247, 252–3, 265, 271, 282, 283, 292, 297, 368–9, 403
Sugana, Luigi 3, 8n12
Svoboda, Josef 190, 207, 217, 242, 253, 322; *Lanterna Magika* (with Radok) 190, 196, 206, 207

Tabaldini, Giovanni 3
Tacitus 12
Tafuri, Manfredo 290
Taganka Theatre, Moscow 320–1
Takemitsu, Toru 469, 476, 491, 497, 499n45
Tallis, Thomas 428, 470
tape recorders 196–8
Tarkovksy, Andrei 246, 468; *Andrei Rublev* 468; *The Sacrifice* 468, 469, 475–7, 491; *Sculpting in Time* (essays) 476
Tartini, Giuseppe 5
Taskova, Slavka 311–2, 313
Taylor, Cecil 342
Teatro Lirico, Milan 330
Tedeschi, Rubens 316, 387
television 286, 479–80
Tempophon (studio device) 298, 307
Thälmann, Ernst 334
Thomas, Ernst 186, 196
time 19–20, 44, 67, 104, 150, 160, 168, 226, 236, 259, 294, 308, 332, 341, 343, 363, 371–2, 374–5, 385, 394, 404, 415
The Times (newspaper) 217, 231, 304
Togliatti, Palmiro 64–5, 112, 216, 246, 279, 286
Togni, Camillo 27, 368, 490
Tokyo, Japan 435–6, 469–70, 476, 497
Tomek, Otto 305
The Toronto Symphony Orchestra, USA 277–9
Trattoria Altanella, Venice 188
Tronti, Mario 237, 283, 288, 375
Tudor, David 157, 176, 186
Turin, Italy 99, 159, 237, 239–40, 286, 288, 323, 328, 338, 448, 468, 469

Tuscany, Italy 2, 309
twelve-note system *see* dodecaphony

Uitti, Frances-Marie 384, 391
Ungaretti, Giuseppe 21, 26, 168–70, 175, 201n58, 206; *Finale* 169–70, 174; *La Taccuino del Vecchio* 175; *La terra promessa* 158, 168–70, 175
Union of Soviet Composers 246
Union of Soviet Socialist Republics (USSR) 176, 204, 231, 246, 270, 280, 287, 289, 320–1, 329, 381, 383, 475–6
l'Unità (communist newspaper) 217, 219, 245, 246, 259, 264, 281, 289, 316, 342, 387
United States of America (USA) 176, 195, 218, 231, 253, 270, 275n171, 279, 281
University of Padova 9, 12–6, 21, 32n12, 33n14, 409
Uruguay 279, 312
USSR *see* Union of Soviet Socialist Republics

Vajont dam disaster (1963) 215, 239
Varèse, Edgard 46, 58, 111, 129, 180, 192, 348; *Ionisation* 46, 58, 348
Vasari, Giorgio 5
Vedova, Emilio 6, 11, 13, 198–9, 203n166, 208, 216, 217, 237, 281, 282, 390–1; ... *Cosidetti Carnevali...* 390–1, 393, 395
Venetian culture 4–5, 7, 8n5, 9–10, 108
Venetian Federation (*Federazione*) 259, 282, 288
Veneto (Venetian dialect) 2, 8n5, 240
Venezuela 285–6
Venice 1–8, 8n29, 16, 64, 84, 105, 123, 148, 187–8, 237, 245, 281–3, 399, 448, 478, 497; *see also specific places in*
Venice Biennale (*La Biennale di Venezia*) 3, 5, 11, 18, 48, 59, 84, 177–8, 198, 207–8, 216, 240, 252, 261, 263, 281–2, 293, 308–9, 320, 376, 382, 387, 407
Venice Cinema Festival 282
Venice Conservatory 15–8, 33n40, 33n43
Venice Film Festival 205, 238, 479
Venice International Theatre Festival 66
Verdi, Giuseppe 2, 25, 65, 308, 328, 343; *Ave Maria* 23, 25, 26, 343, 352, 498; *Nabucco* 328
Vertov, Dziga 323
Vespignani, Arcangelo 11, 12
Vespignani, Luigi and Giovanni 11
Vicentino, Nicola 17, 20, 471
Vicini, Elena 255, 283, 298, 303
Vidolin, Alvise 408
Vienna, Austria 351
Viennese song 141
Vietnam 263–4, 281, 285, 302, 304, 323, 334
Visconti, Luchino 27, 32n6, 66, 209, 286
Vivaldi, Antonio 5, 15, 482, 488

Index

Vlad, Roman 34n55, 309
Von Lewinski, Wolf-Eberhard 123, 175, 186
Vysotsky, Vladimir 321

Wagner, Klaus 304
Wagner, Richard 10
Walton, William and Susana 122
Warsaw Autumn festival, Poland 176, 190, 258–9
Webern, Anton 21, 22, 24, 72, 81n36, 84, 93, 107, 113, 125, 130, 140, 144, 476; *Concerto* op. 24 93; *Variations* op. 30 125, 149
Weimar Republic 66, 254
Weiss, Peter 245, 254, 259, 364–5
Die Welt (newspaper) 63, 123
Wertenson, Birgit Johanna 394, 397n78
West Berlin 253, 280, 289
West German Radio (WDR) 305, 495, 498
West Germany 254
Winckel, Fritz 201n60, 436
Wissenschaftskolleg, Berlin 448, 478–80, 494
Wittgenstein, Ludwig 351–2, 360–1, 389, 401, 403
'workerism' ('operaismo') 288–9, 375

working classes 239, 245, 247, 252, 259–60, 288–90, 291, 310
Wörner, Karl H. 58
Woytowitcz, Stefania 255, 293

Xenakis, Iannis 111, 115, 196, 244

Yates, Frances 462

Zacconi, Lodovico 20
Zamyatin, Yevgeny 10, 32n5
Zarlino, Gioseffo 5, 6, 16, 17, 21, 27
Zattere, Venice 1, 3, 7, 10, 12
Zavattini, Cesare 169
Zehelein, Klaus 349–50
Die Zeitschrift für Musik (journal) 58
Die Zeitschrift für Musiktheorie (journal) 388
Zender, Hans 436
Zimmerman, Bernard 175
Zortzico dance 78, 79
Zuccheri, Marino 180, 196, 197, 203n166, 246–8, 262, 265, 283, 293–4, 311, 334, 338, 368
Zürich, Switzerland 63, 64, 106

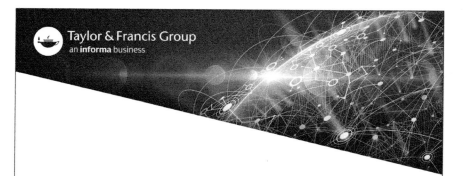